COLONIAL
AMERICAN
WRITING

COLONIAL AMERICAN WRITING

SECOND EDITION

Edited with Introductions by

Roy Harvey Pearce

HOLT, RINEHART AND WINSTON, INC.

New York   Chicago   San Francisco   Atlanta
Dallas   Montreal   Toronto   London

Introduction

The selections in this volume illustrate main aspects of American intellectual and imaginative origins and growth through the third quarter of the eighteenth century. Exhibiting not so much colonial social, institutional, and political forms, as ideas and attitudes which made for such forms, they embody the thought and imagination of those Colonial Americans who were to become Revolutionary Americans. These writings, in fact, point immediately toward the American mind of the Revolutionary period—a mind of the Enlightenment, one which was to center on the notion of the free, rational personality and which was to know that freedom and rationality were embodied in the very nature of things American.

There are represented in this volume some of the origins of that mind and of its drive toward freedom. The Pilgrim idea of freedom through private and separate devotion, the Puritan idea of freedom through work and facing one's fate as a sinful individual, the Virginia idea of freedom through the responsibilities of the ruling gentleman, the Quaker idea of freedom through the inviolable sacredness of the individual, and the frontier idea of freedom through violent self-assertion—all these ultimately found their largest realization in the thoughts, beliefs, and actions of enlightened Americans of the Revolution and beyond. In the writings here selected, we can know these ideas as they came into being and began to be explored and tested and as they made for characteristic attitudes toward life and living.

There is perhaps not enough of what we may, properly speaking, call "literature" in this collection, as there was little of the sustained esthetic attitude in colonial America. Colonial Americans were determined to make a new way of life in a new world—or rather to realize in the best possible way, under the best possible circumstances, the best aspects of the old life which they had left behind them. They had little or no time for that disinterested contemplation which is essential in making works of art. When they did write poetry, it was poetry which had a public, commemorative value, which would recall to them something significant; or it was poetry which showed them that when and if they wished, they could write as well as any gentlemanly Englishman. In their various ways, in their various conditions, with their various beliefs, they took the arts as seriously as they could.

Because they had first of all to survive, they took life with deadly seriousness. And in their seriousness they were able to record memorably life and living as they knew it. When their writing has distinguished style, as it often does, it is style which serves a higher purpose than itself; it is style which expresses the very seriousness of the colonial enterprise. Indeed, when one studies stylistically the best of colonial writing, one is studying the quality of colonial seriousness. The very forms of expression themselves—sermons, histories, diaries, poems, and the like—characterize the men who write, the society to which they write, and the occasion for writing. The difference between the writing of a Mather and of a Byrd, between that of a Sewall and of a Woolman, is in the style and form as well as the content. One can see not only what each believes in, but the quality of the belief. Theirs is the style and form—a mode of conceiving of the self and its world imaginatively—which develop when an idea or an attitude is seriously put into action.

Consideration of style and form—alternative modes of imagination as they are expressed in differing sociocultural contexts—thus returns us to idea and attitude. Basic to that idea and attitude is a search for freedom through order. We can see in these selections widely varying conceptions of what order is and for whom freedom exists, and we can look ahead to the development of such conceptions in the Revolutionary period. Freedom was to come more and more to be the right of all men; a Revolution was to be fought and won; a new world, a new way of thinking, and a new literature were to come into being; new liberties, new responsibilities, new goods and evils, were to develop. The selections printed here show evidence of the beginnings of that development. They should remind us, as we struggle in our time to find freedom through order, that the struggle is eternal; only the conditions of struggle change. They should let us know the past well enough to at once profit from it and to free ourselves from it. Not the least advantage of coming to know these colonial writings is that which accrues when we try to understand our present, for good and bad, as it takes its origins in our past.

Note on the Second Edition

Although I have expanded this edition considerably, dropped some selections, and added others, I have held to the principle according to which the original version was organized: that selections should be long enough to enable a reader to get at more than their substantive concerns. Although they all may not be properly "literary," the pieces here printed all have imaginative power and distinction and can be read and interpreted accordingly. What is at the heart of the matter, at the heart of our coming to know the colonial origins of American life, is a sense of the relationships obtaining among aspects of style—style in writing, in individual lives, and in cultures and subcultures. Bits and pieces do not yield such understanding. Accordingly, I have had to pick and choose carefully, and often enough more or less arbitrarily to anthologize one writer as against a number of others, all perhaps as significant and accomplished as he, all surely as "representative" as he. The important point is that all the writers here anthologized are significant and accomplished, are representative, and are printed at sufficient length—so I hope—that they can be understood in some depth individually and in relation to one another and to the cultural situations in which they lived and wrote. Out of their living came their writing. And we must have enough of their writing to get at the quality of their lives. Finally, I have of course brought the selective bibliographies up to date, used better sources of texts when available, and modified my introductory remarks whenever recent scholarly and critical investigations have demanded. If this is perhaps a somewhat more "literary" collection than the original edition, that is because we now know more about colonial belles lettres than we did when I first put the collection together. The obligation of an

editor of a collection like this one is to mediate between scholarly and critical investigators (himself included) and the reader.
His aim—at least my aim—is to put together not a guidebook
for vacationing tourists but a compendium for travelers who
would go and stay a while.

R. H. P.

May 1968

Bibliographical Note

Bibliographical notes on specific topics will be found following the introductions to each section of this anthology, and bibliographical headnotes precede the individual selections. For a general overview, the best inclusive account of American colonial history is C. M. Andrews, *The Colonial Period of American History*, 4 vols. (New Haven, 1934–1938). A valuable short account is L. B. Wright, *The Atlantic Frontier* (New York, 1947); another is his *Cultural Life of the American Colonies* (New York, 1957). Social history is treated in the second and third volumes of *The History of American Life*, T. J. Wertenbaker's *The First Americans, 1607–1690* (New York, 1927) and J. T. Adam's *Provincial Society, 1690–1732* (New York, 1927). Intellectual history is treated in the opening sections of Merle Curti, *The Growth of American Thought* (New York, 1943) and of Herbert Schneider, *A History of American Philosophy* (New York, 1946). Still the most adequate survey of colonial American literature (understanding "literature" in the broadest sense) is M. C. Tyler, *A History of American Literature, 1607–1765*, 2 vols. (rev. ed., New York, 1897). The first volume of V. L. Parrington, *Main Currents in American Thought* (New York, 1927) suffers most from Parrington's special populist, Jeffersonian bias, but it remains an important and stimulating book, perhaps now a literary work in its own right. The studies of colonial writing in H. M. Jones, *Ideas in America* (Cambridge, 1944) suggest important ways and means of analysis and revaluation, as does his *O Strange New World: American Culture, The Formative Years* (New York, 1964). Parts I and II of Stow Persons, *American Minds* (New York, 1958) offer a sharp summary and analysis of colonial intellectual history. The relevant sections in the first volume of the *Literary History of the United*

States (New York, 1948) offer an invaluable summary of our knowledge of our colonial literature, but do not go very far toward analysis and revaluation; the bibliographies in the third volume and its supplements, however, supersede all others and may be caled definitive for all but the specialist. The essays by Clarence Faust and Leon Howard in *Transitions in American Literary History*, ed. H. H. Clark (Durham, N.C., 1953) do much to suggest the form which future understanding of the period will take.

Textual Note

Whenever possible, texts here printed have been drawn from modern scholarly editions. Where such versions are lacking, texts have been drawn from early editions. Although typographical practice has been modernized, spellings, usages, and locutions have been allowed to stand as in the originals. Obvious errors and omissions have been silently corrected. Unless otherwise noted, dates following titles are those of first publication.

Annotation has been kept to a minimum. Passages in foreign languages have been translated. References to persons, places, and events have been expanded when knowledge of such references is necessary to make sense of passages involved. Proper names occurring in common works of reference, like *Webster's New Collegiate Dictionary* and *The American College Dictionary*, have not been annotated. It has been assumed that the texts can best exhibit themselves without extended commentaries by the editor. Annotation has been directed toward this end.

Grateful acknowledgment is owed the following for permission to reprint versions of texts occurring in books which they have copyrighted: American Book Company, publishers of *The Puritans*, edited by Perry Miller and Thomas Johnson and of *Jonathan Edwards: Representative Selections*, edited by Clarence Faust and Thomas Johnson; American Antiquarian Society, publishers of *The First Century of New England Verse*, edited by Harold Jantz; Princeton University Press, publishers of *The Poetical Works of Edward Taylor*, edited by Thomas Johnson; Yale University Press, publishers of Jonathan Edwards, *Images or Shadows of Divine Things*, edited by Perry Miller; and *The Poems of Edward Taylor*, edited by Donald Stanford; University of North Carolina Press, publishers of Robert Beverly, *The History and Present State of Virginia*, edited by L. B.

Wright; The Arthur H. Clark Company, publishers of *Early Western Travels*, edited by R. G. Thwaites; Harvard University Press, publishers of *Handkerchiefs from Paul*, edited by K. B. Murdock; Harcourt, Brace and World, publishers of *Selections from Cotton Mather*, edited by K. B. Murdock; L. B. Wright and Marion Tinling, editors of *The Secret Diary of William Byrd of Westover, 1709–1712*; Barnes and Noble Inc., publishers of the *Original Narratives of Early American History* series; Columbia University Press, publishers of Mather Byles, *Poems on Several Occasions*, edited by C. L. Carlson and William Dawson, *Poems on Several Occasions*, edited by R. L. Rusk; The Massachusetts Historical Society, publishers of *The Winthrop Papers*; the Henry E. Huntington Library and Art Gallery, publishers of Philip Pain, *Daily Meditations*; Hafner Publishing Company, publishers of *Colonial American Poetry*, edited by Kenneth Silverman.

Contents

IV
THE VIRGINIA GENTLEMAN

V
THE QUAKER

COLONIAL
AMERICAN
WRITING

I

THE VOYAGER

Elizabethan and Stuart voyagers saw in America a land in need of exploitation and a people in need of God and civilization. They felt no contradiction in the union of their ideas of religion and empire; for only in terms of such a union could the voyager—and the planter he became or who came after him—assure himself that his world was ordered and intelligible. It was, as Samuel Purchas said, a "union of spirituals and temporals." The voyager's obsession—a Renaissance obsession—was to make the new world part of the old. If the voyage narratives seldom testify directly to this obsession, they nonetheless furnish us occasional explicit statements of and abundant circumstantial evidence for it. We have to analyze out of the narratives such a valuation of life, its duties, and pleasures precisely because such a valuation is so deeply and integrally imbedded in them.

John Smith is a case in point. A professional soldier turned pamphleteer, not the most modest of men, he published various accounts of his life and adventures, descriptions of lands he had seen, and prescriptions for Englishmen who would go to America. Obviously he is no philosopher. Yet he has a kind of philosophy. And it is that philosophy—one which propagandizes for progress, order, religion, and empire—which holds together his excited accounts of the possibilities of life in a brave new world. The selection from Samuel Purchas, which follows, makes that philosophy explicit. Staying home, he wrote so as to show that America as fact in good part had its origins in America as idea.

Bibliographical Note. The great collections of voyage narratives are Richard Hakluyt's *Principal Navigations* (1598–1600), available in a modern edition in 12 vols. (Glasgow, 1903–1905); and Samuel Purchas's continuation, *Hakluytus Posthumus; or, Purchas His Pilgrimes* (1625), available in a modern edition in 20 vols. (Glasgow, 1905–1907). On the idea of colonization see L. B. Wright, *Religion and Empire* (Chapel Hill, 1943). The monumental study of the idea (European as well as English) of America is Antonello Gerbi, *La Disputa del Nuovo Mundo* (Milan, 1955—in Italian, and Mexico, 1960—in Spanish). Unhappily, no English version is available.

Captain John Smith

(1580–1631)

Bibliographical Note. Smith's writings are collected in E. Arber and A. Bradley, eds., *Travels and Works of Captain John Smith,* 2 vols. (Edinburgh, 1910); the text of the following selection is taken from this edition, I, 187–191 and 208–217. The best account of Smith is in S. E. Morison, *Builders of the Bay Colony* (Boston, 1930), pp. 3–20.

from

A DESCRIPTION OF
NEW ENGLAND (1616)

My first voyage to New England. In the moneth of Aprill, 1614. with two Ships from *London,* of a few Marchants, I chanced to arrive in *New-England,* a parte of *Ameryca*; at the Ile of *Monahigan,* in 43½ of Northerly latitude: our plot was there to take Whales and make tryalls of a Myne of Gold and Copper. If those failed, Fish and Furres was then our refuge, to make our selves savers howsoever. We found this Whale-fishing a costly conclusion: we saw many, and spent much time in chasing them; but could not kill any: they beeing a kinde of Jubartes, and not the Whale that yeelds Finnes and Oyle as wee expected. For our Golde, it was rather the Masters device to get a voyage that projected it, then any

knowledge hee had at all of any such matter. Fish
and Furres was now our guard: and by our late
arrival, and long lingring about the Whale[s], the
prime of both those seasons were past ere wee perceived it; we thinking that their seasons, served
at all times: but wee found it otherwise; for, by
the midst of Iune, the fishing failed. Yet in July
and August some was taken, but not sufficient to
defray so great a charge as our stay required. Of
dry fish we made about 40000., of Cor fish about
7000.

Whilest the sailers fished, my selfe with eight
or nine others of them [that] might best bee
spared; Ranging the coast in a small boat, wee
got for trifles neer 1100 Bcuer skinnes, 100 Martins
[skins], and neer as many Otters; and most of
them within the distancc of twenty leagues.

We ranged the Coast both East and West
much furder; but Eastwards our commodities were
not csteemed, they were so neare the French who
affords them better: and right against us in the
Main [the mainland] was a Ship of Sir Frances
Popphames, that had there such acquaintance,
having many yeares used onely that porte, that the
most parte there, was had by him. And 40 leagues
westwards were two French Ships, that had made
there a great voyage by trade; during the time we
tryed those conclusions, not knowing the Coast,
nor Salvages habitation.

With these Furres, the Trainc [train oil], and
Cor-fish, I returned for England in the Bark:
where within six monthes after our departure from
the Downes, we safe arrived back. The best of this
fish was solde for five pound the hundreth, the
rest by ill usage betwixt three pound and fifty
shillings.

The other ship staied to fit herselfe for Spaine
with the dry fish: which was sould, by the Sailers

reporte that returned, at forty ryalls [20s.] the quintall, each hundred [weight] weighing two quintalls and a halfe.

The situation of New England. New England is that part of America in the Ocean Sea opposite to Nova Albyon [California] in the South Sea, discovered by the most memorable Sir Francis Drake in his voyage about the worlde. In regarde whereto this is stiled New England, beeing in the same latitude. New France, off it, is Northward: Southwardes is Virginia, and all the adioyning Continent, with New Granado, New Spain, New Andolosia, and the West Indies.

Now because I have beene so oft asked such strange questions, of the goodnesse and greatnesse of those spatious Tracts of land, how they can bee thus long unknown, or not possessed by the Spaniard, and many such like demands; I intreat your pardons, if I chance to bee too plaine, or tedious in relating my knowledge for plaine mens satisfaction.

Notes of Florida. Florida is the next adioyning to the Ind[i]es, which unprosperously was attempted to bee planted by the French. A Country farre bigger then England, Scotland, France, and Ireland, yet little knowne to any Christian but by the wonderful ende[a]vours of Ferdinando de Soto, a valiant Spaniard: whose writings in this age is the best guide knowne to search those parts.

Notes of Virginia. Virginia is no Ile (as many doe imagine) but part of the Continent adioyning to Florida; whose bounds may be stretched to the magnitude thereof without offence to any Christian inhabitant. For from the degrees of 30. to 45. his Majestie hath granted his Letters patents, the Coast extending

South-west and North-east aboute 1500 miles; but to follow it aboard, the shore may well be 2000. at the least: of which, 20 miles is the most [that] gives entrance into the Bay of *Chisapeak,* where is the *London* plantation: within which [entrance] is a Country (as you may perceive by the description in a Booke and Map printed in my name of that little I there discovered) [that] may well suffice 300000 people to inhabit.

And Southward adioyneth that part discovered at the charge of Sir *Walter Rawley,* by Sir *Ralph Lane,* and that learned Mathematician Master *Thomas Heryot.*

Northward six or seaven degrees is the River *Sadagahock,* where was planted the Westerne Colony, by that Honourable Patrone of vertue, Sir *Iohn Poppham,* Lord chief Justice of *England.*

Ther[e] is also a relation printed by Captaine *Bartholomew Gosnould,* of *Elizabeths Isles:* and an other by Captaine *Waymouth,* of *Pemmaquid.*

From all these diligent observers, posterity may be bettered by the fruits of their labours. But for divers others that, long before and since, have ranged those parts, within a kenning sometimes of the shore, some touching in one place, some in another, I must entreat them [to] pardon me for omitting them; or if I offend in saying that their true descriptions are concealed, or [were] never well observed, or died with the Authors: so that the Coast is yet still but even as a Coast unknowne and undiscovered.

I have had six or seaven severall plots of those Northern parts, so unlike each to other, and most so differing from any true proportion or resemblance of the Countrey, as they did mee no more good then so much waste paper, though they cost me more. It may be it was not my chance to see the best; but at least others may be deceived as I was, or thro[u]gh dangerous ignorance hazard

themselves as I did, I have drawen a Map from
Point to Point, Ile to Ile, and Harbour to Harbour,
with the Soundings, Sands, Rocks, and Land-
marks as I passed close aboard the Shore in a little
Boat; although there be many things to be observed which the haste of other affaires did cause
me [to] omit. For being sent more to get present
commodities then knowledge by discoveries for
any future good, I had not power to search as I
would: yet it will serve to direct any [that] should
goe that waies, to safe Harbours and the Salvages
habitations. What marchandize and commodities
for their labour they may finde, this following discourse shall plainely demonstrate.

Thus you may see, of this 2000. miles more
then halfe is yet unknowne to any purpose: no,
not so much as the borders of the Sea are yet
certainly discovered. As for the goodness and true
substances of the Land, wee are for [the] most
part yet altogether ignorant of them, unlesse it bee
those parts about the Bay of *Chisapeack,* and
Sagadahock: but onely here and there wee touched
or have seene a little the 'edges of those large
dominions, which doe stretch themselves into the
Maine, God doth know how many thousand miles;
whereof we can yet no more judge, then a stranger
that saileth betwixt *England* and *France* can describe the Harbors and dangers, by landing here or
there in some River or Bay, tell thereby the goodnesse and substances of *Spaine, Italy, Germany,
Bohemia, Hungaria* and the rest. By this you may
perceive how much they erre, that think every one
which hath bin at *Virginia,* understandeth or
knowes what *Virginia* is: Or that the *Spaniards*
know one half quarter of those Territories they
possesse; no, not so much as the true circumference of *Terra Incognita,* whose large dominions
may equalize the greatnesse and goodnes of *America,* for any thing yet known. It is strange with

what small power hee hath raigned in the *East Ind[i]es;* and few will understand the truth of his strength in *America:* where he having so much to keepe with such a pampered force, they neede not greatly feare his furie in the *Bermudas, Virginia, New France,* or *New England.* Beyond whose bounds, *America* doth stretch many thousand miles: into the frozen partes whereof, one Master *Hutson* [*Hudson*], an English Mariner, did make the greatest discoverie of any Christian I know of, where he unfortunately died. For *Affrica,* had not the industrious Portugales ranged her unknowne parts, who would have sought for wealth among those fryed Regions of blacke brutish Negers; where notwithstanding all the wealth and admirable adventures and endeavours more then 140 years [1476–1616], they knowe not one third of those blacke habitations.

But it is not a worke for every one, to manage such an affaire as makes a discoverie, and plants a Colony. It requires all the best parts of Art, Judgement, Courage, Honesty, Constancy, Diligence, and Industrie, to doe but neere well. Some are more proper for one thing then another; and therein are to be imployed: and nothing breedes more confusion then misplacing and misimploying men in their undertakings. *Columbus, Cortez, Pitzara, Soto, Magellanes,* and the rest served more than a prentiship to learne how to begin their most memorable attempts in the *West Ind[i]es:* which to the wonder of all ages successfully they effected, when many hundreds of others, farre above them in the worlds opinion, beeing instructed but by relation, came to shame and confusion in actions of small moment, who doubtlesse in other matters, were both wise, discreet, generous, and couragious. I say not this to detract any thing from their incomparable merits, but to answer those questionlesse questions that keep us back from imitating the worthinesse of their brave spirits that advanced themselves from poore Souldiers to great Captaines, their posterity to great Lords, their King to be one of the greatest Potentates on earth, and the fruites of their labours, his greatest glory, power, and renowne.

. . . . .

A note for men that have great spirits, and smal meanes.

Who can desire more content, that hath small meanes; or but only his merit to advance his fortune, then to tread, and plant that ground hee hath purchased by the hazard of his life? If he have but the taste of virtue and magnanimitie, what to such a minde can bee more pleasant, then planting and building a foundation for his Posteritie, gotte from the rude earth, by Gods blessing and his owne industrie, without preiudice to any? If hee have any graine of faith or zeale in Religion, what can hee doe lesse hurtfull to any: or more agreeable to God, then to seeke to convert those poore Salvages to know Christ, and humanitie, whose labors with discretion will triple requite thy charge and paines? What so truly su[i]tes with honour and honestie, as the discovering things unknowne? erecting Townes, peopling Countries, informing the ignorant, reforming things unjust, teaching virtue; and gaine to our Native mother-countrie a kingdom to attend her: finde imployment for those that are idle, because they know not what to doe: so farre from wronging any, as to cause Posteritie to remember thee; and remembring thee, ever honour that remembrance with praise?

Consider: What were the beginnings and endings of the Monarkies of the *Chaldeans,* the *Syrians,* the *Grecians,* and *Romanes,* but this one rule; What was it they would not doe, for the good of the commonwealth, or their Mother-citie? For ex-

ample: *Rome*, What made her such a Mon-
archesse, but onely the adventures of her youth,
not in riots at home; but in dangers abroade? and
the justice and judgement out of their experience,
when they grewe aged. What was their ruine and
hurt, but this; The excesse of idlenesse, the fond-
nesse of Parents, the want of experience in Magistrates, the admiration of their undeserved honours,
the contempt of true merit, their unjust jeal-
o[u]sies, their politicke incredulities, their hypo-
criticall seeming goodnesse, and their deeds of
secret lewdnesse? finally, in fine, growing onely
formall temporists, all that their predecessors got
in many years, they lost in few daies. Those by
their pain and vertues became Lords of the world;
they by their ease and vices became slaves to their
servants. This is the difference betwixt the use of
Armes in the field, and on the monuments of
stones; the golden age and the leaden age, prosperity and miserie, justice and corruption, substance and shadowes, words and deeds, experience
and imagination, making Commonwealths and
marring Commonwealths, the fruits of vertue and
the conclusions of vice.

Then, who would live at home idly (or thinke
in himselfe any worth to live) onely to eate, drink,
and sleepe, and so die? Or by consuming that
carelessly, his friends got worthily? Or by using
that miserably, that maintained vertue honestly?
Or for being descended nobly, pine with the vaine
vaunt of great kindred, in penurie? Or (to maintaine a silly shewe of bravery) toyle out thy heart,
soule, and time, basely; by shifts, tricks, cards, and
dice? Or by relating newes of others actions, sharke
here or there for a dinner, or supper; deceive thy
friends, by faire promises and dissimulation, in
borrowing where thou never intendest to pay;
offend the lawes, surfeit with excesse, burden thy
Country, abuse thy selfe, despaire in want, and

then couzen thy kindred, yea even thine owne brother, and wish thy parents death (I will not say damnation) to have their estates? though thou seest what honours, and rewards, the world yet hath for them [who] will seeke them and worthily deserve them.

I would be sor[r]y to offend, or that any should mistake my honest meaning: for I wish good to all, hurt to none. But rich men for the most part are growne to that dotage, through their pride in their wealth, as though there were no accident could end it, or their life.

And what hellish care do such take to make it their owne miserie, and their Countries spoile, especially when there is most neede of their imployment? drawing by all manner of inventions, from the Prince and his honest subiects, even the vitall spirits of their powers and estates: as if their Bagges, or Bragges, were so powerfull a defence, the malicious could not assault them; when they are the onely baite, to cause us not to be onely assaulted; but betrayed and murdered in our owne security, ere we well perceive it.

An example of secure coveteousness. May not the miserable ruine of *Constantinople*, their impregnable walles, riches, and pleasures [at] last taken by the *Turke* (which are but a bit, in comparison of their now mightines) remember us of the effects of private covetousness? at which time the good *Emperour* held himselfe rich enough, to have such rich subjects, so formall in all excesse of vanity, all kinde of delicacie and prodigalitie. His povertie when the *Turke* besieged, the citizens (whose marchandizing thoughts were onely to get wealth, little conceiving the desperate resolution of a valiant expert enemy) left the Emp[erour] so long to his conclusions, having spent all he had to pay his young, raw, discontented Souldiers; that sodainly he, they,

and their citie were all a prey to the devouring
Turke. And what they would not spare for the
maintenance of them who adventured their lives
to defend them, did serve onely their enemies to
torment them, their friends, and countrey, and
all Christendome to this present day. Let this
lamentable example remember you that are rich
(seeing there arc such great theeves in the world
to robbe you) not [to] grudge to lend some proportion, to breed them that have little, yet [are]
willing to learne how to defend you: for, it is too
late when the deede is a-doing.

The *Romanes* estate hath beene worse then
this: for, the meere covetousnesse and extortion of
a few of them, so mooved the rest, that not having
any imployment but contemplation; their great
judgements grew to so great malice, as themselves
were sufficient to destroy themselves by faction:
Let this moove you to embrace imployment for
those whose educations, spirits, and judgements
want but your purses; not onely to prevent such
accustomed dangers, but also to gaine more
thereby then you have.

And you fathers, that are either so foolishly
fond, or so miscrably covetous, or so willfully
ignorant, or so negligently carelesse, as that you
will rather maintaine your children in idle wantonness, till they grow your masters; or become so
basely unkinde, as they wish nothing but your
deaths; so that both sorts grow dissolute: and
although you would wish them any where to
escape the gallowes, and ease your cares; though
they spend you here one, two, or three hundred
pound[s] a yeer; you would grudge to give halfe so
much in adventure with them, to obtaine an
estate, which in a small time, but with a little
assistance of your providence, might be better
then your owne. But if an Angell should tell you,
[that] any place yet unknowne can afford such

fortunes; you would not beleeve him, no more
then *Columbus* was beleeved there was any such
Land as is now the well knowne abounding *America*; much lesse such large Regions as are yet
unknowne, as well in *America*, as in *Affrica*, and
Asia, and *Terra incognita*; where were courses for
gentlemen (and them that would be so reputed)
more suiting their qualities, then begging from
their Princes generous disposition, the labours of
his subiects, and the very marrow of his maintenance.

The Authors
conditions.
I have not been so ill bred, but I have tasted of
Plenty and *Pleasure*, as well as *Want* and *Miserie*:
nor doth necessitie yet, or occasion of discontent,
force me to these endeavors: nor am I ignorant
what small thanke I shall have for my paines; or
that many would have the Worlde imagine them
to be of great judgement, that can but blemish
these my designes, by their witty objections and
detractions: yet (I hope) my reasons with my
deeds, will so prevaile with some, that I shall not
want imployment in these affaires, to make the
most blinde see his owne senselessnesse, and in-
credulity; Hoping that gaine will make them
affect that, which Religion, Charity, and the
Common good cannot. It were but a poore device in me, To deceive my selfe; much more the
King, State, my Friends and Countrey, with
these inducements: which, seeing his Majestie
hath given permission, I wish all sorts of worthie,
honest, industrious spirits, would understand: and
if they desire any further satisfaction, I will doe
my best to give it: Not to perswade them to goe
onely; but goe with them: Not leave them there;
but live with them there.

I will not say, but by ill providing and undue
managing, such courses may be taken, [that] may

make us miserable enough: But if I may have the execution of what I have projected; if they want to eate, let them eate or never digest Me. If I performe what I say, I desire but that reward out of the gaines [which] may su[i]te my paines, quality, and condition. And if I abuse you with my tongue, take my head for satisfaction. If any dislike at the yeares end, defraying their charge, by my consent they should freely returne. I feare not want of companie sufficient, were it but knowne what I know of those Countries; and by the proofe of that wealth I hope yearely to returne, if God please to blesse me from such accidents, as are beyond my power in reason to prevent: For, I am not so simple to thinke, that ever any other motive then wealth, will ever erect there a Commonweale; or draw companie from their ease and humours at home, to stay in *New England* to effect my purposes.

And lest any should think the toile might be insupportable, though these things may be had by labour, and diligence: I assure my selfe there are who delight extreamly in vaine pleasure, that take much more paines in *England*, to enjoy it, then I should doe heere [*New England*] to gaine wealth sufficient: and yet I thinke they should not have halfe such sweet content: for, our pleasure here is still gaines; in *England* charges and losse. Heer nature and liberty affords us that freely, which in *England* we want, or it costeth us dearely. What pleasure can be more, then (being tired with any occasion a-shore, in planting Vines, Fruits, or Hearbs, in contriving their owne Grounds, to the pleasure of their owne mindes, their Fields, Gardens, Orchards, Buildings, Ships, and other works, &c.) to recreate themselves before their owne doores, in their owne boates upon the Sea; where man, woman and childe, with a small hooke and

The planters pleasures, and profits.

line, by angling, may take diverse sorts of excellent fish, at their pleasures? And is it not pretty sport, to pull up two pence, six pence, and twelve pence, as fast as you can ha[u]le and veare a line? He is a very bad fisher [that] cannot kill in one day with his hooke and line, one, two, or three hundred Cods: which dressed and dried, if they be sould there for ten shillings the hundred, though in England they will give more than twentie, may not both the servant, the master, and marchant, be well content with this gaine? If a man worke but three dayes in seaven, he may get more then hee can spend, unlesse he will be excessive. Now that Carpenter, Mason, Gardiner, Taylor, Smith, Sailer, Forgers, or what other, may they not make this a pretty recreation though they fish but an houre in a day, to take more then they eate in a weeke? or if they will not eate it, because there is so much better choice; yet sell it, or change it, with the fisher men, or marchants, for any thing they want. And what sport doth yeeld a more pleasing content, and lesse hurt or charge then angling with a hooke; and crossing the sweete ayre from Ile to Ile, over the silent streames of a calme Sea? Wherein the most curious may finde pleasure, profit, and content.

Thus, though all men be not fishers: yet all men, whatsoever, may in other matters doe as well. For necessity doth in these cases so rule a Commonwealth, and each in their severall functions, as their labours in their qualities may be as profitable, because there is a necessary mutuall use of all.

Imploy-
ments for
gentlemen.

For Gentlemen, what exercise should more delight them, then ranging dayly those unknowne parts, using fowling and fishing, for hunting and hawking? and yet you shall see the wilde-haukes give you some pleasure, in seeing them stoope (six

or seaven after one another) an houre or two together, at the skuls of fish in the faire harbours,
as those a-shore at a foule; and never trouble nor
torment yourselues, with watching, mewing, feeding, and attending them: nor kill horse and man
with running and crying, *See you not a hawk?*
For hunting also: the woods, lakes, and rivers
affoord not oncly chase sufficient, for any that
delights in that kinde of toyle, or pleasure; but
such beasts to hunt, that besides the delicacy of
their bodies for food, their skins are so rich, as
may well recompencc thy dayly labour, with a
Captains pay.

For labourers, if those that sowe hemp, rape, tur- *Employ-*
nups, parsnips, carrats, cabidge, and such like; *ments for*
give 20, 30, 40, 50 shillings yearely for an acre of *labourers.*
ground, and meat drinke and wages to use it, and
yet grow rich; when better, or at least as good
ground, may be had, and cost nothing but labour;
it seems strange to me, any such should there
grow poore.

My purpose is not to perswade children from
their parents; men from their wives; nor servants
from their masters: onely, such as with free consent may be spared: But that each parish, or
village, in Citie or Countrey, that will but apparell their fatherlesse children, of thirteene or
fourteen years of age, or young mar[r]ied people,
that have small wealth to live on; heere by their
labour may live exceeding well: provided alwaies
that first there bee a sufficient power to command
them, houses to receive them, meanes to defend
them, and meet provisions for them; for, any
place may bee overlain: and it is most necessarie
to have a fortresse (ere this grow to practice) and
sufficient masters (as, Carpenters, Masons, Fishers, Fowlers, Gardiners, Husbandmen, Sawyers,
Smiths, Spinsters, Taylors, Weavers, and such

like) to take ten, twelve, or twentie, or as ther is occasion, for Apprentises. The Masters by this may quicklie growe rich; these may learne their trades themselves, to doe the like; to a generall and an incredible benefit, for King, and Countrey, Master, and Servant.

Example of the Spanyards. It would bee an historie of a large volume, to recite the adventures of the *Spanyards*, and *Portugals*, their affronts and defeats, their dangers and miseries; which with such incomparable honour and constant resolution, so farre beyond beleefe, they have attempted and indured in their discoveries and plantations, as may well condemne us, of too much imbecillitie, sloth, and negligence: yet the Authors of those new inventions, were held as ridiculous, for a long time, as now are others, that doe but seek to imitate their unparalleled vertues. And though we see daily their mountaines of wealth (sprong from the plants of their generous indevours) yet is our sensualitie and untowardnesse such, and so great, that wee either ignorantly beleeve nothing, or so curiously contest to prevent wee knowe not what future events; that wee either so neglect, or oppresse and discourage the present, as wee spoile all in the making, crop all in the blooming; and building upon faire sand, rather than rough rockes, judge that wee knowe not, governe that wee have not, feare that which is not; and for feare some should doe too well, force such against their willes to be idle or as ill. And who is he [that] hath judgement, courage, and any industrie or qualitie with understanding, will leave his Countrie, his hopes at home, his certaine estate, his friends, pleasures, libertie, and the preferment sweete *England* doth afford to all degrees, were it not to advance his

CAPTAIN JOHN SMITH 19

fortunes by injoying his deserts? whose prosperitie
once appearing will incourage others: but it must
be cherished as a childe, till it be able to goe, and
understand it selfe, and not corrected nor oppressed above it[s] strength, ere it knowe wherefore.

A child can neither performe the office, nor
deedes of a man of strength, nor indure that
affliction He is able; nor can an Apprentice at the
first performe the part of a Maister. And if twentie yeeres bee required to make a child a man,
seven yeares limited [to] an apprentice for his
trade, if scarce an age be sufficient to make a
wise man a States man, and commonly a man
dies ere he hath learned to be discreet: If perfection be so hard to be obtained, as of necessitie
there must bee practice, as well as theorick: Let
no man much condemne this paradox opinion, to
say, that halfe seaven yeeres is scarce sufficient,
for a good capacitie, to learne in these affaires,
how to carrie himselfe: and who ever shall trie
in these remote places the erecting of a Colony,
shall finde at the ende of seaven yeares occasion
enough to use all his discretion: and, in the
Interim all the content, rewardes, gaines, and
hopes will be necessarily required, to be given to
the beginning, till it bee able to creepe, to stand,
and goe, yet time enough to keepe it from running: for there is no feare it wil grow too fast, or
ever to any thing; excepte libertie, profit, honor,
and prosperitie there found, more binde the planters of those affaires, in devotion to effect it; then
bondage, violence, tyranny, ingratitude and such
double dealing, as bindes freemen to become
slaves, and honest men [to] turne knaves: which
hath ever bin the ruine of the most popular com-
mon-weales; and is verie unlikelie ever well to
begin in a new.

The blisse of Who seeth not what is the greatest good of
Spaine. the *Spanyard,* but these new conclusions, in
searching those unknowne parts of the unknowne
world? By which meanes hee dives even into the
verie secrets of all his Neighbours, and the most
part of the world: and when the *Portugale* and
Spanyard had found the *East* and *West Indies;*
how many did condemn themselves, that did not
accept of that honest offer of Noble *Columbus?*
who, upon our neglect, brought them to it, perswading our selves the world had no such places
as they had found: and yet ever since wee finde,
they still (from time to time) have found new
Lands, new Nations, and trades, and still daily
dooe finde both in *Asia, Africa, Terra Incognita,*
and *America;* so that there is neither Soldier nor
Mechanick, from the Lord to the beggar, but
those parts afforde them all imploiment; and
discharge their Native soile, of so many thousands
of all sorts, that else, by their sloth, pride, and
imperfections, would long ere this have troubled
their neighbours, or have eaten the pride of
Spaine it selfe.

Now he knowes little, that knowest not *England* may well spare many more people then
Spaine, and is as well able to furnish them with
all manner of necessaries. And seeing, for all they
have, they cease not still to search for that they
have not, and know not; It is strange we should
be so dull, as not [to] maintaine that which wee
have, and pursue that wee know.

Surely I am sure many would taste it ill, to
bee abridged of the titles and honours of their
predecessors: when if but truly they would judge
themselves; looke how inferior they are to their
noble vertues, so much they are unworthy of their
honours and livings: which never were ordained
for showes and shadowes, to maintaine idlenesse
and vice; but to make them more able to abound

in honor, by heroycall deeds of action, judgement, pietic, and vertue. What was it, they would not doe both in purse and person, for the good of the Commonwealth? which might move them presently to set out their spare kindred in these generous designes.

Religion, aboue all things, should move us (especially the Clergie) if wee were religious, to shewe our faith by our workes; in converting those poore salvages, to the knowledge of God, seeing what paines the *Spanyards* take to bring them to their adulterated faith. Honor might move the Gentrie, the valiant, and industrious; and the hope and assurance of wealth, all; if wee were that we would seeme, and be accounted. Or be we so far inferior to other nations, or our spirits so far dejected, from our auncient predecessors, or our mindes so [set] upon spoile, piracie, and such villany, as to serve the *Portugall*, *Spanyard*, *Dutch*, *French*, or *Turke*, (as to the cost of *Europe*, too many dooe) rather then our God, our King, our Country, and our selves? excusing our idlenesse, and our base complaints, by want of imploiement; when heere is such choise of all sorts, and for all degrees, in the planting and discovering these North parts of *America*.

Samuel Purchas

(1575?–1626)

Bibliographical Note. Purchas edited and wrote much of *Hakluytus Posthumus; or, Purchas His Pilgrimes* (1625). The following selection is taken from the Glasgow, 1906 edition, XIX, pp. 230–238, pp. 242–243.

from

A DISCOURSE ON VIRGINIA (1625)

The workes of God, and varietie there seen set forth his glorie.

God is a Glorious Circle, whose Center is every where, his circumference no where: himselfe to himselfe is Circle and Circumference, the Ocean of Entitie, that very ubique, from whom, to whom (the Centre of unitie) all diversified lines of varietie issue and returne. And although we every where feele his present Deitie, yet the difference of heavenly climate and influence, causing such discording concord of dayes, nights, seasons; such varietie of meteors, elements, aliments; such noveltie in Beasts, Fishes, Fowles; such luxuriant plentie and admirable raritie of Trees, Shrubs, Hearbs: such fertilitie of soyle, insinuation of Seas, multiplicitie of Rivers, safetie of Ports, healthfulnesse of ayre, opportunities of habitation, materialls for action, objects for contemplation, haps in present, hopes of future, worlds of varietie in that diversified world; doe quicken our mindes to apprehend, whet our tongues to declare, and fill both with arguments of divine praise. On the other side considering so good a Countrey, so bad people, having little of Humanitie but shape, ignorant of Civilitie, of Arts, of Religion; more brutish then the beasts they hunt, more wild and unmanly then that unmanned wild Countrey, which they range rather then inhabite; captivated also to Satans tyranny in foolish pieties, mad impieties, wicked idlenesse, busie and bloudy wickednesse: hence have wee fit objects of zcale and pitie, to deliver from the power of darknesse, that where it was said, Yee are not my people, they may bee called the children of the living God: that Justice may so proceed in rooting out those murtherers, that yet in judgement (imitating Gods dealing with us) wee may remember Mercy to such as their owne innocence shall protect, and Hope shall in Charitie judge capable of Christian Faith. And let men know that hee which converteth a sinner from the crrour of his way, shall save a soule from death, and shall hide a multitude of sinnes. And Saviours shall thus come on Mount Zion to judge the Mount of Esau, and the Kingdome (of Virginia) shall be Lord. Thus shall wee at once overcome both Men and Devills, and espouse Virginia to one husband, presenting her as a chast Virgin to Christ. If the eye of Adventurers were thus single, how soone and all the body should be light? But the loving our selves more then God, hath detained so great blessings from us to Virginia, and from Virginia to us. Godlinesse hath the promises of this life, and that which is to come. And if wee be carefull to doe Gods will, he will be ready to doe ours.

All the rich endowments of Virginia, her Virgin-portion from the creation nothing lessened, are wages for all this worke: God in wisedome

Propagation of the Gospell: & rewards thereof.

Ose 2.

Jam. 5. 20.

Obad. ult.

2. Cor. 11.2.
Matth. 6. 22.

1. Tim. 4. 8.

having enriched the Savage Countries, that those
riches might be attractives for Christian suters,
which there may sowe spirituals and reape temporals.

*Answeres to
Objections:
& first to the
want of Gold
and Silver
Mines.*

But what are those riches, where we heare of no
Gold nor Silver, and see more impoverished here
then thence enriched, and for Mines we heare of
none but Iron? Iron mindes! Iron age of the
world! who gave Gold or Silver the Monopoly of
wealth, or made them the Almighties favorites?
Precious perils, specious punishments, whose
originall is neerest hell, whose house is darknesse,
which have no eye to see the heavens, nor admit
heavens eye (guilty malefactors) to see them;
never produced to light but by violence, and convinced, upon records written in bloud, the oc-
casioners of violence in the World; which have
infected the surface of their native earth with deformity and sterility (these Mines being fit em-
blemes of mindes covetous, stored with want, and
ever wanting their owne store) her bowels with
darknesse, damps, deaths, causing trouble to the
neighbour Regions, and mischiefe to the remotest!
Penurious mindes! Is there no riches but Gold
Mines? Are Iron Mines neglected, rejected for
hopes of Silver? What, and who else is the Al-
chymist, and impostor, which turnes the World,
and Men, and all into Iron? And how much Iron-
workes in Warres and Massacres hath American
Gold and Silver wrought thorow all Christendome? Neither speake I this, as if our hopes were
blasted, and growne deplorate and desperate this
way, the Country being so little searched, and the
remote in-land-Mountaines unknowne: but to
shew the sordid tincture and base alloy of these
Mine-mindes. Did not the Spanish Iron (tell me
you that contemne Iron-mines) draw to it the
Indian Silver and Gold? I will not be a Prophet
for Spaine from Virginia. But I cannot forget the

wily apophthegme of the Pilots Boy in the Cacafuego, a great Ship laden with treasure taken in the
South Sea, by Sir Francis Drake; who seeing the
English Ordnance command such treasure from
the Spanish Cacafuego; Our Ship, said he, shall be
called the Cacaplata, and the English may be
named the Cacafuego. I will not be so unmannerly
to give you the homely English; it is enough that
English Iron brought home the Spanish-Indian
Silver and Gold. But let us consult with the wisest
Councellour. Canaan, Abrahams promise, Israels
inheritance, type of heaven, and joy of the earth!
What were her riches? were they not the Grapes
of Eshcol, the balme of Gilead, the Cedary neighbourhood of Libanus, the pastury vale of Jericho,
the dewes of heaven, fertility of soile, temper of
climat, the flowing (not with Golden Sands, but)
with Milke and Hony (necessaries, and pleasures
of life, not bottomelesse gulfes of lust) the commodious scituation for two Seas, and other things
like (in how many inferiour?) to this of Virginia.
What golden Country ever nourished with her
naturall store the hundreth part of men, in so
small a proportion of earth, as David there mus
tered, being 1100000. of Israel, and 500000.[*] of
Juda, not reckoning the Tribes of Levi and Benjamin, all able men for warres? And after him, in
a little part of that little Jehoshaphat (More I
dare say then the Spaniards can finde in one
hundred times so much, of their Mine lands, and
choose their best in Peru, New Spaine, and the
Ilands) the Scriptures containing an infallible
muster-booke of 1160000. able Souldiers in his
small territories?

That then is the richest Land which can feede
most men, Man being a mortall God, the best part
of the best earth, and visible end of the visible
World. What remarkeable Gold or Silver Mines
hath France, Belgia, Lumbardy, or other the rich-

[*] Compare
2. Sam. 24.
with 1.
Chron. 21. It
seemes that
there were
above two
millions of
men besides
women and
children.

est peeces of Europe? what hath Babylonia, Mauritania, or other the best of Asia and Africke? What this our fertile Mother England? Aske our late Travellers which saw so much of Spaine, the most famous part of Europe for Mynes of old, and inriched with the Mynes of the New World, if an Englishman needs to envy a Spaniard, or prefer a Spanish life and happinesse to his owne. Their old Mynes made them the servants of Rome and Carthage: and what their Mynes and mindes doe now I leave them to others. Once, as the Mynes are in barrennest soyle, and covetous men have least, even when they are had of most money (mediis ut Tantalus undis) so I have heard that in Spaine is lesse Gold and Silver, then in other parts of Europe, (I dare not mention the proportions) from both Spanish and English relation: their usuall money also (to meddle with no more) is of base mettall, and their greatest summes computed by Maravedis lesse then our later tokens: except which (devised for poorer uses of the poorest) England of long time knowes no base monyes: and hath seene plentie of Silver and Gold, of Wine and Oyle which (grow not in her) when Spaine, which produceth these, is fed with salads, and drinketh water, helped now and then with Hogges-kinne unsavoury Wine. The Indian Fountaines runne with golden and silver streames (sic vos non vobis) not to themselves, but into that Spanish Cisterne; and these Cisternes are like those of the London Water-house, which hath the Conduit Pipes alway open in the bottome, so that a thousand other Cisternes hold more water then it: so may it be said of the other; it is not Concha but Canalis, a Pipe rather then Cisterne, a Cash-keeper rather then Owner; and (which is spoken of better things) remaining poore, makes many rich. To proceed, are not Myners the most miserable of Slaves, toyled continually, and unto mani-

fold deaths tired for others, in bringing to light
those Treasures of darknesse, and living (if they
live, or if that bee a life) in the suburbs of Hell,
to make others dreame of Heaven? Yea Paradise,
the modell of heaven, had in it no Minerals, nor
was Adam in his innocency, or Noah after the
Worlds recovery, both Lords of all, employed in
Mines, but (in those happy workes which Virginia
inviteth England unto) in Vines, Gardening, and
Husbandry. Neither let any man thinke that I
pleade against the sourenesse of the Grapes, like
the Foxe which could not reach them: but I seriously shew that they are calves and not men,
which adore the golden Calfe, or Nabuchadnezzars
great golden statue, as if the body were not more
then raiment, and those things to be preferred to
money, for whose sake mony (the creature of man;
base Idolatry where the Creator worships his
creature!) was first ordained, and still hath both
use and being.

Doe we not see in this respect, that the Silkes, *Virginias*
Calicos, Drugges, and Spices of the East swallow *high valua-*
up (not to mention the Belgian whirlepoole) all *tion.*
the Mines of the West? and that one Carricke
carrieth more Rials thither, then perhaps some
whole Region in Spaine retaineth for vulgar use?
And whence are English, Portugals, or Dutchmen
fitted for that commerce? as if America had
ominously (for other just reason there is none)
beene called India, as if the West were but drudge
and factor for the East. And what hath dispeopled
the New World, not leaving in some places one
of Millions, but Auri sacra fames, others killing
them in the Mines, or they killing themselves to
prevent the Mines? Let it be riches enough, that
Sir Thomas Dale testified by Letters from thence,
and after his returne to me that foure of the best
Kingdomes of Christendome were not for naturall
endowments comparable to Virginia: and which

Cap. Joh.
Smith.
I have heard of one which hath travelled in all the best Regions of Europe, and hath seene more of Virginia then perhaps any man else, and which needes not speake for any gaine there or thence gotten, as no reputed favourite or favourer of that Society and their actions; that he hath seene no Country to be preferred for soile, nor for commodious Rivers to be compared.

And if successe hath not beene correspondent to English hopes: who seeth not the causes of those diseasters?

Answer to
the objected
ill successes
and causes
thereof.
Division that taile-headed Amphisbæna and many-headed monster, deformed issue of that difformed old Serpent, in some of the Colony there & Company here, hath from time to time thrust in her forged venomous tongue, wherby they have

Jud. 5116.
Prov. 13. 10.
swolne with deadly poison of great thoughts of heart (onely by pride doe men make contention) with blinde-staring eyes of self-love abounding in their own sense: whence suspicions, jealousies, factions, partialities to friends and dependants, wilfull obstinacies, and other furious passions have transported men from Virginias good and their owne. Covetousnesse hath distorted others to minde earth and not heaven, in hastinesse of more then speedy returne and present gaine, forgetting

1. Tim. 6.
that Godlinesse is the best gaine, and that they are planting a Colony, not reaping a harvest, for a publike and not (but in subordinate order) private wealth. A long time Virginia was thought to be much encombered with Englands excrements, some vicious persons, as corrupt levin sowring, or as plague sores infecting others, and that Colony was made a Port Exquiline for such as by ordure or vomit were by good order and physicke worthy to be evacuated from This Body: whence not only lazie drones did not further the Plantation, but wicked Waspes with sharking, and the worst, that is beggerly tyrants, frustrated and supplanted the

labours of others. Cælum non animum mutant
qui trans mare currunt. A prodigious Prodigall
here, is not easily metamorphosed in a Virginian
passage to a thrifty Planter: nor can there neede
wiser choise or more industrious course in any
undertaking, then is requisite in a Christian Colonies plantation amongst Infidels. Which I suppose
hath beene carefully by many Adventurers practised: and whatsoever faults happened by ignorance in the beginnings, neglect of seasons, riot,
sloath, occasionall wants of or in Governours or
Government, abuses of Mariners, trechery of Fugitives, and Savages; and other diseases, which have
in part attended all new Plantations, and consumed many: experience I hope by this time hath
taught to prevent or remedy. The late barbarous
Massacre (hinc illæ lachrymæ) still bleedeth, and
when things were reported to be in better forwardnesse then ever, in great part blasted those hopefull blossomes, disjointed the proceedings in the
Iron workes, Vineyards, Mulberry plants; and in
sudden shifts for life, exposed them to manifold
necessities; insomuch, that many of the Principals
being slain, the rest surprised with feare, reduced
themselves almost from eighty to eight Plantations, whereby pestered with multitude, and destitute of Corne and other forsaken necessaries, they
incurred a grievous and generall sicknesse, which
being increased by infection of some passengers
tainted in their Ship-passage with corrupt Beere,
there followed a mortality which consumed about
five hundred persons, besides three hundred and
fifty or thereabouts murthered in that Savage-
Massacre. All which notwithstanding, there remaine, some have if truely calculated and con-
jectured eighteene hundred persons: for whose security and provision it hath pleased his Majesty to
have a Royall care, as likewise the Honorable
Lords of his Majesties privy Councell, besides the

The massacre hath been the chiefe cause of later miscarying.

This number of 1800. was presented by the Companie to the Lords of the Councell.

honorable endevours of the Councell and well affected members of that Society, which God almighty, the great Founder of Colonies, prosper.

Arguments for Virginian plantation, as being honorable.

Now that I may shew Virginia worthy those princely, honorable and industrious thoughts, I have adventured briefely to point out, rather then to paint out her beauty and attractive ornaments.

1. Religion.

First Religion (as is before observed) inviteth us there to seeke the Kingdome of God first, and all other things shall be ministred to us, and added as advantage to the bargaine: seeke the Kingdome of God, and see an earthly Kingdome in recompence, as the earnest, and the heavenly Kingdome for our full paiment. Of glorifying God in his word and workes in this designe is already spoken.

2. Humanitie.

Secondly, Humanity and our common Nature forbids to turne our eyes from our owne flesh; yea commands us to love our neighbours as our selves, and to play the good Samaritan with these our neighbours (though of another Nation and Religion, as the wounded Jew was to him) to recover them if it be possible, as by Religion, from the power of Sathan to God; so by humanity and civility from Barbarisme and Savagenesse to good manners and humaine polity.

3. Honor of the English Nation.

Thirdly, the Honour of our Nation enjoyneth us not basely to loose the glory of our forefathers acts, which here have beene shewed in King Henry the seventh, King Henry the eight, King Edward the sixt, and Queene Elizabeths times, all which illustrated their names by Discovery of Realmes remote, unknowne parts and ports (and the first, first of all Kings, and the last holding to the last) Discovering and possessing these, and leaving them as just inheritance to his Majesty. What shame to a degenerate posterity, to loose so honorable a claime, and gaine; yea, to neglect that which many English have purchased with doing and suffering so much, and not with their sweate alone, their care and cost, but with their deerest bloud and manifold deaths?

Fourthly, wee may reckon the Honour of our King, and his Royall posterity: to which, in time Virginia may performe as much with equall manuring as ever Britannia and Ireland could promise when first they became knowne to the then civiller World. And were not comparisons odious! I am sure I heard Sir Thomas Dale confidently and seriously exulting in private conference with me, in the hopes of future greatnesse from Virginia, to the English Crowne. And if the wise King wisely said, the honour of a King is in the multitude of his Subjects, loe here the way to preserve, employ, encrease them; and for his Majesty to reach his long royall armes to another World. The Roman Empire sowed Roman Colonies thorow the World, as the most naturall and artificiall way to win and hold the World Romaine.

4. Honour of the King.

Fifthly, the honour of the Kingdome, thus growing and multiplying into Kingdomes, that as Scotland and England seeme sisters, so Virginia, New England, New found Land in the Continent already planted in part with English Colonies, together with Bermuda, and other Ilands may be the adopted and legall Daughters of England. An honorable designe, to which Honor stretcheth her faire hand, the five fingers whereof are adorned with such precious Rings, each enriched with invaluable Jewels of Religion, Humanity, Inheritance, the King, the Kingdome: Honos alit artes, omnesque incenduntur ad studia gloria.

5. Honor of the Kingdome.

6. Argument of profit, generally propounded.

And if Honour hath prevailed with honorable and higher spirits, we shall come laden with arguments of profit to presse meaner hands and hearts to the service of Virginia. Onely I desire that men bring their hearts first, and consider that the very names of a Colony and Plantation doe import a reasonable and seasonable culture, and planting before a Harvest and Vintage can be expected: which if they here exercise our Faith and Hope both for earth and heaven, where all things are prepared; let us not in ruder and cruder foundations and beginnings there, precipitate unto hasty fals.

. . . . .

Arguments of particular comodities and commodiousnesse.

Looke upon Virginia; view her lovely lookes (howsoever like a modest Virgin she is now vailed with wild Coverts and shadie Woods, expecting rather ravishment then Mariage from her Native Savages) survay her Heavens, Elements, Situation; her divisions by armes of Bayes and Rivers into so goodly and well proportioned limmes and members; her Virgin portion nothing empaired, nay not yet improoved, in Natures best Legacies; the neighbouring Regions and Seas so commodious and obsequious; her opportunities for offence and defence; and in all these you shall see, that she is worth the wooing and loves of the best Husband. First, for her Heavens and Climate, she with her Virgin Sisters hath the same (being extended from 30. to 45. degrees of North latitude) with the best parts of Europe, namely the fat of Græcia, Thracia, Spaine, Italie, Morea, Sicilia, (and if we will looke more Northward to the height of France and Britaine, there her Sisters New England, New Scotland, and New-found-land, promise hopefull and kinde entertainment to all Adventurers. If you looke Southwards, you may parallel it with

Barbarie, Egypt, and the fertilest parts of Africke)
and in Asia, all that Chuersonessus, somctime the
seate of foure thousand Cities, and so many Kingdomes, now called Natolia, with her Neighbours
Antiochia, and other Regions of Syria, Damascus,
Libanus, with Babylonia and the glorie of the
Earth: and Types of Heaven, Judea and Paradise;
the Silken Countries also of Persia, China in her
best parts, and Japan, are in the elevation; and
Virginia is Daughter of the same Heavens, which
promise no lesse portion to this Virgin, then those
Matrons had for the foundation-stock of their
wealth and glory.

II
THE PILGRIM

In 1609 a small congregation of Separatists from the village of Scrooby in the west of England managed to flee to Holland, where the members hoped to practice their religion free from all ecclesiastical authority. Hardships, discontent, and fear drove them in 1620 to bargain for land in Virginia; bad seamanship and mismanagement took them, and some adventurers who came along for luck and financial gain, to New England; courage and necessity forced them to take over land to which they had no legal right. Virtually apotheosized in the nineteenth century, they became for us the Pilgrim Fathers. As Separatists, however, they were a minority sect in the Puritan movement. They wanted, simply enough, to be left alone to live and worship as they felt they must. After some early setbacks, their little colony prospered; they raised their crops, dealt in beaver pelts, got along with the Indians, and worshipped as they would; they were even able to buy out London investors in their enterprise. Theirs was to be an independent, communal, almost patriarchal society. But they were gradually drawn into the orbit of the colony established by orthodox Puritans at Massachusetts Bay. They joined the New England Confederacy in 1643, were merged with the Massachusetts Bay Colony in 1684, and so lost their separateness.

What the Plymouth colonists came to be for nineteenth-century Americans is made clearest by the narrative history, *Of Plymouth Plantation*, written by their perennial governor, William Bradford. When it was first printed in 1856, its very grace, dignity, matter-of-fact self-assurance, and simple yet practical idealism made, above all, for the myth and the cult of the Pilgrim Fathers. Myth and cult, however, and attendant snobbishness, sentimentality, and ancestor-worship cannot destroy the strength of Bradford and his fellows. This remains in *Of Plymouth Plantation*.

Bibliographical Note. *Of Plymouth Plantation* (generally called *The History of Plymouth Plantation*) remains the great account of the Pilgrim enterprise; the best edition is that of W. C. Ford, in 2 vols. (Boston, 1912). A more freely, but nonetheless precisely, edited version is *Of Plymouth Plantation, 1620–1647,* ed. Samuel Eliot Morison (New York, 1953). A recent account, valuable because it sets Bradford's narrative in its historical-cultural context, is George F. Willison, *Saints and Strangers* (New York, 1945); it contains a detailed critical bibliography.

William Bradford

(1590–1657)

Bibliographical Note. The most complete edition of *The History of Plymouth Plantation* is that of W. C. Ford, in 2 vols. (Boston, 1912); a more readily accessible scholarly edition is that of W. T. Davis (New York, 1908). The text of the following selections follows that of the Davis edition, pp. 44–48, 92–97, 106–111, 146–147, 390–391. On Bradford, see the article by S. E. Morison in *The Dictionary of American Biography*; on the *History*, see E. F. Bradford, "Conscious Art in Bradford's *History of Plymouth Plantation*," *New England Quarterly.* I (1928), 133–157. The introduction and notes to S. E. Morison's modernized edition of *The History* (New York, 1952) comprise the best introduction to the text.

from

THE HISTORY OF
PLYMOUTH PLANTATION
(WRITTEN 1620–1651)

["*Reasons and Causes of Their Removall*," 1609–1617]

After they had lived in this citie [Leyden] about some 11. or 12. years, (which is the more observable being the whole time of that famose truce[1] between that state and the Spaniards,) and sundrie of them were taken away by death, and many others begane to be well striken in years, the grave mistris Experience

---

[1] This truce, signed April 9, 1609, was to expire in 1621.—*Davis.*

haveing taught them many things, those prudent governours with sundrie of the sagest members begane both deeply to apprehend their present dangers, and wisely to foresee the future, and thinke of timly remedy. In the agitation of their thoughts, and much discours of things hear aboute, at length they began to incline to this conclusion, of remoovall to some other place. Not out of any newfanglednes, or other such like giddie humor, by which men are oftentimes transported to their great hurt and danger, but for sundrie weightie and solid reasons; some of the cheefe of which I will hear breefly touch. And first, they saw and found by experience the hardnes of the place and countrie to be such, as few in comparison would come to them, and fewer that would bide it out, and continew with them. For many that came to them, and many more that desired to be with them, could not endure that great labor and hard fare, with other inconveniences which they underwent and were contented with. But though they loved their persons, approved their cause, and honoured their sufferings, yet they left them as it weer weeping, as Orpah did her mother in law Naomie, or as those Romans did Cato in Utica, who desired to be excused and borne with, though they could not all be Catoes. For many, though they desired to injoye the ordinances of God in their puritie, and the libertie of the gospell with them, yet, alass, they admitted of bondage, with danger of conscience, rather than to indure these hardships; yoa, some prefered and chose the prisons in England, rather then this libertie in Holland, with these afflictions. But it was thought that if a better and easier place of living could be had, it would draw many, and take away these discouragments. Yea, their pastor would often say, that many of those who both wrote and preached now against them, if they were in a place wher they might have libertie and live comfortably, they would then practise as they did.

2ly. They saw that though the people generally bore all these difficulties very cherfully, and with a resolute courage, being in the best and strength of their years, yet old age began to steale on many of them, (and their great and continuall labours, with other crosses and sorrows, hastened it before the time,) so as it was not only probably thought, but apparently seen, that within a few years more they would be in danger to scatter, by necessities pressing them, or sinke under their burdens, or both. And therfore according to the devine proverb, that a wise man seeth the plague when it cometh, and hideth him selfe, Pro. 22. 3., so they like skillfull and beaten souldiers were fearfull either to be intrapped or surrounded by their enimies, so as they should neither be able to fight nor flie; and therfor thought it better to dislodge betimes to some place of better advantage and less danger, if any such could be found. Thirdly; as necessitie was a taskmaster over them, so they were forced to be such, not only to their servants, but in a sorte, to their dearest children; the which as it did not a litle wound the tender harts of many a loving father and mother, so it produced likwise sundrie sad and sorowful effects. For many of their children, that were of best dispositiohs and gracious inclinations, haveing lernde to bear the yoake in their youth, and willing to bear parte of their parents burden, were, often times, so oppressed with their hevie labours, that though their minds were free and willing, yet their bodies bowed under the weight of the same, and became decreped in their early youth; the vigor of nature being consumed in the very budd as it were. But that which was more lamentable, and of all sorowes most heavie to be borne, was that many of their children, by these occasions, and the great licentiousness of youth in that countrie, and the manifold temptations of the place, were drawne away by evill examples into extravagante and dangerous courses, getting the raines off their neks, and departing from their parents. Some became souldiers, others tooke upon them farr viages by sea, and other some worse courses, tending to dissolutnes and the danger of their soules, to the great greefe of their parents and dishonour of God. So that they saw their posteritie would be in danger to degenerate and be corrupted.

Lastly, (and which was not least), a great hope and inward zeall they had of laying some good foundation, or at least to make some way therunto, for the propagating and advancing the gospell of the kingdom of Christ in those remote parts of the world; yea, though they should be but even as steppingstones unto others for the performing of so great a work.

These, and some other like reasons, moved them to undertake this resolution of their removall; the which they afterward prosecuted with so great difficulties, as by the sequell will appeare.

The place they had thoughts on was some of those vast and unpeopled countries of America, which are frutfull and fitt for habitation, being devoyd of all civill inhabitants, wher ther are only salvage and brutish men, which range up and downe, litle otherwise then the wild beasts of the same. This proposition being made publike and coming to the scaning of all, it raised many variable opinions amongst men, and caused many fears and doubts amongst them selves. Some, from their reasons and hops conceived, laboured to stirr up and incourage the rest to undertake and prosecute the same; others, againe, out of their fears, objected against it, and sought to diverte from it, aledging many things, and those neither unreasonable nor unprobable; as that it was a great designe, and subjecte to many unconceivable perills and dangers; as, besids the casulties of the seas (which none can be freed from) the length of the vioage was such, as the weake bodys of women and other persons worne out with age and traville (as many of them were) could never be able to endure. And yet if they should, the miseries of the land which they should be exposed unto, would be to hard to be borne; and lickly, some or all of them togeither, to consume and utterly to ruinate them. For ther they should be liable to famine, and nakednes, and the wante, in a maner, of all things. The chang of aire, diate, and drinking of water, would infecte their bodies with sore sickneses, and greevous diseases. And also those which should escape or overcome these difficulties, should yett be in continuall danger of the salvage people, who are cruell, barbarous, and most trecherous, being most furious in their rage, and merciles wher they overcome; not being contente only to kill, and take away life, but delight to tormente men in the most bloodie manner that may be; fleaing[2] some alive with the shells of fishes, cutting of the members and joynts of others by peesmeale, and broiling on the coles, eate the collops of their flesh in their sight whilst they live; with other cruelties horrible to be related. And surely it could not be thought but the very hearing of these things could not but move the very bowels of

---

[2] Flaying.—*Davis.*

men to grate within them, and make the weake to quake and tremble. It was furder objected, that it would require greater summes of money to furnish such a voiage, and to fitt them with necessaries, then their consumed estats would amounte too; and yett they must as well looke to be seconded with supplies,[3] as presently to be transported. Also many presidents of ill success, and lamentable misseries befalne others in the like designes, were easie to be found, and not forgotten to be aledged; besids their owne experience, in their former troubles and hardships in their removall into Holand, and how hard a thing it was for them to live in that strange place, though it was a neighbour countrie, and a civill and rich comone wealth.

It was answered, that all great and honourable actions are accompanied with great difficulties, and must be both enterprised and overcome with answerable courages. It was granted the dangers were great, but not desperate; the difficulties were many, but not invincible. For though their were many of them likly, yet they were not cartaine; it might be sundrie if the things feared might never befale; others by providente care and the use of good means, might in a great measure be prevented; and all of them, through the help of God, by fortitude and patience, might either be borne, or overcome. True it was, that such atempts were not to be made and undertaken without good ground and reason; not rashly or lightly as many have done for curiositie or hope of gaine, etc. But their condition was not ordinarie; their ends were good and honourable; their calling lawfull, and urgente; and therfore they might expecte the blessing of God in their proceding. Yea, though they should loose their lives in this action, yet might they have comforte in the same, and their endeavors would be honourable. They lived hear but as men in exile, and in a poore condition; and as great miseries might possibly befale them in this place, for the 12. years of truce were now[4] out, and ther was nothing but beating of drumes, and preparing for warr, the events wherof are allway uncertaine. The Spaniard might prove as cruell as the salvages of America, and the famine and pestelence as sore hear as ther,

---

[3] I. e., reinforcements.—Davis.
[4] The truce between the Dutch and Spain would end in April, 1621.—Davis.

and their libertie less to looke out for remedie. After many other perticuler things answered and aledged on both sids, it was fully concluded by the major parte, to put this designe in execution, and to prosecute it by the best means they could.

· · · · ·

[The Voyage, 1620]

. . . now all being compacte togeather in one shipe, they put to sea againe with a prosperus winde, which continued diverce days togeather, which was some incouragmente unto them; yet according to the usuall maner many were afflicted with seasicknes. And I may not omite hear a spetiall worke of Gods providence. Ther was a proud and very profane yonge man, one of the seamen, of a lustie, able body, which made him the more hauty; he would allway be contemning the poor people in their sicknes, and cursing them dayly with greevous execrations, and did not let to tell them, that he hoped to help to cast halfe of them over board before they came to their jurneys end, and to make mery with what they had; and if he were by any gently reproved, he would curse and swear most bitterly. But it plased God before they came halfe seas over, to smite this yong man with a greevous disease, of which he dyed in a desperate maner, and so was him selfe the first that was throwne overbord. Thus his curses light on his owne head; and it was an astonishmente to all his fellows, for they noted it to be the just hand of God upon him.

After they had injoyed faire winds and weather for a season, they were incountred many times with crosse winds, and mette with many feirce stormes, with which the shipe was shroudly⁵ shaken, and her upper works made very leakie; and one of the maine beames in the midd ships was bowed and craked, which put them in some fear that the shipe could not be able to performe the vioage. So some of the cheefe of the company, perceiveing the mariners to feare the suffisiencie of the shipe, as appeared by their mutterings, they entred into serious consullta-

---

⁵ Shrewdly, severely.—Davis.

tion with the m^r and other officers of the ship, to consider in time of the danger; and rather to returne then to cast them selves into a desperate and inevitable perill. And truly ther was great distraction and differance of opinion amongst the mariners them selves; faine would they doe what could be done for their wages sake, (being now halfe the seas over,) and on the other hand they were loath to hazard their lives too desperately. But in examening of all opinions, the m^r and others affirmed they knew the ship to be stronge and firme under water; and for the buckling of the maine beame, ther was a great iron scrue the passengers brought out of Holland, which would raise the beame into his place; the which being done, the carpenter and m^r affirmed that with a post put under it, set firme in the lower deck, and otherways bounde, he would make it sufficiente. And as for the decks and uper workes they would calke them as well as they could, and though with the workeing of the ship they would not longe keepe stanch, yet ther would otherwise be not great danger, if they did not overpress her with sails. So they commited them selves to the will of God, and resolved to proseede. In sundrie of these stormes the winds were so feirce, and the seas so high, as they could not beare a knote of saile, but were forced to hull,[6] for diverce days togither. And in one of them, as they thus lay at hull, in a mighty storme, a lustie yonge man (called John Howland) coming upon some occasion above the grattings, was, with a seele[7] of the shipe throwne into [the] sea; but it pleased God that he caught hould of the top-saile halliards, which hunge over board, and rane out at length; yet he held his hould (though he was sundrie fadomes under water) till he was hald up by the same rope to the brime of the water, and then with a boat hooke and other means got into the shipe againe, and his life saved; and though he was something ill with it, yet he lived many years after, and became a profitable member both in church and commone wealthe. In all this viage ther died but one of the passengers, which was William Butten, a youth, servant to Samuell Fuller, when they drew near the coast. But to omite other things, (that I may be breefe,) after longe

[6] To drift.—*Davis.*
[7] The "seele" of a ship is the toss in a rough sea.—*Davis.*

beating at sea they fell with that land which is called Cape Cod; the which being made and certainly knowne to be it, they were not a litle joyfull. After some deliberation had amongst them selves and with the m^r of the ship, they tacked aboute and resolved to stande for the southward (the wind and weather being faire) to finde some place aboute Hudsons river for their habitation. But after they had sailed that course aboute halfe the day, they fell amongst deangerous shoulds and roring breakers, and they were so farr intangled ther with as they conceived them selves in great danger; and the wind shrinking upon them withall, they resolved to bear up againe for the Cape, and thought them selves hapy to gett out of those dangers before night overtooke them, as by Gods providence they did. And the next day they gott into the Cape-harbor wher they ridd in saftie. A word or too by the way of this cape; it was thus first named by Capten Gosnole and his company, An°: 1602, and after by Capten Smith was caled Cape James; but it retains the former name amongst seamen. Also that pointe which first shewed those dangerous shoulds unto them, they called Pointe Care, and Tuckers Terrour; but the French and Dutch to this day call it Malabarr, by reason of those perilous shoulds, and the losses they have suffered their.

Being thus arived in a good harbor and brought safe to land, they fell upon their knees and blessed the God of heaven, who had brought them over the vast and furious ocean, and delivered them from all the periles and miseries therof, againe to set their feete on the firme and stable earth, their proper elemente. And no marvell if they were thus joyefull, seeing wise Seneca was so affected with sailing a few miles on the coast of his owne Italy; as he affirmed, that he had rather remaine twentie years on his way by land, then pass by sea to any place in a short time; so tedious and dreadfull was the same unto him.

But hear I cannot but stay and make a pause, and stand half amased at this poore peoples presente condition; and so I thinke will the reader too, when he well considers the same. Being thus passed the vast ocean, and a sea of troubles before in their preparation (as may be remembred by that which wente beforc), they had now no friends to wellcome them, nor inns to entertaine or refresh their weatherbeaten bodys, no houses or

much less townes to repaire too, to seeke for succoure. It is recorded in scripture[8] as a mercie to the apostle and his ship-
wraked company, that the barbarians shewed them no smale
kindnes in refreshing them, but these savage barbarians, when
they mette with them (as after will appeare) were readier to fill
their sids full of arrows than otherwise. And for the season it
was winter, and they that know the winters of that cuntrie
know them to be sharp and violent, and subjecte to cruell and
feirce stormes, deangerous to travill to known places, much more
to serch an unknown coast. Besids, what could they see but a
hidious and desolate wildernes, full of wild beasts and willd
men? and what multituds ther might be of them they knew not.
Neither could they, as it were, goe up to the tope of Pisgah, to
vew from this willdernes a more goodly cuntrie to feed their
hops; for which way soever they turnd their eys (save upward to
the heavens) they could have litle solace or content in respecte
of any outward objects. For summer being done, all things stand
upon them with a wetherbeaten face; and the whole countrie,
full of woods and thickets, represented a wild and savage heiw.
If they looked behind them, ther was the mighty ocean which
they had passed, and was now as a maine barr and goulfe to
seperate them from all the civill parts of the world. If it be said
they had a ship to sucour them, it is trew; but what heard they
daly from the m^r and company? but that with speede they
should looke out a place with their shallop, wher they would be
at some near distance; for the season was shuch as he would not
stirr from thence till a safe harbor was discovered by them wher
they would be, and he might goe without danger; and that
victells consumed apace, but he must and would keepe sufficient
for them selves and their returne. Yea, it was muttered by some,
that if they gott not a place in time, they would turne them and
their goods ashore and leave them. Let it also be considred what
weake hopes of supply and succoure they left behinde them,
that might bear up their minds in this sade condition and trialls
they were under; and they could not but be very smale. It is
true, indeed, the affections and love of their brethren at Leyden
was cordiall and entire towards them, but they had litle power

[8] "Act. 28."—*Bradford.*

to help them, or them selves; and how the case stode betweene them and the marchants at their coming away, hath allready been declared. What could now sustaine them but the spirite of God and his grace? May not and ought not the children of these fathers rightly say: *Our faithers were Englishmen which came over this great ocean, and were ready to perish in this willdernes; but they cried unto the Lord, and he heard their voyce, and looked on their adversitie, etc. Let them therfore praise the Lord, because he is good, and his mercies endure for ever. Yea, let them which have been redeemed of the Lord, shew how he hath delivered them from the hand of the oppressour. When they wandered in the deserte willdernes out of the way, and found no citie to dwell in, both hungrie, and thirstie, their sowle was overwhelmed in them. Let them confess before the Lord his loving kindnes, and his wonderfull works before the sons of men.*

. . . . .

[The Mayflower Compact, Early Hardships, and Indian Affairs, 1620–1621]

I shall a litle returne backe and begine with a combination made by them before they came ashore, being the first foundation of their govermente in this place; occasioned partly by the discontented and mutinous speeches that some of the strangers amongst them had let fall from them in the ship—That when they came a shore they would use their owne libertie; for none had power to command them, the patente they had being for Virginia, and not for New-england, which belonged to an other Goverment, with which the Virginia Company had nothing to doe. And partly that shuch an acte by them done (this their condition considered) might be as firme as any patent, and in some respects more sure.

The forme was as followeth.

In the name of God, Amen. We whose names are under-writen, the loyall subjects of our dread soveraigne Lord, King James, by the grace of God, of Great Britaine, Franc, and Ireland king, defender of the faith, etc., haveing undertaken, for the glorie of God, and advancemente of the Christian faith, and honour of our king and countrie, a voyage to plant the first colonie in the Northerne parts of Virginia, doe by these presents solemnly and mutualy in the presence of God, and one of another, covenant and combine our selves togeather into a civill body politick, for our better ordering and preservation and furtherance of the ends aforesaid; and by vertue hearof to enacte, constitute, and frame such just and equall lawes, ordinances, acts, constitutions, and offices, from time to time, as shall be thought most meete and convenient for the generall good of the Colonie, unto which we promise all due submission and obedience. In witnes whereof we have hereunder subscribed our names at Cap-Codd the 11. of November, in the year of the raigne of our soveraigne lord, King James, of England, France, and Ireland the eighteenth, and of Scotland the fiftie fourth. An°: Dom. 1620.

After this they chose, or rather confirmed, Mr. John Carver (a man godly and well approved amongst them) their Governour for that year. And after they had provided a place for their goods, or comone store, (which were long in unlading for want of boats, foulnes of winter weather, and sicknes of diverce,) and begune some small cottages for their habitation, as time would admitte, they mette and consulted of lawes and orders, both for their civill and military Governmente, as the necessitie of their condition did require, still adding therunto as urgent occasion in severall times, and as cases did require.

In these hard and difficulte beginings they found some discontents and murmurings arise amongst some, and mutinous speeches and carriags in other; but they were soone quelled and overcome by the wisdome, patience, and just and equall carrage of things by the Govr and better part, which clave faithfully togeather in the maine. But that which was most sadd and lamentable was, that in 2. or 3. moneths time halfe of their company dyed, espetialy in Jan: and February, being the depth of winter, and wanting houses and other comforts; being infected with the scurvie and other diseases, which this long vioage and their inacomodate condition had brought upon them; so as ther dyed some times 2. or 3. of a day, in the foresaid time; that of 100. and odd persons, scarce 50. remained. And of these in the time of most distres, ther was but 6. or 7. sound persons, who, to their great comendations be it spoken, spared no pains, night nor day, but with abundance of toyle and hazard of their owne health, fetched them woode, made them fires, drest them meat, made their beads, washed their lothsome cloaths, cloathed and uncloathed them; in a word, did all the homly and necessarie offices for them which dainty and quesie stomacks cannot endure to hear named; and all this willingly and cherfully, without any grudging in the least, shewing hercin their true love unto their freinds and bretheren. A rare example and worthy to be remembred. Tow of these 7. were Mr. William Brewster, ther reverend Elder, and Myles Standish, ther Captein and military comander, unto whom my selfe, and many others, were much beholden in our low and sicke condition. And yet the Lord so upheld these persons, as in this generall calamity they were not at all infected either with sicknes, or lamnes. And what I have said of these, I may say of many others who dyed in this generall vissitation, and others yet living, that whilst they had health, yea, or any strength continuing, they were not wanting to any that had need of them. And I doute not but their recompense is with the Lord.

But I may not hear pass by an other remarkable passage not to be forgotten. As this calamitie fell among the passengers that were to be left here to plant, and were hasted a shore and made to drinke water, that the sea-men might have the more bear,[9] and one in his sicknes desiring but a small cann of beere, it was answered, that if he were their owne father he should have none; the disease begane to fall amongst them also, so as allmost halfe of their company dyed before they went away, and many of their officers and lustyest men, as the boatson, gunner, 3. quartermaisters, the cooke, and others. At which the m^r was something strucken and sent to the sick a shore and tould the Govr he should send for beer for them that had need of it, though he drunke water homward bound. But now amongst his company ther was farr another kind of carriage in this miserie then amongst the passengers; for they that before had been boone companions in drinking and joyllity in the time of their health

---

[9] "Which was this author him selfe."—*Bradford*.

and wellfare, begane now to deserte one another in this calamitie, saing they would not hasard ther lives for them, they should
be infected by coming to help them in their cabins, and so, after
they came to dye by it, would doe litle or nothing for them, but
if they dyed let them dye. But such of the passengers as were
yet abord shewed them what mercy they could, which made
some of their harts relente, as the boatson (and some others),
who was a prowd yonge man, and would often curse and scofe
at the passengers; but when he grew weak, they had compassion
on him and helped him; then he confessed he did not deserve
it at their hands, he had abused them in word and deed. O!
saith he, you, I now see, shew your love like Christians indeed
one to another, but we let one another lye and dye like doggs.
Another lay cursing his wife, saing if it had not ben for her he
had never come this unlucky viage, and anone cursing his
felows, saing he had done this and that, for some of them, he
had spente so much, and so much, amongst them, and they were
now weary of him, and did not help him, having need. Another
gave his companion all he had, if he died, to help him in his
weaknes; he went and got a litle spise and made him a mess of
meat once or twise, and because he dyed not so soone as he
expected, he went amongst his fellows, and swore the rogue
would cousen him, he would see him choaked before he made
him any more meate; and yet the pore fellow dyed before morning.

All this while the Indians came skulking about them, and
would sometimes show them selves aloofe of, but when any
aproached near them, they would rune away. And once they
stoale away their tools wher they had been at worke, and were
gone to diner. But about the 16. of March a certaine Indian
came bouldly amongst them, and spoke to them in broken
English, which they could well understand, but marvelled at it.
At length they understood by discourse with him, that he was
not of these parts, but belonged to the eastrene parts, wher some
English-ships came to fhish, with whom he was aquainted, and
could name sundrie of them by their names, amongst whom he
had gott his language. He became proftable to them in aquaint-
ing them with many things concerning the state of the cuntry

in the east-parts wher he lived, which was afterwards profitable
unto them; as also of the people hear, of their names, number,
and strength; of their situation and distance from this place,
and who was cheefe amongst them. His name was Samaset; he
tould them also of another Indian whos name was Squanto, a
native of this place, who had been in England and could speake
better English then him selfe. Being, after some time of enter-
tainmente and gifts, dismist, a while after he came againe, and
5. more with him, and they brought againe all the tooles that
were stolen away before, and made way for the coming of their
great Sachem, called Massasoyt; who, about 4. or 5. days after,
came with the cheefe of his freinds and other attendance, with
the aforesaid Squanto. With whom, after frendly entertainment,
and some gifts given him, they made a peace with him (which
hath now continued this 24. years) in these terms.

1. That neither he nor any of his, should injurie or doe
hurte to any of their peopl.

2. That if any of his did any hurte to any of theirs, he
should send the offender, that they might punish him.

3. That if any thing were taken away from any of theirs, he
should cause it to be restored; and they should doe the like
to his.

4. If any did unjustly warr against him, they would aide
him; if any did warr against them, he should aide them.

5. He should send to his neighbours confederats, to cer-
tifie them of this, that they might not wrong them, but might be
likewise comprised in the conditions of peace.

6. That when ther men came to them, they should leave
their bows and arrows behind them.

After these things he returned to his place caled Sowams,[10]
some 40. mile from this place, but Squanto continued with
them, and was their interpreter, and was a spetiall instrument
sent of God for their good beyond their expectation. He directed them how to set their corne, wher to take fish, and to
procure other comodities, and was also their pilott to bring
them to unknowne places for their profitt, and never left them

---

[10] On the present site of Warren, R. I.—*Davis.*

till he dyed. He was a native of this place, and scarce any left alive besids him selfe.

. . . . .

[Social and Economic Problems, 1623]

. . . they begane to thinke how they might raise as much corne as they could, and obtaine a beter crope then they had done, that they might not still thus languish in miserie. At length, after much debate of things, the Govr (with the advise of the cheefest amongst them) gave way that they should set corne every man for his owne perticuler, and in that regard trust to them selves; in all other things to goe on in the generall way as before. And so assigned to every family a parcell of land, according to the proportion of their number for that end, only for present use (but made no devission for inheritance), and ranged all boys and youth under some familie. This had very good success; for it made all hands very industrious, so as much more corne was planted then other waise would have bene by any means the Govr or any other could use, and saved him a great deall of trouble, and gave farr better contente. The women now wente willingly into the feild, and tooke their litle-ons with them to set corne, which before would aledg weaknes, and inabilitie; whom to have compelled would have bene thought great tiranie and oppression.

The experience that was had in this commone course and condition, tried sundrie years, and that amongst godly and sober men, may well evince the vanitie of that conceite of Platos and other ancients, applauded by some of later times;—that the taking away of propertie, and bringing in communitie into a comone wealth, would make them happy and florishing; as if they were wiser then God. For this comunitie (so farr as it was) was found to breed much confusion and discontent, and retard much imployment that would have been to their benefite and comforte. For the yong-men that were most able and fitte for labour and service did repine that they should spend their time and streingth to worke for other mens wives and children, with out any recompence. The strong, or man of parts, had no more in devission of victails and cloaths, then he that was weake and not able to doe a quarter the other could; this was thought injuestice. The aged and graver men to be ranked and equalised in labours, and victails, cloaths, etc., with the meaner and yonger sorte, thought it some indignite and disrespect unto them. And for mens wives to be commanded to doe servise for other men, as dresing their meate, washing their cloaths, etc., they deemd it a kind of slaverie, neither could many husbands well brooke it. Upon the poynte all being to have alike, and all to doe alike, they thought them selves in the like condition, and one as good as another; and so, if it did not cut of those relations that God hath set amongst men, yet it did at least diminish and take of the mutuall respects that should be preservd amongst them. And would have bene worse if they had been men of another condition. Let none objecte this is men's corruption, and nothing to the course it selfe. I answer, seeing all men have this corruption in them, God in his wisdome saw another course fiter for them.

But to returne. After this course setled, and by that their corne was planted, all ther victails were spente, and they were only to rest on Gods providence; at night not many times knowing wher to have a bitt of any thing the next day. And so, as one well observed, had need to pray that God would give them their dayly brade, above all people in the world. Yet they bore these wants with great patience and allacritic of spirite, and that for so long a time as for the most parte of 2. years; which makes me remember what Peter Martire writs, (in magnifying the Spaniards) in his 5. Decade, pag. 208.[11] *They* (saith he) *led a miserable life for 5. days togeather, with the parched graine of maize only, and that not to saturitie;* and then concluds, *that shuch pains, shuch labours, and shuch hunger, he thought none living which is not a Spaniard could have endured.* But alass! these, when they had maize (that is, Indean corne) they thought it as good as a feast, and wanted not only for 5. days togeather, but some time 2. or 3. months togeather, and neither had bread

---

[11] Peter Martyr of Anghiera, *Decades de Rebus Oceanicis et Novo Orbe,* the great Spanish history of America, translated into English by Richard Eden.—*Davis.*

nor any kind of corne. Indeed, in an other place, in his 2. Decade, page 94. he mentions how others of them were worse put to it, wher they were faine to eate doggs, toads, and dead men, and so dyed almost all. From these extremities they [the] Lord in his goodnes kept these his people, and in their great wants preserved both their lives and healthes; let his name have the praise. Yet let me hear make use of his conclusion, which in some sorte may be applied to this people: *That with their miseries they opened a way to these newlands; and after these stormes, with what ease other men came to inhabite in them, in respecte of the calamities these men suffered; so as they seeme to goe to a bride feaste wher all things are provided for them.*

. . . . .

[The Weakening of the Pilgrim Way, 1644]

Many having left this place (as is before noted) by reason of the straightnes and barrennes of the same, and their finding of better accommodations elsewher, more sutable to their ends and minds; and sundrie others still upon every occasion desiring their dismissions, the church begane seriously to thinke whether it were not better joyntly to remove to some other place, then to be thus weakened, and as it were insensibly dissolved. Many meetings and much consultation was held hearaboute, and diverse were mens minds and opinions. Some were still for staying togeather in this place, aledging men might hear live, if they would be contente with their condition; and that it was not for wante or necessitie so much that they removed, as for the enriching of them selves. Others were resolute upon removall, and so signified that hear they could not stay; but if the church did not remove, they must; insomuch as many were swayed, rather then ther should be a dissolution, to condescend to a removall, if a fitt place could be found, that might more conveniently and comfortablie receive the whole, with such accession of others as might come to them, for their better strength and subsistence; and some such like cautions and limitations. So as, with the afforesaide provissos, the greater parte consented to a removall to a place called Nawsett, which had been superficially viewed and the good will of the purchassers (to whom it belonged) obtained, with some addition thertoo from the Courte. But now they begane to see their errour, that they had given away already the best and most commodious places to others, and now wanted them selves; for this place was about 50. myles from hence, and at an outside of the countrie, remote from all society; also, that it would prove so straite, as it would not be competente to receive the whole body, much less be capable of any addition or increase; so as (at least in a shorte time) they should be worse ther then they are now hear. The which, with sundery other like considerations and inconveniences, made them chaing their resolutions; but such as were before resolved upon removall tooke advantage of this agreemente, and wente on notwithstanding, neither could the rest hinder them, they haveing made some beginning. And thus was this poore church left, like an anciente mother, growne olde, and forsaken of her children, (though not in their affections,) yett in regarde of their bodily presence and personall helpfullness. Her anciente members being most of them worne away by death; and these of later time being like children translated into other families, and she like a widow left only to trust in God. Thus she that had made many rich became her selfe poore.

III

THE PURITAN

The world which Puritans made in New England was under the firm and absolute control of an inscrutable God. It was a world which existed solely for the glorification of that God, a world in which men had to find their place, accept it, and thereby glorify Him. God was all; man had fallen into nothingness and could hope to rise again only if God should so decree. Each man was predestined for eternal salvation or damnation. Although man might feel himself elected to eternal salvation, he could never feel absolutely sure. He could only work and worship, watch and wait, live in this world as God had decreed.

Such was the Puritan's understanding of the world and his place in it. Behind this understanding lay the individualizing forces of the Protestant revolution, the rise of a class of self-made enterprising men, and a revival—principally in the work of Calvin and his followers—of the theology of Saint Augustine. In their sense of themselves as individuals, Puritans were aware of the immense and terrifying gulf between man and God, of human incompleteness and imperfection. This was the sense of sin, and of humility and abasement in the face of that sin. The whole effort of Puritan thinking and living was so to comprehend sin as to live bravely, resignedly, and intelligently with it; so to understand the necessity of living hard in this world, with perhaps only hell in view, as to live righteously; so to justify God's way to man as to build His Commonwealth on the Massachusetts earth.

The devout, upper middle-class Englishmen—headed by learned humanists from Cambridge University—who went to Massachusetts in the 1630's knew that it was their special mission to purify the Church and to restore it to its proper place at the center of society; it was only through the Church and its ministers and teachers that men could learn of their individual sinfulness, of the place of that sinfulness in God's scheme of things, and of the necessity to work and worship in this world. They were so sure of their rightness that they refused to call themselves Separatists (as had the Pilgrims) and insisted that only they were members of the True Church—and thus of the

True Holy Commonwealth. All others had somehow been separated, as they said, from the path of righteousness. If the Puritans were denying the authority of the English Church, its rituals, and its government, they were denying from within the Church, not from without; they could say that their Church had been contaminated and that they would purify it. They were not revolutionaries; they feared and hated dissenters and dissidence. If they were moving away from the authoritarianism of the English Church as the English Church had moved away from the authoritarianism of the Roman Catholic Church, they were not moving into libertarian thinking. Their true church was an absolute church. They could countenance no way but their own.

What the New England Puritans had found was a new principle of order and authority which was to take the place of the old, which should be all the more rigorously held to because it was so much truer than the old. Their new principle stemmed from a new understanding of the nature of the sinful individual and his role in society and in religion. If the individual was free of one kind of external authority, he was in the power of another. This was the authority expressed in the Puritan Theocratic State, certainly as oppressive as the Stuart state which it tried to escape, certainly more oppressive than the Cromwellian state which was its English counterpart. Politically, the record of Puritan New England is one of righteous oppression rising out of righteous authority. Yet, viewed in a twentieth-century perspective, it is the psychological and philosophical source of this authority—the notion of the sinful individual and his duties and destiny, not its expression in social and political forms, which is our heritage from Puritanism and which we should remark as we read the Puritan record, even as we attend duly to the relations between the spiritual and the temporal in Puritan life.

The Puritans possessed a myth which contained the germ of all their truths—theological, philosophic, scientific, political, and esthetic. This was Covenant Theology—a synthesis of their Augustinian, Calvinist Christianity, and their sense of social and economic necessity. In the beginning, according to the myth, God had contracted with Adam in a Covenant of Works; Adam had only to perform certain duties in order to live in his paradise. But, as God had foreknown, Adam willfully broke this contract, gained knowledge but lost his simple clarity of understanding, and so doomed all men after him. Then God's Son contracted with His Father in a Covenant of Grace, by the terms of which He would sacrifice Himself so that God would save a few sons of Adam. As a result, some men were visited with God's irresistible Grace and so elected for eternal salvation. Men had no choice in the matter, only hope. Paradoxically, they might learn more of their hope if they would refine the very instruments of knowledge which, imperfect and misleading, had been gained by Adam in his fall. So it was the duty of men to study, to hope, to wait, and to work—to make themselves more and more aware of their worthlessness, to know that worthlessness so well as to find it overpoweringly right. Thus the sweetness, as it was said, of the sense of sin; thus the hope against hope of election; thus the obligation to accept the authority of those elect in Puritan society; thus the fierce optimism and fortitude—even in the face of damnation; thus the intense and exhilarating certainty that all was right in the world, that everything made sense, that good and bad, sin and sinning, life and death, all were part of that eternal order which glorified God.

New England Puritan society as it took shape was held firmly together by a Civil Convenant which was taken to duplicate the Holy Covenant. Conditions of environment and situation pulled men together into urban and semirural settlements and prospered them in their trading, fishing, farming, and shipbuilding. Theocratically organized, that society was ruled by the Elect who were full church members and who could vote. Practically, worldly goods seemed to go along with spiritual goods; somehow the Elect were also the well-to-do, and work was obviously worship. One who newly felt himself to be of the Elect was required to undergo rigorous examination to prove that he was. Here, if ever, was a stable society.

Yet in the 1650's, as even men who were not of the Elect began to prosper in the new world, work and worship inevitably came to be dissociated; unfranchised Massachusetts citizens felt dissatisfied with the oppressive rule of theocrats; proving oneself to be of the Elect seemed less and less a dire necessity; evidence of eternal salvation and the right to vote no longer seemed necessarily related. A new world of reasonable men, the world of the Enlightenment, of the Royal Society, Newton, and Locke, began slowly but surely to come into the Puritan view. Puritans tried to compromise with that world; but compromise ultimately meant the death of Puritanism, absolute separation of church and state, an optimistic view of human nature, and the birth of democratic liberalism. The initial Puritan move away from religious authority could not itself be halted. Puritanism had established not only the possibility of the primacy of the individual, but even of secular individualism as it was to develop in eighteenth-century America. The existence of a man like Benjamin Franklin was made possible, perhaps necessary.

So the enlightened New Englander of the later eighteenth century could not be a Puritan. It was he, not his Puritan ancestors, who was to help write the Declaration of Independence. In rationalizing Puritan theology and the Puritan sense of sin out of existence, he was to discover a new non-theological basis for individualism and a faith in the possibility of freedom for all; and he was to help found a nation officially and optimistically dedicated to such individualism and such freedom. We can say now what he could not: that the drive towards individualism and freedom was his—and our—heritage from Puritanism. Moreover, recently we have discovered that even if we, like our Revolutionary ancestors, cannot accept the Puritan mythical, theological explanation of the origins of individualism and freedom, we are once more finding it rather easy to accept the Puritan analysis of the risks and uncertainties in them. We are perhaps recovering even something of the Puritan sense of sin.

The selections here printed manifest the Puritan spirit in various forms and under various conditions. John Cotton's *God's Promise to His Plantation* is a utopian, almost primitivist document. The selections (all of them revised sermons) from Thomas Hooker's huge *Application of Redemption* show Puritan theological thinking on its way to becoming dogma; the key to understanding its remarkable style, and the fact that Puritans would willingly work their way through its long length, is the word "application"—theology in action, as it were. John Winthrop's *Model of Christian Charity* and his speech on liberty exhibit the Puritan's total satisfaction in his certainty of the role of sinful individuals in God's world. The piece from the Cotton-Williams debate and the letters of Williams (to the people of Providence and to John Cotton's son) push the libertarian implications of Puritan "individualism" to an extreme which, so almost all Puritans felt, would make life in society impossible; it was Williams' glory that he fully comprehended those implications and their difficulties and, in spite of—indeed, because of—his own ultraorthodoxy in matters theological, was willing to think and live the situation as he saw it all the way through. The selection from Mary Rowlandson's captivity narrative gives us insight into Puritan life on the Indian frontier, as the selection from Samuel Sewall's diary gives us insight into more settled Puritan life. Out of the horrors of her captivity, she makes a full and deep religious experience, and he reveals himself as an eminently practical, full-blooded man, striving above all to be honest with his undoubtedly sinful self. Increase Mather's sermon, coming late in the century, is one of many such—a jeremiad, so-called, in which he would call his audience back to their better days—as would his son, Cotton, in the selection from his *Magnalia*. But the son was also a man touched by the non-Puritan world of the Enlightenment; and in the selection from his *Christian Philosopher* he attempts to prove that the world revealed by the new sciences only demonstrates eternal Christian truth—in effect offering a Puritan view of the argument from design. The selections from Wise and Edwards show the Puritan mind further discovering the world of the Enlightenment. Wise embraces it, and Edwards fights it to a standstill. Edwards is undoubtedly the greatest of Puritan minds, and perhaps the last—committed, in his *Personal Narrative*, to an ultimately mystical sense of religion and religious values, yet capable, in the other selections with their sermonizing rhetoric or keen philosophical and psychological analysis, of demonstrating the absolute primacy of such a mystical sense. In Edwards we can know most fully the Puritan sense of the imperfection of the individual who strives, precisely in the sense of his imperfection, to understand himself and his destiny. Finally, the Puritan poems may serve at once to footnote, develop, and express the complexities of Puritan individualism and its paradoxical relationship to Puritan theological commitments. Above all, the Puritan poems illustrate variously the Puritan faith in the meaningful order of the world and of man's place in it. The anagram drawn from a proper name, the structure of theology, a natural or social event, or a Biblical text—each is to be expanded poetically so as to draw out its full religious significance. The richness of the world, felt fully, contains in itself such a religious significance. Esthetics, as it were, functions as a form of theology, and man's individual creations are shown to be at once totally consonant with and dependent upon God's.

Bibliographical Note. The best guide to the voluminous literature of Puritanism is the collection of texts, with introduction and critical bibliographies, edited by Perry Miller and Thomas Johnson, *The Puritans* (Cincinnati, 1938). Substantially the same selection of texts has been edited by Miller as *The American Puritans* (New York, 1956). Miller has studied Puritan intellectual history in three basic books, *Orthodoxy in Massachusetts* (Cambridge, 1933), *The New England Mind: The Seventeenth Century* (New York, 1939), and *The New England Mind from Colony to Province* (Cambridge, 1953). Important essays of his on Puritans and Puritanism are collected as *Errand into the Wilderness* (Cambridge, 1947). An earlier study, to be modified by Miller's work, is Herbert Schneider, *The Puritan Mind* (New York, 1930). The later history of Puritan theology is examined in Joseph Haroutunian, *Piety and Morality* (New York, 1932). A brilliant brief study of American and English Puritanism, bringing to focus all recent studies of the subject, is Alan Simpson, *Puritanism in Old and New England* (Chicago, 1955). A recent reassessment is Edmund S. Morgan *Visible Saints* (New York, 1963). The great study of the religious-economic significance of Puritanism in western European history is Max Weber, *The Protestant Ethic and the Spirit of Capitalism*, trans. Talcott Parsons (London, 1930); Weber's work is followed by one focused particularly on English (and, incidentally, American) Puritanism, R. H. Tawney, *Religion and the Rise of Capitalism* (New York, 1926). New England Puritan society is best to be seen in two studies by Samuel Eliot Morison, *Builders of the Bay Colony* (Boston, 1930) and *The Puritan Pronaos* (New York, 1936). On the nature and achievement of Puritan literature, see Kenneth Murdock, *Literature and Theology in Colonial New England* (Cambridge, 1949). For a powerful minority report, see Peter Gay, *A Loss of Mastery: Puritan Historians in Colonial America* (Berkeley, 1966).

John Cotton

(1585–1652)

Bibliographical Note. The text here printed follows that of *Old South Leaflet*, No. 53 (1896). The definitive study of Cotton is Larzar Ziff, *The Career of John Cotton*. (Princeton, 1965).

GODS PROMISE TO HIS PLANTATIONS (1630)

2 *Sam.* 7. 10.

Moreover I will appoint a place for my people Israell, and I will plant them, that they may dwell in a place of their owne, and move no more.

In the beginning of this chapter we reade of *Davids* purpose to build God an house, who thereupon consulted with *Nathan* about it, one Prophet standing in neede of anothers help in such waightie matters. *Nathan* incourageth the King unto this worke, verse 3. God the same night meetes *Nathan* and tells him a contrary purpose of his: Wherein God refuseth *Davids* offer, with some kind of earnest and vehement dislike, *verse* 4, 5: Secondly, he refuseth the reason of *Davids* offer, from his long silence. For foure hundred yeares together he spake of no such thing, unto any of the Tribes of *Israel* saying, *Why build you not me an house?* in 6. 7. verses.

Now lest *David* should be discouraged with this answer, the Lord bids *Nathan* to shut up his speech with words of encouragement, and so he remoues his discouragement two wayes.

First, by recounting his former favours dispensed unto *David*. Secondly, by promising the continuance of the like or greater: and the rather, because of this purpose of his. And five blessings God promiseth unto *David*, and his, for his sake.

The first is in the 10. verse: *I will appoint a place for my people Israell*.

Secondly, seeing it was in his heart to build him an house, God would therefore, *build him an house renowned forever*. verse 11.

Thirdly, that he would accept of an house from *Solomon*, verse 12.

Fourthly, hee will be a Father to his sonne, vers. 14. 15.

Fifthly, that he will *establish the throne of his house for ever*.

In this 10 verse is a double blessing promised:

First, the designment of a place for his people.

Secondly, a plantation of them in that place, from whence is promised a threefold blessing.

First, they shall dwell there like Free-holders in a place of their owne.

Secondly, hee promiseth them firme and durable possession, they shall move no more.

Thirdly, they shall have peaceable and quiet resting there, The sonnes of wickedness shall afflict them no more: which is amplified by their former troubles, as before time.

From the appointment of a place for them, which is the first blessing, you may observe this note,

The placing of a people in this or that Countrey is from the appointment of the Lord.

This is evident in the Text, and the Apostle speaks of it as grounded in nature, *Acts* 17. 26. *God hath determined the times before appointed, and the bounds of our habitation. Dut. 2 chap.* 5. 9. God would not have the *Israelites* meddle with the *Edomites*, or the *Moabites*, because he had given them their land for a possession. God assigned out such a land for such a posterity, and for such a time.

Quest. Wherein doth this worke of God stand in appointing a place for a people?

Answ. First, when God espies or discovers a land for a

people, as in *Ezek.* 20. 6. he brought them into a land that he had espied for them: And that is, when either he gives them to discover it themselves, or heare of it discovered by others, and fitting them.

Secondly, after he hath espied it, when he carrieth them along to it, so that they plainly see a providence of God leading them from one Country to another: As in *Exod.* 19. 4. *You have seene how I have borne you as on Eagles wings, and brought you unto my selfe.* So that though they met with many difficulties, yet hee carried them high above them all, like an eagle, flying over seas and rockes, and all hindrances.

Thirdly, when he makes roome for a people to dwell there, as in *Psal.* 80. 9. *Thou preparedst roome for them.* When *Isaac* sojourned among the *Philistines,* he digged one well, and the *Philistines* strove for it, and he called it *Esek.* and he digged another well, and for that they strove also, therefore he called it *Sitnah:* and he removed thence, and digged an other well, and for that they strove not, and he called it *Rohoboth,* and said, *For now the Lord hath made roomee for us, and we shall be fruitfull in the Land.* Now no *Esek,* no *Sitnah,* no quarrel or contention, but now he sits downe in *Rohoboth* in a peaceable roome.

Now God makes room for a people 3 wayes:

First, when he casts out the enemies of a people before them by lawfull warre with the inhabitants, which God cals them unto: as in *Ps.* 44. 2. *Thou didst driue out the heathen before them.* But this course of warring against others, & driving them out withoute provocation, depends upon speciall Commission from God, or else it is not imitable.

Secondly, when he gives a forreigne people favour in the eyes of any native people to come and sit downe with them either by way of purchase, as *Abraham* did obtaine the field of *Machpelah;* or else when they give it in courtesie, as *Pharaoh* did the land of *Goshen* unto the sons of *Jacob.*

Thirdly, when hee makes a Countrey though not altogether void of inhabitants, yet voyd in that place where they reside. Where there is a vacant place, there is liberty for the sonne of *Adam* or *Noah* to come and inhabite, though they neither buy

it, nor aske their leaves. *Abraham* and *Isaac*, when they[1] sojourned amongst the Philistines, they did not buy that land to
feede their cattle, because they said There is roome enough. And
so did *Jacob* pitch his Tent by *Sechem*, *Gen.* 34. 21. There was
roome enough as *Hamor* said, *Let them sit down amongst us.*
And in this case if the people who were former inhabitants did
disturbe them in their possessions, they complained to the King,
as of wrong done unto them: As *Abraham* did because they took
away his well, in *Gen.* 21. 25. For his right whereto he pleaded
not his immediate calling from God, (for that would have
seemed frivolous amongst the Heathen) but his owne industry
and culture in digging the well, verse 30. Nor doth the King reject his plea, with what had he to doe to digge wells in their
soyle? but admitteth it as a Principle in Nature, That in a vacant
soyle, hee that taketh possession of it, and bestoweth culture and
husbandry upon it, his Right it is. And the ground of this is
from the grand Charter given to *Adam* and his posterity in
Paradise, *Gen.* 1. 28. *Multiply, and replenish the earth, and
subdue it.* If therefore any sonne of *Adam* come and finde a
place empty, he hath liberty to come, and fill, and subdue the
earth there. This Charter was renewed to *Noah, Gen.* 9. 1.
Fulfill the earth and multiply: So that it is free from that
comon Grant for any to take possession of vacant Countries.
Indeed no Nation is to drive out another without speciall Commission from heaven, such as the Israelites had, unless the
Natives do unjustly wrong them, and will not recompence the
wrongs done in peaceable fort, & then they may right themselves
by lawfull war, and subdue the Countrey unto themselves.

This placeing of people in this or that Countrey, is from
Gods soveraignty over all the earth, and the inhabitants thereof:
as in *Psal.* 24. 1. *The earth is the Lords, and the fulnesse thereof.*
And in *Ier.* 10. 7. God is there called, *The King of Nations:* and

---

[1] This sojourning was a constant residence there, as in a possession of their
owne; although it be called sojourning or dwelling as strangers, because
they neither had the soveraigne government of the whole Countrey in their
owne hand, nor yet did incorporate themselves into the Commonwealth of
the Natives, to submit themselves into their government. [Cotton's note]

in *Deut*. 10. 14. Therefore it is meete he should provide a place for all Nations to inhabite, and haue all the earth replenished. Onely in the Text here is meant some more speciall appointment, because God tells them it by his owne mouth; he doth not so with other people, he doth not tell the children of *Sier*, that hee hath appointed a place for them: that is, He gives them the land by promise; others take the land by his providence, but Gods people take the land by promise: And therefore the land of *Canaan* is called a land of promise. Which they discerne, first, by discerning themselves to be in Christ, in whom all the promises are yea, and amen.

Secondly, by finding his holy presence with them, to wit, when he plants them in the holy Mountaine of his Inheritance: *Exodus*. 15. 17. And that is when he giveth them the liberty and purity of his Ordinances. It is a land of promise, where they have provision for soule as well as for body. *Ruth* dwelt well for outward respects while shee dwelt in *Moab*, but when shee cometh to dwell in *Israel*, shee is said to come under the wings of God: *Ruth* 2. 12. When God wrappes us in with his Ordinances, and warmes us with the life and power of them as with wings, there is a land of promise.

This may teach us all where we doe now dwell, or where after wee may dwell, be sure you looke at every place appointed to you, from the hand of God: wee may not rush into any place, and never say to God, By your leave; but we must discerne how God appoints us this place. There is poore comfort in sitting down in any place, that you cannot say, This place is appointed me of God. Canst thou say that God spied out this place for thee, and there hath setled thee above all hinderances? didst thou finde that God made roome for thee either by lawfull descent, or purchase, or gift, or other warrantable right? Why then this is the place God hath appointed thee; here hee hath made roome for thee, he hath placed thee in *Rehoboth*, in a peaceable place: This we must discerne, or els we are but intruders upon God. And when wee doe withall discerne, that God giveth us these outward blessings from his love in Christ, and maketh comfortable provision as well for our soule as for our bodies, by the meanes of grace, then doe we enjoy our present possession as well by gracious promise, as by the common, and just, and bountifull providence of the Lord. Or if a man doe remove, he must see that God hath espied out such a Countrey for him.

Secondly, though there be many difficulties yet he hath given us hearts to overlook them all, as if we were carried upon eagles wings.

And thirdly, see God making roome for us by some lawfull means.

Quest. But how shall I know whether God hath appointed me such a place, if I be well where I am, what may warrant my removeall?

Answ. There be foure or five good things, for procurement of any of which I may remove. Secondly, there be some evill things, for avoiding of any of which wee may transplant our selves. Thirdly, if withall we find some speciall providence of God concurring in either of both concerning our selves, and applying general grounds of removall to our personall estate.

First, wee may remove for the gaining of knowledge. Our Saviour commends it in the Queene of the south, that she came from the utmost parts of the earth to heare the wisdom of *Solomon: Matth.* 12. 42. And surely with him she might have continued for the same end, if her personall calling had not re-called her home.

Secondly, some remove and travaile for merchandize and gaine-sake; *Daily bread may be sought from farre, Prov.* 31. 14. Yea our Saviour approveth travaile for Merchants, *Matth.* 13. 45, 46. when hee compareth a Christian to a Merchantman seeking pearles: For he never fetcheth a comparison from any unlawfull thing to illustrate a thing lawfull. The comparison from the unjust Steward, and from the Theefe in the night, is not taken from the injustice of the one, or the theft of the other; but from the wisdome of the one, and the sodainnesse of the other; which in themselves are not unlawfull.

Thirdly, to plant a Colony, that is, a company that agree together to remove out of their owne Country, and settle a Citty or commonwealth elsewhere. Of such a Colony wee reade in *Acts* 16. 12. which God blessed and prospered exceedingly, and made it a glorious Church. Nature teacheth Bees to doe so, when as the hive is too full, they seeke abroad for new dwellings:

So when the hive of the Common wealth is so full, that Tradesmen cannot live one by another, but eate up one another, in this case it is lawfull to remove.

Fourthly, God alloweth a man to remove, when he may employ his Talents and gift better elsewhere, especially when where he is, he is not bound by any speciall engagement. Thus God sent *Ioseph* before to preserve the Church: *Josephs* wisedome and spirit was not fit for a shepheard, but for a Counsellour of State, and therefore God sent him into *Egypt*. *To whom much is given of him God will require the more: Luke.* 12. 48.

Fifthly, for the liberty of the Ordinances. 2 *Chron.* 11. 13, 14, 15. When *Jeroboam* made a desertion from *Judah*, and set up golden Calves to worship, all that were well affected, both Priests and people, sold their possessions, and came to *Ierusalem* for the Ordinances sake. This case was of seasonable use to our fathers in the dayes of Queene *Mary*; who removed to *France* and *Germany* in the beginning of her Reign, upon Proclamation of alteration of religion, before any persecution began.

Secondly, there be evills to be avoyded that may warrant removeall. First, when some grievous sinnes overspread a Country that threaten desolation. *Mic.* 2. 6 to 11 verse: When the people say to them that prophecie, *Prophecie not*; then verse 10. *Arise then, this is not your rest.* Which words though they be a threatning, not a commandement; yet as in a threatning a wise man foreseeth the plague, so in the threatning he seeth a commandement, to hide himselfe from it. This case might have been of seasonable use unto them of the *Palatinate*, when they saw their Orthodox Ministers banished, although themselues might for a while enjoy libertie of conscience.

Secondly, if men be overburdened with debts and miseries, as *Davids* followers were; they may then retire out of the way (as they retired to *David* for safety) not to defraud their creditors (for *God is an avenger of such things*, 1 *Thess.* 4. 6.) but to gaine further opportunity to discharge their debts, and to satisfie their Creditors. 1 *Sam.* 22. 1, 2.

Thirdly, in case of persecution, so did the Apostle in *Acts* 13. 46, 47.

Thirdly, as these generall cases, where any of them doe fall out, doe warrant removeall in generall: so there be some speciall providences or particular cases which may give warrant unto such or such a person to transplant himselfe, and which apply the former generall grounds to particular persons.

First, if soveraigne Authority command and encourage such Plantations by giving way to subjects to transplant themselves, and set up a new Commonwealth. This is a lawfull and expedient case for such particular persons as be designed and sent: *Matth.* 8. 9. and for such as they who are sent, have power to command.

Secondly, when some speciall providence of God leades a man unto such a course. This may also single out particulars. *Psal.* 32. 8. *I will instruct, and guide thee with mine eye.* As the childe knowes the pleasure of his father in his eye, so doth the child of God see Gods pleasure in the eye of his heavenly Fathers providence. And this is done three wayes.

First, if God give a man an inclination to this or that course, for that is the spirit of man; and *God is the father of spirits: Rom.* 1. 11, 12. 1 *Cor.* 16. 12. *Paul* discerned his calling to goe to *Rom*, by his τὸ πρόθυμον, his ready inclination to that voyage; and *Apollos* his loathing to goe to *Corinth, Paul* accepted as a just reason of his refusall of a calling to goe thither. And this holdeth, when in a mans inclination to travaile, his heart is set on no by-respects, as to see fashions, to deceive his Creditours, to fight Duels, or to live idly, these are vaine inclinations; but if his heart be inclined upon right judgement to advance the Gospell, to maintaine his family, to use his Talents fruitfully, or the like good end, this inclination is from God. As the beames of the Moone darting into the Sea leades it to and fro, so doth a secret inclination darted by God into our hearts leade and bowe (as a byas) our whole course.

Secondly, when God gives other men hearts to call us as the men of *Mecedon* did *Paul, Come to us into Macedonia, and helpe us.* When wee are invited by others who have a good calling to reside there, we may goe with them, unlesse we be detained by waightier occasions. One member hath interest in another, to call to it for helpe, when it is not diuerted by greater employment.

Thirdly, there is another providence of God concurring in both these, that is, when a mans calling and person is free, and not tyed by parents, or Magistrates, or other people that have interest in him. Or when abroad hee may doe himselfe and others more good than he can doe at home. Here is then an eye of God that opens a doore there, and sets him loose here, inclines his heart that way, and outlookes all difficulties. When God makes roome for us, no binding here, and an open way there, in such a case God tells them, he will appoint a place for them.

Use. 2. Secondly, this may teach us in every place where God appoints us to sit downe, to acknowledge him as our Landlord. The earth is the Lords and the fullnesse thereof; his are our Countries, our Townes, our houses; and therefore let us acknowledge him in them all. The Apostle makes this use of it amongst the *Athenians, Acts* 17. 26, 27. *He hath appointed the times and places of our habitation; that we might seeke and grope after the Lord.* There is a threefold use thaat we are to make of it, as it appeareth there; Let us seek after the Lord, why? Because if thou commest into an house thou wilt aske for the owner of it: And so if thou commest into a forreigne land, and there findest an house and land provided for thee, wilt thou not enquire, where is the Landlord? where is that God that gave me this house and land? He is missing, and therefore seek after him.

Secondly, thou must feele after him, grope after him by such sensible things, strive to attaine the favour of your Landlord, and labour to be obedient to him that hath given you such a place.

Thirdly, you must labour to finde him in his Ordinances, in prayer and in Christian communion. These things I owe him as my Landlord, and by these I find and enjoy him. This use the very Pagans were to make of their severall Plantations: And if you knew him before, seeke him yet more, and feele after him till you find him in his Ordinances, and in your consciences.

Use 3. Thirdly, when you have found God making way and roome for you, and carrying you by his providence into any place, learne to walke thankfully before him, defraud him not of his rent, but offer yourselves unto his service: Serve that

God, and teach your children to serve him, that hath appointed you and them the place of your habitation.

2 Observation. A *people of Gods plantation shall enjoy their owne place with safety and peace.*

This is manifest in the Text: I will plant them and what followes from thence? They shall dwell in their owne place; But how? Peaceably, they shall not be moved any more. Then they shall dwell safely, then they shall live in peace. The like promise you reade of in *Psal.* 89. 21, 22. *The enemie shall not exact upon them any more. And in Psal.* 92. 13. *Those that be planted in the house of the Lord, shall flourish in the Courts of our God. Gods plantation is a florishing plantation, Amos* 9. 15.

Quest. What is it for God to plant a people?

Answr. It is a Metaphor taken from young Impes; I will plant them, that is, I will make them to take roote there; and that is, where they and their soyle agree well together, when they are well and sufficiently provided for, as a plant suckes nourishment from the soyle that fitteth it.

Secondly, When hee causeth them to grow as plants doe, in *Psal.* 80. 8, 9, 10, 11. When a man growes like a tree in tallnesse and strength, to more firmnesse and eminency, then hee may be said to be planted.

Thirdly, When God causeth them to *fructifie. Psal.* 1. 5.

Fourthly, When he establisheth them there, then he plants, and rootes not up.

But here is something more especiall in this planting; for they were planted before in this land, and yet he promiseth here againe, that he will plant them in their owne land; which doth imply, first, That whatever former good estate they had already, he would prosper it, and increase it.

Secondly, God is said to plant a people more especially, when they become *Trees of righteousnesse, Isay* 61. 3: That they may be called trees of righteousnesse, the planting of the Lord. So that there is implyed not onely a continuance of their former good estate, but that hee would make them a good people, a choice generation: which he did, first, by planting the Ordinances of God amongst them in a more glorious manner, as he did in *Salomons* time.

2. He would give his people *a naile*, and *a place in his Tabernable*, *Isay* 56. 5. And that is to give us part in Christ; for so the Temple typified. So then hee plants us when hee gives us roote in Christ.

Thirdly, When he giveth us to *grow up in him as Calves in the stall*. *Mal.* 4. 2, 3.

Fourthly, & to *bring forth much fruit*, Joh. 15. 1, 2.

Fifthly, and to continue and abide in the state of grace. This is to plant us in his holy Sanctuary, he not rooting us up.

Reasons. This is taken from the kinde acceptance of *Davids* purpose to build God an house, because he saw it was done in the honesty of his heart, therefore he promiseth to give his people a place wherein they should abide forever as in a house of rest.

Secondly, it is taken from the office God takes upon him, when he is our planter, hee becomes our husbandman; and *if he plant us, who shall plucke us up?* *Isay.* 27. 1, 2. *Job.* 34. 29. When he giveth quiet, who can make trouble? If God be the Gardiner, who shall plucke up what he sets down? Every plantation that he hath not planted shall be plucked up, and what he hath planted shall surely be established.

Thirdly, from the nature of the blessing hee conferres upon us: When he promiseth to plant a people, their dayes shall be as the dayes of a Tree, *Isay.* 65. 22: As the Oake is said to be an hundred yeares in growing, and an hundred yeares in full strength, and an hundred yeares in decaying.

Quest: But it may be demanded, how was this promise fulfilled by the people, seeing after this time they met with many persecutions, at home, and abroad, many sources of wickednesse afflicted them; *Jeroboam* was a sonne of wickednesse, and so was *Ahab*, and *Ahaz*, and divers others.

Answ. Because after *Davids* time they had more setlednesse than before.

Secondly, to the godly these promises were fulfilled in Christ.

Thirdly, though this promise was made that others should not wrong them, yet it followes not but that they might wrong themselves by trespassing against God, and so expose themselves to affliction. Whilst they continued Gods plantation, they were a noble Vine, a right seede, but if *Israel* will destroy themselves, the fault is in themselves. And yet even in their captivity the good amongst them God graciously provided for: The *Basket of good figges* God sent into the land of *Caldea* for their good: *Jer.* 24. 5. But if you rebell against God, the same God that planted you will also roote you out againe, for all the evill which you shall doe against your selves: *Jer.* 11. 17. When the Israelites liked not the soile, grew weary of the Ordinances, and forsooke the worship of God, and said, *What part have we in David?* after this they never got so good a King, nor any settled rest in the good land wherein God had planted them. As they waxed weary of God, so hee waxed wearie of thcm, and cast them out of his sight.

Use 1. To exhort all that are planted at home, or intend to plant abroad, to looke well to your plantation, as you desire that the sonnes of wickedness may not afflict you at home, nor enemies abroad, looke that you be right planted, and then you need not to feare, you are safe enough: God hath spoken it, I will plant them, and they shall not be moved, neither shall the sonnes of wickedness afflict them any more.

Quest. What course would you have us take?

Answ. Have speciall care that you ever have the Ordinances planted amongst you, or else never looke for security. As soone as Gods Ordinances cease, your security ceaseth likewise; but if God plant his Ordinances among you, feare not, he will maintaine them. *Isay.* 4. 5,6. V*pon all their glory there shall be a defence;* that is, upon all Gods Ordinances: for so was the Arke called *the Glory of Israel,* 1 *Sam.* 4. 22.

Secondly, have a care to be implanted into the Ordinances, that the word may be ingrafted into you, and you into it: If you take rooting in the ordinances, grow up thereby, bring forth much fruite, continue and abide therein, then you are vineyard of red wine, and the Lord will keepe you, *Isay* 27. 2. 3. that no sonnes of violence shall destroy you. Looke into all the stories whether divine or humane, and you shall never finde that God ever rooted out a people that had the Ordinances planted amongst them, and themselves planted into the Ordinances: never did God suffer such plants to be plucked up; on all thcir glory shall be a defence.

Thirdly, be not unmindfull of our *Jerusalem* at home, whether you leave us, or stay at home with us. *Oh pray for the peace of Jerusalem, they shall prosper that love her. Psal.* 122. 6. *They shall all be confounded and turned backe that hate Sion, Psal.* 129. 5. As God continueth his presence with us, (blessed be his name) so be ye present in spirit with us, though absent in body: Forget not the wombe that bare you and the brest that gave you sucke. Even ducklings hatched under an henne, though they take the water, yet will still have recourse to the wing that hatched them: how much more should chickens of the same feather, and yolke? In the amity and unity of brethren, the Lord hath not onely promised, but commanded a blessing, even life forevermore: *Psal.* 133. 1, 2.

Fourthly, goe forth, every man that goeth, with a publick spirit, looking not on your owne things onely, but also on the things of others: *Phil.* 2. 4. This care of universall helpfullnesse was the prosperity of the first Plantation of the Primitive Church, *Acts* 4. 32.

Fifthly, have a tender care that you looke well to the plants that spring from you, that is, to your children, that they doe not degenerate as the Israelites did; after which they were vexed with afflictions on every hand. How came this to passe? *Ier.* 2. 21. *I planted them a noble Vine, holy, a right seede, how then art thou degenerate into a strange Vine before mee?* Your Ancestours were of a noble divine spirit, but if they suffer their children to degenerate, to take loose courses, then God will surely plucke you up: Otherwise if men have a care to propagate the Ordinances and Religion to their children after them, God will plant them and not roote them up. For want of this, the seede of the repenting *Ninivites* was rooted out.

Sixthly, and lastly, offend not the poore Natives, but as you partake in their land, so make them partakers of your precious faith: as you reape their temporalls, so feede them with your spiritualls: winne them to the love of Christ, for whom Christ died. They never yet refused the Gospell, and therefore more hope they will now receive it. Who knoweth whether God have reared this whole Plantation for such an end:

Use 2. Secondly, for consolation to them that are planted by God in any place, that finde rooting and establishing from

God, this is a cause of much encouragement unto you, that
what hee hath planted he will maintaine, every plantation his
right hand hath not planted shalbe rooted up, but his owne
plantation shall prosper, & flourish. When he promiseth peace
and safety, what enemies shalstbe able to make the promise of
God of none effect? Neglect not walls, and bulwarkes, and
fortifications for your owne defence; but
ever let the name of the Lord be your strong
Tower; and the word of his Promise the
Rocke of your refuge. His word
that made heaven and earth
will not faile, till hea-
ven and earth be
no more
Amen.

FINIS.

Thomas Hooker

(1586–1647)

Bibliographical Note. There is no collection of Hooker's writings. The text which is used here is printed from Hooker's *Application of Redemption By the Effectual Work of the Word, and Spirit of Christ, for the bringing home of Lost Sinners to God, The First Eight Books.* (London, 1656), pp. 205–221; *The Ninth and Tenth Books* (London, 1659), pp. 52–66, pp. 210–217, pp. 619–624. The only modern life of Hooker is G. L. Walker, *Thomas Hooker* (New York, 1891). A significant study of Hooker's supposed liberal tendencies is Perry Miller, "Thomas Hooker and the Democracy of Early Connecticut," *New England Quarterly,* IV (1931), pp. 663–712.

from

THE APPLICATION OF
REDEMPTION (1656, 1659)

A PLAIN AND POWERFUL MINISTERY

Doct. 2: A plain and powerful Ministerie, is the only Ordinary Means to Prepare the heart soundly for Christ.

Hence it is, when our Savior would have this work done, he prepares a workman fit for it, and furnisheth him with abilities, which might enable him to the discharge thereof; the work is great, and the service difficult, and therefore *Elias* is fitted with a Spirit suitable with Power answerable unto that purpose for which he was appointed, an Instrument as we say for the nonce. *John* the Baptist he also inherits these abilities, and that

Minister must be an *Elias*, i.e. must have his Spirit and Power in proportion, if ever this great work of preparation followeth his hand with Comfort and Success; As it was in the Material, so also is it in the building of *this spiritual temple, in which the holy Ghost doth dwell:* The Elect of God are like trees of righteousness, the Word is like the Ax, that must be lifted by a skilful and strong arm of a cunning Minister, who like a Spiritual Artificer must hew and square, and take off the knotty untowardness in the Soul before we can come to touch close and settle upon the Lord Christ as the Cornerstone: *Paul* calls the Saints *Gods husbandry*, 1 Cor. 3.9. A powerful humbling Ministery is like the Plow, to *plow up the fallow ground, the thorny* sensual hearts of sinful men to receive *the immortal seed of the Word of Promise* and the Spirit of Christ thereby.

For the Opening of the Point Two Things are.

1. What is meant by a plain and powerful Ministery, such as that of *Elias*.
2. How this hath force to effect so great a Work.

The plainness of the Ministery appears,

When the Language and Words are such as those of the meanest Capacity have some acquaintance with, and may be able to conceive; when the Preacher accommodates his Speech to the shallow understanding of the Simplest Hearer, so far as in him lies, always avoiding the frothy tinkling of quaint and farfetched Phrases, which take off, and blunt as it were the edge of the blessed Truth and Word of God: Therefore the Apostle rejects *the wisdom of Words* as that which makes the Cross of Christ; that is, the Doctrine of Christ Crucified, revealed in the Gospel, to lose his proper and powerful effect when it is to be preached; where let it be observed that it is not only the vanity and emptiness of Words which is here condemned, but even that pompous gaudiness, and elegancy of Speech, which after an unsuspected manner steals away the mind and affection from the truth, and stayes it with it self, when it should be a means both to convey both Attention and Affection from it self to the truth. He that puts so much Sugar into the Potion, that he hinders the strength, and the work of it by such a kind of mixture, though he please the Pallat of the Patient, yet thereby he wrongs both the Physick, and his Health. So here in Preaching.

For the excellency of Eloquence, and entising words of humane Wisdom which in case were commendable to be used by him who is an Orator, or a Declamor in the School, in the Pulpit becomes ever Fruitless, and many times hurtful and prejudicial to the saving success of the Gospel: Hence the Apostle makes these as Opposite, 2 *Cor.* 2.4. *My Speech and my preaching was not with entising words of mans wisdom, but in the demonstration of the Spirit and of Power:* taking this for granted, as it appears in manner of the Speech, the pompe of entising words must not be discovered if we would have the Spirit in the powerful work of it be demonstrated and made to appear, so much sweetness of words as may make way for the efficacy of the Gospel, may be admitted, and no more. And as all kind of Curiosity and Niceness is to be avoided, so all obscure and unusual Phrases, dark Sentences and Expressions, strange Languages are much more to be rejected, as opposite even to the end of speaking, much more to plainness of the Preaching of the truth. Words are appointed by God in his Providence, to be Carriers as it were, by whose help the thoughts of our minds and the savory apprehensions of truth may be communicated, and conveyed over to the understanding of others; whereas by mystical and dark Sentences he that comes to hear, can by no means profit, because he cannot conceive, and so both Hearer and Speaker must needs miss their end, and lose their labor, since the one doth no good in his Speech, because he so speaks that the other can receive no benefit: He that hath a Pastoral heart must be so affected in dispensing the Doctrine of Grace, as *Paul* was in writing, *Rom.* 1.7. to all that are, *To all that be at Rome,* so should he labor to reach out mercy and comfort to every soul in the congregation, by every sentence he delivers, as much as in him lies, whereas mystical cloudy discourses which exceed the capacity and understanding of most in the assembly, its not possible they should work powerfully upon their Consciences. That which the Mind conceives not, the Heart affects not: Ministers should be, and, if faithful they wil be as nurses to the people, they will prepare milk for the meanest and weakest, and meat for all; but never give dry crust or stones in stead of bread to any; for that was not to feed, but to starve the Child. Hence the Apostle concludes strange Languages in the delivery of the Truth to be a Curse sent of God upon a people, and therefore the Minister that so Communicates the Word, he is the Messenger that brings a Curse to the Congregation, 1 Cor. 14.21,22: *In the Law it is written, with men of other tongues and other lips, will I speak unto this people, wherefore tongues are fore a sign not to them that believe, but to them that believe not:* whereas Prophecying should be in that openness and familiarity of Language, that the unbeleiving, yea, *unlearned should be convinced, and have the secrets of his Heart made manifest to his own Conscience,* that so he may be truly humbled and acknowledge Gods power and presence in the virtue of his own Ordinance blessed by him, 1 Cor. 14.24. It was the complaint of God, *Job* 38.2. *That Counsel was darkened by Words without Knowledg.* It was not allowed in *Jobs* Conference and debate of Questions with his friends, it cannot but be much more condemned in publishing the mysteries of Life and Salvation to others: Its the scope of the Calling and Work of the Ministery *to give the Knowledge of God in the face of Jesus Christ,* 2 Cor. 4.8. To darken Knowledg therefore, is to cross Gods Honor, our own callings, the Comforts of the People over whom we are set, and to be concealers of Gods Mind, not Interpreters and Revealers of his Will.

Object. There is only one Plea here Objected, that carries any appearance of likelihood with it, gathered out of *Eccles.* 12.10. where it is said, *The Preacher sought to find out acceptable words,* and *that that was written, was upright, even words of truth:* Was it *Solomons* Care directed by the Spirit, to study pleasing words to affect his Hearers? Should not his practice be a pattern to all to imitate him in like expressions? Dare any affirm but that he did what he ought? And shall any be so careless or presumptuous as not to endeavor to follow that course recorded with so much Commendation by the Holy Ghost?

Answ. I yeild willingly to all the Truths which the Text holds out unto us; but it shall appear that nothing can from thence by just consequence be Collected, that will cross, but rather confirm, and that undoubtedly what hath been affirmed before. That the Writings of men should be sound, their Speeches acceptable, is granted; but when are they? how shall they be judged to be such? That's the Doubt: which once Cleered, the Objection will be Answered fully: Words then must be judged acceptable, not by the foolish fancies, corrupt and carnal humors of men, but from the warrant they have from the scripture, and the work they have in the hearts of the Hearers for their good, as the 11. vers. of *Eccles.* 12. discovers; it being added as it were by way of Explication, to evidence where that pleasantness of speech lay, *The words of the wise are as Goads and Nails fastened by the Masters of Assemblies which are given by one Shepheard:* As though the Preacher should have expressed himself, more freely and fully thus. If any shall ask, what these acceptable words formerly mentioned are, and how they may be discerned, it is easie for any thus to know them by their working upon the heart: as we judge the goodness and virtue of Physick by its working upon the body, or in the stomach: Those words which are as Goads to awaken and spur on the sluggish and sleepy hearted to the performance of service with greater cheerfulness and speed: those that are as Nails so to fast on the precious truths of God, upon the Consciences of men, that they are kept within the compass of Gods command as Sheep within the fold.

Lastly, Those words which are endited & taught not *by humane wisdom, but by the Spirit of Christ,* 1 Cor. 2.4. who is the only chief Shepheard of his Church, and whose voice should only be heard: such words should be sought out by the speaker, such words deserve to be accounted acceptable by those who hear them. Now how far all quaintness and darkness of speech is from this warrant of the Lord, or this powerfull work in the hearts of his people, let the sluggish and secure courses, the loose lives and conversations of such persons, parishes, places, and congregations, who have, and love such teachers, and such kind of teaching, proclaim and testifie to al the world.

Plainness of Preaching, appears also in the matter that is spoken: when sin and sinners are set out in their native and

natural colours, and carry their proper names, whereby they may
be owned suitable to the loathsomness that is in them, and the
danger of those evils which are their undoubted reward: A
Spade is a Spade, and a Drunkard is a Drunkard, &c. and if he
will have his Sins, he must and shall have Hell with them. Its
Satans Policy (who painter or tyre-maker like, cozens all the
world with colors) to smut and disfigure the beautiful wayes of
Godliness, and the glorious Graces of the Spirit, with the soot
and dirt of reproaches, and base nick-names: Sincerity, he
terms Singularity; Exactness, Puritanism and Hypocrisie; and
so ignorant men (who judge the person by the picture) are
brought out of love and liking with those blessed wayes of
wisdom and holiness. Contrariwise, when he would cast a vaile
over the ugly and deformed face of Vice, and graceless courses
he is forced to lay some false colors of indifferency, delight,
and pleasure; Drunkenness is good fellowship, and neighborhood. Covetousness comes masked under the vizard of frugality
and moderation: Cowardliness is trimmed and decked up in the
robes of discretion, and wariness. If Ministers will not be the
Divels brokers, and followers, their manner of proceeding must
be expresly contrary: When they come to preach, they must
make sin appear truly odious, and fearful to the open view of
all, that all may be afraid and endeavor to avoid it. Those
secret wipes, and witty jerks, and nips at sin, at which the
most prophane are pleased, but not reformed; are utterly unsavory and unseeming the Place, the Person, the Office, of the
Messenger of the Lord of Hosts. What! A Minister a Jester!
O fearful! To make the Pulpit a Stage, to play with sin; when
he should terrifie the Conscience for it? The Lord abominates
the practice, he that knows and fears the Lord should abhor it
with detestation. Thus plainly dealt *Elias* with *Ahab*, 1 *Kings*
18.18. *Its thou and thy Fathers house that have troubled Israel,
because ye have forsaken the Commandments of the Lord, and
followed Baalim.* So also with Israel, 1 *Kings* 18.21. *How long
will you hault between two Opinions? If the Lord be God,
follow him; but if Baal, then follow him.* As if he should have
said, Away with this patching in Profession, either a Saint or a
Devil, make somthing of it, this is down right dealing. And
thus plainly *John* the Baptist who had the same Spirit dealt

with *Herod.* He doth not beat the Bush, and go behind the door to tell him his faults, and mince the matter with some intimations but he speaks out, *Matth.* 14.4. *It is not lawful for thee to have thy Brother* Philips *Wife:* either thou must not have that incestuous Harlot, or thou must not have Grace and Glory. Thus again he dealt with the Sadduces and Pharisees when he saw them come to his baptisms. He saies to them, *Matth.* 3.7. *Oh ye Generation of Vipers, who hath fore-warned you to flee from the wrath to come.* As if he should have said, Egs and Birds, Parents and Posterity, you are a race of venomous, and poysonful wretches: What? A proud Pharisee to listen to the simplicity of the Doctrine of Grace, is it possible? If in sincerity and good earnest, you purpose to embrace the Doctrine of truth, *bring forth then fruits worthy of amendment of life,* vers. 8.

We have done with the Plainness of the Ministery, we are now to enquire wherein the Power of a Ministery Consists: And that appears in Two Things.

There must be soundness of Argument, and undeniable Evidence of Reason out of the Word, which is able to command the Conscience; such strength of truth, which like a mighty stream, may carry an understanding Hearer. When the Apostle was to come amongst the slanting Orators and silken Doctors of Corinth, which so excelled in Eloquence, he brings the tryal of their Ministery unto this touch, 1 Cor. 4.19,20. *I will know not the speech of them that are puffed up, but the power, for the Kingdom of God stands not in word, but in Power.* Its not the flourishes of words, not the sound and tinckling of a company of fine Sentences, like apish toyes and rattles, that will commend our Ministery in the account of God, there is no Kingdom, no Power of the work of the Spirit, the heavenly Majesty of an Ordinance is not seen in such empty shels and shadows: A building with painted walls, and no pillars, would be of little use, and less continuance: A body framed out of Colours, may be a picture of a Bird or Beast, but a living Creature it cannot be, because it wants the soul and substance which should give life and vertue thereunto. So it is when a multitude of gay Sentences are packed together without the sinnews and substance of convicting Arguments: there may be the picture of a Sermon, but the life and power of Preaching there wil not be in any such expressions.

That a Minister may be Powerful, an inward spiritual heat of heart, and holy affection is required, answerable and suitable to the matter, which is to be communicated; and those adde great life and force to the delivery of the truth. *Out of the abundance of the heart the mouth speaks, and a good man out of the good treasure of his heart, brings forth good things,* Mat. 12.35. Where then there is a heart awanting, the chiefest part of Speech, the pith and heart of it is gone; for the several affections out of which the words arise, make an impression, and work a like temper of Spirit in him to whom we utter and express our selves: Thus we speak from heart to heart, and that is the best way to be in the bosome of the Hearer, and the only way to make our words take place and prevail: He that mourns in speaking of sin, makes another mourn for sin committed. An Exhortation that proceeds from the heart, carries a kind of Authority and Commission with it, to make way for it self not to return before it confer with the heart of him that will give attendance to it. Brainish Discourses talk only with the understanding, they go no further, because they rise no deeper than from the understanding of him that speaks. The Doctrine of the Gospel *is like the rain upon the herbs, and the dew upon the grass,* Deut. 32. 2. The strength and stirring of holly affections is like a mighty wind or tempest, makes the truth delivered to press in with more power, and speed, and to soak more deeply, even to the heart root of him that with meekness will receive it.

It may be here enquired for Explication of the Point: How a Ministery thus Plain and Powerful doth work? *Answ.* To speak only so much here as concerns the Place, leaving Particulars until we entreat of the several Parts of Preparation, know we must, the preparing work of a plain and powerful Ministery stands in Two Things.

It discovers the secrets of Sin, makes known the close passages of the Soul to it self, and that in the ugliness thereof: Heb. 4.11. *The Word of God is mighty in Operation, sharper than any two edged sword, divides betwixt the Soul and the Spirit, and is a discerner of the thoughts and intents of the heart.* This was the work that *Paul* aimed at in the dispensation of the Gospel, 2 *Cor.* 4.4. *Handling the Word of God, not deceitfully, but plainly, by manifestation of the truth, he commended himself to every mans Conscience in the sight of God.* As though he had said, Speak Oh ye blessed Saints of Corinth, was not *Paul* in your bosome? Did he not ransack every corner of your Consciences? Certainly you cannot but acknowledge it, your hearts dare not but confess as much.

A lively Ministery over-powers the Corruption, and sets an aw upon the Spirits of such to whom the Word is spoken and blessed. The stout Souldiers, the refuse Publicans, all stoop and stand amazed at the Ministery of *John,* Luke 3.11,12. they all said, *Master, what shall we do? Paul* a Prisoner at the Bar, makes *Felix* (the Judge upon the bench) to tremble. Hence it is, the time of the discovery of the Gospel is called *The great and dreadful day of the Lord,* Mal. 4.5. Hence that of the Apostle, 2 Cor. 10.5. *The weapons of my warfare* (that is, the powerful Ministery of the Word) *are mighty through God, to pull down strong Holds, to cast down imaginations, to captivate every high thought to the Obedience of Christ.*

Therefore our Savior, the *Chief Master of the Assemblies,* is said to speak *with authority, not as the Scribes,* Matt 7.last. Not to tell a man a sleepy tale, a toothless, sapless discourse, so that the hearers when they are gone are never stirred, never troubled for their sins, nor quickened onward in Obedience: But when the power of the Spirit, the presence and majesty of the Lord Christ, appears in his Ordinances, they then carry authority with them and bear down all before them: *Satan falls like lightning,* forsakes his hold, and the stoutest heart is forced to give way to the Government of the King of Saints. Strong Physick either Cures or Kills, either takes away the disease, or life of the Patient, so it is with a spiritual and powerful Ministery, it will work one way or other, either it humbles or hardens, converts or condemns those that live under the stroak thereof. For observe we must, that the Word is but an Instrument in the hand of Christ, who dispenseth the same according to his good pleasure, and the counsel of his own Will, working when, and upon whom he will, and what he will by it. The Sword in the hand of him that wields it may as easily kill as defend another, answerable to the affection of him that strikes therewith:

It is so with the Word which is the Sword of the Spirit, It is the savor of life unto life, but then and to those only to whom the Lord will bless the same; and the savor of death unto death, then and unto those when such a blessing is denied.

Such as be Ministers may hence see the Reason, of that little success we find, that little good we do, in the Vineyard of the Lord: Our Pains prosper not, our Preaching prevails not, with the hearts of men, not one mountain levelled, not a crooked piece squared, not one poor Soul prepared for a Christ, after many months, quarters, years travelling in the work of the Ministery.

The time was *Satan fell like lightning,* suddenly, speedily, when the Disciples of Christ *as Sons of Thunder,* delivered the Gospel in the power and demonstration of the Spirit: But now Satan stands up in his full strength, takes up his stand, maintains his hould in the hearts of men, notwithstanding all that we commonly see done by the most. What is the reason? God is as Merciful as ever, his Word and Ordinances as effectual as ever they were: I need not enquire as he, *Where is the Lord God of* Elias? No, Brethren, I must rather ask, *Where is the Spirit and Power of* Elias? We want Power, and Spirit, and then no wonder we do not, nay, upon these terms in reason we shall never prepare a people for the Lord. The Word of God which is the Sword of the Spirit, is as sharp as ever it was, but our hands are weak, our hearts are feeble, we have no courage, nor power to follow the blow, against the sturdy and base distempers of men: We keep these shameful hidings too much about us, (condemned by the Apostle, 2 *Cor* 4.2.) in the course of our Ministery, loth we are to offend our friend, to displease great ones, to provoke the wicked, and malicious, fear we do, lest their love should be lost, their bounty and kindness taken away, and removed, or else hazard our own earthly comforts, and contents: Its pitty but the tongue of that Minister should cleave to the roof of his mouth, who speaks any thing less than God requires of him; for these base and by respects somtimes Ministers are afraid to speak to the hearts of men, and ashamed to reprove them for those sins which they are not afraid or ashamed to do in the face of the world. Neither do Ministers many times Convince so soundly as they ought, nor gather in those Arguments which may make those truths undeniable, and mens Consciences at a stand. Again, they want that holy spiritual affection, which thcy should deliver Gods Word withal unto his people: And this is the Sum of all, Ministers do not deliver the Word with a heavenly, hearty, violent affection, they do not speak *out of the abundance of their hearts*. If they would speak against sin with a holy indignation, it would make men stand in aw of sin; they talk of it hourly, and say, It is not good to prophane Gods Name, and his Sabboths, and to live an ungodly life, but they do not speak from their hearts in this kind. A sturdy Messenger if he come to a mans house to speak with him, he will not be put off, he will take no denial, but he will speak with him, if it be possible before he goes away: But send a Child of a Message to a man, if a Servant do but tell him, His Master is not at leisure, or that he may speak with him another time, he will easily be put off, and go away before he hath delivered his Message. So it is with a Minister that performs his Office with a hearty affection. For when a man speaks from his heart in this Case, he will have no answer, he will not be dallied withal, he will take no denial but will have that he came for: If a man should say he is not at leisure to speak with him, or to hear him now, he will speak with him another time, he will not go away with this answer, but he will tell him, I came to speak with your hearts, and I will speak with your hearts: He will say to the people, Tell your hearts ye that love the world and the profits and pleasures thereof, (and my heart tells you) did you know the good things that are in Christ Jesus, did you but know what a happy thing it is to have assurance of Gods love, you would never love sin nor delight in wicked deeds, as you have done before: grieve no more for the things of the world, but for your sins. The day is coming when the Heavens shall meet with fire, and you shal hear the voyce of the Archangel, saying, *Arise ye dead and come to judgement*. Where you shall hear that dreadful Sentence, *Depart from me all ye workers of iniquity, I know you not*, Matt.7.23. Oh this may be your case one day. And we that are Ministers of God do mourn for you, and tell your souls, We must have Sorrow from you, we came for Hearts, and must have Hearts before we go. And this is the First Use, shewing the Reason why the Ministers of God do so little good,

It is because this plain and powerful Preaching is so much wanting.

The Second Use discovereth to us the fearful estate and miserable Condition of those that lived a long time under a plain and powerful Ministery, and yet their hearts have not been fitted and prepared for the Lord Jesus. It is a fearful suspicion that the Lord will never bestow any saving Good upon that Soul. He that hath lived under a powerful Ministery many yeers, and yet is not wrought upon thereby, it cannot certainly be concluded, but it is greatly to be suspected, That the means of Grace wil never profit that man. Look as it is with the Master Carpenter, when he hath turned every piece of Timber, and taken what he will for his turn, he tels them that be under him, Let this be hewed, and that be framed and made fit for the building: Afterward he finds one piece broken, and another crackt, and another knotty: Why, what saies he? There is no squaring of these, they are fit for nothing but for burning, they are not fit for any place in the building. Oh! take heed, when Gods Ministers have been cutting, and hewing, now exhorting, now perswading, now cutting the heart with Reproof, and yet finds here a crackt Heart, and there a stubborn Soul, that will not be squared by the Word, lest than the Lord should say, These will never be fitted and prepared for me, they are fit for nothing but the fire. Oh! Take heed of it, for he that will not be fitted for Grace, shall be made a firebrand in Hell for ever. Therefore all you that have lived under a powerful Ministery, and yet are not prepared, go home and reason with your souls, and plead with your own hearts, and say, Lord Why am not I yet humbled and prepared? Shall I thus be alwayes under the hacking and hewing of the Word, and never be framed? Such a man, and such a man was stubborn, and wicked, and prophane, and yet the Lord hath brought him home, and he is become a broken hearted Christian, What shall I think that am not fitted and prepared for Christ by all the means that I have had? Alas! thou maiest justly suspect God never intends good to thy soul: It is no absolute conclusion, but it is a great suspition that those that have lived under a plain and powerful Ministery half a dozen yeers or longer, and have got no good, nor profited under the same, I say, it's a shrewd suspicion, that God will send them down to Hell: Therefore suspect thy own soul and say, Lord, will Exhortations never prevail? Will Instructions never do me good? Will Terrors, and Reproofs never strik my heart? Why, I have heard Sermons that would have shaken the very stones I trod on, that would have moved the seat I sate upon; the very fire of Hell hath flashed in my face, I have seen even the very plagues of hell, I have had many Exhortations, Instructions, Admonitions, and Reproofs, and as powerful means as may be, which yet never did me any good. The Lord be merciful to such a poor soul, and turn his heart that he may lay hold of Mercy in due time.

Exhortation. Is it so, That a plain and powerful Ministery is the means of Preparing the soul of a poor sinner for the Lord Jesus? Why then, when you hear the Word plainly and powerfully preached to you, labor that the Word may be so unto you as it is in it self: It is a preparing Word, labor you that it may prepare your hearts to receive Christ: And you that be Hearers, every one labor to save the Soul of another; let the Father speak concerning his Children, and the Husband concerning his Wife and his Family, and the Wife concerning her Husband, Oh when will it once be, when will the time come that my Child may be fitted for the Lord, when will it be that my poor Family, my poor Wife, my poor Husband shall be prepared for the Lord, the Lord grant, that it may be, if not this Sabbath, yet on another; if not this Sermon, then at the next; Labour therefore to give way unto the Word of God, and suffer your Souls to be wrought upon by it, for the word is powerful to prepare your hearts, but the Minister must hew and square your hearts before they can be prepared for the Lord Jesus, and you must *suffer the words of Exhortation*, (as the Apostle sayes) Heb. 13.22. So likewise suffer the words of Conviction, of Reproof, of Admonition, and hold and keep your hearts under the Words, that you may be wrought upon thereby. And as when men have set Carpenters a work to build an House, then they come every day, and ask them, How doth the work go on? How doth the building go forward? When you are gone home, do you so reason with your selves, and ask your own hearts how the work of the Lord goes forward in you? Is my heart yet humbled? Am I yet fitted and prepared for Christ? I thank God I find some work and power of the Word, and therefore I hope the Building will go forward.

A TRUE SIGHT OF SIN (1659)

Wherein This True Sight, and Apprehension of Sin Properly Discovers It Self.

I answer, A true sight of sin hath two Conditions attending upon it; or it appears in two things: We must see sin, 1. Cleerly. 2. Convictingly, what it is in it self, and what it is to us, not in the appearance and paint of it, but in the power of it; not to fadam it in the notion and conceit only, but to see it with Application.

We must see it cleerly in its own Nature, its Native color and proper hue: It's not every slight conceit, not every general and cursorie, confused thought or careless consideration that will serve the turn, or do the work here, we are all sinners; it is my infirmity, I cannot help it; my weakness, I cannot be rid of it; no man lives without faults and follies, the best have their failings, *In many things we offend all.* But alas all this wind shakes no Corn, it costs more to see sin aright than a few words of course; It's one thing to say sin is thus and thus, another thing to see it to be such; we must look wis[e]ly and steddily upon our distempers, look sin in the face, and discern it to the full; the want whereof is the cause of our mistaking our estates, and not redressing of our hearts and waies, *Gal.* 6. 4. *Let a man prove his own work.* Before the Goldsmith can sever and see the Dross asunder from the Gold, he must search the very bowels of the Mettal, and try it by touch, by tast, by hammer, and by fire; and then he will be able to speak by proof what it is; So here. We perceive sin in the crowd and by hearsay, when we attend some common and customary expressions taken up by persons in their common converse, and so report what others speak, and yet never knew the Truth, what either others or we say, but we do not single out our corruptions and survey the loathsomness of them, as they come naked in their own Natures; this we ought to do: There is great ods betwixt the knowledg of a Traveller, that

in his own person hath taken a view of many Coasts, past
through many Countries, and hath there taken up his abode
some time, and by Experience hath been an Eye-witness of the
extream cold, and scorching heats, hath surveyed the glory and
beauty of the one, the barrenness and meanness of the other; he
hath been in the Wars, and seen the ruin and desolation wrought
there; and another that sits by his fire side, and happily reads
the story of these in a Book, or views the proportion of these in
a Map, the ods is great, and the difference of their knowledg
more than a little: the one saw the Country really, the other
only in the story; the one hath seen the very place, the other
only in the paint of the Map drawn. The like difference is
there in the right discerning of sin; the one hath surveyed the
compass of his whol course, searched the frame of his own
heart, and examined the windings and turnings of his own waies,
he hath seen what sin is, and what it hath done, how it hath
made havock of his peace and comfort, ruinated and laid wast
the very Principles of Reason and Nature, and Morality, and
made him a terror to himself, when he hath looked over the
loathsom abominations that lie in his bosom, that he is afraid
to approach the presence of the Lord to bewail his sins, and to
crave pardon, lest he should be confounded for them, while he
is but confessing of them; afraid and ashamed lest any man
living should know but the least part of that which he knows by
himself, and could count it happy that himself was not, that the
remembrance of those hideous evils of his might be no more;
Another happily hears the like preached or repeated, reads them
writ or recorded in some Authors, and is able to remember and
relate them. The ods is marvelous great. The one sees the
History of sin, the other the Nature of it; the one knows the
relation of sin as it is mapped out, and recorded; the other the
poyson, as by experience he hath found and proved it. It's one
thing to see a disease in the Book, or in a mans body, another
thing to find and feel it in a mans self. There is the report of
it, here the malignity and venom of it.

But how shall we see cleerly the Nature of sin in his naked
hue?

This will be discovered, and may be conceived in the Particulars following. Look we at it: First, As it respects God.

Secondly, As it concerns our selves. As it hath reference to God, the vileness of the nature of sin may thus appear.

It would dispossess God of that absolute Supremacy which is indeed his Prerogative Royal, and doth in a peculiar manner appertayn to him, as the Diamond of his Crown, and Diadem of his Deity, so the Apostle, *He is God over all blessed for ever,* Rom. 9. 5. All from him and all for him, he is the absolute first being, the absolute last end, and herein is the crown of his Glory. All those attributes of Wisdom, Goodness, Holiness, Power, Justice, Mercy, the shine and Concurrency of all these meeting together is to set out the unconceivable excellency of his Glorious name, which exceeds all praise, *Thyne is the kingdom, the power and the glory,* the right of all and so the rule of all and the Glory of all belongs to him.

Now herein lyes the unconceavable hainousness of the hellish nature of sin, it would justle the Almighty out of the Throne of his Glorious Soveraignty, and indeed be above him. For the will of man being the chiefest of all his workmanship, all for his body, the body of the soul, the mind to attend upon the will, the will to attend upon God, and to make choyce of him, and his wil, that is next to him, and he onely above that: and that should have been his Throne and Temple or Chair of State, in which he would have Set his Soveraignty for ever. He did in an Especial manner intend to meet with man, and to communicate himself to man in his righteous Law, as the rule of his Holy and righteous will, by which the will of *Adam* should have been ruled and guided to him, and made happie in him; and all Creatures should have served God in man, and been happy by or through him, serving of God being happy in him; But when the will went from under the government of his rule, by sin, *it would be above God, and be happy without him,* for the rule of the law in each command of it, holds forth a three-fold expression of Soveraignty from the Lord, and therein the Soveraignty of all the rest of his Attributes.

1. The Powerful Supremacy of his just will, as that he hath right to dispose of all and authority to command all at his pleasure; *What if God will? Rom. 9. 22 My Counsel shall stand and I wil do all my pleasure, Isa. 46. 10* And as its true of what shal be done upon us, so his wil hath Soveraignty of Command in

what should be done by us we are to say *the will of the Lord be done; Davids* warrant was *to do all Gods wils* Acts. 13. 22. and our Saviour himself professeth, *John.* 6. 38. *that he came not to do his own will but the will of him that sent him,* and therfore his wrath and jealousie and judgment will break out in case that be disobeyed.

2. There is also a fulness of wisdom in the law of God revealed to guide & direct us in the way we should walk, *Psal.* 19. 7. *the law of God makes wise the simple,* 2. *Tim.* 3. 15. *it's able to make us wise unto Salvation.*

3. There's a Sufficiency of God to content and satisfy us. *Blessed are they who walk in his wayes, and blessed are they that keep his Testimonies. Psal.* 119. 1. 2. *Great prosperity have they that love the law, and nothing shal offend them,* ver. 16. and in truth there can be no greater reward for doing wel, than to be enabled to do well, he that hath attayned his last end he cannot go further, he cannot be better;

Now by sin we justle the law out of its place, and the Lord out of his Glorious Soveraignty, pluck the Crown from his head, and the Scepter out of his hand, and we say and profess by our practice, there is not authority and power there to govern, nor wisdom to guide, nor good to content me, but I will be swayed by mine own wil and led by mine own deluded reason and satisfied with my own lusts. This is the guise of every graceless heart in the commission of sin; *so Pharaoh who is the Lord? I know not the Lord, nor will I lett Israel go. Exod.* 5. 2. in the time of their prosperity see how the Jews turn their backs and shake off the authority of the Lord, *we are Lords* (say they) *we will come no more at thee. Jer.* 2. 31. *and our tongues are our own who shal be Lords over us? Psal.* 12. 4. So for the wisdom of the world, see how they set light by it as not worth the looking after it *Jer.* 18. 12. *we wil walk after our own devices & we wil every one do the imagination of his own evil heart, yea they sett up their own traditions,* their own Idols and delusions, and Lord it over the law, *making the command of God of none effect Math.* 15. 8. 9. So for the goodness of the word; *Job.* 22. 17. *Mat.* 3. 14. *It is in vayn to serve God and what profit is there that we have kept his ordinances, yea his Commandements are ever grievous,* Its a grievous thing to the loose person he cannot have his pleasures but he must have his guilt and gall with them; Its grievous to the worlding that he cannot lay hold on the world by unjust means, but Conscience layes hold upon him as breaking the law. Thou that knowest and keepest thy pride and stubbornness and thy distempers, know assuredly thou dost justle God out of the Throne of his glorious Soveraignty and thou dost profess, Not Gods wil but thine own (which is above his) shall rule thee, thy carnal reason and the folly of thy mind, is above the wisdome of the Lord and that shal guide thee; to please thine own stubborn crooked pervers spirit, is a greater good than to please God and enjoy happines, for this more Contents, thee; That when thou considerest but thy Course, dost thou not wonder that the great and Terrible God doth not pash such a poor insolent worm to pouder, and send thee packing to the pitt every moment.

2. It smiles at the Essence of the Almighty and the desire of the sinner, is not only that God should not be supream but that indeed he should *not be at all,* and therefore it would destroy the being of Jehovah. *Psal.* 81. 15. Sinners are called *the haters of the Lord.* John. 15. 24. *they hated both me and my Father.* Now he that hates endeavours if it be possible the annihilation of the thing hated, and its most certain were it in their power, they would pluck God out of Heaven the light of his truth out of their Consciences, and the law out of the Societies and Assemblies where they live, that they might have elbow room to live as they list. Nay what ever they hate most and intend, and plott more evil against in al the world, they hate God most of all, and intend more evil against him than against all their Enemies besides, because they hate all for his sake, therefore wicked men *are said to destroy the law Psal.* 126. 119 the Adulterer loaths that law that condemns, uncleaness; the Earthworm would destrow that law that forbids Covetousness, they are sayd to *hate the light* John 3. 21. to hate the Saints and Servants of the Lord John 15. 18. *the world hates you,* he that hates the Lanthorn for the lights sake, he hates the light much more, he that hates the faithful because of the Image of God, and the Grace that appears there, he hates the God of all, Grace and Holiness, most of all, so God to *Zenacharib,* Isa. 37. 28. *I know thy going out and thy Comming in, and thy rage*

against me, Oh it would be their content, if there was no God in the world to govern them, no law to curbe them, no justice to punish, no truth to trouble them, Learn therfore to see how far your rebellions reach, It is not arguments you gainsay, not the Counsel of a Minister you reject, the command of a Magistrate ye oppose, evidence of rule or reason ye resist; but be it known to you, you fly in the very face of the Almighty, and it is not the Gospel of Grace ye would have destroyed, but the spirit of Grace, the author of Grace the Lord Jesus, the God of all Grace that ye hate.

It crosseth the whol course of Providence, perverts the work of the Creature and defaceth the beautiful frame, and that sweet correspondence and orderly usefulness the Lord first implanted in the order of things; The Heavens deny their influence, the Earth her strength, the Corn her nourishment, thank sin for that. Weeds come instead of herbs, Cockle and Darnel instead of Wheat, thank sin for that, *Rom.* 8. 22. *The whol Creature* (or Creation) *grones under vanity,* either cannot do what it would or else misseth of that good and end it intended, breeds nothing but vanity, brings forth nothing but vexation, It crooks all things so as that none can straiten them, makes so many wants that none can supply them, *Eccles.* 1. 15. This makes crooked Servants in a family no man can rule them, crooked inhabitants in towns, crooked members in Congregations, ther's no ordering nor joynting of them in that comly accord, and mutual subjection; know they said, *the adversary sin hath done all this.* Man was the mean betwixt God and the Creature to convey all good with all the constancy of it, and therefore when Man breaks, Heaven and Earth breaks all asunder, the Conduit being cracked and displaced there can be no conveyance from the Fountain.

In regard of our selves, see we and consider nakedly the nature of sin, in Four particulars.

Its that which makes a separation between God and the soul, breaks that Union and Communion with God for which we were made, and in the enjoyment of which we should be blessed and happie, *Isai.* 59. 1. 2. *Gods ear is not heavy that it cannot hear nor his hand that it cannot help, but your iniquities have separated betwixt God and you & your sins have hid his*

face that he wil not hear for he professeth, Psal. 5. 4. *that he is
a God that wills not wickedness neither shal iniquity dwell with
him. Into the new Jerusalem shal no unclean thing enter, but
without shal be doggs Rev.* 21. 27. The Dogs to their Kennel,
and Hogs to their Sty and Mire: but if an impenitent wretch
should come into Heaven, the Lord would go out of Heaven;
Iniquity shall not dwell with sin. That then that deprives me of
my greatest good for which I came into the world, and for which
I live and labor in the world, and without which I had better
never to have been born; nay, that which deprives me of an
universal good, a good that hath all good in it, that must needs
be an evil, but have all evil in it: but so doth sin deprive me of
God as the Object of my will, and that wills all good, and
therefore it must bring in Truth all evil with it. Shame takes
away my Honor, Poverty my Wealth, Persecution my Peace,
Prison my Liberty, Death my Life, yet a man may still be a
happy man, lose his Life, and live eternally: But sin takes away
my God, and with him all good goes; Prosperity without God
will be my poyson, Honor without him my bane; nay, the word
without God hardens me, my endeavor without him profits
nothing at all for my good. A Natural man hath no God in any
thing, and therefore hath no good.

It brings an incapability in regard of my selfe to receive
good, and an impossibility in regard of God himself to work my
spiritual good, while my sin Continues, and I Continue impenitent in it. An incapability of a spiritual blessing, *Why transgress ye the Commandement of the Lord that ye cannot prosper
do what ye* can, 2 *Chron.* 24. 20. And *He that being often reproved hardens his heart, shal be consumed suddenly and there
is no remedy,* He that spils the Physick that should cure him,
the meat that should nourish him, there is no remedy but he
must needs dye, so that the Commission of sin makes not only
a separation from God, but obstinate resistance and continuance
in it, maintains an infinit and everlasting distance between God
and the soul: So that so long as the sinful resistance of thy soul
continues; God cannot vouchsafe the Comforting and guiding
presence of his grace; because it's cross to the Covenant of Grace
he hath made, which he will not deny, and his Oath which he
will not alter. So that should the Lord save thee and thy Cor-

ruption, carry thee and thy proud unbeleeving heart to heaven he must nullify the Gospel, (Heb. 5. 9. *He's the Author of Salvation to them that obey him*) and forswear himself, (Heb. 3. 18. *He hath sworn unbeleevers shall not enter into his rest*) he must cease to be just and holy, and so to be God. As *Saul* said to *Jonathan* concerning *David*, 1 Sam. 20. 30, 31. *So long as the Son of* Jesse *lives, thou shalt not be established, nor thy Kingdom:* So do thou plead against thy self, and with thy own soul; So long as these rebellious distempers continue, Grace and Peace, and the Kingdom of Christ can never be established in thy heart For this obstinate resistance differs nothing from the plagues of the state of the damned, when they come to the highest measure, but that it is not yet total and final, there being some kind of abatement of the measure of it, and stoppage of the power of it. Imagine thou sawest the Lord Jesus coming in the clouds, and heardest the last trump blow, *Arise ye dead, and come to Judgment:* Imagine thou sawest the Judg of all the World sitting upon the Throne, thousands of Angels before him, and ten thousands ministring unto him, the Sheep standing on his right hand, and the Goats at the left: Suppose thou heardest that dreadful Sentence, and final Doom pass from the Lord of Life (whose Word made Heaven and Earth, and will shake both) *Depart from me ye cursed*; How would thy heart shake and sink, and die within thee in the thought thereof, wert thou really perswaded it was thy portion? Know, that by thy dayly continuance in sin, thou dost to the utmost of thy power execute that Sentence upon thy soul: It's thy life, thy labor, the desire of thy heart, and thy dayly practice to depart away from the God of all Grace and Peace, and turn the Tomb-stone of everlasting destruction upon thine own soul.

It's the Cause which brings all other evils of punishment into the World, and without this they are not evil, but so far as sin is in them. The sting of a trouble, the poyson and malignity of a punishment and affliction, the evil of the evil of any judgment, it is the sin that brings it, or attends it, *Jer.* 2. 19. *Thine own wickedness shall correct thee, and thy back slidings shall reprove thee, know therefore that it is an evil, and bitter thing that thou hast forsaken the Lord.* Jer. 4. 18. *Thy waies and doings have procured these things unto thee, therefore it is bitter, and reacheth unto the heart.* Take miseries and crosses without sin, they are like to be without a sting, the Serpent without poyson, ye may take them, and make Medicines of them. So *Paul 1 Cor. 15. 55.* he plaies with death it self, sports with the Grave. *Oh death, where is thy sting? Oh Grave where is thy Victory? the sting of death is sin.* All the harmful annoyance in sorrows and punishments, further than either they come from sin, or else tend to it, they are rather improvements of what we have than parting with any thing we do enjoy, we rather lay out our conveniences than seem to lose them, yea, they encrease our Crown, and do not diminish our Comfort. *Blessed are ye when men revile you, and persecute you, and speak all manner of evil of you for my sake, for great is your reward in Heaven:* Matth. 5. 11. There is a blessing in persecutions and reproaches when they be not mingled with the deserts of our sins; yea, our momentary short affliction for a good cause, and a good Conscience, works an excessive exceeding weight of Glory. If then sin brings all evils, and makes all evils indeed to us, then is it worse than all those evils.

It brings a Curse upon all our Comforts, blasts all our blessings, the best of all our endeavors, the use of all the choycest of all Gods Ordinances: it's so evil and vile, that it makes the use of all good things, and all the most glorious, both Ordinances and Improvements evil to us. *Hag.* 2. 13. 14. When the Question was made to the Priest; *If one that is unclean by a dead Body touch any of the holy things, shall it be unclean? And he answered, Yea. So is this People, and so is this Nation before me, saith the Lord; and so is every work of their hands, and that which they offer is unclean:* If any good thing a wicked man had, or any action he did, might be good, or bring good to him, in reason it was the Services and Sacrifices wherein he did approach unto God, and perform Service to him, and yet *the Sacrifice of the wicked is an abomination to the Lord,* Prov. 28. 9. and Tit. 1. 15. *To the pure all things are pure; but to the unbeleeving there is nothing pure, but their very Consciences are defiled.* It is a desperate Malignity in the temper of the Stomach, that should turn our Meat and diet into Diseases, the best Cordials and Preservatives into Poysons, so that what in reason is appointed to nourish a man should kill him. Such is the venom and malignity of sin, makes the use of the best things become evil, nay, the greatest evil to us many times; *Psal.* 109. 7. *Let his prayer be turned into sin.* That which is appointed by God to be the choycest means to prevent sin, is turned into sin out of the corrupt distemper of these carnal hearts of ours.

Hence then it follows; *That sin is the greatest evil in the world, or indeed that can be.* For, That which separates the soul from God, that which brings all evils of punishment, and makes all evils truly evil, and spoils all good things to us, that must needs be the greatest evil, but this is the nature of sin, as hath already appeared.

But that which I will mainly press, is, Sin is only opposite to God, and cross as much as can be to that infinite goodness and holiness which is in his blessed Majesty; it's not the miseries or distresses that men undergo, that the Lord distasts them for, or estrangeth himself from them, he is with *Joseph* in the Prison, with the three Children in the Furnace, with *Lazarus* when he lies among the Dogs, and gathers the Crums from the rich Mans Table, yea with *Job* upon the dung-hil, but he is not able to bear the presence of sin: yea, of this temper are his dearest servants, the more of God is in them, the more opposite they are to sin where ever they find it. It was that he commended in the Church of *Ephesus, That she could not bear those that were wicked,* Rev. 2. 3. As when the Stomach is of a pure temper and good strength, the least surfet or distemper that befals, it presently distasts and disburdens it self with speed. So *David* noted to be *a man after Gods own heart.* He professeth, 101. *Psal.* 3. 7. *I hate the work of them that turn aside, he that worketh deceit shall not dwell in my house, he that telleth lyes, shall not tarry in my sight.* But when the heart becomes like the Stomach, so weak it cannot help it self, nor be helped by Physick, desperate diseases and dissolution of the whol follows, and in reason must be expected. Hence see how God looks at the least connivance, or a faint and feeble kind of opposition against sin, as that in which he is most highly dishonored, and he follows it with most hideous plagues, as that indulgent carriage of *Ely* towards the vile behavior of his Sons for their grosser evils, 1 *Sam.* 2. 23. *Why do you such things, It's not well my Sons that I hear such things: It is not well,* and is that all? why, had they either out of ignorance not known their duty or out of some sudden surprisal of a temptation neglected it, it had not been well, but for them so purposedly to proceed on in the practice of such gross evils, and for him so faintly to reprove: The Lord looks at it as a great sin thus feebly to oppose sin, and therefore verse 29. he tells him, *That he honored his Sons above God,* and therefore he professeth, *Far be it from me to maintain thy house and comfort, for he that honors me I wil honor, and he that despiseth me shall be lightly esteemed,* verse 30. Hence it is the Lord himself is called *the holy one of Israel,* 1. Hab. 12. *Who is of purer eyes than to behold evil, and cannot look upon iniquity,* no not in such as profess themselves Saints, though most deer unto him, no, nor in his Son the Lord Jesus, not in his Saints, *Amos,* 8. 7. *The Lord hath sworn by himself, I abhor the excellency of* Jacob; what ever their excellencies, their priviledges are, if they do not abhor sin, God will abhor them, *Jer.* 22. 24. *Though* Coniah *was as the Signet of my right hand, thence would I pluck him.* Nay, he could not endure the appearance of it in the Lord Christ, for when but the reflection of sin (as I may so say) fell upon our Savior, even the imputation of our transgressions to him, though none iniquity was ever committed by him, the Father withdrew his comforting presence from him, and let loose his infinite displeasure against him, forcing him to cry out, *My God, my God, why hast thou forsaken me?*

Yea, Sin is so evil, (that though it be in Nature, which is the good Creature of God) that there is no good in it, nothing that God will own; but in the evil of punishment it is otherwise, for the torments of the Devils, and punishments of the damned in Hell, and all the plagues inflicted upon the wicked upon Earth, issue from the righteous and revenging Justice of the Lord, and he doth own such execution as his proper work, *Isa.* 45. 7. *Is there any evil in the City,* viz. of punishment, *and the Lord hath not done it? I make peace, I create evil, I the Lord do all these things:* It issues from the Justice of God that he cannot but reward every one according to his own waies and works; those are a mans own, the holy one of Israel hath no hand in them; but he is the just Executioner of the plagues that are inflicted and suffered for these; and hence our blessed Savior becoming our Surety, and standing in our room, he endured the pains of the Second death, even the fierceness of the fury of an offended God; and yet it was impossible he could commit the least sin, or be tainted with the least corrupt distemper. And it's certain it's better to suffer all plagues without any one sin, than to commit the least sin, and to be freed from all plagues. Suppose that all miseries and sorrows that ever befel all the wicked in Earth and Hell, should meet together in one soule, as all waters gathered together in one Sea: Suppose thou heardest the Devils roaring, and sawest Hell gaping, and flames of everlasting burnings flashing before thine eyes; it's certain it were better for thee to be cast into those inconceivable torments than to commit the least sin against the Lord: Thou dost not think so now, but thou wilt find it so one day.

Meditation

Meditation *is a serious intention of the mind whereby wee come to search out the truth, and settle it effectually upon the heart.*

An intention of the mind; when one puts forth the strength of their understanding about the work in hand, takes it as an especial task whereabout the heart should be taken up and that which wil require the whol man, and that to the bent of the best ability he hath, so the word is used *Jos.* 1. 8. *thou shalt not suffer the word to depart out of thy mind, but thou shalt meditate therein day and night,* when either the word would depart away or our corruptions would drive it away, meditation layes hold upon it and wil not let it go, but exerciseth the strength of the attention of his thoughts about it, makes a buisiness of it as that about which he might do his best, and yet fals short of what he should do in it. So *David* when he would discover where the stream and overflowing strength of his affections vented themselves, he points at this practice as that which employes the mind to the ful. *Psal* 119. 197. *Oh how I love thy law, it is my meditation all the day,* love is the great wheel of the soul that sets al on going, and how doth that appear? it is my meditation day and night; the word in the original signifyeth to swim, a man spreads the breadth of his understanding about that work, and layes out himself about the service wherein there is both difficulty and worth.

Serious.] Meditation is not a flourishing of a mans wit, but hath a set bout at the search of the truth, beats his brain as wee use to say, hammers out a buisiness, as the Gouldsmith with his mettal, he heats it and beats it turnes it on this side and then on that, fashions it on both that he might frame it to his mind; meditation is hammering of a truth or poynt propounded, that he may carry and conceive the frame and compass in his mind,

not salute a truth as we pass by occasionally but solemnly entertain it into our thoughts; Not look upon a thing presented as a
spectator or passenger that goes by: but lay other things aside,
and look at this as the work and employment for the present to
take up our minds. It's one thing in our diet to take a snatch and
away, another thing to make a meal, and sit at it on purpose until wee have seen al set before us and we have taken our fil of al,
so we must not cast an eye or glimpse at the truth by some sudden or fleighty apprehension, a snatch and away, but we must
make a meal of musing. Therefore the Psalmist makes it the
main trade that a Godly man drives, professedly opposite to the
carriage of the wicked, whether in his outward or inward work,
in his disposition or expression of himself in his common
practice; whereas they walk in the corrupt counsels of their own
hearts, stand in the way of sinners, not only devise what is
naught, but practice and persevere in what they have devised,
and sit in the seat of the scorners; A blessed man his rode in
which he travels, his set trade *he meditates in the Law of God
day and night*: that is the counsel in which he walks, the way in
which he stands, the seat in which he sits. Look at this work as a
branch of our Christian calling, not that which is left to our
liberty, but which is of necessity to be attended and that in good
earnest as a Christian duty, which God requires, not a little
available to our spiritual welfare.

The end is doubly expressed in the other part of the
description.

1. *The searching of the truth.*
2. *The effectual setling of it upon the heart.*

The search of the truth: Meditation is a coming in with the
truth or any cause that comes to hand, that we may enquire the
ful state of it before our thoughts part with it, so that we see
more of it or more clearly and fully than formerly we did, this
is one thing in that of the Prophet *Hos. 6. 3. Then shall yee
know if you follow on to know,* when we track the footsteps of
the truth, in al the passages, until we have viewed the whol prog-
resse of it, from truth to truth from point to point. *This it is to
dig for wisdom, Prov. 2. 2.* When men have found a mine or a
veyn of Silver, they do not content themselves, to take that

which is uppermost and next at hand within sight which offers it self upon the surface of the Earth, but they dig further as hoping to find more, because they see somewhat. So meditation rests not in what presents it self to our consideration, but digs deeper gathers in upon the truth, and gaynes more of it then did easily appear at the first, and this it doth.

1. *When it recals things formerly past, sets them in present view before our consideration and judgment* Meditation sends a mans thoughts afar off, cals over and revives the fresh apprehension of things done long before, marshals them al in rank together, brings to mind such things which were happily quite out of memory, & gone from a man, which might be of great use and special help to discover our condition according to the quality of it; may be Conscience starts the consideration but of one sin, but meditation looks abroad, and brings to hand many of the same, and of the like kind and that many dayes past and long ago committed, This distemper now sticks upon a man and brings him under the arrest of Conscience and the condemnation thereof. But saies meditation let me mind you of such and such sins at such and such times, in such and such companies, committed and multiplycd both more and worse than those that now appear so loathsom and so troublesom to you; meditation is as it were the register and remembrancer, that looks over the records of our daily corruptions, and keeps them upon file, and brings them into court and fresh consideration *Job.* 13. 26. *Thou makest me to possess the sins of my youth:* This makes a man to renew the sins of his youth, makes them fresh in our thoughts, as though new done before our eyes. This Interpreters make the meaning of that place *Job.* 14. 17. *My trangression is sealed up in a bag, and thou sewest up mine iniquity,* though God do thus, yet he doth it by this means in the way of his Providence, *i.e.* by recounting and recalling our corruptions to mind, by serious meditation we sew them all up together, we look back to the linage and pedegree of our lusts, and track the abominations of our lives, step by step, until we come to the very nest where they are hatched and bred, even of our original corruption, and body of death, where they had their first breath and being, links al our distempers together from our infancy to

our youth, from youth to riper age, from thence to our declining daies. So *David*, from the vileness of his present lusts is led to the wickedness in *which he was warmed*, Psal. 51. 5. This was typed out in the old Law by *the chewing of the cud;* Meditation cals over again those things that were past long before, and not within a mans view and consideration.

Meditation *takes a special Survey of the compass of our present condition, and the Nature of those corruptions that come to be considered:* It's the traversing of a mans thoughts, the coasting of the mind and imagination into every crevis and corner, pryes into every particular, takes a special view of the borders and confines of any corruption or condition that comes to be scanned, *Psal.* 119. 59. *I considered my waies, and turned my feet unto thy testimonies;* he turned them upside down, looked through them as it were; a present apprehension peeps in as it were through the crevis or key-hole, looks in at the window as a man passeth by: but Meditation lifts up the latch and goes into each room, pries into every corner of the house, and surveyes the composition and making of it, with all the blemishes in it. Look as the Searcher at the Sea-Port, or Custom-house, or Ships, satisfies himself not to over-look carelessly in a sudden view, but unlocks every Chest, romages every corner, takes a light to discover the darkest passages. So is it with Meditation, it observes the woof and web of wickedness, the ful frame of it, the very utmost Selvage and out-side of it, takes into consideration all the secret conveyances, cunning contrivements, all bordering circumstances that attend the thing, the consequences of it, the nature of the causes that work it, the several occasions and provocations that lead to it, together with the end and issue that in reason is like to come of it, *Dan.* 12. 4. *Many shall run to and fro, and knowledg shall encrease:* Meditation goes upon discovery, toucheth at every coast, observes every creek, maps out the dayly course of a mans conversation and disposition.

The second End of Meditation is, *It settles it effectually upon the heart.* It's not the pashing of the water at a sudden push, but the standing and soaking to the root, that loosens the weeds and thorns, that they may be plucked up easily. It's not the laying of Oyl upon the benummed part, but the chafing of it in, that suppleth the Joynts, and easeth the pain. It is so in the soul; Application laies the Oyl of the Word that is searching and savory, Meditation chafeth it in, that it may soften and humble the hard and stony heart: Application is like the Conduit or Channel that brings the stream of the Truth upon the soul; but Meditation stops it as it were, and makes it soak into the heart, that so our corruptions may be plucked up kindly by the Roots.

This settling upon the heart appears in a three-fold work.

It affects the heart with the Truth attended, and leaves an Impression upon the Spirit answerable to the Nature of the thing which is taken into Meditation: 2 *Pet.* 2. 8. It's said of *Lot, in seeing and hearing, he vexed his righteous soul.* Many saw and heard the hideous abominations, and were not touched nor affected therewith. No more had he been, but that he vexed and troubled his own righteous soul, because he was driven to a dayly consideration of them which cut him to the quick. The word is observable, it signifies to try by a touch-stone, and to examine, and then upon search to bring the soul upon the rack: therefore the same word is used, *Matth.* 14. 24. *The Ship was tossed by the waves;* the consideration of the abominations of the place raised a tempest of trouble in *Lots* righteous soul. This the wise man calls *laying to the heart,* Eccles. 7. 1, 2. *It's better to go to the house of mourning than to the house of laughter; for this is the end of all men, and the living will lay it to his heart.* When the Spectacle of Misery and Mortality is laid in the grave, yet savory Meditation laies it to a mans heart, and makes it real there in the work of it. The Goldsmith observes that it is not the laying of the fire, but the blowing of it that melts the Mettal: So with Meditation, it breaths upon any Truth that is applied, and that makes it really sink and soak into the soul; and this is the reason why in an ordinary and common course of Providence, and Gods dealing with sinners, (leaving his own exceptions to his own good pleasure) that the most men in the time and work of Conversion have that scorn cast upon them, *that they grow melancholly.* And it's true thus far in the course of ordinary appearance; The Lord usually never works upon the soul by the Ministry of the Word to make it effectual, but he drives the sinner to sad thoughts of heart, and makes him keep an audit in his own soul by serious meditation, and pondering of his waies; otherwise the Word neither affects throughly, nor works kindly upon him.

It keeps the heart under the heat and authority of the Truth that it's taken up withal, by constant attendance of his thoughts. Meditation keeps the Conscience under an arrest, so that it cannot make an escape from the Evidence and Authority of the Truth, so that there is no way, but either to obey the Rule of it, or else be condemned by it. But escape it cannot, Meditation meets and stops al the evasions and sly pretences the fals-hearted person shal counterfeit. If a man should deny his fault, and himself guilty, Meditation will evidence it beyond all gainsaying, by many testimonies which Meditation wil easily cal to mind; remember ye not in such and such a place: upon such an occasion, you gave way to your wicked heart to do thus and thus; you know it, and God knows it, and I have recorded it: If the sinner would lessen his fault, Meditation aggravates it; or if he seem to slight it, and look at it as a matter of no moment, yet Meditation will make it appear, there is greater evil in it, and greater necessity to bestow his thoughts upon it than he is aware of.

Hence it is Meditation laies siege unto the soul, and cuts off al carnal pretences that a wretched self-deceiving hypocrite would relieve himself by; and stil lies at the soul, this you did, at that time, in that place, after that manner; so that the soul is held fast prisoner, and cannot make an escape; but as *David* said, *Psal.* 51. 3. *My sins are ever before me:* Consideration keeps them within view, and will not suffer them to go out of sight and thoughts; and therefore it is *Paul* joyns those two together, 1 *Tim.* 3. 15. *Meditate in these things, and be in them.*

It provokes a man (by a kind of over-bearing power) to the practice of that with which he is so affected: A settled and serious Meditation of any thing, is as the setting open of the Flood-gates, which carries the soul with a kind of force and violence, to the performance of what he so bestows his mind upon; as a mighty stream let out turns the mill. *Phil.* 4. 9. *Think of these things, and do them:* thinking men are doing men. *Psal.* 39. 3. *While I was thus musing, the fire broke out, and I spake:* the busie stirring of Meditation is like the raising of a tempest in the heart, that carries out all the actions of the man by an uncontroulable command. *I considered my waies, and turned my feet unto thy Statutes:* right Consideration, brings in a right Reformation with it.

True Contrition

Doct.   *They who are truly pierced with Godly sorrow for their sins are willing openly to confess them, when they are called thereunto. Or. True contrition is accompanied with confession when God calls thereunto.*

So do these converts here in the place, they come here of their own accord, they do not stay til they be arrested and summoned to the court; but they readily arrest, indite, arraign and accuse themselves before *Peter* and the rest of the Apostles. Men and bretheren you have discovered many sins and the dreadful condition of the sinners who are guilty thereof, loe we are the men, thus and thus we have done. By us the Lord Jesus was opposed and pursued, by us he was derided, rayled upon and blasphemed, by us it was that he was murthered, and we are they that have embrewed our hands in his most precious blood: we are they that cryed it and desired it, *Crucified him, away with him, not him, but Barabbas.* Nay they roundly, readily, told al, this in secret we plotted against his life and liberty, thus we consented unto those that should attempt the treason and attachment and encouraged them in their cruelty and trayterous proceeding, we are they that gloryed and rejoyced in the unrighteous murther of the innocent son of God, we applauded our selves in that we so prospered in our unjust practises, Oh so would we have it. Men and bretheren we plainly here profess it, we openly and nakedly acknowledge it, they are our sins which you have discovered, and we are

the sinners against whom you have truly proclaimed the judgments of God our sins intolerable,
and our condition miserable, we are the men, we
are those accursed, cruel wretches whereof you
speak *and what shal we do?* Observe the like expression in the like estate and condition, when al
sorts of people came to the Baptists ministery, and
the Lord was pleased to direct him to pierce their
hearts by the preaching of the truth; they lay open
their sins and sores before him and crave succor
and relief, as it appears by receits he gives, he
applies several directions according to the several
diseases *Luk.* 3. 12. 13. Then came *the Publicans,*
anon *the Souldiers* saying *what shal WE do?* and
he answers suitably: they made known their mala-
dies and he applyes the cure. As it is in an inward
cankerd sore, if it be lanced throughly and to the
quick, it then bleeds kindly and freely: so with
the soul, If the heart feel the sin really, the tongue
wil freely express it, when the season shal require
the point is clear, we wil see if we can make it
plain.

. . . . .

*Before I can come to lay forth the ful breadth
of the truth I must premise two things.*
  That sins are of three sorts, as they come to
our present consideration, in the case at hand.
  *First, some are publick and notorious done in
the light of the sun,* open unto the view of al, that
are in the place to see it, or come to the hearing of
it. Such are practises which are impudent when
men are fearless and shameless in their way, *They
declare their sin as* Sodom *Isa.* 3. 9. al may see,
and they pass not much what they do, so in the
case of *Eli's* sons. I *Sam.* 2. 17. 23.
  Secondly, *Some are private between party and*
party to which none are privy but themselves,
either the offence don to another. As Josephs *mis-*

tress when they were alone inticeth him. Gen. 39.
7. The Adulterous woman meets with the young
man, allures, yea tempts him impudently by her
loose speech and behavior. Or elss they are So-
ciates together in the same evil, as of Simeon *and*
Levy; *bretheren in iniquity,* Gen. 49. 5.

Thirdly *Some sins are secret when no eyes
sees,* no living man apprehends, but a mans heart
and conscience, he commits the evil alone, and he
alone knows it and God onely who knows the
secret of al hearts.

By *open confession,* I understand, the discovery and acknowledgment of the sin to any who
knew not of it, before, whether it be publickely
to many or privately to some one; because a man
is brought thus, to open himself to such, and to
make them privy to that which by way of preparation premised, the answer to the first question
wil be referred unto three heads, touching publick,
and private and secret sins; in al which particulars
there be particular directions to settle a mans
judgment, and to order his practices, in a right
way.

*Touching publick sins, the rule is here; what
ever sins have been publickly committed or being
private come to be made publick, of such God
requires publick acknowledgment and confession,*
two branches here I wil touch both.

*If the publick scandals and evil which have
broke out in our practice* to the offence of others,
and stumbling of the weak, the grief of the good,
the encouragement of the wicked, who may be
provoked in the like carriages or confirmed in them
by reason of our example; *then its requisite and
necessary, men should take open shame by sollemn
acknowledgment.* Its the rule which Christ hath
left unto the Church, *who sin openly rebuk openly*
I *Tim.* 5. 20. and if a rebuk according to the rule of

God ought to be dispensed, it ought to be received. And that is a main end which on both hands ought to be looked at, both in giving and receiving publick censure, that the delinquent be ashamed, and brought to acknowledg his sin & judg himself for it. So *Joshua* to *Achan* Jos. 7. 19. *tel me what hast thou done?* I Thes. 4. 14. *If any man obey not the Gospel, note such a man,* set a brand upon him by a sad censure *that he may be ashamed* and to see his evil and come to acknowledgment of it. And hence men should lay shame upon him and he answerably ought to take it. And when men are out of the Church that the power thereof cannot reach them, the connivence and feeblness of humane lawes, wil not see execution done upon them; Its commonly the way of providence, that the Lord doth force men to do that out of horror or conscience which they wil not do out of Conscience to Gods holy command. Sometimes the Lord arrests men upon their sick beds and constraineth them to bear the shame of that, which they would not be brought to see in the dayes of their folly. Then send for such and such who have been deeply wronged by me, for such who have been corrupted by my example, The evil counsel that I have given, the loathsom carriages and unsavory language, and speeches that I have expressed, those subtil insinuations, and baits that I have layd to entice and entangle them, I desire now that God would pardon and they forgive: yea such who have been ringleaders to their wicked and leud courses they were not able to abide their persons and practice, either take him away, or remove me hence sayes the sick party *thus they brought their books and burnt them openly in the view of all,* when once God brought their hearts to a through sight and sorrow for their sin *Acts.* 19. 19. Sometimes upon the place of execution God constrains me to vomit out their wretchedness, to

leave shame upon themselves, and to leave their
names for a reproach and curse behind them and
to confess now to be condemned, when they would
not confess in humility to seek and receive mercy
to be pardoned. Oh beware by my example that
you never rebel against Parents, reject the counsel
and command of Governors, that was my sin, hath
been my bane, and made me rush on headily to
mine own ruin and confusion, Nay.

Secondly, *If the commission of them were
private and yet they be made publick by any way
in a course of providence, stil God calls for confession answerable, as the season shal require and
opportunity suit,* As suppose a mans secret fact
come to open view, either by others care, or by the
weakness of any according to my defect, in al these
cases open acknowledgment is requisite, as for instance in the severals, The house if broke, the
goods stoln, conveyed and hid, at length the owner
sees, challengeth, pursues him in the open court of
Justice and yet righteously; and that which was
cunningly carryed before comes now openly to be
censured again: suppose that there is an offence
given to a brother in Church Covenant and while
the case is in debate and depending between them
two, the party offended against the rule of our
savior, carelessly and heedelessly relates this to
several persons, some without, some within the
Church and they also report it heedlessly to others,
so that it growes common and the report publick
Matth. though they of the Church (for the rule of our
18. 15. Savior binds them properly because they have
16. 17. power to reforme or prevent evil, and doth not in
many cases reach others out of that relation)
though they I say, did sinfully and disorderly make
it publick, and that according to Gods Command,
to take the open shame of the evil, as seeing Gods
hand so pursuing of him, for purposes best known
to his Majesty; for the reality and venom of the

scandal, issues properly from his sin, though the report came occasionally and disorderly from others.

Since then the Scandal goes so far, and the hurt like to be so common by means of his sin, it's requisite the salve should be as large as the sore, that the report of the confession for the recovery of the evil, may go as far as the infection hath done by the report of the evil committed. Nay, if through my just desert, it be made publick, when private Counsels take not place, nor admonitions awe, nor reasons prevail, when no private means that the Lord Jesus hath appointed, and have been improved, do good, but that they are constrained to appeal to the publick; this shews the strength of the distemper, and the danger of it; and therefore the sinner needs more deeply to be affected with it, and with greater shame and sorrow to bewail it: As when the Offender wil not hear one, nor yet two or three, that the stiffness and obstinacy grows so high that the Brethren are constrained to call in the help of the whol Congregation, and our Savior is constrained to raise the whol Army, the Body of the Church, to make head against an evil, it argues the corruption grows malignant and deadly, and the condition dangerous and desperate, and therefore the Confession must be suitable, must lie in soak, and be of more than usual efficacy, or else it wil in reason be no way satisfactory.

John Winthrop

(1588–1649)

Bibliographical Note. Winthrop's *Journal,* which covers his lifetime, is available in a two-volume edition, ed. James Savage (Boston, 1853) and in another two-volume edition, ed. J. K. Hosmer (New York, 1908); it is now being printed definitively as part of the *Winthrop Papers,* published by the Massachusetts Historical Society. The text of *A Model of Christian Charity* is that of *Winthrop Papers,* II (Boston, 1931), pp. 282–295. The text of the selection from the *Journal* follows that in Perry Miller and Thomas Johnson, eds., *The Puritans* (New York, 1938), pp. 205–207, which in turn derives from Savage's text of the *Journal.* On Winthrop see R. C. Winthrop, *Life and Letters of John Winthrop,* 2 vols. (Boston 1864–1867); S. E. Morison, *Builders of the Bay Colony* (Boston, 1930), pp. 51–104; S. Gray, "The Political Thought of John Winthrop," *New England Quarterly,* III (1930), pp. 681–705; and Edmund S. Morgan, *The Puritan Dilemma* (Boston, 1958).

Written On Boarde the Arrabella, On the Attlantick Ocean. By the Honorable JOHN WINTHROP *Esquire. In His passage, (with the great Company of Religious people, of which Christian Tribes he was the Brave Leader and famous Governor;) from the Island of Great Brittaine, to New-England in the North America. Anno 1630.*

CHRISTIAN CHARITIE.

A MODELL HEREOF.

God Almightie in his most holy and wise providence hath soe disposed of the Condicion of mankinde, as in all times some must be rich some poore, some highe and eminent in power and dignitie; others meane and in subjeccion.

THE REASON HEREOF.

1. REAS: *First*, to hold conformity with the rest of his workes, being delighted to shewe forthe the glory of his wisdome in the variety and differance of the Creatures and the glory of his power, in ordering all these differences for the preservacion and good of the whole, and the glory of his greatnes that as it is the glory of princes to have many officers, soe this great King will have many Stewards counting himselfe more honoured in dispenceing his guifts to man by man, then if hee did it by his owne immediate hand.

2. REAS: *Secondly*, That he might have the more occasion to manifest the worke of his Spirit: first, upon the wicked in moderateing and restraineing them: soe that the riche and mighty should not eate upp the poore, nor the poore, and dispised rise upp against theire superiours, and shake off theire yoake; 2ly in the regenerate in exerciseing his graces in them, as in the greate ones, theire love mercy, gentlenes, temperance etc., in the poore and inferiour sorte, theire faithe patience, obedience etc:

3. REAS: Thirdly, That every man might have need of other, and from hence they might be all knitt more nearly together in the Bond of brotherly affeccion: from hence it appeares plainely that noe man is made more honourable then another or more wealthy etc., out of any perticuler and singuler respect to himselfe but for the glory of his Creator and the Common good of the Creature, Man; Therefore God still reserves the propperty of these guifts to himselfe as Ezek: 16. 17. he there calls wealthe his gold and his silver etc. Prov: 3. 9. he claimes theire service as his due honour the Lord with thy riches etc. All men being thus (by divine providence) rancked into two sortes, riche and poore; under the first, are comprehended all such as are able to live comfortably by theire owne meanes duely improved; and all others are poore according to the former distribution. There are two rules whereby wee are to walke one towards another: JUSTICE

and MERCY. These are allwayes distinguished in theire Act and in theire object, yet may they both concure in the same Subject in eache respect; as sometimes there may be an occasion of shewing mercy to a rich man, in some sudden danger of distresse, and allsoe doeing of meere Justice to a poor man in regard of some perticuler contract etc. There is likewise a double Lawe by which wee are regulated in our conversacion one towardes another: in both the former respects, the lawe of nature and the lawe of grace, or the morrall lawe or the lawe of the gospell, to omitt the rule of Justice as not propperly belonging to this purpose otherwise then it may fall into consideracion in some perticuler Cases: By the first of these lawes man as he was enabled soe withall [is] commaunded to love his neighbour as himselfe upon this ground stands all the precepts of the morrall lawe, which concernes our dealings with men. To apply this to the works of mercy this lawe requires two things first that every man afford his help to another in every want or distresse Secondly, That hee performe this out of the same affeccion, which makes him carefull of his owne good according to that of our Saviour Math: [7.12] Whatsoever ye would that men should doe to you. This was practised by Abraham and Lott in entertaineing the Angells and the old man of Gibea.

The Lawe of Grace or the Gospell hath some differance from the former as in these respectes first the lawe of nature was given to man in the estate of innocency; this of the gospell in the estate of regeneracy: 2ly, the former propounds one man to another, as the same fleshe and Image of god, this as a brother in Christ allsoe, and in the Communion of the same spirit and soe teacheth us to put a difference betweene Christians and others. Doe good to all especially to the household of faith; upon this ground the Israelites were to putt a difference betweene the brethren of such as were strangers though not of the Canaanites. 3ly. The Lawe of nature could give noe rules for dealeing with enemies for all are to be considered as freinds in the estate of innocency, but the Gospell commaunds love to an enemy. Proofe. If thine Enemie hunger feede him; Love your Enemies doe good to them that hate you Math: 5. 44.

This Lawe of the Gospell propoundes likewise a difference of seasons and occasions there is a time when a christian must sell all and give to the poore as they did in the Apostlcs times. There is a tyme allsoe when a christian (though they give not all yet) must give beyond theire abillity, as they of Macedonia. Cor: 2. 6. likewise community of perills calls for extraordinary liberallity and soe doth Community in some speciall service for the Churche. Lastly, when there is noe other meanes whereby our Christian brother may be releived in this distresse, wee must help him bcyond oui ability, rather then tempt God, in putting him upon help by miraculous or extraordinary meanes.

This duty of mercy is exercised in the kindes, Giveing, lending, and forgiveing.

Quest. What rule shall a man observe in giveing in respect of the measure?

Ans. If the time and occasion be ordinary he is to give out of his aboundance—let him lay aside, as god hath blessed him. If the time and occasion bc extraoidinary he must be ruled by them; takeing this withall, that then a man cannot likely doe too much especially, if he may leave himselfe and his family under probable meanes of comfortable subsistance.

Objection. A man must lay upp for posterity, the fathers lay upp for posterity and children and he is worse than an Infidell that providcth not for his owne.

Ans. For the first, it is plaine, that it being spokcn by way of Comparison it must be meant of the ordinary and usuall course of fathcrs and cannot extend to times and occasions extraordinary; for the other place the Apostlc speakes against such as walked inordinately, and it is without question, that he is worse then an Infidell whoe throughe his owne Sloathe and volupluousnes shall neglect to provide for his family.

Objection. The wisc mans Eies are in his head (saith Salomon) and foreseeth the plague, therefore wee must forecast and lay upp against evil times when hee or his may stand in need of all he can gather.

Ans: This very Argument Salomon useth to perswade to liberallity. Eccle: [11.1.] cast thy bread upon the waters etc.: for thou knowest not what evil may come upon the land Luke 16. make you freinds of the riches of Iniquity; you will aske how this shall be? very well. for first he that gives to the poorc lends to the lord, and he will repay him even in this life an hundred fold to

him or his. The righteous is ever mercifull and lendeth and his
seed enjoyeth the blessing; and besides wee know what advantage it will be to us in the day of account, when many such
Witnesses shall stand forthe for us to witnesse the improvement
of our Tallent. And I would knowe of those whoe pleade soe
much for layeing up for time to come, whether they hold that to
be Gospell Math: 16. 19. Lay not upp for yourselves Treasures
upon Earth etc. if they acknowledge it what extent will they
allowe it; if onely to those primitive times lett them consider
the reason whereupon our Saviour groundes it, the first is that
they are subject to the moathe, the rust the Theife. Secondly,
They will steale away the hearte, where the treasure is there will
the heart be allsoe. The reasons are of like force at all times
therefore the exhortacion must be generall and perpetuall which
[applies] allwayes in respect of the love and affeccion to riches
and in regard of the things themselves when any speciall
service for the churche or perticuler distresse of our brother
doe call for the use of them; otherwise it is not onely lawfull
but necessary to lay upp as Joseph did to have ready uppon
such occasions, as the Lord (whose stewards wee are of them)
shall call for them from us: Christ gives us an Instance of the
first, when hee sent his disciples for the Asse, and bidds them
answer the owner thus, the Lord hath need of him; soe when
the Tabernacle was to be builte his [servant] sends to his people
to call for their silver and gold etc.; and yeildes them noe other
reason but that it was for his worke, when Elisha comes to the
widowe of Sareptah and findes her prepareing to make ready
her pittance for herselfe and family, he bids her first provide
for him, he challengeth first gods parte which shee must first
give before shee must serve her owne family, all these teache
us that the lord lookes that when hee is pleased to call for his
right in any thing wee have, our owne Interest wee have must
stand aside, till his turne be served, for the other wee need
looke noe further then to that of John 1. he whoe hath this
worlds goodes and seeth his brother to neede, and shutts upp
his Compassion from him, how dwelleth the love of god in
him, which comes punctually to this Conclusion: if thy brother
be in want and thou canst help him, thou needst not make

doubt, what thou shouldst doe, if thou lovest god thou must help him.

QUEST: What rule must wee observe in lending?

ANS: Thou must observe whether thy brother hath present or probable, or possible meanes of repayeing thee, if ther be none of these, thou must give him according to his necessity, rather than lend him as hee requires; if he hath present meanes of repayeing thee, thou art to looke at him, not as an Act of mercy, but by way of Commerce, wherein thou arte to walke by the rule of Justice, but, if his meanes of repayeing thee be onely probable or possible then is hee an object of thy mercy thou must lend him, though there be danger of looseing it Deut: 15. 7. If any of thy brethren be poore etc. thou shalt lend him sufficient that men might not shift off this duty by the apparant hazzard, he tells them that though the Yeare of Jubile were at hand (when he must remitt it, if hee were not able to rcpay it before) yet he must lend him and that chearefully: it may not greive thee to give him (saith hee) and because some might object, why soe I should soone impoverishe my selfe and my family, he adds with all thy Worke etc. for our Saviour Math: 5. 42. From him that would borrow of thee turne not away.

QUEST: What rule must wee observe in forgiveing?

ANS: Whether thou didst lend by way of Commerce or in mercy, if he have noething to pay thee [thou] must forgive him (except in cause where thou hast a surety or a lawfull pleadge) Deut. 15. 2. Every seaventh yeare the Creditor was to quitt that which hee lent to his brother if hee were poore as appeares ver: 8[4]: save when there shall be noe poore with thee. In all these and like Cases Christ was a generall rule Math: 7. 22. Whatsoever ye would that men should doe to you doe yee the same to them allsoe.

QUEST: What rule must wee observe and walke by in cause of Community of perill?

ANS: The same as before, but with more enlargement towardes others and lesse respect towards our selves, and our owne right hence it was that in the primitive Churche they sold all had all things in Common, neither did any man say that

that which he possessed was his owne likewise in theire returne
out of the Captivity, because the worke was greate for the
restoreing of the church and the danger of enemies was Common to all Nehemiah exhortes the Jewes to liberallity and
readines in remitting theire debtes to theire brethren, and dis-
poseth liberally of his owne to such as wanted and stands not
upon his owne due, which hee might have demaunded of them,
thus did some of our forefathers in times of persecucion here
in England, and soe did many of the faithful in other Churches
whereof wee keepe an honourable remembrance of them, and
it is to be observed that both in Scriptures and latter stories
of the Churches that such as have beene most bountifull to
the poore Saintes especially in these extraordinary times and
occasions god hath left them highly Commanded to posterity,
as Zacheus, Cornelius, Dorcas, Bishop Hooper, the Cuttler of
Brussells and divers others observe againe that the scripture
gives noe causion to restraine any from being over liberall this
way; but all men to the liberall and cherefull practise hereof
by the sweetest promises as to instance one for many, Isaiah
58. 6: Is not this the fast that I have chosen to loose the bonds
of wickednes, to take off the heavy burdens to lett the oppressed goe free and to breake every Yoake, to deale thy bread
to the hungry and to bring the poore that wander into thy
house, when thou seest the naked to cover them etc. then shall
thy light breake forthe as the morneing, and thy healthe shall
growe speedily, thy righteousnes shall goe before thee, and the
glory of the lord shall embrace thee, then thou shalt call and
the lord shall Answer thee etc. 2. 10: If thou power out thy
soule to the hungry, then shall thy light spring out in darknes,
and the lord shall guide thee continually, and satisfie thy Soule
in draught, and make fatt thy bones, thou shalt be like a
watered Garden, and they shall be of thee that shall build
the old wast places etc. on the contrary most heavy cursses are
layd upon such as are straightened towards the Lord and his
people Judg: 5. [23] Cursse ye Meroshe because the [y] came
not to help the Lord etc. Pro: [21. 13] Hee whoe shutteth his
eares from hearing the cry of the poore, he shall cry and shall
not be heard: Math: 25. [41] Goe ye cussed into everlasting

fire etc. [42.] I was hungry and ye fedd mee not. Cor: 2. 9. 16.
[6.] He that soweth spareingly shall reape spareingly.

Haveing allready sett forth the practise of mercy according to the rule of gods lawe, it will be usefull to lay open the
groundes of it allsoe being the other parte of the Commaunde-
ment and that is the affeccion from which this exercise of
mercy must arise, the Apostle tells us that this love is the
fullfilling of the lawe, not that it is enough to love our brother
and soe noe further but in regard of the excellency of his partes
giveing any motion to the other as the Soule to the body and
the power it hath to sett all the faculties on worke in the outward exercise of this duty as when wee bid one make the
clocke strike he doth not lay hand on the hammer which is the
immediate instrument of the sound but setts on worke the
first mover or maine wheele, knoweing that will certainely
produce the sound which hee intends; soe the way to drawe
men to the workes of mercy is not by force of Argument from
the goodnes or necessity of the worke, for though this course
may enforce a rationall minde to some present Act of mercy as
is frequent in experience, yet it cannot worke such a habit in
a Soule as shall make it prompt upon all occasions to produce
the same effect but by frameing these affeccions of love in the
hearte which will as natively bring forthe the other, as any cause
doth produce the effect.

The diffinition which the Scripture gives us of love is this
Love is the bond of perfection. First, it is a bond, or ligament.
2ly, it makes the worke perfect. There is noe body but consistes
of partes and that which knitts these partes together gives the
body its perfeccion, because it makes eache parte soe contiguous
to other as thereby they doe mutually participate with eache
other, both in strengthe and infirmity in pleasure and paine, to
instance in the most perfect of all bodies, Christ and his church
make one body: the severall partes of this body considered
aparte before they were united were as disproportionate and as
much disordering as soe many contrary quallities or elements
but when christ comes and by his spirit and love knitts all
these partes to himselfe and each to other, it is become the
most perfect and best proportioned body in the world Eph:

4. 16. "Christ by whome all the body being knitt together by
every joynt for the furniture thereof according to the effectuall
power which is in the measure of every perfeccion of partes a
glorious body without spott or wrinckle the ligaments hereof
being Christ or his love for Christ is love 1 John: 4. 8. Soe this
definition is right Love is the bond of perfeccion.

From hence wee may frame these Conclusions.

1 first all true Christians are of one body in Christ. 1. Cor.
12. 12. 13. 17. [27.] Ye are the body of Christ and members of
[your?] parte.

2ly. The ligamentes of this body which knitt together are
love.

3ly. Noe body can be perfect which wants its propper ligamentes.

4ly. All the partes of this body being thus united are made
soe contiguous in a speciall relacion as they must needes partake
of each others strength and infirmity, joy, and sorrowe, weale
and woe. 1 Cor: 12. 26. If one member suffers all suffer with it,
if one be in honour, all rejoyce with it.

5ly. This sensiblenes and Sympathy of each others Condicions will necessarily infuse into each parte a native desire
and endeavour, to strengthen defend preserve and comfort the
other.

To insist a little on this Conclusion being the product of
all the former the truthe hereof will appeare both by precept
and patterne i. John. 3. 10. yee ought to lay downe your lives
for the brethren Gal: 6. 2. beare ye one anothers burthens and
soe fulfill the lawe of Christ.

For patterns wee have that first of our Saviour whoe out
of his good will in obedience to his father, becomeing a parte
of this body, and being knitt with it in the bond of love, found
such a native sensiblenes of our infirmities and sorrowes as hee
willingly yeilded himself to deathe to ease the infirmities of
the rest of his body and soe heale theire sorrowes: from the
like Sympathy of partes did the Apostles and many thousands
of the Saintes lay downe theire lives for Christ againe, the like
wee may see in the members of this body among themselves.
1. Rom. 9. Paule could have beene contented to have beene
seperated from Christ that the Jewes might not be cutt off

from the body: It is very observable which hee professeth of his affectionate part[ak]eing with every member: whoe is weake (saith hee) and I am not weake? whoe is offended and I burne not; and againe. 2 Cor: 7. 13. therefore wee are comforted because yee were comforted. of Epaphroditus he speaketh Phil: 2. 30. that he regarded not his owne life to [do] him service soe Phebe. and others are called the servantes of the Churche, now it is apparant that they served not for wages or by Constrainte but out of love, the like wee shall finde in the histories of the churche in all ages the sweete Sympathie of affeccions which was in the members of this body one towardes another, theire chearfullnes in serveing and suffering together how liberall they were without repineing harbourers without grudgeing and helpfull without reproacheing and all from hence they had fervent love amongst them which onely make [s] the practise of mercy constant and easie.

The next consideracion is how this love comes to be wrought; Adam in his first estate was a perfect modell of mankinde in all theire generacions, and in him this love was perfected in regard of the habit, but Adam Rent in himselfe from his Creator, rent all his posterity allsoe one from another, whence it comes that every man is borne with this principle in him, to love and seeke himselfe onely and thus a man continueth till Christ comes and takes possession of the soule, and infuseth another principle love to God and our brother. And this latter haveing continuall supply from Christ, as the head and roote by which hee is united get the predominency in the soule, soe by little and little expells the former 1 John 4. 7. love cometh of god and every one that loveth is borne of god, soe that this love is the fruite of the new birthe, and none can have it but the new Creature, now when this quallity is thus formed in the soules of men it workes like the Spirit upon the drie bones Ezek. 37. [7] bone came to bone, it gathers together the scattered bones or perfect old man Adam and knitts them into one body againe in Christ whereby a man is become againe a liveing soule.

The third Consideracion is concerning the exercise of this love, which is twofold, inward or outward, the outward hath beene handled in the former preface of this discourse, for un-

folding the other wee must take in our way that maxime of
philosophy, Simile simili gaudet or like will to like; for as it is
things which are carved with disafeccion to eache other, the
ground of it is from a dissimilitude or [blank] ariseing from the
contrary or different nature of the things themselves, soe the
ground of love is an apprehension of some resemblance in the
things loved to that which affectes it, this is the cause why the
Lord loves the Creature, soe farre as it hath any of his Image
in it, he loves his elect because they are like himself, he beholds
them in his beloved sonne: soe a mother loves her childe,
because shee throughly conceives a resemblance of herselfe in
it. Thus it is betweene the members of Christ, each discernes
by the worke of the spirit his owne Image and resemblance in
another, and therefore cannot but love him as he loves himselfe: Now when the soule which is of a sociable nature findes
any thing like to it selfe, it is like Adam when Eve was brought
to him, shee must have it one with herselfe this is fleshe of my
fleshe (saith shee) and bone of my bone shee conceives a great
delighte in it, therefore shee desires nearenes and familiarity
with it: shee hath a greate propensity to doe it good and receives
such content in it, as feareing the miscarriage of her beloved
shee bestowes it in the inmost closett of her heart, shee will
not endure that it shall want any good which shee can give it,
if by occasion shee be withdrawne from the Company of it,
shee is still lookeing towardes the place where shee left her
beloved, if shee heare it groane she is with it presently, if shee
finde it sadd and disconsolate shee sighes and mournes with it,
shee hath noe such joy, as to see her beloved merry and thrive-
ing, if shee see it wronged, shee cannot beare it without passion, shee setts noe boundes of her affeccions, nor hath any
thought of reward, shee findes recompence enoughe in the
exercise of her love towardes it, wee may see this Acted to life
in Jonathan and David. Jonathan a valiant man endued with
the spirit of Christ, soe soone as hee Discovers the same spirit
in David had presently his hearte knitt to him by this linement
of love, soe that it is said he loved him as his owne soule, he
takes soe great pleasure in him that hee stripps himselfe to
adorne his beloved, his fathers kingdome was not soe precious

to him as his beloved David, David shall have it with all his hearte, himself desires noe more but that hee may be neare to him to rejoyce in his good hee chooseth to converse with him in the wildernesse even to the hazzard of his owne life, rather then with the greate Courtiers in his fathers Pallace; when hee sees danger towards him, hee spares neither care paines, nor perill to divert it, when Injury was offered his beloved David, hee could not beare it, though from his owne father, and when they must parte for a Season onely, they thought theire heartes would have broake for sorrowe, had not theire affeccions found vent by aboundance of Teares: other instances might be brought to shewe the nature of this affeccion as of Ruthe and Naomi and many others, but this truthe is cleared enough. If any shall object that it is not possible that love should be bred or upheld without hope of requitall, it is graunted but that is not our cause, for this love is allwayes under reward it never gives, but it allwayes receives with advantage: first, in regard that among the members of the same body, love and affection are reciprocall in a most equall and sweete kinde of Commerce. 2ly [3ly], in regard of the pleasure and content that the exercise of love carries with it as wee may see in the naturall body the mouth is at all the paines to receive, and mince the foode which serves for the nourishment of all the other partes of the body, yet it hath noe cause to complaine; for first, the other partes send backe by secret passages a due proporcion of the same nourishment in a better forme for the strengthening and comforteing the mouthe. 2ly the labour of the mouthe is accompanied with such pleasure and content as farre exceedes the paines it takes: soe is it in all the labour of love, among christians, the partie loveing, reapes love againe as was shewed before, which the soule covetts more than all the wealthe in the world. 2ly [4ly]. noething yeildes more pleasure and content to the soule then when it findes that which it may love fervently, for to love and live beloved is the soules paradice, both heare and in heaven: In the State of Wedlock there be many comfortes to beare out the troubles of that Condicion; but let such as have tryed the most, say if there be any sweetnes in that Condicion comparable to the exercise of mutuall love.

From the former Consideracions ariseth these Conclusions.
1 First, This love among Christians is a reall thing not
Imaginarie.

2ly. This love is as absolutcly necessary to the being of
the body of Christ, as the sinewes and other ligaments of a
naturall body are to the being of that body.

3ly. This love is a divine spirituall nature free, active strong
Couragious permanent under valueing all things beneathe its
proper object, and of all the graces this makes us nearer to
resemble the virtues of our heavenly father.

4ly. It restes in the love and wellfare of its beloved, for
the full and certaine knowledge of these truthes concerning
the nature use, [and] excellency of this grace, that which the
holy ghost hath left recorded 1. Cor. 13. may give full satisfac-
cion which is needfull for every true member of this lovely body
of the Lord Jesus, to worke upon theire heartes, by prayer
meditacion continuall exercise at least of the speciall [power]
of this grace till Christ be formed in them and they in him
all in eache other knitt together by this bond of love.

It rests now to make some applicacion of this discourse
by the present designe which gave the occasion of writeing of it.
Herein are 4 things to be propounded: first the persons, 2ly,
the worke, 3ly, the end, 4ly the meanes.

1. For the persons, wee are a Company professing our
selves fellow members of Christ, In which respect onely though
wee were absent from eache other many miles, and had our
imploymentes as farre distant, yet wee ought to account our
selves knitt together by this bond of love, and live in the excer-
cise of it, if wee would have comforte of our being in Christ,
this was notorious in the practise of the Christians in former
times, as is testified of the Waldenses from the mouth of one
of the adversaries Aeneas Sylvius, mutuo [solent amare] penè
antequam norint, they use to love any of theire owne religion
even before they were acquainted with them.

2ly. for the worke wee have in hand, it is by a mutuall
consent through a speciall overruleing providence, and a more
then an ordinary approbation of the Churches of Christ to
seeke out a place of Cohabitation and Consorteshipp under
a due forme of Government both civill and ecclesiasticall. In

such cases as this the care of the publique must oversway all private respects, by which not onely conscience, but meare Civill pollicy doth binde us; for it is a true rule that perticuler estates cannott subsist in the ruine of the publique.

3ly. The end is to improve our lives to doe more service to the Lord the comforte and encrease of the body of christe whereof wee are members that our selves and posterity may be the better preserved from the Common corrupcions of this evill world to serve the Lord and worke out our Salvacion under the power and purity of his holy Ordinances.

4ly. for the meanes whereby this must bee effected, they are 2fold, a Conformity with the worke and end wee aime at, these wee see are extraordinary, therefore wee must not content our selves with usuall ordinary meanes whatsoever wee did or ought to have done when wee lived in England, the same must wee doe and more allsoe where wee goe: That which the most in theire Churches maineteine as a truthe in profession onely, wee must bring into familiar and constant practise, as in this duty of love wee must love brotherly without dissimulation, wee must love one another with a pure hearte fervently wee must beare one anothers burthens, wee must not looke onely on our owne things, but allsoe on the things of our brethren, neither must wee think that the lord will beare with such faileings at our hands as hee dothe from those among whome we have lived, and that for 3 Reasons.

1. In regard of the more neare bond of mariage, betweene him and us, wherein he hath taken us to be his after a most strickt and peculiar manner which will make him the more Jealous of our love and obedience soe he tells the people of Israell, you onely have I knowne of all the families of the Earthe therefore will I punishe you for your Transgressions.

2ly, because the lord will be sanctified in them that come neare him. Wee know that there were many that corrupted the service of the Lord some setting upp Alters before his owne, others offering both strange fire and strange Sacrifices allsoe; yet there came noe fire from heaven, or other sudden Judgement upon them as did upon Nadab and Abihu whoe yet wee may thinke did not sinne presumptuously.

3ly, When God gives a speciall Commission he lookes to

have it stricktly observed in every Article, when hee gave Saule a Commission to destroy Amaleck hee indented with him upon certaine Articles and because hee failed in one of the least, and that upon a faire pretence, it lost him the kingdome, which should have beene his reward, if hee had observed his Commission: Thus stands the cause betweene God and us, wee are entered into Covenant with him for this worke, wee have taken out a Commission, the Lord hath given us leave to drawe our owne Articles wee have professed to enterprise these Accions upon these and these ends, wee have hereupon besought him of favour and blessing: Now if the Lord shall please to heare us, and bring us in peace to the place wee desire, then hath hee ratified this Covenant and sealed our Commission, [and] will expect a strickt performance of the Articles contained in it, but if wee shall neglect the observacion of these Articles which are the ends wee have propounded, and dissembling with our God, shall fall to embrace this present world and prosecute our carnall intencions, seekeing great things for our selves and our posterity, the Lord will surely breake out in wrathe against us be revenged of such a perjured people and make us knowe the price of the breache of such a Covenant.

Now the onely way to avoyde this shipwracke and to provide for our posterity is to followe the Counsell of Micah, to doe Justly, to love mercy, to walke humbly with our God, for this end, wee must be knitt together in this worke as one man, wee must entertaine each other in brotherly Affeccion, wee must be willing to abridge our selves of our superfluities, for the supply of others necessities, wee must uphold a familiar Commerce together in all meekenes, gentlenes, patience and liberallity, wee must delight in eache other, make others Condicions our owne rejoyce together, mourne together, labour, and suffer together, allwayes haveing before our eyes our Commission and Community in the worke, our Community as members of the same body, soe shall wee keepe the unitie of the spirit in the bond of peace, the Lord will be our God and delight to dwell among us, as his owne people and will commaund a blessing upon us in all our wayes, soe that wee shall see much more of his wisdome power goodnes and truthe then formerly wee have beene acquainted with, wee shall finde that the God of Israell

is among us, when tenn of us shall be able to resist a thousand
of our enemies, when hee shall make us a prayse and glory,
that men shall say of succeeding plantacions: the lord make it
like that of New England: for wee must Consider that wee
shall be as a Citty upon a Hill, the eies of all people are uppon
us; soe that if wee shall deale falsely with our god in this worke
wee have undertaken and soe cause him to withdrawe his present
help from us, wee shall be made a story and a by-word through
the world, wee shall open the mouthes of enemies to speake
evill of the wayes of god and all professours for Gods sake; wee
shall shame the faces of many of gods worthy servants, and
cause theire prayers to be turned into Cursses upon us till wee
be consumed out of the good land whether wee arc goeing:
And to shutt upp this discourse with that exhortacion of Moses
that faithfull servant of the Lord in his last farewell to Israell
Deut. 30. Beloved there is now sett before us life, and good,
deathe and evill in that wee are Commaunded this day to love
the Lord our God, and to love one another to walke in his
wayes and to keepe his Commaundements and his Ordinance,
and his lawes, and the Articles of our Covenant with him that
wee may live and be multiplyed, and that the Lord our God
may blesse us in the land whether wee goe to possesse it: But if
our heartes shall turne away soe that wee will not obey, but
shall be seduced and worshipp [serve *cancelled*] other Gods
our pleasures, and proffitts, and serve them; it is propounded
unto us this day, wee shall surely perishe out of the good Land
whether wee passe over this vast Sea to possesse it;

> Therefore lett us choose life,
> that wee, and our Seede,
> may live; by obeyeing his
> voyce, and cleaveing to him,
> for hee is our life, and
> our prosperity.

from

THE JOURNAL*

[SPEECH TO THE GENERAL COURT, JULY 3, 1645]

I suppose something may be expected from me, upon this charge that is befallen me,[1] which moves me to speak now to you; yet I intend not to intermeddle in the proceedings of the court, or with any of the persons concerned therein. Only I bless God, that I see an issue of this troublesome business. I also acknowledge the justice of the court, and, for mine own part, I am well satisfied, I was publicly charged, and I am publicly and legally acquitted, which is all I did expect or desire. And though this be sufficient for my justification before men, yet not so before the God, who hath seen so much amiss in my dispensations (and even in this affair) as calls me to be humble. For to be publicly and criminally charged in this court, is matter of humiliation, (and I desire to make a right use of it,) notwithstanding I be thus acquitted. If her father had spit in her face, (saith the Lord concerning Miriam,) should she not have been ashamed seven days? Shame had lien upon her, whatever the occasion had been. I am unwilling to stay you from your urgent affairs, yet give me leave (upon this special occasion) to speak a little more to this assembly. It may be of some good use, to inform and rectify the judgments of some of the people, and may prevent such distempers as have arisen amongst us. The great questions that have troubled the country, are about the authority of the magistrates and the liberty of the people. It is yourselves who have called us to this office, and being called by you, we have our authority from

---

* Reprinted from *The Puritans*, edited by Perry Miller and Thomas Johnson and used with permission of the American Book Company.
[1] Winthrop had been acquitted of charges that he had exceeded his authority as a magistrate.

God, in way of an ordinance, such as hath the image of God eminently stamped upon it, the contempt and violation whereof hath been vindicated with examples of divine vengeance. I entreat you to consider, that when you choose magistrates, you take them from among yourselves, men subject to like passions as you are. Therefore when you see infirmities in us, you should reflect upon your own, and that would make you bear the more with us, and not be severe censurers of the failings of your magistrates, when you have continual experience of the like infirmities in yourselves and others. We account him a good servant, who breaks not his covenant. The covenant between you and us is the oath you have taken of us, which is to this purpose, that we shall govern you and judge your causes by the rules of God's laws and our own, according to our best skill. When you agree with a workman to build you a ship or house, etc., he undertakes as well for his skill as for his faithfulness, for it is his profession, and you pay him for both. But when you call one to be a magistrate, he doth not profess nor undertake to have sufficient skill for that office, nor can you furnish him with gifts, etc., therefore you must run the hazard of his skill and ability. But if he fail in faithfulness, which by his oath he is bound unto, that he must answer for. If it fall out that the case be clear to common apprehension, and the rule clear also, if he transgress here, the error is not in the skill, but in the evil of the will: it must be required of him. But if the case be doubtful, or the rule doubtful, to men of such understanding and parts as your magistrates are, if your magistrates should err here, yourselves must bear it.

For the other point concerning liberty, I observe a great mistake in the country about that. There is a twofold liberty, natural (I mean as our nature is now corrupt) and civil or federal. The first is common to man with beasts and other creatures. By this, man, as he stands in relation to man simply, hath liberty to do what he lists; it is a liberty to evil as well as to good. This liberty is incompatible and inconsistent with authority, and cannot endure the least restraint of the most just authority. The exercise and maintaining of this liberty makes men grow more evil, and in time to be worse than brute beasts: omnes sumus licentia deteriores. This is that great enemy of truth and peace, that wild beast, which all the ordinances of God are bent against, to restrain and subdue it. The other kind of liberty I call civil or federal, it may also be termed moral, in reference to the covenant between God and man, in the moral law, and the politic covenants and constitutions, amongst men themselves. This liberty is the proper end and object of authority, and cannot subsist without it; and it is a liberty to that only which is good, just, and honest. This liberty you are to stand for, with the hazard (not only of your goods, but) of your lives, if need be. Whatsoever crosseth this, is not authority, but a distemper thereof. This liberty is maintained and exercised in a way of subjection to authority; it is of the same kind of liberty wherewith Christ hath made us free. The woman's own choice makes such a man her husband; yet being so chosen, he is her lord, and she is to be subject to him, yet in a way of liberty, not of bondage; and a true wife accounts her subjection her honor and freedom, and would not think her condition safe and free, but in her subjection to her husband's authority. Such is the liberty of the church under the authority of Christ, her king and husband; his yoke is so easy and sweet to her as a bride's ornaments; and if through forwardness or wantonness, etc., she shake it off, at any time, she is at no rest in her spirit, until she take it up again; and whether her lord smiles upon her, and embraceth her in his arms, or whether he frowns, or rebukes, or smites her, she apprehends the sweetness of his love in all, and is refreshed, supported, and instructed by every such dispensation of his authority over her. On the other side, ye know who they are that complain of this yoke and say, let us break their bands, etc., we will not have this man to rule over us. Even so, brethren, it will be between you and your magistrates. If you stand for your natural corrupt liberties, and will do what is good in your own eyes, you will not endure the least weight of authority, but will murmur, and oppose, and be always striving to shake off that yoke; but if you will be satisfied to enjoy such civil and lawful liberties, such as Christ allows you, then will you quietly and cheerfully submit unto that authority which is set over you, in all the administrations of it, for your good. Wherein, if we fail at any time, we hope we shall be willing (by God's assistance) to hearken to good advice from any of you, or in any other way of God; so shall your liberties be preserved, in upholding the honor and power of authority amongst you.

Roger Williams

(c. 1603–1683)

Bibliographical Note. Williams' writings have been collected in *Publications of the Narragansett Club*, I–VI (1866–1874); a seventh volume, edited by Perry Miller was added in 1963, when the whole was reprinted. The texts here printed follow this edition, IV, 493–501 and VI, pp. 263–265, 278–286, pp. 351–357. The best biography remains that by S. H. Brockunier, *The Irrepressible Democrat: Roger Williams* (New York, 1940), although it is corrected in some details and emphases by Ola Elizabeth Winslow, *Master Roger Williams* (New York, 1957). The pioneering study of Williams' thought, although it is too unsympathetic towards Williams' adversaries, is J. E. Ernst, *The Political Thought of Roger Williams* (Seattle, 1929). A brilliant, though tendentious, brief study is Perry Miller, *Roger Williams* (Indianapolis, 1953). Miller's account is to be set against and balanced by Sacvan Bercovitch, "Typology in Puritan New England: The Williams-Cotton Controversy Reassessed," *American Quarterly*, XIX (1967), 166–191.

from

THE BLOODY TENENT YET MORE BLOODY (1651)

["THE PORTRAITURE OF THE BLOUDIE TENENT"]

The Portraiture of the *Bloudie Tenent.*

Truth. Christ Jesus the *Sun* of *Righteousnesse* hath broke forth, and dayly, will, to a *brighter* and *brighter Discoverie* of this deformed *Ethiopian:* And for my selfe I must proclaime, before

[136]

the most holy God, *Angells* and *Men,* that (what
ever other *white* and heavenly *Tenents* Mr *Cotton*
houlds)[1] yet this is a *fowle,* a *black,* and a *bloudie
Tenent.*

A *Tenent* of high *Blasphemie* against the
God of *Peace,* the God of *Order,* who hath of
one *Bloud,* made all *Mankinde,* to dwell upon
the face of the Earth, now, all *confounded* and
destroyed in their *Civill Beings* and *Subsistences,*
by mutuall flames of *warre* from their severall respective *Religions* and *Consciences.*

A *Tenent warring* against the *Prince* of *Peace,
Christ Jesus,* denying his *Appearance* and *Comming* in the *Flesh,* to put an end to, and *abolish*
the *shadowes* of that *ceremoniall* and *typicall*
Land of *Canaan.*

A *Tenent* fighting against the sweete *end* of
his *comming,* which was not to destroy mens
Lives, for their *Religions,* but to save them, by the
meeke and peaceable *Invitations* and *perswasions*
of his peaceable *wisdomes Maidens.*

A *Tenent* fowly charging his *Wisedome,
Faithfullnes* and *Love,* in so poorly providing such
Magistrates and *Civill Powers* all the *World* over,
as might effect so great a *charge* pretended to be
committed to them.

A *Tenent* lamentably guilty of his most precious *bloud,* shed in the *bloud* of so many hundreth thousand of his poore *servants* by the *civill
powers* of the *World,* pretending to suppresse
Blasphemies, Heresies, Idolatries, Superstition, &c.

A *Tenent* fighting with the *Spirit* of *Love,
Holines,* and *Meeknes,* by kindling fiery *Spirits of*

Luc. 9.
Prov. 9.

---

[1] This passage, in which Truth and Peace speak, concludes the tract, which
is itself the last in a series of debates between Williams and John Cotton
on freedom of belief and worship. Cotton had defended Puritan persecution
of those who would not conscientiously subscribe to Puritan beliefs.
Williams here is searching out the full implications of this "bloudie tenent
of persecution for cause of conscience."

false zeale and *Furie,* when yet such *Spirits* know not of what *Spirit* they are.

A *Tenent* fighting with those mighty *Angels* who stand up for the peace of the *Saints,* against *Persia, Grecia,* &c. and so consequently, all other *Nations,* who fighting for their severall *Religions,* and against the *Truth,* leave no *Roome* for such as feare and love the *Lord* on the Earth.

A *Tenent,* against which the blessed *Soules* under the *Altar* cry loud for *vengeance,* this *Tenent* having cut their *Throats,* torne out their *Hearts,* and powred forth their *Bloud* in all *Ages,* as the onely *Hereticks* and *Blasphemers* in the World.

A *Tenent* which no *Uncleannes,* no *Adulterie, Incest, Sodomie,* or *Beastialitie* can equall, this *ravishing* and forcing (*explicitly* or *implicitly*) the very *Soules* and *Consciences* of all the *Nations* and *Inhabitants* of the *World.*

A *Tenent* that puts out the very *eye* of all true *Faith,* which cannot but be as free and voluntarie as any *Virgin* in the *World,* in *refusing* or *embracing* any *Spirituall offer* or *object.*

A *Tenent* loathsome and ugly (in the eyes of the *God* of *Heaven,* and serious sonnes of men) I say, loathsome with the palpable *filths* of *grosse dissimulation* and *hypocrisie:* Thousands of *Peoples* and whole *Nations,* compelld by this *Tenent* to put on the sowle *vizard* of *Religious hypocrisie,* for feare of *Lawes, losses* and *punishments,* and for the keeping and hoping for of *favour, libertie, worldly commoditie,* &c.

A *Tenent* wofully guiltie of hardning all false and *deluded Consciences* (of whatsoever *Sect, Faction, Heresie,* or *Idolatrie,* though never so horrid and *blasphemous*) by *cruelties* and *violences* practiced against them: all false *Teachers* and their *Followers* (ordinarily) contracting a

Brawnie and *steelie hardnesse* from their *sufferings* for their *Consciences*.

A *Tenent* that shuts and bars out the gracious *prophecies* and *promises* and *discoveries* of the most glorious *Sun* of *Righteousnes, Christ Jesus,* that burnes up the holy *Scriptures,* and forbids them (upon the point) to be read in *English,* or that any *tryall* or *search,* or (truly) free *disquisition* be made by them: when the most able, diligent and conscionable *Readers* must pluck forth their own *eyes,* and be forced to reade by the (which foever *prædominant*) *Cleargies Spectacles.*

A *Tenent* that *seales up* the spirituall *graves* of all men, *Jewes* and *Gentiles,* (and consequently stands guiltie of the *damnation* of all men) since no *Preachers,* nor *Trumpets of Christ* himselfe may call them out, but such as the severall and respective *Nations* of the *World* themselves allow of.

A *Tenent* that fights against the *common principles* of all *Civilitie,* and the very *civill being* and *combinations* of *men* in *Nations, Cities,* &c. by commixing (*explicitly* or *implicitly*) a *spirituall* and *civill State* together, and so confounding and overthrowing the *puritie* and *strength* of both.

A *Tenent* that kindles the devouring *flames* of *combustions* and *warres* in most *Nations* of the *World,* and (if *God* were not infinitely gracious) had almost ruind the *English, French,* the *Scotch* and *Irish,* and many other *Nations, Germane, Polonian, Hungarian, Bohemian,* &c.

A *Tenent* that bowes downe the *backs* and *necks* of all *civill States* and *Magistrates, Kings* and *Emperours,* under the proud feete of that *man* and *monster* of *sinne* and *pride* the *Pope,* and all *Popish* and proud *Cleargie-men* rendring such *Laicks* and *Seculars* (as they call them) but slavish *Executioners* (upon the point) of their most imperious *Synodicall Decrees* and *Sentences.*

A *Tenent* that renders the highest *civill Magistrates* and *Ministers* of *Justice* (the *Fathers* and *Gods* of their *Countries*) either odious or lamentably grievous unto the very best *Subjects* by either clapping or keeping on, the *iron yoakes* of *cruellest oppression.* No *yoake* or *bondage* comparably so grievous, as that upon the Soules necke of mens *Religion* and *Consciences.*

A *Tenent*, all besprinckled with the *bloudie murthers, stobs, poysonings, pistollings, powderplots,* &c. against many famous *Kings, Princes,* and *States,* either actually performed or attempted, in *France, England, Scotland, Low-Countries,* and other *Nations.*

A *Tenent* all *red* and *bloudie* with those most *barbarous* and *Tyger*-like *Massacres,* of so many thousand and ten thousands formerly in *France,* and other parts, and so lately and so horribly in *Ireland:* of which, what ever causes be assigned, this chiefly will be found the true, and while this continues (to wit, *violence* against *Conscience*) this *bloudie Issue,* sooner or later, must *breake forth* againe (except *God* wonderfully stop it) in *Ireland* and other places too.

A *Tenent* that *stunts* the *growth* and *flourishing* of the most likely and hopefullest *Commonweales* and *Countries,* while *Consciences,* the *best,* and the *best* deserving *Subjects* are forct to flie (by enforced or voluntary *Banishment*) from their native *Countries;* The lamentable proofe whereof *England* hath felt in the flight of so many worthy *English,* into the *Low Countries* and *New England,* and from *New England* into old againe and other forraigne parts.

A *Tenent* whose grosse partialitie denies the *Principles of common Justice,* while *Men* waigh out to the *Consciences* of all others, that which

they judge not fit nor right to be waighed out to
their owne: Since the *persecutours Rule* is, to
take and persecute all *Consciences*, onely, *himselfe*
must not be touched.

A *Tenent* that is but *Machevilisme*, and
makes a *Religion*, but a *cloake* or *stalking horse*
to *policie* and *private Ends* of *Jeroboams Crowne*,
and the *Priests Benefice*, &c.

A *Tenent* that *corrupts* and *spoiles* the very
Civill Honestie and *Naturall Conscience* of a
Nation. Since *Conscience* to *God* violated, proves
(without *Repentance*) ever after, a very *Jade*, a
Drug, loose and *unconscionable* in all converse
with men.

Lastly, a *Tenent* in *England* most unseasonable, as powring *Oyle* upon those *Flames* which
the high *Wisdome* of the *Parliament*, (by easing
the yoakes on Mens *Consciences*) had begun to
quench.

In the sad Consideration of all which (Deare
Peace) let *Heaven* and *Earth* judge of the *washing* and *colour* of this *Tenent*. For thee *sweete
heavenly Guest*) goe lodge thee in the *breasts* of
the *peaceable* and humble *Witnesses* of *Jesus*,
that love the *Truth* in *peace!* Hide thee from the
Worlds *Tumults* and *Combustions*, in the breasts
of thy truely *noble children*, who professe and
endeavour to breake the *irony* and insupportable
yoakes upon the *Soules* and *Consciences* of any
of the sonnes of Men.

Peace her Repose and Tabernacle.

Peace. Me-thinkes (Deare *Truth*) if any of the
least of these deepe charges be found against
this *Tenent*, you doe not wrong it when you stile
it *bloudie*: But since, in the wofull proofe of all
Ages past, since *Nimrod* (the *Hunter* or *persecu-
tour* before the *Lord*) these and more are lamentably evident and undeniable: it gives me wonder
that so many and so excellent *eyes* of *Gods*

servants should not espie so fowle a *monster*, especially considering the *universall opposition* this *Tenent* makes against *Gods Glory*, and the *Good* of all mankinde.

The Bloudie Tenant *of persecution compared.*

Truth. There hath been many fowle *opinions*, with which the *old Serpent* hath infected and bewitched the sonnes of men (touching *God, Christ*, the *Spirit*, the *Church*, against *Holines*, against *Peace*, against *civill Obedience*, against *chastitie*) in so much, that even *Sodomie* it selfe hath been a *Tenent* maintained in print by some of the very *pillars* of the *Church* of *Rome*: But this *Tenent* is so universally opposite to *God* and *man*, so pernicious and destructive to both (as hath been declared) that like the *Powder-plot*, it threatens to blow up all *Religion*, all *civilitie*, all *humanitie*, yea the very *Being* of the *World*, and the *Nations* thereof at once.

Peace. He that is the *Father* of *Lies*, and a *murtherer* from the beginning, he knowes this well, and this ugly *Blackmore* needs a *maske* or *vizard*.

The maskes and vizards of the bloudie Tenent.

Truth. Yea the *bloudines* and *inhumantie* of it is such, that not onely Mr *Cottons* more tender and holy Breast, but even the most bloudie *Bonners* and *Gardiners* have been forced to arme themselves with the faire *shewes* and glorious *pretences*, of the *Glory* of *God*, and *zeale* for that *Glory*, the *Love* of his *Truth*, the *Gospel* of *Christ Jesus*, *love* and *pitie* to mens soules, the *peace* of the *Church*, *uniformitie*, *Order*, the *peace* of the *Commonweale*, the *Wisedome of the State*, the *Kings*, *Queenes* and *Parliaments* proceedings, the *odiousnesse* of *Sects*, *Heresies*, *Blasphemies*, *Novelties*, *Seducers*, and their *Infections*: the *obstinacie* of *Hereticks*, after all *Meanes*, *Disputations*, *Exami-*

nations, *Synods*, yea and after *Conviction* in the poore *Hereticks* owne *Conscience:* Add to these the flattring sound of those glosing *Titles,* the *Godly Magistrate,* the *Christian Magistrate,* the *Nurcing Fathers* and *Mothers* of the *Church, Christian Kings* and *Queenes.* But all other *Kings* and *Magistrates* (even all the *Nations* of the *World* over, as Mr *Cotton* pleads) must suspend and hould their hands, and not meddle in *matters* of *Religion,* untill they be informed, &c.

Peace. The dreadfull righteous hand of *God,* the *Eternall* and avenging *God,* is pulling off these *maskes* and *vizards,* that *thousands,* and the *World* may see this *bloudie Tenents Beautie.*

Truth. But see (my *heavenly Sister* and true *stranger* in this Sea-like restles, raging *World*) see here what *Fires* and *Swords* are come to part us! Well; Our *meetings* in the Heavens shall not thus be interrupted, our *Kisses* thus *distracted,* and our *eyes* and *cheekes* thus *wet, unwiped:* For me, though *censured, threatned, persecuted,* I must *professe,* while *Heaven* and *Earth lasts,* that no one *Tenent* that either *London, England,* or the *World* doth harbour, is so *hereticall, blasphemous, seditious,* and *dangerous* to the *corporall,* to the *spirituall,* to the *present,* to the *Eternall* Good of all Men, as the *bloudie Tenent* (how ever *wash't* and *whited*) I say, as is the *bloudie Tenent* of *persecution* for cause of *Conscience.*

Truth & Peace, *their meetings seldome and short.*

[TWO LETTERS TO THE TOWN OF PROVIDENCE: AN APOLOGIA]

[*Providence, August, 1654.*]

WELL-BELOVED FRIENDS AND NEIGHBORS,—I am like a man in a great fog. I know not well how to steer. I fear to run upon the rocks at home, having had trials abroad. I fear to run quite backward, as men in a mist do, and undo all that I have been a long time undoing myself to do, viz.: to keep up the name of a people, a free people, not enslaved to the bondages and iron yokes of the great (both soul and body) oppressions of the English and barbarians about us, nor to the divisions and disorders within ourselves. Since I set the first step of any English foot into these wild parts, and have maintained a chargeable and hazardous correspondence with the barbarians, and spent almost five years' time with the state of England, to keep off the rage of the English against us, what have I reaped of the root of being the stepping-stone of so many families and towns about us, but grief, and sorrow, and bitterness? I have been charged with folly for that freedom and liberty which I have always stood for; I say liberty and equality, both in land and government. I have been blamed for parting with Moshasuck, and afterward Pawtuxet, (which were mine own as truly as any man's coat upon his back,) without reserving to myself a foot of land, or an inch of voice in any matter, more than to my servants and strangers. It hath been told me that I labored for a licentious and contentious people; that I have foolishly parted with town and colony advantages, by which I might have preserved both town and colony in as good order as any in the country about us. This, and ten times more, I have been censured for, and at this present am called a traitor by one party, against the state of England, for not maintaining the charter and the colony; and it is said I am as good as banished by yourselves, and that both sides wished that I might never have landed, that the fire of contention might have had no stop in burning. Indeed, the words have been so sharp between myself and some lately, that at last I was forced to say, they might well silence all complaints if I once began to complain, who was unfortunately fetched and drawn from my employment, and sent to so vast distance from my family, to do your work of a high and costly nature, for so many days and weeks and months together, and there left to starve, or steal, or beg or borrow. But blessed be God, who gave me favor to borrow one while, and to work another, and thereby to pay your debts there, and to come over with your credit and honor, as an agent from you, who had, in your name, grappled with the agents and friends of all your enemies round about you. I am told that your opposites thought on me, and provided, as I may say, a sponge to wipe off your scores and debts in England, but that it was obstructed by yourselves, who rather meditated on means and new agents to be sent over, to cross what Mr. Clarke and I obtained. But, gentlemen, blessed be God, who faileth not, and blessed be his name for his wonderful PROVI-DENCES, by which alone this town and colony, and that grand cause of TRUTH AND FREEDOM OF CONSCIENCE, hath been upheld to this day. And blessed be his name who hath again quenched so much of our fires hitherto, and hath brought your names and his own name thus far out of the dirt and scorn, reproach, &c. I find among yourselves and your opposites that of Solomon true, that the contentions of brethren (some that lately were so) are the bars of a castle, and not easily broken; and I have heard some of both sides zealously talking of undoing them-selves by a trial in England. Truly, friends, I cannot but fear you lost a fair wind lately, when this town was sent to for its deputies, and you were not pleased to give an overture unto the rest of the inhabitants about it; yea, and when yourselves thought that I invited you to some conference tending to reconciliation, before the town should act in so fundamental a business, you were pleased to forestall that, so that being full of grief, shame and astonishment, yea, and fear that all that is now done, espe-cially in our town of Providence, is but provoking the spirits of men to fury and desperation, I pray your leave to pray you to remember (that which I lately told your opposites) *only by pride cometh contention.* If there be humility on the one side, yet there is pride on the other, and certainly the eternal God will engage against the proud. I therefore pray you to examine, as I have done them, your proceedings in this first particular. Secondly, Love covereth a multitude of sins. Surely your charges and complaints each against other, have not hid nor covered any thing, as we use to cover the nakedness of those we love. If you will now profess not to have disfranchised humanity and love, but that, as David in another case, you will sacrifice to the common peace, and common safety, and common credit, that which may be said to cost you something, I pray your loving leave to tell you, that if I were in your soul's case, I would send unto your opposites such a line as this: "Neighbors, at the constant request, and upon the constant mediation which our neighbor Roger Williams, since his arrival, hath used to us, both for pacification and accommodation of our sad differences, and also upon the late endeavors in all the other towns for an union, we are persuaded to remove our obstruction, viz.: that paper of contention between us, and to deliver it into the hands of our aforesaid neighbor and to obliterate that order, which that paper did occasion. This removed, you may be pleased to meet with, and debate freely, and vote in all matters with us, as if such grievances had not been amongst us. Secondly, if yet aught remain grievous, which we ourselves, by free debate and conference, cannot compose we offer to be judged and censured by four men, which out of any part of the colony you shall choose two, and we the other.

Gentlemen, I only add, that I crave your loving pardon to your bold but true friend.

ROGER WILLIAMS.

[LETTER TO THE TOWN OF PROVIDENCE, JANUARY 1655, ON THE LIMITS OF FREEDOM]

That ever I should speak or write a tittle, that tends to such an infinite liberty of conscience, is a mistake, and which I have ever disclaimed and abhorred. To prevent such mistakes, I shall at present only propose this case: There goes many a ship to sea, with many hundred souls in one ship, whose weal or woe is common, and is a true picture of a commonwealth, or a human combination or society. It hath fallen out sometimes, that both papists and protestants, Jews and Turks, may be embarked in one ship; upon which supposal I affirm, that all the liberty of conscience, that ever I pleaded for, turns upon these two hinges —that none of the papists, protestants, Jews, or Turks, be forced to come to the ship's prayers or worship, nor compelled from their own particular prayers or worship, if they practice any. I further add, that I never denied, that notwithstanding this liberty, the commander of this ship ought to command the ship's course, yea, and also command that justice, peace and sobriety, be kept and practiced, both among the seamen and all the passengers. If any of the seamen refuse to perform their services, or passengers to pay their freight; if any refuse to help, in person or purse, towards the common charges or defence; if any refuse to obey the common laws and orders of the ship, concerning their common peace or preservation; if any shall mutiny and rise up against their commanders and officers; if any should preach or write that there ought to be no commanders or officers, because all are equal in Christ, therefore no masters nor officers, no laws nor orders, nor corrections nor punishments;—I say, I never denied, but in such cases, whatever is pretended, the commander or commanders may judge, resist, compel and punish such transgressors, according to their deserts and merits. This if seriously and honestly minded, may, if it so please the Father of lights, let in some light to such as willingly shut not their eyes.

I remain studious of your common peace and liberty.

ROGER WILLIAMS

[LETTER TO JOHN COTTON[1]: AN APOLOGIA]

Roger Williams to John Cotton,
of Plymouth.
Providence, 25 March, 1671.

SIR,—Loving respects premised. About three weeks since, I received yours, dated in December, and wonder not that prejudice, interest, and passion have lift up your feet thus to trample on me as on some Mahometan, Jew, or Papist; some common thief or swearer, drunkard or adulterer; imputing to me the odious crimes of blasphemies, reproaches, slanders, idolatries; to be in the Devil's kingdom; a graceless man, &c.; and all this without any Scripture, reason, or argument, which might enlighten my conscience as to any error or offence to God or your dear father. I have now much above fifty years humbly and earnestly begged of God to make me as vile as a dead dog in my own eye, so that I might not fear what men should falsely say or cruelly do against me; and I have had long experience of his merciful answer to me in men's false charges and cruelties against me to this hour.

My great offence (you so often repeat) is my wrong to your dear father,—your glorified father, &c. But the truth is, the love and honor which I have always showed (in speech and writing) to that excellently learned and holy man, your father,

---

[1] This John Cotton was the son of the John Cotton against whose writings Williams' *Bloody Tenent* had been directed.

have been so great, that I have been censured by divers for it. God knows, that, for God's sake, I tenderly loved and honored his person (as I did the persons of the magistrates, ministers, and members whom I knew in Old England, and knew their holy affections, and upright aims, and great self-denial, to enjoy more of God in this wilderness); and I have therefore desired to waive all personal failings, and rather mention their beauties, to prevent the insultings of the Papists or profane Protestants, who used to scoff at the weaknesses—yea, and at the divisions—of those they use to brand for Puritans. The holy eye of God hath seen this the cause why I have not said nor writ what abundantly I could have done, but have rather chose to bear all censures, losses, and hardships, &c.

This made that honored father of the Bay, Mr. Winthrop, to give me the testimony, not only of exemplary diligence in the ministry (when I was satisfied in it), but of patience also, in these words in a letter to me: "Sir, we have often tried your patience, but could never conquer it." My humble desire is still to bear, not only what you say, but, when power is added to your will, an hanging or burning from you, as you plainly intimate you would long since have served my book, had it been your own, as not being fit to be in the possession of any Christian, as you write.

Alas! Sir, what hath this book merited, above all the many thousands full of old Romish idols' names, &c., and new Popish idolatries, which are in Christians' libraries, and use to be alleged in testimony, argument, and confutation?

What is there in this book but presseth holiness of heart, holiness of life, holiness of worship, and pity to poor sinners, and patience toward them while they break not the civil peace? 'Tis true, my first book, the "Bloody Tenent," was burnt by the Presbyterian party (then prevailing); but this book whereof we now speak (being my Reply to your father's Answer) was received with applause and thanks by the army, by the Parliament, professing that, of necessity,—yea, of Christian equity,—there could be no reconciliation, pacification, or living together, but by permitting of dissenting consciences to live amongst them; insomuch that that excellent servant of God, Mr. John Owen (called Dr. Owen), told me before the General (who sent for me about that very business), that before I landed, himself and many others had answered Mr. Cotton's book already. The first book, and the point of permitting Dissenters, his Majesty's royal father assented to; and how often hath the son, our sovereign, declared himself indulgent toward Dissenters, notwithstanding the clamors and plottings of his self-seeking bishops! And, Sir, (as before and formerly), I add, if yourself, or any in public or private, show me any failing against God or your father in that book, you shall find me diligent and faithful in weighing and in confessing or replying in love and meekness.

Oh! you say, wrong to a father made a dumb child speak, &c. Sir, I pray forget not that your father was not God, but man,—sinful, and failing in many things, as we all do, saith the Holy Scripture. I presume you know the scheme of Mr. Cotton's Contradictions (about Church-discipline), presented to the world by Mr. Daniel Cawdrey, a man of name and note. Also, Sir, take heed you prefer not the earthen pot (though your excellent father) before his most high eternal Maker and Potter. Blessed that you were born and proceeded from him, if you honor him more for his humility and holiness than for outward respect, which some (and none shall justly more than myself) put upon him.

Sir, you call my three proposals, &c., abominable, false, and wicked; but, as before, thousands (high and holy, too, some of them) will wonder at you. Captain Gookins, from Cambridge, writes me word that he will not be my antagonist in them, being candidly understood. Your honored Governor tells me there is no foundation for any dispute with Plymouth about those proposals; for you force no men's conscience. But, Sir, you have your liberty to prove them abominable, false, and wicked, and to disprove that which I have presented in the book concerning the New England churches to be but parochial and national, though sifted with a finer sieve, and painted with finer colors.

You are pleased to count me excommunicate; and therein you deal more cruelly with me than with all the profane, and Protestants and Papists too, with whom you hold communion in the parishes, to which (as you know) all are forced by the bishops. And yet you count me a slave to the Devil, because, in conscience to God, and love to God and you, I have told you of it. But, Sir, the truth is (I will not say I excommunicate you, but), I first withdrew communion from yourselves for halting between Christ and Antichrist,—the parish churches and Christian congregations. Long after, when you had consultations of killing me, but some rather advised a dry pit of banishment, Mr. Peters advised an excommunication to be sent me (after the manner of Popish bulls, &c.); but this same man, in London, embraced me, and told me he was for liberty of conscience, and preached it; and complained to me of Salem for excommunicating his distracted wife, and for wronging him in his goods which he left behind him.

Sir, you tell me my time is lost, &c., because (as I conceive you) not in the function of ministry. I confess the offices of Christ Jesus are the best callings; but generally they are the worst trades in the world, as they are practised only for a maintenance, a place, a living, a benefice, &c. God hath many employments for his servants. Moses forty years, and the Lord Jesus thirty years, were not idle, though little known what they did as to any ministry; and the two prophets prophesy in sackcloth, and are Christ Jesus his ministers, though not owned by the public ordinations. God knows, I have much and long and conscientiously and mournfully weighed and digged into the differences of the Protestants themselves about the ministry. He knows what gains and preferments I have refused in universities, city, country, and court, in Old England, and something in New England, &c., to keep my soul undefiled in this point, and not to act with a doubting conscience, &c. God was pleased to show me much of this in Old England; and in New, being unanimously chosen teacher at Boston (before your dear father came, divers years), I conscientiously refused, and withdrew to Plymouth, because I durst not officiate to an unseparated people, as, upon examination and conference, I found them to be. At Plymouth, I spake on the Lord's days and week days, and wrought hard at the hoe for my bread (and so afterward at Salem), until I found them both professing to be a separated people in New England (not admitting the most godly to communion without a covenant), and yet communicating with the parishes in Old by their members repairing on frequent occasions thither.

Sir, I heartily thank you for your conclusion,—wishing my conversion and salvation; without which, surely vain are our privileges of being Abraham's sons, enjoying the covenant, holy education, holy worship, holy church or temple; of being adorned with deep understanding, miraculous faith, angelical parts and utterance; the titles of pastors or apostles; yea, of being sacrifices in the fire to God.

Sir, I am unworthy (though desirous to be),

Your friend and servant,

ROGER WILLIAMS.

Mrs. Mary Rowlandson

(c. 1635–c. 1678)

Bibliographical Note. The text printed below follows that of the second edition "Corrected and amended." No copy of the first edition, issued the same year as the second, is known. On Mrs. Rowlandson and the tradition of the captivity narrative, see R. H. Pearce, "The Significances of the Captivity Narrative," *American Literature*, XIX (1947), 1–20.

from

THE SOVERAIGNTY AND GOODNESS OF GOD, TOGETHER WITH THE FAITHFULNESS OF HIS PROMISES DISPLAYED; BEING A NARRATIVE OF THE CAPTIVITY AND RESTAURATION OF MRS. MARY ROWLANDSON

(1682)

On the tenth of February 1675, Came the Indians with great numbers upon Lancaster: Their first coming was about Sunrising; hearing the noise of some Guns, we looked out; several Houses were burning, and the Smoke ascending to Heaven. There were five persons taken in one house, the Father, and the

Mother and a sucking Child, they knockt on the head; the other two they took and carried away alive. Their were two others, who being out of their Garison upon some occasion were set upon; one was knockt on the head, the other escaped: Another their was who running along was shot and wounded, and fell down; he begged of them his life, promising them Money (as they told me) but they would not hearken to him but knockt him in head, and stript him naked, and split open his Bowels. Another seeing many of the Indians about his Barn, ventured and went out, but was quickly shot down. There were three others belonging to the same Garison who were killed; the Indians getting up upon the roof of the Barn, had advantage to shoot down upon them over their Fortification. Thus these murtherous wretches went on, burning, and destroying before them.

At length they came and beset our own house, and quickly it was the dolefullest day that ever mine eyes saw. The House stood upon the edg of a hill; some of the Indians got behind the hill, others into the Barn, and others behind any thing that could shelter them; from all which places they shot against the House, so that the Bullets seemed to fly like hail; and quickly they wounded one man among us, then another, and then a third, About two hours (according to my observation, in that amazing time) they had been about the house before they prevailed to fire it (which they did with Flax and Hemp, which they brought out of the Barn, and there being no defence about the House, only two Flankers at two opposite corners and one of them not finished) they fired it once and one ventured out and quenched it, but they quickly fired it again, and that took. Now is the dreadful hour come, that I have often heard of (in time of War, as it was the case of others) but now mine eyes see it. Some in our house were fighting for their lives, others wallowing in their blood, the House on fire over our heads, and the bloody Heathen ready to knock us on the head, if we stirred out. Now might we hear Mothers and Children crying out for themselves, and one another, Lord, What shall we do? Then I took my Children (and one of my sisters, hers) to go forth and leave the house: but as soon as we came to the dore and appeared, the Indians shot so thick that the bulletts rattled against the House, as if one had taken an handfull of stones and threw them, so that we were fain to give back. We had six stout Dogs belonging to our Garrison, but none of them would stir, though another time, if any Indian had come to the door, they were ready to fly upon him and tear him down. The Lord hereby would make us the more to acknowledge his hand, and to see that our help is always in him. But out we must go, the fire increasing, and coming along behind us, roaring, and the Indians gaping before us with their Guns, Spears and Hatchets to devour us. No sooner were we out of the House, but my Brother in Law (being before wounded, in defending the house, in or near the throat) fell down dead, wherat the Indians scornfully shouted, and hallowed, and were presently upon him, stripping off his cloaths, the bulletts flying thick, one went through my side, and the same (as would seem) through the bowels and hand of my dear Child in my arms. One of my elder Sisters Children, named William, had then his Leg broken, which the Indians perceiving, they knockt him on head. Thus were we butchered by those merciless Heathen, standing amazed, with the blood running down to our heels. My eldest Sister being yet in the House, and seeing those wofull sights, the Infidels haling Mothers one way, and Children another, and some wallowing in their blood: and her elder Son telling her that her Son William was dead, and my self was wounded, she said, And, Lord, let me dy with them; which was no sooner said, but she was struck with a Bullet, and fell down dead over the threshold. I hope she is reaping the fruit of her good labours, being faithful to the service of God in her place. In her younger years she lay under much trouble upon spiritual accounts, till it pleased God to make that precious Scripture take hold of her heart, 2 Cor. 12. 9. *And he said unto me, my Grace is sufficient for thee.* More then twenty years after I have heard her tell how sweet and comfortable that place was to her. But to return: The Indians laid hold of us, pulling me one way, and the Children another, and said, Come go along with us; I told them they would kill me: they answered, If I were willing to go along with them, they would not hurt me.

Oh the dolefull sight that now was to behold at this House! *Come, behold the works of the Lord, what dissolations he has made in the Earth.* Of thirty seven persons who were in this one House, none escaped either present death, or a bitter captivity, save only one, who might say as he, Job 1. 15, *And I only am escaped alone to tell the News*. There were twelve killed, some shot, some stab'd with their Spears, some knock'd down with their Hatchets. When we are in prosperity, Oh the little that we think of such dreadfull sights, and to see our dear Friends, and Relations ly bleeding out their heart-blood upon the ground. There was one who was chopt into the head with a Hatchet, and stript naked, and yet was crawling up and down. It is a solemn sight to see so many Christians lying in their blood, some here, and some there, like a company of Sheep torn by Wolves, All of them stript naked by a company of hellhounds, roaring, singing, ranting and insulting, as if they would have torn our very hearts out; yet the Lord by his Almighty power preserved a number of us from death, for there were twenty-four of us taken alive and carried Captive.

I had often before this said, that if the Indians should come, I should chuse rather to be killed by them then taken alive but when it came to the tryal my mind changed; their glittering weapons so daunted my spirit, that I chose rather to go along with those (as I may say) ravenous Beasts, then that moment to end my dayes; and that I may the better declare what happened to me during that grievous Captivity, I shall particularly speak of the severall Removes we had up and down the Wilderness.

The First Remove

Now away we must go with those Barbarous Creatures, with our bodies wounded and bleeding, and our hearts no less than our bodies. About a mile we went that night, up upon a hill within sight of the Town, where they intended to lodge. There was hard by a vacant house (deserted by the English before, for fear of the Indians). I asked them whither I might not lodge in the house that night to which they answered, what will you love English men still? this was the dolefullest night that ever my eyes saw. Oh the roaring, and singing and danceing, and yelling of those black creatures in the night, which made the place a lively resemblance of hell. And as miserable was the wast that was there made, of Horses, Cattle, Sheep, Swine, Calves, Lambs, Roasting Pigs, and Fowl (which they had plundered in the Town) some roasting, some lying and burning, and some boyling to feed our merciless Enemies; who were joyful enough though we were disconsolate. To add to the dolefulness of the former day, and the dismalness of the present night: my thoughts ran upon my losses and sad bereaved condition. All was gone, my Husband gone (at least separated from me, he being in the Bay; and to add to my grief, the Indians told me they would kill him as he came homeward) my Children gone, my Relations and Friends gone, our house and home and all our comforts within door, and without, all was gone, (except my life) and I knew not but the next moment that might go too. There remained nothing to me but one poor wounded Babe, and it seemed at present worse than death that it was in such a pitiful condition, bespeaking Compassion, and I had no refreshing for it, nor suitable things to revive it. Little do many think what is the savageness and brutishness of this barbarous Enemy, I even those that seem to profess more than others among them, when the English have fallen into their hands.

Those seven that were killed at Lancaster the summer before upon a Sabbath day, and the one that was afterward killed upon a week day, were slain and mangled in a barbarous manner, by one-ey'd John, and Marlborough's Praying Indians, which Capt. Mosely brought to Boston, as the Indians told me.

The Second Remove

But now, the next morning, I must turn my back upon the Town, and travel with them into the vast and desolate Wilderness, I knew not whither. It is not my tongue, or pen can express the sorrows of my heart, and bitterness of my spirit, that I had at this departure: but God was with me, in a wonderfull manner, carrying me along, and bearing up my spirit, that it did not quite fail. One of the Indians carried my poor wounded Babe upon a horse, it went moaning all along, I shall dy, I shall dy. I went on foot after it, with sorrow that cannot be exprest. At length I took it off the horse, and carried it in my arms till my strength failed, and I fell down with it: Then they set me upon a horse with my wounded Child in my lap, and there being no furniture upon the horse back, as we were going down a steep hill, we both fell over the horses head, at which they like inhumane creatures laught, and rejoyced to see it, though I thought we should there have ended our dayes, as overcome with so many difficulties. But the Lord renewed my strength still, and carried me along, that I might see more of his Power; yea, so much that I could never have thought of, had I not experienced it.

After this it quickly began to snow, and when night came on, they stopt: and now down I must sit in the snow, by a little fire, and a few boughs behind me, with my sick Child in my lap; and calling much for water, being now (through the wound) fallen into a violent Fever. My own wound also growing so stiff, that I could scarce sit down or rise up, yet so it must be, that I must sit all this cold winter night upon the cold snowy ground, with my sick Child in my armes, looking that every hour would be the last of its life; and having no Christian friend near me, either to comfort or help me. Oh, I may see the wonderfull power of God, that my Spirit did not utterly sink under my affliction: still the Lord upheld me with his gracious and merciful Spirit, and we were both alive to see the light of the next morning.

The Third Remove

The morning being come, they prepared to go on their way. One of the Indians got up upon a horse, and they set me up behind him, with my poor sick Babe in my lap. A very wearisome and tedious day I had of it; what with my own wound, and my Childs being so exceeding sick, and in a lamentable condition with her wound. It may be easily judged what a poor feeble condition we were in, there being not the least crumb of refreshing that came within either of our mouths, from Wednesday night to Saturday night, except only a little cold water. This day in the afternoon, about an hour by Sun, we came to the place where they intended, *viz.* an Indian Town, called Wenimesset, Norward of Quabaug. When we were come, Oh the number of Pagans (now merciless enemies) that there came about me, that I may say as David, Psal. 27. 13, *I had fainted, unless I had believed,* etc.[1] The next day was the Sabbath: I then remembered how careless I had been of Gods holy time, how many Sabbaths I had lost and mispent, and how evily I had walked in Gods sight; which lay so close unto my spirit, that it was easie for me to see how righteous it was with God to cut off the thread of my life, and cast me out of his presence for ever. Yet the Lord still shewed mercy to me, and upheld me; and as he wounded me with one hand, so he healed me with the other. This day there came to me one Robbert Pepper (a man belonging to Roxbury) who was taken in Captain Beers his Fight, and had been now a considerable time with the Indians; and up with them almost as far as Albany, to see king Philip, as he told me, and was now very lately come into these parts. Hearing, I say, that I was in this Indian Town, he obtained leave to come and see me. He told me, he himself was wounded in the leg at Captain Beers his fight; and was not able some time to go, but as they carried him, and as he took Oaken leaves and laid to his wound, and through the blessing of God he was able to travel again. Then I took Oaken leaves and laid to my side, and with the blessing of God it cured me also; yet before the cure was wrought, I may say, as it is in Psal. 38. 5, 6. *My wounds stink and are corrupt, I am troubled, I am bowed down greatly, I go mourning all the day long.* I sat much alone with a poor wounded Child in my lap, which moaned night and day, having nothing to revive the body, or cheer the spirits of her, but in stead of that, sometimes one Indian would come and tell me one hour, that your Master will knock your Child in the head, and then a second, and then a third, your Master will quickly knock your Child in the head.

This was the comfort I had from them, miserable comforters are ye all, as he said. Thus nine dayes I sat upon my knees, with my Babe in my lap, till my flesh was raw again; my Child being even ready to depart this sorrowfull world, they bade me carry it out to another Wigwam (I suppose because they would not be troubled with such spectacles) Whither I went with a very heavy heart, and down I sat with the picture of

---

[1] "Unless I had believed to see the goodness of the Lord in the land of the living."—*1682 edition.*

death in my lap. About two houres in the night, my sweet Babe like a Lambe departed this life, on Feb. 18, 1675. It being about six yeares, and five months old. It was nine dayes from the first wounding, in this miserable condition, without any refreshing of one nature or other, except a little cold water. I cannot, but take notice, how at another time I could not bear to be in the room where any dead person was, but now the case is changed; I must and could ly down by my dead Babe, side by side all the night after. I have thought since of the wonderfull goodness of God to me, in preserving me in the use of my reason and senses, in that distressed time, that I did not use wicked and violent means to end my own miserable life. In the morning, when they understood that my child was dead they sent for me home to my Masters Wigwam: (by my Master in this writing, must be understood Quanopin, who was a Saggamore, and married King Phillips wives Sister; not that he first took me, but I was sold to him by another Narrhaganset Indian, who took me when first I came out of the Garison). I went to take up my dead child in my arms to carry it with me, but they bid me let it alone: there was no resisting, but goe I must and leave it. When I had been at my masters wigwam, I took the first opportunity I could get, to go look after my dead child: when I came I askt them what they had done with it? then they told me it was upon the hill: then they went and shewed me where it was, where I saw the ground was newly digged, and there they told me they had buried it: There I left that Child in the Wilderness, and must commit it, and my self also in this Wilderness-condition, to him who is above all.

. . . . .

The Seventh Remove

After a restless and hungry night there, we had a wearisome time of it the next day. The Swamp by which we lay, was, as it were, a deep Dungeon, and an exceeding high and steep hill before it. Before I got to the top of the hill, I thought my heart and legs, and all would have broken, and failed me. What through faintness, and soreness of body, it was a grievous day of travel to me. As we went along, I saw a place where English Cattle had been: that was comfort to me, such as it was: quickly after that we came to an English Path, which so took with me, that I thought I could have freely lyen down and dyed. That day, a little after noon, we came to Squaukheag, where the Indians quickly spread themselves over the deserted English Fields, gleaning what they could find; some pickt up ears of Wheat that were crickled down, some found ears of Indian Corn, some found Ground-nuts, and others sheaves of Wheat that were frozen together in the shock, and went to threshing of them out. My self got two ears of Indian Corn, and whilst I did but turn my back, one of them was stolen from me, which much troubled me. There came an Indian to them at that time, with a basket of Horse-liver. I asked him to give me a piece: What, sayes he, can you eat Horse-liver? I told him, I would try, if he would give a piece, which he did, and I laid it on the coals to rost; but before it was half ready they got half of it away from me, so that I was fain to take the rest and eat it as it was, with the blood about my mouth, and yet a savoury bit it was to me: *For to the hungry Soul every bitter thing is sweet.* A solemn sight methought it was, to see Fields of wheat and Indian Corn forsaken and spoiled: and the remainders of them to be food for our merciless Enemies. That night we had a mess of wheat for our Supper.

The Eighth Remove

On the morrow morning we must go over the River, *i.e.* Connecticot, to meet with King Philip; two Cannoos full, they had carried over, the next Turn I my self was to go; but as my foot was upon the Cannoo to step in, there was a sudden out-cry among them, and I must step back; and instead of going over the River, I must go four or five miles up the River farther Northward. Some of the Indians ran one way, and some another. The cause of this rout was, as I thought, their espying some English Scouts, who were thereabout. In this travel up the River, about noon the Company made a stop, and sate down; some to eat, and others to rest them. As I sate amongst them, musing of things past, my Son Joseph unexpectedly came to me:

we asked of each others welfare, bemoaning our dolefull condition, and the change that had come upon uss. We had Husband and Father, and Children, and Sisters, and Friends, and Relations, and House, and Home, and many Comforts of this Life: but now we may say, as Job, *Naked came I out of my Mothers Womb, and naked shall I return: The Lord gave, and the Lord hath taken away, Blessed be the Name of the Lord.* I asked him whither he would read; he told me, he earnestly desired it, I gave him my Bible, and he lighted upon the comfortable Scripture, Psal. 118. 17, 18. I shall not dy but live, and declare the works of the Lord: the Lord hath chastened me sore, yet he hath not given me over to death. Look here, Mother (says he) did you read this? And here I may take occasion to mention one principall ground of my setting forth these Lines: even as the Psalmist sayes, To declare the Works of the Lord, and his wonderful Power in carrying us along, preserving us in the Wilderness, while under the Enemies hand, and returning of us in safety again, And His goodness in bringing to my hand so many comfortable and suitable Scriptures in my distress. But to Return, We travelled on till night; and in the morning, we must go over the River to Philip's Crew. When I was in the Cannoo, I could not but be amazed at the numerous crew of Pagans that were on the Bank on the other side. When I came ashore, they gathered all about me, I sitting alone in the midst: I observed they asked one another questions, and laughed, and rejoyced over their Gains and Victories. Then my heart began to fail: and I fell a weeping which was the first time to my remembrance, that I wept before them. Although I had met with so much Affliction, and my heart was many times ready to break, yet could I not shed one tear in their sight: but rather had been all this while in a maze, and like one astonished: but now I may say as, Psal. 137. 1. *By the Rivers of Babylon, there we sate down: yea, we wept when we remembered Zion.* There one of them asked me, why I wept, I could hardly tell what to say: yet I answered, they would kill me: No, said he, none will hurt you. Then came one of them and gave me two spoon-fulls of Meal to comfort me, and another gave me half a pint of Pease; which was more worth than many Bushels at another time. Then I went to see King Philip, he bade me come in and sit down, and asked me whether I woold smoke it (a usual Complement nowadayes amongst Saints and Sinners) but this no way suited me. For though I had formerly used Tobacco, yet I had left it ever since I was first taken. It seems to be a Bait, the Devil layes to make men loose their precious time: I remember with shame, how formerly, when I had taken two or three pipes, I was presently ready for another, such a bewitching thing it is: But I thank God, he has now given me power over it; surely there are many who may be better imployed than to ly sucking a stinking Tobacco-pipe.

Now the Indians gather their Forces to go against North-Hampton: over-night one went about yelling and hooting to give notice of the design. Whereupon they fell to boyling of Ground-nuts, and parching of Corn (as many as had it) for their Provision: and in the morning away they went. During my abode in this place, Philip spake to me to make a shirt for his boy, which I did, for which he gave me a shilling: I offered the mony to my master, but he bade me keep it: and with it I bought a piece of Horse flesh. Afterwards he asked me to make a Cap for his boy, for which he invited me to Dinner. I went, and he gave me a Pancake, about as big as two fingers; it was made of parched wheat, beaten, and fryed in Bears grease, but I thought I never tasted pleasanter meat in my life. There was a Squaw who spake to me to make a shirt for her *Sannup*, for which she gave me a piece of Bear. Another asked me to knit a pair of Stockins, for which she gave me a quart of Pease: I boyled my Pease and Bear together, and invited my master and mistress to dinner, but the proud Gossip, because I served them both in one Dish, would eat nothing, except one bit that he gave her upon the point of his knife. Hearing that my son was come to this place, I went to see him, and found him lying flat upon the ground: I asked him how he could sleep so? he answered me, That he was not asleep, but at Prayer; and lay so, that they might not observe what he was doing. I pray God he may remember these things now he is returned in safety. At this Place (the Sun now getting higher) what with the beams and heat of the Sun, and the smoak of the Wigwams, I thought I should have been blind. I could scarce discern one Wigwam from another. There was here one Mary Thurston of Medfield, who seeing how it was with me, lent me a Hat to wear: but as soon as I was gone, the Squaw (who owned that Mary Thurston) came running after me, and got it away again. Here was the Squaw that gave me one spoonfull of Meal. I put it in my Pocket to keep it safe: yet notwithstanding some body stole it, but put five Indian Corns in the room of it: which Corns were the greatest Provisions I had in my travel for one day.

The Indians returning from North-Hampton, brought with them some Horses, and Sheep, and other things which they had taken: I desired them, that they would carry me to Albany, upon one of those Horses, and sell me for Powder: for so they had sometimes discoursed. I was utterly hopless of getting home on foot, the way that I came. I could hardly bear to think of the many weary steps I had taken, to come to this place.

. . . . .

The Sixteenth Remove

We began this Remove with wading over Baquag River: the water was up to the knees, and the stream very swift, and so cold that I thought it would have cut me in sunder. I was so weak and feeble, that I reeled as I went along, and thought there I must end my dayes at last, after my bearing and getting thorough so many difficulties; the Indians stood laughing to see me staggering along: but in my distress the Lord gave me experience of the truth, and goodness of that promise, Isai. 43. 2. *When thou passest thorough the Waters, I will be with thee, and through the Rivers, they shall not overflow thee.* Then I sat down to put on my stockins and shoos, with the teares running down mine eyes, and many sorrowfull thoughts in my heart, but I gat up to go along with them. Quickly there came up to us an Indian, who informed them, that I must go to Wachusit to my master, for there was a Letter come from the Council to the Saggamores, about redeeming the Captives, and that there would be another in fourteen dayes, and that I must be there ready. My heart was so heavy before that I could scarce speak or go in the path; and yet now so light, that I could run.

My strength seemed to come again, and recruit my feeble knees, and aking heart: yet it pleased them to go but one mile that night, and there we stayed two dayes. In that time came a company of Indians to us, near thirty, all on horseback. My heart skipt within me, thinking they had been English-men at the first sight of them, for they were dressed in English Apparel, with Hats, white Neckcloths, and Sashes about their wasts, and Ribbonds upon their shoulders: but when they came near, their was a vast difference between the lovely faces of Christians, and the foul looks of those Heathens, which much damped my spirit again.

．　．　．　．　．

The Eighteenth Remove

We took up our packs and along we went, but a wearisome day I had of it. As we went along I saw an English-man stript naked, and lying dead upon the ground, but knew not who it was. Then we came to another Indian Town, where we stayed all night. In this Town there were four English Children, Captives; and one of them my own Sisters. I went to see how she did, and she was well, considering her Captive-condition. I would have tarried that night with her, but they that owned her would not suffer it. Then I went into another Wigwam, where they were boyling Corn and Beans, which was a lovely sight to see, but I could not get a taste thereof. Then I went to another Wigwam, where there were two of the English Children; the Squaw was boyling Horses feet, then she cut me off a little piece, and gave one of the English Children a piece also. Being very hungry I had quickly eat up mine, but the Child could not bite it, it was so tough and sinewy, but lay sucking, gnawing, chewing and slabbering of it in the mouth and hand, then I took it of the Child, and eat it my self, and savoury it was to my taste. Then I may say as Job, Chap. 6. 7. *The things that my soul refused to touch, are as my sorrowfull meat.* Thus the Lord made that pleasant refreshing, which another time would have been an abomination. Then I went home to my mistresses Wigwam;

and they told me I disgraced my master with begging, and if I did so any more, they would knock me in head: I told them, they had as good knock me in head as starve me to death.

The Twentieth Remove

It was their usual manner to remove, when they had done any mischief, lest they should be found out: and so they did at this time. We went about three or four miles, and there they built a great Wigwam, big enough to hold an hundred Indians, which they did in preparation to a great day of Dancing. They would say now amongst themselves, that the Governour would be so angry for his loss at Sudbury, that he would send no more about the Captives, which made me grieve and tremble. My Sister being not far from the place where we now were, and hearing that I was here, desired her master to let her come and see me, and he was willing to it, and would go with her: but she being ready before him, told him she would go before, and was come within a Mile or two of the place; Then he overtook her, and began to rant as if he had been mad; and made her go back again in the Rain; so that I never saw her till I saw her in Charlestown. But the Lord requited many of their ill doings, for this Indian her Master, was hanged afterward at Boston. The Indians now began to come from all quarters, against their merry dancing day. Among some of them came one Goodwife Kettle: I told her my heart was so heavy that it was ready to break: so is mine too said she, but yet said, I hope we shall hear some good news shortly. I could hear how earnestly my Sister desired to see me, and I as earnestly desired to see her: and yet neither of us could get an opportunity. My Daughter was also now about a mile off, and I had not seen her in nine or ten weeks, as I had not seen my Sister since our first taking. I earnestly desired them to let me go and see them: yea, I intreated, begged, and perswaded them, but to let me see my Daughter; and yet so hard hearted were they, that they would not suffer it. They made use of their tyrannical power whilst they had it: but through the Lords wonderfull mercy, their time was now but short.

On a Sabbath day, the Sun being about an hour high in the

afternoon, came Mr. John Hoar (the Council permitting him, and his own foreward spirit inclining him) together with the two forementioned Indians, Tom and Peter, with their third Letter from the Council. When they came near, I was abroad: though I saw them not, they presently called me in, and bade me sit down and not stir. Then they catched up their Guns, and away they ran, as if an Enemy had been at hand; and the Guns went off apace. I manifested some great trouble, and they asked me what was the matter? I told them, I thought they had killed the English-man (for they had in the mean time informed me that an English-man was come) they said, No; They shot over his Horse and under, and before his Horse; and they pusht him this way and that way, at their pleasure: shewing what they could do: Then they let them come to their Wigwams. I begged of them to let me see the English-man, but they would not. But there was I fain to sit their pleasure. When they had talked their fill with him, they suffered me to go to him. We asked each other of our welfare, and how my Husband did, and all my Friends? He told me they were all well, and would be glad to see me. Amongst other things which my Husband sent me, there came a pound of Tobacco: which I sold for nine shillings in Money: for many of the Indians for want of Tobacco, smoaked Hemlock, and Ground-Ivy. It was a great mistake in any, who thought I sent for Tobacco: for through the favour of God, that desire was overcome. I now asked them, whither I should go home with Mr. Hoar? They answered No, one and another of them: and it being night, we lay down with that answer; in the morning, Mr. Hoar invited the Saggamores to Dinner; but when we went to get it ready, we found that they had stollen the greatest part of the Provision Mr. Hoar had brought, out of his Bags, in the night. And we may see the wonderfull power of God, in that one passage, in that when there was such a great number of the Indians together, and so greedy of a little good food; and no English there, but Mr. Hoar and my self: that there they did not knock us in the head, and take what we had: there being not only some Provision, but also Trading-cloth, a part of the twenty pounds agreed upon: But instead of doing us any mischief, they seemed to be ashamed of the fact, and said, it were some Matchit

Indian[2] that did it. Oh, that we could believe that there is no thing too hard for God! God shewed his Power over the Heathen in this, as he did over the hungry Lyons when Daniel was cast into the Den. Mr. Hoar called them betime to Dinner, but they ate very little, they being so busie in dressing themselves, and getting ready for their Dance: which was carried on by eight of them, four Men and four Squaws: My master and mistress being two. He was dressed in his Holland shirt, with great Laces sewed at the tail of it, he had his silver Buttons, his white Stockins, his Garters were hung round with Shillings, and he had Girdles of Wampom upon his head and shoulders. She had a Kersey Coat, and covered with Girdles of Wampom from the Loins upward: her armes from her elbows to her hands were covered with Bracelets; there were handfulls of Necklaces about her neck, and severall sorts of Jewels in her ears. She had fine red Stokins, and white Shoos, her hair powdered and face painted Red, that was always before Black. And all the Dancers were after the same manner. There were two other singing and knocking on a Kettle for their musick. They kept hopping up and down one after another, with a Kettle of water in the midst, standing warm upon some Embers, to drink of when they were dry. They held on till it was almost night, throwing out Wampom to the standers by. At night I asked them again, if I should go home? They all as one said No, except my Husband would come for me. When we were lain down, my Master went out of the Wigwam, and by and by sent in an Indian called James the Printer, who told Mr. Hoar, that my Master would let me go home to morrow, if he would let him have one pint of Liquors. Then Mr. Hoar called his own Indians, Tom and Peter, and bid them go and see whither he would promise it before them three: and if he would, he should have it; which he did, and he had it. Then Philip smeling the business cal'd me to him, and asked me what I would give him, to tell me some good news, and speak a good word for me. I told him, I could not tell what to give him, I would any thing I had, and asked him what he would have? He said, two Coats and twenty shillings in Mony, and half a bushel of seed Corn, and some Tobacco. I thanked him for

---

[2] *I.e.*, bad Indian.—*1682 edition.*

his love: but I knew the good news as well as the crafty Fox. My Master after he had had his drink, quickly came ranting into the Wigwam again, and called for Mr. Hoar, drinking to him, and saying, He was a good man: and then again he would say, Hang him Rogue: Being almost drunk, he would drink to him, and yet presently say he should be hanged. Then he called for me. I trembled to hear him, yet I was fain to go to him, and he drank to me, shewing no incivility. He was the first Indian I saw drunk all the while that I was amongst them. At last his Squaw ran out, and he after her, round the Wigwam, with his mony jingling at his knees: But she escaped him: But having an old Squaw he ran to her: and so through the Lords mercy, we were no more troubled that night. Yet I had not a comfortable nights rest: for I think I can say, I did not sleep for three nights together. The night before the Letter came from the Council, I could not rest, I was so full of feares and troubles, God many times leaving us most in the dark, when deliverance is nearest: yea, at this time I could not rest night nor day. The next night I was overjoyed, Mr. Hoar being come, and that with such good tidings. The third night I was even swallowed up with the thoughts of things, *viz.* that ever I should go home again; and that I must go, leaving my Children behind me in the Wilderness; so that sleep was now almost departed from mine eyes.

On Tuesday morning they called their General Court (as they call it) to consult and determine, whether I should go home or no: And they all as one man did seemingly consent to it, that I should go home; except Philip, who would not come among them.

But before I go any further, I would take leave to mention a few remarkable passages of providence, which I took special notice of in my afflicted time.

1. Of the fair opportunity lost in the long March, a little after the Fort-fight, when our English Army was so numerous, and in pursuit of the Enemy, and so near as to take several and destroy them: and the Enemy in such distress for food, that our men might track them by their rooting in the earth for Ground-nuts, whilest they were flying for their lives. I say, that then our Army should want Provision, and be forced to leave their pursuit and return homeward: and the very next week the Enemy came

upon our Town, like Bears bereft of their whelps, or so many ravenous Wolves, rending us and our Lambs to death. But what shall I say? God seemed to leave his People to themselves, and order all things for his own holy ends. *Shal there be evil in the City and the Lord hath not done it? They are not grieved for the affliction of Joseph, therefore shal they go Captive, with the first that go Captive.* It is the Lords doing, and it should be marvelous in our eyes.

2. I cannot but remember how the Indians derided the slowness, and dulness of the English Army, in its setting out. For after the desolations at Lancaster and Medfield, as I went along with them, they asked me when I thought the English Army would come after them? I told them I could not tell: It may be they will come in May, said they. Thus did they scoffe at us, as if the English would be a quarter of a year getting ready.

3. Which also I have hinted before, when the English Army with new supplies were sent forth to pursue after the enemy, and they understanding it, fled before them till they came to Baquaug River, where they forthwith went over safely: that that River should be impassable to the English. I can but admire to see the wonderfull providence of God in preserving the heathen for farther affliction to our poor Countrey. They could go in great numbers over, but the English must stop: God had an over-ruling hand in all those things.

4. It was thought, if their Corn were cut down, they would starve and dy with hunger: and all their Corn that could be found, was destroyed, and they driven from that little they had in store, into the Woods in the midst of Winter; and yet how to admiration did the Lord preserve them for his holy ends, and the destruction of many still amongst the English! strangely did the Lord provide for them; that I did not see (all the time I was among them) one Man, Woman, or Child, die with hunger.

Though many times they would eat that, that a Hog or a Dog would hardly touch; yet by that God strengthened them to be a scourge to his People.

The chief and commonest food was Ground-nuts: They eat also Nuts and Acorns, Harty-choaks, Lilly roots, Ground-beans, and several other weeds and roots, that I know not.

They would pick up old bones, and cut them to pieces at the joynts, and if they were full of wormes and magots, they would scald them over the fire to make the vermine come out, and then boile them, and drink up the Liquor, and then beat the great ends of them in a Morter, and so eat them. They would eat Horses guts, and ears, and all sorts of wild Birds which they could catch: also Bear, Vennison, Beaver, Tortois, Frogs, Squirrels, Dogs, Skunks, Rattle-snakes; yea, the very Bark of Trees; besides all sorts of creatures, and provision which they plundered from the English. I can but stand in admiration to see the wonderful power of God, in providing for such a vast number of our Enemies in the Wilderness, where there was nothing to be seen, but from hand to mouth. Many times in a morning, the generality of them would eat up all they had, and yet have some forther supply against they wanted. It is said, Psal. 81. 13, 14. *Oh, that my People had hearkned to me, and Israel had walked in my wayes, I should soon have subdued their Enemies, and turned my hand against their Adversaries.* But now our perverse and evil carriages in the sight of the Lord, have so offended him, that instead of turning his hand against them, the Lord feeds and nourishes them up to be a scourge to the whole Land.

5. Another thing that I would observe is, the strange providence of God, in turning things about when the Indians was at the highest, and the English at the lowest. I was with the Enemy eleven weeks and five dayes, and not one Week passed without the fury of the Enemy, and some desolation by fire and sword upon one place or other. They mourned (with their black faces) for their own lossess, yet triumphed and rejoyced in their inhumane, and many times devilish cruelty to the English. They would boast much of their Victories; saying, that in two hours time they had destroyed such a Captain, and his Company at such a place; and such a Captain and his Company in such a place; and such a Captain and his Company in such a place: and boast how many Towns they had destroyed, and then scoffe, and say, They had done them a good turn, to send them to Heaven so soon. Again, they would say, This Summer that they would knock all the Rogues in the head, or drive them into the Sea, or make them flie the Countrey: thinking surely, Agag-

like, *The bitterness of Death is past*.[3] Now the Heathen begins to think all is their own, and the poor Christians hopes to fail (as to man) and now their eyes are more to God, and their hearts sigh heavenward: and to say in good earnest, *Help Lord, or we perish:* When the Lord had brought his people to this, that they saw no help in any thing but himself: then he takes the quarrel into his own hand: and though they had made a pit, in their own imaginations, as deep as hell for the Christians that Summer, yet the Lord hurll'd them selves into it. And the Lord had not so many wayes before to preserve them, but now he hath as many to destroy them.

But to return again to my going home, where we may see a remarkable change of Providence: At first they were all against it, except my Husband would come for me; but afterwards they assented to it, and seemed much to rejoyce in it; some askt me to send them some Bread, others some Tobacco, others shaking me by the hand, offering me a Hood and Scarfe to ride in; not one moving hand or tongue against it. Thus hath the Lord answered my poor desire, and the many earnest requests of others put up unto God for me. In my travels an Indian came to me, and told me, if I were willing, he and his Squaw would run away, and go home along with me: I told him No: I was not willing to run away, but desired to wait Gods time, that I might go home quietly, and without fear. And now God hath granted me my desire. O the wonderfull power of God that I have seen, and the experience that I have had: I have been in the midst of those roaring Lyons, and Salvage Bears, that feared neither God, nor Man, nor the Devil, by night and day, alone and in company: sleeping all sorts together, and yet not one of them ever offered me the least abuse of unchastity to me, in word or action. Though some are ready to say, I speak it for my own credit; But I speak it in the presence of God, and to his Glory. Gods Power is as great now, and as sufficient to save, as when he preserved Daniel in the Lions Den; or the three Children in the fiery Furnace. I may well say as his Psal. 107. 12, *Oh give thanks unto the Lord for he is good, for his mercy endureth for ever.* Let the Redeemed of the Lord say so, whom he hath redeemed

---

[3] I Samuel xv. 32.—*1682 edition.*

from the hand of the Enemy, especially that I should come away in the midst of so many hundreds of Enemies quietly and peaceably, and not a Dog moving his tongue. So I took my leave of them, and in coming along my heart melted into tears, more then all the while I was with them, and I was almost swallowed up with the thoughts that ever I should go home again.

. . . . .

I can remember the time, when I used to sleep quietly without workings in my thoughts, whole nights together, but now it is other wayes with me. When all are fast about me, and no eye open, but his who ever waketh, my thoughts are upon things past, upon the awfull dispensation of the Lord towards us; upon his wonderfull power and might, in carrying of us through so many difficulties, in returning us in safety, and suffering none to hurt us. I remember in the night season, how the other day I was in the midst of thousands of enemies, and nothing but death before me: It is then hard work to perswade my self, that ever I should be satisfied with bread again. But now we are fed with the finest of the Wheat, and, as I may say, With honey out of the rock: In stead of the Husk, we have the fatted Calf: The thoughts of these things in the particulars of them, and of the love and goodness of God towards us, make it true of me, what David said of himself, Psal. 6. 5. *I watered my Couch with my tears.* Oh! the wonderfull power of God that mine eyes have seen, affording matter enough for my thoughts to run in, that when others are sleeping mine eyes are weeping.

I have seen the extreme vanity of this World: One hour I have been in health, and wealth, wanting nothing: But the next hour in sickness and wounds, and death, having nothing but sorrow and affliction.

Before I knew what affliction meant, I was ready sometimes to wish for it. When I lived in prosperity, having the comforts of the World about me, my relations by me, my Heart chearfull, and taking little care for any thing; and yet seeing many, whom I preferred before my self, under many tryals and afflictions, in sickness, weakness, poverty, losses, crosses, and cares of the World, I should be sometimes jealous least I should have my portion in this life, and that Scripture would come to my mind, Heb. 12. 6. *For whom the Lord loveth he chasteneth, and scourgeth every Son whom he receiveth.* But now I see the Lord had his time to scourge and chasten me. The portion of some is to have their afflictions by drops, now one drop and then another; but the dregs of the Cup, the Wine of astonishment, like a sweeping rain that leaveth no food, did the Lord prepare to be my portion. Affliction I wanted, and affliction I had, full measure (I thought) pressed down and running over; yet I see, when God calls a Person to any thing, and through never so many difficulties, yet he is fully able to carry them through and make them see, and say they have been gainers thereby. And I hope I can say in some measure, As David did, *It is good for me that I have been afflicted.* The Lord hath shewed me the vanity of these outward things. That they are the Vanity of vanities, and vexation of spirit; that they are but a shadow, a blast, a bubble, and things of no continuance. That we must rely on God himself, and our whole dependance must be upon him. If trouble from smaller matters begin to arise in me, I have something at hand to check my self with, and say, why am I troubled? It was but the other day that if I had had the world, I would have given it for my freedom, or to have been a Servant to a Christian. I have learned to look beyond present and smaller troubles, and to be quieted under them, as Moses said, Exod. 14. 13. *Stand still and see the salvation of the Lord.*

Increase Mather

(1639–1723)

Bibliographical Note. The text here printed is that of the original edition (London, 1674), in which two sermons were published— one having been delivered in the morning, one in the afternoon. On Increase Mather, see the wonderfully full account in Kenneth Murdock, *Increase Mather: the Foremost American Puritan* (Cambridge, 1925). On the jeremiad—the type of sermon this represents —see Perry Miller, *The New England Mind from Colony to Province* (Cambridge, 1953).

THE DAY OF TROUBLE IS NEAR, SERMON II (1674)

Whence is it that the Lord doth sometimes bring dayes of great trouble upon his own people? *Ans.* The Reasons may be referred unto two Heads:

1. The Lord doth this with respect unto Himself.

2. With respect unto his people. As indeed all the Providences of God, all that he doth in the world, may be referred unto those two Heads, the Lord therein aimeth at his own glory, and his peoples good.

1. *The Lord hath respect unto Himself, in those troubles which come upon the Church.* Hereby his Faithfulness is manifested and glorified: therefore *David saith, Psal. 119.75. I know, O Lord, that thy judgements are right, and that thou in faithfulness hast afflicted me.* The Lord sheweth his great Faithfulness as to the time, the kinde, the measure, the manner, the duration of whatever afflictions may befall any of his faithful

Servants. And his Power also is hereby discovered: it is a glorious evidence of the wonderful Power of God, that the Church should be upheld and preserved in the world, notwithstanding the troubles and miseries thereof. The Church's being continued in the world, is one of the great Wonders of divine Providence, wherein the mighty Power of God is seen. It is said, that the children of *Israel* were *like two little flocks of Kids* before the Syrians, 1 Kings 20, 27. Should we see a little flock of Kids, or of Sheep, in the midst of Wolves and devourers, and yet not destroyed, we should say, The finger of God is here. Truly thus it is: The Church is a *little-little flock* of Sheep, and that in the midst of thousands of Wolves and Tygers, yet this flock is saved alive; so then the Power of God is seen and glorified. *Moses* did sometimes marvel at this thing, *Exod.3.2.3. And he looked, and behold the Bush burned with fire, and the Bush was not consumed; and Moses said, I will now turn aside, and see this great sight, why the Bush is not burnt.* The children of *Israel* were the Bush that was all on fire, in respect of the *Egyptian* Persecution, which then they were under; but the Lord by a mighty hand of Providence upheld them, so that the fire did not consume them. Moreover, the Saints are wont to glorifie God more in a day of trouble, then at other times: *Isa.24.15. Glorifie ye the Lord in the fires,* so are the Saints wont to do, when in the fires of affliction, they bring more glory to God, it may be in one day, then in many years of prosperity. How was the Name of Christ advanced, and his Interest promoted in the world in the Primitive Times? and the reason was, because those were times of great Suffering. Hence then the Lord brings such times upon his people.

2. *God brings dayes of trouble with respect to his people.* And that especially on a fourfold account. 1. For their Probation. 2. For their Instruction. 3. For their Correction. 4. In order to their Purgation.

1. *The Lord aimeth at the Probation of his people,* in those troubles which befall them in the world. Hence *Ezek.* 21.13. the Prophet there speaking of the same day of trouble which the Text hath reference unto, *saith, Because it is a triall,&c.* So *Rev.2.10. Fear none of those things thou shalt suffer; behold, the Devil shall cast some of you into prison, that ye may be*

Tried. Hence the afflictions of Gods children are compared to a refining Furnace, or to a calcining Pot, wherein Metals are *Tried,* 1 Pet.1.7. *The triall of your Faith,&c.* The Greek word (τὸ δοχιμιον)[1] signifieth a Furnace wherein Goldsmiths try Metals; even so the Lord by afflictions Trieth what Metal men are made of, whether they be Gold or Dross, whether they be Silver, or Lead onely. The Faith and Patience of his Servants are hereby put to the Trial: therefore John speaking concerning the troubles which should come upon the Church under Antichrist, saith, *Here is the Patience and Faith of the Saints,* Rev.13.10. that is to say, by these troubles it is exercised and manifested. By this means the Lord Trieth the sincerity and fidelity of his Servants; yea, and what measure of grace they have too. If they faint in the day of adversity, their strength is small; but they hold out faithfully and couragiously in times of great trouble, have received a good measure of grace.

2. *The Lord by bringing dayes of trouble upon his Servants, aimeth at their Instruction.* Psal.94.12. *Blessed is the man whom thou chastenest, O Lord, and teachest him out of thy Law.* Therefore doth the Lord bring his precious ones under chastening dispensations of Providence sometimes, that so he may Teach them, yea, and many a blessed lesson doth he teach them thereby. Afflicting times are not only Trying times, but also Teaching times: *Psal. 19.71. It is good for me that I have been afflicted, that I might learn thy statutes.* Hereby the children of God *learn,* yea they learn to know more of God, and of themselves too: as we see in *Job,* who after his troubles could say, *Mine eye seeth thee;* and, *I abhor my self in dust and ashes.* By afflictions, men are taught to know that God is God, and that sin is sin. Ever since that day of trouble which the Text speaketh of, the Jews have dreaded that sin which was the principal Cause of all their miseries.

3. *The Lord in afflicting his people, aimeth at their Correction.* Hence affliction is called a Rod, *Ezek, 21,10. It is the Rod of my son, contemning every tree. Israel* was Gods son, as the Lord said to *Pharaoh, Israel is my son, my first-born;* now the *Caldeans* were a Rod, whereby God scourged that son of his.

---

[1] "Proof."

It is true, that personal afflictions oftentimes come onely or chiefly in a way of Trial, but publick Calamities are wont to come as Corrections and just Punishment for sin: *Jer.30.15. Why criest thou for thine affliction? for the multitude of thine iniquities, because thy sins were increased, have I done these things unto thee.* And to the like purpose doth the Lord speak by the Prophet *Micah*, Chap.1.ver.5. *For the transgression of Jacob is all this, and for the sins of the house of Israel.*

Quest. But you will say, What sins are they for which God is wont to bring dayes of trouble upon his people?

Ans. We shall here take notice onely of such sins as are mentioned in this Context, as the Procuring Cause of that day of Calamity here threatned. And they are three:

(1.) *The not ordering matters aright, respecting the Worship of God,* was the principal Crime which brought this trouble. Idolatry was the sin, that at this time above others, troubled *Israel.* Hence it is said, *ver.3,4. I will recompence upon thee all thine abominations;* h.e. I will punish you for your Idols: for usually in the Scripture, *Idols* are called *Abominations.* It is said, *Rev.21.27. He that maketh an abomination,* that is, he that maketh an Idol, shall not enter into the Heavenly *Jerusalem.* That sin of corrupting the Worship of God, hath been the grand Procuring Cause of those astonishing and desolating Plagues that have come upon the earth. If men worship a false God, their sorrows shall be multiplied; or if they worship the true God in false Wayes, by means which he never appointed, and which never came into his heart, that's a sin that procureth great wrath. If men shall adde unto what the Lord hath commanded, and so corrupt his pure Worship with their own devices, vengeance will come for it: *Psal.99.8. Thou tookest vengeance of their inventions;* Hos. 11.6. *The Sword shall abide on his Cities, because of their own counsels;* that is to say, because they corrupted the Worship of God with inventions of their own. So on the other hand, if there be a *taking from* the Word of God, in matters referring to his Worship, dayes of trouble will come. In case Churches shall not come up fully to practice the Institutions of Christ; and to stand perfect and compleat in all the will of God, the Lord will punish them for their neglects; as we see in the Jewish Church, who met with sore troubles after the return from Captivity, and the reason of it was, because they did not carry on Temple-work to that perfection which should have been, *Hag.*1.4. Yea moreover, if men grow careless as to the manner of their worshipping God, (though Object and Means should be according to his Will) the Lord will visit for that iniquity. When the *Corinthians* were not duely careful as to the manner of worshipping, *for this cause many were weak and sick amongst them*, 1 Cor.11.30. It is (as was hinted but now) conceived by some Expositors, that the Lord sent the Plague amongst them, for that sin. We reade in *Ezekiel*, that *fire was taken from between the Cherubims*, i.e. from off the Incense Altar, *and scattered over the City*, Chap.10.2. Why? to signifie that here was the cause wherefore the City was burnt, it was the Lords Controversie respecting his Altar, his Worship that is, which brought that famous City into ruinous heaps. So again, *Isai.* 29.1. it is there said, *Wo to Ariel, to Ariel the City where David dwelt.* Ariel signifieth the Lion of God, and may intend the Altar, which like a Lion did devour the Sacrifices offered thereon: here then was the true Cause of that Wo which befell that City and Nation, in that matters respecting *Ariel*, even the Altar and Worship of God, were not as should have been. Look as when things are managed aright as to Divine Worship, great prosperity is wont to follow, *Ezra 3.3. They set the Altar upon his Bases, for fear was upon them, because of the people of those Countreys:* They knew that that was the way to engage the Lord to be with them, and to defend them against their Enemies, even to set the Altar upon his right Bases; so the contrary is to be affirmed, when the Altar is not set upon his Bases, great troubles are then like to come.

(2.) *Pride is another sin* here mentioned, as the Cause of this day of trouble: ver.10. *Behold the day, behold it is come, the morning is gone forth, the Rod hath blossomed, Pride hath budded:* The buddings of Pride, do cause the Rod to blossome against a people. Hence the morning, even the fatall day came upon *Sodom*, Ezek. 16.49. *This was the iniquity of Sodom, Pride, fullness of bread, and abundance of Idleness.* Pride is mentioned in the first place, because that indeed was the first firebrand which set *Sodom* on fire. It was for that sin in special, that those Proud Cities were brought down into ashes.

(3.) *Oppression is another Evil* mentioned, as the Procuring Cause of this trouble, *ver.11. Violence is risen up into a Rod of wickedness.* Violence, Oppression that is, brought the wicked *Caldeans* upon the *Jews.* There seems to be a marvellous Elegancy in the Prophets words: The *Tribe* (the same Hebrew word signifieth a Rod, and a Tribe) of *Judah* is compared unto a *Rod;* now what were the Buds that grew upon this Rod? even Pride and Oppression: therefore did the day of trouble draw near. Thus we see the Lord brings troubles upon his people, that so he may correct them for their sins.

4. *God herein also aimeth at their Purgation.* So is it said concerning the day of trouble that was inflicted on the Church by the *Babilonians, Isa.27.9. By this shall the iniquity of Jacob be purged, and this is all the fruit, to take away his sin.* And concerning the troubles under *Antiochus,* of which *Daniel* speaketh, *Chap.11.35. Some of them understanding shall fall, to try them, and to purge, and to make them white.* To the same purpose is that, *Zech.13.9. And I will bring the third part through the fire, and will refine them as silver is refined,&c.* So then, that which the Lord intends by bringing his people into the Furnace of Affliction, is that he may make pure Metal of them, yea, that they may be purged and sanctified, and become vessels meet for their Masters use.

We have done with the *Doctrinal handling* of the Truth before us, the *Uses* of it follow.

USE I. If the Lord doth sometimes bring dayes of great trouble upon his own people, then *we ought not to think it strange, or to be any wayes dismayed at it, if we see it so now:* I say we should not think it strange. So doth the Apostle instruct us, 1 Pet. 4.12. *Beloved, think it not strange concerning the fiery triall which is to try you, as though some strange thing happened to you.* Why, this is no more then what hath been in almost all Ages of the Church, and will be to the worlds end, and therefore why should we strain at it? Nor should we be dismayed thereat, but rather say as the Church doth, in Psal.46. *God is very a present help in trouble, therefore we will not fear though the earth be removed, and though the waters roar and be troubled, though the mountains shake with the swelling thereof. Selah.* Truly thus it is at this day, the multitude of many people make a noise like the noise of the seas: we have heard the rushing of the Nations; yea, we have heard the sea and the waves thereof roaring. What roarings have there been on the sea, in these late dayes? and the Mountains begin to shake with the swelling thereof. Kingdoms shake, Nations shake, yet let us not be dismayed, for the Lord will carry on his own good work and glorious designs, in the midst of these troubles. It is said, *Deut.9.25.* that the City should be *built in troublous times.* The Lord is carrying on the building of his own House even in these troublous times. And why should we be dismayed? for all these Affairs are ordered and managed by the hand of him that is our Mediator. Therefore in *Ezekiels* Vision of the Wheel, that is, the Wheel of Providence, it is indeed said, that the *rings were high and dreadful,* Chap.I.ver.18. but it is said, ver.26. *There is a Man above upon the Throne,* that is to say, Jesus Christ, who is Man as well as God, even He as Mediator doth order all the Affairs and Motions of that Wheel of Providence, which is matter of wonderful encouragement, when the Revolutions thereof are dreadful for us to behold. Christ is become Head of all things to his Church; All power in Heaven and in Earth is given to him, that so he might manage all things, so as shall be for the good of his Church, as well as for his Fathers glory. And therefore though troubles come, why should we be dismayed thereat? yea, why should we be dismayed thereat? for a glorious issue and happy deliverance out of all these troubles, shall certainly arise to the Church in due time: *Jer.30.7. It is even the time of Jacobs trouble, but he shall be saved out of it.*

USE II. If the Lord bring dayes of trouble upon his people, *what will he do unto his and their Enemies?* If trouble may come upon *Israel,* what then will become of *Babylon?* If this be done to the green Tree, what shall be done to the dry, that is fit for nothing else but the fire? To this purpose doth the Prophet speak unto *Moab,* Jer.49.12. *Behold, they whose judgement was not to drink of the Cup, have assuredly drunken, and art thou he that shalt altogether go unpunished? thou shalt not go unpunished, but thou shalt surely drink of it.* Jewish Expositors (and that not altogether without reason) when *Moab* is spoken of in the Scripture, are wont to apply it unto *Rome:*

for indeed the *Moabites* were Types of the present *Antichristian generation.* Why, behold at this day, they whose Judgement it was not to drink of the Cup, have assuredly drunk thereof; the Lord we see hath begun with *Protestant Nations,* and hath made them to drink deep of the Cup of his indignation, in this day wherein he is giving of the Cup to the Nations round, beginning at *Jerusalem.* And art thou he, O *Moab?* Art thou he, O *Roman Antichrist,* that shalt escape? thou shalt not escape, but shalt certainly drink thereof, yea drink thereof untill thou spue, and fall, and rise no more.

And this we see is the use which the Apostle Peter maketh of this Doctrine, I. *Pet.*4.17.18. *For the time is come that judgement must begin at the house of God: and if it first begin at us, what shall the end be of them that obey not the Gospel of God? And if the righteous scarcely be saved, where shall the ungodly and sinner appear?* This might be applied to publick and professed Enemies to the Cause and Kingdome of the Lord Jesus; where shall they appear? The Seventh Trumpet (which is the last of the Wo-Trumpets) will sound quickly, and the *Woes* thereof will light upon the Heads of the Antichristian Party in the world. Wo, wo be to them, saith the Lord. This might also be applied unto every ungodly sinner: All you that continue in your sins, *what will your end be?* Troubles may come upon the Lords people, but they shall soon be over: but as for thee, if thou diest in thy sins, without Repentance, and without an interest in Jesus Christ by Faith unfeigned in his Name, thy sorrows shall never have an end.

USE III. If God doth sometimes bring dayes of trouble upon his own people, here then is matter of solemn Awakening unto us; *It concerns us well to consider, whether there be not a day of trouble near unto us.* For Awakening here, I shall mention some things, which look awfully upon us. Some *Arguments* let us here take notice of, which seem to speak as if *a day of trouble* were *near unto us,* yea and *not the sounding again of the Mountains.*

1. (To begin with that which is most general) *There is a day of trouble coming upon all the World;* and such trouble too, as the like hath not been: for I am perswaded that Scrip-

ture is yet to be fulfilled, even that *Dan.12.1.* where it is said, *There shall be a time of trouble, such as never was since there was a Nation, to that same time.* We are in expectation of glorious times, wherein Peace and Prosperity shall run down like a River, and like a mighty stream over all the earth; but immediately before those dayes, there will be such horrible Combustions and Confusions, as the like never was. It is said, *Psal. 46.9. He maketh Wars to cease unto the end of the earth:* but the words immediately foregoing are, *Come, behold the works of the Lord, what desolations he hath made in the earth.* Before the dayes come, wherein the Nations shall learn war no more, O what desolations wil the Lord make in the earth? We look that the Church shall be in its *Philadelphian state,* when Enemies shall come and *bow before the feet* of *Jerusalem,* as Christ speaketh in his Epistle to the Church of *Philadelphia,* but first there will *an hour of Temptation come upon all the world,* Rev.3.10. We look that the *Jews* shall be *Converted;* I know, and am persuaded by the Lord Jesus, that it shall be so in the appointed time. We look that *Chittim* and *Ashur* (that is, *Pope* and *Turk*) shall perish for ever; but is it not said, *Alas, who shall live when God doth these things?* Numb.24.23. We know that in *Abrahams* Vision, *when the Sun was going down, an horrour of great darkness fell upon him,* Gen.15.12. Why so? but to signifie, that when the Sun is going down, even in the end of the World, when Christ is ready to come and set up his Kingdome, and judge the earth, there shall be great horrour of darkness and misery upon the world: Darkness shall then cover the earth, and gross darkness the people.

2. *Our eyes see, and our ears hear of the beginnings of sorrows.* That which Christ spake with immediate reference to the troubles preceding the destruction of the *Jewish* Church and State, may be applied to the troubles of the last times, the former being a type of the latter, *Matt.24.6,7,8. And ye shall hear of wars, rumours of wars, see that you be not troubled, for all these things must come to pass, but the end is not yet: for Nation shall rise against Nation, and Kingdom against Kingdom, and there shall be Famines, and Pestilences, and Earthquakes in divers places: All these are the beginnings of sorrows.* What do we hear of at this day, but Wars, and rumours of

Wars? and Nation rising up against Nation, and Kingdome against Kingdome? Now if these are the beginnings of sorrows, what, and where, and when will the end be? There's an over-flowing scourge breaking in upon the world, even a Judgement, that will not keep within ordinary banks or bounds, but shall pass over into many Lands. And how far will it go? where will the Tayle of this Storm fall at last, do we think? How if it should fall upon *America*? Will not some drops at least light upon *New-England*? We may speak in the words of the Prophet in my Text, and say, *The morning is come,* The day of trouble begins to dawn upon the world. Alas for this day, it is great, there is none like it. It is then high time for us to awake out of sleep.

3. To come nearer home; *The fatal Strokes which have been amongst us speak ominously.* Is not that a plain Scripture, *Isa.57.1. The righteous is taken away from the evil to come?* The Lord hath been taking away many righteous ones from the midst of us; yea righteous ones, that should have stood in the gap, now when the waters of many Troubles are breaking in upon us, whereby he hath *made a way to his anger,* Psal.78.50. How many Magistrates, and Ministers especially, hath the Lord bereaved us of? When Kings call home their Ambassadors, it's a sign they will proclaim War. God hath called home many of his Ambassadors of late, and that's a sign that War is determined in Heaven against us. Our Enemies are coming, and our Chariots and our Horsmen are gone. *Ah! poor* New-England, *thy Chariots and thy Horsmen are gone from thee, and now thine Enemies are coming against thee.* And I would not pass by in silence, the observable Providence of God, who hath so ordered, that many Ancient Christians have been taken away of late, as it were together. I have made some Enquiry about that matter, and finde it to be a general observation, That in many Plantations round about, in one or two years time, a great number of aged Christians have been hid in their graves. *The taking away of the Ancient,* is mentioned as an ominous sign, *Isa.3.2. Methuselah* was the oldest man in the old world, and he died the year before the Flood come. Inasmuch as many of our *Methuselahs* are lately gone, and that so near together, we may fear that a Flood is coming. It's a sign of a Winter at hand, that

so many aged ones should drop down into the grave together. Nor would I omit here, the sudden Deaths whereby many have been snatched away. When Christ was told of some that were taken away by sudden death, he replied, *I tell you, Nay: except you repent, ye shall all likewise perish,* Luke 13.3. As if the Lord had said, I would have you take these sudden destructions which befall some, as an *Item* unto you, that your Enemies will come and make a general laughter amongst you, except you do by Repentance prevent it. And in the 4th of *Amos*, it is set down as a sign fore-running a day of great and general trouble, *ver.11. I have overthrown some of you, as God overthrew Sodom and Gomorrah.* And how did God overthrow *Sodom* and *Gomorrah?* Was it not with Thunder and Lightning from Heaven? Many amongst us of late years have been so overthrown: yea this year, at least four persons have been so, and sundry of them good men, which maketh the Strokes the more awful and ominous.

4. *There are manifold transgressions, and mighty sins amongst us.* And here if I should leave off speaking, and we should all of us joyn together in weeping and lamenting, it would be the best course that could be taken. Brethren, what shall I say? As to *matters of Religion,* things are not as should be. There is a great decay as to the power of godliness amongst us. Professors are many of them of a loose, carnal, ungirt Conversation. We can now see little difference between Churchmembers and other men, as to their discourses, or their spirits, or their walking, or their garb, but Professors of Religion *fashion themselves according to the world.* And what *Pride* is there? Spiritual Pride, in Parts and common Gifts of the Spirit, and in Spiritual Priviledges; yea carnal, shameful, foolish Pride, in Apparel, Fashions, and the like. Whence is all that rising up, and disobedience in Inferiours towards Superiours, in Families, in Churches, and in the Commonwealth, but from the unmortified Pride which is in the hearts of the sons and daughters of men? And is there not Oppression amongst us? Are there no biting Usurers in *New-England?* Are there not those that grinde the faces of the poor? A poor man cometh amongst you, and he must have a Commodity whatever it cost him, and you will make him give whatever you please, and put what price you

please upon what he hath to give too, without respecting the just value of the thing. Verily I am afraid, that the *Oppressing Sword* will come upon us, because of the Oppressions and Extortions which the eyes of the Lords glory have seen amongst us. And are there not *Contentions and Divisions* amongst us? It is in vain for us to go about to palliate this matter, or to cover this sure, for the shame of our nakedness doth appear, so as that we are become a derision amongst our Enemies. We are divided in our Judgements; and if that were all, the matter were not much: but we are divided in our Affections, divided in our Prayers, divided in our Counsels: And will not an House divided be brought to desolation? We may say as that blessed *Burroughs* once complained, W*e have been so divided, that it is the infinite Mercy of God that our Enemies have not come in at our breaches, and divided all amongst themselves.* Alas! that Gods Diamonds should be cutting one another. I do believe, that one reason why the Lord threatneth to send upon us that Calamity of War at this day, is because of wars and fightings which he hath seen, and been provoked with in the midst of us. If you will needs be fighting (saith God) I'le send those upon you, that shall give you enough of it, *Jam.*4.1. The Clashings and *Tumults* which have been amongst us, may cause us to fear, that such a *day of Tumult* as the Text speaketh of, is hastening upon us. And what a *woful worldly spirit* is there in many? Hence God, and Christ, and Heaven, and the Concernments of mens own Souls, are not minded: yea, duties of Communion with the Lord are either totally neglected, or slubbered over. Some don't pray in their Families above once a day: Why? they have not time, they say. Why not? how is your time taken up? Is it in doing publick service for God or for his people? If it were so, we must have a care that it be not said to us, *Thou wast made the keeper of the Vineyard, but thy own Vineyard thou hast not kept.* But that's not the reason why men neglect duty; no, it is because they have not time for their worldly occasions. *O this World! this World!* undoeth many a man, that thinks he shall go to Heaven when he dieth. And in this respect our Land is full of Idolatry. What is like to come on us? Alas we have changed our Interest. The Interest of *New-England* was Religion, which did distinguish us from other *English*

Plantations, they were built upon a Worldly design, but we upon a Religious design, when-as now we begin to spouse a Worldly Interest, and so to chuse a new God, therefore no wonder that War is like to be in the gates. I cannot but admire the Providence of God, that he should threaten to punish us with a generation of men that are notorious for that sin of Worldliness, as if the Lord would make us see what our great sin is, in the Instruments of our trouble. *David* might see by the Instrument of his trouble, what sin it was which God afflicted him for, when *Achitophel*, who was *Bathshebah's* Grandfather, rose up against him. Truly so may we in the Instruments of our present affliction, reade what our sin hath been. And is there not woful *Covenant-breaking* amongst us? Men when they come into the Church, enter into the solemnest Covenant that can be; They promise in the presence of God, Angels and Saints, that they will watch over one anothers Souls: But how little is that Christian and Brotherly Watchfulness attended ever after? Indeed, if men fall out one with another, then they can watch for Haltings, and prosecute to the utmost, which is to serve themselves, and their own vile lusts and passions, upon Christ and his holy Ordinance; but otherwise, there are too many that can see one another sin, and never attend the Rules of Christ appointed for the healing of every sinning, offending Brother. This is lamentable! And as for the *Children of the Covenant*, as the Scripture calls them, are not they lamentably neglected? Me-thinks it is a very solemn Providence, that the Lord should seem at this day to be *numbering many of the Rising Generation for the Sword*; as if the Lord should say, I will bring a Sword to avenge the quarrel of a *neglected Covenant*. Churches have not so performed Covenant-duties towards their Children, as should have been, and especially, the Rising Generation have many of them broken the Covenant themselves, in that they do not endeavour to come up to that which their solemn Vow in Baptism doth engage them to before the Lord, even *to know and serve the Lord God of their Fathers*. Yet again, *How unfruitfull have we been under precious Means of Grace?* How hath the Lord been disappointed in his righteous and reasonable Expectations concerning us? We have not in this our day known the things that do belong unto our peace, and therefore now things look as if the dayes of our peace were ended. It is not long since that Scripture was opened and applied in the hearing of many of you, *Luke* 19.43.44. *The dayes shall come upon thee, that thine Enemies shall keep thee in on every side, because thou knewest not the time of thy visitation.* How righteous is it, that the Lord should make us to know the difference that is between the service of the Lord, and the service of *Shishak?* 2 Chron.12.8. *O Ntw England,* because thou servedst not the Lord thy God with joyfulness, and with gladnes of heart, for the abundance of all things, therefore it is just with God to say, Thou shalt serve thy Enemies which the Lord shall send against thee, in hunger, and in thirst, and in nakedness, and in Want of all things, *Deut.*28.47,48.

5. *Signs have appeared in Heaven and Earth, presaging sad Mutations to be at hand.* By *Signs,* I mean *Prodigies,* which the Scripture calls Signs. It is a celebrated Saying, *That God never brings great judgements upon any place, but he first giveth Warning of it, by some portentous Signs.* So did the Lord deal by *Egypt* in the dayes of old: and so it was with *Jerusalem,* a few years before the *Roman* destruction. Therefore Christ said, *Luke* 21.17. *Fearful sights, and great signs shall there be from Heaven.* Josephus doth relate at large, what terrible Prodigies appeared before those miserable dayes. The like also happened before the troubles under *Antiochus,* as the Historiographers of that Age have declared. "There appeared Troops of Horsemen in array, "encountering and running one against another, with shaking of "Shields, and multitude of Pikes, and drawing of Swords, *etc.* Something like unto that, is said to have been amongst us. I confess I am very slow to give credit to reports of that nature: but it is credibly reported, that in sundry places Volleys of small Shot have been heard in the Air, yea and great Pieces of Ordnance discharged, when there hath been no such thing in reality. And I think God would not have us altogether slight that *bloody Prodigie* which hapned about this time Twelve-moneth (as Eye-witnesses have affirmed) in that Neighbouring place, which since is fallen into the hands of our Enemies. However, it puts me in minde of what I have read, *viz.* that in *York* in England it rained blood, a little before the *Danes* entrance into the Land. Moreover, we have all seen and felt *Blazing Stars,*

Earthquakes, Prodigious Thunders, and Lightnings, and Tempests. We may here make use of that Scripture, which though it have a spirituall meaning, yet some good Interpreters do not reject a literal Sense of the words, *Isa.29.6. And thou shalt be visited of the Lord of Hosts with Thunder, and with Earthquake, and great noise, with storm, and tempest, and the flame of devouring fire.* Hath it not been so with us? We have been visited with great noise, and with the devouring flame, that is, with terrible Thunders and Lightnings, and with *Earthquakes*, which are often a Prognostick of *State-quakes*, yea and *Heartquakes*, not far off; and with Storms and Tempests, and that too upon Lords-dayes, in a very dismall manner. Now let us not be of those, that regard not the work of the Lord, nor the operation of his hands.

6. *There is a black Cloud over our heads, which begins to drop upon us.* Providence hath so ordered, that our Enemies are come near, and may we not then think that trouble is near? The Lord hath been whetting his glittering Sword a long time, we have heard a noise, and a dismall din hath been in our ears, but now the Sword seems to be facing and marching directly towards us: yea, we see *Jerusalem* compassed about with Enemies. Christ said unto his Disciples, *Luke 21.20. When ye shall see Jerusalem compassed with Enemies, then know that the desolation thereof is nigh.* Is not our *Jerusalem* compassed with Armies? There are pretended Friends at our backs, and professed Enemies before our faces. The sky looketh red and lowring, we may therefore fear, that foul Weather is at hand: As once that Prophet said, There is a sound of an abundance of Rain, and in the meanwhile, *the Heaven was black with Clouds.* Truly so it is at this day, the Heavens are black over our heads. The Clouds begin to gather thick in our Horizon: yea, there is a Cloud of Blood, which begins to drop upon us. When once a Cloud begins to drop, you know that a Shower is wont to follow. The Cloud of Blood over our heads begins to drop, there was one drop fell the other day, witness the man that was slain upon the Coasts: the Lord grant that a Shower of Blood may not follow. What need have we to pray, that this Cloud may blow over, and pass away.

7. *Without doubt the Lord Jesus hath a peculiar respect unto this place, and for this people.* This is *Immanuels* Land.

Christ by a wonderful Providence hath dispossessed Satan, who raigned securely in these Ends of the Earth, for Ages the Lord knoweth how many, and here the Lord hath caused as it were *New Jerusalem* to come down from Heaven; He dwels in this place: therefore we may conclude that he will scourge us for our backslidings. So doth he say, *Rev*.3.19. *As many as I love, I rebuke and chasten.* It is not onely true concerning particular persons, but as to Churches, (those words were spoken to a Church) that if Christ hath a peculiar love unto them, then he will rebuke and chasten them, as there shall be cause for it. Indeed we may therefore hope that the Lord will not destroy us. Through the grace of Christ, I am not at all afraid of that. The Lord will not as yet destroy this place: Our Fathers have built Sanctuaries for his Name therein, and therefore he will not destroy us. The Planting of these Heavens, and the laying the Foundations of this Earth, is one of the Wonders of this last Age. As *Moses* said, *Ask now of the dayes that are past, ask from one side of Heaven to the other, hath God essayed to go and take him a Nation out of the midst of a Nation?* Deut. 4.32.34. God hath culled out a people, even out of all parts of a Nation, which he hath also had a great favour towards, and hath brought them by a mighty hand, and an out-stretched arm, over a greater then the Red Sea, and here hath he planted them, and hath caused them to grow up as it were into a little Nation: And shall we think that all this is to destroy them within forty or fifty years? Destruction shall not as yet be. Nevertheless, the Lord may greatly afflict us, and bring us very low. It is a notable Observation, which I remember a *Jewish* Writer hath, who lived in the dayes of the second Temple: "The dealings of God with "our Nation (saith he) and with the Nations of the world, is "very different: for other Nations may sin and do wickedly, and "God doth not punish them, untill they have filled up the "measure of their sins, and then he utterly destroyeth them; but "if our Nation forsake the God of their Fathers never so little, "God presently cometh upon us with one Judgement or other, "that so he may prevent our destruction. So let me say, Neighbouring Plantations about us may possibly sin grievously, and yet it may be long before the Lord taketh them to do, because it may be he'll reckon with them once for all at last; but if *New-England* shall forsake the Lord, Judgement shall quickly overtake us, because the God of our Fathers is not willing to destroy us their Children.

These things then are enough to awaken us out of our Security. I have thought of three other Signs of approaching misery, which I shall not mention at this time, albeit they are (in my apprehension) no less ominous, then any thing that hath been spoken.

USE IV. I conclude with a word of Exhortation. *Let us carry our selves as doth become those that have a day of trouble near unto them; yea, so as that we may prevent the troubles which seem to be near.* I need not say much by way of Motive. Remember the *Arguments* mentioned in the last Use; and the *Signs* of Troubles being near, insisted on in the former part of the day. And consider, that if we carry our selves in a suitable manner, we may possibly escape those Evils, that otherwise are like to overtake us. It is possible that this Cloud may blow over, *Amos* 5.15. *It may be the Lord of Hosts will be gracious to the remnant of Joseph.* Truly we are the remnant of *Joseph*; we are (as *Joseph* was) *separated from our Brethren,* who can tell but that the Lord may be gracious to us? *Zeph.*2.3. *Seek ye the Lord, all the meek of the earth; seek righteousness, seek meekness: it may be ye shall be hid in the day of the Lords anger.* Nay, if we carry our selves as doth become us in a day of trouble, it's past a *may be,* that we shall be hid in the day of the Lords anger.

Quest. But *how ought we to carry our selves now that trouble is near unto us?*

Ans. 1. *It doth concern us and become us to be an humble people.* As sometimes the Lord said to his people of old, *Now put off thy Ornaments, that I may know what to do unto thee,* Exod.33.5. so doth the Lord by his Providence speak to us, Put off thy Ornaments, O *New-England,* that I may know what to do unto thee, that I may know whether I had best spare thee, or punish thee. Prepare to meet thy God, even to meet him as sometimes *Abigall* did *David,* with Confessions, and humble Supplications. And if we humble our selves deeply and unfeignedly, God cannot finde in his heart to destroy us. It is a wonderful Scripture which we have, 1 *Chron*,21.16. *David lift up his eyes, and saw the Angel of the Lord stand between the Earth and the Heaven; having a drawn Sword in his hand, stretched out over Jerusalem; then David and the Elders of Israel, who were clothed in sackcloth, fell upon their faces.* Indeed the Angel of the Lord is standing over us with a drawn Sword in his hand, but if we fall upon our faces before the Lord, as doth become us, God will say, Let it be enough that the Sword is held over this people, stay thine hand, put up the Sword.

2. *It becometh us in such a day as this, to be a very Heavenly people.* As *Elisha* said, *Is it a time to receive money, and garments, and olive yards, etc?* So, is it now a time for us to set our mindes upon the world, and the things of the world? We should now remember what the Prophet *Jeremiah* said to *Baruch*, Chap.45.5. *And seekest thou great things for thy self? Seek them not: for behold, I will bring evil upon all flesh, saith the Lord.* Now will nothing serve you but the world, in this day wherein God is shaking all Nations, yea shaking Heaven and Earth, and Sea and dry Land? What is the voice of God to us in these dreadful dispensations, but this, See that your hearts be taken off from the world, and set them more upon those things that cannot be shaken?

3. *We should be a Believing people.* That's the way to be delivered out of trouble: *Psal.*22.4. *Our fathers trusted in thee; they trusted, and thou didst deliver them.* O the mighty things that Faith can do! It is said, *Heb.*11.34. *By Faith they escaped the edge of the Sword, and turned to flight the Armies of the aliens.* Though Armies should come against us, the Spirit of Faith may turn them back. In the times of the *Maccabees* (for unto those troubles doth the Apostle there allude) sometimes a small handfull, worsted great Armies that came against them, because they acted Faith upon the Name of the Lord. Or if troubles should overtake us, Faith will help us to suffer, as well as to do great things for God.

4. *It concerns us in this day of trouble to be a Reforming people.* Let us *amend our wayes and our doings, and the Lord will cause us to dwell in this place*, Jer.7.3. Certainly we need Reformation. Where is the old *New-England Spirit*, that once

was amongst us? Where is our first love? Where is our Zeal for
God, especially in matters respecting the first Table, which once
was our glory? What is become of that life and power of godliness, that hath been in this place? Now if the Lord help us to
reform whatever is amiss, he will still do us good, notwithstanding all our sins, which have provoked him, and caused him to
frown upon us. We have a plain text for this, Jer.18.7,8. *At what
instant I shall speak concerning a Nation, and concerning a
Kingdome, to pluck up, and to pull down, and to destroy it; if
that Nation against whom I have pronounced, turn from their
evil, then will I repent of the evil which I thought to do unto
them.*

5. *It concerns us and becomes us, now that trouble is near,
to be a United people:* otherwise our Enemies will say, that we
are under a penal Infatuation. We may well say as that worthy
Divine was wont to express, *Haec non sunt litigandi, sed orandi
tempora;* These are not times for us to be contending one against
another but rather to be praying one with another, and one for
another. Shall we be worse then dumb, and brute, and savage
Creatures have sometimes been? It is a memorable Passage,
which some Historians make mention of, That once in *Somer-
setshire* in *England,* when there was a sudden Flood, wherein
many men were drowned, the dumb Creatures ran to the top of
an Hill, that so They might escape the fury and destruction of
the Flood; and there such Creatures as had an Antipathy in
their Natures, even Dogs and Hares, yea Cats and Mice, could
sit quietly together, and never offter to molest one another. Why
behold, there is a Flood coming in upon us, And shall we not
now live quietly by one another? Shall we not at such a time as
this lay aside our Animosities and Variances about matters,
which it's great pity that ever a Contention should be upheld
amongst good men, about such small differences? Naturalists
write concerning the Stone *Tyrrhenus,* that if it be cast upon the
water whole, it will swim, but if it be broken it will sink presently. Would we sink, or would we swim in this Sea of trouble
that is a coming? If we break, we shall sink; if we divide, we
perish, and are like to be an undone people: But if we be *whole,*
if we unite, we shall *swim,* our heads will then be above water,

let what troubles can come: yea, and we shall then be a burthen-some stone to all that shall burthen themselves with us. If we do but become one with God and one another, as we ought to be, we need not fear all the world. Oh that our Divisions, and other Evils that are amongst us, might be repented of, and then I dare speak it boldly before all this Congregation, God will make *New England* a burthensome stone, yea though all the Nations of the Earth should be gathered together against it, they shall be broken in pieces.

6. *We should be a Praying people, Psal.50.15. Call upon me in the day of trouble.* Thus *David, Psal.22.11. Be not far from me, for trouble is near.* In a time when trouble was near, he doth betake himself to God by Faith and Prayer. What people under Heaven have ever had more encouragement unto Prayer, then we have had? Know it Enemies to your terrour; Know it all the World, That the Lords poor *New-England People,* have ever found him to be a *God that heareth Prayer:* and therefore let's be at that work still. And truly, there is as much need now as ever. We may even say, as sometimes that blessed Martyr did, *Pray, pray, pray, never more need then now.* Alas, that we are no oftener in such a solemn manner, as at this day before the Lord! We may here allude to that which is spoken, *Rev.8.* we there reade that there was *silence in Heaven half an hour,* and then followeth an *Earthquake.* It's sad to consider, that there hath been so great a silence in Heaven amongst us: I have thought on it with some grief of heart, that there hath not been so much Fasting and Praying in *New-England* of late years, as sometimes formerly, though never so much need as now. Who knoweth, but the Lord may bring these troubles within our sight, that so we may seek him early, yea that so the Spirit of Prayer may be awakened amongst us? There are some that cannot pray, all unregenerate sinners are destitute of the Spirit of Prayer; many poor miserable Souls, that keep their Prayers and Tears till such time as they will do them no good. But I know that there are many, Scores, Hun-dreds here this day, that have an Interest in Heaven, and know how to improve it. Why then, up and be doing. If thou hast but one Tear in thy eyes, if thou hast but one Prayer in thy heart,

spend it now. And let us remember the words of the Lord Jesus, *Luke* 21.36. *Watch ye therefore, and pray alwayes, that ye may be counted worthy to escape all these things which shall come to pass.*

Samuel Sewall

(1652–1730)

Bibliographical Note. Sewall's diary is printed in the *Collections of the Massachusetts Historical Society,* 5th ser., V–VII (1878–1882). The selections here printed follow that text; V, 44, 342, 369–370, 419–420, 442–445, VI, 343, VII, 262–276. The best general account of Sewall is N. H. Chamberlain, *Samuel Sewall and the World He Lived In* (Boston, 1897). The diarist, however, reveals himself as no one else can.

from

THE DIARY
[WRITTEN 1673-1729]

Jan. 13, 167⁶⁄₇. Giving my chickens meat, it came to my mind that I gave them nothing save Indian corn and water, and yet they eat it and thrived very well, and that that food was necessary for them, how mean soever, which much affected me and convinced what need I stood in of spiritual food, and that I should not nauseat daily duties of Prayer, &c.

. . . . .

March 19, 169⁰⁄₁. Mr. C. Mather preaches the Lecture from Mat. 24., and appoint his portion with the Hypocrites: In his proem said, *Totus mundus agit histrionem.* Said one sign of a hypocrit was for a man to strain at a Gnat and swallow a Camel. Sign in 's Threat discovered him; To be zealous against an iñoccnt fashion, taken up and used by the best of men; and yet make no Conscience of being guilty of great Immoralities. Tis supposed means wearing of Perriwigs: said would deny themselves in any thing but parting with an oportunity to do God service; that so might not offend good Christians. Meaning, I suppose, was fain to wear a Perriwig for his health. I expected not to hear a vindication of Perriwigs in Boston Pulpit by Mr. Mather; however, not from that Text. The Lord give me a good Heart and help to know, and not only to know but also to doe his Will; that my Heart and Head may be his.

Nov. 6. Joseph threw a knop of Brass and hit his Sister Betty on the forhead so as to make it bleed and swell; upon which, and for his playing at Prayer-time, and eating when Return Thanks, I whipd him pretty smartly. When I first went in (call'd by his Grandmother) he sought to shadow and hide himself from me behind the head of the Cradle: which gave me the sorrowfull remembrance of Adam's carriage.

. . . . .

Nov. 22, 1692. I prayd that God would pardon all my Sinfull Wanderings, and direct me for the future. That God would bless the Assembly in their debates, and that would chuse and assist our Judges, &c., and save New England as to Enemies and Witchcrafts, and vindicate the late Judges, consisting with his Justice and Holiness, &c., with Fasting. Cousin Anne Quinsy visited me in the Evening, and told me of her children's wellfare. Now about, Mercy Short grows ill again, as formerly.

. . . . .

[Jan. 13, 169⅚.]

. . . . .

When I came in, past 7. at night, my wife met me in the Entry and told me Betty had surprised them. I was surprised with the abruptness of the Relation. It seems Betty Sewall had given some signs of dejection and sorrow; but a little after diñer she burst out into an amazing cry, which caus'd all the family to cry too; Her Mother ask'd the reason; she gave none; at last said she was afraid she should goe to Hell, her Sins were not pardon'd. She was first wounded by my reading a Sermon of Mr. Norton's, about the 5th. of Jan. Text Jno 7. 34. Ye shall seek me and shall not find me. And those words in the Sermon, Jno 8. 21. Ye shall seek me and shall die in your sins, ran in her mind, and terrified her greatly. And staying at home Jan. 12. she read out of Mr. Cotton Mather—Why hath Satan filled thy heart, which increas'd her Fear. Her Mother ask'd her whether she pray'd. She answer'd, Yes; but feared her prayers were not heard because her Sins not pardon'd. Mr. Willard though sent for timelyer, yet not being told of the message, till bruised Dinsdals [?] was given him; He came not till after I came home. He discoursed with Betty who could not give a distinct account, but was confused as his phrase was, and as had experienced in himself. Mr. Willard pray'd excellently. The Lord bring Light and Comfort out of this dark and dreadful Cloud, and Grant that Christ's being formed in my dear child, may be the issue of these painfull pangs.

. . . . .

Decr. 21 [1696.]   A very great Snow is on the Ground. I go in the morn to Mr. Willard, to entreat him to chuse his own time to come and pray with little Sarah: He comes a little before night, and prays very fully and well. Mr. Mather, the President, had prayd with her in the time of the Courts sitting. Decr. 22. being Catechising day, I give Mr. Willard a note to pray for my daughter publickly, which he did. Note, this morn Madam Elisa Bellingham came to our house and upbraided me with setting my hand to pass Mr. Wharton's acco- to the Court, where he obtain'd a Judgmt for Eustace's farm. I was wheadled and hector'd into that business, and have all along been uneasy in the remembrance of it: and now there is one come who will not spare to lay load. The Lord take away my filthy garments, and give me change of Rayment. This day I remove poor little Sarah into my Bed-chamber, where about Break of Day Decr. 23. she gives up the Ghost in Nurse Cowell's Arms. Born, Nov. 21, 1694. Neither I nor my wife were by: Nurse not expecting so sudden a change, and having promis'd to call us. I thought of Christ's Words, could you not watch with me one hour! and would fain have sat up with her: but fear of my wives illness, who is very valetudinarious, made me to lodge with her in the new Hall, where was call'd by Jane's Cry, to take notice of my dead daughter. Nurse did long and pathetically ask our pardon that she had not call'd us, and said she was surpriz^d. Thus this very fair day is rendered fowl to us by reason of the general Sorrow and Tears in the family. Master Chiever was here the evening before, I desir'd him to pray for my daughter. The Chapt^r read in course on Decr. 23. m. was Deut. 22. which made me sadly reflect that I had not been so thorowly tender of my daughter; nor so effectually carefull of her Defence and preservation as I should have been. The good Lord pity and pardon and help for the future as to those God has still left me.

Dec^r- 24. Sam. recites to me in Latin, Mat. 12. from the 6th. to the end of the 12th. v. The 7th. verse did awfully bring to mind the Salem Tragedie.

6th. day, Decr. 25, 1696. We bury our little daughter. In the chamber, Joseph in course reads Ecclesiastes 3^d. a time to be born and a time to die—Elisabeth, Rev. 22. Hanah, the 38th- Psalm. I speak to each, as God helped, to our mutual comfort I hope. I order'd Sam. to read the 102. Psalm. Elisha Cooke, Edw. Hutchinson, John Baily, and Josia Willard bear my little daughter to the Tomb.

Note. Twas wholly dry, and I went at noon to see in what order things were set; and there I was entertain'd with a view of, and converse with, the Coffins of my dear Father Hull, Mother Hull, Cousin Quinsey, and my Six Children: for the little posthumous was now took up and set in upon that that stands on John's: so are three, one upon another twice, on the bench at the end. My Mother ly's on a lower bench, at the end, with head to her Husband's head: and I order'd little Sarah to be set on her Grandmother's feet. 'Twas an awfull yet pleasing Treat; Having said, The Lord knows who shall be brought hither next, I came away.

. . . . .

[Jan. 14, 1697.]

．　．　．　．　．

Copy of the Bill I put up on the Fast day;[1] giving it to Mr. Willard as he pass'd by, and standing up at the reading of it, and bowing when finished; in the Afternoon.

Samuel Sewall, sensible of the reiterated strokes of God upon himself and family; and being sensible, that as to the Guilt contracted upon the opening of the late Comission of Oyer and Terminer at Salem (to which the order for this Day relates) he is, upon many accounts, more concerned than any that he knows of, Desires to take the Blame and shame of it, Asking pardon of men, And especially desiring prayers that God, who has an Unlimited Authority, would pardon that sin and all other his sins; personal and Relative: And according to his infinite Benignity, and Sovereignty, Not Visit the sin of him, or of any other, upon himself or any of his, nor upon the Land: But that He would powerfully defend him against all Temptations to Sin, for the future; and vouchsafe him the efficacious, saving Conduct of his Word and Spirit.

．　．　．　．　．

Sixth-day, April, 11 [1712]. I saw Six Swallows together flying and chipering very rapturously.

．　．　．　．　．

Sept. 30, 1720. Mr. Colman's Lecture: Daughter Sewall acquaints Madam Winthrop that if she pleas'd to be within at 3. p.m. I would wait on her. She answer'd she would be at home.

Oct. 1, 1720. Satterday, I dine at Mr. Stoddard's: from thence I went to Madam Winthrop's just at 3. Spake to her, saying, my loving wife died so soon and suddenly, 'twas hardly convenient for me to think of Marrying again; however I came

---

[1] This day was officially appointed as one of public fasting, prayer, and contrition over the Witchcraft Trials of 1692, in which Sewall had participated.

to this Resolution, that I would not make my Court to any person without first Consulting with her. Had a pleasant discourse about 7 Single persons sitting in the Fore-seat 7ʳ 29ᵗʰ, viz. Madᵐ Rebekah Dudley, Catharine Winthrop, Bridget Usher, Deliverance Legg, Rebekah Loyd, Lydia Colman, Elizabeth Bellingham. She propounded one and another for me; but none would do, said Mrs. Loyd was about her Age.

Oct. 3, 1720. Waited on Madam Winthrop again; 'twas a little while before she came in. Her daughter Noyes being there alone with me, I said, I hoped my Waiting on her Mother would not be disagreeable to her. She answer'd she should not be against that that might be for her Comfort. I Saluted her, and told her I perceiv'd I must shortly wish her a good Time; (her mother had told me, she was with Child, and within a Moneth or two of her Time). By and by in came Mr. Airs, Chaplain of the Castle, and hang'd up his Hat, which I was a little startled at, it seeming as if he was to lodge there. At last Madam Winthrop came too. After a considerable time, I went up to her and said, if it might not be inconvenient I desired to speak with her. She assented, and spake of going into another Room; but Mr. Airs and Mrs. Noyes presently rose up, and went out, leaving us there alone. Then I usher'd in Discourse from the names in the Fore-seat; at last I pray'd that Katharine [Mrs. Winthrop] might be the person assign'd for me. She instantly took it up in the way of Denyal, as if she had catch'd at an Opportunity to do it, saying she could not do it before she was asked. Said that was her mind unless she should Change it, which she believed she should not; could not leave her Children. I express'd my Sorrow that she should do it so Speedily, pray'd her Consideration, and ask'd her when I should wait on her agen. She setting no time, I mention'd that day Sennight. Gave her Mr. Willard's Fountain open'd with the little print and verses; saying, I hop'd if we did well read that book, we should meet together hereafter, if we did not now. She took the Book, and put it in her Pocket. Took Leave.

Oct. 6, 1720. A little after 6. p.m. I went to Madam Winthrop's. She was not within. I gave Sarah Chickering the Maid 2ˢ, Juno, who brought in wood, 1ˢ. Afterward the Nurse came in, I gave her 18ᵈ. having no other small Bill. After awhile

Dr. Noyes came in with his Mother; and quickly after his wife came in: They sat talking, I think, till eight a-clock. I said I fear'd I might be some Interruption to their Business: Dr. Noyes reply'd pleasantly: He fear'd they might be an Interruption to me, and went away. Madam seem'd to harp upon the same string. Must take care of her Children; could not leave that House and Neighbourhood where she had dwelt so long. I told her she might doe her children as much or more good by bestowing what she laid out in Hous-keeping, upon them. Said her Son would be of Age the 7th of August. I said it might be inconvenient for her to dwell with her Daughter-in-Law, who must be Mistress of the House. I gave her a piece of Mr. Belcher's Cake and Ginger-Bread wrapped up in a clean sheet of Paper; told her of her Father's kindness to me when Treasurer, and I Constable. My Daughter Judith was gon from me and I was more lonesom—might help to forward one another in our Journey to Canaan.—Mr. Eyre came within the door; I saluted him, ask'd how Mr. Clark did, and he went away. I took leave about 9 aclock. I told [her] I came now to refresh her Memory as to Monday-night; said she had not forgot it. In discourse with her, I ask'd leave to speak with her Sister; I meant to gain Mad^m Mico's favour to persuade her Sister. She seem'd surpris'd and displeas'd, and said she was in the same condition!

Oct. 10, 1720. In the Evening I visited Madam Winthrop, who treated me with a great deal of Curtesy; Wine, Marmalade. I gave her a News-Letter about the Thanksgiving Proposals, for sake of the verses for David Jeffries. She tells me Dr. Increase Mather visited her this day, in Mr. Hutchinson's Coach.

Oct. 11, 1720. I writ a few Lines to Madam Winthrop to this purpose: "Madam, These wait on you with Mr. Mayhew's Sermon, and Account of the state of the Indians on Martha's Vinyard. I thank you for your Unmerited Favours of yesterday; and hope to have the Happiness of Waiting on you to-morrow before Eight a-clock after Noon. I pray God to keep you, and give you a joyfull entrance upon the Two Hundred and twenty ninth year of Christopher Columbus his Discovery; and take Leave, who am, Madam, your humble Servt. S.S.

Oct. 12, 1720. Mrs. Anne Cotton came to door (twas before 8.) said Madam Winthrop was within, directed me into the little Room, where she was full of work behind a Stand; Mrs. Cotton came in and stood. Madam Winthrop pointed to her to set me a Chair. Madam Winthrop's Countenance was much changed from what 'twas on Monday, look'd dark and lowering. At last, the work, (black stuff or Silk) was taken away, I got my Chair in place, had some Converse, but very Cold and indifferent to what 'twas before. Ask'd her to acquit me of Rudeness if I drew off her Glove. Enquiring the reason, I told her twas great odds between handling a dead Goat, and a living Lady. Got it off. I told her I had one Petition to ask of her, that was, that she would take off the Negative she laid on me the third of October; She readily answer'd she could not, and enlarg'd upon it; She told me of it so soon as she could; could not leave her house, children, neighbours, business. I told her she might do som Good to help and support me. Mentioning Mrs. Gookin, Nath, the widow Weld was spoken of; said I had visited Mrs. Denison. I told her Yes! Afterward I said, If after a first and second Vagary she would Accept of me returning, Her Victorious Kindness and Good Will would be very Obliging. She thank'd me for my Book, (Mr. Mayhew's Sermon), But said not a word of the Letter. When she insisted on the Negative, I pray'd there might be no more Thunder and Lightening, I should not sleep all night. I gave her Dr. Preston, The Church's Marriage and the Church's Carriage, which cost me 6ª at the Sale. The door standing open, Mr. Airs came in, hung up his Hat, and sat down. After awhile, Madam Winthrop moving, he went out. Jnº Eyre look'd in, I said How do ye, or, your servant Mr. Eyre: but heard no word from him. Sarah fill'd a Glass of Wine, she drank to me, I to her, She sent Juno home with me with a good Lantern, I gave her 6ᵈ and bid her thank her Mistress. In some of our Discourse, I told her I had rather go to the Stone-House adjoining to her, than to come to her against her mind. Told her the reason why I came every other night was lest I should drink too deep draughts of Pleasure. She had talk'd of Canary, her Kisses were to me better than the best Canary. Explain'd the expression Concerning Columbus.

Oct. 13. I tell my Son and daughter Sewall, that the Weather was not so fair as I apprehended.

Oct. 17. In the Evening I visited Madam Winthrop, who

Treated me Courteously, but not in Clean Linen as sometimes. She said, she did not know whether I would come again, or no. I ask'd her how she could so impute inconstancy to me. (I had not visited her since Wednesday night being unable to get over the Indisposition received by the Treatment received that night, and I *must* in it seem'd to sound like a made piece of Formality.) Gave her this day's Gazett. Heard David Jeffries say the Lord's Prayer, and some other portions of the Scriptures. He came to the door, and ask'd me to go into Chamber, where his Grandmother was tending little Katee, to whom she had given Physick; but I chose to sit below. Dr. Noyes and his wife came in, and sat a Considerable time; had been visiting Son and dâter Cooper. Juno came home with me.

Oct. 18, 1720. Visited Madam Mico, who came to me in a splendid Dress. I said, It may be you have heard of my Visiting Madam Winthrop, her Sister. She answered, Her Sister had told her of it. I ask'd her good Will in the Affair. She answer'd, If her Sister were for it, she should not hinder it. I gave her Mr. Homes's Sermon. She gave me a Glass of Canary, entertain'd me with good Discourse, and a Respectfull Remembrance of my first Wife. I took Leave.

Oct. 19, 1720. Midweek, Visited Madam Winthrop; Sarah told me she was at Mr. Walley's, would not come home till late. I gave her Hannah 3 oranges with her Duty, not knowing whether I should find her or no. Was ready to go home: but said if I knew she was there, I would go thither. Sarah seem'd to speak with pretty good Courage, She would be there. I went and found her there, with Mr. Walley and his wife in the little Room below. At 7 a-clock I mentioned going home; at 8. I put on my Coat, and quickly waited on her home. She found occasion to speak loud to the servant, as if she had a mind to be known. Was Courteous to me; but took occasion to speak pretty earnestly about my keeping a Coach: I said 'twould cost £100. per annum: she said twould cost but £40. . . . Exit. Came away somewhat late.

Oct. 20, 1720. . . . Madam Winthrop not being at Lecture, I went thither first; found her very Serene with her dâter Noyes, Mrs. Dering, and the widow Shipreev sitting at a little Table, she in her arm'd Chair. She drank to me, and I to Mrs.

Noyes. After awhile pray'd the favour to speak with her. She took one of the Candles, and went into the best Room, clos'd the shutters, sat down upon the Couch. She told me Madam Usher had been there, and said the Coach must be set on Wheels, and not by Rusting. She spake somthing of my needing a Wigg. Ask'd me what her Sister said to me. I told her, She said, If her Sister were for it, She would not hinder it. But I told her, she did not say she would be glad to have me for her Brother. Said, I shall keep you in the Cold, and asked her if she would be within to morrow night, for we had had but a running Feat. She said she could not tell whether she should, or no. I took Leave. As were drinking at the Governour's, he said: In England the Ladies minded little more than that they might have Money, and Coaches to ride in. I said, And New-England brooks its Name. At which Mr. Dudley smiled. Govr said they were not quite so bad here.

Oct. 21, 1720. Friday, My Son, the Minister, came to me p.m. by appointment and we pray one for another in the Old Chamber; more especially respecting my Courtship. About 6. a-clock I go to Madam Winthrop's; Sarah told me her Mistress was gon out, but did not tell me whither she went. She presently order'd me a Fire; so I went in, having Dr. Sibb's Bowels with me to read. I read the two first Sermons, still no body came in: at last about 9. a-clock Mr. Jn° Eyre came in; I took the opportunity to say to him as I had done to Mrs. Noyes before, that I hoped my Visiting his Mother would not be disagreeable to him; He answered me with much Respect. When twas after 9. a-clock He of himself said he would go and call her, she was but at one of his Brothers: A while after I heard Madam Winthrop's voice, enquiring somthing about John. After a good while and Clapping the Garden door twice or thrice, she came in. I mentioned something of the lateness; she banter'd me, and said I was later. She receiv'd me Courteously. I ask'd when our proceedings should be made publick: She said They were like to be no more publick than they were already. Offer'd me no Wine that I remember. I rose up at 11 a-clock to come away, saying I would put on my Coat, She offer'd not to help me. I pray'd her that Juno might light me home, she open'd the Shutter, and said twas pretty light abroad, Juno was weary and gon to bed.

So I came hôm by Star-light as well as I could. At my first coming in, I gave Sarah five Shillings. I writ Mr. Eyre his Name in
his book with the date Octob^r 21. 1720. It cost me 8^s. Jehovah
jireh! Madam told me she had visited M. Mico, Wendell, and
Wm Clark of the South [Church].

Oct. 22, 1720. Dâter Cooper visited me before my going out
of Town, staid till about Sun set. I brought her going near as
far as the Orange Tree. Coming back, near Leg's Corner, Little
David Jeffries saw me, and looking upon me very lovingly, ask'd
me if I was going to see his Grandmother? I said, Not to-night.
Gave him a peny, and bid him present my Service to his Grandmother.

Oct. 24, 1720. I went in the Hackny Coach through the
Common, stop'd at Madam Winthrop's (had told her I would
take my departure from thence). Sarah came to the door with
Katee in her Arms: but I did not think to take notice of the
Child. Call'd her Mistress. I told her, being encourag'd by David
Jeffries loving eyes, and sweet Words, I was come to enquire
whether she could find in her heart to leave that House and
Neighbourhood, and go and dwell with me at the Southend; I
think she said softly, Not yet. I told her It did not ly in my Lands
to keep a Coach. If I should, I should be in danger to be brought
to keep company with her Neighbour Brooker, (he was a little
before sent to prison for Debt). Told her I had an Antipathy
against those who would pretend to give themselves; but nothing
of their Estate. I would a proportion of my Estate with my self.
And I suppos'd she would do so. As to a Perriwig, My best and
greatest Friend, I could not possibly have a greater, began to find
me with Hair before I was born, and had continued to do so
ever since; and I could not find in my heart to go to another. She
commended the book I gave her, Dr. Preston, the Church
Marriage; quoted him saying 'twas inconvenient keeping out of
a Fashion commonly used. I said the Time and Tide did circum-
scribe my Visit. She gave me a Dram of Black-Cherry Brandy,
and gave me a lump of the Sugar that was in it. She wish'd me
a good Journy. I pray'd God to keep her, and came away. Had
a very pleasant Journy to Salem.

Oct. 31, 1720. At night I visited Madam Winthrop about
5. p.m. They told me she was gon to Madam Mico's. I went

thither and found she was gon; so return'd to her house, read the Epistles to the Galatians, Ephesians in Mr. Eyre's Latin Bible. After the Clock struck 8. I began to read the 103. Psalm. Mr. Wendell came in from his Warehouse. Ask'd me if I were alone? Spake very kindly to me, offer'd me to call Madam Winthrop. I told him, She would be angry, had been at Mrs. Mico's; he help'd me on with my Coat and I came home: left the Gazett in the Bible, which told Sarah of, bid her present my Service to Mrs. Winthrop, and tell her I had been to wait on her if she had been at home.

Nov. 1, 1720. I was so taken up that I could not go if I would.

Nov. 2, 1720. Midweek, went again, and found Mrs. Alden there, who quickly went out. Gave her about ½ pound of Sugar Almonds, cost 3ˢ per £. Carried them on Monday. She seem'd pleas'd with them, ask'd what they cost. Spake of giving her a Hundred pounds per anum if I dy'd before her. Ask'd her what sum she would give me, if she should dy first? Said I would give her time to Consider of it. She said she heard as if I had given all to my Children by Deeds of Gift. I told her 'twas a mistake, Point-Judith was mine &c. That in England, I own'd, my Father's desire was that it should go to my eldest Son; 'twas 20£ per annum; she thought 'twas forty. I think when I seem'd to excuse pressing this, she seem'd to think twas best to speak of it; a long winter was coming on. Gave me a Glass or two of Canary.

Nov. 4, 1720. Friday, Went again about 7. a-clock; found there Mr. John Walley and his wife: sat discoursing pleasantly. I shew'd them Isaac Moses's [an Indian] Writing. Madam W. serv'd Comfeits to us. After awhile a Table was spread, and Supper was set. I urg'd Mr. Walley to Crave a Blessing; but he put it upon me. About 9. they went away. I ask'd Madam what fashioned Necklace I should present her with, She said, None at all. I ask'd her Whereabout we left off last time; mention'd what I had offer'd to give her; Ask'd her what she would give me; She said she could not Change her Condition: She had said so from the beginning; could not be so far from her Children, the Lecture. Quoted the Apostle Paul affirming that a single Life was better than a Married. I answer'd That was for the present

Distress. Said she had not pleasure in things of that nature as formerly: I said, you are the fitter to make me a Wife. If she hald in that mind, I must go home and bewail my Rashness in making more haste than good Speed. However, considering the Supper, I desired her to be within next Monday night, if we liv'd so long. Assented. She charg'd me with saying, that she must put away Juno, if she came to me: I utterly deny'd it, it never came in my heart; yet she insisted upon it; saying it came in upon discourse about the Indian woman that obtained her Freedom this Court. About 10. I said I would not disturb the good orders of her House, and came away. She not seeming pleas'd with my Coming away. Spake to her about David Jeffries, had not seen him.

Nov. 7, 1720. My Son pray'd in the Old Chamber. Our time had been taken up by Son and Daughter Cooper's Visit; so that I only read the 130th and 143 Psalm. Twas on the Account of my Courtship. I went to Mad. Winthrop; found her rocking her little Katee in the Cradle. I excus'd my Coming so late (near Eight). She set me an arm'd Chair and Cusheon; and so the Cradle was between her arm'd Chair and mine. Gave her the remnant of my Almonds; She did not eat of them as before; but laid them away; I said I came to enquire whether she had alter'd her mind since Friday, or remained of the same mind still. She said, Thereabouts. I told her I loved her, and was so fond as to think that she loved me: She said had a great respect for me. I told her, I had made her an offer, without asking any advice; she had so many to advise with, that twas a hindrance. The Fire was come to one short Brand besides the Block, which Brand was set up in end; at last it fell to pieces, and no Recruit was made: She gave me a Glass of Wine. I think I repeated again that I would go home and bewail my Rashness in making more haste than good Speed. I would endeavour to contain myself, and not go on to sollicit her to do that which she could not Consent to. Took leave of her. As came down the steps she bid me have a Care. Treated me Courteously. Told her she had enter'd the 4th year of her Widowhood. I had given her the News-Letter before; I did not bid her draw off her Glove as sometime I had done. Her Dress was not so clean as somtime it had been. Jehovah jireh!

Nov. 9, 1720. Dine at Bro^r Stoddard's: were so kind as to enquire of me if they should invite M'^{m} Winthrop; I answer'd No. Thank'd my Sister Stoddard for her Courtesie; . . . She sent her servant home with me with a Lantern. Madam Winthrop's Shutters were open as I pass'd by.

John Wise

(1652–1725)

Bibliographical Note. There is no modern edition of Wise's writings. The selection here printed follows the text of A *Vindication of the Government of New England Churches* (Boston, 1772), pp. 21–48; this was the text used as an anti-British, democratic tract. There is no large general study of Wise. The most satisfactory essay is C. L. Rossiter, "John Wise: Colonial Democrat," *New England Quarterly*, XII (1949), 3–32.

from

A VINDICATION
OF THE GOVERNMENT
OF NEW ENGLAND CHURCHES
(1717)

[*On Natural Law and the Government of Men and Churches*]

CHAP. I

The divine establishment in providence of the [New England] churches, in their order is apparently the royal assent of the supream monarch of the churches, to the grave decisions of reason in favour of mans natural state of being, and original freedom. For if we should make a new *survey* of the institution before named under the brightest light of nature, there is no greater example of natural wisdom in any settlement on earth; for the present and future security of human beings in all that is most valuable and grand, than in this. That it seems to me as though wise and provident nature by the dictates of right reason excited by the moving suggestions of humanity; and awed with the just demands of natural liberty, equity, equality, and principles of self-preservation, originally drew up the scheme, and then obtained the royal approbation. And certainly it is agreeable that we attribute it to God whether we receive it nextly from reason or revelation, for that each is equally an emanation of his wisdom, *Prov.* 20. 27. The spirit of man is the candle of the Lord, searching all the inward parts of the belly. There be many larger volumes in this dark recess called the belly to be read by that candle God has lighted up. And I am very well assured the forenamed constitution is a transcript out of some of their pages, John I. 4, 9. *And the life was the light of men, which lighteth every man which cometh into the world.* This admirable effect of Christ's creating power in hanging out so many lights to guide man through a dark world, is as applicable to the light of reason, as to that of revelation. For that the light of reason as a law and rule of right, is an effect of Christ's goodness, care and creating power, as well as of revelation; though revelation is natures law in a fairer and brighter edition. This is granted by the *London* ministers, *p.* 8. *C.* 3. 'That, that which is evident by, and consonant to the true light of nature, or natural reason, is to be accounted, *Jure Divino*, in matters of religion.' But in the further and more distinct management of this plea; I shall,

1. Lay before the reader several principles [of] natural knowledge.

2. Apply or improve them in ecclesiastical affairs.

3. Infer from the premises, a demonstration that these churches, if not properly formed; yet are fairly established in their present order by the law of nature.

CHAP. II

1. I shall disclose several principles of natural knowledge; plainly discovering the law of nature; or the true sentiments of natural reason, with respect to mans being and government. And in this essay I shall peculiarly confine the discourse to two heads, *viz.*

1. Of the natural (in distinction to the civil) and then,
2. Of the civil being of man. And I shall principally take baron *Puffendorff* for my chief guide and spokes-man.

1. I shall consider man in a state of natural being, as a freeborn subject under the crown of heaven, and owing homage to none but God himself. It is certain civil government in general, is a very admirable result of providence, and an incomparable benefit to mankind, yet must needs be acknowledged to be the effect of human free-compacts and not of divine institution; it is the produce of mans reason, of human and rational combinations, and not from any direct orders of infinite wisdom, in any positive law wherein is drawn up this or that scheme of civil government. Government (says the Lord *Warrington*)[1] is necessary—in that no society of men can subsist without it; and that particular form of government is necessary which best suits the temper and inclination of a people. Nothing can be God's ordinance, but what he has particularly declared to be such; there is no particular form of civil government described in God's word, neither does nature prompt it. The government of the *Jews* was changed five times. Government is not formed by nature, as other births or productions; if it were, it would be the same in all countries; because nature keeps the same method, in the same thing, in all climates. If a common-wealth be changed into a monarchy, is it nature that forms, and brings forth the monarch? Or if a royal family be wholly extinct (as in *Noah's* case, being not heir apparent from descent from *Adam*) is it nature that must go to work (with the kings bees, who themselves alone preserve the royal race in that empire)

---

[1] Henry Booth, Earl of Warrington (1652–1694), known for his defense of civil and religious liberty against royal prerogative. His *Works*, principally political speeches and pamphlets, were published in 1694.

to breed a monarch before the people can have a king, or a government sent over them? And thus we must leave kings to resolve which is their best title to their crowns, whether natural right, or the constitution of government settled by human compacts, under the direction and conduct of reason. But to proceed under the head of a state of natural being, I shall more distinctly explain the state of human nature in its original capacity, as man is placed on earth by his maker, and cloathed with many investitures, and immunities which properly belong to man separately considered. As,

1. The prime immunity in mans state, is that he is most properly the subject of the law of nature. He is the favourite animal on earth; in that this part of God's image, *viz.* reason is congenate with his nature, wherein by a law immutable, instampt upon his frame, God has provided a rule for men in all their actions, obliging each one to the performance of that which is right, not only as to justice, but likewise as to all other moral virtues, the which is nothing but the dictate of right reason founded in the soul of man. *Molloy, De Mao, Præf.*[2] That which is to be drawn from mans reason, flowing from the true current of that faculty, when unperverted, may be said to be the law of nature, on which account, the holy scriptures declare it written on mens hearts. For being endowed with a soul, you may know from yourself, how, and what you ought to act, Rom. 2. 14. *These having not a law, are a law to themselves.* So that the meaning is, when we acknowledge the law of nature to be the dictate of right reason, we must mean that the understanding of man is endowed with such a power, as to be able, from the contemplation of human condition to discover a necessity of living agreably with this law: And likewise to find out some principle, by which the precepts of it, may be clearly and solidly demonstrated. The way to discover the law of nature in our own state, is by a narrow watch, and accurate contemplation of our natural condition, and propensions. Others say this is the way to find out the law of nature. *scil.* If a man any ways doubts, whether what

---

[2] A reference to the discussion of natural law in Charles Molloy, *De Jure Maritimo* (1676), a standard legal treatise often reprinted in Wise's lifetime.

he is going to do to another man be agreable to the law of
nature, then let him suppose himself to be in that other mans
room; and by this rule effectually executed. A man must be a
very dull scholar to nature not to make proficiency in the
knowledge of her laws. But more particularly in pursuing our
condition for the discovery of the law of nature, this is very
obvious to view, *viz.*

1. A principal of self love, and self preservation, is very predominant in every mans being.

2. A sociable disposition.

3. An affection or love to mankind in general. And to give
such sentiments the force of a law, we must suppose a God who
takes care of all mankind, and has thus obliged each one, as a
subject of higher principles of being, than meer instincts. For
that all law properly considered, supposes a capable subject, and
a superiour power, and the law of God which is binding, is
published by the dictates of right reason as other ways: Therefore
says *Plutarch, to follow God and obey reason is the same thing.*
But moreover that God has established the law of nature, as the
general rule of government, is further illustrable from the many
sanctions in providence, and from the peace and guilt of conscience in them that either obey, or violate the law of nature.
But moreover, the foundation of the law of nature with relation
to government, may be thus discovered. *scil.* Man is a creature
extreamly desirous of his own preservation; of himself he is
plainly exposed to many wants, unable to secure his own safety,
and maintenance without assistance of his fellows; and he is
also able of returning kindness by the furtherance of mutual
good; but yet man is often found to be malicious; insolent, and
easily provoked, and as powerful in effecting mischief, as he is
ready in designing it. Now that such a creature may be preserved,
it is necessary that he be sociable; that is, that he be capable and
disposed to unite himself to those of his own species, and to
regulate himself towards them, that they may have no fair
reason to do him harm; but rather incline to promote his
interests, and secure his rights and concerns. This then is a
fundamental law of nature, that every man as far as in him lies,
do maintain a sociableness with others, agreable with the main

end and disposition of human nature in general. For this is very apparent, that reason and society render man the most potent of all creatures. And finally, from the principles of sociableness it follows as a fundamental law of nature, that man is not so wedded to his own interest, but that he can make the common good the mark of his aim: And hence he becomes capacitated to enter into a civil state by the law of nature; for without this property in nature, *viz.* Sociableness, which is for cementing of parts, every government would soon moulder and dissolve.

2. The second great immunity of man is an original liberty instampt upon his rational nature. He that intrudes upon this liberty, violates the law of nature. In this discourse I shall wave the consideration of mans moral turpitude, but shall view him physically as a creature which God has made and furnished essentially with many enobling immunities, which render him the most august animal in the world, and still, whatever has happened since his creation, he remains at the upper-end of nature, and as such is a creature of a very noble character. For as to his dominion, the whole frame of the lower part of the universe is devoted to his use, and at his command; and his liberty under the conduct of right reason, is equal with his trust. Which liberty many be briefly considered, internally as to his mind, and externally as to his person.

1. The native liberty of man's nature implies, a faculty of doing or omitting things according to the direction of his judgment. But in a more special meaning, this liberty does not consist in a loose and ungovernable freedom, or in an unbounded license of acting. Such licence is disagreeing with the condition and dignity of man, and would make man of a lower and meaner constitution than bruit creatures; who in all their liberties are kept under a better and more rational government, by their instincts. Therefore as *Plutarch* says, *Those persons only who live in obedience to reason, are worthy to be accounted free: They alone live as they will, who have learnt what they ought to will.* So that the true natural liberty of man, such as really and truely agrees to him, must be understood, as he is guided and restrained by the tyes of reason, and laws of nature; all the rest is brutal, if not worse.

2. Mans external personal, natural liberty, antecedent to all human parts, or alliances must also be considered. And so every man must be conceived to be perfectly in his own power and disposal, and not to be controuled by the authority of any other. And thus every man, must be acknowleded equal to every man, since all subjection and all command are equally banished on both sides; and considering all men thus at liberty, every man, has a prerogative to judge for himself, *viz.* What shall be most for his behoof, happiness and well-being.

3. The third capital immunity belonging to mans nature, is an equality amongst men; which is not to be denied by the law of nature, till man has resigned himself with all his rights for the sake of a civil state; and then his personal liberty and equality is to be cherished, and preserved to the highest degree, as will consist with all just distinctions amongst men of honor, and shall be agreable with the public good. For man has a high valuation of himself, and the passion seems to lay its first foundation (not in pride, but) really in the high and admirable frame and constitution of human nature. The word man, says my author, is thought to carry somewhat of dignity in its sound; and we commonly make use of this as the most proper and prevailing argument against a rude insulter, *viz. I am not a beast or a dog. But am a man as well as yourself.* Since then human nature agrees equally with all persons; and since no one can live a sociable life with another that does not own or respect him as a man; It follows as a command of the law of nature, that every man esteem and treat another as one who is naturally his equal, or who is a man as well as he. There be many popular, or plausible reasons that greatly illustrate this equality, *viz.* that we all derive our being from one stock, the same common father of human race. On this consideration *Bœthius* checks the pride of the insulting nobility.

> *Quid Genus et Proavos Strepitis?*
> *Si Primordia Vestra,*
> *Auteremque Deum Spectas,*
> *Nullus Degener Extat*
> *Nisi vitiis Pejora fovens,*
> *Proprium Deserat Orturn.*

Fondly our first descent we boast;
  If whence at first our breath we draw,
  The common springs of life we view,
The airy Notion soon is lost.
  The almighty made us equal all:
  But he that slavishly complys
  To do the drudgery of vice,
Denyes his high original.

And also that our bodies are composed of matter, frail, brittle, and lyable to be destroyed by thousand accidents; we all owe our existence to the same method of propagation. The noblest mortal in his entrance on the stage of life, is not distinguished by any pomp or of passage from the lowest of mankind; and our life hastens to the same general mark: Death observes no ceremony, but knocks as loud at the barriers of the court, as at the door of the cottage. This equality being admitted, bears a very great force in maintaining peace and friendship amongst men. For that he who would use the assistance of others, in promoting his own advantage, ought as freely to be at their service, when they want his help on the like occasions. *One good turn requires another,* is the common proverb; for otherwise he must need esteem others unequal to himself, who constantly demands their aid, and as constantly denies his own. And whoever is of this insolent temper, cannot but highly displease those about him, and soon give occasion of the breach of the common peace. It was a manly reproof which *Charactacus* gave the *Romans. Num Si vos Omnibus &c.* What! because you desire to be masters of all men, does it follow therefore that all men should desire to be your slaves, for that it is a command of natures law, that no man that has not obtained a particular and special right, shall arrogate to himself a larger share than his fellows, but shall admit others to equal priviledges with himself. So that the principle of equality in a natural state, is peculiarly transgressed by pride, which is when a man without sufficient reason prefers himself to others. And though as *Hensius,* paraphrases upon *Aristotle's* politicks to this purpose. *viz. Nothing is more suitable to nature, then that those who excel in understanding and pru-*

dence, should rule and controul those who are less happy in those advantages, &c. Yes we must note, that there is room for an answer, *scil.* That it would be the greatest absurdity to believe, that nature actually invests the wise with a sovereignity over the weak; or with a right of forcing them against their wills; for that no sovereignity can be established, unless some human deed, or covenant precede: Nor does natural fitness for government make a man presently governor over another; for that as *Ulpian* says, *by a natural right all men are born free;* and nature having set all men upon a level and made them equals, no servitude or subjection can be conceived without inequality; and this cannot be made without usurpation or force in others, or voluntary compliance in those who resign their freedom, and give away their degree of natural being. And thus we come,

2. To consider man in a civil state of being; wherein we shall observe the great difference between a natural, and political state; for in the latter state many great disproportions appear, or at least many obvious distinctions are soon made amongst men; which doctrine is to be laid open under a few heads.

1. Every man considered in a natural state, must be allowed to be free, and at his own dispose; yet to suit mans inclinations to society; and in a peculiar manner to gratify the necessity he is in of public rule and order, he is impelled to enter into a civil community; and divests himself of his natural freedom, and puts himself under government; which amongst other things comprehends the power of life and death over him; together with authority to anjoyn him some things to which he has an utter aversion, and to prohibit him other things, for which he may have as strong an inclination; so that he may be often under this authority, obliged to sacrifice his private, for the public good. So that though man is inclined to society, yet he is driven to a combination by great necessity. For that the true and leading cause of forming governments, and yielding up natural liberty, and throwing mans equality into a common pile to be new cast by the rules of fellowship; was really and truly to guard themselves against the injuries men were lyable to interchangeably; for none so good to man, as man, and yet none a greater enemy. So that,

2. The first human subject and original of civil power is the people. For as they have a power every man over himself in a natural state, so upon a combination they can and do bequeath this power unto others; and settle it according as their united discretion shall determine. For that this is very plain, that when the subject of sovereign power is quite extinct, that power returns to the people again. And when they are free, they may set up what species of government they please; or if they rather incline to it, they may subside into a state of natural being, if it be plainly for the best. In the *Eastern* country of the *Mogul*, we have some resemblance of the case; for upon the death of an absolute monarch, they live so many days without a civil head; but in that *Interregnum*, those who survive the vacancy, are glad to get into a civil state again; and usually they are in a very bloody condition when they return under the covert of a new monarch; this project is to indear the people to a tyranny, from the experience they have so lately had of an anarchy.

3. The formal reason of government is the will of a community, yielded up and surrendered to some other subject, either of one particular person, or more, conveyed in the following manner.

Let us conceive in our mind a multitude of men, all naturally free and equal; going about voluntarily, to erect themselves into a new common-wealth. Now their condition being such, to bring themselves into a politick body, they must needs enter into divers covenants.

1. They must interchangeably each man covenant to joyn in one lasting society, that they may be capable to concert the measures of their safety, by a publick vote.

2. A vote or decree must then nextly pass to set up some particular species of government over them. And if they are joyned in their first compact upon absolute terms to stand to the decision of the first vote concerning the species of government: Then all are bound by the majority to acquiesce in that particular form thereby settled, though their own private opinion, incline them to some other model.

3. After a decree has specified the particular form of government, then there will be need of new covenant, whereby

those on whom sovereignty is conferred, engage to take care of the common peace, and welfare. And the subjects on the other head, to yield them faithful obedience. In which covenant is included that submission and union of wills, by which a state may be conceived to be but one person. So that the most proper definition of a civil state, is this, *viz.* A civil state is a compound moral person. Whose will (united by those covenants before passed) is the will of all; to the end it may use, and apply the strength and riches of private persons towards maintaining the common peace, security, and well-being of all, which may be conceived as tho' the whole state was now become but one man; in which the aforesaid covenants may be supposed under God's providence, to be the divine *Fiat*, pronounced by God, let us make man. And by way of resemblance the aforesaid being may be thus anatomized.

1. The sovereign power is the soul infused, giving life and motion to the whole body.

2. Subordinate officers are the joynts by which the body moves.

3. Wealth and riches are the strength.

4. Equity and laws are the reason.

5. Councellors the memory.

6. *Salus Populi*, or the happiness of the people, is the end of its beings: or main business to be attended and done.

7. Concord amongst the members, and all estates, is the health.

8. Sedition is sickness, and civil war death.

9. The parts of sovereignty may be considered: So,

1. As it prescribes the rule of action: It is rightly termed legislative power.

2. As it determines the controversies of subjects by the standard of those rules. So is it justly termed judiciary power.

3. As it arms the subjects against foreigners, or forbids hostility, so its called the power of peace and war.

4. As it takes in ministers for the discharge of business, so it is called the right of appointing magistrates. So that all great officers and public servants, must needs owe their original to the creating power of sovereignty. So that those whose right it is to create, may dissolve the being of those who are

created, unless they cast them into an immortal frame. And yet must needs be dissoluble if they justly forfeit their being to their creators.

5. The chief end of civil communities, is, that men thus conjoyned, may be secured against the injuries, they are liable to from their own kind. For if every man could secure himself singly; it would be great folly for him, to renounce his natural liberty, in which every man is his own king and protector.

6. The sovereign authority besides, that it inheres in every state as in a common and general subject. So farther according as it resides in some one person, or in a council (consisting of some select persons, or of all the members of a community) as in a proper and particular subject, so it produceth different forms of common-wealths, *viz.* Such as are either simple and regular, or mixt.

1. The forms of a regular state are three only, which forms arise from the proper and particular subject, in which the supream power resides. As,

1. A democracy, which is when the sovereign power is lodged in a council consisting of all the members, an where every member has the privilege of a vote. This form of government, appears in the greatest part of the world to have been the most ancient. For that reason seems to shew it to be most probable, that when men (being originally in a condition of natural freedom and equality) had thoughts of joyning in a civil body, would without question be inclined to administer their common affairs, by their common judgment, and so must necessarily to gratify that inclination established a democracy; neither can it be rationally imagined, that fathers of families being yet free and independent, should in a moment, or little time take off their long delight in governing their own affairs, and devolve all upon some single sovereign commander; for that it seems to have been thought more equitable, that what belonged to all should be managed by all, when all had entered by compact into one community. The original of our government, says *Plato*, (speaking of the *Athenian* commonwealth) was taken from the equality of our race. Other states there are composed of different blood, and of unequal lines, the consequence of which are disproportionable soveraignty,

tyranical or oligarchycal sway; under which men live in such a manner, as to esteem themselves partly lords, and partly slaves to each other. But we and our countrymen, being all born brethren of the same mother, do not look upon ourselves, to stand under so hard a relation, as that of lords and slaves; but the parity of our descent incline us to keep up the like parity of our laws, and to yield the precedency to nothing but to superior virtue and wisdom. And moreover it seems very manifest that most civil communities arose at first from the union of families, that were nearly allyed in race and blood. And though ancient story make frequent mention of kings, yet it appears that most of them were such that had an influence rather in perswading, then in any power of commanding. So *Justin* discribes that kind of government, as the most primitive, which *Aristotle* stiles an heroical kingdom. *viz.* Such as is no ways inconsistent with a democratical state. *De princip. Reru.* 1. *L.* 1. *C.*

A democracy is then erected, when a number of free persons, do assemble together, in order to enter into a covenant for uniting themselves in a body: And such a preparative assembly hath some appearance already of a democracy; it is a democracy in *embrio*, properly in this respect, that every man hath the priviledge freely to deliver his opinion concerning the common affairs. Yet he who dissents from the vote of the majority, is not in the least obliged by what they determine, till by a second covenant, a popular form be actually established; for not before then can we call it a democratical government, *viz.* Till the right of determining all matters relating to the public safety, is actually placed in a general assembly of the whole people; or by their own compact and mutual agreement, determine themselves the proper subject for the exercise of sovereign power. And to compleat this state, and render it capable to exert its power to answer the end of a civil state: These conditions are necessary.

1. That a certain time and place be assigned for assembling.

2. That when the assembly be orderly met, as to time and place, that then the vote of the majority must pass for the vote of the whole body.

3. That magistrates be appointed to exercise the authority

of the whole for the better dispatch of business, of every days occurence; who also may with more mature diligence, search into more important affairs; and if in case any thing happens of greater consequence, may report it to the assembly; and be peculiarly serviceable in putting all public decrees into execution. Because a large body of people is almost useless in respect of the last service, and of many others as to the more particular application and exercise of power. Therefore it is most agreable with the law of nature, that they institute their officers to act in their name, and stead.

2. The second species of regular government, is an aristocracy; and this is said then to be constituted when the people, or assembly united by a first covenant, and having thereby cast themselves into the first rudiments of a state; do then by common decree, devolve the sovereign power, on a council consisting of some select members; and these having accepted of the designation, are then properly invested with sovereign command; and then an aristocracy is formed.

3. The third species of a regular government, is a monarchy which is settled when the sovereign power is conferred on some one worthy person. It differs from the former, because a monarch who is but one person in natural, as well as in moral account, and so is furnished with an immediate power of excercising sovereign command in all instances of government; but the forenamed must needs have particular time and place assigned; but the power and authority is equal in each.

2. Mixt governments, which are various and of diversd kinds (not now to be enumerated) yet possibly the fairest in the world is that which has a regular monarchy; settled upon a noble democracy as its basis. And each part of the government is so adjusted by pacts and laws that renders the whole constitution an *elisium*. It is said of the British empire, that it is such a monarchy, as that by the necessary subordinate concurrence of the lords and commons, in the making and repealing all statutes or acts of parliament; it hath the main advantages of an aristocracy, and of a democracy, and yet free from the disadvantages and evils of either. It is such a monarchy, as by most admirable temperament affords very much to the industry, liberty, and happiness of the subject, and reserves enough for

the majesty and prerogative of any king, who will own his people as subjects, not as slaves. It is a kingdom, that of all the kingdoms of the world, is most like to the kingdom of Jesus Christ, whose yoke is easy, and burden light. Present state of England 1st part 64 *p*. Thus having drawn up this brief scheme concerning man, and the nature of civil government, he is become sole subject of. I shall nextly proceed to make improvements of the premises, to accommodate the main subject under our consideration.

2. I shall now make some improvement of the foregoing principles of civil knowledge, fairly deduced from the law of nature. And I shall peculiarly refer to ecclesiastical affairs, whereby we may in probability discover more clearly the kind, and something of the nature of that government, which Christ has placed in and over his church. The learned debates of men, and divine writ sometimes seems to cast such a grandure on the church and its officers, as tho' they stood in peerage with civil empire. *Rev.* 1. 6, 9. 1, *Pet.* 2. 9. 1 *Cor.* 4. 8. 1 *Cor.* 12. 28. 2 *Cor.* 10. 8. But all such expressions must needs be otherways interpreted. God is the highest cause that acts by council; and it must needs be altogether repugnant, to think he should forecast the state of this world by no better a scheme, than to order two sovereign powers, in the same grand community, which would be like placing two suns in the firmament, which would be to set the universe into a flame: That should such an error happen, one must needs be forthwith extinguished, to bring the frame of nature into a just temper and keep it out of harms way. But to proceed with my purpose I shall go back upon the civil scheme, and inquire after two things: First of rebellion against government in general, and then in special; whether any of the aforesaid species of regular government can be predicable of the church of God on earth.

1. In general concerning rebellion against government for particular subjects to break in upon regular communities duly established, is from the premises to violate the law of nature; and is a high usurpation upon the first grand immunities of mankind. Such rebels in states, and usurpers in churches affront the world, with a presumption that the best of the brotherhood are a company of fools, and that themselves have fairly monop-

olized all the reason of human nature. Yea, they take upon them the boldness to assume a prerogative of trampling under foot the natural original equality and liberty of their fellows; for to push the proprietors of settlements out of possession of their old, and impose new schemes upon them, is vertually to declare them in a state of vassalage, or that they were born so; and therefore will the usurper be so gracious as to insure them they shall not be sold at the next market: They must esteem it a favour, for by this time all the original prerogatives of mans nature are intentionally a victim, smoaking to satiate the usurpers ambition. It is a very tart observation on an *English* monarch, and where is may by proportion be applied to a subject must needs sink very deep, and serve for evidence under this head. It is in the secret history of K. C. 2. and K. J. 2. *p.* 2. says my author, Where the constitution of a nation is such, that the laws of the land are the measures both of the sovereigns commands, and the obedience of the subjects, whereby it is provided; that as the one are not to invade what by concessions and stipulations is granted to the ruler; so the other is not to deprive them of their lawful and determined rights and liberties; then the prince who strives to subvert the fundamental laws of the society, is the traytor and the rebel, and not the people, who endeavour to preserve and defend their own. It's very applicable to particular men in their rebellions or usurpations in church or state.

2. In special I shall now proceed to enquire, whether any of the aforesaid species of regular, unmixt governments can with any good shew of reason be predicable of the church of Christ on earth. If the churches of Christ, as churches, are either the object or subject of a sovereign power intrusted in the hands of men, then most certainly one of the fore-cited schemes of a perfect government will be applicable to it.

Before I pursue the enquiry, it may not be improper to pause, and make some caution here, by distinguishing between that which may have some resemblance of civil power, and the thing itself; and so the power of churches is but a faint resemblance of civil power; it comes in reality nothing near to the thing itself; for the one is truly coercive, the other persuasive; the one is sovereign power, the other is delegated and ministerial: But not to delay, I shall proceed with my enquiry, and therein shall endeavour to humour the several great claimers of government in the church of Christ. And,

1. I shall begin with a monarchy. It's certain, his holiness, either by reasonable pleas, or powerful cheats, has assumed an absolute and universal sovereignty; this fills his cathedral chair, and is adorned with a triple crown, and in defence thereof does protect, The Almighty has made him both key-keeper of heaven and hell, with the adjacent territories of purgatory, and vested in him an absolute sovereignty over the christian world. And his right has so far prevailed, that princes and civil monarchs hold their crowns and donations as his dutiful sons, and loyal subjects; he therefore decks himself with the spoils of the divine attributes, stiling himself, our Lord God, *optimum, maximum et supremum numen in Terris*; a God on earth, a visible deity, and that his power is absolute, and his wisdom infallible. And many of the great potentates of the earth have paid their fealty, as though it was really so. One of them clad in canvas, going bare-foot in the depth of winter, (in obedience to the decree, stinting the penance in proportion to the wickedness of princes) has waited many days for absolution at his pious gates. Another has thrown himself down prostrate a humble penitent before him: He has placed his holy foot on the monarchs profane neck as crushing a vermine, crawling out of the stable of his sovereignty; and others frequently kiss his toes with very profound devotion. These and such like triumphant signals of his sovereign power does he wear. And indeed if he is the universal monarch of the catholic church, princes that are members of it must needs knock under; for that in one world there cannot possibly be two *Most High's*, any more than two *Infinites*. Thus you see the clergy, or gospel ministry of the christian world have so wisely, handled business, and managed the gospel, that they have fairly (as they avouch) found a sovereign power bequeathed in it to the ministry of Christ, and romaging more warily and nicely, at last found a spiritual monarch, very compleatly furnished with the keys of all sorts of power hanging at his girdle; an may we not pronounce the wiser they! seeing the world growing weary of religion, was willing to loll itself down to sleep, and leave them in sole trust with the whole interest of

God's kingdom. But the sad enquiry is, whether this sort of government has not plainly subverted the design of the gospel, and the end for which Christ's government was ordained, *viz.* the moral, spiritual, and eternal happiness of men?

But I have no occasion to pursue this remark with tedious demonstrations: It's very plain, it's written with blood in capital letters, to be read at midnight by the flames of *Smithfield,* and other such like consecrated fires. That the government of this ecclesiastical monarch has instead of sanctifying, absolutely debauched the world, and subverted all good christianity in it. So that without the least shew of any vain presumption we may infer, that God and wise nature were never propitious to the birth of this monster.

An aristocracy which places the supream power in a select company of choice persons. Here I freely acknowledge were the gospel ministry established the subject of this power, *viz.* To will and do, in all church affairs without controul, &c. This government might do to support the church in its most valuable rights, &c. If we could be assured they would make the scripture, and not their private will the rule of their personal and ministerial actions: and indeed upon these terms any species of government, might serve the great design of redemption; but considering how great an interest is embarked, and how frail a bottom we trust, though we should rely upon the best of men, especially if we remember what is in the hearts of good men, (*viz.* much ignorance, abundance of small ends, many times cloked with a high pretence in religion; pride skulking and often breeding revenge upon a small affront; and blown up by a pretended zeal; yet really and truly by nothing more divine than interest, or ill nature) and also considering how very uncertain we are of the real goodness of those we esteem good men; and also how impossible it is to secure the intail of it to successors: and also if we remind how christianity by the foresaid principle has been peel'd, rob'd and spoiled already; it cannot consist with the light of nature to venture again upon such perils, especially if we can find a safer way home. More distinctly.

It is very plain (allowing me to speak emblematically) the primitive constitution of the churches was a democracy, as appears by the foregoing parallel. But after the christian churches were received into the favour of the imperial court, under the dominion of *Constantine* the great; there being many præliminaries which had furnished the ministers with a disposition thereunto, they quickly deprived the fraternities of their rights in the government of the churches, when they were once provided of a plentiful maintenance through the liberality of *Constantine*, that when christianity was so luxuriantly treated, as by his great bounty, and noble settlement, it is said there was a voice heard from heaven, saying, Now is poyson poured into the church. But the subversion of the constitution, is a story too long now to tell. Take therefore part of it, out of a late author well versed in antiquity, which may give some brief image of the whole.

Nun multa secula jus Plebis Illasum Mansit, neque Aliter Evenire Potuit, Quin Illud, vel amittatur, vel saltem diminuatur, &c. De Ordina; Diss. Hystorica. P. 36. 40. 41.

The right of the people did not remain unhurt through many ages; neither could it well be otherways, but that it must be lost, or much diminished. *Zonaras*[3] does confess that heretofore bishops were chosen by the suffrage of the people. But many seditions happening among them; it was decreed that every bishop should hereafter be chosen by the authority of the bishops of every province. The cause seemed to be so very specious, that nothing could be more decent, or more conducive to the safety of the commonwealth.

Yet (says my author) if you do well weigh the business, you must needs acknowledge nothing could have happened more pernicious or destructive to the church of God. For soon after these things came to pass, it is very obvious, that tyranny over the consciences of the faithful; and an intolerable pride every where grew rampant among the guides of the church. Yet there was one thing still very needful to be done; and that was to establish or confirm the power which the metropolitans, and bishops had acquired to themselves. Therefore they fell to it tooth and nail to drive away the fraternity from all interest in

---

[3] John Zonaras, from whom Wise has just quoted and translated, a twelfth-century Byzantine historian.

elections: And alas poor hearts! They began to sleep with both ears; that then was scarce any enemy left to interrupt, or controul the conquerors. This was the manner of the clergy till they had made themselves the subjects of all power and then acted arbitrarily, and did what they pleased in the church of God.

But let the learned, knowing world, consider, what the issue of all this was, *scil.* what a wretched capacity the drowsiness and cowardise of the people; and the usurpation and ambition of the ministry brought the professing world into. If those who were truely godly on both sides had in a few ages lookt down from heaven, and had eyed the following centuries, they might have beheld a world of matter for sorrowful impressions; to think that they themselves had occasioned the ruin of millions, by their remis and passive temper in one sort; and too much humouring, and nourishing pride, and high conceits of themselves and others, in the other; when as if they had stood firm to the government as left settled by the apostles; they had certainly prevented an apostacy that has damncd, and confounded a great part of about thirty generations of men, women, and children. That for my own part I can upon experience, in some measure truly say (to the history of the primitive churches in the loss of their government; and the consequents which followed, when I am impelled to repeat it to myself) as onc *Eneas* said to queen *Dido,*

Infandum Regina Jubes Renovare Dolorem
—— Quis tulia fando
Temperet e Lacrimis! ——

So doleful a contemplation is it to think the world should be destroyed by those men, who by God were ordained to save it!

In a word, an aristocracy is a dangerous constitution in the church of Christ, as it possesses the presbytery of all church power: What has been observed sufficiently evinces it. And not only so but from the nature of the constitution, for it has no more barrier to it, against the ambition, insults, and arbitrary measures of men, then an absolute monarchy. But to abbreviate; it seems most agreable with the light of nature, that if there be any of the regular government settled in the church of God it must needs be,

3. A democracy. This is a form of government, which the light of nature does highly value, and often directs to as most agreable to the just and natural prerogatives of human beings. This was of great account, in the early times of the world. And not only so, but upon the experience of several thousand years, after the world had been tumbled, and tost from one species of government to another, at a great expence of blood and treasure, many of the wise nations of the world have sheltered themselves under it again; or at least have blendished, and balanced their governments with it.

It is certainly a great truth, *scil*. That mans original liberty after it is resigned, (yet under due restrictions) ought to be cherished in all wise governments; or otherwise a man in making himself a subject, he alters himself from a freeman, into a slave, which to do is repugnant to the law of nature. Also the natural equality of men amongst men must be duly favored; in that government was never established by God or nature, to give one man a prerogative to insult over another; therefore in a civil, as well as in a natural state of being, a just equality is to be indulged so far as that every man, is bound to honor every man, which is agreable both with nature and religion, 1. Pet. 2.17. *Honor all men.*—The end of all good government is to cultivate humanity, and promote the happiness of all, and the good of every man in all his rights, his life, liberty, estate, honor, &c. without injury or abuse done to any. Then certainly it cannot easily be thought, that a company of men, that shall enter into a voluntary compact, to hold all power in their own hands, thereby to use and improve their united force, wisdom, riches and strength for the common and particular good of every member, as is the nature of a democracy; I say it cannot be that this sort of constitution, will so readily furnish those in government with an appetite, or disposition to prey upon each other, or imbezle the common stock; as some particular persons may be apt to do when set off, and intrusted with the same power. And moreover this appears very natural, that when the aforesaid government or power, settled in all, when they have elected certain capable persons to minister in their affairs, and the said ministers remain accountable to the assembly; these officers must needs be under the influence of many wise cautions from their own thoughts (as well as under confinement by their commission) in their whole administration: And from thence it must needs follow that they will be more apt, and inclined to steer right for the main point, *viz.* The peculiar good, and benefit of the whole, and every particular member fairly and sincerely. And why may not these stand for very rational pleas in church order?

For certainly if Christ has settled any form of power in his church he has done it for his churches safety, and for the benefit of every member: Then he must needs be presumed to have made choice of that government as should least expose his people to hazard, either from the fraud, or arbitrary measures of particular men. And it is as plain as day light, there is no species of government like a democracy to attain this end. There is but about two steps from an aristocracy, to a monarchy, and from thence but one to a tyranny; an able standing force, and an ill-nature, *Ipso facto,* turns an absolute monarch into a tyrant; this is obvious among the Roman *Cæsars,* and through the world. And all these direful transmutations are easier in church affairs (from the different qualities of things) then in civil states. For what is it that cunning and learned men can't make the world swallow as an article of their creed, if they are once invested with an uncontroulable power, and are to be the standing orators to mankind in matters of faith and obedience? indeed some very wise and learned men are pleased to inveigh, and reproach the notion of a democracy in the church, which makes the *Cetu fidelium* or community of the faithful the first subject of the power of government. This they say tends to *Brownism,* and abhorred anarchy, and then they say they upon such præmises, it must needs follow that every member of the body must be an officer; and then every one must preach and dispence the sacraments, &c.

Reply. Certainly such gentlemen, either designs to pose and baffle their reader with falacy; or they themselves never took up, or understood the true ideas of the several species of government; in that a democracy is as regular a form, and as particular as any other.

For,

1. An absolute or limited monarch can't manage the power or government devolved upon him, without the great officers of the crown, or a large sett of ministers; though possible he may with the quicker dispatch issue out his degrees, yet he must execute all by his ministry. And why may not a democracy be indulged the same liberty? And this will prevent all anarchy or confusion most apparently. But,

2. The bitter pill to swallow in this doctrine of a democracy in the church, is the terrible power of life and death; or the accountableness of particular members to the assembly, and especially those in the ministry; but yet this is agreable with the nature of the constitution, and easily managed without anarchy, or popular confusion also, which would be made very evident, if we should but run the parallel in all points between the democracy of the state and church. But nextly from the premises, I shall

3. Infer, That if these churches are not properly formed, yet are fairly established in their present order by the law of nature. And will they be advised, I would exhort them to try who will be so bold as to dare to disseize them. A monarchy has been tryed in the church with a witness, but it has absolutely failed us. An aristocracy in a deep calm threw the democracy overboard, and took not only the helm in hand, but seized ship and cargo as their right and title; but after some time brought all to shipwreck, and that in a good harbour too.

A democracy was the noble government which beat out in all the bad weather of ten bloody persecutions under the management of antiquity. And this is our constitution, and what can't we be pleased? This constitution is as agreable with the light and laws of nature as any other whatsoever, as has been fairly laid down and fully evinced, and more accommodated to the concerns of religion than any other. Therefore I shall now conclude my demonstration with this brief appeal to the common reason of mankind, *viz.*

How can it consist with the honourable terms man holds upon here on earth; that the best sort of men that we can find in the world; such men are as adorned with a double sett of enobling immunities, the first from nature, the other from grace;

that these men when they enter into charter-party to manage
a trade for heaven, must *ipso facto* be clapt under a government, that is arbitrary and dispotick; yea that carries the plain
symptoms of a tyranny in it, when the light of nature knows of
a better species, and frequently has made use of it? It wants no
farther demonstration, for it's most apparent, that nature is so
much mistress of herself, that man in a natural state of being,
is under God the first subject of all power, and therefore can
make his own choice, and by deliberate compacts settles his
own conditions for the government of himself in a civil state
of being: And when a government so settled shall throw itself
from its foundations, or the subjects of sovereign power shall
subvert or confound the constitution, they then degrade themselves; and so all power returns again to the people, who are the
first owners. And what! Is man become so unfortunate, de-
graded and debased, as to be without all power in settling a
government over himself, relating to the matters of his eternal
well-being? Or when he comes back to a fathers house, must
he fall into the capacity of a meer passive being, and be put
under such tutors, as can easily turn tyrants over him, and no
relief left for him in his own hands; this is certainly most repugnant to the light of nature, and very disagreable with the liberty
and free genius of a gospel state. Nay, in a word, it the government of the churches be settled by God, either in the hands
of a church monarch, or aristocracy, and the people are no ways
the subject of church-power: Nay, if they are not under Christ,
the fountain of power; then the reformation so called, is but a
meer cheat, a schism, and notorious rebellion; neither is there
room left for the least paliation, or shadow of excuse, for the
reformers in renouncing their obedience to their publick governors. And the Martyrologies which pretend to immortalize the
fame of eminent heroes, must be changed into chronicles, handling along an account of the just and deserved fate of a crew
of rebels against God and government; for what business had
such a company of illeterate crack brain'd fellows to meddle
with their rulers, or examine into their administrations? For
if they have no right of power in government, they stand absolutely bound to yield a passive obedience and non-resistance;
and if they are so hardy and daring as to oppose their lawful

rulers, the sharpest penality in this world, is too easy for them; the inquisition is but dallying and playing with them; hell is their desert. But how it comes about that a state of grace, when in want of a suitable government, it become such a vassil, and wise and cunning nature is by her creator intrusted, and adorned with more enobling prerogatives, I must leave, and resign unto those learned men to solve, who plead for an aristocracy in the churches of Christ.

But to wind up the whole discourse in a few words, I acknowledge many objections may be here made, and several questions of moment might here fall under debate; but having obtained what I have principally sought for, in traversing the paths of nature, in the three following particulars; therefore with them, and with one objection answered; and also with some brief improvement of the grand hypothesis in this demonstration, I shall finish the argument.

1. Three particulars; or so many golden maxims, securing the honor of congregational churches.

Particular 1. That the people or fraternity under the gospel, are the first subject of power; or else religion sinks the dignity of human nature into a baser capacity with relation to ecclesiasitical, then it is in, in a natural state of being with relation to civil government.

Particular 2. That a democracy in church or state, is a very honorable and regular government according to the dictates of right reason. And therefore,

Particular 3. That these churches of *New-England*, in their ancient constitution of church order; it being a democracy, are manifestly justified and defended by the law and light of nature.

2. The objection. The plea from the law of nature for a democracy in the church, is as forceable for any other species of government; because nature is furnished with such a variety of schemes as has been pleaded to: And why may not the wise christian nations take which likes them best?

Answ. We must distinguish between man left solely to the direction of the law of nature, and as the subject of revelation, wherein divine wisdom may interpose; and determine on some particular species, without hurting or crossing the law of nature. Therefore,

1. I readily grant and acknowledge, a christian people may settle what species of government they please, when they are solely left to determine by the law of nature, what government in the church they will have. But then we must remember, that by the argument or concession, the power is originally in the people; and then our own case is secure and safe enough; both on the account of the reversion of power, and especially, for that the people the first subjects of power, have been pleased to settle a democracy for their government, in the churches of this country. And if after the peaceable possession of about an hundred years, any persons can persuade them to alter their government into any other species, this will be less worthy of blame, than craftily, or unfairly to force it out of their hands.

2. It's granted, that according to the light of nature, there be various regular models of government; but if divine wisdom is pleased to interpose and over-rule natures agitations, and cast the scales for this or that particular form, nature will be but fair manuered to submit to its author and rector. So that if we find that God has disclosed his mind by revelation, that his churches be the subjects of a democracy, than all stand obliged to comply under a double bond. And so we come under a proper crisis to enquire in the next place for scripture-evidence in the justification of these churches.

But before I proceed to it, I shall

3. Make some brief improvement of the main *Hypothesis* in the demonstration; that is to say, if the government of the gospel churches, be a democracy, these consequences must necessarily follow, *scil.*

1. *Cons.* That the right of convoking councils ecclesiastical, is in the churches.

2. *Cons.* That such a council has only consultative not a juridical power in it. A juridical power comitted to such a representative body is both needless, and also dangerous to the distinct and perfect states they derive from. Compleat states settled upon a body of immutiable and imperial laws as its basis, may want council; but to create a new subject of juridical power, is some way to endanger the being of the creators.

3. *Cons.* That all the members of an ecclesiastical council, deriving from a democracy are subjects of equal power. What-

ever the power is, the several delegates must from the nature of the government they derive from, be equal sharers in it. Democratical states, in their representative body can make but one house, because they have but one subject of supream power in their nature, and therefore their delegates, let them be who or what they may be, are under equal trust; so that none can justly claim superiority over their fellows, or pretend to a higher power in their suffrage. Indeed in such kingdoms, where the sovereign power is distributed and settled in divers subjects, that the ballance of power may be more even, for the safety of the whole, and of all parts under all acts of sovereign power: From such a settlement of power, there arises several distinct states in the same government, which when convened as one subject of sovereign power, they make different houses in their grand sessions; and so one house or state can negative another. But in every distinct house of these states, the members are equal in their vote; the most ayes makes the affirmative vote, and most no's the negative: They don't weigh the intellectual furniture, or other distinguishing qualifications of the several voters in the scales of the golden rule of fellowship; they only add up the ayes, and the no's, and so determine the suffrage of the house.

Cotton Mather

(1663–1728)

Bibliographical Note. There is no collected edition of Mather's 444 known printed works; these are listed masterfully, however, in T. J. Holmes, *Cotton Mather: A Bibliography of His Works,* 3 vols. (Cambridge, 1940). The only scholarly edition of Mather's writings is Kenneth Murdock, ed. *Selections from Cotton Mather* (New York, 1926). The selections here printed follow Murdock's text, pp. 1–36, 40–51, 58–84, 285–302, 349–362.* The best biographies of Mather are Barrett Wendell, *Cotton Mather: The Puritan Priest* (1891) and Kenneth Murdock's sketch in the *Dictionary of American Biography.* Murdock's introduction to his *Selections* is the most adequate general study of Mather as a man of letters. On the form and function of the *Magnalia,* see Sacvan Bercovitch, "New England Epic: Cotton Mather's *Magnalia* . . . ," *ELH,* XXXIII (1968), 337–350.

---

* Notes by Kenneth Murdock, Copyright 1926, and used with his permission.

from

THE MAGNALIA CHRISTI AMERICANA[1]

(1702)

A GENERAL INTRODUCTION

Ἐρῶ δὲ τοῦτο, τῆς τῶν ἐντευξαμένων ᾽ωφελείας ἕνεκα.

Dicam hoc propter utilitatem eorum qui Lecturi sunt hoc opus.
Theodorit.[2]

§ 1. I write the *Wonders* of the CHRISTIAN RELIGION, flying from the Depravations of *Europe*, to the *American Strand:* And, assisted by the Holy Author of that *Religion*, I do, with all Conscience of *Truth*, required therein by Him, who is the *Truth* it self, Report the *Wonderful Displays* of His Infinite Power, Wisdom, Goodness, and Faithfulness, wherewith His Divine Providence hath *Irradiated* an *Indian Wilderness.*

I Relate the *Considerable Matters*, that produced and attended the First Settlement of COLONIES, which have been Renowned for the Degree of REFORMATION, Professed and Attained by *Evangelical Churches*, erected in those *Ends of the Earth:* And a *Field* being thus prepared, I proceed unto a Relation of the *Considerable Matters* which have been acted thereupon.

I first introduce the *Actors*, that have, in a more exemplary manner served those *Colonies;* and give *Remarkable Occurrences*, in the exemplary LIVES of many *Magistrates*, and of more *Ministers*, who so *Lived*, as to leave unto Posterity, *Examples* worthy of *Everlasting Remembrance.*

I add hereunto, the *Notables* of the only *Protestant Uni-*

---

[1] The American Annals of Christ, i.e., American Ecclesiastical History.
[2] "I say this for the benefit of those who are readers of this book." Theodoret was one of the early fathers of the Church, c. 393–457.—*Murdock.*

versity, that ever shone in that Hemisphere of the *New World*; with particular Instances of *Criolians*,[3] in our *Biography*, provoking the *whole World*, with vertuous Objects of Emulation.

I introduce then, the *Actions* of a more Eminent Importance, that have signalized those *Colonies*; Whether the *Establishments*, directed by their *Synods*; with a Rich Variety of *Synodical* and *Ecclessiastical* Determinations; or, the *Disturbances*, with which they have been from all sorts of *Temptations* and *Enemies* Tempestuated; and the *Methods* by which they have still weathered out each *Horrible Tempest*.

And into the midst of these *Actions*, I interpose an entire *Book*, wherein there is, with all possible Veracity, a *Collection* made, of *Memorable Occurrences*, and amazing *Judgments* and *Mercies*, befalling many *particular Persons* among the People of *New-England*.

Let my Readers expect all that I have promised them, in this *Bill of Fare*; and it may be they will find themselves entertained with yet many other Passages, above and beyond their Expectation, deserving likewise a room in *History*: In all which, there will be nothing, but the *Author's* too mean way of preparing so great Entertainments, to Reproach the Invitation.

§ 2. The Reader will doubtless desire to know, what it was that

> ———tot *Volvere casus*
> *Insignes Pietate Viros, tot adire Labores,*
> *Impulerit.*[4]

And our *History* shall, on many fit Occasions which will be therein offered, endeavour, with all *Historical* Fidelity and Simplicity, and with as little Offence as may be, to satisfy him. The Sum of the Matter is, That from the very Beginning of the

---

[3] Criolians or Creolians, an obsolete word for persons born or naturalized in America but of European race. . . . —*Murdock*.
[4] "Drove men eminent in piety to endure so many calamities and to undertake so many hardships." The quotation is slightly altered from the *Æneid*, I, 9–11.—*Murdock*.

REFORMATION in the *English Nation*, there hath always been a Generation of *Godly Men*, desirous to pursue the *Reformation of Religion, according to the word of God, and the Example of the best Reformed Churches*; and answering the Character of *Good Men*, given by *Josephus*, in his Paraphrase on the words of *Samuel* to *Saul*, μηδὲν ἄλλο πραχθήσεσθαι καλῶς ὑφ᾽ ἑαυτῶν νομίζοντες ἢ ὅτι ἂν ποιήσωσι τοῦ θεοῦ κεκελευκότος. *They think they do nothing Right in the Service of God, but what they do according to the Command of God.* And there hath been another Generation of Men, who have still employed the *Power* which they have generally still had in their Hands, not only to stop the Progress of the Desired *Reformation*, but also, with Innumerable Vexations, to Persecute those that most Heartily wished well unto it. There were many of the *Reformers*, who joyned with the Reverend *JOHN FOX*, in the *Complaints* which he then entred in his *Martyrology*, about the *Baits of Popery* yet left in the Church; and in his *Wishes, God take them away, or ease us from them, for God knows, they be the Cause of much Blindness and Strife amongst Men!* They Zealously decried the *Policy* of complying always with the *Ignorance* and *Vanity* of the *People*; and cried out earnestly for *Purer Administrations* in the House of God, and more *Conformity* to the *Law of Christ*, and *Primitive Christianity*: While others would not hear of going any further than the *First Essay of Reformation.* 'Tis very certain, that the *First Reformers* never intended, that what *They* did, should be the *Absolute Boundary of Reformation*, so that it should be a Sin to proceed any further; as, by their own going beyond *Wicklift*, and *Changing* and *Growing* in their own *Models* also, and the Confessions of *Cranmer*, with the *Scripta Anglicana* of *Bucer*, and a thousand other things, was abundantly demonstrated. But after a Fruitless Expectation, wherein the truest Friends of the *Reformation* long waited, for to have that which *Heylin* himself [5] owns to have been the Design of the *First Reformers*, followed as it should have been, a Party very unjustly arrogating to themselves, the Venerable Name of, *The Church of* England, by

---

[5] Peter Heylyn, 1600–1662, an Anglican divine and historian, defended Bishop Laud, and wrote often against the Puritans. . . . —Murdock.

Numberless Oppressions, grievously *Smote those their Fellow-Servants*. Then 'twas that, as our Great OWEN hath expressed it,[6] *Multitudes of Pious, Peaceable Protestants, were driven, by their Severities, to leave their Native Country, and seek a Refuge for their Lives and Liberties, with Freedom, for the Worship of God, in a Wilderness, in the Ends of the Earth.*

§ 3. It is the History of these PROTESTANTS, that is here attempted: PROTESTANTS that highly honoured and affected *The Church of* ENGLAND, and humbly Petition to be a *Part* of it: But by the Mistake of a few powerful *Brethren*, driven to seek a place for the Exercise of the *Protestant Religion*, according to the Light of their Consciences, in the Desarts of *America*. And in this Attempt I have proposed, not only to preserve and secure the Interest of *Religion*, in the Churches of that little Country NEW-ENGLAND, so far as the Lord Jesus Christ may please to Bless it for that End, but also to offer unto the Churches of the *Reformation*, abroad in the World, some small *Memorials*, that may be serviceable unto the Designs of *Reformation*, whereto, I believe, they are quickly to be awakened. I am far from any such Boast, concerning these Churches, *That they have Need of Nothing*, I wish their *Works* were more *perfect before God*. Indeed, that which Austin called *The Perfection of Christians*, is like to be, until the Term for the *Antichristian Apostasie* be expired, *The Perfection of Churches* too; *Ut Agnoscant se nunquam esse perfectas*.[7] Nevertheless, I perswade my selfe, that *so far as they have attained*, they have given *Great Examples* of the *Methods* and *Measures*, wherein an *Evangelical Reformation* is to be prosecuted, and of the *Qualifications* requisite in the Instruments that are to prosecute it, and of the *Difficulties* which may be most likely to obstruct it, and the most likely *Directions* and *Remedies* for those Obstructions. It may be, 'tis not possible for me to do a greater Service unto the Churches on the *Best*

---

[6] John Owen, 1616–1683, usually called one of the three greatest English Puritans. . . . —*Murdock.*
[7] "That they may acknowledge themselves to be by no means perfect."— *Murdock.*

Island of the Universe, than to give a distinct Relation of those *Great Examples* which have been occurring among Churches of *Exiles*, that were driven out of that *Island*, into an horrible *Wilderness*, meerly for their being Well-willers unto the *Reformation*. When that Blessed Martyr *Constantine* was carried, with other Martyrs, in a *Dung-Cart*, unto the place of Execution, he pleasantly said, *Well, yet we are a precious Odour to God in Christ*. Tho' the *Reformed Churches* in the *American Regions*, have, by very Injurious Representations of their Brethren (all which they desire to Forget and Forgive!) been many times thrown into a *Dung-Cart*; yet, as they have been a *precious Odour to God in Christ*, so, I hope, they will be a *precious Odour* unto *His People*; and not only *Precious*, but *Useful* also, when the *History* · of them shall come to be considered. A *Reformation of the Church* is coming on, and I cannot but thereupon say, with the dying *Cyrus* to his Children in *Xenophon*, Ἐκ τῶν προγεγεννημένων μανθάνετε αὐτὴ γὰρ ἀρίστη διδασκαλία. *Learn from the things that have been done already, for this is the best way of Learning*. The Reader hath here an Account of *The Things that have been done already*. *Bernard* upon that Clause in the *Canticles*, [*O thou fairest among Women*] has this ingenious Gloss, *Pulchram, non omnimode quidem, sed pulchram inter mulieres eam docet, videlicet cum Distinctione, quatenus ex hoc amplius reprimatur, & sciat quid desit sibi.*[8] Thus I do not say, That the Churches of *New-England* are the most *Regular* that can be; yet I do say, and am sure, That they are very like unto those that were in the *First Ages* of Christianity. And if I assert, That in the *Reformation* of the Church, the State of it in those *First Ages*, is to be not a little considered, the Great *Peter Ramus*,[9] among others, has emboldened me. For when the Cardinal of *Lorrain*, the *Mæcenas* of that Great Man, was offended at him, for turning *Protestant*, he replied, *Inter Opes illas, quibus me ditasti, has etiam in æternum re-*

---

[8] "He teaches that she is fair, not in a universal sense, but fair among women, plainly with a distinction, to which extent his praise is qualified, and she may know what is lacking to her."—*Murdock.*

[9] This opponent of Aristotelianism, an educational reformer, who lived 1515–1572, was much read by the Puritans. . . . —*Murdock.*

cordabor, quod Beneficio, Poessiacæ Responsionis tuæ didici, de Quindecim a Christo sæculis, primum vere esse aureum, Reliqua, quo longius abscederent esse nequiora, atque deteriora: Tum igitur cum fieret optio, Aureum sæculum delegi.[10] In short, The *First Age* was the *Golden Age*: To return unto *That*, will make a Man a *Protestant*, and I may add, a *Puritan*. 'Tis possible, That our Lord Jesus Christ carried some Thousands of *Reformers* into the Retirements of an *American Desart*, on purpose, that, with an opportunity granted unto many of his Faithful Servants, to enjoy the precious *Liberty* of their *Ministry*, tho' in the midst of many *Temptations* all their days, He might there, *To* them first, and then *By* them, give a *Specimen* of many Good Things, which He would have His Churches elsewhere aspire and arise unto: And *This* being done, He knows whether there be not *All done*, that *New-England* was planted for; and whether the Plantation may not, soon after this, *Come to Nothing*. Upon that Expression in the Sacred Scripture, *Cast the unprofitable Servant into Outer Darkness*, it hath been imagined by some, That the *Regiones Exteræ* of America, are the *Tenebræ Exteriores*, which the *Unprofitable* are there condemned unto. No doubt, the Authors of those Ecclesiastical Impositions and Severities, which drove the English Christians into the *Dark Regions* of America, esteemed those *Christians* to be a very *unprofitable* sort of Creatures. But behold, ye *European* Churches, There are *Golden Candlesticks* [more than *twice Seven times Seven!*] in the midst of this *Outer Darkness;* Unto the *upright* Children of *Abraham*, here hath arisen *Light in Darkness*. And let us humbly speak it, it shall be *Profitable* for you to consider the *Light*, which from the midst of this *Outer Darkness*, is now to be Darted over unto the other side of the *Atlantick Ocean*. But we must therewithal ask your Prayers, that these *Golden Candlesticks* may not *quickly* be *Removed out of their place!*

---

[10] "Among those riches, with which you enriched me, this I was mindful of always, which I learned from your reply at Poissy—that of the fifteen centuries since Christ, the first is truly golden. The rest, the farther they are removed from the first, are the more worthless and degenerate. Therefore when choice was to be made, I chose the golden age."—*Murdock*.

§ 4. But whether *New-England* may *Live* any where else or no, it must *Live* in our *History!*

HISTORY, in general, hath had so many and mighty Commendations from the Pens of those Numberless Authors, who, from *Herodotus* to *Howel*,[11] have been the professed Writers of it, that a tenth part of them Transcribed, would be a Furniture for a *Polyanthea in Folio*.[12] We, that have neither liberty, nor occasion, to quote those Commendations of *History*, will content our selves with the Opinion of one who was not much of a *profess'd Historian*, expressed in that passage, whereto all Mankind subscribe, *Historia est Testis temporum, Nuntia vetustatis, Lux veritatis, vita memoriæ, magistra vitæ*.[13] But of all *History* it must be confessed, that the *Palm* is to be given unto *Church History*; wherein the *Dignity*, the *Suavity*, and the *Utility* of the *Subject* is transcendent. I observe, that for the Description of the *whole World* in the Book of *Genesis*, that *First-born of all Historians*, the great *Moses*, employes but *one* or *two* Chapters, whereas he implies,[14] it may be *seven times* as many Chapters, in describing that one little *Pavilion*, *The Tabernacle*. And when I am thinking, what may be the Reason of this *Difference*, methinks it intimates unto us, That the *Church* wherein the Service of God is performed, is much more Precious than the *World*, which was indeed created for the Sake and Use of the *Church*. 'Tis very certain, that the greatest Entertainments must needs occur in the History of the *People*, whom the *Son* of God hath *Redeemed* and *Purified* unto himself, as a *Peculiar People*, and whom the *Spirit* of God, by *Supernatural Operations* upon their Minds, does cause to live like *Strangers* in *this World*, conforming themselves unto the *Truths* and *Rules* of his Holy Word, in Expectation of a *Kingdom*, whereto they shall be in another and a better *World*

---

[11] William Howell, 1638–1680, author of *An Institution of General History*, 1661. . . . —*Murdock*.
[12] *I.e.*, a large collection of select quotations, an anthology.—*Murdock*.
[13] "History is the witness of periods of time, the messenger of antiquity, the light of truth, the life of memory, the instructress of life." Cotton Mather here quotes Cicero (*De Oratore*, II, 9) but fails to preserve the original order. . . . —*Murdock*.
[14] Employes?—*Murdock*.

advanced. Such a *People* our Lord Jesus Christ hath procured
and preserved in all Ages *visible;* and the Dispensations of his
wonderous Providence towards this People (for, *O Lord, thou
do'st lift them up, and cast them down!*) their Calamities, their
Deliverances, the Dispositions which they have still discovered,
and the considerable *Persons* and *Actions* found among them,
cannot but afford Matters of *Admiration* and *Admonition,*
above what any other Story can pretend unto: 'Tis nothing but
Atheism in the Hearts of Men, that can perswade them otherwise. Let any Person of good Sense peruse the History of
Herodotus, which, like a River taking Rise, where the *Sacred
Records* of the *Old Testament* leave off, runs along smoothly
and sweetly, with Relations that sometimes perhaps want an
Apology, down until the *Grecians* drive the *Persians* before
them. Let him then peruse *Thucydides,* who from *Acting* be-
took himself to *Writing,* and carries the ancient State of the
Grecians, down to the twenty first Year of the *Peloponnesian
Wars* in a manner, which *Casaubon* judges to be *Mirandum
potius quam imitandum.*[15] Let him next Revolve *Xenophon,*
that *Bee* of *Athens,* who continues a Narrative of the *Greek
Affairs,* from the *Peloponnesian Wars,* to the Battle of *Man-
tinea,* and gives us a *Cyrus* into the bargain, at such a rate, that
Lipsius reckons the Character of a *Suavi, Fidus & Circumspec-
tus Scriptor,*[16] to belong unto him. Let him from hence proceed
unto *Diodorus Siculus,* who, besides a rich Treasure of *Egyptian,
Assyrian, Lybian* and *Grecian,* and other *Antiquities,* in a
Phrase, which according to *Photius's* Judgment, is 'ἱστορία
μάλιστα πρεπούσῃ, *of all most becoming an Historian,*[17] carries
on the Thread begun by his Predecessors, until the End of the
Hundred and nineteenth *Olympiad;* and where he is defective,
let it be supplied from *Arianus,* from *Justin,* and from *Curtius,*
who in the relish of *Colerus* is, *Quovis melle dulcior.*[18] Let him

---

[15] "To be admired rather than imitated."—*Murdock.*
[16] "An agreeable, faithful and careful writer." Justus Lipsius, 1547–1606,
was a learned critic, and editor of classical texts.—*Murdock.*
[17] Photius, patriarch of Constantinople in the second half of the ninth
century.—*Murdock.*
[18] "More sweet than honey." Colerus is probably Johann Coler, a German
theological writer of the sixteenth century.—*Murdock.*

hereupon consult *Polybius,* and acquaint himself with the Birth and Growth of the *Roman Empire,* as far as 'tis described, in *Five* of the *Forty* Books composed by an Author, who with a Learned *Professor of History* is, *Prudens Scriptor, si quis alius.*[19] Let him now run over the Table of the *Roman* Affairs, compendiously given by *Lucius Florus,* and then let him consider the Transactions of above three hundred Years reported by *Dionysius Halicarnassæus,* who, if the Censure of *Bodin* may be taken, *Græcos omnes & Latinos superasse videatur.*[20] Let him from hence pass to *Livy,* of whom the famous Critick says, *Hoc solum ingenium (de Historicis Loquor) populus Romanus par Imperio suo habuit,*[21] and supply those of his *Decads* that are lost, from the best Fragments of Antiquity, in others (and especially *Dion* and *Salust*) that lead us on still further in our way. Let him then proceed unto the Writers of the *Cesarean* times, and first revolve *Suetonius,* then *Tacitus,* then *Herodian,* then a whole Army more of *Historians,* which now crowd into our *Library;* and unto all the rest, let him not fail of adding the Incomparable *Plutarch,* whose Books they say, *Theodore Beza* preferred above any in the World, next unto the Inspired Oracles of the *Bible:* But if the Number be still too little to satisfie an *Historical Appetite,* let him add *Polyhistor* unto the number, and all the *Chronicles* of the following Ages. After all, he must sensibly acknowldge, that the two short Books of *Ecclesiastical History,* written by the Evangelist *Luke,* hath given us more *glorious Entertainments,* than all these voluminous Historians if they were put all together. The *Atchievements* of one *Paul* particularly, which that Evangelist hath *Emblazon'd,* have more *True Glory* in them, than all the Acts of those Execrable *Plunderers* and *Murderers,* and irresistible *Banditti* of the World, which have ben dignified with the Name of *Conquerors. Tacitus* counted *Ingentia bella, Expugnationes urbium, fusos captosque Reges,*[22] the Ravages of *War,* and the

---

[19] "A discreet writer, if there ever was one."—*Murdock.*
[20] "Seems to have surpassed all the Greeks and Latins."—*Murdock.*
[21] "As for historians, the Romans had this one genius worthy of their empire."—*Murdock.*
[22] "Vast wars, captures of cities, kings captured or in flight."—*Murdock.*

glorious *Violences*, wherof great Warriors make a wretched Ostentation, to be the *Noblest Matter* for an *Historian*. But there is a *Nobler*, I humbly conceive, in the planting and forming of *Evangelical Churches*, and the *Temptations*, the *Corruptions*, the *Afflictions*, which assault them, and their *Salvations* from those Assaults, and the Exemplary *Lives* of those that Heaven employs to be Patterns of *Holiness* and *Usefulness* upon Earth: And unto such it is, that I now invite my Readers; Things, in comparison whereof, the Subjects of many other Histories, are of as little weight, as the Questions about Z, the last Letter of our Alphabet, and whether H is to be pronounced with an Aspiration, where about whole Volumes have been written, and of no more Account, than the Composure of *Didymus*.[23] But for the *manner* of my treating this *Matter*, I must now give some account unto him.

§ 5. *Reader!* I have done the part of an *Impartial Historian*, albeit not without all occasion perhaps, for the Rule which a worthy Writer, in his *Historica*, gives to every Reader, *Historici Legantur cum Moderatione & venia, & cogitetur fieri non posse ut in omnibus circumstantiis sint Lyncei.*[24] *Polybius* complains of those *Historians*, who always made either the *Carthagenians* brave, and the *Romans* base, or è *contra*, in all their Actions, as their Affection for their own *Party* led them. I have endeavoured, with all *good Conscience*, to decline this writing meerly for a *Party*, or doing like the Dealer in History, whom *Lucian* derides, for always calling the Captain of his own Party an *Achilles*, but of the adverse Party a *Thersites:* Nor have I added unto the just Provocations for the Complaint made by the Baron *Maurier*,[25] That the *greatest part of Histories* are but so many *Panegyricks* composed by *Interested Hands*, which *elevate Iniquity to the Heavens, like Paterculus*, and like *Machiavel*, who propose *Tiberius Cesar*, and *Cesar Borgia*, as Examples fit

[23] Alexandrian grammarian of the time of Cicero. . . . —*Murdock*.
[24] "Historians are to be read with moderation and indulgence, and it is to be remembered that they cannot in everything be as keen-sighted as Lynceus."—*Murdock*.
[25] Probably Louis Aubery, Seigneur du Maury, d. 1687, writer of several historical works.—*Murdock*.

for *Imitation,* whereas *True History* would have Exhibited them as Horrid *Monsters* as very *Devils*. 'Tis true, I am not of the Opinion, that one cannot merit the Name of an *Impartial Historian,* except he write bare *Matters of Fact,* without all *Reflection;* for I can tell where to find this given as the Definition of *History, Historia est rerum gestarum, cum laude aut vituperatione, Narratio.*[26] And if I am not altogether a *Tacitus,* when *Vertues* or *Vices* occur to be matters of *Reflection,* as well as of *Relation,* I will, for my Vindication, appeal to *Tacitus* himself, whom *Lipsius* calls one of the *Prudentest* (tho' *Tertullian,* long before, counts him the *Lyingest*) of them who have Inriched the World with *History:* He says, *Præcipuum munus Annalium reor, ne virtutes sileantur, utque pravis Dictis, Factisque ex posteritate & Infamia metus sit.*[27] I have not *Commended* any Person, but when I have really judg'd, not only *That* he *Deserved* it, but also that it would be a Benefit unto Posterity to know, Wherein he deserved it: And my Judgment of *Desert,* hath not been *Biassed,* by Persons being of my own particular Judgment in matters of *Disputation,* among the Churches of God. I have been as willing to wear the Name of *Simplicius Verinus,*[28] throughout my whole undertaking, as he that, before me, hath assumed it: Nor am I like Pope *Zachary,* impatient so much as to hear of any *Antipodes.*[29] The Spirit of a *Schusselbergius,*[30] who falls foul with Fury and Reproach on all who differ from him; The Spirit of an *Heylin,* who seems to count no Obloquy too hard for a *Reformer;* and the Spirit of those (*Folio-writers* there are, some of them, in the English

---

[26] "History is the story of events, with praise or blame."—*Murdock.*

[27] "I regard it as history's highest function not to let virtues be uncelebrated, and to hold up as a terror the censure of posterity for bad words and deeds." (Tacitus, *Annals,* iii, 65.)—*Murdock.*

[28] Simplicius Verinus was the name assumed at times by Claude Saumaise (Salmasius), 1588–1653, a French classical scholar, famous for his controversy with Milton.—*Murdock.*

[29] Pope Zacharias, bishop of Rome from 741 to 752, directed that there be expelled from the church one Virgilius who held that there was another world below the earth.—*Murdock.*

[30] Konrad Schlüsselburg, 1543–1619, Lutheran writer and controversialist.—*Murdock.*

Nation!) whom a Noble Historian Stigmatizes, as, *Those Hot-headed, Passionate Bigots, from whom, 'tis enough, if you be of a Religion contrary unto theirs, to be defamed, condemned and pursued with a thousand Calumnies.* I thank Heaven I Hate it with all my Heart. But how can the *Lives* of the *Commendable* be written without *Commending* them? Or, is that Law of *History* given in one of the eminentest pieces of *Antiquity* we now have in our hands, wholly antiquated, *Maxime proprium est Historiæ, Laudem rerum egregie gestarum persequi?* [31] Nor have I, on the other side, forbore to mention many *Censurable* things, even in the Best of my Friends, when the things, in my opinion, were *not Good*; or so bore away for *Placentia*, in the course of our Story, as to pass by *Verona*; but been mindful of the Direction which *Polybius* gives to the Historian, *It becomes him that writes an History, sometimes to extol Enemies in his Praises, when their praise-worthy Actions bespeak it, and at the same time to reprove the best Friends, when their Deeds appear worthy of a reproof; in-as much as History is good for nothing, if Truth (which is the very Eye of the Animal) be not in it.* Indeed I have thought it my duty upon all accounts, (and if it have proceeded unto the degree of a *Fault*, there is, it may be, something in my *Temper* and *Nature*, that has betray'd me therein) to be more sparing and easie, in thus mentioning of *Censurable* things, than in my other *Liberty:* A writer of *Church-History*, should, I know, be like the *builder of the Temple*, one of the *Tribe of Naphthali*; and for this I will also plead my *Polybius* in my Excuse; *It is not the Work of an Historian, to commemorate the Vices and Villanies of Men, so much as their just, their fair, their honest Actions: And the Readers of History get more good by the Objects of their Emulation, than of their Indignation.* Nor do I deny, that tho' I cannot approve the Conduct of *Josephus*, (whom *Jerom* not unjustly nor ineptly calls, *The Greek Livy*) when he left out of his *Antiquities*, the Story of the *Golden Calf*, and I don't won-

---

[31] "It is in the highest degree the property of history to record praise of good deeds."—*Murdock.*

der to find *Chamier*, and *Rivet*,[32] and others, taxing him for his *Partiality* towards his Country-men; yet I have left unmentioned some *Censurable Occurrences* in the *Story* of our *Colonies*, as things no less *Unuseful* than *Improper* to be raised out of the Grave, wherein *Oblivion* hath now buried them; lest I should have incurred the *Pasquil* bestowed upon Pope *Urban*, who employing a *Committee* to Rip up the *Old Errors* of his Predecessors, one clap'd a pair of Spurs upon the heels of the Statue of *St. Peter*; and a Label from the Statue of St. *Paul* opposite thereunto, upon the Bridge, ask'd him, *Whither he was bound?* St. *Peter* answered, *I apprehend some Danger in staying here; I fear they'll call me in Question for denying my Master*. And St. *Paul* replied, *Nay, then I had best be gone too, for they'll question me also, for Persecuting the Christians before my Conversion.* Briefly, My Pen shall Reproach none, that can give a Good Word unto any Good Man that is not of their *own Faction*, and shall *Fall out* with none, but those that can *Agree* with no body else, except those of their own *Schism*. If I draw any sort of Men with *Charcoal*, it shall be, because I remember a notable passage of the *Best Queen* that ever was in the World, our late *Queen Mary*. Monsieur *Jurieu*, that he might Justifie the Reformation in *Scotland*, made a very black Representation of their old Queen *Mary*; for which, a certain *Sycophant* would have incensed our Queen *Mary* against that Reverend Person, saying, *Is it not a Shame that this Man, without any Consideration for your Royal Person, should dare to throw such Infamous Calumnies upon a Queen, from whom your Royal Highness is descended?* But that Excellent Princess replied, *No, not at all; Is it not enough that by fulsome Praises great Persons be lull'd asleep all their Lives; But must Flattery accompany them to their very Graves? How should they fear the Judgment of Posterity, if Historians be not allowed to speak the Truth after their Death?* But whether I do my self *Commend*, or whether I give my Reader an opportunity to *Censure*, I am careful above all things to do it with *Truth*; and as I have considered the words of *Plato, Deum indigne & graviter ferre,*

---

[32] Daniel Chamier, 1570?–1621, French Protestant writer, and André Rivet, 1573–1651, French Calvinist theologian.—*Murdock*.

cum quis ei similem hoc est, virtute præstantem, vituperet, aut laudet contrarium.[33] So I have had the *Ninth Commandment* of a greater *Law-giver* than Plato, to preserve my care of *Truth* from first to last. If any Mistake have been any where committed, it will be found meerly *Circumstantial*, and wholly *Involuntary;* and let it be remembred, that tho' no *Historian* ever merited better than the Incomparable *Thuanus*,[34] yet learned Men have said of *his* Work, what they never shall truly say of *ours*, that it contains *multa falsissima & indigna.*[35] I find *Erasmus* himself mistaking *One* Man for *Two*, when writing of the Ancients. And even our own English Writers too are often mistaken, and in Matters of a very late Importance, as *Baker*, and *Heylin*, and *Fuller*, (professed Historians) tell us, that *Richard Sutton*, a single Man, founded the *Charter-House;* whereas his Name was *Thomas*, and he was a married Man. I think I can Recite such Mistakes, it may be *Sans* Number occurring in the most credible Writers; yet I hope I shall *commit* none such. But altho' I thus challenge, as my due, the Character of an *Impartial*, I doubt I may not challenge *That* of an *Elegant Historian*. I cannot say, whether the *Style*, wherein this *Church-History* is written, will please the Modern *Criticks·* But if I seem to have used ἁπλουστάτῃ συντάξει γραφῆς,[36] a Simple, Submiss, Humble *Style*, 'tis the same that *Eusebius* affirms to have been used by *Hegesippus*, who, as far as we understand, was the first Author (after *Luke*) that ever composed an entire Body of *Ecclesiastical History*, which he divided into *Five Books*, and Entitled, ὑπομνήματα των εηηλησιαστιηων πράξεων.[37] Whereas *others*, it may be, will reckon the Style Embellished with too much of *Ornament*, by the multiplied References to other and former Concerns, closely couch'd, for the Observation of the *Attentive*, in almost every Paragraph;

---

[33] "It is to act unworthily and offensively toward God, to abuse anyone who is like him excelling in virtue, or to praise the opposite of such a one."—*Murdock*.

[34] Jacques Auguste de Thou, French historian and poet, 1553–1617.—*Murdock*.

[35] "Much that is most false and unworthy."—*Murdock*.

[36] "The most simple style of writing."—*Murdock*.

[37] "Memorials of ecclesiastical transactions."—*Murdock*.

252   THE PURITAN

but I must confess, that I am of his mind who said, *Sicuti sal modice cibis aspersus Condit, & gratiam saporis addit, ita si paulum Antiquitatis admiscueris, Oratio fit venustior.*[38] And I have seldom seen that Way of Writing faulted, but by those, who, for a certain odd Reason, sometimes find fault, *That the Grapes are not ripe.* These *Embellishments* (of which yet I only —*Veniam pro laude peto*)[39] are not the puerile Spoils of *Polyanthea's;* but I should have asserted them to be as choice *Flowers* as most that occur in Ancient or Modern Writings, almost unavoidably putting themselves into the Authors Hand, while about his Work, if those words of *Ambrose* had not a little frightened me, as well as they did *Baronius, Unumquemque Fallunt sua scripta.*[40] I observe that Learned Men have been so terrified by the Reproaches of *Pedantry*, which little Smatterers at Reading and Learning have, by their *Quoting Humours* brought upon themselves, that, for to avoid all Approaches towards that which those Feeble Creatures have gone to imitate, the best way of Writing has been most injuriously deserted. But what shall we say? The Best way of Writing, under Heaven, shall be the Worst, when *Erasmus* his Monosyllable Tyrant[41] will have it so! And if I should have resign'd my self wholly to the Judgment of *others*, What way of Writing to have taken, the Story of the two Statues made by *Policletus* tells me, what may have been the Issue:[42] He contrived one of them according to the Rules that best pleased himself, and the other according to the Fancy of every one that look'd upon his Work: The former was afterwards Applauded by all, and the latter Derided by those very Persons who had given their Directions for it. As for such *Unaccuracies* as the *Critical* may discover, *Opere in*

---

[38] "Just as salt discreetly spread on food seasons it, and increases its flavor, so to mix in a little of antiquity makes style more pleasing."—*Murdock.*
[39] "I ask pardon for this praise."—*Murdock.*
[40] "Everyone errs about his own writings."—*Murdock.*
[41] "Our speech at this day (for the most part) consisteth of words of one sillable. Which thing Erasmus observing, merily in his Ecclesiast, compareth the English toong to a Dogs barking, that soundeth nothing els, but Baw, waw, waw, in Monosillable." William Lambarde, *Perambulation of Kent,* p. 233 (ed. 1826). This was written in 1570.—*Murdock.*
[42] The story which follows occurs in Ælian, and, doubtless, elsewhere.—*Murdock.*

longo,[43] I appeal to the *Courteous,* for a favourable Construction of them; and certainly they will be favourably Judged of, when there is considered the *Variety* of my *other Employments,* which have kept me in continual Hurries, I had almost said, like those of the *Ninth Sphere,*[44] for the few Months in which this Work has been *Digesting.* It was a thing well thought, by the wise Designers of *Chelsey-Colledge,* wherein able *Historians* were one sort of Persons to be maintained;[45] That the Romanists do in one Point condemn the Protestants; for among the Romanists, they don't burden their *Professors* with any *Parochial Incumbrances;* but among the *Protestants,* the very same *Individual* Man must *Preach, Catechize,* Administer the *Sacraments,* Visit the Afflicted, and manage all the parts of *Church-Discipline;* and if any *Books* for the Service of Religion, be written, Persons thus *extreamly incumbred* must be the Writers. Now, of all the Churches under Heaven, there are none that expect so much *Variety* of Service from their Pastors, as those of *New-England;* and of all the Churches in *New-England,* there are none that require more, than those in *Boston,* the Metropolis of the English *America;* whereof *one* is, by the Lord Jesus Christ, committed unto the Care of the unworthy Hand, by which this *History* is compiled. Reader, Give me leave humbly to mention, with him in *Tully, Antequam de Re, Pauca de Me!* [46] Constant *Sermons,* usually more than once, and perhaps three or four times, in a Week, and all the other Duties of a *Pastoral Watchfulness,* a very *large Flock* has all this while demanded of me; wherein, if I had been furnished with as many *Heads* as a *Typheus,* as many *Eyes* as an *Argos,* and as many *Hands* as a *Briareus,* I might have had Work enough to have employ'd them all; nor hath my *Station* left me free from Obligations to spend very much time in the *Evangelical Service* of *others* also. It would have been a great *Sin* in me, to have *Omitted,* or *Abated,* my Just Cares, to *fulfil my Ministry in*

---

[43] "In a long work."—*Murdock.*
[44] The ninth or "Crystalline Sphere" in the Ptolemaic system of astronomy. —*Murdock.*
[45] King James' College, Chelsea, founded 1609.—*Murdock.*
[46] "Before coming to the subject, a little about myself."—*Murdock.*

these things, and in a manner *Give my self wholly to them*. All
the time I have had for my *Church-History*, hath been perhaps
only, or chiefly, that, which I might have taken else for less
profitable Recreations; and it hath all been done by *Snatches*.
My Reader will not find me the Person intended in his *Littany*,
when he says, *Libera me ab homine unius Negotis*:[47] Nor have
I spent *Thirty Years* in shaping this my *History*, as *Diodorus
Siculus* did for his, [and yet both *Bodinus* and *Sigonius*[48] complain of the Σφαλματα[49] attending it.] But I wish I could have
enjoy'd entirely for this *Work*, one quarter of the little more
than *Two Years* which have roll'd away since I began it; whereas
I have been forced sometimes wholly to throw by the Work
whole Months together, and then resume it, but by a stolen
hour or two in a day, not without some hazard of incurring the
Title which *Coryat* put upon his History of his Travels, *Crudi-
ties hastily gobbled up in five Months*. *Protogenes* being seven
Years in drawing a Picture, *Apelles* upon the sight of it, said,
*The Grace of the Work was much allay'd by the length of the
Time*. Whatever else there may have been to take off the *Grace
of the Work*, now in the Readers hands, (whereof the *Pictures*
of Great and Good Men make a considerable part) I am sure
there hath not been the *length of the Time* to do it. Our English Martyrologer, counted it a sufficient *Apology*, for what
Meanness might be found in the first Edition of his *Acts and
Monuments*, that it was *hastily rashed up in about fourteen
Months*: And I may Apologize for this Collection of our *Acts
and Monuments*, that I should have been glad, in the little
more than *Two Years* which have ran out, since I enter'd upon
it, if I could have had one half of *About fourteen Months* to
have entirely devoted thereunto. But besides the *Time*, which
the *Daily Services* of *my own* first, and then many *other*
Churches, have necessarily call'd for, I have lost abundance of
precious *Time*, thro' the feeble and broken State of my *Health*,
which hath unfitted me for *Hard Study*; I can do nothing to purpose at *Lucubrations*. And yet, in this *Time* also of the two or

[47] "Deliver me from a man of but one interest."—*Murdock.*
[48] Charles Sigonius (Carlo Sigonio), 1524–1585, Italian writer and philolo-
gist.—*Murdock.*
[49] "Errors."—*Murdock.*

three Years last past, I have not been excused from the further Diversion of *Publishing* (tho' not so many as they say *Mercurius Trismegistus* did, yet) more than a *Score* of other Books, upon a copious Variety of other Subjects, besides the composing of several more, that are not yet published. Nor is this neither all the *Task* that I have in this while had lying upon me; for (tho' I am very sensible of what *Jerom* said, *Non bene fit, quod occupato Animo fit;*[50] and of *Quintilian's* Remark, *Non simul in multa intendere Animus totum potest,*)[51] when I applied my mind unto this way of serving the Lord JESUS CHRIST in my Generation, I set upon another and a greater, which has had, I suppose, more of my *Thought* and *Hope* than this, and wherein there hath passed me, for the most part, *Nulla dies sine linea.*[52] I considered, That all sort of *Learning* might be made gloriously Subservient unto the *Illustration* of the *Sacred Scripture;* and that no *professed Commentaries* had hitherto given a thousandth part of so much *Illustration* unto it, as might be given. I considered, that Multitudes of *particular Texts,* had, especially of later Years, been more notably *Illustrated* in the *Scattered Books* of Learned Men, than in any of the *Ordinary Commentators.* And I consider'd, That the *Treasures* of *Illustration* for the Bible, dispersed in many hundred Volumes, might be fetch'd all together by a Labour that would resolve to *Conquer all things;* and that all the *Improvements* which the *Later-ages* have made in the *Sciences,* might be also, with an inexpressible Pleasure, call'd in, to Assist the *Illustration* of the *Holy Oracles,* at a Rate that hath not been attempted in the vulgar *Annotations;* and that a common degree of *Sense,* would help a Person, who should converse much with these things, to attempt sometimes also an *Illustration* of his own, which might expect some Attention. Certainly, it will not be ungrateful unto good Men, to have innumerable *Antiquities, Jewish, Chaldee, Arabian, Grecian* and *Roman,* brought home unto us, with a *Sweet Light* Reflected from them on the *Word,* which is our *Light:* Or, To have all the *Typical* Men and things in our *Book of Mysteries,* accom-

---

[50] "What is done with an occupied mind, is not well done."—*Murdock.*
[51] "One cannot put his whole mind on many things at the same time."—*Murdock.*
[52] "No day without a line."—*Murdock.*

modated with their *Antitypes*: Or, To have many Hundreds of References to our dearest *Lord Messiah*, discovered in the Writings which *Testifie of Him*, oftner than the most of Mankind have hitherto imagined: Or, To have the *Histories* of all Ages, coming in with punctual and surprising *Fulfillments* of the Divine *Prophecies*, as far as they have been hitherto fulfilled; and not meer *Conjectures*, but even Mathematical and Incontestable *Demonstrations*, given of *Expositions* offered upon the *Prophecies*, that yet remain to be accomplished: Or, To have in *One Heap*, Thousands of those *Remarkable Discoveries of the deep things of the Spirit of God*, whereof *one* or *two*, or a few, sometimes, have been, with good Success accounted Materials enough to advance a Person into *Authorism*; or to have the delicious *Curiosities* of *Grotius*, and *Bochart*, and *Mede*, and *Lightfoot*, and *Selden*, and *Spencer*[53] (carefully selected and corrected) and many more Giants in Knowledge, all set upon one Table. Travellers tell us, That at *Florence* there is a rich Table, worth a thousand Crowns, made of Precious Stones neatly inlaid; a Table that was fifteen Years in making, with no less than Thirty Men daily at work upon it; even such a Table could not afford so rich Entertainments, as one that should have the Soul-feasting Thoughts of those Learned Men together set upon it. Only 'tis pitty, that instead of one poor feeble *American*, overwhelm'd with a thousand other Cares, and capable of touching this Work no otherwise than in a Digression, there be not more than Thirty Men daily employ'd about it. For, when the excellent Mr. *Pool*[54] had finished his Laborious and Immortal Task, it was noted by some considerable Persons, *That wanting Assistance to Collect for him many miscellaneous Criticisms, occasionally scattered in other Authors, he left many better Things behind him than he found.* At more than all this, our *Essay* is levell'd, if it be not anticipated with that Epitaph,

---

[53] Grotius, 1583–1645, the great Dutch lawyer and theologian; Samuel Bochart, 1599–1667, French Protestant scholar; Joseph Mede, 1586–1638, English theologian; John Lightfoot, 1602–1675, learned English divine; John Selden, 1584–1654, statesman, political writer and archæologist; and John Spencer, 1630–1695, theologian and Hebraist, were all men whose works Cotton Mather knew well.—*Murdock*.

[54] Matthew Poole, 1624–1709, compiled a famous *Synopsis* of the various biblical commentators.—*Murdock*.

magnis tamen excidit ausis.[55] Designing accordingly, to give the Church of God such displays of his blessed Word, as may be more Entertaining for the Rarity and Novelty of them, than any that have hitherto been seen together in any *Exposition*; and yet such as may be acceptable unto the most Judicious, for the Demonstrative Truth of them, and unto the most Orthodox, for the regard had unto the *Analogy of Faith* in all, I have now, in a few Months, got ready an huge number of *Golden Keys* to open the *Pandects* of Heaven, and some thousands of charming and curious and singular Notes, by the *New Help* whereof, the *Word* of CHRIST *may run and be glorified.* If the *God of my Life*, will please to spare my Life [my yet Sinful, and Slothful, and thereby Forfeited Life!] as many years longer as the *Barren Fig-tree* had in the Parable, I may make unto the Church of God, an humble Tender of our BIBLIA AMERICANA, a Volumn enrich'd with better things than all the Plate of the *Indies*; YET NOT I, BUT THE GRACE OF CHRIST WITH ME. My Reader sees, why I commit the Fault of a περιαυτία,[56] which appears in the mention of these Minute-passages; 'tis to excuse whatever other Fault of Inaccuracy, or Inadvertency, may be discovered in an History, which hath been a sort of Rapsody made up (like the Paper whereon 'tis written!) with many little Rags, torn from an Employment, multifarious enough to over-whelm one of my small Capacities.

> *Magna dabit, qui magna potest; mihi parva potenti,*
> *Parvaque poscenti, parva dedisse sat est.*[57]

§ 6. But shall I prognosticate thy Fate, now that,

> *Parve (sed invideo) ne me, Liber, ibis in Urbem.*[58]

Luther, who was himself owner of such an Heart, advised every Historian to get the *Heart of a Lion*; and the more I consider

---

[55] "Yet he fell short of what he had ventured to attempt."—*Murdock.*
[56] "Discussion about myself."—*Murdock.*
[57] "He will give great things, who is able; for me, who am able to do little, and who ask for little, it is enough to have given a little."—*Murdock.*
[58] "O little book, though I envy you, not I, shall go forth to the world."— *Murdock.*

of the Provocation, which this our *Church-History* must needs give to that Roaring Lion, who has, through all Ages hitherto, been tearing the Church to pieces, the more occasion I see to wish my self a *Cœur de Lion*. But had not my Heart been Trebly Oak'd and Brass'd for such Encounters as this our History may meet withal, I would have worn the Silk-worms Motto, *Operitur dum Operatur*,[59] and have chosen to have written *Anonymously*; or, as *Claudius Salmasius* calls himself *Walo Messalinus*, as *Ludovicus Molinæus* calls himself *Ludiomæus Colvinus*, as *Carolus Scribanius* calls himself *Clarus Bonarscius*, (and no less Men than *Peter du Moulin*, and Dr. *Henry More*, stile themselves, the one *Hippolytus Fronto*, the other *Franciscus Paleopolitanus*.)[60] Thus I would have tried, whether I could not have Anagrammatized my Name into some Concealment; or I would have referr'd it to be found in the second Chapter of the second Syntagm of *Selden de Diis Syris*.[61] Whereas now I freely confess, 'tis COTTON MATHER that has written all these things;

Me, me, ad sum qui scripsi; in me convertite Ferrum.[62]

I hope 'tis a right Work that I have done; but we are not yet arrived unto the *Day, wherein God will bring every Work into Judgment* (the Day of the *Kingdom* that was promised unto *David*) and a Son of *David* hath as Truly as Wisely told us, that until the arrival of that Happy Day, this is one of the *Vanities* attending Humane Affairs; *For a right Work a Man shall be envied of His Neighbour*. It will not be so much a surprise unto me, if I should live to see our *Church-History* vexed with *Aniemad-versions* of Calumnious Writers, as it would have been unto *Virgil*, to read his *Bucolicks* reproached by the *Antibucolica* of a

---

[59] "It is hidden while it works."—*Murdock*.
[60] Louis Molinæus, or Moulin, was an English physician, born about 1603; Charles Scribani, or Scribanius, was a Jesuit historian, living 1561–1629; Peter du Moulin was an English theologian, and Henry More was one of the English "Cambridge Platonists."—*Murdock*.
[61] The name Mather occurs in the book of John Selden referred to (p. 165 of the London 1617 edition).—*Murdock*.
[62] "It is I who have written; turn the sword against me." This is an alteration of the *Æneid*, ix, 427.—*Murdock*.

Nameless Scribbler, and his *Æneids* travestied by the *Æneido-mastix* of *Carbilius:* Or *Herennius* taking pains to make a Collection of the *Faults*, and *Faustinus* of the *Thefts*, in his incomparable Composures: Yea, *Pliny*, and *Seneca* themselves, and our *Jerom*, reproaching him, as a Man of no Judgment, nor Skill in Sciences; while *Pædianus* affirms of him, that he was himself, *Usque adeo invidiæ Expers, ut si quid erudite dictum inspiceret alterius, non minus gauderet ac si suum esset.*[63] How should a Book, no better laboured than this of ours, escape *Zoilian*[64] Outrages, when in all Ages, the most exquisite Works have been as much vilified, as *Plato's* by *Scaliger*, and *Aristotle's* by *Lactantius?* In the time of our K. *Edward* VI. there was an Order to bring in all the Teeth of St. *Apollonia*, which the People of his one Kingdom carried about them for the Cure of the *Tooth ach;* and they were so many, that they almost fill'd a Tun. Truly *Envy* hath as many *Teeth* as Madam *Apollonia* would have had, if all those pretended Reliques had been really hers. And must all these *Teeth* be fastned on thee, *O my Book?* It may be so! And yet the *Book*, when ground between these *Teeth*, will prove like *Ignatius* in the *Teeth* of the furious Tygers, *The whiter Manchet for the Churches of God.* The greatest and fiercest Rage of *Envy*, is that which I expect from those IDUMÆANS, whose Religion is all Ceremony, and whose Charity is more for them who deny the most Essential things in the Articles and Homilies of the Church of *England*, than for the most Conscientious Men in the World, who manifest their being so, by their Dissent in some little Ceremony: Or those Persons whose Hearts are notably expressed in those words used by one of them ['tis *Howel* in his *Familiar Letters*, Vol. 1. Sect. 6. Lett. 32.] *I rather pitty, than hate, Turk or Infidel, for they are of the same Metal, and bear the same Stamp, as I do, tho' the Inscriptions differ; If I hate any, 'tis those Schismaticks that puzzle the sweet Peace of our Church; so that I could be con-*

---

[63] "Ever so very free of envy, that when he examined anything learnedly written by another, he was not less delighted than as if it were his own." —*Murdock.*

[64] Zoilus, a fourth century Greek rhetorician, so severely criticized Homer as to be known as the "Scourge of Homer."—*Murdock.*

tent to see an Anabaptist go to Hell on a Brownists Back.[65] The
Writer whom I last quoted, hath given us a Story of a young
Man in *High-Holbourn,* who being after his death Dissected,
there was a Serpent with divers tails, found in the left Ventricle
of his Heart. I make no question, that our Church-History will
find some Reader disposed like that Writer, with an Heart as
full of Serpent and Venom as ever it can hold: Nor indeed will
they be able to hold, but the Tongues and Pens of those angry
Folks, will scourge me as with Scorpions, and cause me to feel
(if I will feel) as many Lashes as *Cornelius Agrippa* expected
from their Brethren, for the Book in which he exposed their
Vanities.[66] A Scholar of the great JUELS, made once about
fourscore Verses, for which the Censor of *Corpus Christi*
Colledge in the beginning of Queen *Maries* Reign, publickly
and cruelly scourged him, with one Lash for every Verse.[67] Now
in those Verses, the young Man's Prayers to the Lord JESUS
CHRIST, have this for part of the answer given to them.

> *Respondet Dominus, spectans de sedibus altis,*
> *Ne dubites recte credere, parve puer.*
> *Olim sum passus mortem, nunc occupo dextram*
> *Patris, nunc summi sunt mea regna poli.*
> *Sed tu, crede mihi, vires Scriptura resumet,*
> *Tolleturque suo tempore missa nequam.*

In English.

> The Lord beholding from his Throne, reply'd,
> Doubt not, O *Youth,* firmly in me confide.
> I dy'd long since, now sit at the Right Hand
> Of my bless'd Father, and the World command.
> Believe me, *Scripture* shall regain her sway,
> And wicked *Mass* in due time fade away.

---

[65] The Brownists were those who followed the beliefs of Robert Brown—in
general, they were the more extreme Independents among the English
Puritans. . . .—*Murdock.*
[66] Heinrich Cornelius Agrippa, 1487–1535, published in 1531 his *De Vani-
tate et Incertitude Scientiarum,* which brought him into difficulties with
the Inquisition.—*Murdock.*
[67] Bishop John Jewel of Salisbury, 1522–1571. . . .—*Murdock.*

Reader, I also expect nothing but *Scourges* from that Generation, to whom the *Mass book* is dearer than the Bible. But I have now likewise confessed another Expectation, that shall be my Consolation under all. They tell us, That on the highest of the *Caspian* Mountains in *Spain*, there is a Lake, whereinto if you throw a Stone, there presently ascends a Smoke, which forms a dense Cloud, from whence issues a Tempest of Rain, Hail, and horrid Thunder-claps, for a good quarter of an hour. Our Church-History will be like a Stone cast into that Lake, for the furious Tempest which it will raise among some, whose Ecclesiastical Dignities have set them, as on the top of Spanish Mountains. The Catholick Spirit of Communion wherewith 'tis written, and the Liberty which I have taken, to tax the Schismatical Impositions and Persecutions of a Party, who have always been as real Enemies to the English Nation, as to the Christian and Protestant Interest, will certainly bring upon the whole Composure, the quick Censures of that Party, at the first cast of their look upon it. In the Duke of *Alva's* Council of twelve Judges, there was one *Hessels* a *Flemming*, who slept always at the Trial of Criminals, and when they wak'd him to deliver his Opinion, he rub'd his Eyes, and cry'd between sleeping and waking, *Ad patibulum! ad Patibulum!* To the Gallows with 'em! [And, by the way, this Blade was himself, at the last, condemned unto the Gallows, without an Hearing!] As quick Censures must this our Labour expect from those who will not bestow waking thoughts upon the Representations of Christianity here made unto the World; but have a Sentence of Death always to pass, or at least, Wish, upon these Generous Principles, without which, 'tis impossible to maintain the Reformation: And I confess, I am very well content, that this our Labour takes the Fate of those Principles: Nor do I dissent from the words of the Excellent *Whitaker* upon *Luther, Fœlix ille, quem Dominus eo Honore dignatus est, ut Homines nequissimos suos haberet inimicos.*[68] But if the old Epigrammatist, when he saw Guilty Folks raving Mad at his Lines, could say——

---

[68] "Happy is he, whom God has deemed worthy of the honor that he may have the worst of men for his enemies."—*Murdock.*

Hoc volo; nunc nobis carmina nostra placent:[69]

Certainly an Historian should not be displeased at it, if the Enemies of Truth discover their Madness at the true and free Communications of his History: and therefore the more Stones they throw at this Book, there will not only be the more Proofs, that it is a Tree which hath good Fruits growing upon it, but I will build my self a Monument with them, whereon shall be inscribed, that Clause in the Epitaph of the Martyr *Stephen:*

Excepit Lapides, cui petra Christus erat:[70]

Albeit perhaps the *Epitaph,* which the old *Monks* bestow'd upon *Wickliff,* will be rather endeavour'd for me, (*If I am thought worth one!*) by the Men, who will, with all possible *Monkery,* strive to stave off the approaching *Reformation.*

But since an Undertaking of this Nature, must thus encounter so much Envy, from those who are under the Power of the *Spirit that works in the Children of Unperswadeableness,* methinks I might perswade my self, that it will find another sort of Entertainment from those Good Men who have a better Spirit in them: For, as the Apostle *James* hath noted, (so with Monsieur *Claude* I read it) *The Spirit that is in us, lusteth against Envy;* and yet even in *us* also, there will be the *Flesh,* among whose Works, one is *Envy,* which will be *Lusting* against the *Spirit.* All Good Men will not be satisfied with every thing that is here set before them. In my own Country, besides a considerable number of loose and vain Inhabitants risen up, to whom the Congregational Church-Discipline, which cannot Live well, where the Power of Godliness dyes, is become distasteful for the Purity of it; there is also a number of eminently Godly Persons, who are for a Larger way, and unto these my Church-History will give distast, by the things which it may happen to utter, in favour of that Church-Discipline on some few occasions; and the Discoveries which I may happen to make of my Apprehensions, that *Scripture,* and *Reason,* and *Antiquity*

---

[69] "This is what I wish; now my songs please me."—*Murdock.*
[70] . . . "He died by *stoning,* but his *Rock* was Christ."—*Murdock.*

is for it; and that it is not far from a glorious Resurrection. But that, as the Famous Mr. *Baxter*, after Thirty or Forty Years hard Study, about the true Instituted Church-Discipline, at last, not only own'd, but also invincibly prov'd, That it is *The Congregational*; so, The further that the *Unprejudiced Studies* of Learned Men proceed in this Matter, the more generally the *Congregational Church-Discipline* will be pronounced for. On the other side, There are some among us, who very strictly profess the *Congregational Church-Discipline*, but at the same time they have an unhappy Narrowness of Soul, by which they confine their value and Kindness too much unto their own Party; and unto those my *Church History* will be offensive, because my Regard unto our own declared Principles, does not hinder me from giving the Right-hand of Fellowship unto the valuable Servants of the Lord Jesus Christ, who find not our Church-Discipline as yet agreeable unto their present Understandings and Illuminations. If it be thus in my own Country, it cannot be other wise in That whereto I send this account of my own. Briefly, as it hath been said, That if all *Episcopal* Men were like Archbishop *Usher*, and all *Presbyterians* like *Stephen Marshal*, and all *Independents* like *Jeremiah Burroughs*, the Wounds of the Church would soon be healed;[71] my Essay to carry that Spirit through this whole Church-History, will bespeak Wounds for it, from those that are of another Spirit. And there will also be in every Country those Good Men, who yet have not had the Grace of Christ so far prevailing in them, as utterly to divest them of that piece of Ill Nature which the Comedian resents, *In homine Imperito, quo nil quicquam Injustius, quia nisi quod ipse facit, nil recte factum putat.*[72]

However, All these things, and an hundred more such things which I think of, are very small Discouragements for such a Service as I have here endeavoured. I foresee a Recompence,

---

[71] James Ussher, Archbishop of Armagh, an Anglican, liberal toward Puritanism, 1581–1656; Marshall, 1594?–1655, and Burroughs, 1599–1646, were men of breadth of view and wide influence.—*Murdock*.

[72] "Nothing is more unjust than an inexperienced man, who thinks nothing is right except what he has done himself." (Terence, *Adelphi*, ll. 98–99.) —*Murdock*.

which will abundantly swallow up all Discouragements! It may be *Strato* the Philosopher counted himself well recompensed for his Labours, when *Ptolemy* bestow'd fourscore Talents on him. It may be Archimelus the Poet counted himself well recompensed, when Hiero sent him a thousand Bushels of Wheat for one little Epigram: And *Saleius* the Poet might count himself well recompensed, when Vespasian sent him twelve thousand and five hundred *Philippicks*; and *Oppian* the Poet might count himself well recompensed, when Caracalla sent him a piece of Gold for every Line that he had inscribed unto him. As I live in a Country where such Recompences never were in fashion; it hath no Preferments for me, and I shall count that I am well Rewarded in it, if I can escape without being heavily Reproached, Censured and Condemned, for what I have done: So I thank the Lord, I should exceedingly Scorn all such mean Considerations, I seek not out for Benefactors, to whom these Labours may be Dedicated: There is ONE to whom all is due! From Him I shall have a Recompence: And what Recompence? The Recompence, whereof I do, with inexpressible Joy, assure my self, is this, *That these my poor Labours will certainly serve the Churches and Interests of the Lord Jesus Christ.* And I think I may say, That I ask to live no longer, than I count a Service unto the Lord Jesus Christ, and his Churches, to be it self a glorious Recompence for the doing of it. When *David* was contriving to build the House of God, there was that order given from Heaven concerning him, *Go tell* David, *my Servant.* The adding of *that* more than *Royal Title* unto the Name of David, was a sufficient Recompence for all his Contrivance about the House of God. In our whole *Church-History*, we have been at work for the House of the Lord Jesus Christ, [Even that *Man* who is the *Lord God*, and whose *Form* seems on that occasion represented unto His *David*] And herein 'tis Recompence enough, that I have been a *Servant* unto that heavenly Lord. The greatest *Honour*, and the sweetest *Pleasure*, out of *Heaven*, is to Serve our Illustrious Lord JESUS CHRIST, who hath *loved us, and given himself for us*; and unto whom it is infinitely reasonable that we should *give our selves*, and all that we *have* and *Are*: And it may be the *Angels* in *Heaven* too, aspire not after an higher Felicity.

Unto thee, therefore, O thou Son of God, and King of
Heaven, and Lord of all things, whom all the Glorious Angels
of Light, unspeakably love to Glorifie; I humbly offer up a poor
History of Churches, which own thee alone for their Head, and
Prince, and Law-giver; Churches which thou hast purchas'd
with thy own Blood, and with wonderful Dispensations of thy
Providence hitherto protected and preserved; and of a People
which thou didst Form for thy self, to shew forth thy Praises. I
bless thy great Name, for thy inclining of me to, and carrying
of me through, the Work of this History: I pray thee to sprinkle
the Book of this History with thy Blood, and make it acceptable
and profitable unto thy Churches, and serve thy Truths and
ways among thy People, by that which thou hast here prepared;
for 'tis THOU that hast prepar'd it for them. Amen.

Quid sum? Nil. Quis sum? Nullus. Sed Gratia CHRISTI,
Quod sum, quod Vivo, quodque Laboro, facit.[73]

. . . . .

BOOK II, CHAPTER I. THE LIFE OF WILLIAM BRADFORD

Omnium Somnos, illius vigilantia defendit, omnium otium illius
Labor, omnium Delitias illius Industria, omnium vacationem
illius occupatio.[1]

§ 1. It has been a Matter of some Observation, that although
Yorkshire be one of the largest Shires in England, yet, for all
the Fires of Martyrdom which were kindled in the Days of
Queen Mary, it afforded no more Fuel than one poor Leaf;
namely, John Leaf, an Apprentice, who suffered for the Doctrine of the Reformation at the same Time and Stake with the

---

[73] "What am I? Nothing. Who am I? No one. But the Grace of Christ
makes what I am, my life, and what I do."—Murdock.
[1] "His vigilance defends the sleep of all; his labor, their rest; his industry,
their pleasures; and his diligence, their leisure."—Murdock.

Famous *John Bradford*. But when the Reign of Queen *Eliza-beth* would not admit the *Reformation* of *Worship* to proceed unto those Degrees, which were proposed and pursued by no small number of the Faithful in those Days, *Yorkshire* was not the least of the Shires in *England* that afforded Suffering *Wit-nesses* thereunto. The *Churches* there *gathered* were quickly molested with such a raging *Persecution*, that if the Spirit of *Separation* in them did carry them unto a further *Extream* than it should have done, one blameable Cause thereof will be found in the *Extremity* of that *Persecution*. Their *Troubles* made that *Cold* Country too *Hot* for them, so that they were under a necessity to *seek* a Retreat in the *Low Countries;* and yet the watchful Malice and Fury of their Adversaries rendred it almost impossible for them to *find* what they sought. For them to leave their *Native Soil*, their *Lands* and their *Friends*, and go into a *Strange Place*, where they must hear *Forreign Language*, and live *meanly* and *hardly*, and in other Imploy-ments than that of *Husbandry*, wherein they had been Edu-cated, *these* must needs have been such *Discouragements* as could have been Conquered by none, save those who *sought first the Kingdom of God, and the Righteousness thereof*. But that which would have made these Discouragements the more Unconquerable unto an ordinary Faith, was the terrible Zeal of their Enemies to Guard all *Ports*, and Search all *Ships*, that none of them should be carried off. I will not relate the *sad things* of this kind, then *seen* and *felt* by this People of God; but only exemplifie those *Trials* with one short Story. Divers of this People having Hired a *Dutchman* then lying at *Hull*, to carry them over to *Holland*, he promised faithfully to take them in between *Grimsly* and *Hull*;[2] but *they* coming to the Place a Day or Two too soon, the appearance of such a Multi-tude alarmed the *Officers* of the Town adjoining, who came with a great Body of *Soldiers* to seize upon them. Now it hap-pened that one Boat full of *Men* had been carried Aboard, while the *Women* were yet in a *Bark* that lay Aground in a Creek at Low-Water. The *Dutchman* perceiving the *Storm* that was thus beginning *Ashore*, swore by the *Sacrament* that he

---

[2] *I.e.*, Grimsby.—*Murdock*.

would stay no longer for any of them; and so taking the Advantage of a Fair Wind then Blowing, he put out to *Sea* for *Zealand*. The Women thus left near *Grimsly-Common*, bereaved of their Husbands, who had been hurried from them, and forsaken of their Neighbours, of whom none durst in this Fright stay with them, were a very rueful Spectacle; some crying for *Fear*, some shaking for *Cold*, all dragg'd by Troops of *Armed* and *Angry* Men from one Justice to another, till not knowing what to do with them, they e'en dismiss'd them to shift as well as they could for themselves. But by their singular *Afflictions*, and by their Christian *Behaviours*, the *Cause* for which they exposed themselves did gain considerably. In the mean time, the Men at Sea found Reason to be glad that their Families were not with them, for they were surprized with an *horrible Tempest*, which held them for Fourteen Days together, in Seven whereof they saw not *Sun, Moon,* or *Star,* but were driven upon the Coast of *Norway.* The *Mariners* often despaired of Life, and once with doleful shrieks gave over all, as thinking the Vessel was Foundred: But the Vessel rose again, and when The *Mariners* with sunk Hearts often cried out, *We Sink! We Sink!* The Passengers without such Distraction of Mind, even while the Water was running into their Mouths and Ears, would chearfully Shout, *Yet Lord, thou canst save! Yet Lord, thou canst save!* And the Lord accordingly brought them at last safe unto their *Desired Haven:* And not long after helped their Distressed Relations thither after them, where indeed they found upon almost all Accounts *a new World,* but a World in which they found that they must live like *Strangers* and *Pilgrims.*

§ 2. Among those Devout People was our *William Bradford,* who was Born *Anno* 1588. in an obscure Village call'd *Ansterfield,* where the People were as unacquainted with the *Bible,* as the *Jews* do seem to have been with *part* of it in the Days of *Josiah;* a most Ignorant and Licentious *People,* and *like unto their Priest.* Here, and in some other Places, he had a Comfortable *Inheritance* left him of his Honest Parents, who died while he was yet a Child, and cast him on the Education, first of his *Grand Parents,* and then of his *Uncles,* who devoted him, like his Ancestors, unto the Affairs of *Husbandry.* Soon and long Sickness kept him, as he would afterwards thankfully say, from the *Vanities of Youth*, and made him the fitter for what he was afterwards to undergo. When he was about a Dozen Years Old, the Reading of the *Scriptures* began to cause great Impressions upon him; and those Impressions were much assisted and improved, when he came to enjoy Mr. *Richard Clifton's*[3] Illuminating Ministry, not far from his Abode; he was then also further befriended, by being brought into the Company and Fellowship of such as were then called *Professors;*[4] though the Young Man that brought him into it, did after become a Prophane and Wicked *Apostate*. Nor could the *Wrath* of his *Uncles*, nor the *Scoff* of his *Neighbours* now turn'd upon him, as one of the *Puritans*, divert him from his Pious Inclinations.

§ 3. At last beholding how fearfully the Evangelical and Apostolical *Church-Form*, whereinto the Churches of the *Primitive Times* were cast by the good Spirit of God, had been *Deformed* by the *Apostacy* of the *Succeeding Times*; and what little Progress the *Reformation* had yet made in many Parts of *Christendom* towards its Recovery, he set himself by Reading, by Discourse, by Prayer, to learn whether it was not his Duty to *withdraw* from the Communion of the *Parish-Assemblies*, and *engage* with some *Society* of the Faithful, that should keep close unto the *Written Word* of God, as the *Rule* of their *Worship*. And after many Distresses of Mind concerning it, he took up a very Deliberate and Understanding *Resolution* of doing so; which *Resolution* he chearfully Prosecuted, although the provoked *Rage* of his Friends tried all the ways imaginable to reclaim him from it, unto all whom his Answer was, *Were I like to endanger my Life, or consume my Estate by any ungodly Courses, your Counsels to me were very seasonable: But you know that I have been Diligent and Provident in my Calling, and not only desirous to augment what I have, but also to enjoy it in your Company; to part from which will be as great a Cross as can befal me. Nevertheless, to keep a good Conscience, and walk in such a Way as God has prescribed in his Word, is a*

---

[3] Richard Clifton, a Puritan, minister at Scrooby and later in Amsterdam. He died in 1610.—*Murdock*.
[4] *I.e.*, those who professed to have religious faith.—*Murdock*.

*thing which I must prefer before you all, and above Life it self.
Wherefore, since 'tis for a good Cause that I am like to suffer
the Disasters which you lay before me, you have no Cause to
be either angry with me, or sorry for me; yea, I am not only
willing to part with every thing that is dear to me in this World
for this Cause, but I am also thankful that God has given me
an Heart so to do, and will accept me so to suffer for him.* Some
lamented him, *some* derided him, *all* disswaded him: Nevertheless the more they did it, the more fixed he was in his Purpose
to seek the Ordinances of the Gospel, where they should be
dispensed with most of the *Commanded Purity*; and the *sudden Deaths* of the chief Relations which thus lay at him,
quickly after convinced him what a Folly it had been to have
quitted his *Profession*, in Expectation of any Satisfaction from
them. So to *Holland* he attempted a removal.

§ 4. Having with a great Company of Christians Hired a
Ship to Transport them for *Holland*, the Master perfidiously
betrayed them into the Hands of those *Persecutors*, who Rifled
and Ransack'd their Goods, and clapp'd their Persons into
Prison at *Boston*, where they lay for a Month together. But Mr.
Bradford being a Young Man of about *Eighteen*, was dismissed
sooner than the rest, so that within a while he had Opportunity
with some others to get over to *Zealand*, through *Perils* both by
Land and *Sea* not inconsiderable; where he was not long Ashore
e're a *Viper* seized on his Hand, that is, an Officer, who carried
him unto the Magistrates, unto whom an envious Passenger
had accused him as having *fled* out of *England*. When the
Magistrates understood the True Cause of his coming thither,
they were well satisfied with him; and so he repaired joyfully
unto his Brethren at *Amsterdam*, where the Difficulties to
which he afterwards stooped in Learning and Serving of a
Frenchman at the Working of *Silks*, were abundantly Compensated by the *Delight* wherewith he sat under the *Shadow*
of our Lord in his purely dispensed Ordinances. At the end of
Two Years, he did, being of Age to do it, convert his Estate in
England into Money; but Setting up for himself, he found
some of his Designs by the *Providence* of God frowned upon,
which he judged a *Correction* bestowed by God upon him for
certain Decays of *Internal Piety*, whereinto he had fallen; the

Consumption of his *Estate* he thought came to prevent a *Consumption* in his *Virtue*. But after he had resided in *Holland* about half a Score Years, he was one of those who bore a part in that Hazardous and Generous Enterprize of removing into *New-England*, with part of the *English* Church at *Leyden*, where at their first Landing, his dearest Consort accidentally falling Overboard, was drowned in the *Harbour*; and the rest of his Days were spent in the Services, and the Temptations, of that *American Wilderness*.

§ 5. Here was Mr. *Bradford* in the Year 1621. Unanimously chosen the *Governour* of the Plantation: The Difficulties whereof were such, that if he had not been a Person of more than Ordinary Piety, Wisdom and Courage, he must have sunk under them. He had with a Laudable Industry been laying up a Treasure of *Experiences*, and he had now occasion to use it: Indeed nothing but an *Experienced* Man could have been suitable to the Necessities of the People. The Potent Nations of the *Indians*, into whose Country they were come, would have cut them off, if the Blessing of God upon *his* Conduct had not quell'd them; and if his Prudence, Justice and Moderation had not overruled them, they had been ruined by their own *Distempers*. One *Specimen* of his Demeanour is to this Day particularly spoken of. A Company of Young Fellows that were newly arrived, were very unwilling to comply with the Governour's Order for *Working* abroad on the Publick Account; and therefore on *Christmass-Day*, when he had called upon them, they excused themselves, with a pretence that it was against their *Conscience* to *Work* such a Day. The Governour gave them no Answer, only that he would spare them till they were better informed; but by and by he found them all at *Play* in the Street, sporting themselves with various Diversions; whereupon Commanding the Instruments of their Games to be taken from them, he effectually gave them to understand, *That it was against his Conscience that they should play whilst others were at* Work; *and that if they had any Devotion to the Day, they should show it at Home in the Exercises of Religion, and not in the Streets with Pastime and Frolicks;* and this gentle Reproof put a final stop to all such Disorders for the future.

§ 6. For Two Years together after the beginning of the
Colony, whereof he was now Governour, the poor People had a
great Experiment of *Man's not living by Bread alone;* for when
they were left all together without one Morsel of *Bread* for
many Months one after another, still the good Providence of
God relieved them, and supplied them, and this for the most
part out of the *Sea.* In this low Condition of Affairs, there was
no little Exercise for the *Prudence* and *Patience* of the Governour, who chearfully bore his part in all: And that *Industry*
might not flag, he quickly set himself to settle *Propriety*[5]
among the New-Planters; foreseeing that while the whole Country labour'd upon a *Common Stock,* the *Husbandry* and *Business* of the Plantation could not *flourish,* as *Plato* and others
long since dream'd that it would, if a *Community* were established. Certainly, if the Spirit which dwelt in the *Old Puritans,*
had not inspired these *New-Planters,* they had sunk under the
Burden of these Difficulties; but our *Bradford* had a *double
Portion* of that Spirit.

§ 7. The Plantation was quickly thrown into a *Storm* that
almost overwhelmed it, by the unhappy Actions of a Minister
sent over from *England* by the *Adventurers* concerned for the
Plantation; but by the Blessing of Heaven on the Conduct of
the Governour, they Weathered out that *Storm.* Only the *Adventurers* hereupon breaking to pieces, threw up all their Concernments with the *Infant Colony;* whereof they gave this as
one Reason, *That the Planters dissembled with His Majesty,
and their Friends in their Petition, wherein they declared for a
Church-Discipline, agreeing with the* French *and others of the
Reforming Churches in* Europe. Whereas 'twas now urged, that
they had admitted into their Communion a Person, who at his
Admission utterly *renounced* the Churches of *England,* (which
Person by the way, was *that* very Man who had made the Complaints against them) and therefore though they denied the
Name of *Brownists* yet they were the *Thing.* In Answer here-
unto, the very Words written by the Governour were these;
Whereas you Tax us with dissembling about the French Dis-
cipline, *you do us wrong, for we both hold and practice the*

---

[5] *I.e.,* property.—*Murdock.*

Discipline *of the* French *and other* Reformed *Churches* (*as they have published the same in the* Harmony of Confessions) *according to our Means, in Effect and Substance. But whereas you would tie us up to the* French Discipline *in every Circumstance, you derogate from the* Liberty *we have in Christ Jesus. The Apostle* Paul *would have none* to follow him *in any thing, but wherein he* follows Christ; *much less ought any Christian or Church in the* World *to do it. The* French *may err, we may err, and other Churches may err, and doubtless do in many* Circumstances. *That Honour therefore belongs only to the* Infallible Word of God, *and* pure Testament of Christ, *to be propounded and followed as the* only *Rule and Pattern for Direction herein to all Churches and Christians. And it is too great* Arrogancy *for any Men or Church to think, that he or they have so sounded the* Word *of God unto the bottom, as precisely to set down the Churches Discipline without Error in Substance or Circumstance, that no other without blame may digress or differ in any thing from the same. And it is not difficult to shew that the* Reformed Churches *differ in many* Circumstances *among themselves.* By which Words it appears how far he was free from that *Rigid Spirit* of *Separation,* which broke to pieces the *Separatists* themselves in the *Low Countries,* unto the great Scandal of the *Reforming Churches.* He was indeed a Person of a *well-temper'd Spirit,* or else it had been scarce possible for him to have kept the Affairs of *Plymouth* in so good a *Temper* for *Thirty Seven* Years together; in every one of which he was chosen their Governour, except the *Three Years,* wherein Mr. *Winslow,* and the *Two Years,* wherein Mr. *Prince,* at the choice of the People, took a *turn* with him.

§ 8. The *Leader* of a People in a *Wilderness* had need be a *Moses;* and if a *Moses* had not led the People of *Plymouth-Colony,* when this Worthy Person was their Governour, the People had never with so much Unanimity and Importunity still called *him* to lead them. Among many Instances thereof, let this one piece of *Self denial be told for a Memorial of him, wheresoever this History shall be considered.* The Patent of the Colony was taken in *his* Name, running in these Terms, *To* William Bradford, *his Heirs, Associates and Assigns:* But when the number of the *Freemen* was much Increased, and many New *Townships* Erected, the *General Court* there desired of Mr. *Bradford,* that he would make a Surrender of the same into *their Hands,* which *he* willingly and presently assented unto, and confirmed it according to their Desire by his *Hand* and *Seal,* reserving no more for himself than was his *Proportion,* with others, by *Agreement.* But as he found the Providence of Heaven many ways *Recompencing* his many Acts of *Self-denial,* so he gave this Testimony to the Faithfulness of the Divine Promises; *That he had forsaken Friends, Houses and Lands for the sake of the Gospel, and the Lord gave them him again. Here* he prospered in his *Estate;* and besides a Worthy *Son* which he had by a former Wife, he had also Two Sons and a Daughter by another, whom he Married in this Land.

§ 9. He was a Person for *Study* as well as *Action;* and hence, notwithstanding the Difficulties through which he passed in his Youth, he attained unto a notable Skill in *Languages;* the *Dutch* Tongue was become almost as Vernacular to him as the *English;* the *French* Tongue he could also manage; the *Latin* and the *Greek* he had Mastered; but the *Hebrew* he most of all studied, *because,* he said, *he would see with his own Eyes the Ancient Oracles of God in their Native Beauty.* He was also well skill'd in *History,* in *Antiquity,* and in *Philosophy;* and for *Theology* he became so versed in it, that he was an *Irrefragable Disputant* against the *Errors,* especially those of *Anabaptism,* which with Trouble he saw rising in his Colony; wherefore he wrote some Significant things for the Confutation of those Errors. But the *Crown* of all was his Holy, Prayerful, Watchful and Fruitful *Walk with God,* wherein he was very Exemplary.

§ 10. At length he fell into an Indisposition of Body, which rendred him unhealthy for a whole *Winter;* and as the *Spring* advanced, his Health yet more declined; yet he felt himself not what he counted *Sick,* till one *Day;* in the *Night* after which, the God of Heaven so fill'd his Mind with *Ineffable Consolations,* that he seemed little short of *Paul,* rapt up unto the *Unutterable* Entertainments of *Paradise.* The next Morning he told his Friends, *That the good Spirit of God had given him a Pledge of his Happiness in another World, and the Firstfruits of his Eternal Glory:* And on the Day following he died,

May 9. 1657. in the 69th Year of his Age. Lamented by all the Colonies of *New-England*, as a Common Blessing and Father to them all.

O mihi si Similis Contingat Clausula Vitæ! [6]

Plato's brief Description of a *Governour*, is all that I will now leave as his Character, in an

EPITAPH.

Νομεὺς Τροφός ἀγέλης ἀνθρωπίνης. [7]

MEN *are but* FLOCKS: BRADFORD *beheld their Need, And long did them at once both* Rule *and* Feed.

. . . . .

BOOK II, CHAPTER IV. THE LIFE OF JOHN WINTHROP

Quicunq; Venti erunt, Ars nostra certe non aberit. Cicer.[8]

§ 1. Let *Greece* boast of her patient *Lycurgus*, the *Lawgiver*, by whom *Diligence, Temperance, Fortitude* and *Wit* were made the *Fashions* of a therefore Long-lasting and Renowned Commonwealth: Let *Rome* tell of her Devout *Numa*, the *Lawgiver*, by whom the most Famous Commonwealth saw *Peace* Triumphing over extinguished *War*, and cruel *Plunders*, and *Murders* giving place to the more mollifying Exercises of his *Religion*. Our *New-England* shall tell and boast of her WINTHROP, a *Lawgiver*, as patient as *Lycurgus*, but not admitting any of *his* Criminal Disorders; as Devout as *Numa*, but not liable to any

---

[6] "Oh, may a similar ending of life come to me."—*Murdock.*
[7] "Shepherd and feeder of the human herd."—*Murdock.*
[8] "Whatever winds shall blow, our art surely shall not die."—*Murdock.*

of *his* Heathenish Madnesses; a *Governour* in whom the Excellencies of *Christianity* made a most improving Addition unto the *Virtues*, wherein even without *those* he would have made a *Parallel* for the Great Men of *Greece*, or of *Rome*, which the Pen of a *Plutarch* has Eternized.

§ 2. A stock of *Heroes* by right should afford nothing but what is *Heroical*; and nothing but an extream Degeneracy would make any thing less to be expected from a Stock of *Winthrops*. Mr. *Adam Winthrop*, the Son of a Worthy Gentleman wearing the same Name, was himself a Worthy, a Discreet, and a Learned Gentleman, particularly Eminent for *Skill* in the *Law*, nor without Remark for *Love* to the *Gospel*, under the Reign of King *Henry* VIII. And Brother to a Memorable *Favourer* of the *Reformed Religion* in the Days of Queen *Mary*, into whose Hands the Famous Martyr *Philpot* committed his *Papers*, which afterwards made no Inconsiderable part of our *Martyr-Books*. This Mr. *Adam Winthrop* had a Son of the same Name also, and of the same Endowments and Imployments with his Father; and this Third *Adam Winthrop* was the Father of that Renowned *John Winthrop*, who was the Father of *New-England*, and the Founder *of a Colony*, which upon many Accounts, like *him* that Founded it, may challenge the *First Place* among the *English* Glories of *America*. Our *JOHN WINTHROP* thus Born at the Mansion-House of his Ancestors, at *Groton* in *Suffolk*, on *June* 12. 1587. enjoyed afterwards an agreeable Education. But though he would rather have Devoted himself unto the Study of Mr. *John Calvin*, than of Sir *Edward Cook*; nevertheless, the Accomplishments of a *Lawyer*, were those wherewith Heaven made his chief Opportunities to be Serviceable.

§ 3. Being made, at the unusually early Age of *Eighteen*, a *Justice of Peace*, his Virtues began to fall under a more general Observation; and he not only so *Bound himself to the Behaviour* of a *Christian*, as to become Exemplary for a Conformity to the *Laws* of *Christianity* in his own Conversation, but also discovered a more than ordinary Measure of those Qualities, which adorn an *Officer of Humane Society*. His *Justice* was Impartial, and used the *Ballance* to weigh not the *Cash*, but the *Case* of those who were before him: *Prosopolatria*, he reckoned as bad as *Idololatria*:[9] His *Wisdom* did exquisitely Temper things according to the *Art of Governing*, which is a Business of more Contrivance than the *Seven Arts* of the *Schools*: *Oyer* still went before *Terminer* in all his Administrations:[10] His *Courage* made him *Dare to do right*, and fitted him to stand among the *Lions*, that have sometimes been the *Supporters* of the Throne: All which Virtues he rendred the more Illustrious, by *Emblazoning* them with the Constant *Liberality* and *Hospitality* of a *Gentleman*. This made him the *Terror* of the Wicked, and the *Delight* of the Sober, the *Envy* of the many, but the *Hope* of those who had any *Hopeful Design* in Hand for the Common Good of the Nation, and the Interests of Religion.

§ 4. Accordingly when the *Noble Design* of carrying a Colony of *Chosen People* into an *American* Wilderness, was by *some* Eminent Persons undertaken, *This* Eminent Person was, by the Consent of all, *Chosen* for the *Moses*, who must be the Leader of so great an Undertaking: And indeed nothing but a *Mosaic Spirit* could have carried him through the *Temptations*, to which either his *Farewel* to his *own Land*, or his *Travel* in a *Strange Land*, must needs expose a Gentleman of his *Education*. Wherefore having Sold a fair Estate of Six or Seven Hundred a Year, he Transported himself with the Effects of it into *New-England* in the Year 1630. where he spent it upon the Service of a famous Plantation founded and formed for the Seat of the most *Reformed Christianity*: And continued there, conflicting with *Temptations* of all sorts, as many Years as the *Nodes* of the *Moon* take to dispatch a Revolution.[11] Those Persons were never concerned in a *New-Plantation*, who know not that the unavoidable Difficulties of such a thing, will call for all the *Prudence* and *Patience* of a Mortal Man to Encounter therewithal; and they must be very insensible of the Influence, which the *Just Wrath* of Heaven has permitted the *Devils* to have upon *this World*, if they do not think that the

---

[9] "Worship of persons" as bad as "worship of idols."—*Murdock*.
[10] "Hearing" before "judging."—*Murdock*.
[11] The time required for a revolution of the nodes of the moon is 18.6 years.—*Murdock*.

Difficulties of a *New-Plantation*, devoted unto the *Evangelical Worship* of our Lord Jesus Christ, must be yet more than Ordinary. How *Prudently*, how *Patiently*, and with how much Resignation to our Lord Jesus Christ, our brave *Winthrop* waded through these *Difficulties*, let Posterity Consider with Admiration. And know, that as the *Picture* of this their *Governour*, was, after his *Death*, hung up with Honour in the *State-House* of his Country, so the *Wisdom*, *Courage*, and Holy *Zeal* of his *Life*, were an Example well-worthy to be Copied by all that shall succeed in *Government*.

§ 5. Were he now to be consider'd only as a *Christian*, we might therein propose him as greatly Imitable. He was a very *Religious* Man; and as he strictly kept his *Heart*, so he kept his *House*, under the Laws of *Piety*; *there* he was every Day constant in Holy Duties, both Morning and Evening, and on the *Lord's Days*, and *Lectures*; though he *wrote* not after the Preacher, yet such was his *Attention*, and such his *Retention* in *Hearing*, that he repeated unto his *Family* the *Sermons* which he had heard in the Congregation. But it is chiefly as a *Governour* that he is now to be consider'd. Being the *Governour* over the considerablest Part of *New-England*, he maintain'd the Figure and Honour of his Place with the Spirit of a true *Gentleman*; but yet with such obliging *Condescention* to the Circumstances of the Colony, that when a certain troublesome and malicious Calumniator, well known in those Times, printed his Libellous *Nick-Names* upon the chief Persons here, the worst *Nich-Name* [sic] he could find for the Governour, was *John Temper-well*; and when the Calumnies of that ill Man caused the Arch-Bishop to Summon one Mr. *Cleaves* before the King, in hopes to get some Accusation from him against the Country, Mr. *Cleaves* gave such an Account of the Governour's laudable Carriage in all Respects, and the serious Devotion wherewith Prayers were both publickly and privately made for His Majesty, that the King expressed himself most highly *Pleased* therewithal, only *Sorry* that so Worthy a Person should be no better Accommodated than with the Hardships of *America*. He was, indeed, a *Governour*, who had most exactly studied that Book, which pretending to Teach *Politicks*, did only contain *Three Leaves*, and but *One Word* in each of those Leaves, which Word was, MODERATION. Hence, though he were a Zealous Enemy to all *Vice*, yet his *Practice* was according to his *Judgment* thus expressed; *In the Infancy of Plantations, Justice should be administred with more Lenity than in a settled State; because People are more apt then to Transgress; partly out of Ignorance of new Laws and Orders, partly out of Oppression of Business, and other Straits.* [LENTO GRADU [12]] *was the old Rule; and if the Strings of a new Instrument be wound up unto their heighth, they will quickly crack.* But when some Leading and Learned Men took Offence at his Conduct in this Matter, and upon a *Conference* gave it in as their Opinion, *That a stricter Discipline was to be used in the beginning of a Plantation, than after its being with more Age established and confirmed,* the Governour being readier to see *his own* Errors than *other Mens*, professed his Purpose to endeavour their Satisfaction with less of *Lenity* in his Administrations. At that *Conference* there were drawn up several other *Articles* to be observed between the Governour and the rest of the Magistrates, which were of this Import: *That* the *Magistrates*, as far as might be, should aforehand ripen their *Consultations*, to produce that *Unanimity* in their *Publick* Votes, which might make them liker to the *Voice of God; that if Differences* fell out among them in their Publick Meetings, they should speak only to the *Case*, without any Reflection, with all due *Modesty*, and but by way of *Question;* or Desire the deferring of the *Cause* to further time; and after *Sentence* to intimate privately no *Dislike; that* they should be more *Familiar*, Friendly and Open unto each other, and more frequent in their *Visitations*, and not any way expose each other's *Infirmities*, but seek the *Honour* of each other, and all the Court; *that* One Magistrate shall not *cross* the Proceedings of another, without first advising with him; and *that* they should in all their Appearances abroad, be so circumstanced as to prevent all Contempt of Authority; and *that* they should Support and Strengthen all *Under Officers.* All of which *Articles* were observed by no Man more than by the *Governour* himself.

§ 6. But whilst he thus did as our *New-English Nehemiah*,

---

[12] "By slow degrees."—*Murdock.*

the part of a *Ruler* in Managing the Public Affairs of our *American Jerusalem*, when there were *Tobijahs* and *Sanballats* enough to vex him, and give him the Experiment of *Luther's* Observation, *Omnis qui regit, est tanquam signum, in quod omnia Jacula, Satan & Mundus dirigunt;*[13] he made himself still an exacter *Parallel* unto that Governour of *Israel*, by doing the part of a *Neighbour* among the distressed People of the *New-Plantation*. To teach them the *Frugality* necessary for those times, he abridged himself of a Thousand comfortable things, which he had allow'd himself elsewhere: His *Habit* was not that *soft Raiment*, which would have been disagreeable to a *Wilderness*; his *Table* was not covered with the *Superfluities* that would have invited unto *Sensualities*: *Water* was commonly his *own Drink*, though he gave Wine to *others*. But at the same time his *Liberality* unto the Needy was even beyond measure Generous; and therein he was continually causing *The Blessing of him that was ready to Perish to come upon him, and the Heart of the Widow and the Orphan to sing for Joy*: But none more than those of Deceas'd *Ministers*, whom he always treated with a very singular Compassion; among the Instances whereof we still enjoy with us the Worthy and now Aged Son of that Reverend *Higginson*, whose Death left his Family in a wide World soon after his arrival here, publickly acknowledging the Charitable *Winthrop* for his *Foster-Father*. It was often-times no small Trial unto his *Faith*, to think, *How a Table for the People should be furnished when they first came into the Wilderness!* And for very many of the People, his *own good Works* were needful, and accordingly employed for the answering of his *Faith*. Indeed, for a while the Governour was the *Joseph*, unto whom the whole Body of the People repaired when their *Corn* failed them: And he continued Relieving of them with his *open-handed Bounties*, as long as he had any Stock to do it with; and a lively *Faith* to *see* the return of the *Bread after many Days*, and not *Starve* in the Days that were to pass till that *return* should be *seen*, carried him chearfully through those Expences. Once it was observable, that on *Feb.* 5. 1630.

---

[13] "Everyone who rules is like a target against which Satan and the World aim all their darts."—*Murdock*.

when he was distributing the last Handful of *the Meal in the Barrel* unto a Poor Man distressed by the Wolf *at the Door,* at that Instant they spied a Ship arrived at the Harbour's Mouth Laden with *Provisions* for them all. Yea, the Governour sometimes made his own *private Purse* to be the *Publick*; not by *sucking* into it, but by *squeezing* out of it; for when the *Publick Treasure* had nothing in it, he did himself defray the Charges of the *Publick.* And having learned that Lesson of our Lord, *That it is better to Give, than to Receive,* he did, at the General Court when he was a Third time chosen Governour, make a Speech unto this purpose, *That he had received Gratuties from divers Towns, which he accepted with much Comfort and Content; and he had likewise received Civilities from particular Persons, which he could not refuse without Incivility in himself: Nevertheless, he took them with a trembling Heart, in regard of Gods Word, and the Conscience of his own Infirmities; and therefore he desired them that they would not hereafter take it Ill if he refused such Presents for the time to come.* 'Twas his Custom also to send some of his Family upon Errands, unto the Houses of the Poor about their *Mealtime,* on purpose to *spy* whether they *wanted*; and if it were found that they *wanted,* he would make *that* the Opportunity of sending Supplies unto them. And there was one Passage of his *Charity* that was perhaps a little *unusual:* In an hard and long Winter, when Wood was very scarce at *Boston,* a Man gave him a private *Information,* that a needy Person in the Neighbourhood stole Wood sometimes from *his* Pile; whereupon the Governour in a seeming Anger did reply, *Does he so? I'll take a Course with him; go, call that Man to me, I'll warrant you I'll cure him of Stealing!* When the Man came, the Governour considering that if he had *Stoln,* it was more out of *Necessity* than *Disposition,* said unto him, *Friend, It is a severe Winter, and I doubt you are but meanly provided for Wood; wherefore I would have you supply your self at my Wood-Pile till this cold Season be over.* And he then Merrily asked his Friends, *Whether he had not effectually cured this Man of Stealing his Wood?*

§ 7. One would have imagined that so *good* a Man could have had no *Enemies*; if we had not had a daily and woful

Experience to Convince us, that *Goodness* it self will *make* Enemies. It is a wonderful Speech of *Plato,* (in one of his Books, *De Republica*) *For the trial of true Vertue, 'tis necessary that a good Man* μηδὲν ἀδικῶν, δόξαν ἔχει την μεγίστην ἀδικιας. *Tho' he do no unjust thing, should suffer the Infamy of the greatest Injustice.* The Governour had by his unspotted *Integrity,* procured himself a great Repntation [*sic*] among the *People;* and then the Crime of Popularity was laid unto his Charge by such, who were willing to deliver him from the Danger of having *all Men speak well of him.* Yea, there were Persons eminent both for Figure and for Number, unto whom it was almost *Essential* to *dislike* every thing that came from *him;* and yet *he* always maintained an Amicable Correspondence with them; as believing that they acted according to their Judgment and Conscience, or that their Eyes were held by some *Temptation* in the worst of all their Oppositions. Indeed, his *right Works* were so many, that they exposed him unto the *Envy* of his Neighbours; and of such *Power* was that *Envy,* that somctimes he could not *stand before it;* but it was by *not standing* that he most effectually *withstood* it all. Great Attempts were sometimes made among the *Freemen,* to get him left out from his Place in the *Government* upon little Pretences, lest by the too *frequent Choice* of One Man, the *Government* should ccase to be by *Choice;* and with a particular aim at *him,* Sermons were Preached at the Anniversary Court of *Election,* to disswade the *Freemen* from chusing *One Man* Twice together. This was the Reward of his *extraordinary Serviceableness!* But when these Attempts *did* succeed, as they sometimes *did,* his Profound *Humility* appeared in that *Equality of Mind,* wherewith he applied himself cheerfully to serve the Country in whatever Station their *Votes* had allotted for him. And one Year when the *Votes* came to be Numbered, there were found Six less for Mr. *Winthrop,* than for another Gentleman who then stood in Competition: But several other Persons regularly Tendring their *Votes* before the *Election* was published, were, upon a very frivolous Objection, refused by some of the Magistrates, that were afraid lest the *Election* should at last fall upon Mr. *Winthrop:* Which though it was well perceived, yet such was the *Self-denial,* of this *Patriot,* that he would not permit any Notice to be taken of the Injury. But these *Trials* were nothing in Comparison of those harsher and harder *Treats*, which he sometimes had from the *Froward-ness* of not a few in the Days of their *Paroxisms;* and from the *Faction* of some against him, not much unlike that of the *Piazzi* in *Florence* against the Family of the *Medices:* All of which he at last Conquered by Conforming to the Famous *Judges* Motto, *Prudens qui Patiens.*[14] The Oracles of God have said, *Envy is rottenness to the Bones;* and *Gulielmus Parisiensis*[15] applies it unto Rulers, who are as it were the *Bones* of the Societies which they belong unto: *Envy,* says he, *is often found among them, and it is rottenness unto them.* Our *Winthrop* Encountred this *Envy* from others, but Conquered it, by being free from it himself.

§ 8. Were it not for the sake of introducing the Exemplary Skill of this Wise Man, *at giving soft Answers,* one would not chuse to Relate those Instances of *Wrath,* which he had some-times to Encounter with; but he was for his *Gentleness,* his *Forbearance,* and his *Longanimity,* a Pattern so worthy to be Written *after,* that something must here be Written *of* it. He seemed indeed never to speak any other Language than that of *Theodosius, If any Man speak evil of the Governour, if it be thro' Lightness, 'tis to be contemned; if it be thro' Madness, 'tis to be pitied; if it be thro' Injury, 'tis to be remitted.* Be-hold, Reader, the *Meekness of Wisdom* notably exemplified! There was a time when he received a very sharp Letter from a Gentleman, who was a Member of the Court, but he de-livered back the Letter unto the Messengers that brought it with such a Christian Speech as this, *I am not willing to keep such a matter of Provocation by me!* Afterwards the same Gentleman was compelled by the scarcity of Provisions to send unto him that he would Sell him some of his Cattel; where-upon the Governour prayed him to accept what he had sent for as a *Token* of his Good Will; but the Gentleman returned him this Answer, *Sir, your overcoming of your self hath over-come me;* and afterwards gave Demonstration of it. The

---

[14] "He is prudent who is patient."—*Murdock.*
[15] William, who became Bishop at Paris, in 1228.—*Murdock.*

French have a saying, That *Un Honeste Homme, est un Homme mesle!* A *good* Man is a *mixt Man;* and there hardly ever was a more sensible *Mixture* of those Two things, *Resolution* and *Condescention,* than in this good Man. There was a time when the Court of *Election,* being for fear of Tumult, held at *Cambridge,* May 17. 1637. The Sectarian part of the Country, who had the Year before gotten a *Governour* more unto their Mind, had a Project now to have confounded the *Election,* by demanding that the *Court* would consider a *Petition* then tendered before their Proceeding thereunto. Mr. *Winthrop* saw that this was only a Trick to throw all into Confusion, by putting off the *Choice* of the *Governour* and *Assistents* until the *Day* should be over; and therefore he did, with a strenuous *Resolution,* procure a disappointment unto that mischievous and ruinous Contrivance. Nevertheless, Mr. *Winthrop* himself being by the Voice of the Freemen in this Exigence chosen the *Governour,* and all of the other Party left out, that ill-affected Party discovered the *Dirt* and *Mire,* which remained with them, after the *Storm* was over; particularly the *Serjeants,* whose Office 'twas to attend the *Governour,* laid down their *Halberts;* but such was the *Condescention* of this Governour, as to take no present Notice of this Anger and Contempt, but only Order some of his own Servants to take the *Halberts:* And when the Country manifested their deep Resentments of the Affront thus offered him, *he* prayed them to *overlook* it. But it was not long before a Compensation was made for these things by the *doubled Respects* which were from all Parts paid unto him. Again, there was a time when the Suppression of an *Antinomian* and *Familistical* Faction, which extreamly threatned the Ruin of the Country, was generally thought much owing unto this Renowned Man;[16] and therefore when the Friends of that Faction could not wreak their Displeasure on him with any *Politick* Vexations, they set themselves to do it by *Ecclesiastical* ones. Accordingly when a Sentence of *Banishment* was passed on the Ringleaders of those Disturbances, who

---

[16] This refers to the "persecution" of Anne Hutchinson for her nonconformity to Puritan ideas . . . —*Murdock.*

—*Maria & Terras, Cælumq; profundum,*
Quippe ferant, Rapidi, secum, vertantq; per Auras;[17]

many at the Church of *Boston,* who were then that way too
much inclined, most earnestly solicited the Elders of that
Church, whereof the Governour was a *Member,* to call him
forth as an *Offender* for passing of that Sentence. The *Elders*
were unwilling to do any such thing; but the Governour understanding the *Ferment* among the *people,* took that occasion to
make a Speech in the Congregation to this Effect. 'Brethren,
'Understanding that some of you have desired that I should
'Answer for an *Offence* lately taken among you; had I been
'called upon so to do, I would, *First,* Have advised with the
'Ministers of the Country, whether the *Church* had Power to
'call in Question the *Civil Court;* and I would, *Secondly,* Have
'advised with the rest of the *Court,* whether I might discover
'their Counsels unto the *Church.* But though I know that the
'Reverend *Elders* of this Church, and some others, do very well
'apprehend that the *Church* cannot enquire into the Proceed-
'ings of the *Court;* yet for the Satisfaction of the weaker who
'do not apprehend it, I will declare my Mind concerning it.
'If the *Church* have any such Power, they have it from the
'Lord Jesus Christ; but the Lord Jesus Christ hath disclaimed
'it, not only by *Practice,* but also by *Precept,* which we have
'in his Gospel, *Mat.* 20. 25, 26. It is true indeed, that *Magis-*
'*trates,* as they are *Church-Members,* are accountable unto the
'*Church* for their Failings; but that is when they are out of
'their Calling. When *Uzziah* would go offer Incense in the
'*Temple,* the Officers of the *Church* called him to an account,
'and withstood him; but when *Asa* put the Prophet in Prison,
'the Officers of the *Church* did not call *him* to an account for
'*that.* If the *Magistrate* shall in a *private way* wrong any Man,
'the *Church* may call him to an Account for it; but if he be
'in Pursuance of a Course of *Justice,* though the thing that he
'does be *unjust,* yet he is not accountable for it before the
'*Church.* As for my self I did nothing in the Causes of any of

---

[17] "Swift bear with them sea and earth and the lofty sky, and drive them
through the air."—*Murdock.*

'the *Brethren,* but by the Advice of the *Elders* of the *Church.*
'Moreover, in the *Oath* which I have taken there is this Clause,
'*In all Causes wherein you are to give your* Vote, *you shall do*
'*as in your Judgment and Conscience you shall see to be Just,*
'*and for the publick Good.* And I am satisfied, it is most for
'the Glory of God, and the *publick Good,* that there has been
'such a *Sentence* passed; yea, those *Brethren* are so divided from
'the *rest* of the Country in their Opinions and Practices, that
'it cannot stand with the *publick Peace* for them to continue
'with us; *Abraham* saw that *Hagar* and *Ishmael* must be sent
'away. By such a Speech he marvellously convinced, satisfied
and mollified the *uneasie Brethren* of the Church; *Sic cunctus
Pelagi cecidit Fragor*—.[18] And after a little patient waiting, the
differences all so wore away, that the Church, meerly as a
Token of Respect unto the Governour, when he had newly
met with some *Losses* in his Estate, sent him a Present of
several *Hundreds* of Pounds. Once more there was a time,
when some active Spirits among the *Deputies* of the Colony,
by their endeavours not only to make themselves a *Court of
Judicature,* but also to take away the *Negative* by which the
Magistrates might check their *Votes,* had like by over-driving
to have run the whole Government into something too *Democratical.* And if there were a Town in *Spain* undermined by
Coneys, another Town in *Thrace* destroyed by *Moles,* a Third
in *Greece* ranversed by *Frogs,* a Fourth in *Germany* subverted
by *Rats;* I must on this Occasion add, that there was a Country
in *America* like to be confounded by a *Swine.* A certain *stray
Sow* being found, was claimed by Two several Persons with a
Claim so equally maintained on both sides, that after Six or
Seven Years *Hunting* the Business, from one Court unto another, it was brought at last into the *General Court,* where the
final Determination was, *that it was impossible to proceed unto
any Judgment in the Case.* However in the debate of this
Matter, the *Negative* of the *Upper-House* upon the *Lower* in
that Court was brought upon the Stage; and agitated with so
hot a Zeal, that a *little more and all had been in the Fire.* In
these Agitations the Governour was informed that an offence

[18] "So all the din of the sea subsided."—*Murdock.*

had been taken by some eminent Persons, at certain Passages in a Discourse by him written thereabouts; whereupon with his usual *Condescendency,* when he next came into the General Court, he made a Speech of this Import. 'I understand, that 'some have *taken* Offence at something that I have lately 'written; which *Offence* I desire to remove now, and begin this 'Year in a reconciled State with you all. As for the *Matter* of 'my Writing, I had the Concurrence of my *Brethren;* it is a 'Point of *Judgment* which is not at my own disposing. I have 'examined it over and over again, by such *Light* as God has 'given me, from the Rules of *Religion, Reason,* and *Custom;* 'and I see no cause to Retract any thing of it: Wherefore I 'must enjoy my *Liberty* in *that,* as *you* do your selves. But for 'the *Manner, this,* and all that was blame-worthy in it, was 'wholly *my own;* and whatsoever I might alledge for my own 'Justification therein before *Men,* I wave it, as now setting my 'self before another *Judgment-Seat.* However, what I wrote was 'upon *great Provocation,* and to vindicate my self and others 'from great Aspersion; yet that was no sufficient Warrant for 'me to allow any *Distemper of Spirit* in my self; and I doubt 'I have been too prodigal of my *Brethren's Reputation;* I might 'have maintained my Cause without casting any Blemish upon 'others, when I made that my Conclusion, *And now let Re-* '*ligion and sound Reason give Judgment in the Case;* it look'd 'as if I arrogated too much unto *my self,* and too little to 'others. And when I made that Profession, *That I would main-* '*tain what I wrote before all the World,* though such Words 'might modestly be spoken, yet I perceive an unbeseeming '*Pride* of my own Heart breathing in them. For these Failings 'I ask Pardon both of God and Man.

> *Sic ait, & dicto citius Tumida Æquora placat,*
> *Collectasq; fugat Nubes, Solemq; reducit.*[19]

This *acknowledging Disposition* in the Governour, made them all *acknowledge,* that he was truly *a Man of an excellent Spirit.*

---

[19] "So he spoke, and thus quickly calmed the swelling sea, put to rout the gathered clouds, and brought back the sun."—*Murdock.*

In fine, the *Victories* of an *Alexander*, an *Hannibal*, or a *Cæsar*
over *other Men*, were not so Glorious, as the *Victories* of this
great Man over *himself*, which also at last prov'd *Victories* over
other Men.

§ 9. But the stormiest of all the *Trials* that ever befel this
Gentleman, was in the Year 1645. when he was in *Title* no
more than *Deputy-Governour* of the Colony. If the famous
Cato were Forty-four times call'd into Judgment, but as often
acquitted; let it not be wondred, and if our Famous *Winthrop*
were one time so. There hapning certain Seditious and Mutinous Practices in the Town of *Hingham*, the *Deputy-Governour* as legally as prudently interposed his *Authority* for the
checking of them: Whereupon there followed such an *En-
chantment* upon the minds of the *Deputies* in the General
Court, that upon a scandalous Petition of the Delinquents
unto *them*, wherein a pretended Invasion made upon the
Liberties of the *People* was complained of the *Deputy-Governour*, was most Irregularly call'd forth unto an Ignominous
Hearing before them in a vast Assembly; whereto with a
Sagacious Humility he *consented*, although he shew'd them
how he might have *Refused* it. The result of that *Hearing* was,
That notwithstanding the touchy *Jealousie* of the *People* about
their *Liberties* lay at the bottom of all this Prosecution, yet
Mr. *Winthrop* was publickly Acquitted, and the Offenders were
severally Fined and Censured. But Mr. *Winthrop* then resum-
ing the Place of *Deputy-Governour* on the Bench, saw cause
to speak unto the *Root of the Matter* after this manner. 'I
'shall not now speak any thing about the past *Proceedings* of
'this Court, or the *Persons* therein concerned. Only I bless God
'that I see an Issue of this troublesome Affair. I am well satis-
'fied that I was publickly *Accused*, and that I am now publickly
'*Acquitted*. But though I am justified before *Men*, yet it may
'be the *Lord* hath seen so much amiss in my Administrations,
'as calls me to be *humbled*; and indeed for me to have been
'thus charged by *Men*, is it self a Matter of *Humiliation*,
'whereof I desire to make a right use before the *Lord*. If
'*Miriam's* Father spit in her Face, she is to be *Ashamed*. But
'give me leave before you go, to say something that may rectifie
'the *Opinions* of many *People*, from whence the *Distempers*

'have risen that have lately prevailed upon the *Body* of *this*
'People. The Questions that have troubled the Country have
'been about the *Authority of the Magistracy,* and the *Liberty*
'*of the People.* It is *You* who have called *us* unto this Office;
'but being thus *called,* we have our *Authority* from God; it is
'the *Ordinance* of God, and it hath the *Image* of God stamped
'upon it; and the contempt of it has been vindicated by *God*
'with terrible Examples of his Vengeance. I intreat you to
'consider, That when you chuse *Magistrates,* you take them
'from among your selves, *Men subject unto like Passions with*
'*your selves.* If you see *our* Infirmities, reflect on *your own,* and
'you will not be so severe Censurers of *Ours.* We count him
'*a good Servant* who *breaks not his Covenant:* The *Covenant*
'between *Us* and *You,* is the *Oath* you have taken of *us,* which
'is to this Purpose, *That we shall govern you, and judge your*
'*Causes, according to God's Laws, and our own, according to*
'*our best Skill.* As for our *Skill,* you must run the hazard of it;
'and if there be an Error, not in the *Will,* but only in the
'*Skill,* it becomes *you* to bear it. Nor would I have you to
'mistake in the Point of your own *Liberty.* There is a *Liberty*
'of corrupt Nature, which is affected both by *Men* and *Beasts,*
'to do what they list; and this *Liberty* is inconsistent with
'*Authority,* impatient of all Restraint; by this *Liberty, Sumus*
'*Omnes Deteriores;*[20] 'Tis the Grand Enemy of *Truth* and
'*Peace,* and all the *Ordinances* of God are bent against it. But
'there is a Civil, a Moral, a Federal *Liberty,* which is the
'proper End and Object of *Authority;* it is a *Liberty* for that
'only which is *just* and *good;* for this *Liberty* you are to stand
'with the hazard of your very *Lives;* and whatsoever Crosses it,
'is not *Authority,* but a *Distemper* thereof. This *Liberty* is
'maintained in a way of *Subjection* to *Authority;* and the
'*Authority* set over you, will in all Administrations for your
'good be quietly submitted unto, by all but such as have a
'Disposition to *shake off the Yoke,* and lose their true *Liberty,*
'by their murmuring at the Honour and Power of *Authority.*'
    The *Spell* that was upon the Eyes of the People being thus

---

[20] "We are all the worse."—*Murdock.*

dissolved, their *distorted* and *enraged* notions of things all vanished; and the People would not afterwards entrust the Helm of the *Weather-beaten* Bark in any other Hands, but Mr. *Winthrop's,* until he Died.

§ 10. Indeed such was the *Mixture* of *distant Qualities* in him, as to make a most admirable *Temper;* and his having a certain *Greatness of Soul,* which rendered him Grave, Generous, Courageous, Resolved, Well-applied, and every way a *Gentleman* in his Deameanour, did not hinder him from taking sometimes the old *Romans* way to avoid Confusions, namely, *Cedendo;*[21] or from discouraging some things which are agreeable enough to most that wear the Name of *Gentlemen.* Hereof I will give no Instances, but only *oppose* two Passages of his Life.

In the Year 1632: the Governour, with his Pastor Mr. *Wilson,* and some other Gentlemen, to settle a good understanding between the Two Colonies, travelled as far as *Plymouth,* more than Forty Miles, through an Howling Wilderness, no better accommodated in those early Days, than the *Princes* that in *Solomon's* time saw *Servants on Horseback,* or than *Genus* and *Species* in the old Epigram, *going on Foot.* The difficulty of the *Walk,* was abundantly compensated by the Honourable, *first* Reception, and *then* Dismission, which they found from the Rulers of *Plymouth;* and by the good Correspondence thus established between the New Colonies, who were like the floating Bottels wearing this Motto, *Si Collidimur, Frangimur.*[22] But there were at this time in *Plymouth* two Ministers, leavened so far with the Humours of the *Rigid Separation,* that they insisted vehemently upon the Unlawfulness of calling any *unregenerate* Man by the Name of *Good-man such an One,* until by their indiscreet urging of this Whimsey, the place began to be disquieted. The wiser People being troubled at these Trifles, they took the opportunity of Governour *Winthrop's* being *there,* to have the thing publickly propounded in the Congregation; who in answer

---

[21] "By yielding."—*Murdock.*
[22] "If we collide, we break."—*Murdock.*

thereunto, distinguished between a *Theological* and a *Moral Goodness;* adding, that when *Juries* were first used in *England,* it was usual for the *Crier,* after the Names of Persons fit for that Service were called over, to bid them all, *Attend, Good Men, and True;* whence it grew to be a *Civil Custom* in the *English Nation,* for Neighbours living by one another, to call one another *Good-man such an One:* And it was pity now to make a stir about a *Civil Custom,* so innocently introduced. And that Speech of Mr. *Winthrop's* put a lasting stop to the Little, Idle, Whimsical *Conceits,* then beginning to grow Obstreperous. Nevertheless there was one *Civil Custom* used *in* (and in few *but*) the *English Nation,* which this Gentleman did endeavour to abolish in *this Country;* and that was, *The usage of Drinking to one another.* For although by *Drinking to one another,* no more is meant than an act of *Courtesie,* when one going to *Drink,* does Invite another to do so too, for the same Ends with himself; nevertheless the Governour (not altogether unlike *to Cleomenes,* of whom 'tis reported by *Plutarch,* ἄγοντι οὐδεὶς ποτήριον προσέορε, *Nolenti poculum nunquam præbuit,*[23]) considered the *Impertinency* and *Insignificancy* of this Usage, as to any of *those Ends* that are usually pretended for it; and that indeed it ordinarily served for *no Ends* at all, but only to provoke Persons unto *unseasonable,* and perhaps *unreasonable* Drinking, and at last produce that abominable *Health-Drinking,* which the *Fathers* of old so severely rebuked in the *Pagans,* and which the *Papists* themselves do Condemn, when their Casuists pronounce it, *Peccatum mortale, provocare ad Æquales Calices, & Nefas Respondere.*[24] Wherefore in his own most Hospitable House he left it off, not out of any silly or stingy *Fancy,* but meerly that by his *Example* a greater *Temperance,* with *Liberty* of *Drinking,* might be Recommended, and sundry *Inconveniences* in Drinking avoided; and his *Example* accordingly began to be much followed by the sober People in *this Country,* as it now also begins to be among

---

[23] "Never offered drink to one who was unwilling."—*Murdock.*
[24] "It is a mortal sin to challenge anyone to a drinking match, and wrong to accept such a challenge."—*Murdock.*

Persons of the *Highest* Rank in the *English Nation* it self; until an *Order of Court* came to be made against that *Ceremony* in Drinking, and then the *old Wont* violently returned, with a *Nitimur in Vetitum.*[25]

§ 11. *Many were the Afflictions of this Righteous Man!* He lost much of his Estate in a Ship, and in an *House,* quickly after his coming to *New-England,* besides the Prodigious Expence of it in the Difficulties of his first coming hither. Afterwards his assiduous Application unto the Publick *Affairs,* (wherein *Ipse se non habuit, postquam Respublica eum Gubernatorem habere capit*)[26] made him so much to neglect his own *private Interests,* that an *unjust Steward* ran him 2500 *l.* in Debt before he was aware; for the Payment whereof he was forced, many Years before his Decease, to sell the most of what he had left unto him in the Country. Albeit, by the observable Blessing of God upon the *Posterity* of this *Liberal Man,* his Children all of them came to fair Estates, and lived in good Fashion and Credit. Moreover, he successively Buried Three *Wives;* the First of which was the Daughter and Heiress of Mr. *Forth, of Much Stambridge* in *Essex,* by whom he had *Wisdom with an Inheritance;* and an excellent Son. The Second was the Daughter of Mr. *William Clopton,* of *London,* who Died with her Child, within a very little while. The Third was the Daughter of the truly Worshipful Sir *John Tyndal,* who made it her whole Care to please, First *God,* and then her *Husband;* and by whom he had Four Sons, which Survived and Honoured their Father. And unto all these, the Addition of the *Distempers,* ever now and then raised in the *Country,* procured unto him a very singular share of Trouble; yea, so hard was the Measure which he found even among Pious Men, in the Temptations of a *Wilderness,* that when the *Thunder* and *Lightning* had smitten a *Wind-mill,* whereof he was Owner, some had *such things in their Heads,* as publickly to Reproach this *Charitablest* of Men, as if the *Voice of the Almighty* had rebuked, I know not what *Oppression,* which

---

[25] "We strive for what is forbidden."—*Murdock.*
[26] "He did not possess himself after the state began to possess him as governor."—*Murdock.*

they *judged* him Guilty of: Which things I would not have mentioned, but that the Instances may fortifie the Expectations of my *best Readers* for such Afflictions.

§ 12. He that had been for his Attainments, as they said of the blessed *Macarius*, a Παιδαριογερων *An old Man, while a young One*, and that had in his *young Days* met with many of those *Ill Days*, whereof he could say, he had *little Pleasure in them*; now found *old Age* in its Infirmities advancing *Earlier* upon him, than it came upon his much longer lived Progenitors. While he was yet Seven Years off of that which we call *the grand Climacterical*,[27] he felt the Approaches of his *Dissolution*; and finding he could say,

> Non Habitus, non ipse Color non Gressus Euntis,
> Non Species Eadem, quæ fuit ante, manet.[28]

he then wrote this account of himself, *Age now comes upon me, and Infirmities therewithal, which makes me apprehend that the time of my departure out of this World is not far off. However our times are all in the Lord's Hand, so as we need not trouble our Thoughts how long or short they may be, but how we may be found Faithful when we are called for.* But at last when *that Year* came, he took a *Cold* which turned into a *Feaver*, whereof he lay *Sick* about a Month, and in that *Sickness*, as it hath been observed, that there was allowed unto the *Serpent* the *bruising of the Heel*; and accordingly at the *Heel* or the *Close* of our Lives the *old Serpent* will be *Nibbling* more than ever in our Lives before; and when the Devil sees that we shall shortly be, *where the wicked cease from troubling*, that *wicked One* will *trouble* us more than ever; so this eminent Saint now underwent sharp Conflicts with the *Tempter*, whose *Wrath* grew *Great*, as the *Time* to exert it grew *Short*; and he was Buffetted with the Disconsolate Thoughts of Black and Sore *Desertions*, wherein he could use that sad Representation of his own Condition.

---

[27] The sixty-third year of life.—*Murdock.*
[28] "There remains not the appearance, not even the color, nor the way of life, and not the same aspect, of that which was before."—*Murdock.*

Nuper Eram Judex; Jam Judicor; Ante Tribunat,
Subsistens paveo, Judicor ipse modo.[29]

But it was not long before those *Clouds* were Dispelled, and he enjoyed in his Holy Soul the *Great Consolations of God!* While he thus lay *Ripening* for Heaven, he did out of Obedience unto the *Ordinance* of our Lord, send for the *Elders of the Church* to *Pray* with him; yea, they and the whole Church *Fasted* as well as *Prayed* for him; and in that *Fast* the venerable *Cotton*[30] Preached on *Psal.* 35. 13, 14. *When they were Sick, I humbled my self with Fasting; I behaved my self as though he had been my Friend or Brother; I bowed down heavily, as one that Mourned for his Mother:* From whence I find him raising that Observation, *The Sickness of one that is to us as a Friend, a Brother, a Mother, is a just occasion of deep humbling our Souls with Fasting and Prayer;* and making this Application, 'Upon this Occasion we are now 'to attend this Duty for a *Governour,* who has been to us as 'a *Friend* in his *Counsel* for all things, and *Help* for our *Bodies* 'by *Physick,* for our *Estates* by *Law,* and of whom there was 'no fear of his becoming an *Enemy,* like the *Friends* of *David:* 'A *Governour* who has been unto us as a *Brother;* not usurping 'Authority over the Church; often speaking his *Advice,* and 'often contradicted, even by Young Men, and some of low 'degree; yet not replying, but offering Satisfaction also when 'any supposed *Offences* have arisen; a *Governour* who has been 'unto us as a *Mother,* Parent-like distributing his *Goods* to 'Brethren and Neighbours at his first coming: and *gently* 'bearing our *Infirmities* without taking notice of them.' *Such* a *Governour* after he had been more than *Ten* several times by the People chosen their *Governour,* was *New-England* now to lose; who having, like *Jacob,* first left his *Council* and *Blessing* with his *Children* gathered about his Bed-sides; and, like *David, served his Generation by the Will of God,* he *gave up the Ghost* and *fell asleep* on *March* 26.

---

[29] "Once I was a judge, now I am judged. I stand trembling before the tribunal, now I myself am judged."—*Murdock.*
[30] Rev. John Cotton, grandfather of Cotton Mather.—*Murdock.*

1649. Having, like the dying Emperour *Valentinian*, this above all his other *Victories* for his Triumphs, *His overcoming of himself*.

The Words of *Josephus* about *Nehemiah*, the Governour of *Israel*, we will now use upon this Governour of *New-England*, as his

EPITAPH.

Ἀνὴρ ἐγένετο χρηστὸς τὴν φύσιν, καὶ δίκαιος,
Καὶ περὶ τοὺς ὁμοεθνεῖς φιλοτιμότατος·
Μνημεῖον αἰώνιον ἀυτω καταλιπὼν τὰ τῶν
Ἱεροσολύμων τείχη[31]

VIR FUIT INDOLE BONUS, AC JUSTUS:
ET POPULARIUM GLORIÆ AMANTISSIMUS:
QUIBUS ETERNUM RELIQUIT MONUMENTUM,
          Novanglorum MOENIA.

---

[31] "He was a man by nature good and just, and most zealous for honor for his countrymen, leaving for them an eternal memorial—the walls of Jerusalem." The Latin paraphrase which follows substitutes New England for Jerusalem.—*Murdock*.

from

THE CHRISTIAN PHILOSOPHER
(1721)

THE PREFACE

RELIGIO PHILOSOPHICA;[1]

OR, THE

Christian Philosopher:

BEING

A Commentary, of the more Modern and Certain
PHILOSOPHY,[2] upon that Instruction,

JOB. xxxvi. 24.

Remember that thou magnify His Work which Men behold.

The Works of the Glorious GOD in the *Creation* of the
World, are what I now propose to exhibit; in brief *Essays* to
enumerate *some of them*, that He may be glorified in them:
And indeed my *Essays* may pretend unto no more than *some
of them*; for, *Theophilus*[3] writing, *of the Creation*, to his
Friend *Antolycus*, might very justly say, That if he should have
a *Thousand Tongues*, and live a *Thousand Years*, yet he were
not able to describe the admirable Order of the Creation,
διὰ τὸ ὑπερβάλλον μεγεθὸς καὶ τὸν πλοῦτον σοφίας τοῦ Θεοῦ.
*Such a Transcendent Greatness of God, and the Riches of his
Wisdom appearing in it!*

    Chrysostom, I remember, mentions a *Twofold Book* of
GOD; the Book of the *Creatures*, and the Book of the *Scriptures*: GOD having taught first of all us διὰ πραγμάτων,

---

[1] "Philosophic (or Scientific) Religion."—*Murdock.*
[2] Philosophy in the sense of science in general.—*Murdock.*
[3] Theophilus of Antioch, died 190 A.D.—*Murdock.*

by his *Works*, did it afterwards διὰ γραμμάτων, by his *Words*. We will now for a while read the *Former* of these *Books*, 'twill help us in reading the *Latter*: They will admirably assist one another. The *Philosopher* being asked, What his *Books* were; answered, *Totius Entis Naturalis Universitas*.[4] All Men are accommodated with that *Publick Library*. *Reader,* walk with me into it, and see what we shall find so legible there, *that he that runs may read it.* Behold, a Book, whereof we may agreeably enough use the words of honest *Ægardus*; *Lectu hic omnibus facilis, etsi nunquam legere didicerint, & communis est omnibus, omniumque oculis expositus.*[5]

The Introduction

The *Essays* now before us will demonstrate, that *Philosophy* is no *Enemy*, but a mighty and wondrous *Incentive* to *Religion*; and they will exhibit that PHILOSOPHICAL RELIGION, which will carry with it a most sensible *Character*, and victorious *Evidence* of a *reasonable Service*. GLORY TO GOD IN THE HIGHEST, and GOOD-WILL TOWARDS MEN, animated and exercised; and a Spirit of *Devotion* and of *Charity* inflamed, in such Methods as are offered in these *Essays*, cannot but be attended with more Benefits, than any *Pen* of ours can declare, or any *Mind* conceive.

In the *Dispositions* and *Resolutions* of PIETY thus enkindled, a *Man* most effectually *shews himself a* MAN, and with unutterable Satisfaction answers the grand END of his Being, which is, *To glorify GOD.* He discharges also the Office of a *Priest* for the *Creation*, under the Influences of an admirable Saviour, and therein asserts and assures his Title unto that *Priesthood*, which the Blessedness of the *future State* will very much consist in being advanced to. The whole *World* is indeed a *Temple* of GOD, *built* and *filled* by that Almighty *Architect*; and in this *Temple*, every such one, affecting him-

---

[4] "The natural university of all the existing universe."—*Murdock.*
[5] "Here is reading easy for everyone even though they have not learned to read, and it is open to all, and set out before everyone's eyes."—*Murdock.*

self with the Occasions for it, will *speak of His Glory*. He will also rise into that *Superior Way* of *Thinking* and of *Living*, which the *Wisest* of Men will chuse to take; which the more *Polite Part* of Mankind, and the *Honourable of the Earth*, will esteem it no Dishonour for them to be acquainted with. Upon that Passage occurring in the best of Books, *Ye Sons of the Mighty, ascribe unto the Lord Glory and Strength*; it is a Gloss and an Hint of *Munster*, which carries with it a Cogency: *Nihil est tam sublime, tanque magnificum, quod non teneatur laudare & magnificare Deum Creatorem suum.*[6] Behold, a *Religion*, which will be found *without Controversy*; a *Religion*, which will challenge all possible Regards from the *High*, as well as the *Low*, among the People; I will resume the Term, a PHILOSOPHICAL RELIGION: And yet how *Evangelical!*

In prosecuting this *Intention*, and in introducing almost every *Article* of it, the Reader will continually find some *Author* or other *quoted*. This constant Method of *Quoting*, 'tis to be hoped, will not be censured, as proceeding from an *Ambition to intimate and boast a Learning*, which the *Messieurs du Port-Royal*[7] have rebuked; and that the Humour for which *Austin* reproached *Julian*, will not be found in it: *Quis hæc audiat, & non ipso nominum strepitu terreatur, si est ineruditus, qualis est hominum multitudo, & existimet te aliquem magnum qui hæc scire potueris?*[8] Nor will there be discernible any Spice of the impertinent Vanity, which *La Bruyere* hath so well satirized: '*Herillus* will always *cite*, whether he speaks or writes. 'He makes the *Prince of Philosophers* to say, *That Wine ine-*'*briates*; and the *Roman Orator*, *That Water temperates it*. If 'he talks of *Morality*, it is not he, but the Divine *Plato*, who 'affirms, *That Virtue is amiable, and Vice odious*. The most 'common and trivial things, which he himself is able to think 'of, are ascribed by him to *Latin* and *Greek* Authors.' But in

---

[6] "Nothing is so sublime or magnificent as not to be bound to magnify and praise the Lord, its creator."—*Murdock*.
[7] Port-Royal, a famous community in France, including among its members some of the most learned men of the 17th century.—*Murdock*.
[8] "Who can hear this and not be frightened by the very sound of the names—provided he is not learned, as most men are not—and who but will consider you great because you know so much?"—*Murdock*.

these *Quotations,* there has been proposed, first, a due *Grati-tude* unto those, who have been my *Instructors;* and indeed, *something within me* would have led me to it, if *Pliny,* who is one of them, had not given me a Rule; *Ingenuum est profiteri per quos profeceris.*[9] It appears also but a piece of *Justice,* that the *Names* of those whom the Great GOD has distinguished, by employing them to make those *Discoveries* which are here collected, should live and shine in every such Collection. Among these, let it be known, that there are especially Two, unto whom I have been more indebted, than unto many others; the Indus-trious Mr. RAY, and the Inquisitive Mr. DERHAM; *Fratrum dulce par:*[10] upon whom, in divers Paragraphs of this *Rhap-sody,*[11] I have had very much of my Subsistence; (I hope with-out doing the part of a *Fidentinus* upon them) and I give thanks to Heaven for them.

'Tis true, some Scores of other *Philosophers* have been consulted on this Occasion; but an *Industry* so applied, has in it very little to bespeak any *Praises* for him that has used it: He earnestly renounces them, and sollicits, that not only *he,* but the *Greater Men,* who have been his *Teachers,* may disappear before the Glorious GOD, whom these *Essays* are all written to represent as *worthy to be praised,* and by whose *Grace we are what we are;* nor have we *any thing but what we have received* from Him.

A considerable Body of Men (if the *Jansenists*[12] may now be thought so) in *France,* have learnt of Monsieur *Pascal,* to de-note themselves by the *French* Impersonal Particle *On;* and it was his opinion, that an honest Man should not be found of *naming himself,* or using the word I, and ME; that *Christian Piety* will annihilate our I, and ME, and *Human Civility* will suppress it, and conceal it.

Most certainly there can be very little Pretence to an I, or ME, for what is done in these *Essays.* '*Tis done,* and entirely, *by the Help of* God: This is all that can be pretended to.

---

[9] "It is noble to acknowledge by whom you have profited."—*Murdock.*
[10] "A sweet pair of brothers." . . .—*Murdock.*
[11] A collection, a literary work without definite form.—*Murdock.*
[12] A school of Roman Catholic theologians, whose views dominated Port-Royal.—*Murdock.*

There is very little, that may be said, really to be performed by the Hand that is now writing; but only the *Devotionary Part* of these *Essays*, tho they are not altogether destitute of *American* Communications: And if the *Virtuoso's*, and all the *Genuine Philosophers* of our Age, have approved the Design of the devout RAY and DERHAM, and others, in their Treatises; it cannot be distasteful unto them, to see what was more *generally hinted at* by those Excellent Persons, here more *particularly carried on*, and the more *special Flights* of the true PHILOSOPHICAL RELIGION exemplified. Nor will they that value the Essays of the memorable Antients, *Theodoret*, and *Nazianzen*, and *Ambrose*, upon *the Works of the six Days*, count it a Fault, if among lesser Men in our Days, there be found those who say, *Let me run after them*. I remember, when we read, *Praise is comely for the Upright*, it is urged by *Kimchi*, that the Word which we render *comely*, signifies *desirable*, and *acceptable*; and the Sense of that Sentence is, that *Qui recti sunt, aliud nihil desiderant quam Laudem & Gloriam Dei*.[13] Sure I am, such *Essays* as these, to observe, and proclaim, and publish the *Praises* of the Glorious GOD, will be *desirable* and *acceptable* to all that have a *right Spirit* in them; the rest, who are *blinded*, are Fools, and unregardable: As little to be regarded as a *Monster* flourishing a *Broomstick! Vix illis optari quidquam pejus potest, quam ut fatuitate sua fruantur*.[14] For such *Centaurs* to be found in the Tents of professed *Christianity!*—Good God, unto what Times hast thou reserved us! If the *self taught Philosopher* will not, yet *Abubeker*, a *Mahometan* Writer, by whom such an one was exhibited more than five hundred Years ago, will *rise up in the Judgment with this Generation, and condemn it*. Reader, even a *Mahometan* will shew thee one, without any *Teacher*, but *Reason* in a serious View of *Nature*, led on to the Acknowledgment of a Glorious GOD. Of a Man, supposed as but using his *Rational Faculties* in viewing the Works of GOD, even the *Mahometan* will tell thee; 'There ap-'peared unto him those Fooststeps of Wisdom and Wonders in

---

[13] "The righteous desire nothing but the praise and glory of God."—*Murdock*.
[14] "Hardly anything worse can be hoped for them, than that they may have the fruit of their folly."—*Murdock*.

'the *Works of Creation*, which affected his Mind with an exces-
'sive Admiration; and he became hereby assured, that all these
'things must proceed from such a *Voluntary Agent* as was *infi-*
'*nitely perfect*, yea, above all Perfection: such an one to whom
'the Weight of the least Atom was not unknown, whether in
'Heaven or Earth. Upon his viewing of the *Creatures*, whatever
'*Excellency* he found of any kind, he concluded, it must needs
'proceed from the Influence of that *Voluntary Agent*, so illustri-
'ously glorious, the *Fountain* of *Being*, and of *Working*. He
'knew therefore, that whatsoever Excellencies were by Nature in
'*Him*, were by so much the greater, the more perfect, and the
'more lasting; and that there was no proportion between those
'*Excellencies* which were in *Him*, and those which were found
'in the *Creatures*. He discerned also, by the virtue of that more
'Noble Part of his, whereby he knew the *necessarily existent*
'*Being*, that there was in him a certain Resemblance thereof:
'And he saw, that it was his Duty to labour by all manner of
'Means, how he might obtain the Properties of that *Being*, put
'on *His Qualities*, and imitate *His Actions*; to be diligent and
'careful also in promoting *His Will*; to commit all his Affairs
'unto *Him*, and heartily to acquiesce in all those *Decrees* of *His*
'which concerned him, either from within, or from without: so
'that he pleased himself in *Him*, tho he should *afflict* him, and
'even *destroy* him.' I was going to say, *O Mentis aureæ Verba
bracteata!* [15] But the Great *Alsted* instructs me, that we *Christians*, in our valuable Citations from them that are Strangers to
Christianity, should seize upon the Sentences as containing *our
Truths*, detained in the hands of *Unjust Possessors*; and he
allows me to say, *Audite Ciceronem, quem Natura docuit*.[16]
However, this I may say, *God has thus far taught a* Mahometan!
And this I will say, *Christian*, beware lest a *Mahometan* be
called in for thy *Condemnation!*

    Let us conclude with a Remark of *Minutius Fælix*:[17] 'If so
'much Wisdom and Penetration be requisite to *observe* the
'wonderful Order and Design in the Structure of the World,

---

[15] "O golden words of a golden mind."—*Murdock*.
[16] "Hear Cicero, whom Nature taught."—*Murdock*.
[17] Marcus Minucius Felix, Latin apologist for Christianity, in the third
century.—*Murdock*.

'how much more were necessary to *form* it!' If Men so much admire Philosophers, because they *discover* a small Part of the *Wisdom* that made all things; they must be stark blind, who do not admire that *Wisdom* itself!

· · · · ·

Essay XXIII. of the Earth.

The Lord by Wisdom has founded the Earth. A poor Sojourner on the *Earth* now thinks it his Duty to behold and admire the *Wisdom* of his glorious Maker there.

The *Earth*, which is the Basis and Support of so many Vegetables and Animals, and yields the alimentary Particles, whereof *Water* is the Vehicle, for their Nourishment: *Quorum omnium* (as *Tully* saith well) *incredibilis Multitudo, insatiabili Varietate distinguitur.*[18]

The various Moulds and Soils of the Earth declare the admirable Wisdom of the Creator, in making such a provision for a vast variety of Intentions. *God said, Let the Earth bring forth!* And yet,

> *Nec vero Terræ ferre omnes omnia possunt.*[19]

It is pretty odd; they who have written *de Arte Combinatoria,* reckon of no fewer than one hundred and seventy-nine Millions, one thousand and sixty different sorts of Earth: But we may content ourselves with Sir *John Evelyn's* Enumeration, which is very short of *that.*[20]

However, the *Vegetables* owe not so much of their Life and Growth to the *Earth* itself, as to some agreeable Juices or Salts lodg'd in it. Both Mr. *Boyle* and *Van Helmont*, by Experiments, found the Earth scarce at all diminished when *Plants*, even *Trees*, had been for divers Years growing in it.

---

[18] "Of all these an incredible number, divided with inexhaustible variety."—*Murdock.*
[19] "Not all lands can bear all things."—*Murdock.*
[20] Mather here draws on Evelyn's *Terra,* whence he takes his reference to the *De Arte Combinatoria.*—*Murdock.*

The *Strata* of the Earth, its *Lays* and *Beds*, afford surprizing Matters of Observation: the *Objects* lodged in them: the *Uses* made of them; and particularly the *Passage* they give to *sweet Waters*, as being the *Calanders*[21] wherein they are sweetned. It is asserted that these are found all to lie very much according to the Laws of *Gravity*. Mr. *Derham* went far to demonstrate this Assertion.

The *vain Colts of Asses*, that *fain would be wise*, have cavill'd at the *unequal Surface of the Earth*, have open'd against the *Mountains*, as if they were *superfluous Excrescences*; but *Warts* deforming the Face of the Earth, and Proofs the *Earth* is but an Heap of Rubbish and Ruins. *Pliny* had more of Religion in him.

The sagacious Dr. *Halley* has observed, That the Ridges of *Mountains* being placed thro the midst of their Continents, do serve as *Alembicks*, to distil fresh Waters in vast Quantities for the Use of the World: And their *Heights* give a Descent unto the *Streams*, to run gently, like so many Veins of the *Macrocosm*, to be the more beneficial to the Creation. The generation of *Clouds*, and the distribution of *Rains*, accommodated and accomplished by the *Mountains*, is indeed so observable, that the learned *Scheuchzer* and *Creitlovius* can't forbear breaking out upon it with a *Mirati summam Creatoris Sapientiam!* [22]

What *Rivers* could there be without those admirable *Tools of Nature!*

Vapours being raised by the *Sun*, acting on the Surface of the *Sea*, as a *Fire* under an Alembick, by rarefying of it, makes the lightest and freshest Portions thereof to rise first; which *Rarefaction* is made (as Dr. *Cheyne* observes)[23] by the insinuation of its active Particles among the porous Parts thereof, whereby they are put into a violent Motion many different ways, and so are expanded into little Bubbles of larger Dimensions than formerly they had; and so they become specifically

---

[21] *I.e.*, colanders, strainers.—*Murdock.*
[22] "Wonderful is the lofty wisdom of the Creator." The quotation and the names of the two authorities, are taken direct from Derham.—*Murdock.*
[23] Mather refers to Dr. George Cheyne's *Philosophical Principles of Religion, Natural and Revealed.—Murdock.*

lighter, and the weightier *Atmosphere* buoys them up. The Streams of these *Vapours* rest in places where the Air is of equal *Gravity* with them, and are carried up and down the *Atmosphere* by the course of that Air, till they hit at last against the sides of the *Mountains*, and by this Concussion are condensed, and thus become heavier than the Air they swum in, and so gleet down the rocky Caverns of these *Mountains*, the inner parts whereof being hollow and stony, afford them a *Bason*, until they are accumulated in sufficient Quantities, to break out at the first *Crany*: whence they descend into Plains, and several of them uniting, form Rivulets; and many of those uniting, do grow into *Rivers*. This is the story of them; this their *Pedigree!*

Minerals are dug out of *Mountains*; which, if they were sought only in level Countries, the Delfs would be so flown with Waters, that it would be impossible to make *Addits* or *Soughs* to drein them.[24] Here is, as *Olaus Magnus* expresses it, *Inexhausta pretiosorum Metallorum ubertas.*[25]

A *German* Writer, got upon the *Mountains*, gives this Account of them: *Sunt ceu tot naturales Fornaces Chymicæ, in quibus Deus varia Metalla & Mineralia excoquit & maturat.*[26]

The *Habitations* and *Situations* of Mankind are made vastly the more comfortable for the *Mountains*. There is a vast Variety of *Plants* proper to the *Mountains:* and many Animals find the *Mountains* their most proper places to breed and feed in. *The highest Hills a Refuge to the wild Goats!* A Point Mr. *Ray* has well spoken to.

They report that *Hippocrates* did usually repair to the *Mountains* for the *Plants*, by which he wrought the chief of his Cures.

Mountains also are the most convenient Boundaries to Territories, and afford a Defence unto them. One calls them *the Bulwarks of Nature, cast up at the Charges of the Almighty;*

---

[24] Delf = a ditch; addits and soughs = drains, gutters.—*Murdock.*
[25] "Inexhaustible plenty of precious minerals."—*Murdock.*
[26] "They are like so many natural chemical furnaces in which God tempers and ripens various metals and minerals."—*Murdock.*

the Scorns of the most victorious Armies. The *Barbarians* in *Curtius*[27] were confidently sensible of this!

Yea, we may appeal to the Senses of all Men, whether the grateful Variety of *Hills* and *Dales* be not more pleasing than the largest continued *Plains.*

'Tis also a *salutary Conformation* of the Earth; some Constitutions are best suited *above,* and others *below.*

Truly these massy and lofty Piles can by no means be spared.

Galen, thou shalt chastize the *Pseudo-Christians,* who reproach the Works of God. Say! —— *Accusandi sanè meâ Sententiâ hic sunt Sophistæ, qui cùm nondum invenire neque exponere Opera Naturæ queant, eam tamen inertia atque inscitia condemnant.*[28]

Say now, O *Man,* say, under the sweet Constraints of Demonstration, *Great* GOD, *the Earth is full of thy Goodness!*

And Dr. *Grew* shall carry on the more general Observation for us. 'How little is the Mischief which the *Air, Fire,* or *Water* 'sometimes doth, compared with the innumerable *Uses* to 'which they daily serve? Besides the *Seas* and *Rivers,* how many 'wholesome *Springs* are there for one that is *poisonous?* Are the 'Northern Countries subject to *Cold?* They have a greater plenty 'of *Furs* to keep the People warm. Would those under or near 'the Line be subject to *Heat?* They have a constant *Easterly* '*Breeze,* which blows strongest in the Heat of the Day, to refresh 'them: And with this Refreshment *without,* they have a variety 'of excellent *Fruits* to comfort and cool them *within.* How ad'mirably are the *Clouds* fed with Vapours, and carried about 'with the *Winds,* for the gradual, equal, and seasonable watering 'of most Countries? And in those which have less *Rain,* how 'abundantly is the want of that supplied with noble *Rivers?*'

Even the subterraneous *Caverns* have their Uses. And so have the *Ignivomous Mountains:* Those terrible things are *Spiracles,* to vent the *Vapours,* which else might make a dismal

---

[27] Quintus Curtius, historian.—*Murdock.*
[28] "Those sophists are blameable, who, since they cannot discover or make clear the works of nature, condemn it from laziness and ignorance."—*Murdock.*

Havock. Dr. *Woodward* observes, That tho Places which are
very subject unto *Earthquakes* usually have these *Volcano's,* yet
without these *fiery Vents* their *Earthquakes* would bring more
tremendous Desolations upon them.

Those two flammivomous Mountains, *Vesuvius* and *Ætna,*
have sometimes terrified the whole World with their tremendous
Eruptions. *Vesuvius* transmitted its frightful Cinders as far as
Constantinople, which obliged the Emperor to leave the City;
and Historians tell us there was kept an Anniversary Commemo-
ration of it. *Kircher* has given us a Chronicle of what furious
things have by done by *Ætna;* the melted Matter which one
time it poured forth, spreading in breadth six Miles, ran down
as far as *Catanea,*[29] and forced a Passage into the Sea.

Asia abounds in these *Volcano's. Africa* is known to have
eight at least. In *America* 'tis affirmed that there are not less
than fifteen, among that vast Chain of Mountains called the
Andes. One says, 'Nature seems here to keep house under
'ground, and the Hollows of the *Mountains* to be the *Funnels*
'or *Chimneys,* by which the fuliginous Matter of those everlast-
'ing Fires ascends.'

The *North* too, that seems doom'd unto *eternal Cold,* has
its famous *Hecla.* And *Bartholomew Zenet*[30] found one in
Greenland, yet nearer to the Pole; the Effects whereof are very
surprizing.

A reasonable and religious Mind cannot behold these formidable *Mountains,* without some Reflections of this importance:
*Great GOD, who knows the Power of thine Anger? Or what
can stand before the powerful Indignation of that God, who can
kindle a Fire in his Anger that shall burn to the lowest Hell, and
set on fire the Foundations of the Mountains!*

The *Volcano's* would lead us to consider the *Earthquakes,*
wherein the *Earth* often suffers violent, and sometimes very destructive Concussions.

The History of Earthquakes would be a large, as well as a

---

[29] Catania.—*Murdock.*
[30] Possibly a reference to Nicolo Zeno, who, in the 14th century is said to
have gone to Greenland, and to have discovered a volcano there.—*Murdock.*

sad Volume. Whether a *Colluctation*[31] *of Minerals* in the Bowels of the *Earth* is the cause of those direful Convulsions, may be considered: As we know a Composition of Gold which *Aqua Regia* has dissolved; *Sal Armoniack,* and *Salt of Tartar,* set on fire, will with an horrible crack break thro all that is in the way. But Mankind ought herein to tremble before the Justice of God. Particular *Cities* and *Countries,* what fearful Desolations have been by Earthquakes brought upon them!

The old sinking of *Helice* and *Buris,* absorbed by *Earthquakes* into the Sea, mention'd by *Ovid,* or the twelve Cities that were so swallow'd up in the Days of *Tiberius,* are small things to what *Earthquakes* are to do on our Globe; yea, have already done. I know not what we shall think of the huge *Atlantis,* mentioned by *Plato,* now at the bottom of the *Atlantick* Ocean: But I know *Varenius* thinks it probable, that the Northern Part of *America* was joined unto *Ireland,* till Earthquakes made the vast and amazing Separation. Others have thought so of *England* and *France;* of *Spain* and *Africa;* of *Italy* and *Sicily.*

Ah, *Sicily!* Art thou come to be spoken of? No longer ago than t'other day what a rueful Spectacle was there exhibited in the Island of *Sicily* by an *Earthquake,*[32] in which there perished the best part of two hundred thousand Souls!

Yea, *Ammianus Marcellinus* tells us, in the Year 365, *Horrendi Tremores per omnem Orbis Ambitum grassati sunt.*[33]

O Inhabitants of the Earth, how much ought you to fear the things that will bring you into ill Terms with the Glorious GOD! *Fear,* lest the *Pit* and the *Snare* be upon you! Against all other Strokes there may some Defence or other be thought on: There is none against an *Earthquake!* It says, *Tho they hide in the top of* Carmel, *I will find them there!*

But surely the *Earthquakes* I have met with will effectually instruct me to avoid the Folly of setting my Heart inordinately on any *Earthly* Possessions or Enjoyments. Methinks I hear Heaven saying *Surely he will receive this Instruction!*

A modern Philosopher speaks at this rate, 'We do not know

---

[31] Conflict.—*Murdock.*
[32] Probably the earthquakes in January, 1693.—*Murdock.*
[33] "Fearful shakings went through all the surface of the earth."—*Murdock.*

'when and where we stand upon *good Ground:* It would amaze
'the stoutest Heart, and make him ready to die with Fear, if he
'could see into the *subterraneous World,* and view the dark Re-
'cesses of Nature under ground; and behold, that even the strong-
'est of our Piles of Building, whose Foundation we think is laid
'firm and fast, yet are set upon an Arch or Bridge, made by the
'bending Parts of the Earth one upon another, over a prodigious
'Vault, at the bottom of which there lies an unfathomable Sea,
'but its upper Hollows are filled with stagnating Air, and with
'Expirations of sulphureous and bituminous Matter. Upon such
'a *dreadful Abyss* we walk, and ride, and sleep; and are sustained
'only by an *arched Roof,* which also is not in all places of an
'equal Thickness.'

Give me leave to say, I take *Earthquakes* to be very *moving
Preachers* unto *worldly-minded Men:* Their Address may be very
agreeably put into the Terms of the Prophet; O *Earth, Earth,
Earth, hear the Word of the Lord!*

'Chrysostom did well, among his other Epithets, to call the
'Earth *our Table;* but it shall *teach* me as well as *feed* me: May
'I be a *Deipnosophist*[34] upon it.

'Indeed, what is the Earth but a *Theatre,* as has been long
'since observed? *In quo Infinita & Illustria, Providentiæ, Boni-
'tatis, Potentiæ ac Sapientiæ Divinæ Spectacula contem-
'planda!* [35] But I must not forget 'that this *Earth* is very shortly
'to be my *sleeping-place;* it has a *Grave* waiting for me: I *will
'not fear to go down, for thou has promised, O my Saviour, to
'bring me up again.'

Appendix

§. Having arrived thus far, I will here make a Pause, and acknowledge the shine of Heaven on *our Parts of the Earth,* in the
Improvements of our *modern Philosophy.*

To render us the more sensible hereof, we will propose a
few Points of the *Mahometan Philosophy,* or Secrets reveal'd

---

[34] "A master of the art of dining."—*Murdock.*
[35] "In which are to be contemplated infinite and glorious spectacles of the
Divine providence, goodness, power, and wisdom."—*Murdock.*

unto *Mahomet,* which none of his Followers, who cover so much of the Earth at this Day, may dare to question.

The *Winds*; 'tis an *Angel* moving his *Wings* that raises them.

The *Flux* and *Reflux* of the *Sea,* is caused by an *Angel's* putting his Foot on the middle of the *Ocean,* which compressing the Waves, the Waters run to the Shores; but being removed, they retire into their proper Station.

Falling Stars are the *Firebrands* with which the *good Angels* drive away the *bad,* when they are too saucily inquisitive, and approach too near the Verge of the Heavens, to eves-drop the Secrets there.

Thunder is nothing else but the cracking of an *Angel's Whip,* while he slashes the dull Clouds into such and such places, when they want *Rains* to fertilize the Earth.

Eclipses are made thus: The *Sun* and *Moon* are shut in a *Pipe,* which is turned up and down; from each Pipe is a Window, by which they enlighten the World; but when God is angry at the Inhabitants of it for their Transgressions, He bids an *Angel* clap to the Window, and so turn the Light towards Heaven from the Earth: for this Occasion *Forms of Prayer* are left, that the Almighty would avert his Judgments, and restore Light unto the World.

The thick-skull'd Prophet sets another *Angel* at work for *Earthquakes*; he is to hold so many *Ropes* tied unto every Quarter of the Globe, and when he is commanded, he is to pull; so he shakes that part of the Globe: and if a City, or Mountain, or Tower, is to be overturned, then he tugs harder at the Pulley, till the Rivers dance, and the Valleys are filled with Rubbish, and the Waters are swallowed up in the Precipices.

May our Devotion exceed the Mahometan *as much as our Philosophy!*

. . . . .

Essay XXXII. of Man.

[. *Hear now the Conclusion of the Matter.* To enkindle the *Dispositions* and the *Resolutions* of PIETY in my Brethren, is the *Intention* of all my ESSAYS, and must be the *Conclusion* of them.

Atheism is now for ever chased and hissed out of the World, every thing in the World concurs to a Sentence of *Banishment* upon it. *Fly, thou Monster, and hide, and let not the darkest Recesses of* Africa *itself be able to cherish thee; never dare to shew thyself in a World where every thing stands ready to overwhelm thee!* A BEING that must be *superior* to *Matter*, even the *Creator* and *Governor* of all *Matter*, is every where so conspicuous, that there can be nothing more *monstrous* than *to deny the God that is above.* No *System* of *Atheism* has ever yet been offered among the Children of Men, but what may presently be convinced of such *Inconsistences*, that a Man must ridiculously believe *nothing certain* before he can imagine them; it must be a *System* of *Things which cannot stand together!* A Bundle of *Contradictions* to themselves, and to all *common Sense.* I doubt it has been an *inconsiderate* thing to pay so much of a Compliment to *Atheism*, as to bestow solemn *Treatises* full of learned *Arguments* for the Refutation of a *delirious Phrenzy*, which ought rather to be put out of countenance with the most *contemptuous Indignation.* And I fear such Writers as have been at the pains to put the *Objections* of *Atheism* into the most plausible Terms, that they may have the honour of *laying a Devil when they have raised him*, have therein done too *unadvisedly.* However, to so much notice of the raving *Atheist* we may condescend while we go along, as to tell him, that for a Man to question the *Being of a* GOD, who requires from us an *Homage* of *Affection*, and *Wonderment*, and Obedience to Himself, and a perpetual Concern for the Welfare of the *Human Society*, for which He has in our *Formation* evidently *suited* us, would be an *exalted Folly*, which undergoes especially two Condemnations; it is first condemned by this, that every Part of the *Universe* is continually *pouring in* something for the *confuting* of it; there is not a Corner of the whole World but what supplies a *Stone* towards the Infliction of such a *Death* upon the *Blasphemy* as justly belongs to it: and it has also this condemning of it, that Men would soon become *Canibals* to one another by embracing it; Men being utterly destitute of any Principle to keep them *honest in the Dark*, there would be no *Integrity* left in the World, but they would be as the *Fishes of the Sea to one another*, and worse than *the creeping Things, that have no Ruler over them.* Indeed from every thing in the World there is this Voice more audible than the loudest Thunder to us; *God hath spoken, and these two things have I heard!* First, *Believe and adore a glorious GOD, who has made all these Things, and know thou that He will bring thee into Judgment!* And then *be careful to do nothing but what shall be for the Good of the Community which the glorious GOD has made thee a Member of.* Were what God *hath spoken* duly regarded, and were these *two things* duly complied with, the World would be soon revived into a desirable *Garden of God,* and Mankind would be fetch'd up into very comfortable Circumstances; till *then* the World continues in a wretched Condition, *full of doleful Creatures,* with *wild Beasts crying* in its *desolate Houses, Dragons* in its most *pleasant Palaces.* And now declare, *O every thing that is reasonable,* declare and pronounce upon it whether it be possible that *Maxims* absolutely *necessary* to the *Subsistence* and *Happiness* of Mankind, can be *Falsities?* There is no possibility for this, that *Cheats* and *Lyes* must be so *necessary,* that the *Ends* which alone are worthy of a glorious GOD, cannot be attain'd without having *them* imposed upon us!

Having dispatch'd the *Atheist,* with bestowing on him *not many* Thoughts, yet *more* than could be deserved by such an *Idiot;* I will proceed now to propose two general Strokes of *Piety,* which will appear to a *Christian Philosopher* as unexceptionable as any Proposals that ever were made to him.

First, the Works of the glorious God exhibited to our View, 'tis most certain they do *bespeak,* and they should *excite* our *Acknowledgments of His Glories* appearing in them: the Great GOD is infinitely *gratified* in beholding the Displays of His own infinite *Power,* and *Wisdom,* and *Goodness,* in the Works which He has made; but it is also a most acceptable Gratification to Him, when such of His Works as are the *rational Beholders* of themselves, and of the rest, shall with devout Minds *acknowledge* His Perfections, which they see shining there. Never does one endued with *Reason* do anything more evidently *reasonable,* than when he makes every thing that occurs to him in the vast Fabrick of the World, an *Incentive* to some agreeable Efforts and Salleys of *Religion*. What can any Man living object against the *Piety* of a Mind awaken'd by the sight of God in His Works, to such Thoughts as these: V*erily, there is a glorious GOD! Verily, the GOD who does these things is worthy to be feared, worthy to be loved, worthy to be relied on! Verily, all possible Obedience is due to such a GOD; and most abominable, most inexcusable is the Wickedness of all Rebellion against Him!* A Mind kept under the Impression of such Thoughts as these, is an *holy* and a *noble* Mind, a *Temple* of God, a *Temple filled with the Glory of God*. There is nothing but what will afford an *Occasion* for the *Thoughts*; the oftner a Man improves the *Occasion*, the more does he *glorify* GOD, and answer the *chief End of Man*; and why should he not *seek occasion* for it, by visiting for this purpose the several *Classes* of the Creatures (for *Discipulus in hâc Scholâ erit Peripateticus*)[36] as he may have opportunity for so generous an Exercise! But since the horrid Evil of all *Sin* is to be inferred from this; *it is a Rebellion against the Laws of the glorious GOD, who is the Maker and the Ruler of all Worlds*; and *it is a disturbance of the good Order wherein the glorious Maker and Ruler of all Things has placed them all*; how much ought a quickned Horror of *Sin* to accompany this Contemplation, and produce this most agreeable Resolution, *My God, I will for ever fear to offend thy glorious Majesty!* Nor is this all the *Improvement* which we are to make of what we see in the *Works of God*; in our *improving* of them, we are to accept of the *Rebuke* which they give to our *Presumption*, in pretending to criticize upon the *dark things* which occur in the Dispensations of His *Providence*; there is not any one of all the *Creatures* but what has those *fine things* in the *Texture* of it, which have never yet been reached by our *Searches*, and we are as much at a loss about the *Intent* as about the *Texture* of them; *as yet* we know not what the glorious God *intends* in His forming of those *Creatures*, nor what *He has to do* in them, and with them; He therein proclaims this Expectation, *Surely they will fear me, and receive Instruction*. And the Point wherein we are now instructed is this: 'What! Shall I be 'so vain as to be *dissatisfied* because I do not *understand* what is

[36] "A disciple of this school must be a Peripatetic."– *Murdock*.

'done by the glorious GOD in the Works of His *Providence!*' O *my Soul, hast thou not known, hast thou not heard concerning the everlasting God, the Lord, the Creator of the Ends of the Earth, that there is no searching of His Understanding?* And then, secondly, the CHRIST of God must not be forgotten, who is *the Lord of all. I am not ashamed of the Gospel of CHRIST,* of which I will *affirm constantly,* that if the *Philosopher* do not call it in, he *paganizes,* and leaves the finest and brightest Part of his Work unfinished. Let *Colerus*[37] persuade us if he can, that in .the Time of *John Frederick* the Elector of *Saxony* there was dug up a *Stone,* on which there was a Representation of our *crucified Saviour;* but I cannot forbear saying, there is not a *Stone* any where which would not look *black* upon me, and *speak* my Condemnation, if my *Philosophy* should be so *vain* as to make me lay aside my Thoughts of my *enthroned Saviour.* Let *Lambecius,*[38] if he please, employ his Learning upon the Name of our Saviour CHRIST, found in Letters naturally engraven at the bottom of a large *Agate-Cup,* which is to be seen among the Emperor's Curiosities; I have never drank in that *Cup,* however I can more easily believe it than I can the *Crucifixus ex Radice Crambres enatus,*[39] or the *Imago Virginis cum Filiolo, in Minerâ Ferri expressa,*[40] and several more such things, which the Publishers of the *German Ephemerides*[41] have mingled with their better Entertainments: but I will assert, that a glorious CHRIST is more to be considered in the *Works of Nature* than the *Philosopher* is generally aware of; and my CHRISTIAN *Philosopher* has not fully done his Part, till He who is *the First-born of every Creature* be come into Consideration with him. *Alsted* mentions a *Siclus Judæo-Christianus,*[42]

---

[37] Johann Jacob Coler, 16th century German theologian and writer.—*Murdock.*

[38] Peter Lambeck, 1628–80, German historian.—*Murdock.*

[39] "The crucifix springing from a cabbage root." Mather misprints "crambres" for "crambes."—*Murdock.*

[40] "Image of the Virgin and Child moulded in iron ore."—*Murdock.*

[41] The "German Ephemerides" was a scientific periodical in Germany, *Miscellanea Curiosa sive Ephemeridum Medico-Physicarum Germanicarum,* etc. Cotton Mather refers to articles in the volume for 1670.—*Murdock.*

[42] "A Jewish-Christian shekel (coin)."—*Murdock.*

which had on one side the Name *JESUS*, with the Face of our *Saviour*, and on the other the Words that signify *the King Messiah comes with Peace, and God becomes a Man*; and Leusden[43] says he had a couple of these *Coins* in his possession. I have nothing to say on the behalf of the *Zeal* in those *Christianized Jews*, who probably were the Authors of these *Coins*, a *Zeal* that *boil'd* into so needless an Expression of an Homage, that indeed cannot be too much expressed in the *instituted ways* of it to a Redeemer, whose *Kingdom is not of this World*: but this I will say, *all the Creatures in this World are part of His Kingdom*; there are no *Creatures* but what are His *Medals*, on every one of them the Name of JESUS is to be found inscribed. Celebrate, *O Danhaver*,[44] thy *Granatilla*, the *Peruvian Plant*, on which a strong Imagination finds a Representation of the *Instruments* employed in the *Sufferings* of our Saviour, and especially the *bloody Sweat* of His Agonies; were the Representation as really and lively made as has been imagined, I would subscribe to the Epigram upon it, which concludes:

Flos hic ità formâ vincit omnes Flosculos,
Ut totus optet esse Spectator Oculus.[45]

But I will, with the Exercise of the most *solid Reason*, by every part of the World, as well as the *Vegetables*, be led to my Saviour.

A *View of the Creation* is to be taken, with suitable Acknowledgments of the glorious CHRIST, in whom the *eternal Son of God* has personally united Himself to ONE of His *Creatures*, and becomes on *his* account propitious to *all the rest*; our *Piety* indeed will not be *Christianity* if HE be left unthought upon.

This is HE, of whom we are instructed, *Col*. 1. 16, 17. *All things were created by Him, and for Him; and He is before all things, and by Him all things consist.* It is no contemptible

---

[43] Johann Leusden, 1624–1699, Dutch scholar, and friend of Cotton Mather's father.—*Murdock*.
[44] Johann Conrad Danhawer, 1603–1666, German theologian.—*Murdock*.
[45] "This flower so surpasses all others in its form that every eye may wish to see it."—*Murdock*.

Thought wherewith *De Sabunde* has entertained us: *Productio Mundi à Deo facta de Nihilo, arguit aliam productionem, summam, occultam, & æternam in Deo, quæ est de sua propria Natura, in qua producitur Deus de Deo, & per quam ostenditur summa Trinitas in Deo.*[46] And certainly he that as a *Father* does produce a *Son,* but as an *Artist* only produce an *House,* has a Value for the *Son* which he has not for the *House;* yea, we may say, if GOD had not first, and from Eternity, been a *Father* to our *Saviour,* He would never have exerted Himself as an *Artist* in that *Fabrick,* which He has built *by the Might of His Power, and for the Honour of His Majesty!*

The Great Sir *Francis Bacon* has a notable Passage in his *Confession of Faith: I believe that God is so holy, as that it is impossible for Him to be pleased in any Creature, tho the Work of his own Hands, without beholding of the same in the Face of a Mediator; —— without which it was impossible for Him to have descended to any Work of Creation, but He should have enjoyed the blessed and individual Society of three Persons in the Godhead for ever; but out of His eternal and infinite Goodness and Love purposing to become a Creature, and communicate with His Creatures, He ordained in His eternal Counsel that one Person of the Godhead should be united to one Nature, and to one particular of His Creatures; that so in the Person of the Mediator the true Ladder might be fixed, whereby God might descend to His Creatures, and His Creatures ascend to Him.*

It was an high Flight of *Origen,*[47] who urges, that our *High-Priest's* having *tasted of Death,* ὑπὲρ παντος, FOR ALL, is to be extended even to the very *Stars,* which would otherwise have been *impure* in the sight of God; and thus are ALL THINGS restored to the *Kingdom* of the Father. Our Apostle *Paul* in a famous Passage to the *Colossians* [i. 19, 20.] may seem highly to favour this Flight. One says upon it, 'If this be so, we need not 'break the Glasses of *Galilæo,* the *Spots* may be washed out of

---

[46] "The creation of the world, made by God from nothing, shows that there is another creation, high, secret, and eternal, in God, which is of His own nature, in which God is created from God, and by which is made plain the Trinity in God." Raymond de Sebonde, d. 1432, was a Spanish physician, author of *Theologia Naturalis.—Murdock.*

[47] Alexandrian Christian writer of the 2d and 3d centuries.—*Murdock.*

'the *Sun*, and *total Nature* sanctified to God that made it.'

Yea, the sacred Scriptures plainly and often invite us to a Conception, which Dr. *Goodwin* has chosen to deliver in such Terms as these: 'The *Son of God* personally and actually existing 'as the Son of God with God, afore the World or any Creature 'was made, He undertaking and convenanting with God to be- 'come a *Man*, yea, *that Man* which He hath now taken up into 'one Person with Himself, as well for *this End*, as for *other* '*Ends* more glorious; God did in the Foreknowledge of *that*, 'and in the Assurance of that *Covenant* of His, proceed to 'the *creating* of all things which He hath made; and without the 'Intuition of *this*, or having *this* in His Eye, He would not have 'made any thing which He hath made.'

O CHRISTIAN, *lift up now thine Eyes, and look from the place where thou art* to all Points of the Compass, and concerning *whatever thou seest*, allow that all these things were formed *for the Sake* of that Glorious-One, who is now *God manifest in the Flesh* of our JESUS; 'tis on *His* Account that the eternal Godhead has the *Delight* in all these things, which preserves them in their Being, and grants them the *Help*, in the *obtaining* whereof they *continue to this day*.

But were they not all made *by the hand*, as well as *for the Sake* of that Glorious-ONE? They were verily so. *O my JESUS, it was that Son of God who now dwells in thee, in and by whom the Godhead exerted the Power, which could be exerted by none but an all-powerful GOD, in the creating of the World!* He is that WORD of GOD *by whom all things were made, and without whom was not any thing made that was made.*

This is not all that we have to think upon; we see an incomparable *Wisdom* of GOD in His *Creatures*; one cannot but presently infer, *What an incomprehensible Wisdom then in the Methods and Affairs of that Redemption, whereof the glorious GOD has laid the Plan in our JESUS!* Things which the *Angels* desire to look into. But, O *evangelized Mind*, go on, mount up, soar higher, think at this rate; *the infinite Wisdom which formed all these things is peculiarly seated in the Son of God;* He is that *reflexive Wisdom* of the eternal *Father*, and that *Image of the invisible God, by whom all things were created;* in *Him* there is after a peculiar manner the original *Idea* and *Archetype*

of every thing that offers the infinite *Wisdom* of God to our
Admiration. Wherever we see the *Wisdom* of God admirably
shining before us, we are invited to such a Thought as this; *this
Glory is originally to be found in thee, O our Immanuel!* 'Tis in
Him *transcendently*. But then 'tis impossible to stop without
adding, *How glorious, how wondrous, how lovely art thou, O
our Saviour!*

Nor may we lay aside a grateful Sense of this, that as the
Son of God is *the Upholder of all Things in all Worlds,* thus,
that it is owing to his potent *Intercession* that the *Sin of Man*
has made no more havock on this *our World*. This *our World*
has been by the *Sin of Man* so perverted from the *true Ends* of
it, and rendred full of such loathsome and hateful Regions, and
such *Scelerata Castra,*[48] that the Revenges of God would have
long since rendred it as a *fiery Oven,* if our blessed JESUS had
not *interceded* for it: *O my Saviour, what would have become
of me, and of all that comforts me, if thy Interposition had not
preserved us!*

We will add one thing more: Tho the one GOD in His
three Subsistences be the *Governor* as well as the *Creator* of the
World, and so the *Son* of God ever had what we call the *natural
Government* of the World, yet upon the *Fall* of Mankind there
is a *mediatory Kingdom* that becomes expedient, that so *guilty
Man,* and that which was *lost,* may be brought to God; and the
singular Honour of this *mediatory Kingdom* is more *immediately*
and most *agreeably* assign'd to the *Son of God,* who assumes the
Man JESUS into His own Person, and has *all Power in Heaven
and Earth given to Him;* all things are now commanded and
ordered by the *Son of God* in the *Man upon the Throne,* and
this *to the Glory of the Father,* by whom the *mediatory Kingdom* is erected, and so conferred. This *peculiar Kingdom* thus
managed by the *Son of God* in our JESUS, will cease when the
illustrious Ends of it are all accomplished, and *then* the *Son of
God* no longer having such a *distinct Kingdom* of His own, shall
return to those eternal Circumstances, wherein He shall reign
with the *Father* and the *Holy Spirit,* one God, blessed for ever.
In the mean time, what Creatures can we behold without being

---

[48] "Wicked settlements."—*Murdock.*

obliged to some such Doxology as this; *O Son of God, incarnate and enthroned in my JESUS, this is part of thy Dominion! What a great King art thou, and what a Name hast thou above every Name, and how vastly extended is thy Dominion! Dominion and Fear is with thee, and there is no Number of thine Armies! All the Inhabitants of the Earth, and their most puissant Emperors, are to be reputed as nothing before thee!*

But then at last I am losing myself in such Thoughts as these: *Who can tell* what *Uses* our Saviour will put all these *Creatures* to at the *Restitution of all things,* when He comes to rescue them from the *Vanity* which as yet captivates them and incumbers them; and His raised People in the *new Heavens* will make their Visits to a *new Earth,* which they shall find flourishing in *Paradisaick* Regularities? *Lord, what thou meanest in them, I know not now, but I shall know hereafter!* I go on, *Who can tell* how sweetly our Saviour may *feast* His *chosen People* in the *Future* State, with Exhibitions of all these *Creatures,* in their various *Natures,* and their curious *Beauties* to them? *Lord, I hope for an eternally progressive Knowledge, from the Lamb of God successively leading me to the Fountains of it!*

I recover out of my more *conjectural Prognostications,* with resolving what may *at present* yield to a serious Mind a *Satisfaction,* to which this World knows none superior: When in a way of *occasional Reflection* I employ the *Creatures* as my *Teachers,* I will by the *Truths* wherein those ready *Monitors* instruct me, be led to my glorious JESUS; I will consider the *Truths as they are in JESUS,* and count my *Asceticks* deficient, till I have some Thoughts of HIM and of His *Glories* awakened in me. To conclude, It is a good Passage which a little Treatise entitled, *Theologia Ruris,* or, *The Book of Nature,* breaks off withal, and I might make it my Conclusion: 'If we mind *Heaven* 'whilst we live here upon *Earth,* this *Earth* will serve to conduct 'us to *Heaven,* thro the Merits and Mediation of the *Son of God,* 'who was made the *Son of Man,* and came thence on purpose 'into this lower World to convey us up thither.'

I will finish with a Speculation, which my most valuable Dr. *Cheyne* has a little more largely prosecuted and cultivated. All *intelligent compound Beings* have their whole Entertainment in these three Principles, the DESIRE, the OBJECT, and the SENSATION arising from the *Congruity* between them; this *Analogy* is preserved full and clear thro the *Spiritual World*, yea, and thro the *material* also; so *universal* and *perpetual* an *Analogy* can arise from nothing but its *Pattern* and *Archetype* in the infinite God or Maker; and could we carry it up to the Source of it, we should find the TRINITY of Persons in the eternal GODHEAD admirably exhibited to us. In the GOD-HEAD we may first apprehend a *Desire*, an infinitely active, ardent, powerful *Thought*, proposing of *Satisfaction*; let this represent GOD the FATHER: but it is not possible for any Object but God Himself to *satisfy Himself*, and fill His *Desire* of Happiness; therefore HE Himself *reflected* in upon Himself, and contemplating His own infinite Perfections, even the *Brightness of His Glory*, and the *express Image of His Person*, must answer this glorious Intention; and this may represent to us GOD the SON. Upon this Contemplation, wherein GOD Himself does behold, and possess, and enjoy Himself, there cannot but arise a *Love*, a *Joy*, an *Acquiescence* of God Himself within Himself, and worthy of a God; this may shadow out to us the third and the last of the Principles in this *mysterious Ternary*, that is to say, the Holy SPIRIT. Tho these *three Relations* of the Godhead in itself, when derived analogically down to Creatures, may appear but *Modifications* of a *real Subsistence*, yet in the supreme Infinitude of the Divine Nature, they must be infinitely *real* and *living* Principles. Those which are but *Relations* when transferred to *created Beings*, are glorious REALITIES in the infinite God. And in this View of the Holy Trinity, low as it is, it is impossible the SON should be without the FATHER, or the FATHER without the SON, or both without the Holy SPIRIT; it is impossible the SON should not be necessarily and eternally begotten of the FATHER, or that the HOLY SPIRIT should not necessarily and eternally proceed both from Him and from the SON. Thus from what occurs throughout the whole Creation, *Reason* forms an imperfect Idea of this incomprehensible Mystery.

But it is time to stop here, and indeed how can we go any further!

Jonathan Edwards

(1703–1758)

Bibliographical Note. The best edition of Edwards' writings is Samuel Austin, ed., *The Works of President Edwards* (Worcester, 1808–1809). Thus far there have been issued two volumes (New Haven, 1957–1959) of a modern scholarly edition, *The Works of Jonathan Edwards.* An excellent selection, immaculately edited, is C. H. Faust and T. H. Johnson, *Jonathan Edwards: Representative Selections* (New York, 1935); this edition contains a careful critical bibliography. Perry Miller has edited from manuscript Edwards' important *Images or Shadows of Divine Things* (New Haven, 1948). The selections printed below follow the texts of Faust and Johnson's *Representative Selections*, pp. 52–72, 155–172, and 231–249 and of Miller's edition of the *Images*, pp. 43–44, 48–49, 69–70, 79, 94–95, 97, 102, 104–105, 109, 135–137. For Edwards' life see Ola E. Winslow, *Jonathan Edwards* (New York, 1940); on his mind, see the introduction to the Faust and Johnson *Representative Selections* and, most important, Perry Miller, *Jonathan Edwards* (New York, 1949). See also H. G. Townsend, ed., *The Philosophy of Jonathan Edwards from His Private Notebooks* (Eugene, 1955).

PERSONAL NARRATIVE*

(*Written after* 1739)

I had a variety of concerns and exercises about my soul from my childhood; but had two more remarkable seasons of awakening, before I met with that change by which I was brought to

---

* Reprinted from *Jonathan Edwards: Representative Selections*, edited by C. H. Faust and T. H. Johnson and used with permission of the American Book Company.

those new dispositions, and that new sense of things, that I have since had. The first time was when I was a boy, some years before I went to college, at a time of remarkable awakening in my father's congregation, I was then very much affected for many months, and concerned about the things of religion, and my soul's salvation; and was abundant in duties. I used to pray five times a day in secret, and to spend much time in religious talk with other boys; and used to meet with them to pray together. I experienced I know not what kind of delight in religion. My mind was much engaged in it, and had much self-righteous pleasure; and it was my delight to abound in religious duties. I with some of my schoolmates joined together, and built a booth in a swamp, in a very retired spot, for a place of prayer. And besides, I had particular secret places of my own in the woods, where I used to retire by myself; and was from time to time much affected. My affections seemed to be lively and easily moved, and I seemed to be in my element when engaged in religious duties. And I am ready to think, many are deceived with such affections, and such a kind of delight as I then had in religion, and mistake it for grace.

But in process of time, my convictions and affections were off; and I entirely lost all those affections and delights and left off secret prayer, at least as to any constant performance of it; and returned like a dog to his vomit, and went on in the ways of sin. Indeed I was at times very uneasy, especially towards the latter part of my time at college; when it pleased God, to seize me with a pleurisy; in which he brought me nigh to the grave, and shook me over the pit of hell. And yet, it was not long after my recovery, before I fell again into my old ways of sin. But God would not suffer me to go on with any quietness; I had great and violent inward struggles, till, after many conflicts with wicked inclinations, repeated resolutions, and bonds that I laid myself under by a kind of vows to God, I was brought wholly to break off all former wicked ways, and all ways of known outward sin; and to apply myself to seek salvation, and practise many religious duties; but without that kind of affection and delight which I had formerly experienced. My concern now wrought more by inward struggles and conflicts, and selfreflections. I made seeking my salvation the main business of my life. But yet, it seems to me, I sought after a miserable manner; which has made me sometimes since to question, whether ever it issued in that which was saving; being ready to doubt, whether such miserable seeking ever succeeded. I was indeed brought to seek salvation in a manner that I never was before; I felt a spirit to part with all things in the world, for an interest in Christ. My concern continued and prevailed, with many exercising thoughts and inward struggles; but yet it never seemed to be proper to express that concern by the name of terror.

From my childhood up, my mind had been full of objections against the doctrine of God's sovereignty, in choosing whom he would to eternal life, and rejecting whom he pleased; leaving them eternally to perish, and be everlastingly tormented in hell. It used to appear like a horrible doctrine to me. But I remember the time very well, when I seemed to be convinced, and fully satisfied, as to this sovereignty of God, and his justice in thus eternally disposing of men, according to his sovereign pleasure. But never could give an account, how, or by what means, I was thus convinced, not in the least imagining at the time, nor a long time after, that there was any extraordinary influence of God's Spirit in it; but only that now I saw further, and my reason apprehended the justice and reasonableness of it. However, my mind rested in it; and it put an end to all those cavils and objections. And there has been a wonderful alteration in my mind, in respect to the doctrine of God's sovereignty, from that day to this; so that I scarce ever have found so much as the rising of an objection against it, in the most absolute sense, in God's shewing mercy to whom he will shew mercy, and hardening whom he will. God's absolute sovereignty and justice, with respect to salvation and damnation, is what my mind seems to rest assured of, as much as of any thing that I see with my eyes; at least it is so at times. But I have often, since that first conviction, had quite another kind of sense of God's sovereignty than I had then. I have often since had not only a conviction, but a delightful conviction. The doctrine has very often appeared exceeding pleasant, bright, and sweet. Absolute sovereignty is what I love to ascribe to God. But my first conviction was not so.

The first instance that I remember of that sort of inward, sweet delight in God and divine things that I have lived much in since, was on reading those words, I Tim. i. 17. *Now unto the King eternal, immortal, invisible, the only wise God, be honor and glory for ever and ever, Amen.* As I read the words, there came into my soul, and was as it were diffused through it, a sense of the glory of the Divine Being; a new sense, quite different from any thing I ever experienced before. Never any words of scripture seemed to me as these words did. I thought with myself, how excellent a Being that was, and how happy I should be, if I might enjoy that God, and be rapt up to him in heaven, and be as it were swallowed up in him for ever! I kept saying, and as it were singing over these words of scripture to myself; and went to pray to God that I might enjoy him, and prayed in a manner quite different from what I used to do; with a new sort of affection. But it never came into my thought, that there was any thing spiritual, or of a saving nature in this.

From about that time, I began to have a new kind of apprehensions and ideas of Christ, and the work of redemption, and the glorious way of salvation by him. An inward, sweet sense of these things, at times, came into my heart; and my soul was led away in pleasant views and contemplations of them. And my mind was greatly engaged to spend my time in reading and meditating on Christ, on the beauty and excellency of his person, and the lovely way of salvation by free grace in him. I found no books so delightful to me, as those that treated of these subjects. Those words Cant. ii. 1, used to be abundantly with me, *I am the Rose of Sharon, and the Lilly of the valleys.* The words seemed to me, sweetly to represent the loveliness and beauty of Jesus Christ. The whole book of Canticles used to be pleasant to me, and I used to be much in reading it, about that time; and found, from time to time, an inward sweetness, that would carry me away, in my contemplations. This I know not how to express otherwise, than by a calm, sweet abstraction of soul from all the concerns of this world; and sometimes a kind of vision, or fixed ideas and imaginations, of being alone in the mountains, or some solitary wilderness, far from all mankind, sweetly conversing with Christ, and wrapt and swallowed up in God. The sense I had of divine things, would often of a sudden kindle up, as it were, a sweet burning in my heart; an ardor of soul, that I know not how to express.

Not long after I first began to experience these things, I gave an account to my father of some things that had passed in my mind. I was pretty much affected by the discourse we had together; and when the discourse was ended, I walked abroad alone, in a solitary place in my father's pasture, for contemplation. And as I was walking there, and looking up on the sky and clouds, there came into my mind so sweet a sense of the glorious *majesty* and *grace* of God, that I know not how to express. I seemed to see them both in a sweet conjunction; majesty and meekness joined together; it was a sweet, and gentle, and holy majesty; and also a majestic meekness; an awful sweetness; a high, and great, and holy gentleness.

After this my sense of divine things gradually increased, and became more and more lively, and had more of that inward sweetness. The appearance of every thing was altered; there seemed to be, as it were, a calm, sweet cast, or appearance of divine glory, in almost every thing. God's excellency, his wisdom, his purity and love, seemed to appear in every thing; in the sun, moon, and stars; in the clouds, and blue sky; in the grass, flowers, trees; in the water, and all nature; which used greatly to fix my mind. I often used to sit and view the moon for continuance; and in the day, spent much time in viewing the clouds and sky, to behold the sweet glory of God in these things; in the mean time, singing forth, with a low voice my contemplations of the Creator and Redeemer. And scarce any thing, among all the works of nature, was so sweet to me as thunder and lightning; formerly, nothing had been so terrible to me. Before, I used to be uncommonly terrified with thunder, to be struck with terror when I saw a thunder storm rising; but now, on the contrary, it rejoiced me. I felt God, so to speak, at the first appearance of a thunder storm; and used to take the opportunity, at such times, to fix myself in order to view the clouds, and see the lightnings play, and hear the majestic and awful voice of God's thunder, which oftentimes was exceedingly entertaining, leading me to sweet contemplations of my great and glorious God. While thus engaged, it always seemed natural to me to sing, or chant for my meditations; or, to speak my thoughts in soliloquies with a singing voice.

I felt then great satisfaction, as to my good state; but that did not content me. I had vehement longings of soul after God and Christ, and after more holiness, wherewith my heart seemed to be full, and ready to break; which often brought to my mind the words of the Psalmist, Psal. cxix. 28. *My soul breaketh for the longing it hath.* I often felt a mourning and lamenting in my heart, that I had not turned to God sooner, that I might have had more time to grow in grace. My mind was greatly fixed on divine things; almost perpetually in the contemplation of them. I spent most of my time in thinking of divine things, year after year; often walking alone in the words, and solitary places, for meditation, soliloquy, and prayer, and converse with God; and it was always my manner, at such times, to sing forth my contemplations. I was almost constantly in ejaculatory prayer, wherever I was. Prayer seemed to be natural to me, as the breath by which the inward burnings of my heart had vent. The delights which I now felt in the things of religion, were of an exceeding different kind from those before mentioned, that I had when a boy; and what I then had no more notion of, than one born blind has of pleasant and beautiful colors. They were of a more inward, pure, soul animating and refreshing nature. Those former delights never reached the heart; and did not arise from any sight of the divine excellency of the things of God; or any taste of the soul satisfying and life-giving good there is in them.

My sense of divine things seemed gradually to increase, until I went to preach at Newyork, which was about a year and a half after they began; and while I was there, I felt them, very sensibly, in a much higher degree than I had done before. My longings after God and holiness, were much increased. Pure and humble, holy and heavenly Christianity, appeared exceeding amiable to me. I felt a burning desire to be in every thing a complete Christian; and conformed to the blessed image of Christ; and that I might live, in all things, according to the pure, sweet and blessed rules of the gospel. I had an eager thirsting after progress in these things; which put me upon pursuing and pressing after them. It was my continual strife day and night, and constant inquiry, how I should *be* more holy, and *live* more holily, and more becoming a child of God, and a disciple of Christ. I now sought an increase of grace and holiness, and a holy life, with much more earnestness, than ever I sought grace before I had it. I used to be continually examining myself, and studying and contriving for likely ways and means, how I should live holily, with far greater diligence and earnestness, than ever I pursued any thing in my life; but yet with too great a dependence on my own strength; which afterwards proved a great damage to me. My experience had not then taught me, as it has done since, my extreme feebleness and impotence, every manner of way; and the bottomless depths of secret corruption and deceit there was in my heart. However, I went on with my eager pursuit after more holiness, and conformity to Christ.

The heaven I desired was a heaven of holiness; to be with God, and to spend my eternity in divine love, and holy communion with Christ. My mind was very much taken up with contemplations on heaven, and the enjoyments there; and living there in perfect holiness, humility and love: And it used at that time to appear a great part of the happiness of heaven, that there the saints could express their love to Christ. It appeared to me a great clog and burden, that what I felt within, I could not express as I desired. The inward ardor of my soul, seemed to be hindered and pent up, and could not freely flame out as it would. I used often to think, how in heaven this principle should freely and fully vent and express itself. Heaven appeared exceedingly delightful, as a world of love; and that all happiness consisted in living in pure, humble, heavenly, divine love.

I remember the thoughts I used then to have of holiness; and said sometimes to myself, "I do certainly know that I love holiness, such as the gospel prescribes." It appeared to me, that there was nothing in it but what was ravishingly lovely; the highest beauty and amiableness . . . a *divine* beauty; far purer than any thing here upon earth; and that every thing else was like mire and defilement, in comparison of it.

Holiness, as I then wrote down some of my contemplations on it, appeared to me to be of a sweet, pleasant, charming, serene, calm nature; which brought an inexpressible purity, brightness, peacefulness and ravishment to the soul. In other words, that it made the soul like a field or garden of God, with all manner of pleasant flowers; all pleasant, delightful, and undisturbed; enjoying a sweet calm, and the gently vivifying beams of the sun. The soul of a true Christian, as I then wrote my meditations, appeared like such a little white flower as we see in the spring of the year; low and humble on the ground, opening its bosom to receive the pleasant beams of the sun's glory; rejoicing as it were in a calm rapture; diffusing around a sweet fragrancy; standing peacefully and lovingly, in the midst of other flowers round about; all in like manner opening their bosoms, to drink in the light of the sun. There was no part of creature holiness, I had so great a sense of its loveliness, as humility, brokenness of heart and poverty of spirit; and there was nothing that I so earnestly longed for. My heart panted after this, to lie low before God, as in the dust; that I might be nothing, and that God might be ALL, that I might become as a little child.

While at Newyork, I was sometimes much affected with reflections of my past life,considering how late it was before I began to be truly religious; and how wickedly I had lived till then; and once so as to weep abundantly, and for a considerable time together.

On *January* 12, 1723, I made a solemn dedication of myself to God, and wrote it down; giving up myself, and all that I had to God; to be for the future, in no respect, my own; to act as one that had no right to himself, in any respect. And solemnly vowed, to take God for my whole portion and felicity; looking on nothing else, as any part of my happiness, nor acting as if it were; and his law for the constant rule of my obedience: engaging to fight, with all my might, against the world, the flesh, and the devil, to the end of my life. But I have reason to be infinitely humbled, when I consider, how much I have failed, of answering my obligation.

I had, then, abundance of sweet, religious conversation, in the family where I lived, with Mr. John Smith, and his pious mother. My heart was knit in affection, to those, in whom were appearances of true piety; and I could bear the thoughts of no other companions, but such as were holy, and the disciples of the blessed Jesus. I had great longings, for the advancement of Christ's kingdom in the world; and my secret prayer used to be, in great part, taken up in praying for it. If I heard the least hint, of any thing that happened, in any part of the world, that appeared, in some respect or other, to have a favourable aspect, on the interests of Christ's kingdom, my soul eagerly catched at it; and it would much animate and refresh me. I used to be eager to read public news-letters, mainly for that end; to see if I could not find some news, favourable to the interest of religion in the world.

I very frequently used to retire into a solitary place, on the banks of Hudson's River, at some distance from the city, for contemplation on divine things and secret converse with God: and had many sweet hours there. Sometimes Mr. Smith and I walked there together, to converse on the things of God; and our conversation used to turn much on the advancement of Christ's kingdom in the world, and the glorious things that God would accomplish for his church in the latter days. I had then, and at other times, the greatest delight in the holy scriptures, of any book whatsoever. Oftentimes in reading it, every word seemed to touch my heart. I felt a harmony between something in my heart, and those sweet and powerful words. I seemed often to see so much light exhibited by every sentence, and such a refreshing food communicated, that I could not get along in reading; often dwelling long on one sentence, to see the wonders contained in it; and yet almost every sentence seemed to be full of wonders.

I came away from Newyork in the month of April, 1723, and had a most bitter parting with Madam Smith and her son. My heart seemed to sink within me, at leaving the family and city, where I had enjoyed so many sweet and pleasant days. I went from Newyork to Wethersfield, by water; and as I sailed away, I kept sight of the city as long as I could. However, that night after this sorrowful parting, I was greatly comforted in God at Westchester, where we went ashore to lodge: and had a pleasant time of it all the voyage to Saybrook. It was sweet to me to think of meeting dear christians in heaven, where we should never part more. At Saybrook we went ashore to lodge on Saturday, and there kept the Sabbath; where I had a sweet and refreshing season, walking alone in the fields.

After I came home to Windsor, I remained much in a like frame of mind, as when at Newyork; only sometimes I felt my heart ready to sing, with the thoughts of my friends at Newyork. My support was in contemplations on the heavenly state; as I find in my Diary of May 1, 1723. It was a comfort to think of that state, where there is fulness of joy; where reigns heavenly calm, and delightful love, without alloy; where there are continually the dearest expressions of this love; where is the enjoyment of the persons loved, without ever parting; where those persons who appear so lovely in this world, will really be inexpressibly more lovely, and full of love to us. And how sweetly will the mutual lovers join together, to sing the praises of God and the Lamb! How will it fill us with joy to think, that this enjoyment, these sweet exercises, will never cease, but will last to all eternity. . . . I continued much in the same frame, in the general, as when at Newyork, till I went to Newhaven, as Tutor of the College: particularly, once at Bolton, on a journey from Boston, while walking out alone in the fields. After I went to Newhaven, I sunk in religion; my mind being diverted from my eager pursuits after holiness, by some affairs, that greatly perplexed and distracted my thoughts.

In September, 1725, I was taken ill at Newhaven, and while endeavouring to go home to Windsor, was so ill at the North Village, that I could go no farther; where I lay sick, for about a quarter of a year. In this sickness, God was pleased to visit me again, with the sweet influences of his Spirit. My mind was greatly engaged there, on divine and pleasant contemplations, and longings of soul. I observed, that those who watched with me, would often be looking out wishfully for the morning; which brought to my mind those words of the Psalmist, and which my soul with delight made its own language, *My soul waiteth for the Lord, more than they that watch for the morning; I say, more than they that watch for the morning;* and when the light of day came in at the window, it refreshed my soul, from one morning to another. It seemed to be some image of the light of God's glory.

I remember, about that time, I used greatly to long for the

conversion of some, that I was concerned with; I could gladly
honour them, and with delight be a servant to them, and lie at
their feet, if they were but truly holy. But some time after this,
I was again greatly diverted with some temporal concerns, that
exceedingly took up my thoughts, greatly to the wounding of
my soul; and went on, through various exercises, that it would be
tedious to relate, which gave men much more experience of my
own heart, than I ever had before.

Since I came to this town, I have often had sweet com-
placency in God, in views of his glorious perfections and the
excellency of Jesus Christ. God has appeared to me a glorious
and lovely Being, chiefly on account of his holiness. The holiness of God has always appeared to me the most lovely of all
his attributes. The doctrines of God's absolute sovereignty, and
free grace, in shewing mercy to whom he would shew mercy;
and man's absolute dependence on the operations of God's
Holy Spirit, have very often appeared to me as sweet and glorious doctrines. These doctrines have been much my delight.
God's sovereignty has ever appeared to me, great part of his
glory. It has often been my delight to approach God, and adore
him as a sovereign God, and ask sovereign mercy of him.

I have loved the doctrines of the gospel; they have been
to my soul like green pastures. The gospel has seemed to me
the richest treasure; the treasure that I have most desired, and
longed that it might dwell richly in me. The way of salvation
by Christ has appeared, in a general way, glorious and excellent,
most pleasant and most beautiful. It has often seemed to me,
that it would in a great measure spoil heaven, to receive it in
any other way. That text has often been affecting and delightful to me, Isa. xxxii. 2. *A man shall be an hiding place from the
wind, and a covert from the tempest, &c.*

It has often appeared to me delightful, to be united to
Christ; to have him for my head, and to be a member of his
body; also to have Christ for my teacher and prophet. I very
often think with sweetness, and longings, and pantings of soul,
of being a little child, taking hold of Christ, to be led by him
through the wilderness of this world. That text, Math. xviii. 3,
has often been sweet to me, *except ye be converted and become
as little children, &c.* I love to think of coming to Christ, to

receive salvation of him, poor in spirit, and quite empty of self, humbly exalting him alone; cut off entirely from my own root, in order to grow into, and out of Christ; to have God in Christ to be all in all; and to live by faith in the son of God, a life of humble, unfeigned confidence in him. That scripture has often been sweet to me, Psal. cxv. 1. *Not unto us, O Lord, not unto us, but unto thy name give glory, for thy mercy, and for thy truth's sake.* And those words of Christ, Luke x. 21. *In that hour Jesus rejoiced in spirit, and said, I thank thee, O Father, Lord of heaven and earth, that thou hast hid these things from the wise and prudent, and hast revealed them unto babes: Even so, Father, for so it seemed good in thy sight.* That sovereignty of God which Christ rejoiced in, seemed to me worthy of such joy; and that rejoicing seemed to shew the excellency of Christ, and of what spirit he was.

Sometimes, only mentioning a single word caused my heart to burn within me; or only seeing the name of Christ, or the name of some attribute of God. And God has appeared glorious to me, on account of the Trinity. It has made me have exalting thoughts of God, that he subsists in three persons; Father, Son and Holy Ghost. The sweetest joys and delights I have experienced, have not been those that have arisen from a hope of my own good estate; but in a direct view of the glorious things of the gospel. When I enjoy this sweetness, it seems to carry me above the thoughts of my own estate; it seems at such times a loss that I cannot bear, to take off my eye from the glorious, pleasant object I behold without me, to turn my eye in upon myself, and my own good estate.

My heart has been much on the advancement of Christ's kingdom in the world. The histories of the past advancement of Christ's kingdom have been sweet to me. When I have read histories of past ages, the pleasantest thing in all my reading has been, to read of the kingdom of Christ being promoted. And when I have expected, in my reading, to come to any such thing, I have rejoiced in the prospect, all the way as I read. And my mind has been much entertained and delighted with the scripture promises and prophecies, which relate to the future glorious advancement of Christ's kingdom upon earth.

I have sometimes had a sense of the excellent fulness of

Christ, and his meetness and suitableness as a Saviour; whereby he has appeared to me, far above all, the chief of ten thousands. His blood and atonement have appeared sweet, and his righteousness sweet; which was always accompanied with ardency of spirit; and inward strugglings and breathings, and groanings that cannot be uttered, to be emptied of myself, and swallowed up in Christ.

Once, as I rode out into the woods for my health, in 1737, having alighted from my horse in a retired place, as my manner commonly has been, to walk for divine contemplation and prayer, I had a view that for me was extraordinary, of the glory of the Son of God, as Mediator between God and man, and his wonderful, great, full, pure and sweet grace and love, and meek and gentle condescension. This grace that appeared so calm and sweet, appeared also great above the heavens. The person of Christ appeared ineffably excellent with an excellency great enough to swallow up all thought and conception . . . which continued as near as I can judge, about an hour; which kept me the greater part of the time in a flood of tears, and weeping aloud. I felt an ardency of soul to be, what I know not otherwise how to express, emptied and annihilated; to lie in the dust, and to be full of Christ alone; to love him with a holy and pure love; to trust in him; to live upon him; to serve and follow him; and to be perfectly sanctified and made pure, with a divine and heavenly purity. I have, several other times, had views very much of the same nature, and which have had the same effects.

I have many times had a sense of the glory of the third person in the Trinity, in his office of Sanctifier in his holy operations, communicating divine light and life to the soul. God, in the communications of his Holy Spirit, has appeared as an infinite fountain of divine glory and sweetness; being full, and sufficient to fill and satisfy the soul; pouring forth itself in sweet communications; like the sun in its glory, sweetly and pleasantly diffusing light and life. And I have sometimes had an affecting sense of the excellency of the word of God, as a word of life; as the light of life; a sweet, excellent lifegiving word; accompanied with a thirsting after that word, that it might dwell richly in my heart.

Often, since I lived in this town, I have had very affecting views of my own sinfulness and vileness; very frequently to such a degree as to hold me in a kind of loud weeping, sometimes for a considerable time together; so that I have often been forced to shut myself up. I have had a vastly greater sense of my own wickedness, and the badness of my heart, than ever I had before my conversion. It has often appeared to me, that if God should mark iniquity against me, I should appear the very worst of all mankind; of all that have been, since the beginning of the world to this time; and that I should have by far the lowest place in hell. When others, that have come to talk with me about their soul concerns, have expressed the sense they have had of their own wickedness, by saying that it seemed to them, that they were as bad as the devil himself; I thought their expressions seemed exceeding faint and feeble, to represent my wickedness.

My wickedness, as I am in myself, has long appeared to me perfectly ineffable, and swallowing up all thought and imagination; like an infinite deluge, or mountain over my head. I know not how to express better what my sins appear to me to be, than by heaping infinite upon infinite, and multiplying infinite by infinite. Very often, for these many years, these expressions are in my mind, and in my mouth, "Infinite upon infinite . . . Infinite upon infinite!" When I look into my heart, and take a view of my wickedness, it looks like an abyss infinitely deeper than hell. And it appears to me, that were it not for free grace, exalted and raised up to the infinite height of all the fulness and glory of the great Jehovah, and the arm of his power and grace stretched forth in all the majesty of his power, and in all the glory of his sovereignty, I should appear sunk down in my sins below hell itself; far beyond the sight of every thing, but the eye of sovereign grace, that can pierce even down to such a depth. And yet it seems to me, that my conviction of sin is exceeding small, and faint; it is enough to amaze me, that I have no more sense of my sin. I know certainly, that I have very little sense of my sinfulness. When I have had turns of weeping and crying for my sins I thought I knew at the time, that my repentance was nothing to my sin.

I have greatly longed of late, for a broken heart, and to lie low before God; and, when I ask for humility, I cannot bear the thoughts of being no more humble than other Christians. It seems to me, that though their degrees of humility may be suitable for them, yet it would be a vile selfexaltation in me, not to be the lowest in humility of all mankind. Others speak of their longing to be "humbled to the dust;" that may be a proper expression for them, but I always think of myself, that I ought, and it is an expression that has long been natural for me to use in prayer, "to lie infinitely low before God." And it is affecting to think, how ignorant I was, when a young Christian, of the bottomless, infinite depths of wickedness, pride, hypocrisy and deceit, left in my heart.

I have a much greater sense of my universal, exceeding dependence on God's grace and strength, and mere good pleasure, of late, than I used formerly to have; and have experienced more of an abhorrence of my own righteousness. The very thought of any joy arising in me, on any consideration of my own amiableness, performances, or experiences, or any goodness of heart or life, is nauseous and detestable to me. And yet I am greatly afflicted with a proud and selfrighteous spirit, much more sensibly than I used to be formerly. I see that serpent rising and putting forth its head continually, every where, all around me.

Though it seems to me, that, in some respects, I was a far better Christian, for two or three years after my first conversion, than I am now; and lived in a more constant delight and pleasure; yet, of late years, I have had a more full and constant sense of the absolute sovereignty of God, and a delight in that sovereignty; and have had more of a sense of the glory of Christ, as a Mediator revealed in the gospel. On one Saturday night, in particular, I had such a discovery of the excellency of the gospel above all other doctrines, that I could not but say to myself, "This is my chosen light, my chosen doctrine"; and of Christ, "This is my chosen Prophet." It appeared sweet, beyond all expression, to follow Christ, and to be taught, and enlightened, and instructed by him; to learn of him, and live to him. Another Saturday night, (*January* 1739) I had such a sense, how sweet and blessed a thing it was to walk in the way of duty; to do that which was right and meet to be done, and agreeable to the holy mind of God; that it caused me to break forth into a kind of loud weeping, which held me some time, so that I was forced to shut myself up, and fasten the doors. I could not but, as it were, cry out, "How happy are they which do that which is right in the sight of God! They are blessed indeed, they are the happy ones!" I had, at the same time, a very affecting sense, how meet and suitable it was that God should govern the world, and order all things according to his own pleasure; and I rejoiced in it, that God reigned, and that his will was done.

SINNERS IN THE HANDS OF AN ANGRY GOD*
(Preached 1741)

Deut. XXXII. 35

—Their foot shall slide in due time.—

In this verse is threatened the vengeance of God on the wicked unbelieving Israelites, who were God's visible people, and who lived under the means of grace; but who, notwithstanding all God's wonderful works towards them, remained (as ver. 28.) void of counsel, having no understanding in them. Under all the cultivations of heaven, they brought forth bitter and poisonous fruit; as in the two verses next preceding the text.—The expression I have chosen for my text, *Their foot shall slide in due time,* seems to imply the following things, relating to the punishment and destruction to which these wicked Israelites were exposed.

1. That they were always exposed to *destruction;* as one that stands or walks in slippery places is always exposed to fall. This is implied in the manner of their destruction coming upon them, being represented by their foot sliding. The same is expressed, Psalm lxxiii. 18. "Surely thou didst set them in slippery places; thou castedst them down into destruction."

---

* Reprinted from *Jonathan Edwards: Representative Selections,* edited by C. H. Faust and T. H. Johnson and used with permission of the American Book Company.

2. It implies, that they were always exposed to sudden unexpected destruction. As he that walks in slippery places is every moment liable to fall, he cannot foresee one moment whether he shall stand or fall the next; and when he does fall, he falls at once without warning: Which is also expressed in Psalm lxxiii. 18, 19. "Surely thou didst set them in slippery places; thou castedst them down into destruction: How are they brought into desolation as in a moment!"

3. Another thing implied is, that they are liable to fall *of themselves*, without being thrown down by the hand of another; as he that stands or walks on slippery ground needs nothing but his own weight to throw him down.

4. That the reason why they are not fallen already, and do not fall now, is only that God's appointed time is not come. For it is said, that when that due time, or appointed times comes, *their foot shall slide*. Then they shall be left to fall, as they are inclined by their own weight. God will not hold them up in these slippery places any longer, but will let them go; and then, at that very instant, they shall fall into destruction; as he that stands on such slippery declining ground, on the edge of a pit, he cannot stand alone, when he is let go he immediately falls and is lost.

The observation from the words that I would now insist upon is this.—"There is nothing that keeps wicked men at any one moment out of hell, but the mere pleasure of God"—By the *mere* pleasure of God, I mean his *sovereign* pleasure, his arbitrary will, restrained by no obligation, hindered by no manner of difficulty, any more than if nothing else but God's mere will had in the least degree, or in any respect whatsoever, any hand in the preservation of wicked men one moment.—The truth of this observation may appear by the following considerations.

1. There is no want of *power* in God to cast wicked men into hell at any moment. Men's hands cannot be strong when God rises up. The strongest have no power to resist him, nor can any deliver out of his hands.—He is not only able to cast wicked men into hell, but he can most easily do it. Sometimes an earthly prince meets with a great deal of difficulty to subdue a rebel, who has found means to fortify himself, and has made

himself strong by the numbers of his followers. But it is not so with God. There is no fortress that is any defence from the power of God. Though hand join in hand, and vast multitudes of God's enemies combine and associate themselves, they are easily broken in pieces. They are as great heaps of light chaff before the whirlwind; or large quantities of dry stubble before devouring flames. We find it easy to tread on and crush a worm that we see crawling on the earth; so it is easy for us to cut or singe a slender thread that any thing hangs by: thus easy is it for God, when he pleases, to cast his enemies down to hell. What are we, that we should think to stand before him, at whose rebuke the earth trembles, and before whom the rocks are thrown down?

2. They *deserve* to be cast into hell; so that divine justice never stands in the way, it makes no objection against God's using his power at any moment to destroy them. Yea, on the contrary, justice calls aloud for an infinite punishment of their sins. Divine justice says of the tree that brings forth such grapes of Sodom, "Cut it down, why cumbereth it the ground?" Luke xiii. 7. The sword of divine justice is every moment brandished over their heads, and it is nothing but the hand of arbitrary mercy, and God's mere will, that holds it back.

3. They are already under a sentence of *condemnation* to hell. They do not only justly deserve to be cast down thither, but the sentence of the law of God, that eternal and immutable rule of righteousness that God has fixed between him and mankind, is gone out against them, and stands against them; so that they are bound over already to hell. John iii. 18. "He that believeth not is condemned already." So that every unconverted man properly belongs to hell; that is his place; from thence he is, John viii. 23. "Ye are from beneath:" And thither he is bound; it is the place that justice, and God's word, and the sentence of his unchangeable law assign to him.

4. They are now the objects of that very same *anger* and wrath of God, that is expressed in the torments of hell. And the reason why they do not go down to hell at each moment, is not because God, in whose power they are, is not then very angry with them; as he is with many miserable creatures now tormented in hell, who there feel and bear the fierceness of his

wrath. Yea, God is a great deal more angry with great numbers that are now on earth: yea, doubtless, with many that are now in this congregation, who it may be are at ease, than he is with many of those who are now in the flames of hell.

So that it is not because God is unmindful of their wickedness, and does not resent it, that he does not let loose his hand and cut them off. God is not altogether such an one as themselves, though they may imagine him to be so. The wrath of God burns against them, their damnation does not slumber; the pit is prepared, the fire is made ready, the furnace is now hot, ready to receive them; the flames do now rage and glow. The glittering sword is whet, and held over them, and the pit hath opened its mouth under them.

5. The *devil* stands ready to fall upon them, and seize them as his own, at what moment God shall permit him. They belong to him; he has their souls in his possession, and under his dominion. The scripture represents them as his goods, Luke xi. 12. The devils watch them; they are ever by them at their right hand; they stand waiting for them, like greedy hungry lions that see their prey, and expect to have it, but are for the present kept back. If God should withdraw his hand, by which they are restrained, they would in one moment fly upon their poor souls. The old serpent is gaping for them; hell opens its mouth wide to receive them; and if God should permit it, they would be hastily swallowed up and lost.

6. There are in the souls of wicked men those hellish *principles* reigning, that would presently kindle and flame out into hell fire, if it were not for God's restraints. There is laid in the very nature of carnal men, a foundation for the torments of hell. There are those corrupt principles, in reigning power in them, and in full possession of them, that are seeds of hell fire. These principles are active and powerful, exceeding violent in their nature, and if it were not for the restraining hand of God upon them, they would soon break out, they would flame out after the same manner as the same corruptions, the same enmity does in the hearts of damned souls, and would beget the same torments as they do in them. The souls of the wicked are in scripture compared to the troubled sea, Isa., lvii. 20. For the present, God restrains their wickedness by his mighty power,

as he does the raging waves of the troubled sea, saying, "Hitherto shalt thou come, but no further;" but if God should withdraw that restraining power, it would soon carry all before it. Sin is the ruin and misery of the soul; it is destructive in its nature; and if God should leave it without restraint, there would need nothing else to make the soul perfectly miserable. The corruption of the heart of man is immoderate and boundless in its fury; and while wicked men live here, it is like fire pent up by God's restraints, whereas if it were let loose, it would set on fire the course of nature; and as the heart is now a sink of sin, so if sin was not restrained, it would immediately turn the soul into a fiery oven, or a furnace of fire and brimstone.

7. It is no security to wicked men for one moment, that there are no visible means of death at hand. It is no security to a natural man, that he is now in health, and that he does not see which way he should now immediately go out of the world by any accident, and that there is no visible danger in any respect in his circumstances. The manifold and continual experience of the world in all ages, shows this is no evidence, that a man is not on the very brink of eternity, and that the next step will not be into another world. The unseen, unthought-of ways and means of persons going suddenly out of the world are innumerable and inconceivable. Unconverted men walk over the pit of hell on a rotten covering, and there are innumerable places in this covering so weak that they will not bear their weight, and these places are not seen. The arrows of death fly unseen at noon-day; the sharpest sight cannot discern them. God has so many different unsearchable ways of taking wicked men out of the world and sending them to hell, that there is nothing to make it appear, that God had need to be at the expence of a miracle, or go out of the ordinary course of his providence, to destroy any wicked man, at any moment. All the means that there are of sinners going out of the world, are so in God's hands, and so universally and absolutely subject to his power and determination, that it does not depend at all the less on the mere will of God, whether sinners shall at any moment go to hell, than if means were never made use of, or at all concerned in the case.

8. Natural men's prudence and care to preserve their own

lives, or the care of others to preserve them, do not secure them a moment. To this, divine providence and universal experience do also bear testimony. There is this clear evidence that men's own wisdom is no security to them from death; that if it were otherwise we should see some difference between the wise and politic men of the world, and others, with regard to their liableness to early and unexpected death: but how is it in fact? Eccles. ii. 16. "How dieth the wise man? even as the fool."

9. All wicked men's pains and *contrivance* which they use to escape hell, while they continue to reject Christ, and so remain wicked men, do not secure them from hell one moment. Almost every natural man that hears of hell, flatters himself that he shall escape it; he depends upon himself for his own security; he flatters himself in what he has done, in what he is now doing, or what he intends to do. Every one lays out matters in his own mind how he shall avoid damnation, and flatters himself that he contrives well for himself, and that his schemes will not fail. They hear indeed that there are but few saved, and that the greater part of men that have died heretofore are gone to hell; but each one imagines that he lays out matters better for his own escape than others have done. He does not intend to come to that place of torment; he says within himself, that he intends to take effectual care, and to order matters so for himself as not to fail.

But the foolish children of men miserably delude themselves in their own schemes, and in confidence in their own strength and wisdom; they trust to nothing but a shadow. The greater part of those who heretofore have lived under the same means of grace, and are now dead, are undoubtedly gone to hell; and it was not because they were not as wise as those who are now alive: it was not because they did not lay out matters as well for themselves to secure their own escape. If we could speak with them, and inquire of them, one by one, whether they expected, when alive, and when they used to hear about hell, ever to be the subjects of that misery: we doubtless, should hear one and another reply, "No, I never intended to come here: I had laid out matters otherwise in my mind; I thought I should contrive well for myself: I thought my scheme good. I intended to take effectual care; but it came upon me unexpected; I did not look for it at that time, and in that manner; it came as a thief: Death outwitted me: God's wrath was too quick for me. Oh, my cursed foolishness! I was flattering myself, and pleasing myself with vain dreams of what I would do hereafter; and when I was saying, Peace and safety, then suddenly destruction came upon me."

10. God has laid himself under *no obligation*, by any promise to keep any natural man out of hell one moment. God certainly has made no promises either of eternal life, or of any deliverance or preservation from eternal death, but what are contained in the covenant of grace, the promises that are given in Christ, in whom all the promises are yea and amen. But surely they have no interest in the promises of the covenant of grace who are not the children of the covenant, who do not believe in any of the promises, and have no interest in the Mediator of the covenant.

So that, whatever some have imagined and pretended about promises made to natural men's earnest seeking and knocking, it is plain and manifest, that whatever pains a natural man takes in religion, whatever prayers he makes, till he believes in Christ, God is under no manner of obligation to keep him a moment from eternal destruction.

So that, thus it is that natural men are held in the hand of God, over the pit of hell; they have deserved the fiery pit, and are already sentenced to it; and God is dreadfully provoked, his anger is as great towards them as to those that are actually suffering the executions of the fierceness of his wrath in hell, and they have done nothing in the least to appease or abate that anger, neither is God in the least bound by any promise to hold them up one moment; the devil is waiting for them, hell is gaping for them, the flames gather and flash about them, and would fain lay hold on them, and swallow them up; the fire pent up in their own hearts is struggling to break out: and they have no interest in any Mediator, there are no means within reach that can be any security to them. In short, they have no refuge, nothing to take hold of; all that preserves them every moment is the mere arbitrary will, and uncovenanted, unobliged forbearance of an incensed God.

Application

The use of this awful subject may be for awakening unconverted persons in this congregation. This that you have heard
is the case of every one of you that are out of Christ.—That
world of misery, that lake of burning brimstone, is extended
abroad under you. There is the dreadful pit of the glowing
flames of the wrath of God; there is hell's wide gaping mouth
open; and you have nothing to stand upon, nor any thing to
take hold of; there is nothing between you and hell but the *p. 55*
air; it is only the power and mere pleasure of God that holds
you up.

You probably are not sensible of this; you find you are kept
out of hell, but do not see the hand of God in it; but look at
other things, as the good state of your bodily constitution, your
care of your own life, and the means you use for your own preservation. But indeed these things are nothing; if God should withdraw his hand, they would avail no more to keep you from
falling, than the thin air to hold up a person that is suspended
in it.

Your wickedness makes you as it were heavy as lead, and
to end downwards with great weight and pressure towards hell;
and if God should let you go, you would immediately sink and
swiftly descend and plunge into the bottomless gulf, and your
healthy constitution, and your own care and prudence, and best
contrivance, and all your righteousness, would have no more
influence to uphold you and keep you out of hell, than a spider's
web would have to stop a fallen rock. Were it not for the
sovereign pleasure of God, the earth would not bear you one
moment; for you are a burden to it; the creation groans with
you; the creature is made subject to the bondage of your corruption, not willingly; the sun does not willingly shine upon
you to give you light to serve sin and Satan; the earth does not
willingly yield her increase to satisfy your lusts; nor is it willingly a stage for your wickedness to be acted upon; the air does
not willingly serve you for breath to maintain the flame of life
in your vitals, while you spend your life in the service of God's
enemies. God's creatures are good, and were made for men to

serve God with, and do not willingly subserve to any other purpose, and groan when they are abused to purposes so directly contrary to their nature and end. And the world would spew you out, were it not for the sovereign hand of him who hath subjected it in hope. There are black clouds of God's wrath now hanging directly over your heads, full of the dreadful storm, and big with thunder; and were it not for the restraining hand of God, it would immediately burst forth upon you. The sovereign pleasure of God, for the present, stays his rough wind; otherwise it would come with fury, and your destruction would come like a whirlwind, and you would be like the chaff of the summer threshing floor.

The wrath of God is like great waters that are damned for the present; they increase more and more, and rise higher and higher, till an outlet is given; and the longer the stream is stopped, the more rapid and mighty is its course, when once it is let loose. It is true, that judgment against your evil works has not been executed hitherto; the floods of God's vengeance have been withheld; but your guilt in the mean time is constantly increasing, and you are every day treasuring up more wrath; the waters are constantly rising, and waxing more and more mighty; and there is nothing but the mere pleasure of God, that holds the waters back, that are unwilling to be stopped, and press hard to go forward. If God should only withdraw his hand from the flood-gate, it would immediately fly open, and the fiery floods of the fierceness and wrath of God, would rush forth with inconceivable fury, and would come upon you with omnipotent power; and if your strength were ten thousand times greater than it is, yea ten thousand times greater than the strength of the stoutest, sturdiest devil in hell, it would be nothing to withstand or endure it.

The bow of God's wrath is bent, and the arrow made ready on the string, and justice bends the arrow at your heart, and strains the bow, and it is nothing but the mere pleasure of God, and that of an angry God, without any promise or obligation at all, that keeps the arrow one moment from being made drunk with your blood. Thus all you that never passed under a great change of heart, by the mighty power of the Spirit of God upon your souls; all you that were never born again, and made new creatures, and raised from being dead in sin, to a state of new, and before altogether unexperienced light and life, are in the hands of an angry God. However you may have reformed your life in many things, and may have had religious affections, and may keep up a form of religion in your families and closets, and in the house of God, it is nothing but his mere pleasure that keeps you from being this moment swallowed up in everlasting destruction. However unconvinced you may now be of the truth of what you hear, by and by you will be fully convinced of it. Those that are gone from being in the like circumstances with you, see that it was so with them; for destruction came suddenly upon most of them; when they expected nothing of it, and while they were saying, Peace and safety: now they see, that those things on which they depended for peace and safety, were nothing but thin air and empty shadows.

The God that holds you over the pit of hell, much as one holds a spider, or some loathsome insect over the fire, abhors you, and is dreadfully provoked: his wrath towards you burns like fire; he looks upon you as worthy of nothing else, but to be cast into the fire; he is of purer eyes than to bear to have you in his sight; you are ten thousand times more abominable in his eyes, than the most hateful venomous serpent is in ours. You have offended him infinitely more than ever a stubborn rebel did his prince; and yet it is nothing but his hand that holds you from falling into the fire every moment. It is to be ascribed to nothing else, that you did not go to hell the last night; that you was suffered to awake again in this world, after you closed your eyes to sleep. And there is no other reason to be given, why you have not dropped into hell since you arose in the morning, but that God's hand has held you up. There is no other reason to be given why you have not gone to hell, since you have sat here in the house of God, provoking his pure eyes by your sinful wicked manner of attending his solemn worship. Yea, there is nothing else that is to be given as a reason why you do not this very moment drop down into hell.

O sinner! Consider the fearful danger you are in: it is a great furnace of wrath, a wide and bottomless pit, full of the fire of wrath, that you are held over in the hand of that God, whose wrath is provoked and incensed as much against you, as against many of the damned in hell. You hang by a slender thread, with the flames of divine wrath flashing about it, and ready every moment to singe it, and burn it asunder; and you have no interest in any Mediator, and nothing to lay hold of to save yourself, nothing to keep off the flames of wrath, nothing of your own, nothing that you ever have done, nothing that you can do, to induce God to spare you one moment.— And consider here more particularly,

1. Whose wrath it is: it is the wrath of the infinite God. If it were only the wrath of man, though it were of the most potent prince, it would be comparatively little to be regarded. The wrath of kings is very much dreaded, especially of absolute monarchs, who have the possessions and lives of their subjects wholly in their power, to be disposed of at their mere will. Prov. xx. 2. "The fear of a king is as the roaring of a lion: Whoso provoketh him to anger, sinneth against his own soul." The subject that very much enrages an arbitrary prince, is liable to suffer the most extreme torments that human art can invent, or human power can inflict. But the greatest earthly potentates in their greatest majesty and strength, and when clothed in their greatest terrors, are but feeble, despicable worms of the dust, in comparison of the great and almighty Creator and King of heaven and earth. It is but little that they can do, when most enraged, and when they have exerted the utmost of their fury. All the kings of the earth, before God, are as grasshoppers; they are nothing, and less than nothing: both their love and their hatred is to be despised. The wrath of the great King of kings, is as much more terrible than theirs, as his majesty is greater. Luke xii. 4, 5. "And I say unto you, my friends, Be not afraid of them that kill the body, and after that, have no more that they can do. But I will forewarn you whom you shall fear: fear him, which after he hath killed, hath power to cast into hell: yea, I say unto you, Fear him."

2. It is the fierceness of his wrath that you are exposed to. We often read of the fury of God; as in Isaiah lix. 18. "According to their deeds, accordingly he will repay fury to his adversaries." So Isaiah lxvi. 15. "For behold, the Lord will come with fire, and with his chariots like a whirlwind, to render his anger with fury, and his rebuke with flames of fire." And in many

other places. So, Rev. xix. 15. we read of "the wine press of the fierceness and wrath of Almighty God." The words are exceeding terrible. If it had only been said, "the wrath of God," the words would have implied that which is infinitely dreadful: but it is "the fierceness and wrath of God." The fury of God! the fierceness of Jehovah! Oh, how dreadful must that be! Who can utter or conceive what such expressions carry in them! But it is also "the fierceness and wrath of *Almighty* God." As though there would be a very great manifestation of his almighty power in what the fierceness of his wrath should inflict, as though omnipotence should be as it were enraged, and exerted, as men are wont to exert their strength in the fierceness of their wrath. Oh! then, what will be the consequence! What will become of the poor worms that shall suffer it! Whose hands can be strong? And whose heart can endure? To what a dreadful, inexpressible, inconceivable depth of misery must the poor creature be sunk who shall be the subject of this!

Consider this, you that are here present, that yet remain in an unregenerate state. That God will execute the fierceness of his anger, implies, that he will inflict wrath without any pity. When God beholds the ineffable extremity of your case, and sees your torment to be so vastly disproportioned to your strength, and sees how your poor soul is crushed, and sinks down, as it were, into an infinite gloom; he will have no compassion upon you, he will not forbear the executions of his wrath, or in the least lighten his hand; there shall be no moderation or mercy, nor will God then at all stay his rough wind; he will have no regard to your welfare, nor be at all careful lest you should suffer too much in any other sense, than only that you shall *not suffer beyond what strict justice requires.* Nothing shall be withheld, because it is so hard for you to bear. Ezek. viii. 18. "Therefore will I also deal in fury: mine eye shall not spare, neither will I have pity; and though they cry in mine ears with a loud voice, yet I will not hear them." Now God stands ready to pity you; this is a day of mercy; you may cry now with some encouragement of obtaining mercy. But when once the day of mercy is past, your most lamentable and dolorous cries and shrieks will be in vain; you will be wholly lost and thrown away of God, as to any regard to your welfare. God will have no other use to put you to, but to suffer misery; you shall be continued in being to no other end; for you will be a vessel of wrath fitted to destruction; and there will be no other use of this vessel, but to be filled full of wrath. God will be so far from pitying you when you cry to him, that it is said he will only "laugh and mock," Prov. i. 25, 26, &c.

How awful are those words, Isa. lxiii. 3, which are the words of the great God. "I will tread them in mine anger, and will trample them in my fury, and their blood shall be sprinkled upon my garments, and I will stain all my raiment." It is perhaps impossible to conceive of words that carry in them greater manifestations of these three things, *viz.* contempt, and hatred, and fierceness of indignation. If you cry to God to pity you, he will be so far from pitying you in your doleful case, or showing you the least regard or favour, that instead of that, he will only tread you under foot. And though he will know that you cannot bear the weight of omnipotence treading upon you, yet he will not regard that, but he will crush you under his feet without mercy; he will crush out your blood, and make it fly, and it shall be sprinkled on his garments, so as to stain all his raiment. He will not only hate you, but he will have you, in the utmost contempt: no place shall be thought fit for you, but under his feet to be trodden down as the mire of the streets.

3. The *misery* you are exposed to is that which God will inflict to that end, that he might show what that wrath of Jehovah is. God hath had it on his heart to show to angels and men, both how excellent his love is, and also how terrible his wrath is. Sometimes earthly kings have a mind to show how terrible their wrath is, by the extreme punishments they would execute on those that would provoke them. Nebuchadnezzar, that mighty and haughty monarch of the Chaldean empire, was willing to show his wrath when enraged with Shadrach, Meshech, and Abednego; and accordingly gave orders that the burning fiery furnace should be heated seven times hotter than it was before; doubtless, it was raised to the utmost degree of fierceness that human art could raise it. But the great God is also willing to show his wrath, and magnify his awful majesty and mighty power in the extreme sufferings of his enemies. Rom. ix. 22. "What if God, willing to show his wrath, and to

makc his power known, endure with much long-suffering the vessels of wrath fitted to destruction?" And seeing this is his design, and what he has determined, even to show how terrible the unrestrained wrath, the fury and fierceness of Jehovah is, he will do it to effect. There will be something accomplished and brought to pass that will be dreadful with a witness. When the great and angry God hath risen up and executed his awful vengeance on the poor sinner, and the wretch is actually suffering the infinite weight and power of his indignation, then will God call upon the whole universe to behold that awful majesty and mighty power that is to be seen in it. Isa. xxxiii. 12–14. "And the people shall be as the burnings of lime, as thorns cut up shall they be burnt in the fire. Hear ye that are far off, what I have done; and ye that are near, acknowledge my might. The sinners in Zion are afraid; fearfulness hath surprised the hypocrites," &c.

Thus it will be with you that are in an unconverted state, if you continue in it; the infinite might, and majesty, and terribleness of the omnipotent God shall be magnified upon you, in the ineffable strength of your torments. You shall be tormented in the presence of the holy angels, and in the presence of the Lamb; and when you shall be in this state of suffering, the glorious inhabitants of heaven shall go forth and look on the awful spectacle, that they may see what the wrath and fierceness of the Almighty is; and when they have seen it, they will fall down and adore that great power and majesty. Isa. lxvi. 23, 24. "And it shall come to pass, that from one new moon to another, and from one sabbath to another, shall all flesh come to worship before me, saith the Lord. And they shall go forth and look upon the carcasses of the men that have transgressed against me; for their worm shall not die, neither shall their fire be quenched, and they shall be an abhorring unto all flesh."

4. It is *everlasting* wrath. It would be dreadful to suffer this fierceness and wrath of Almighty God one moment; but you must suffer it to all eternity. There will be no end to this exquisite horrible misery. When you look forward, you shall see a long for ever, a boundless duration before you, which will swallow up your thoughts, and amaze your soul; and you will absolutely despair of ever having any deliverance, any end, any

mitigation, any rest at all. You will know certainly that you must wear out long ages, millions of millions of ages, in wrestling and conflicting with this almighty merciless vengeance; and then when you have so done, when so many ages have actually been spent by you in this manner, you will know that all is but a point to what remains. So that your punishment will indeed be infinite. Oh, who can express what the state of a soul in such circumstances is! All that we can possibly say about it, gives but a very feeble, faint representation of it; it is inexpressible and inconceivable: For "who knows the power of God's anger?"

How dreadful is the state of those that are daily and hourly in the danger of this great wrath and infinite misery! But this is the dismal case of every soul in this congregation that has not been born again, however moral and strict, sober and religious, they may otherwise be. Oh that you would consider it, whether you be young or old! There is reason to think, that there are many in this congregation now hearing this discourse, that will actually be the subjects of this very misery to all eternity. We know not who they are, or in what seats they sit, or what thoughts they now have. It may be they are now at ease, and hear all these things without much disturbance, and are now flattering themselves that they are not the persons, promising themselves that they shall escape. If we knew that there was one person, and but one, in the whole congregation, that was to be the subject of this misery, what an awful thing would it be to think of! If we knew who it was, what an awful sight would it be to see such a person! How might all the rest of the congregation lift up a lamentable and bitter cry over him! But, alas! instead of one, how many is it likely will remember this discourse in hell? And it would be a wonder, if some that are now present should not be in hell in a very short time, even before this year is out. And it would be no wonder if some persons, that now sit here, in some seats of this meeting-house, in health, quiet and secure, should be there before to-morrow morning. Those of you that finally continue in a natural condition, that shall keep out of hell longest will be there in a little time! your damnation does not slumber; it will come swiftly, and, in all probability, very suddenly upon many of you. You have reason to wonder that you are not already in hell. It is doubtless the case of some whom you have seen and known, that never deserved hell more than you, and that heretofore appeared as likely to have been now alive as you. Their case is past all hope; they are crying in extreme misery and perfect despair; but here you are in the land of the living and in the house of God, and have an opportunity to obtain salvation. What would not those poor damned hopeless souls give for one day's opportunity such as you now enjoy!

And now you have an extraordinary opportunity, a day wherein Christ has thrown the door of mercy wide open, and stands in calling and crying with a loud voice to poor sinners; a day wherein many are flocking to him, and pressing into the kingdom of God. Many are daily coming from the east, west, north and south; many that were very lately in the same miserable condition that you are in, are now in a happy state, with their hearts filled with love to him who has loved them, and washed them from their sins in his own blood, and rejoicing in hope of the glory of God. How awful is it to be left behind at such a day! To see so many others feasting, while you are pining and perishing! To see so many rejoicing and singing for joy of heart, while you have cause to mourn for sorrow of heart, and howl for vexation of spirit! How can you rest one moment in such a condition? Are not your souls as precious as the souls of the people at Suffield,* where they are flocking from day to day to Christ?

Are there not many here who have lived long in the world, and are not to this day born again? and so are aliens from the commonwealth of Israel, and have done nothing ever since they have lived, but treasure up wrath against the day of wrath? Oh, sirs, your case, in an especial manner, is extremely dangerous. Your guilt and hardness of heart is extremely great. Do you not see how generally persons of your years are passed over and left, in the present remarkable and wonderful dispensation of God's mercy? You had need to consider yourselves, and awake thoroughly out of sleep. You cannot bear the fierceness and wrath of the infinite God.—And you, young men, and young

---

* A town in the neighbourhood. [Edwards's note.]

women, will you neglect this precious season which you now enjoy, when so many others of your age are renouncing all youthful vanities, and flocking to Christ? You especially have now an extraordinary opportunity; but if you neglect it, it will soon be with you as with those persons who spent all the precious days of youth in sin, and are now come to such a dreadful pass in blindness and hardness.—And you, children, who are unconverted, do not you know that you are going down to hell, to bear the dreadful wrath of that God, who is now angry with you every day and every night? Will you be content to be the children of the devil, when so many other children in the land are converted, and are become the holy and happy children of the King of kings?

And let every one that is yet of Christ, and hanging over the pit of hell, whether they be old men and women, or middle aged, or young people, or little children, now hearken to the loud calls of God's word and providence. This acceptable year of the Lord, a day of such great favours to some, will doubtless be a day of as remarkable vengeance to others. Men's hearts harden, and their guilt increases apace at such a day as this, if they neglect their souls; and never was there so great danger of such persons being given up to hardness of heart and blindness of mind. God seems now to be hastily gathering in his elect in all parts of the land; and probably the greater part of adult persons that ever shall be saved, will be brought in now in a little time, and that it will be as it was on the great outpouring of the Spirit upon the Jews in the apostles' days: the election will obtain, and the rest will be blinded. If this should be the case with you, you will eternally curse this day, and will curse the day that ever you was born, to see such a season of the pouring out of God's Spirit, and will wish that you had died and gone to hell before you had seen it. Now undoubtedly it is, as it was in the days of John the Baptist, the axe is in an extraordinary manner laid at the root of the trees, that every tree which brings not forth good fruit, may be hewn down and cast into the fire.

Therefore, let every one that is out of Christ, now awake and fly from the wrath to come. The wrath of Almighty God is now undoubtedly hanging over a great part of this congregation: Let every one fly out of Sodom: "Haste and escape for your lives, look not behind you, escape to the mountain, lest you be consumed."

from

A TREATISE CONCERNING RELIGIOUS AFFECTIONS* (1746).

PART III

Showing What Are Distinguishing Signs of Truly Gracious and Holy Affections

I come now to the second thing appertaining to the trial of religious affections, which was proposed, viz., To take notice of some things, wherein those affections that are spiritual and gracious, do differ from those that are not so.

. . . . .

I. Affections that are truly spiritual and gracious, do arise from those influences and operations on the heart, which are spiritual, supernatural and divine.

I will explain what I mean by these terms, whence will appear their use to distinguish between those affections which are spiritual, and those which are not so.

We find that true saints, or those persons who are sanctified by the Spirit of God, are in the New Testament called spiritual persons. And their being spiritual is spoken of as their peculiar character, and that wherein they are distinguished from

* Reprinted from *Jonathan Edwards: Representative Selections*, edited by C. H. Faust and T. H. Johnson and used with permission of the American Book Company.

those who are not sanctified. This is evident, because those who are spiritual are set in opposition to natural men, and carnal men. Thus the spiritual man and the natural man are set in opposition one to another, 1 Cor. ii. 14, 15: "The natural man receiveth not the things of the Spirit of God; for they are foolishness unto him; neither can he know them, because they are spiritually discerned. But he that is spiritual judgeth all things." The Scripture explains itself to mean an ungodly man, or one that has no grace, by a natural man: thus the Apostle Jude, speaking of certain ungodly men, that had crept in unawares among the saints, ver. 4, of his epistle, says, v. 19, "These are sensual, having not the Spirit." This the apostle gives as a reason why they behaved themselves in such a wicked manner as he had described. Here the word translated *sensual*, in the original is ψυχικοι, which is the very same, which in those verses in 1 Cor. chap. ii. is translated *natural*. In the like manner, in the continuation of the same discourse, in the next verse but one, spiritual men are opposed to carnal men; which the connection plainly shows mean the same, as spiritual men and natural men, in the foregoing verses; "And I, brethren, could not speak unto you, as unto spiritual, but as unto carnal;" i. e., as in a great measure unsanctified. That by carnal the apostle means corrupt and unsanctified, is abundantly evident, by Rom. vii. 25, and viii. 1, 4, 5, 6, 7, 8, 9, 12, 13, Gal. v. 16, to the end, Col. ii. 18. Now therefore, if by natural and carnal in these texts, be intended unsanctified, then doubtless by spiritual, which is opposed thereto, is meant sanctified and gracious.

. . . . .

1. The Spirit of God is given to the true saints to dwell in them, as his proper lasting abode; and to influence their hearts, as a principle of new nature, or as a divine supernatural spring of life and action. The Scriptures represent the Holy Spirit not only as moving, and occasionally influencing the saints, but as dwelling in them as his temple, his proper abode, and everlasting dwelling place, 1 Cor. iii. 16, 2 Cor. vi. 16, John xiv. 16, 17. And he is represented as being there so united to the facul-

ties of the soul, that he becomes there a principle or spring of new nature and life.

So the saints are said to live by Christ living in them, Gal. ii. 20. Christ by his Spirit not only *is* in them, but *lives* in them; and so that they live by his life; so is his Spirit united to them, as a principle of life in them; they do not only drink living water, but this "living water becomes a well or fountain of water," in the soul, "springing up into spiritual and everlasting life," John iv. 14, and thus becomes a principle of life in them. This living water, this evangelist himself explains to intend the Spirit of God, chap. vii. 38, 39. The light of the Sun of righteousness does not only shine upon them, but is so communicated to them that they shine also, and become little images of that Sun which shines upon them; the sap of the true vine is not only conveyed into them, as the sap of a tree may be conveyed into a vessel, but is conveyed as sap is from a tree into one of its living branches, where it becomes a principle life. The Spirit of God being thus communicated and united to the saints, they are from thence properly denominated from it, and are called *spiritual*.

On the other hand, though the Spirit of God may many ways influence natural men; yet because it is not thus communicated to them, as an indwelling principle, they do not derive any denomination or character from it: for, there being no union, it is not their own. The light may shine upon a body that is very dark or black; and though that body be the subject of the light, yet, because the light becomes no principle of light in it, so as to cause the body to shine, hence that body does not properly receive its denomination from it, so as to be called a lightsome body. So the Spirit of God acting upon the soul only, without communicating itself to be an active principle in it, cannot denominate it spiritual. A body that continues black, may be said not to have light, though the light shines upon it: so natural men are said "not to have the Spirit," Jude 19, sensual or natural (as the word is elsewhere rendered), having not the Spirit.

2. Another reason why the saints and their virtues are called spiritual (which is the principal thing) is, that the Spirit

of God, dwelling as a vital principle in their souls, there produces those effects wherein he exerts and communicates himself in his own proper nature. Holiness is the nature of the Spirit of God, therefore he is called in Scripture the Holy Ghost. Holiness, which is as it were the beauty and sweetness of the divine nature, is as much the proper nature of the Holy Spirit, as heat is the nature of fire, or sweetness was the nature of that holy anointing oil, which was the principal type of the Holy Ghost in the Mosaic dispensation; yea, I may rather say, that holiness is as much the proper nature of the Holy Ghost, as sweetness was the nature of the sweet odor of that ointment. The Spirit of God so dwells in the hearts of the saints, that he there, as a seed or spring of life, exerts and communicates himself, in this his sweet and divine nature, making the soul a partaker of God's beauty and Christ's joy, so that the saint has truly fellowship with the Father, and with his Son Jesus Christ, in thus having the communion or participation of the Holy Ghost. The grace which is in the hearts of the saints, is of the same nature with the divine holiness, as much as it is possible for that holiness to be, which is infinitely less in degree; as the brightness that is in a diamond which the sun shines upon, is of the same nature with the brightness of the sun, but only that it is as nothing to it in degree. Therefore Christ says, John iii. 6, "That which is born of the Spirit, is spirit"; i.e., the grace that is begotten in the hearts of the saints, is something of the same nature with that Spirit, and so is properly called a spiritual nature; after the same manner as that which is born of the flesh is flesh, or that which is born of corrupt nature is corrupt nature.

But the Spirit of God never influences the minds of natural men after this manner. Though he may influence them many ways, yet he never, in any of his influences, communicates himself to them in his own proper nature. Indeed he never acts disagreeably to his nature, either on the minds of saints or sinners: but the Spirit of God may act upon men agreeably to his own nature, and not exert his proper nature in the acts and exercises of their minds: the Spirit of God may act so, that his actions may be agreeable to his nature, and yet may not at all communicate himself in his proper nature, in the effect of that action. Thus, for instance, the Spirit of God moved upon the face of the waters, and there was nothing disagreeable to his nature in that action; but yet he did not at all communicate himself in that action, there was nothing of the proper nature of the Holy Spirit in that motion of the waters. And so he may act upon the minds of men many ways, and not communicate himself any more than when he acts on inanimate things.

Thus not only the manner of the relation of the Spirit, who is the operator, to the subject of his operations, is different; as the Spirit operates in the saints, as dwelling in them, as an abiding principle of action, whereas he doth not so operate upon sinners; but the influence and operation itself is different, and the effect wrought exceeding different. So that not only the persons are called *spiritual*, as having the Spirit of God dwelling in them; but those qualifications, affections, and experiences, that are wrought in them by the Spirit, are also *spiritual*, and therein differ vastly in their nature and kind from all that a natural man is or can be the subject of, while he remains in a natural state; and also from all that men or devils can be the authors of. It is a spiritual work in this high sense; and therefore above all other works is peculiar to the Spirit of God.

. . . . .

From these things it is evident, that those gracious influences which the saints are subjects of, and the effects of God's Spirit which they experience, are entirely above nature, altogether of a different kind from any thing that men find within themselves by nature, or only in the exercise of natural principles; and are things which no improvement of those qualifications, or principles that are natural, no advancing or exalting them to higher degrees, and no kind of composition of them, will ever bring men to; because they not only differ from what is natural, and from every thing that natural men experience, in degree and circumstances, but also in kind; and are of a nature vastly more excellent. And this is what I mean, by supernatural, when I say that gracious affections are from those influences that are supernatural.

From hence it follows, that in those gracious exercises and

affections which are wrought in the minds of the saints, through the saving influences of the Spirit of God, there is a new inward perception or sensation of their minds, entirely different in its nature and kind, from any thing that ever their minds were the subjects of before they were sanctified. For doubtless if God by his mighty power produces something that is new, not only in degree and circumstances, but in its whole nature, and that which could be produced by no exalting, varying, or compounding of what was there before, or by adding any thing of the like kind; I say, if God produces something thus new in a mind, that is a perceiving, thinking, conscious thing; then doubtless something entirely new is felt, or perceived, or thought; or, which is the same thing, there is some new sensation or perception of the mind, which is entirely of a new sort, and which could be produced by no exalting, varying, or compounding of that kind of perceptions or sensations which the mind had before; or there is what some metaphysicians call a new simple idea. If grace be, in the sense above described, an entirely new kind of principle, then the exercises of it are also entirely a new kind of exercises. And if there be in the soul a new sort of exercises which it is conscious of, which the soul knew nothing of before, and which no improvement, composition, or management of what it was before conscious or sensible of, could produce, or any thing like it; then it follows that the mind has an entirely new kind of perception or sensation; and here is, as it were, a new spiritual sense that the mind has, or a principle of a new kind of perception or spiritual sensation, which is in its whole nature different from any former kinds of sensation of the mind, as tasting is diverse from any of the other senses; and something is perceived by a true saint, in the exercise of this new sense of mind, in spiritual and divine things, as entirely diverse from any thing that is perceived in them, by natural men, as the sweet taste of honey is diverse from the ideas men have of honey by only looking on it, and feeling of it. So that the spiritual perceptions which a sanctified and spiritual person has, are not only diverse from all that natural men have after the manner that the ideas or perceptions of the same sense may differ one from another, but rather as the ideas and sensations of different senses do differ. Hence the work of the Spirit of God in regeneration is often in

Scripture compared to the giving a new sense, giving eyes to see, and ears to hear, unstopping the ears of the deaf, and opening the eyes of them that were born blind, and turning from darkness unto light. And because this spiritual sense is immensely the most noble and excellent, and that without which all other principles of perception, and all our faculties are useless and vain; therefore the giving this new sense, with the blessed fruits and effects of it in the soul, is compared to a raising the dead, and to a new creation.

This new spiritual sense, and the new dispositions that attend it, are no new faculties, but are new principles of nature. I use the word principles for want of a word of a more determinate signification. By a principle of nature in this place, I mean that foundation which is laid in nature, either old or new, for any particular manner or kind of exercise of the faculties of the soul; or a natural habit or foundation for action, giving a personal ability and disposition to exert the faculties in exercises of such a certain kind; so that to exert the faculties in that kind of exercises may be said to be his nature. So this new spiritual sense is not a new faculty of understanding, but it is a new foundation laid in the nature of the soul, for a new kind of exercises of the same faculty of understanding. So that new holy disposition of heart that attends this new sense is not a new faculty of will, but a foundation laid in the nature of the soul, for a new kind of exercises of the same faculty of will.

The Spirit of God, in all his operations upon the minds of natural men, only moves, impresses, assists, improves, or some way acts upon natural principles; but gives no new spiritual principle. Thus when the Spirit of God gives a natural man visions, as he did Balaam, he only impresses a natural principle, viz., the sense of seeing, immediately exciting ideas of that sense; but he gives no new sense; neither is there any thing supernatural, spiritual, or divine in it. So if the Spirit of God impresses on a man's imagination, either in a dream, or when he is awake, any outward ideas of any of the senses, either voices, or shapes and colors, it is only exciting ideas of the same kind that he has by natural principles and senses. So if God reveals to any natural man any secret fact: as, for instance, something that he shall hereafter see or hear; this is not infusing or exercising any new spiritual principle, or giving the ideas of any new spiritual sense; it is only impressing, in an extraordinary manner, the ideas that will hereafter be received by sight and hearing.—So in the more ordinary influences of the Spirit of God on the hearts of sinners, he only assists natural principles to do the same work to a greater degree, which they do of themselves by nature. Thus the Spirit of God by his common influences may assist men's natural ingenuity, as he assisted Bezaleel and Aholiab in the curious works of the tabernacle: so he may assist men's natural abilities in political affairs, and improve their courage and other natural qualifications, as he is said to have put his spirit on the seventy elders, and on Saul, so as to give him another heart: so God may greatly assist natural men's reason, in their reasoning about secular things, or about the doctrines of religion, and may greatly advance the clearness of their apprehensions and notions of things of religion in many respects, without giving any spiritual sense. So in those awakenings and convictions that natural men may have, God only assists conscience, which is a natural principle, to do that work in a further degree, which it naturally does. Conscience naturally gives men an apprehension of right and wrong, and suggests the relation there is between right and wrong, and a retribution: the Spirit of God assists men's consciences to do this in a greater degree, helps conscience against the stupefying influence of worldly objects and their lusts. And so many other ways might be mentioned wherein the Spirit acts upon, assists, and moves natural principles; but after all it is no more than nature moved, acted and improved; here is nothing supernatural and divine. But the Spirit of God in his spiritual influences on the hearts of his saints, operates by infusing or exercising new, divine, and supernatural principles; principles which are indeed a new and spiritual nature, and principles vastly more noble and excellent than all that is in natural men.

From what has been said it follows, that all spiritual and gracious affections are attended with and do arise from some apprehension, idea, or sensation of mind, which is in its whole nature different, yea, exceeding different, from all that is, or can be in the mind of a natural man; and which the natural man discerns nothing of, and has no manner of idea of (agreeable to 1

Cor. ii. 14), and conceives of no more than a man without the sense of tasting can conceive of the sweet taste of honey, or a man without the sense of hearing can conceive of the melody of a tune, or a man born blind can have a notion of the beauty of the rainbow.

But here two things must be observed, in order to the right understanding of this.

1. On the one hand it must be observed, that not every thing which in any respect appertains to spiritual affections, is new and entirely different from what natural men can conceive of, and do experience; some things are common to gracious affections with other affections; many circumstances, appendages and effects are common. Thus a saint's love to God has a great many things appertaining to it, which are common with a man's natural love to a near relation; love to God makes a man have desires of the honor of God, and a desire to please him; so does a natural man's love to his friend make him desire his honor, and desire to please him; love to God causes a man to delight in the thoughts of God, and to delight in the presence of God, and to desire conformity to God, and the enjoyment of God; and so it is with a man's love to his friend; and many other things might be mentioned which are common to both. But yet that idea which the saint has of the loveliness of God, and that sensation, and that kind of delight he has in that view, which is as it were the marrow and quintessence of his love, is peculiar, and entirely diverse from any thing that a natural man has, or can have any notion of. And even in those things that seem to be common, there is something peculiar; both spiritual and natural love cause desires after the object beloved; but they be not the same sort of desires: there is a sensation of soul in the spiritual desires of one that loves God, which is entirely different from all natural desires: both spiritual love and natural love are attended with delight in the object beloved; but the sensations of delight are not the same, but entirely and exceedingly diverse. Natural men may have conceptions of many things about spiritual affections; but there is something in them which is as it were the nucleus, or kernel of them, that they have no more conception of, than one born blind, has of colors.

It may be clearly illustrated by this: we will suppose two

men; one is born without the sense of tasting, the other has it; the latter loves honey, and is greatly delighted in it, because he knows the sweet taste of it; the other loves certain sounds and colors; the love of each has many things that appertain to it, which is common; it causes both to desire and delight in the object beloved, and causes grief when it is absent, &c., but yet that idea or sensation which he who knows the taste of honey has of its excellency and sweetness, that is the foundation of his love, is entirely different from any thing the other has or can have; and that delight which he has in honey is wholly diverse from any thing that the other can conceive of, though they both delight in their beloved objects. So both these persons may in some respects love the same object: the one may love a delicious kind of fruit, which is beautiful to the eye, and of a delicious taste; not only because he has seen its pleasant colors, but knows its sweet taste; the other, perfectly ignorant of this, loves it only for its beautiful colors: there are many things seen, in some respect, to be common to both; both love, both desire, and both delight; but the love and desire, and delight of the one, is altogether diverse from that of the other. The difference between the love of a natural man and a spiritual man is like to this; but only it must be observed, that in one respect it is vastly greater, viz., that the kinds of excellency which are perceived in spiritual objects, by these different kinds of persons, are in themselves vastly more diverse than the different kinds of excellency perceived in delicious fruit, by a tasting and a tasteless man; and in another respect it may not be so great, viz., as the spiritual man may have a spiritual sense or taste, to perceive that divine and most peculiar excellency but in small beginnings, and in a very imperfect degree.

2. On the other hand, it must be observed that a natural man may have those religious apprehensions and affections, which may be in many respects very new and surprising to him, and what before he did not conceive of; and yet what he experiences be nothing like the exercises of a principle of new nature, or the sensations of a new spiritual sense; his affections may be very new, by extraordinarily moving natural principles in a very new degree, and with a great many new circumstances, and a new cooperation of natural affections, and a new composition of

ideas; this may be from some extraordinary powerful influence of Satan, and some great delusion; but there is nothing but nature extraordinarily acted. As if a poor man that had always dwelt in a cottage, and had never looked beyond the obscure village where he was born, should in a jest be taken to a magnificent city and prince's court, and there arrayed in princely robes, and set on the throne, with the crown royal on his head, peers and nobles bowing before him, and should be made to believe that he was now a glorious monarch; the ideas he would have, and the affections he would experience, would in many respects be very new, and such as he had no imagination of before; but all this is no more than extraordinarily raising and exciting natural principles, and newly exalting, varying, and compounding such sort of ideas, as he has by nature; here is nothing like giving him a new sense.

Upon the whole, I think it is clearly manifest, that all truly gracious affections do arise from special and peculiar influences of the Spirit, working that sensible effect or sensation in the souls of the saints, which are entirely different from all that is possible a natural man should experience, not only different in degree and circumstances, but different in its whole nature; so that a natural man not only cannot experience that which is individually the same, but cannot experience any thing but what is exceeding diverse, and immensely below it, in its kind; and that which the power of men or devils is not sufficient to produce the like of, or any thing of the same nature.

I have insisted largely on this matter, because it is of great importance and use evidently to discover and demonstrate the delusions of Satan, in many kinds of false religious affections, which multitudes are deluded by, and probably have been in all ages of the Christian church; and to settle and determine many articles of doctrine, concerning the operations of the Spirit of God, and the nature of true grace.

Now, therefore, to apply these things to the purpose of this discourse.

From hence it appears, that impressions which some have made on their imagination, or the imaginary ideas which they have of God or Christ, or heaven, or any thing appertaining to religion, have nothing in them that is spiritual, or of the nature of true grace. Though such things may attend what is spiritual, and be mixed with it, yet in themselves they have nothing that is spiritual, nor are they any part of gracious experience.

Here, for the sake of common people, I will explain what is intended by impressions on the imagination and imaginary ideas. The imagination is that power of the mind whereby it can have a conception, or idea of things of an external or outward nature (that is, of such sort of things as are the objects of the outward senses) when those things are not present, and be not perceived by the senses. It is called imagination from the word *image*; because thereby a person can have an image of some external thing in his mind, when that thing is not present in reality, nor any thing like it. All such things as we perceive by our five external senses, seeing, hearing, smelling, tasting, and feeling, are external things: and when a person has an idea or image of any of these sorts of things in his mind, when they are not there, and when he does not really see, hear, smell, taste, nor feel them; that is to have an imagination of them, and these ideas are imaginary ideas: and when such kinds of ideas are strongly impressed upon the mind, and the image of them in the mind is very lively, almost as if one saw them, or heard them, &c., that is called an impression on the imagination. Thus colors and shapes, and a form of countenance, they are outward things; because they are that sort of things which are the objects of the outward sense of seeing; and therefore when any person has in his mind a lively idea of any shape, or color, or form of countenance; that is to have an imagination of those things. So if he has an idea, of such sort of light or darkness, as he perceives by the sense of seeing; that is to have an idea of outward light, and so is an imagination. So if he has an idea of any marks made on paper, suppose letters and words written in a book; that is to have an external and imaginary idea of such kind of things as we sometimes perceive by our bodily eyes. And when we have the ideas of that kind of things which we perceive by any of the other senses, as of any sounds or voices, or words spoken; this is only to have ideas of outward things, viz., of such kind of things as are perceived by the external sense of hearing, and so that also is imagination: and when these ideas are lively impressed, almost as if they were really heard with the ears, this is to have an impression on the imagination. And so I might go on, and instance in the ideas of things appertaining to the other three senses of smelling, tasting, and feeling.

Many who have had such things have very ignorantly supposed them to be of the nature of spiritual discoveries. They have had lively ideas of some external shape, and beautiful form of countenance; and this they call spiritually seeing Christ. Some have had impressed upon them ideas of a great outward light; and this they call a spiritual discovery of God's or Christ's glory. Some have had ideas of Christ's hanging on the cross, and his blood running from his wounds; and this they call a spiritual sight of Christ crucified, and the way of salvation by his blood. Some have seen him with his arms open ready to embrace them; and this they call a discovery of the sufficiency of Christ's grace and love. Some have had lively ideas of heaven, and of Christ on his throne there, and shining ranks of saints and angels; and this they call seeing heaven opened to them. Some from time to time have had a lively idea of a person of a beautiful countenance smiling upon them; and this they call a spiritual discovery of the love of Christ to their souls, and tasting the love of Christ. And they look upon it as sufficient evidence that these things are spiritual discoveries, and that they see them spiritually, because they say they do not see these things with their bodily eyes, but in their hearts; for they can see them when their eyes are shut. And in like manner, the imaginations of some have been impressed with ideas of the sense of hearing; they have had ideas of words, as if they were spoken to them, sometimes they are the words of Scripture, and sometimes other words. they have had ideas of Christ's speaking comfortable words to them. These things they have called having the inward call of Christ, hearing the voice of Christ spiritually in their hearts, having the witness of the Spirit, and the inward testimony of the love of Christ, &c.

The common and less considerate and understanding sort of people, are the more easily led into apprehensions that these things are spiritual things, because spiritual things being invisible, and not things that can be pointed forth with the finger, we are forced to use figurative expressions in speaking of them, and to borrow names from external and sensible objects to signify them by. Thus we call a clear apprehension of things spiritual by the name of *light*; and a having such an apprehension of such or such things, by the name of *seeing* such things; and the conviction of the judgment, and the persuasion of the will, by the word of Christ in the gospel, we signify by spiritually hearing the call of Christ: and the Scripture itself abounds with such like figurative expressions. Persons hearing these often used, and having pressed upon them the necessity of having their eyes opened, and having a discovery of spiritual things, and seeing Christ in his glory, and having the inward call, and the like, they ignorantly look and wait for some such external discoveries, and imaginary views as have been spoken of; and when they have them are confident, that now their eyes are opened, now Christ has discovered himself to them, and they are his children; and hence are exceedingly affected and elevated with their deliverance and happiness, and many kinds of affections are at once set in a violent motion in them.

But it is exceedingly apparent that such ideas have nothing in them which is spiritual and divine, in the sense wherein it has been demonstrated that all gracious experiences are spiritual and divine. These external ideas are in no wise of such a sort, that they are entirely, and in their whole nature diverse from all that men have by nature, perfectly different from, and vastly above any sensation which it is possible a man should have by any natural sense or principle, so that in order to have them, a man must have a new spiritual and divine sense given him, in order to have any sensations of that sort: so far from this, that they are ideas of the same sort which we have by the external senses, that are some of the inferior powers of the human nature; they are merely ideas of external objects, or ideas of that nature, of the same outward, sensitive kind; the same sort of sensations of mind (differing not in degree, but only in circumstances) that we have by those natural principles which are common to us with the beasts, viz., the five external senses. This is a low, miserable notion of spiritual sense, to suppose that it is only a conceiving or imagining that sort of ideas which we have by our animal senses, which senses the beasts have in as great perfection as we; it is, as it were, a turning

Christ, or the divine nature in the soul, into a mere animal. There is nothing wanting in the soul, as it is by nature, to render it capable of being the subject of all these external ideas, without any new principles. A natural man is capable of having an idea, and a lively idea of shapes, and colors, and sounds, when they are absent, and as capable as a regenerate man is: so there is nothing supernatural in them. And it is known by abundant experience, that it is not the advancing or perfecting human nature, which makes persons more capable of having such lively and strong imaginary ideas, but that on the contrary, the weakness of body and mind, and distempers of body, make persons abundantly more susceptive of such impressions.[1]

As to a truly spiritual sensation, not only is the manner of its coming into the mind extraordinary, but the sensation itself is totally diverse from all that men have, or can have, in a state of nature, as has been shown. But as to these external ideas, though the way of their coming into the mind is sometimes unusual, yet the ideas in themselves are not the better for that; they are still of no different sort from what men have by their senses; they are of no higher kind, nor a whit better. For instance, the external idea a man has now of Christ hanging on the cross, and shedding his blood, is no better in itself, than the external idea that the Jews his enemies had, who stood round his cross, and saw this with their bodily eyes. The imaginary idea which men have now of an external brightness and glory of God, is no better than the idea the wicked congregation in the wilderness had of the external glory of the Lord at Mount Sinai, when they saw it with their bodily eyes; or any better than that idea which millions of cursed reprobates will have of the external glory of Christ at the day of judgment, who shall see, and have a very lively idea of ten thousand times

---

[1] Conceits and whimsies abound most in men of weak reason; children, and such as are cracked in their understanding, have most of them; strength of reason banishes them, as the sun does mists and vapors. But now the more rational any gracious person is, by so much more is he fixed and settled, and satisfied in the grounds of religion; yea, there is the highest and purest reason in religion; and when this change is wrought upon men, it is carried on in a rational way. Isa. i. 18, John xix. 9." *Flavel's Preparation for Sufferings*, Chap. vi. [Edwards's note.]

greater external glory of Christ, than ever yet was conceived in any man's imagination:[2] yea, the image of Christ, which men conceive in their imaginations, is not in its own nature of any superior kind to the idea the Papists conceive of Christ, by the beautiful and affecting images of him which they see in their churches (though the way of their receiving the idea may not be so bad); nor are the affections they have, if built primarily on such imaginations, any better than the affections raised in the ignorant people, by the sight of those images, which oftentimes are very great; especially when these images, through the craft of the priests, are made to move, and speak, and weep, and the like.[3] Merely the way of persons receiving these imaginary ideas, does not alter the nature of the ideas themselves that are received; let them be received in what way they will, they are still but external ideas, or ideas of outward appearances, and so are not spiritual. Yea, if men should actually receive such external ideas by the immediate power of the most high God upon their minds, they would not be spiritual, they would be no more than a common work of the Spirit of God; as is

[2] "If any man should see, and behold Christ really and immediately, this is not the saving knowledge of him. I know the saints do know Christ as if immediately present; they are not strangers by their distance: if others have seen him more immediately, I will not dispute it. But if they have seen the Lord Jesus as immediately as if here on earth, yet Capernaum saw him so; nay, some of them were disciples for a time, and followed him, John vi. And yet the Lord was hid from their eyes. Nay, all the world shall see him in his glory, which shall amaze them; and yet this is far short of having the saving knowledge of him, which the Lord doth communicate to the elect. So that though you see the Lord so really, as that you become familiar with him, yet, Luke xiii, 26: 'Lord have we not eat and drank,' &c.—and so perish." Shepard's Par. of the Ten Virgins, Part I, p. 197, 198. [Edwards's note.]
[3] "Satan is transformed into an angel of light: and hence we have heard that some have heard voices; some have seen the very blood of Christ dropping on them, and his wounds in his side: some have seen a great light shining in the chamber; some have been wonderfully affected with their dreams; some in great distress have had inward witness, 'Thy sins are forgiven'; and hence such liberty and joy, that they are ready to leap up and down the chamber. O adulterous generation! this is natural and usual with men, they would fain see Jesus, and have him present to give them peace; and hence Papists have his images. Wo to them that have no other manifested Christ, but such a one." Shepard's Parable of the Ten Virgins, Part I, p. 198. [Edwards's note.]

evident in fact, in the instance of Balaam, who had impressed on his mind, by God himself, a clear and lively outward representation or idea of Jesus Christ, as "the Star rising out of Jacob, when he heard the words of God, and knew the knowledge of the Most High, and saw the vision of the Almighty, falling into a trance," Numb. xxiv. 16, 17, but yet had no manner of spiritual discovery of Christ; that Day Star never spiritually rose in his heart, he being but a natural man.

And as these external ideas have nothing divine or spiritual in their nature and nothing but what natural men, without any new principles, are capable of; so there is nothing in their nature which requires that peculiar, inimitable and unparalleled exercise of the glorious power of God, in order to their production, which it has been shown there is in the production of true grace. There appears to be nothing in their nature above the power of the devil. It is certainly not above the power of Satan to suggest thoughts to men; because otherwise he could not tempt them to sin. And if he can suggest any thoughts or ideas at all, doubtless imaginary ones, or ideas of things external, are not above his power;[4] for the external ideas men have are the lowest sort of ideas. These ideas may be raised only by impressions made on the body, by moving the animal spirits, and impressing the brain.—Abundant experience does certainly show, that alterations in the body will excite imaginary or external ideas in the mind; as often, in the case of a high fever, melancholy, &c. These external ideas are as much below the more intellectual exercises of the soul, as the body is a less noble part of man than the soul.

And there is not only nothing in the nature of these external ideas or imaginations of outward appearances, from whence we can infer that they are above the power of the devil; but it is certain also that the devil can excite, and often hath excited such ideas. They were external ideas which he excited in the

---

[4] "Consider how difficult, yea and impossible it is to determine that such a voice, vision, or revelation is of God, and that Satan cannot feign or counterfeit it: seeing he hath left no certain marks by which we may distinguish one spirit from another." *Flavel's Causes and Cures of Mental Terrors*, clause 14. [Edwards's note.]

dreams and visions of the false prophets of old, who were under the influence of lying spirits, that we often read of in Scripture, as Deut. xiii. 1, 1 Kings xxii. 22, Isa. xxviii. 7, Ezek. xiii. 7. And they were external ideas that he often excited in the minds of the heathen priests, magicians and sorcerers, in their visions and ecstasies, and they were external ideas that he excited in the mind of the man Christ Jesus, when he showed him all the kingdoms of the world, with the glory of them, when those kingdoms were not really in sight.

And if Satan or any created being, has power to impress the mind with outward representations, then no particular sort of outward representations can be any evidence of a divine power. Almighty power is no more requisite to represent the shape of man to the imagination, than the shape of anything else: there is no higher kind of power necessary to form in the brain one bodily shape or color than another: it needs a no more glorious power to represent the form of the body of a man, than the form of a chip or block; though it be of a very beautiful human body, with a sweet smile in his countenance, or arms open, or blood running from the hands, feet and side: that sort of power which can represent black or darkness to the imagination, can also represent white and shining brightness: the power and skill which can well and exactly paint a straw, or a stick of wood, on a piece of paper or canvass; the same in kind, only perhaps further improved, will be sufficient to paint the body of a man, with great beauty and in royal majesty, or a magnificent city, paved with gold, full of brightness, and a glorious throne, &c. So it is no more than the same sort of power that is requisite to paint one as the other of these on the brain. The same sort of power that can put ink upon paper, can put on leaf gold. So that it is evident to a demonstration, if we suppose it to be in the devil's power to make any sort of external representation at all on the fancy (as without doubt it is, and never any one questioned it who believed there was a devil, that had any agency with mankind): I say, if so, it is demonstrably evident, that a created power may extend to all kinds of external appearances and ideas in the mind. From hence it again clearly appears, that no such things have any thing in them that is spiritual, supernatural, and divine, in the sense in which it has been proved that all truly gracious experiences have. And though external ideas, through man's make and frame, do ordinarily in some degree attend spiritual experiences, yet these ideas are no part of their spiritual experience, any more than the motion of the blood, and beating of the pulse, that attend experiences, are a part of spiritual experience. And though undoubtedly, through men's infirmity in the present state, and especially through the weak constitution of some persons, gracious affections which are very strong, do excite lively ideas in the imagination; yet it is also undoubted, that when persons' affections are founded on imaginations, which is often the case, those affections are merely natural and common, because they are built on a foundation that is not spiritual; and so are entirely different from gracious affections, which, as has been proved, do evermore arise from those operations that are spiritual and divine.

These imaginations do oftentimes raise the carnal affections of men to an exceeding great height: and no wonder, when the subjects of them have an ignorant, but undoubting persuasion, that they are divine manifestations, which the great Jehovah immediately makes to their souls, therein giving them testimonies in an extraordinary manner, of his high and peculiar favor.

Again, it is evident from what has been observed and proved of the manner in which gracious operations and effects in the heart are spiritual, supernatural and divine, that the immediate suggesting of the words of Scripture to the mind has nothing in it which is spiritual.

from

IMAGES OR SHADOWS
OF DIVINE THINGS*

[*On the Nature of Images*]

25. There are many things in the constitution of the world that are not properly shadows and images of divine things that yet are significations of them, as children's being born crying is a signification of their being born to sorrow. A man's coming into the world after the same manner as the beasts is a signification of the ignorance and brutishness of man, and his agreement in many things with the beasts.

. . . . .

70. If we look on these shadows of divine things as the voice of God purposely by them teaching us these and those spiritual and divine things, to show of what excellent advantage it will be, how agreeably and clearly it will tend to convey instruction to our minds, and to impress things on the mind and to affect the mind, by that we may, as it were, have God speaking to us. Wherever we are, and whatever we are about, we may see divine things excellently represented and held forth. And it will abundantly tend to confirm the Scriptures, for there is an excellent agreement between these things and the holy Scripture.

. . . . .

118. Images of divine things. It is with many of these images as it was with the sacrifices of old: they are often repeated,

---

* Reprinted from *Images or Shadows of Divine Things* by Jonathan Edwards. Edited by Perry Miller and used with permission of the Yale University Press.

whereas the antitype is continual and never comes to pass but once. Thus sleep is an image of death that is repeated every night; so the morning is the image of the resurrection; so the spring of the year is the image of the resurrection which is repeated every year. And so of many other things that might be mentioned, they are repeated often, but the antitype is but once. The shadows are often repeated to show t[w]o things, viz., [1.] that the thing shadowed is not yet fulfilled, and 2. to signify the great importance of the antitype that we need to be so renewedly and continually put in mind of it.

· · · · ·

156. The book of Scripture is interpreter of the book of nature two ways, viz., by declaring to us those spiritual mysteries that are indeed signified and typified in the constitution of the natural world; and secondly, in actually making application of the signs and types in the book of nature as representations of those spiritual mysteries in many instances.

[On the Meaning of Some Images]

4. The heavens' being filled with glorious, luminous bodies is to signify the glory and happiness of the heavenly inhabitants, and amongst these the sun signifies Christ and the moon the church.

· · · · ·

26. Christ often makes use of representations of spiritual things in the constitution of the [world] for argument, as thus: the tree is known by its fruit. These things are not merely mentioned as illustrations of his meaning, but as illustrations and evidences of the truth of what he says.

· · · · ·

79. The whole material universe is preserved by gravity or attraction, or the mutual tendency of all bodies to each other.

One part of the universe is hereby made beneficial to another; the beauty, harmony, and order, regular progress, life, and motion, and in short all the well-being of the whole frame depends on it. This is a type of love or charity in the spiritual world.

. . . . .

129. That a child needs correction, and the benefit of correcting children is a type of what is true with respect to God's children.

. . . . .

146. The late invention of telescopes, whereby heavenly objects are brought so much nearer and made so much plainer to sight and such wonderfull discoveries have been made in the heavens, is a type and forerunner of the great increase in the knowledge of heavenly things that shall be in the approaching glorious times of the Christian church.

. . . . .

152. The changes that pass on the face of the earth by the gradual approach of the sun is a remarkeable type of what will come to pass in the visible church of God and world of mankind in the approach of the church's latter day glory. The latter will be gradual, as the former is. The light and warmth of the sun in the former is often interrupted by return of clouds and cold, and the fruits of the earth kept back from a too sudden growth and a too quick transition from the dead state in winter to their summer's glory, which in the end would be hurtfull to them and would kill them. So it is in the spiritual world: if there should be such warm weather constantly without interruption as we have sometimes in Feb., March, and April, the fruits of the earth would flourish mightily for a little while, but would not be prepared for the summer's heat, but that would kill them. This is typical of what is true concerning the church of God and particular souls. The earth being stripped of its white winter garments in which all looked clean, but all

was dead, and the making of it so dirty as it is early in the spring in order to fit it for more beautifull clothing in a living state in summer, is also typical of what passes in the spiritual change of the world and also a particular soul. The surface of the earth is, as it were, dissolved in the spring; the ground is loosened and broke up and soften[ed] with moisture, and its filthiness never so much appears as then, and then is the most windy, turbulent season of all.

. . . . .

[The Beauty of the World]

The beauty of the world consists wholly of sweet mutual consents, either within itself or with the supreme being. As to the corporeal world, though there are many other sorts of consents, yet the sweetest and most charming beauty of it is its resemblance of spiritual beauties. The reason is that spiritual beauties are infinitely the greatest, and bodies being but the shadows of beings, they must be so much the more charming as they shadow forth spiritual beauties. This beauty is peculiar to natural things, it surpassing the art of man.

Thus there is the resemblance of a decent trust, dependence and acknowledgment in the planets continually moving round the sun, receiving his influences by which they are made happy, bright and beautiful: a decent attendance in the secondary planets, an image of majesty, power, glory, and beneficence in the sun in the midst of all, and so in terrestrial things, as I have shown in another place.

It is very probable that that wonderful suitableness of green for the grass and plants, the blues of the skie, the white of the clouds, the colours of flowers, consists in a complicated proportion that these colours make one with another, either in their magnitude of the rays, the number of vibrations that are caused in the atmosphere, or some other way. So there is a great suitablenes between the objects of different senses, as between sounds, colours, and smells; as between colours of the woods and flowers and the smells and the singing of birds, which it is probable consist in a certain proportion of the vibrations that are made in the different organs. So there are innumerable other agreeablenesses of motions, figures, etc. The gentle motions of waves, of [the] lily, etc., as it is agreeable to other things that represent calmness, gentleness, and benevolence, etc. the fields and woods seem to rejoice, and how joyfull do the birds seem to be in it. How much a resemblance is there of every grace in the field covered with plants and flowers when the sun shines serenely and undisturbedly upon them, how a resemblance, I say, of every grace and beautifull disposition of mind, of an inferiour towards a superiour cause, preserver, benevolent benefactor, and a fountain of happiness.

How great a resemblance of a holy and virtuous soul is a calm, serene day. What an infinite number of such like beauties is there in that one thing, the light, and how complicated an harmony and proportion is it probable belongs to it.

There are beauties that are more palpable and explicable, and there are hidden and secret beauties. The former pleases, and we can tell why; we can explain the particular point for the agreement that renders the thing pleasing. Such are all artificial regularities; we can tell wherein the regularity lies that affects us. [The] latter sort are those beauties that delight us and we cannot tell why. Thus, we find ourselves pleased in beholding the colour of the violets, but we know not what secret regularity or harmony it is that creates that pleasure in our minds. These hidden beauties are commonly by far the greatest, because the more complex a beauty is, the more hidden is it. In this latter fact consists principally the beauty of the world, and very much in light and colours. Thus mere light is pleasing to the mind. If it be to the degree of effulgence, it is very sensible, and mankind have agreed in it: they all represent glory and extraordinary beauty by brightness. The reason of it is either that light or our organ of seeing is so contrived that an harmonious motion is excited in the animal spirits and propagated to the brain. That mixture we call white is a proportionate mixture that is harmonious, as Sir Isaac Newton has shown, to each particular simple colour, and contains in it some harmony or other that is delightfull. And each sort of rays play a distinct tune to the soul, besides those lovely mixtures that are found in nature. Those beauties, how lovely is the green of the face of the earth in all manner of colours, in flowers, the colour of the skies, and lovely tinctures of the morning and evening.

Corollary: Hence the reason why almost all men, and those that seem to be very miserable, love life, because they cannot bear to lose sight of such a beautiful and lovely world. The ideas, that every moment whilst we live have a beauty that we take not distinct notice of, brings a pleasure that, when we come to the trial, we had rather live in much pain and misery than lose.

PURITAN POETRY

Bibliographical Note. The best general study of Puritan poetry remains K. B. Murdock, *Literature and Theology in Colonial New England* (Cambridge, 1949), pp. 137–172. Invaluable for newly discovered texts and for bibliographies are: H. S. Jantz, *The First Century of New England Verse* (Worcester, 1944) and Kenneth Silverman, ed., *Colonial American Poetry* (New York, 1968). For general historical-critical introductions, see Roy Harvey Pearce, *The Continuity of American Poetry* (Princeton, 1961), pp. 17–58; Norman S. Grabo, "The Veiled Vision: The Role of Aesthetics in Early American Intellectual History," *William and Mary Quarterly*, XIX (1962), 493–510; and Hyatt Waggoner, "Puritan Poetry," *Criticism*, VI (1964), 291–312. Studies of individual poets are listed in Leo Lemay, "Seventeenth-Century American Poetry: A Bibliography of the Scholarship, 1943 to 1966," *Early American Literature Newsletter*, I (1966), 9–18. Sources for texts here printed are given in a headnote to each poem, which is dated wherever bibliographical information allows.

from

THE WHOLE BOOK OF PSALMS FAITHFULLY TRANSLATED INTO ENGLISH METER (1640)

Text: *The Bay Psalm Book, ed. Zoltan Haraszti*
(*Chicago, 1956*)

FROM THE PREFACE

The singing of Psalms, though it breathe forth nothing but holy harmony, and melody: yet such is the subtlety of the enemy, and the enmity of our nature against the Lord, & his ways, that our hearts can find matter of discord in this harmony, and crotchets of division in this holy melody. For there have been three questions especially stirring concerning singing. First, what psalms are to be sung in churches? whether David's and other scripture psalms, or the psalms invented by the gifts of godly men in every age of the church. Secondly, if scripture psalms, whether in their own words, or in such meter as English poetry is wont to run in? Thirdly, by whom are they to be sung? whether by the whole churches together with their voices? or by one man singing alone and the rest joining in silence, & in the close saying amen.

   Touching the first, certainly the singing of David's psalms was an acceptable worship of God, not only in his own, but in succeeding times. . . . So that if the singing David's psalms be a moral duty & therefore perpetual; then we under the New Testament are bound to sing them as well as they under the Old: and if we are expressly commanded to sing Psalms, Hymns, and spiritual songs, then either we must sing David's psalms, or else may affirm they are not spiritual songs: which being penned by an extraordinary gift of the Spirit, for the sake especially of God's spiritual Israel, not to be read and preached only (as other parts of holy writ) but to be sung also, they are therefore most spiritual, and still to be sung of all the Israel of God: . . .

As for the scruple that some take at the translation of the book of psalms into meter, because David's psalms were sung in his own words without meter: we answer—First. There are many verses together in several psalms of David which run in rhythms (as those that know the Hebrew and as Buxtorf shows *Thesau*. pa. 029) which shows at least the lawfulness of singing psalms in English rhythms.

Secondly. The psalms are penned in such verses as are suitable to the poetry of the Hebrew language, and not in the common style of such other books of the Old Testament as are not poetical; now no Protestant doubteth but that all the books of the scripture should by God's ordinance be extant in the mother tongue of each nation, that they may be understood of all, hence the psalms are to be translated into our English tongue; and if in our English tongue we are to sing them, then as all our English songs (according to the course of our English poetry) do run in meter, so ought David's psalms to be translated into meter, that so we may sing the Lord's songs, as in our English tongue so in such verses as are familiar to an English ear which are commonly metrical: and as it can be no just offense to any good conscience, to sing David's Hebrew songs in English words, so neither to sing his poetical verses in English poetical meter: men might as well stumble at singing the Hebrew psalms in our English tunes (and not in the Hebrew tunes) as at singing them in English meter, (which are our verses) and not in such verses as are generally used by David according to the poetry of the Hebrew language: but the truth is, as the Lord hath hid from us the Hebrew tunes, lest we should think ourselves bound to imitate them; so also the course and frame (for the most part) of their Hebrew poetry, that we might not think ourselves bound to imitate that, but that every nation without scruple might follow as the grave sort of tunes of their own country songs, so the graver sort of verses of their own country poetry.

Neither let any think, that for the meter's sake we have

taken liberty or poetical license to depart from the true and proper sense of David's words in the Hebrew verses, no; but it hath been one part of our religious care and faithful endeavor, to keep close to the original text.

As for other objections taken from the difficulty of Ainsworth's tunes, and the corruptions in our common psalm books, we hope they are answered in this new edition of psalms which we here present to God and his Churches. For although we have cause to bless God in many respects for the religious endeavors of the translators of the psalms into meter usually annexed to our Bibles, yet it is not unknown to the godly learned that they have rather presented a paraphrase than the words of David translated according to the rule 2 *Chron.* 29. 30. and that their addition to the words, detractions from the words are not seldom and rare, but very frequent and many times needless, (which we suppose would not be approved of if the psalms were so translated into prose) and that their variations of the sense, and alterations of the sacred text too frequently, may justly minister matter of offense to them that are able to compare the translation with the text; of which failings, some judicious have oft complained, others have been grieved, whereupon it hath been generally desired, that as we do enjoy other, so (if it were the Lord's will) we might enjoy this ordinance also in its native purity: we have therefore done our endeavor to make a plain and familiar translation of the psalms and words of David into English meter, and have not so much as presumed to paraphrase to give the sense of his meaning in other words; we have therefore attended herein as our chief guide the original, shunning all additions, except such as even the best translators of them in prose supply, avoiding all material detractions from words or sense. The word ו which we translate *and* as it is redundant sometime in the Hebrew, so sometimes (though not very often) it hath been left out and yet not then, if the sense were not fair without it.

As for our translations, we have with our English Bibles (to which next to the Original we have had respect) used the Idioms of our own tongue instead of Hebraisms, lest they might seem English barbarisms. Synonymies we use indifferently: as *folk* for *people,* and *Lord* for *Jehovah,* and sometime (though

seldom) *God* for *Jehovah*; for which (as for some other inter-
pretations of places cited in the New Testament) we have the
scriptures' authority *Ps.* 14. with 53. *Heb.* 1. 6. with *Psalm* 97. 7.
Where a phrase is doubtful we have followed that which (in
our own apprehension) is most genuine & edifying:

Sometime we have contracted, sometime dilated the same
Hebrew word, both for the sense and the verse's sake: which
dilatation we conceive to be no paraphrastical addition no more
than the contraction of a true and full translation to be any
unfaithful detraction or diminution: as when we dilate *who
healeth* and say *he it is who healeth*; so when we contract, *those
that stand in awe of God* and say *God's fearers.*

Lastly. Because some Hebrew words have a more full and
emphatical signification than any one English word can or doth
sometime express, hence we have done that sometime which
faithful translators may do, viz. not only to translate the word
but the emphasis of it; as אל *mighty God,* for *God.* בדך
humbly bless for *bless; rise to stand, Psalm* 1. for *stand, truth
and faithfulness* for *truth.* Howbeit, for the verse's sake we do
not always thus, yet we render the word truly though not fully;
as when we sometimes say *rejoice* for *shout for joy.*

As for all other changes of numbers, tenses, and characters
of speech, they are such as either the Hebrew will unforcedly
bear, or our English forcibly calls for, or they no way change
the sense; and such are printed usually in another character.

If therefore the verses are not always so smooth and elegant
as some may desire or expect; let them consider that God's
Altar needs not our polishings: *Ex.* 20. for we have respected
rather a plain translation, than to smooth our verses with the
sweetness of any paraphrase, and so have attended Conscience
rather than Elegance, fidelity rather than poetry, in translating
the Hebrew words into English language, and David's poetry
into English meter; that so we may sing in Sion the Lord's songs
of praise according to his own will; until he take us from hence,
and wipe away all our tears, & bid us enter into our master's joy
to sing eternal Hallelujahs.

PSALME 23
A PSALM OF DAVID

The Lord to me a shepherd is,
    want therefore shall not I.
2. He in the folds of tender grass,
    doth cause me down to lie:
To waters calm me gently leads
3   Restore my soul doth he:
he doth in paths of righteousness:
    for his name's sake lead me.
4 Yea though in valley of death's shade
    I walk, none ill I'll fear:
because thou art with me, thy rod,
    and staff my comfort are.
5 For me a table thou hast spread,
    in presence of my foes:
thou dost anoint my head with oil.
    my cup it overflows.
6 Goodness & mercy surely shall
    all my days follow me:
and in the Lord's house I shall dwell
    so long as days shall be.

PSALME 90
A PRAYER OF MOSES
THE MAN OF GOD.

O Lord, thou hast been unto us
    from generation,
to generation, a place
    of fixed mansion.
2 Before the mountaines were brought forth,
    ere earth & world by thee o Lord

were form'd: thou art eternally
      God to eternitee.
3 Thou dost unto destruction
      turne miserable men:
   and then thou sayst yee sonnes of men
      doe yee returne agen.
4 For why o Lord, a thousand yeares
      are but within thy sight
   as yesterday when it is past:
      and as a watch by night.
5 By thee like as it were a flood
      they quite away are borne,
   they like a sleep, & as the grasse
      that grows up in the morne.
6 It in the morning flourisheth,
      it also up doth grow;
   it in the ev'ning is cut downe
      it withereth also.
7 Because wee by thine anger are
      consumed speedily:
   and by thy sore displeasure wee
      are troubled suddenly.
8 Thou hast set our iniquityes
      before thee in thy sight:
   our secret evills are within
      thy countenances light.
9 Because in thine exceeding wrath
      our dayes all passe away:
   our years wee have consumed quite,
      ev'n as a tale *are they*.
10 Threescore & ten yeares are the dayes
      of our yeares which remaine,
   & if through strength they fourscore be,
      their strength is grief & paine:
   For it's cut off soone, & wee flye
11   away: Who is't doth know
   thine angers strength? according as
      thy feare, thy wrath is so.

12 Teach us to count our dayes: our hearts
          so wee'l on wisdome set.
13 Turne Lord, how long? of thy servants
          let it repent thee yet?
14 O give us satisfaction
          betimes with thy mercee:
    that so rejoyce, & be right glad,
          through all our dayes may wee.
15 According to the dayes *wherin*
          affliction wee have had,
    and yeares *wherin* wee have seen ill,
          now also make us glad.
16 Unto those that thy servants be
          doe thou thy work declare:
    also thy comely glory to
          those that thy children are.
    Let our Gods beauty be on us,
          our handy works also
    stablish on us; our handy work
          establish it doe thou.

PSALME 137

    The rivers on of Babilon
          there when wee did sit downe:
    yea even then wee mourned, when
          wee remembred Sion.
 2 Our Harps wee did hang it amid,
          upon the willow tree.
 3 Because there they that us away
          led in captivitee,
    Requir'd of us a song, & thus
          askt mirth: us waste who laid,
    sing us among a Sions song,
          unto us then they said.
 4 The lords song sing can wee? being
 5   in strangers land. Then let

loose her skill my right hand, if I
    Jerusalem forget.
6 Let cleave my tongue my pallate on,
    if minde thee doe not I:
if chiefe joyes or'e I prize not more
    Jerusalem my joy.
7 Remember Lord, Edoms sons word,
    unto the ground said they,
it rase, it rase, when as it was
    Jerusalem her day.
8 Blest shall hee bee, that payeth thee,
    daughter of Babilon,
whom must be waste: that which thou hast
    rewarded us upon.
9 O happie hee shall surely bee
    that taketh up, that eke
thy little ones against the stones
    doth into pieces breake.

PSALME 141

A psalme of David.
O GOD, my Lord, on thee I call,
    doe thou make hast to mee:
and harken thou unto my voice,
    when I cry unto thee.
2 And let my pray'r directed be
    as incense in thy sight:
and the up-lifting of my hands
    as sacrifice at night.
3 Jehovah, oh that thou would'st set
    a watch my mouth before:
as also of my lips with care
    o doe thou keepe the dore.
4 Bow not my heart to evill things:
    to doe the wicked deed
with wicked workers: & let not
    mee of their dainties feed.

5 Let just-men smite mee, kindenes 'tis;
    let him reprove mee eke,
it shall be such a pretious oyle,
    my head it shall not breake:
For yet my prayr's ev'n in their woes.
6   When their judges are cast
on rocks, then shall they heare my words,
    for they are sweet to taste.
7 Like unto one who on the earth
    doth cutt & cleave the wood,
ev'n so our bones at the graves mouth
    are scattered abroad.
8 But unto thee o God, the Lord
    directed are mine eyes:
my soule o leave not destitute,
    on thee my hope relyes.
9 O doe thou keepe mee from the snare
    which they have layd for mee;
& also from the grins of those
    that work iniquitee.
10 Together into their owne nets
    o let the wicked fall:
untill such time that I escape
    may make from them withall.

John Wilson

(1588–1661)

CLAUDIUS GILBERT [1]
ANAGRAM. TIS BRAUL I CUDGEL.*
(1657)

Text: *Harold Jantz*, The First Century of
New England Verse (*Worcester, 1944*), *p. 34.*

[Tis Braul I Cudgel.] Ranters, Quakers Braul,
Divels, and Jesuites, Founders of them all.
Their Brauling Questions whosoever reades
may soone perceive, These are their proper heades.
What Better Cudgels, then Gods holy word,
(For Brauls so cursed,) and the Civil sword?
By God Ordained to suppresse such evils,
Which God Abhorreth as he doth the Devils.
Oh! Lett these blessed Cudgels knocke them downe.
Lett Sathan fall, that Christ may weare the Crowne.
Let Baal pleade for Baal; who are Christs,
Abhorr, oppose, Confound these Antichrists.
yea Lett the Lord confound them, who with spight
Against his Truth maliciously Fight.

---

* Reprinted by courtesy of the American Antiquarian Society.
[1] Gilbert was the author of a book attacking that sect so hated by the
Puritans, the Quakers. Wilson, as Puritan minister, is celebrating Gilbert's
holy work.

Anonymous

"ANAGRAM ON THOMAS DUDLEY"*
(1645?)

Text: Jantz, The First Century, *p. 34.*

> Thomas Dudley
> ah! old, must dye
> A deaths head on your hand you neede not weare
> a dying hand you on your shoulders beare
> you nccd not one to minde you, you must dye
> you in your name may spell mortalitye
> younge men may dye, but old men these dye must
> t'will not be long before you turne to dust.
> before you turne to dust! ah! must; old! dye!
> what shall younge doe, when old in dust doe lye?
> when old in dust lyc, what N. England doe?
> when old in dust doe lye, it's best dye too.

---

* Reprinted by courtesy of the American Antiquarian Society.

John Fiske

(1608–1677)

"UPON THE DECEASE OF THE REVEREND MR. THO: HOOKER &C"*
(1647)

Text: Jantz, The First Century, *p. 123.*

Thomas Hooker
Anagr.
A Rest; oh com'! oh

A Rest's at hand after thy weary dayes
After thy Tossings heere in wilderness:

A rest is it? oh com'! oh, no delayes
let bee! of this life end the wretchednes.

---

* Reprinted by courtesy of the American Antiquarian Society and the Brown University Library.

"UPON THE MUCH-TO BE LAMENTED DESEASE OF THE REVEREND MR. JOHN COTTON LATE TEACHER TO THE CHURCH AT BOSTON N. E. WHO DEPARTED THIS LIFE 23 OF 10. 52."*

Text: Jantz, The First Century, pp. 118–121.

JOHN ⎰ COTTON
⎱ *KOTTON AFTER THE*
  OLD ENGLISH WRITING

ANAGR:
O, HONIE KNOTT

> With Joy erst while, (when knotty doubts arose)
> To Thee we calld, o Sir, the knott disclose:
> But now o and alasse to thee to call
> In vayne tis thou no Answer give or shall.
> Could loud Shrickes, could crys recall thee back
> From deaths estate we wold our eye ne're slack
> O, this our greife it is, lament shall we
> A Father in our Israel's cea'st to be
> even hee that in the Church a pillar was
> A gurdeon knot of sweetest graces as
> He who set fast to Truths so clossly knitt
> as loosen him could ne're the keene witt
> Hee who his Flesh together bound ful-fast

---

* Reprinted by courtesy of the American Antiquarian Society.

no knott more sure whilest his life did last
Hee who the knotts of Truth, of Mysteries
sacred, most cleerely did ope' fore our eyes
even hee who such a one, is ceas'd to bee
'twixt whose life, death, the most sweete harmony
Knotts we doe meet with many a cue daily
which crabbed anggry tough unpleasing bee
But we as in a honi-comb a knott
of Hony sweete, here had such sweetenes Gott
the knotts and knobbs that on the Trees doe grow
the bitterest excressences we know.

  his soule Embalmd with grace
   was fit to soare on high
  and to receive its place
   above the starry skie.
  now grant O G[od that we]
   may follow afte[r him]
  surviving worlds ocean unto thee
   our passage safe may swim.

A vine tree seene, a plant of Gods owne hand
In it this knott of sweetest parts did stand.
The knott sometimes seems a deformity
It's a mistake, tho such be light set by
The knott it is the Joynt, the strength of parts
the bodies-beauty, so this knott out-starts
What others in that place, they ought to bee
even such a knott exemplar'ly was hee
Knotts now adayes affrayd of are most men
of Hony if expose'd feare none would then
I guesse why knotty Learning downe does goe
'twould not, if as in him 'twere sweetned soe
Meeknes Humility forbearance too
this lovely knott to love the most did woe
In knotts what greate adoe to gayne the hearte
yee had it heere, he did it free impart
When knotty theames and paynes some meet with then
as knotty and uncouth their tongue and pen

so 'twas not heere, he caus'd us understand
and tast the sweetnes of the knott in hand.
When knotty querks and quiddities broacht were
by witt of man he sweetely Breathed there.
His charity his wisdom meeknes eke
left none that loved light, in knotts to seeke
Hee tho invincible thrô softnes did
the knottiest peeces calme and cleave amid
Such was hee of such use in these last dayes
Whose want bewayle, o, and alas alwaies
This knott so we have seen lien broknly
By knotts so breathlesse, so crookt, crackt, or fly
This knott thereof so surfetted we see
By hony surfetted we know som bee
The cause nor in the knott nor hony say
Thrô Temper bad, unskilfulnes this may
O knott of Hony most delightfull when
Thou livd'st, thi death a sad presage hath ben
Have Ben? yea is, and is, and is alas
For woe to us, so greate a Breach when was
Woe to that knotty pride hee ne're subdude
Woe they who doe his Truthes dispenct exclude
and woe to them that factions there contrive
woe them whose wayes unrighteous survive
Woe they that by him warning did not take
Woe to us all if mercy us forsake
A Mercy once New England thou hast had
(you Boston cheifly) in thi Cotton clad
Some 'gan to count't too meane a dresse and sought
Silk Velvetts Taffeties best could be bought
these last will soyle, if first doe soyle also
how can wc think but Naked we shall goe
must silken witts, must velvet tongues be had
and shall playne preaching be accounted bad
I feare a famine, pinching times t'ensue
Time Such may have, slighted mercy to Rue
My wakened muse to rest, my moystned pen
mye eye, my hearte which powred out this have ben

cease try no more, for Hee hath gayn'd his prize
His heavenly mansion 'bove the starry skie
Returne thee home and wayle the evills there
Repent breake off thi sins Jehovah feare

O Jehovah feare: this will thi wisdom bee
And thou his waies of mercy yet maust see
Returne thou mee;   And turned bie
Lord unto thee: even so shall I.
                            Jo: Fiske

Anne Bradstreet

(1612–1672)

"THE FOUR SEASONS OF
THE YEAR"

(1650)

Text: The Works of Anne Bradstreet,
ed. John Harvard Ellis (Charlestown, 1867),
pp. 168–179.*

SPRING

Another four I've left yet to bring on,
Of four times four the last *Quaternion*,
The Winter, Summer, Autumn & the Spring,
In season all these Seasons I shall bring:
Sweet Spring like man in his Minority,
At present claim'd, and had priority.
With smiling face and garments somewhat green,
She trim'd her locks, which late had frosted been,
Nor hot nor cold, she spake, but with a breath,
Fit to revive, the nummed earth from death.
Three months (quoth she) are 'lotted to my share
March, April, May of all the rest most fair.
Tenth of the first, *Sol* into *Aries* enters,

---

* Here and in what follows I have used Ellis' text in preference to the
modernized text in Jeanine Hensley, ed., *The Works of Anne Bradstreet*
(Cambridge, 1967).

And bids defiance to all tedious winters,
Crosseth the Line, and equals night and day,
(Stil adds to th' last til after pleasant *May*)
And now makes glad the darkned northern wights
Who for some months have been but starry lights.
Now goes the Plow-man to his merry toyle,
He might unloose his winter locked soyl:
The Seeds-man too, doth lavish out his grain,
In hope the more he casts, the more to gain:
The Gardner now superfluous branches lops,
And poles erects for his young clambring hops.
Now digs then sowes his herbs, his flowers & roots
And carefully manures his trees of fruits.
The *Pleiades their influence* now give,
And all that seem'd as dead afresh doth live.
The croaking frogs, whom nipping winter kil'd
Like birds now chirp, and hop about the field,
The Nightingale, the black-bird and the Thrush
Now tune their layes, on sprayes of every bush.
The wanton frisking Kid, and soft-fleec'd Lambs
Do jump and play before their feeding Dams,
The tender tops of budding grass they crop,
They joy in what they have, but more in hope:
For though the frost hath lost his binding power,
Yet many a fleece of snow and stormy shower
Doth darken *Sol*'s bright eye, makes us remember
The pinching North-west wind of cold *December*.
My second moneth is *April*, green and fair,
Of longer dayes, and a more temperate Air:
The Sun in *Taurus* keeps his residence,
And with his warmer beams glanceth from thence
This is the month whose fruitful showrs produces
All set and sown for all delights and uses:
The Pear, the Plum, the Apple-tree now flourish
The grass grows long the hungry beast to nourish.
The Primrose pale, and azure violet
Among the virduous grass hath nature set,
That when the Sun on's Love (the earth) doth shine
These might as lace set out her garment fine.

The fearfull bird his little house now builds
In trees and walls, in Cities and in fields.
The outside strong, the inside warm and neat;
A natural Artificer compleat.
The clocking hen her chirping chickins leads
With wings & beak defends them from the gleads
My next and last is fruitfull pleasant *May*,
Wherein the earth is clad in rich aray,
The Sun now enters loving *Gemini*,
And heats us with the glances of his eye,
Our thicker rayment makes us lay aside
Lest by his fervor we be torrifi'd.
All flowers the Sun now with his beams discloses,
Except the double pinks and matchless Roses.
Now swarms the busy, witty, honey-Bee,
VVhose praise deserves a page from more then me
The cleanly Huswifes Dary's now in th' prime,
Her shelves and firkins fill'd for winter time.
The meads with Cowslips, Honey-suckles dight,
One hangs his head, the other stands upright·
But both rejoyce at th' heavens clear smiling face,
More at her showers, which water them a space.
For fruits my Season yields the early Cherry,
The hasty Peas, and wholsome cool Strawberry.
More solid fruits require a longer time,
Each Season hath his fruit, so hath each Clime:
Each man his own peculiar excellence,
But none in all that hath preheminence.
Sweet fragrant Spring, with thy short pittance fly
Let some describe thee better then can I.
Yet above all this priviledg is thine,
Thy dayes still lengthen without least decline:

SUMMER

When *Spring* had done, the *Summer* did begin,
With melted tauny face, and garments thin,
Resembling Fire, Choler, and Middle age,

As *Spring* did Air, Blood, Youth in's equipage.
Wiping the sweat from of her face that ran,
With hair all wet she puffing thus began;
Bright *June, July* and *August* hot are mine,
In'th first *Sol* doth in crabbed *Cancer* shine.
His progress to the North now's fully done,
Then retrograde must be my burning Sun,
Who to his southward Tropick still is bent,
Yet doth his parching heat but more augment
Though he decline, because his flames so fair,
Have throughly dry'd the earth, and heat the air.
Like as an Oven that long time hath been heat,
Whose vehemency at length doth grow so great,
That if you do withdraw her burning store,
Tis for a time as fervent as before.
Now go those frolick Swains, the Shepherd Lads
To wash the thick cloth'd flocks with pipes full glad
In the cool streams they labour with delight
Rubbing their dirty coats till they look white:
Whose fleece when finely spun and deeply dy'd
With Robes thereof Kings have been dignifi'd.
Blest rustick Swains, your pleasant quiet life,
Hath envy bred in Kings that were at strife,
Careless of worldly wealth you sing and pipe,
Whilst they'r imbroyl'd in wars & troubles rife:
VVhich made great *Bajazet* cry out in's woes,
Oh happy shepherd which hath not to lose.
Orthobulus, nor yet *Sebastia* great,
But whist'leth to thy flock in cold and heat.
Viewing the Sun by day, the Moon by night
Endimions, Dianaes dear delight,
Upon the grass resting your healthy limbs,
By purling Brooks looking how fishes swims.
If pride within your lowly Cells ere haunt,
Of him that was Shepherd then King go vaunt.
This moneth the Roses are distil'd in glasses,
VVhose fragrant smel all made perfumes surpasses
The Cherry, Gooseberry are now in th' prime,

And for all sorts of Pease, this is the time.
July my next, the hott'st in all the year,
The sun through *Leo* now takes his Career,
VVhose flaming breath doth melt us from afar,
Increased by the star Canicular.
This Month from *Julius Cæsar* took its name,
By Romans celebrated to his fame.
Now go the Mowers to their slashing toyle,
The Meadowes of their riches to dispoyle,
VVith weary strokes, they take all in their way,
Bearing the burning heat of the long day.
The forks and Rakes do follow them amain,
VVhich makes the aged fields look young again.
The groaning Carts do bear away this prize.
To Stacks and Barns where it for Fodder lyes.
My next and last is *August* fiery hot
(For much, the *Southward* Sun abateth not)
This Moneth he keeps with *Virgo* for a space,
The dryed Earth is parched with his face.
August of great *Augustus* took its name,
Romes second Emperour of lasting fame,
With sickles now the bending Reapers goe
The russling tress of *terra* down to mowe;
And bundles up in sheaves, the weighty wheat,
Which after Manchet makes for Kings to eat:
The Barly, Rye and Pease should first had place,
Although their bread have not so white a face.
The Carter leads all home with whistling voyce,
He plow'd with pain, but reaping doth rejoyce;
His sweat, his toyle, his careful wakeful nights,
His fruitful Crop abundantly requites.
Now's ripe the Pear, Pear-plumb, and Apricock,
The prince of plumbs, whose stone's as hard as Rock
The Summer seems but short, the Autumn hasts
To shake his fruits, of most delicious tasts
Like good old Age, whose younger juicy Roots
Hath still ascended, to bear goodly fruits.
Until his head be gray, and strength be gone.

Yet then appears the worthy deeds he'th done:
To feed his boughs exhausted hath his sap,
Then drops his fruits into the eaters lap.

AUTUMN

Of *Autumn* moneths *September* is the prime,
Now day and night are equal in each Clime,
The twelfth of this *Sol* riseth in the Line,
And doth in poizing *Libra* this month shine.
The vintage now is ripe, the grapes are prest,
Whose lively liquor oft is curs'd and blest:
For nought so good, but it may be abused,
But its a precious juice when well its used.
The raisins now in clusters dryed be,
The Orange, Lemon dangle on the tree:
The Pomegranate, the Fig are ripe also,
And Apples now their yellow sides do show.
Of Almonds, Quinces, Wardens, and of Peach,
The season's now at hand of all and each.
Sure at this time, time first of all began,
And in this moneth was made apostate Man:
For then in *Eden* was not only seen,
Boughs full of leaves, or fruits unripe or green,
Or withered stocks, which were all dry and dead,
But trees with goodly fruits replenished;
Which shews nor Summer, Winter nor the Spring
Our Grand-Sire was of Paradice made King:
Nor could that temp'rate Clime such difference make,
If scited as the most Judicious take.
October is my next, we hear in this
The Northern winter-blasts begin to hiss.
In *Scorpio* resideth now the Sun,
And his declining heat is almost done.
The fruitless Trees all withered now do stand,
Whose sapless yellow leavs, by winds are fan'd,
Which notes when youth and strength have past their prime
Decrepit age must also have its time.

The Sap doth slily creep towards the Earth
There rests, until the Sun give it a birth.
So doth old Age still tend unto his grave,
Where also he his winter time must have;
But when the Sun of righteousness draws nigh,
His dead old stock, shall mount again on high.
November is my last, for Time doth haste,
We now of winters sharpness 'gins to tast.
This moneth the Sun's in *Sagitarius*,
So farre remote, his glances warm not us.
Almost at shortest is the shorten'd day,
The *Northern* pole beholdeth not one ray.
Now Greenland, Groanland, Finland, Lapland, see
No Sun, to lighten their obscurity:
Poor wretches that in total darkness lye,
With minds more dark then is the dark'ned Sky.
Beaf, Brawn, and Pork are now in great request,
And solid meats our stomacks can digest.
This time warm cloaths, full diet, and good fires,
Our pinched flesh, and hungry mawes requires:
Old, cold, dry Age and Earth *Autumn* resembles,
And Melancholy which most of all dissembles.
I must be short, and shorts, the short'ned day,
What winter hath to tell, now let him say.

WINTER

Cold, moist, young flegmy winter now doth lye
In swadling Clouts, like new born Infancy
Bound up with frosts, and furr'd with hail & snows,
And like an Infant, still it taller grows;
December is my first, and now the Sun
To th' Southward *Tropick*, his swift race doth run:
This moneth he's hous'd in horned *Capricorn*,
From thence he 'gins to length the shortned morn,
Through *Christendome* with great Feastivity,
Now's held, (but ghest) for blest Nativity.
Cold frozen *January* next comes in,

Chilling the blood and shrinking up the skin;
In *Aquarius* now keeps the long wisht Sun,
And Northward his unwearied Course doth run:
The day much longer then it was before,
The cold not lessened, but augmented more.
Now Toes and Ears, and Fingers often freeze,
And Travellers their noses sometimes leese.
Moist snowie *February* is my last,
I care not how the winter time doth haste.
In *Pisces* now the golden Sun doth shine,
And Northward still approaches to the Line,
The Rivers 'gin to ope, the snows to melt,
And some warm glances from his face are felt;
Which is increased by the lengthen'd day,
Until by's heat, he drive all cold away,
And thus the year in Circle runneth round:
Where first it did begin, in th' end its found.

> *My Subjects bare, my Brain is bad,*
> *Or better Lines you should have had:*
> *The first fell in so nat'rally,*
> *I knew not how to pass it by;*
> *The last, though bad I could not mend,*
> *Accept therefore of what is pen'd,*
> *And all the faults that you shall spy*
> *Shall at your feet for pardon cry.*

"THE FLESH AND THE SPIRIT"
(1650)

Text: *Works, pp. 381–385.*

> In secret place where once I stood
> Close by the Banks of *Lacrim* flood
> I heard two sisters reason on

Things that are past, and things to come;
One Flesh was call'd, who had her eye
On worldly wealth and vanity;
The other Spirit, who did rear
Her thoughts unto a higher sphere:
Sister, quoth Flesh, what liv'st thou on
Nothing but Meditation?
Doth Contemplation feed thee so
Regardlesly to let earth goe?
Can Speculation satisfy
Notion without Reality?
Dost dream of things beyond the Moon
And dost thou hope to dwell there soon?
Hast treasures there laid up in store
That all in th' world thou count'st but poor?
Art fancy sick, or turn'd a Sot
To catch at shadowes which are not?
Come, come, Ile shew unto thy sence,
Industry hath its recompence.
What canst desire, but thou maist see
True substance in variety?
Dost honour like? acquire the same,
As some to their immortal fame:
And trophyes to thy name erect
Which wearing time shall ne're deject.
For riches dost thou long full sore?
Behold enough of precious store.
Earth hath more silver, pearls and gold,
Then eyes can see, or hands can hold.
Affect's thou pleasure? take thy fill,
Earth hath enough of what you will.
Then let not goe, what thou maist find,
For things unknown, only in mind.
Spir. Be still thou unregenerate part,
Disturb no more my setled heart,
For I have vow'd, (and so will doe)
Thee as a foe, still to pursue.
And combate with thee will and must,
Untill I see thee laid in th' dust.

Sisters we are, ye twins we be,
Yet deadly feud 'twixt thee and me;
For from one father are we not,
Thou by old Adam wast begot,
But my arise is from above,
Whence my dear father I do love.
Thou speakst me fair, but hatst me sore,
Thy flatt'ring shews Ile trust no more.
How oft thy slave, hast thou me made,
when I believ'd, what thou hast said,
And never had more cause of woe
Then when I did what thou bad'st doe.
Ile stop mine ears at these thy charms,
And count them for my deadly harms.
Thy sinfull pleasures I doe hate,
Thy riches are to me no bait,
Thine honours doe, nor will I love;
For my ambition lyes above.
My greatest honour it shall be
When I am victor over thee,
And triumph shall, with laurel head,
When thou my Captive shalt be led,
How I do live, thou need'st not scoff,
For I have meat thou know'st not off;
The hidden Manna I doe eat,
The word of life it is my meat.
My thoughts do yield me more content
Then can thy hours in pleasure spent.
Nor are they shadows which I catch,
Nor fancies vain at which I snatch,
But reach at things that are so high,
Beyond thy dull Capacity;
Eternal substance I do see,
With which inriched I would be:
Mine Eye doth pierce the heavens, and see
What is Invisible to thee.
My garments are not silk nor gold,
Nor such like trash which Earth doth hold,
But Royal Robes I shall have on,

More glorious then the glistring Sun;
My Crown not Diamonds, Pearls, and gold,
But such as Angels heads infold.
The City where I hope to dwell,
There's none on Earth can parallel;
The stately Walls both high and strong,
Are made of pretious *Jasper* stone;
The Gates of Pearl, both rich and clear,
And Angels are for Porters there;
The Streets thereof transparent gold,
Such as no Eye did e're behold,
A Chrystal River there doth run,
Which doth proceed from the Lambs Throne:
Of Life, there are the waters sure,
Which shall remain for ever pure,
Nor Sun, nor Moon, they have no need,
For glory doth from God proceed:
No Candle there, nor yet Torch light,
For there shall be no darksome night.
From sickness and infirmity,
For evermore they shall be free,
Nor withering age shall e're come there,
But beauty shall be bright and clear;
This City pure is not for thee,
For things unclean there shall not be:
If I of Heaven may have my fill,
Take thou the world, and all that will.

THE AUTHOR TO HER BOOK

Text: Works, pp. 389–390.

Thou ill-form'd offspring of my feeble brain,
Who after birth did'st by my side remain,
Till snacht from thence by friends, less wife then true

Who thee abroad, expos'd to publick view,
Made thee in raggs, halting to th' press to trudg,
Where errors were not lessened (all may judg)
At thy return my blushing was not small,
My rambling brat (in print) should mother call,
I cast thee by as one unfit for light,
Thy Visage was so irksome in my fight;
Yet being mine own, at length affection would
Thy blemishes amend, if so I could:
I wash'd thy face, but more defects I saw,
And rubbing off a spot, still made a flaw.
I stretcht thy joynts to make thee even feet,
Yet still thou run'st more hobling then is meet;
In better dress to trim thee was my mind,
But nought save home-spun Cloth, i'th' house I find
In this array, 'monst Vulgars mayst thou roam
In Criticks hands, beware thou dost not come;
And take thy way where yet thou are not known,
If for thy Father askt, say, thou hadst none:
And for thy Mother, she alas is poor,
Which caus'd her thus to send thee out of door.

"BEFORE THE BIRTH OF ONE OF HER CHILDREN."
(1678)

Text: Works, p. 393.

All things within this fading world hath end,
Adversity doth still our joyes attend;
No tyes so strong, no friends so dear and sweet,
But with deaths parting blow is sure to meet.
The sentence past is most irrovocable,

A common thing, yet oh inevitable;
How soon, my Dear, death may my steps attend,
How soon't may be thy Lot to lose thy friend,
We both are ignorant, yet love bids me
These farewell lines to recommend to thee,
That when that knot's unty d that made us one,
I may seem thine, who in effect am none.
And if I see not half my dayes that's due,
What nature would, God grant to yours and you;
The many faults that well you know I have,
Let be interr'd in my oblivions grave;
If any worth or virtue were in me,
Let that live freshly in thy memory
And when thou feel'st no grief, as I no harms,
Yet love thy dead, who long lay in thine arms:
And when thy loss shall be repaid with gains
Look to my little babes my dear remains.
And if thou love thy self, or loved'st me
These O protect from step Dames injury.
And if chance to thine eyes shall bring this verse,
With some sad sighs honour my absent Herse;
And kiss this paper for thy love's dear sake,
Who with salt tears this last Farewel did take.

"TO MY DEAR AND
LOVING HUSBAND"
(1678)

Text: Works, p. 394.

> If ever two were one, then surely we.
> If ever man were lov'd by wife, then thee;
> If ever wife was happy in a man,

Compare with me ye women if you can.
I prize thy love more then whole Mines of gold,
Or all the riches that the East doth hold.
My love is such that Rivers cannot quench,
Nor ought but love from thee, give recompence.
Thy love is such I can no way repay,
The heavens reward thee manifold I pray.
Then while we live, in love lets so persever,
That when we live no more, we may live ever.

ON MY DEAR GRAND-CHILD
SIMON BRADSTREET, *
WHO DYED ON *16. NOVEMB. 1669.*
BEING BUT A MONETH,
AND ONE DAY OLD.

Text: Works, p. 406.

No sooner come, but gone, and fal'n asleep,
Acquaintance short, yet parting caus'd us weep,
Three flours, two fearcely blown, the last i'th' bud,
Cropt by th' Almighties hand; yet is he good,
With dreadful awe before him let's be mute,
Such was his will, but why, let's not dispute,
With humble hearts and mouths put in the dust,
Let's say he's merciful as well as just.
He will return, and make up all our losses,
And smile again, after our bitter crosses.
Go pretty babe, go rest with Sisters twain
Among the blest in endless joyes remain.

                                        A. B.

---

* The fourth child of her eldest son, Samuel.

Samuel Danforth

(d. 1674)

from

AN ALMANACK FOR THE YEAR OF OUR LORD 1647*

Text: K. B. Murdock, ed. Handkerchiefs for Paul (*Cambridge, 1927*), *pp. 101–104.*

[March]

> A Coal-white Bird appears this spring
> That neither cares to sigh or sing.
> This when the merry Birds espy,
> They take her for some enemy.
> Why so, when as she humbly stands
> Only to shake you by your hands?

[April]

> That which hath neither tongue nor wings
> This month how merrily it sings:
> To see such, out for dead who lay
> To cast their winding sheets away?
> Friends! would you live? some pils then take
> When head and stomack both doe ake.

---

* Reprinted from *Handkerchiefs for Paul*, edited by K. B. Murdock and used with permission of the Harvard University Press.

[*June*]

Who dig'd this spring of Gardens here,
Whose mudded streames at last run cleare?
But why should we such water drink?
Give loosers what they list to think,
Yet know, one God, one Faith profest
To be New-Englands interest.

[*July*]

The wooden Birds are now in sight,
Whose voices roare, whose wings are white,
Whose mawes are fill'd with hose and shooes,
With wine, cloth, sugar, salt and newes,
When they have eas'd their stomacks here
They cry, farewell untill next yeare.

[*August*]

Many this month I doe fore-see
Together by the eares will bee:
Indian and English in the field
To one another will not yeild.
Some weeks continue will this fray,
Till they be carted all away.

[*September*]

Four heads should meet and counsell have,
The chickens from the kite to save,
The idle drones away to drive,
The little Bees to keep i'th hive.
How hony m[a]y be brought to these
By making fish to dance on trees.

[*October*]

If discontented Bellyes shall
Wish that the highest now might fall:

Their wish fulfilled they shall see,
Whenas within the woods they bee.
Poor Tinker think'st our shrubs will sing:
The Bramble here shall be our King.

[*November*]

None of the wisest now will crave
To know what winter we shall have.
If shall be milde, let such be told.
If that it be not over cold.
Nor over cold shall they it see,
If very temperate it bee

[*December*]

It maybe now some enemy—
Not see, but felt, will make you fly.
Where is it best then to abide:
I think close by the fier side.
If you must fight it out i'the field,
Your hearts let woollen breast-plates shield.

[*January*]

Great bridges shall be made alone
Without ax, timber, earth or stone,
Of chrystall metall, like to glasse;
Such wondrous works soon come to passe,
If you may then have such a way,
The Ferry-man you need not pay.

[*February*]

Our Lillyes which refus'd to spin
All winter past, shall now begin
To feel the lash of such a Dame,
Whom some call Idleness by name.
Excepting such who all this time
Had reason good against my rime.

Urian Oakes

(1631–1681)

"AN ELEGY UPON THE DEATH OF THE REVEREND MR THOMAS SHEPARD"*

(1677)

Text: Perry Miller and T. H. Johnson, eds., The Puritans (New York, 1938), pp. 641–650.

[1]

Oh! that I were a Poet now in grain!
How would I invocate the Muses all
To deign their presence, lend their flowing Vein,
And help to grace dear *Shepard's* Funeral!
   How would I paint our griefs, and succours borrow
   From Art and Fancy, to limn out our sorrow!

---

* Reprinted from *The Puritans*, edited by Perry Miller and T. H. Johnson and used with permission of the American Book Company.

[2]

Now could I wish (if wishing would obtain)
The sprightli'est Efforts of Poetick Rage,
To vent my Griefs, make others feel my pain,
For this loss of the Glory of our Age.
  Here is a subject for the loftiest Verse
  That ever waited on the bravest Hearse.

[3]

And could my Pen ingeniously distill
The purest Spirits of a sparkling wit
In rare conceits, the quintessence of skill
In *Elegiack Strains*; none like to it:
  I should think all too little to condole
  The fatal loss (to us) of such a Soul.

[4]

Could I take highest Flights of Fancy, soar
Aloft; If Wits Monopoly were mine:
All would be much too low, too light, too poor,
To pay due tribute to this great Divine.
  Ah! Wit avails not, when th'Heart's like to break,
  Great griefs are Tongue-ti'ed, when the lesser speak.

[5]

Away loose rein'd Careers of Poetry,
The celebrated Sisters may be gone;
We need no *Mourning Women's* Elegy,
No forc'd, affected, artificial Tone.
  Great and good *Shepard's* Dead! Ah! this alone
  Will set our eyes abroach, dissolve a stone.

[6]

Poetick Raptures are of no esteem,
Daring *Hyperboles* have here no place,

Luxuriant Wits on such a copious Theme,
Would shame themselves, and blush to shew their face
   Here's worth enough to overmatch the skill
   Of the most stately Poet *Laureat's Quill.*

[7]

Exube'rant Fancies useless here I deem,
Transcendent vertue scorns feign'd Elogies:
He that gives *Shepard* half his due, may seem,
If Strangers hear it, to Hyperbolize.
   Let him that can, tell what his vertues were,
   And say, this Star mov'd in no common Sphere.

[8]

Here need no Spices, Odours, curious Arts,
No skill of *Egypt,* to embalm the Name
Of such a Worthy: let men speak their hearts,
They'l say, He merits an Immortal Fame.
   When *Shepard* is forgot, all must conclude,
   This is prodigious ingratitude.

[9]

But live he shall in many a gratefull Breast,
Where he hath rear'd himself a Monument,
A Monument more stately than the best,
On which Immensest Treasures have been spent.
   Could you but into th'Hearts of thousands peep,
   There would you read his Name engraven deep.

[10]

Oh! that my head were Waters, and mine Eyes
A flowing Spring of Tears, still issuing forth
In streams of bitterness, to solemnize
   The *Obits* of this Man of matchless worth!

Next to the Tears our sins do need and crave,
I would bestow my Tears on *Shepards* Grave.

[*11*]

Not that he needs our Tears: for he hath dropt
His measure full; not one Tear more shall fall
Into God's Bottle from his eyes; *Death* stopt
That water-course, his sorrows ending all.
    He Fears, he Cares, he Sighs, he Weeps no more:
    Hee's past all storms, Arriv'd at th'wished Shoar.

[*12*]

Dear *Shepard* could we reach so high a strain
Of pure Seraphick love, as to devest
Our selves, and love, of self-respects, thy gain
Would joy us, though it cross our interest.
    Then would we silence all compaints with this,
    Our Dearest Friend is doubtless gone to Bliss.

[*13*]

Ah! but the Lesson's hard, thus to deny
Our own dear selves, to part with such a Loan
Of Heaven (in time of such necessity)
And love thy comforts better than our own.
    Then let us moan our loss, adjourn our glee,
    Till we come thither to rejoice with thee.

[*14*]

As when some formidable Comets blaze,
As when Portentous Prodigies appear,
Poor Mortals with amazement stand and gaze,
With hearts affrighted, and with trembling fear:
    So are we all amazed at this blow,
    Sadly portending some approaching woe.

[15]

We shall not summon bold Astrologers,
To tell us what the Stars say in the case,
(Those Cousin-Germans to black Conjurers)
We have a sacred Oracle that says,
    When th'Righteous perish, men of mercy go,
    It is a sure presage of coming wo.

[16]

He was (ah woful word! to say he was)
Our wrestling *Israel*, second unto none,
The man that stood i'th'gap, to keep the pass,
To stop the Troops of Judgments rushing on.
    This Man the honour had to hold the hand
    Of an incensed God against our Land.

[17]

When such a Pillar's faln (Oh such an one!)
When such a glorious, shining Light's put out,
When Chariot and Horsemen thus are gone;
Well may we fear some Downfal, Darkness, Rout.
    When such a Bank's broke down, there's sad occasion
    To wail, and dread some grievous Inundation.

[18]

What! must we with our God, and Glory part?
Lord! Is thy Treaty with *New-England* come
Thus to an end? And is War in thy Heart?
That this Ambassadour is called home.
    So Earthly Gods (Kings) when they War intend,
    Call home their Ministers, and Treaties end.

[19]

Oh for the Raptures, Transports, Inspirations
Of *Israel's Singers* when his *Jon'athan's* Fall

So tun'd his mourning Harp! what Lamentations
Then would I make for *Shepards* Funerall
   How truly can I say, as well as He?
   My *Dearest Brother I'am distress'd for thee.*

[20]

How Lovely, Worthy, Peerless, in my view?
How Precious, Pleasant hast thou been to me?
How Learned, Prudent, Pious, Grave, and True?
And what a Faithful Friend? who like to thee?
   Mine Eye's desire is vanish'd: who can tell
   Where lives my dearest *Shepard's* Parallel?

[21]

'Tis strange to think: but we may well believe,
That not a few of different Perswasions
From this great Worthy, do now truly grieve
I'th'Mourning croud, and joyn their Lamentations.
   Such Powers Magnetick had He to draw to Him
   The very Hearts, and Souls, of all that knew Him!

[22]

Art, Nature, Grace, in Him were all combin'd
To shew the World a matchless *Paragon:*
In whom of Radiant Virtues no less shin'd,
Than a whole Constellation: but hee's gone!
   Hee's gone alas! Down in the Dust must ly
   As much of this rare Person as could dy.

[23]

If to have solid Judgement, Pregnant Parts,
A piercing Wit, and comprehensive Brain;
If to have gone the *Round* of all the Arts,
Immunity from Deaths Arrest would gain,
   Shepard would have been Death-proof, and secure
   From that All conquering Hand, I'm very sure.

[24]

If Holy Life, and Deeds of Charity,
If Grace illustrious, and Virtue tri'ed,
If modest Carriage, rare Humility,
Could have brib'd Death, good *Shepard* had not di'ed.
    Oh! but inexorable Death attacks
    The best Men, and promiscu'ous havock makes.

[25]

Come tell me, Criticks, have you ever known
Such Zeal, so temper'd well with moderation?
Such Prudence, and such Inno'cence met in one?
Such Parts, so little Pride and Ostentation?
    Let *Momus* carp, and *Envy* do her worst,
    And swell with *Spleen* and *Rancour* till she burst.

[26]

To be descended well, doth *that* commend?
Can Sons their Fathers Glory call their own?
Our *Shepard* justly might to this pretend,
(His Blessed Father was of high Renown,
    Both *Englands* speak him great, admire his Name)
    But his own pers'onal worth's a better claim.

[27]

Great was the Father, once a glorious Light
Among us, Famous to an high Degree:
Great was this Son: indeed (to do him right)
As Great and Good (to say no more) as He.
    A double portion of his Fathers Spirit
    Did this (his Eldest) Son, through Grace, inherit.

[28]

His Look commanded Reverence and Awe,
Though Mild and Amiable, not Austere:

Well Humour'd was He (as I ever saw)
And rul'd by Love and Wisdome, more than Fear.
  The Muses, and the Graces too, conspir'd
  To set forth this Rare Piece, to be admir'd.

[29]

He govern'd well the Tongue (that busie thing,
Unruly, Lawless and Pragmatical)
Gravely Reserv'd, in Speech not lavishing,
Neither too sparing, nor too liberal.
  His Words were few, well season'd, wisely weigh'd,
  And in his Tongue the Law of kindness sway'd.

[30]

Learned he was beyond the common Size,
Befriended much by Nature in his Wit,
And Temper, (Sweet, Sedate, Ingenious, Wise)
And (which crown'd all) he was Heav'ens Favourite:
  On whom the God of all Grace did command,
  And show'r down Blessings with a lib'eral hand.

[31]

Wise He, not wily, was; Grave, not Morose;
Not stiffe, but steady; Seri'ous, but not Sowre;
Concern'd for all, as if he had no Foes;
(Strange if he had!) and would not wast an Hour.
  Thoughtful and Active for the common good:
  And yet his own place wisely understood.

[32]

Nothing could make him stray from Duty; Death
Was not so frightful to him, as Omission
Of Ministerial work; he fear'd no breath
Infecti'ous, i'th'discharge of his Commission.

Rather than run from's work, he chose to dy,
Boldly to run on Death, than duty fly.

[33]

(Cruel Disease! that didst (like *High-way-men*)
Assault the honest Trav'eller in his way,
And rob dear *Shepard* of his life (Ah!) then,
When he was on the Road, where Duty lay.
    Forbear, bold Pen! 'twas God that took him thus,
    To give him great Reward, and punish us.)

[34]

Zealous in God's cause, but meek in his own;
Modest of Nature, bold as any Lion,
Where Consc'ience was concern'd: and there were none
More constant Mourners for afflicted Sion:
    So gene'ral was his care for th'Churches all,
    His Spirit seemed Apostolical.

[35]

Large was his Heart, to spend without regret,
Rejoycing to do good: not like those *Moles*
That root i'th'Earth, or roam abroad, to get
All for themselves (those sorry, narrow Souls!)
    But He, like th'Sun (i'th'Center, as some say)
    Diffus'd his Rayes of Goodness every way.

[36]

He breath'd Love, and pursu'd Peace in his day,
As if his Soul were made of Harmony:
Scarce ever more of Goodness crouded lay
In such a piece of frail Mortality.
    Sure Father *Wilsons* genuine Son was he,
    New-England's Paul had such a *Timothy*.

[37]

No slave to th' Worlds grand *Idols;* but he flew
At *Fairer Quarries,* without stooping down
To Sublunary prey: his great Soul knew
Ambition none, but of the Heave'nly Crown.
   Now he hath won it, and shall wear't with Honour,
   Adoring Grace, and God in Christ, the Donour.

[38]

A Friend to Truth, a constant Foe to Errour,
Pow'erful i'th'*Pulpit,* and sweet in converse,
To weak ones gentle, to th'Profane a Terrour.
Who can his vertues, and good works rehearse?
   The Scripture-Bishops-Character read o'er,
   Say this was *Shepards:* what need I say more?

[39]

I say no more: let them that can declare
His rich and rare endowments, paint this Sun,
With all its dazling Rayes: But I despair,
Hopeless by any hand to see it done.
   They that can *Shepards* goodness well display,
   Must be as good as he: But who are they?

[40]

See where our Sister *Charlstown* sits and Moans!
Poor Widowed *Charlstown!* all in Dust, in Tears!
Mark how she wrings her hands! hear how she groans!
See how she weeps! what sorrow like to hers!
   Charlstown, that might for joy compare of late
   With all about her, now looks desolate.

[41]

As you have seen some Pale, Wan, Ghastly look,
When grisly Death, that will not be said nay,

Hath seiz'd all for it self, Possession took,
And turn'd the Soul out of its house of Clay:
    So Visag'd is poor *Charlstown* at this day;
    Shepard, her very Soul, is torn away.

[42]

Cambridge groans under this so heavy cross,
And Sympathizes with her Sister dear;
Renews her Griefs afresh for her old loss
Of her own *Shepard,* and drops many a Tear.
    Cambridge and *Charlstown* now joint Mourners are,
    And this tremendous loss between them share.

[43]

Must Learnings Friend (Ah! worth us all) go thus?
That Great Support to *Harvards* Nursery!
Our *Fellow* (that no Fellow had with us)
Is gone to Heave'ns great University.
    Our's now indeed's a lifeless *Corporation,*
    The Soul is fled, that gave it *Animation!*

[44]

Poor *Harvard's* Sons are in their Mourning Dress:
Their sure Friend's gone! their Hearts have *put on Mourning;*
Within their Walls are Sighs, Tears, Pensiveness;
Their new Foundations dread an overturning.
    Harvard! where's such a fast Friend left to thee!
    Unless thy great Friend, *Leveret,* it be.

[45]

We must not with our greatest Soveraign strive,
Who dare find fault with him that is most High?
That hath an absolute Prerogative,
And doth his pleasure: none may ask him, why?
    We're Clay-lumps, Dust-heaps, nothings in his sight:
    The Judge of all the Earth doth always right.

[46]

Ah! could not Prayers and Tears prevail with God!
Was there no warding off that dreadful Blow!
And was there no averting of that Rod!
Must *Shepard* dy! and that good Angel go!
  Alas! Our heinous sins (more than our haits)
  It seems, were louder, and out-crie'd our Prayers.

[47]

See what our sins have done! what Ruines wrought
And how they have pluck'd out our very eyes!
Our sins have slain our *Shepard!* we have bought,
And dearly paid for, our Enormities.
  Ah Cursed sins! that strike at God, and kill
  His *Servants,* and the Blood of *Prophets* spill.

[48]

As you would loath the Sword that's warm and red,
As you would hate the hands that are embru'd
I'th'Hearts-blood of your dearest Friends: so dread,
And hate your sins; Oh! let them be pursu'd:
  Revenges take on bloody sins: for there's
  No refuge-City for these Murtherers.

[49]

In vain we build the Prophets Sepulchers,
In vain bedew their Tombs with Tears, when Dead;
In vain bewail the Deaths of Ministers,
Whilst Prophet-killing sins are harboured.
  Those that these Murth'erous Traitors favour, hide;
  Are with the blood of Prophets deeply di'ed.

[50]

New-England! know thy Heart-plague: feel this blow;
A blow that sorely wounds both Head and Heart,

A blow that reaches All, both high and low,
A blow that may be felt in every part.
  Mourn that this *Great Man's* faln in *Israel:*
  Lest it be said, *with him New-England fell!*

[51]

Farewel, Dear *Shepard!* Thou art gone before,
Made free of *Heaven,* where thou shalt sing loud *Hymns*
Of *High triumphant Praises* evermore,
In the sweet Quire of *Saints* and *Seraphims.*
  Lord! look on us here, clogg'd with sin and clay,
  And we, through Grace, shall be as happy as they.

[52]

My Dearest, Inmost, Bosome-Friend, is Gone!
Gone is my sweet Companion, Soul's delight!
Now in an Huddling Croud I'm all alone,
And almost could bid all the World *Goodnight:*
  Blest be my Rock! God lives: Oh let him be,
  As He is, so All in All to me.

The Bereaved, Sorrowful

URIAN OAKES

John Saffin

(1632–1710)

Text: John Saffin: His Book (1665–1708),
ed., Caroline Hazard (New York, 1928), pp. 11–12.

MARTHA SAFFIN

Text: His Book, p. 11.

Anagr: { 1 In hart am Saff
{ 2 Ah! firm an fast

In hart am Saff ha firm and fast
To my Beloved to my Last
or
Am Safe in heart, ah firm and fast
To my Beloved to my Last

AN ELEGIE ON HIS DEAR AND TRUELY PIOUS MOTHER MRS GRACE SAFFIN ALIAS ELSWORTH WHO DEPARTED THIS LIFE IN LONDON IN A GOOD OLD AGE. ANNO

Text: His Book, *pp.* 15–16.

Anag: { Grace Ellsworth / Sel grace worth } alias—Saffin

Sel grace worth money; more worth one little graine
then all the Incomes of the King of Spaine:
yea the whole world: since greatest Monarchs high
with all their wealth, the least graine cannot buy.
Then surely you were here Exceeding Rich,
That of free Grace you truely own'd so much,
Yet tis no wonder, since you Ere did love
that grace God gave you Ever to Improve:
to best advantage, so that many a year,
you did improve your Gracious Talent here;
in use of meanes you Dayly did frequent
unto Gods Glory, and your Soules Content.
Cherish That Heaven-born Soul of yours, did allways
with the fathings of Gods house which made it florish
Like a green Bay Tree: which was ne'r beguild
of its due moysture: Since you from a Child
did know the Holy Scripture: in that Station
Learnd'st that, which made you wise unto Salvation.
Nor did you onely tread Gods holy wayes:
Just in the prime, and morning of your Dayes;
But allso persever'd; being truly Sage
did bring forth fruit to God in your Old age.

So that this Honour's your undoubted Due,
of being a young Saint, and an Old one too.

A LAMENTATION ON MY DEAR SON SIMON WHO DYED OF THE SMALL POX ON THE 23 NOVEMBER 1678

Text: His Book, pp. 21–22.

> Simon my son, son of my Nuptiall knott
> ah! Simon's gone, Simon my son is not
> whose Heaven-born Soul in full ripe fruit appears
> wherein he liv'd an age above his years.
> whose pregnant witt, quick Genius, parts sublime
> facill'd his Books, made him Pernassus clime
> and Dare Apelles so were he alive
> Who best should . . . or Rarest piece contrive
> He unappall'd with humble Confidence
> could to's Superiours speak without Offence
> So free and unconcern'd as one had been
> conversing with his Equalls Dayly seen
> his Towering Fancy, and his quaint invention
> Excell'd most of his Standing and prctcntion
> Lovely in's features his Complection fair
> of comely Jeasture, flaxen was his haire
> But that which Crowneth all the Rest
> In his own language better is Exprest.

When he was goeing on in the Thirteenth year of his life he was in the month of November visited with that sore and then Epidemicall Distemper of the small pox, and have-

ing very patiently layen under Burthen thereof about 15 Days
(all hopes of his recovery being all most gone) Docter Cook
(who was his Physician) came to him and asked him how he
did, Simon answered never better in all my life. Docter How
so Simon. Simon why Because I shall be blessed to all Eternity.
The Docter (thinkeing he might be in a Dilerium) Replyed
But Simon how do you know you shall be blessed to all
Eternity. Simon. Jesus Christ hath told me so, and I Dare not
but beleive him, the like and more he said to the same purpose
he said to Mr Willard the Minister who came after and often
to see him. And so he went on & continued with Soul-Ravish-
ing Expressions till his Speech faild him to the Comfort and
Admiration of all that heard him, and
on the 23th of November 1678 he went Tryumphantly to
Heaven. He allso often said Mother Brother John, come away
make hast adding, that they must follow, and that Mr Thatcher
did look and waite for . . . and that there was Room Enough
for them all in Heaven.

FROM VIRGINIA, 1654

Text: His Book, *pp. 181–182.*

> Sweetly (my Dearest) I left thee asleep
> Which Silent parting made my heart to weep,
> Faine would I wake her, but Love did Reply
> O wake her not, So sweetly let her Lye.
> But must I goe, ô must I Leave her So,
> So ill at Ease: invovl'd in Slumbering wo
> Must I goe hence: and thus my Love desert
> Unknown to Her, ô must I now Depart;
> Thus was I hurried with such thoughts as these,
> Yet loath to Rob the of thy prefent Ease,
> or rather senceless payn: farewell thought I,
> My Joy my Deare in whom I live or Dye

Farewell Content, farewell fare Beauty's light
And the most pleasing Object of my Sight;
I must begone, Adeiu my Dear, Adieu
Heavens grant good Tideings I next heare from you
Thus in sad Silence I alone and mute,
My lips bad thee farewell, with a Salute.
And so went from thee; turning back againe
I thought one kiss to little then Stole twaine
And then another: but no more of this,
Count with your Self how many of them you miss.
And now my love soon let me from the heare
Of thy good health, that may my Spirits Cheare
Acquaint me with such passages as may
present themselves since I am come away
And above all things let me thee Request
To bee both Chearfull quiet and at Rest
In thine own Spirit, and let nothing move
Thee unto Discontent my Joy my Love.
Hopeing that all things shall at last Conduce
Unto our Comfort and a Blessed use
Considering that those things are hardly gain'd
Are most Delightfull when they are Attain'd.
Gold Crowns are heavy: Idalian Burn's
And Lovers Days are good, and bad by turn's
But yet the Consumnation will Repay
The Debt that's due many a happy Day
Which that it may so be, Ile Heaven Implore
To grant the same henceforth forever more
And so farewell, farewell fair Beautys light
Ten thousand times Adieu my Dear Delight.
    Your Ever loveing friend whilest Hee
    Desolved is: or Cease to bee.

TO HER COMING HOME

Text: His Book, *p. 182.*

Sayle gentle Pinnace Zepherus doth not faile
with prosperous gales, Saile Gentle Pinnace Sayle
Proud Neptune Stoops, and freely Condescends
For's foremer Roughness, now to make amends;
Thetis with her green Mantle sweetly Glides
With smileing Dimples Singing by our Sides
Sayle Gentle Pinnace Zepherus does not faile
With Prosperous gales, Sayle Gentle Pinnace Sayle.

AN EPITHALMIUM OR
WEDDING SONG

Text: His Book, *p. 191.*

Come Brave Gallants come away,
it quickly will be Break of Day;
Sweet virgins and fair Ladys all
hark: for it is the Bridgrooms Call;
hast, if you will be Dignifid
t' attend the Bridegroom and the Bride:
with all your Rich Attire, and Dress,
See who can best, their love Express;
for Neptune now hath lay'd aside
His Seagreen Mantle, Thetis pride:
to grace the Bride with good Intents
be take them Silver ornaments;
the pretty Birds, that Sing most rare:
Retaine their Notes, and lend an Eare

to hear the sweet Hermonious Noise,
of the fair Bride, and Bridegrooms voice;
and Everything doth motion move,
with awefull due Respect, and Love
To Honour this their Nuptiall Tye
that thence may Spring a Progenie
which may in vertue Ever Shine
like Pha'bus in Meridian line;
meanwhile wee'll Sing on Every side
Joyes to the Bridegroom & the Bride.

ON A ROGUE THAT ABUS'D THE PEOPLE OF N. E. OF ALL RANKS AND SEXES, IN A PRINTED SCURRILLOUS PAMPHLETT

Text: His Book, *p. 192.*

This Indigent Romantick Lowsey Lecher,
Be lyes both sexes, Magistrate, & preacher;
So gross, malicious Serpentinely-fell:
Proceeding from Abaddon, hatch'd in Hell.

John James

(1633–1729)

"OF JOHN BUNYANS LIFE &C"*
(1702)

Text: Jantz, The First Century, *p. 150.*

Wel mended Tinker! sans dispute
Brasse into Gold Grace can transmute.
Its hammer rings upon thy breast
so sanctifyed wert and blest
In thee an happy change was made
And thou becamest an other blad
Unswaupt, instampt & meliorate
By such means was thy wretched state
So sovereigne a Mastery
Has Grace to cure debauchery.

                                        Nov-8-1702

---

* Reprinted by courtesy of the American Antiquarian Society.

Philip Pain

(d. *c.* 1668)

from

DAILY MEDITATIONS: OR, QUOTIDIAN PREPARATIONS FOR, AND CONSIDERATIONS OF DEATH AND ETERNITY

(1668)

Text: Daily Meditations
(*San Marino, California*, 1936).*

SEVEN

> Death puts an end to every thing below,
> It gives the killing wound, the fatall blow,
> Of those that here awhile did but reside,
> But for a time, the last act is, They dy'd.
>   Then grant, O Lord, that I may act this Part
>   Well on the Stage; then Death, lo here's my ♥.

---

* Used with permission of the Henry E. Huntington Library and Art Gallery.

EIGHT

Scarce do I pass a day, but that I hear
Some one or other's dead; and to my ear
Me thinks it is no news: but Oh! did I
Think deeply on it, what it is to dye,
    My Pulses all would bear, I should not be
    Drown'd in this Deluge of Security.

NINETEEN

How bruitish, Oh how sensless are all those,
Who the World do so themselves dispose,
As if there were no God to serve, no Death
That's coming to deprive them of their breath?
    Lord help me so to live, that I may bee
    Never forgetful of my Death or Thee.

THIRTY-ONE

We have no License from our God to waste
One day, one hour, one moment, that do haste
So swiftly from us in our sinful pleasures,
But rather to lay up for lasting treasures.
    Lord, Spare me yet a little, that I may
    Prepare for Death, and for the Judgement-day.

FORTY-NINE

In Heaven are eternal joyes; and sure
In that place there are Remedies to cure
Our here Sin-sick'ned Souls: but Oh shall I
Be made a Patient of this Remedy?
    Lord, I believe a Heaven there is; but this
    The Question is, Shall I enjoy that bliss?

FIFTY

In Hell are Torments, Torments without end;
And them I must endure, if that no friend
I have of Jesus. O my Soul, must I
Go from PAIN here, to Pain eternally?
    I know there is a Hell: Lord, grant that I
    May go from Earth to Heaven when I dye.

Benjamin Tompson

(1642–1714)

GULIELMI TOMPSONI BRAINTREENSIS ECCLESIAE PASTORIS IN ANGLIA UTRAQUE CELEBERIMI VICE. EPITAPHIUM

Text: Benjamin Tompson, 1642–1714,
ed., Howard J. Hall (*Boston*, 1924), *pp*. 107–108.

Judicious Zeale: New-Englands Boanerges
Lies Tombles: not to spare the Churches Charges
But that the world may know he lacks no Tomb
Who in Ten thousand hearts commanded room
While thus the thundring Textman hidden lies
Some Virgins slumber: Others wantonize.

"UPON THE SETTING
OF THAT OCCIDENTAL STAR
JOHN WINTHROP *ESQ*;"

Text: Benjamin Tompson, *pp*. 84–86.

Nine Muses, get you all but one to sleep,
But spare *Melpomene*, with me to weep.
From you whose bleared Eyes have Lectures read,
Of many of our *English* Heroe's dead.
I beg a glance from Spectacles of Woe,
(Quotidian Gazets) Brave *Winthrop* to.
Whose death Terrestrial Comets did portend,
To every one who was his Countreys friend.
The Blaze of Towns was up like Torches light,
To guide him to his Grave, who was so fit
To rule, or to obey, to live or die:
(A special Favorite of the Most High)
Monarch of Natures Secrets, who did hold,
Its grand Elixir named the *Star* of GOLD.
Or else the World mistakes, and by his deeds,
Of Daily Charities Expence he needs.
But had he it, he wiser was than so,
That every Ape of Artists should it know.
He had the System of the Universe,
Too Glorious for any to Rehearse.
As *Moses* took the Law in Clouds and Fire;
Which Vulgars barr'd at distance much admire
Thus was he taught the precious Art of healing,
(Judge we but by success) at Gods revealing.
He mounted up the Stairs of Sciences,
Unto the place of Visions which did please.
Where on the Pinacle of worldly skill,
On Kingdoms of all Arts, he gaz'd his fill.
Into his Thoughts Alembick we may think,
He crouded Stars to make a Diet Drink.
(I mean) Terrestrial Stars which in the Earth,

Receive their vitals and a Mineral Birth:
That *Proteus, Mercury,* he could compel,
Most soberly well fixt at home to dwell.
Of Salt (which Cooks do use for Eggs and Fishes)
He made a Balsom better than all Riches;
And Sulphur too provided for mens woe,
He made an Antidote Diseases to.
This Terrene three, were made by Fire his friends,
To bring about his ARCHIATRICK ends.
He saw the World, which first had only shade,
And after rich Embroideries on it laid,
Of Glorious Light; how the Homogeneal spark,
Did first Rebell against the Central dark.
He saw the Jemms how first they budded, and
The Birth of Minerals, which put to stand
Natures grand Coartiers. He knew the Womb
From whom the Various Tribes of Herbs did come.
He had been round the Philosophick sea,
And knew the Tincture if there any be:
But all his Art must lie, there's no Disease
Predominant, where he doth take his Ease:
Outliving *Theophrast,* he shew'd thereby
Himself Hermetick, more surpassing high
TRISMEGESTOS I'll stile him; first in Grace,
Thrice great in ART, the next deserving place;
Thrice High in humble Carriage, and who,
Would not to Highest Meekness ready bow?
England and *Holland* did great *Winthrop* woe;
Both had experienc'd Wonders he could doe.
But poor *New-England* stole his humble Heart,
From whose deep Wounds he never would depart:
His Councel Balsome like, he poured in,
And plaistred up its Breaches made by sin.
Natives themselves, in parlies would confess,
Brave *Winthrops* Charity and Holiness.
The Time he rul'd, War never toucht his bound,
When Fire, and Sword, and Death, raged all around.
Above whose reach he reigns in Glories Rays,
Singing with all the Saints his Makers praise.

Edward Taylor

(1642–1729)

"PROLOGUE" TO PREPARATORY MEDITATIONS BEFORE MY APPROACH TO THE LORDS SUPPER. CHIEFLY UPON THE DOCTRINE PREACHED UPON THE DAY OF ADMINISTRATION

Text: The Poems of Edward Taylor,
ed., Donald E. Stanford (*New Haven*, 1960), *p. 1*.

> Lord, Can a Crumb of Dust the Earth outweigh,
>   Outmatch all mountains, nay the Chrystall Sky?
> Imbosom in't designs that shall Display
>   And trace into the Boundless Deity?
>   Yea hand a Pen whose moysture doth guild ore
>   Eternall Glory with a glorious glore.
>
> If it its Pen had of an Angels Quill,
>   And sharpend on a Pretious Stone ground tite,
> And dipt in Liquid Gold, and mov'de by Skill
>   In Christall leaves should golden Letters write
>   It would but blot and blur yea jag, and jar
>   Unless thou mak'st the Pen, and Scribener.

[439]

I am this Crumb of Dust which is design'd
  To make my Pen unto thy Praise alone,
And my dull Phancy I would gladly grinde
  Unto an Edge on Zions Pretious Stone.
  And Write in Liquid Gold upon thy Name
  My Letters till thy glory forth doth flame.

Let not th'attempts breake down my Dust I pray
  Nor laugh thou them to scorn but pardon give.
Inspire this Crumb of Dust till it display
  Thy Glory through't: and then thy dust shall live.
  Its failings then thou'lt overlook I trust,
  They being Slips slipt from thy Crumb of Dust.

Thy Crumb of Dust breaths two words from its breast,
  That thou wilt guide its pen to write aright
To Prove thou art, and that thou art the best
  And shew thy Properties to shine most bright.
  And then thy Works will shine as flowers on Stems
  Or as in Jewellary Shops, do jems.

MEDITATION SIX
(FIRST SERIES)
(WRITTEN 1683?)

Canticles II: I: I Am . . . The Lily
of the Valleys.
Text: Poems, p. 16.

    Am I thy Gold? Or Purse, Lord, for thy Wealth;
      Whether in mine, or mint refinde for thee?
    Ime counted so, but count me o're thyselfe,
      Lest gold washt face, and brass in Heart I bee.
      I Feare my Touchstone touches when I try
      Mee, and my Counted Gold too overly.

Am I new minted by thy Stamp indeed?
   Mine Eyes are dim; I cannot clearly see.
Be thou my Spectacles that I may read
   Thine Image, and Inscription stampt on mee.
   If thy bright Image do upon me stand.
   I am a Golden Angell in thy hand.

Lord, make my Soule thy Plate: thine Image bright
   Within the Circle of the same enfoile.
And on its brims in golden Letters write
   Thy Superscription in an Holy style.
   Then I shall be thy Money, thou my Hord:
   Let me thy Angell bee, bee thou my Lord.

MEDITATION EIGHT
(FIRST SERIES)
(WRITTEN 1684)

John VI:51: I am the Living Bread.
Text: Poems, *p.* 18–19.

I kening through Astronomy Divine
   The Woilds bright Battlement, wherein I spy
A Golden Path my Pensill cannot line,
   From that bright Throne unto my Threshold ly.
   And while my puzzled thoughts about it pore,
   I find the Bread of Life in't at my doore.

When that this Bird of Paradise put in
   This Wicker Cage (my Corps) to tweedle praise
Had peckt the Fruite forbad: and so did fling
   Away its Food; and lost its golden dayes,
   It fell into Celestiall Famine sore:
   And never could attain a morsell more.

Alas! alas! Poore Bird, what wilt thou doe?
　This Creatures field no food for Souls e're gave:
And if thou knock at Angells dores they show
　An Empty Barrell: they no soul bread have.
　Alas! Poore Bird, the Worlds White Loafe is done.
　And cannot yield thee here the smallest Crumb.

In this sad state, Gods Tender Bowells run
　Out streams of Grace: And he to end all strife,
The Purest Wheate in Heaven, his deare-dear Son
　Grinds, and kneads up into this Bread of Life:
　Which Bread of Life from Heaven down came and stands
　Disht on thy Table up by Angells Hands.

Did God mould up this Bread in Heaven, and bake,
　Which from his Table came, and to thine goeth?
Doth he bespeake thee thus, This Soule Bread take.
　Come, Eate thy fill of this, thy Gods White Loafe?
　Its Food too fine for Angells; yet come, take
　And Eate thy fill Its Heavens Sugar Cake.

What Grace is this knead in this Loafe? This thing
　Souls are but petty things it to admire.
Yee Angells, help: This fill would to the brim
　Heav'ns whelm'd-down Chrystall meele Bowle, yea and higher.
　This Bread of Life dropt in thy mouth doth Cry:
　Eate, Eate me, Soul, and thou shalt never dy.

MEDITATION THIRTY-TWO
(FIRST SERIES)
(WRITTEN 1689)

I Corinthians 3.22: *For All Things Are Yours,*
Whether Paul, or Apollos, or Cephas,
or the World, or Life, or Death, or Things

Present, or Things to Come; All Are Yours;
and We Are Christ's; and Christ is God's.
Text: Poems, *pp. 51–52.*

> Thy Grace, Dear Lord's my golden Wrack, I finde
>   Screwing my Phancy into ragged Rhimes,
> Tuning thy Praises in my feeble minde
>   Untill I come to strike them on my Chimes.
>   Were I an Angell bright, and borrow could
>   King Davids Harp, I would them play on gold.
>
> But plung'd I am, my minde is puzzled,
>   When I would spin my Phancy thus unspun,
> In finest Twine of Praise I'm muzzled.
>   My tazzled Thoughts twirld into Snick-Snarls run.
>   Thy Grace, my Lord, is such a glorious thing,
>   It doth Confound me when I would it sing.
>
> Eternall Love an Object mean did smite
>   Which by the Prince of Darkness was beguilde,
> That from this Love it ran and sweld with spite
>   And in the way with filth was all defilde
>   Yet must be reconcild, cleansd, and begrac'te
>   Or from the fruits of Gods first Love displac'te.
>
> Then Grace, my Lord, wrought in thy Heart a vent,
>   Thy Soft Soft hand to this hard worke did goe,
> And to the Milke White Throne of Justice went
>   And entred bond that Grace might overflow.
>   Hence did thy Person to my Nature ty
>   And bleed through humane Veans to satisfy.
>
> Oh! Grace, Grace, Grace! this Wealthy Grace doth lay
>   Her Golden Channells from thy Fathers throne,
> Into our Earthen Pitchers to Convay
>   Heavens Aqua Vitae to us for our own.
>   O! let thy Golden Gutters run into
>   My Cup this Liquour till it overflow.
>
> Thine Ordinances, Graces Wine-fats where
>   Thy Spirits Walkes, and Graces runs doe ly
> And Angells waiting stand with holy Cheere

From Graces Conduite Head, with all Supply.
These Vessells full of Grace are, and the Bowls
In which their Taps do run, are pretious Souls.

Thou to the Cups dost say (that Catch this Wine,)
This Liquour, Golden Pipes, and Wine-fats plain,
Whether Paul, Apollos, Cephas, all are thine.
Oh Golden Word! Lord speake it ore again.
Lord speake it home to me, say these are mine.
My Bells shall then thy Praises bravely chime.

MEDITATION FORTY-ONE
(FIRST SERIES)
(WRITTEN 1691)

John. 14.2: I Go to Prepare a Place for You.
Text: Poems, p. 67.

A Clew of Wonders! Clusterd Miracles!
Angells, come whet your sight hereon. Here's ground.
Sharpen your Phansies here, ye Saints in Spiricles.
Here is enough in Wonderment to drownd's.
Make here the Shining dark or White on which
Let all your Wondring Contemplations pitch.

The Magnet of all Admiration's here.   ·
Your tumbling thoughts turn here. Here is Gods Son,
Wove in a Web of Flesh, and Bloode rich geere.
Eternall Wisdoms Huswifry well spun.
Which through the Laws pure Fulling mills did pass.
And so went home the Wealthy'st Web that was.

And why thus shew? Hark, harke, my Soule. He came
To pay thy Debt. And being come most Just

The Creditor did sue him for the same,
    Did winn the Case, and in the grave him thrust.
Who having in this Prison paid the Debt.
And took a Quittance, made Death's Velvet fret.

He broke her Cramping tallons did unlute
    The sealed Grave, and gloriously up rose.
Ascendeth up to glory on this Sute,
    Prepares a place for thee where glorie glowes.
    Yea yea for thee, although thy griefe out gush
    At such black Sins at which the Sun may blush.

What Wonder's here? Big belli'd Wonders in't
    Remain, though wrought for Saints as white as milk.
But done for me whose blot's as black as inke.
    A Clew of Wonders finer far than Silke.
    Thy hand alone that wound this Clew I finde
    Can to display these Wonders it unwinde.

Why didst thou thus? Reason stands gasterd here.
    She's overflown: this Soares above her Sight.
Gods onely Son for Sinners thus appeare,
    Prepare for Durt a throne in glory bright!
    Stand in the Doore of Glory to imbrace
    Such dirty bits of Dirt, with such a grace!

Reason, lie prison'd in this golden Chain.
    Chain up thy tongue, and silent stand a while.
Let this rich Love thy Love and heart obtain
    To tend thy Lord in all admiring Style.
    Lord screw my faculties up to the Skill
    And height of praise as answers thy good Will.

Then while I eye the Place thou hast prepar'de
    For such as I, I'le sing thy glory out
Untill thou welcome me, as 'tis declar'de
    In this sweet glory runing rounde about.
    I would do more but can't, Lord help me so
    That I may pay in glory what I owe.

MEDITATION FIFTY-SIX
(SECOND SERIES)
(WRITTEN 1703)

John XV: 24: If I Had Not Done Among Them
the Works Which None Other Man Did,
They Had Not Had Sin: but Now Have They
Both Seen and Hated Both Me and My Father.
Text: Poems, pp. 179–181.

Should I with silver tooles delve through the Hill
    Of Cordilera for rich thoughts, that I
My Lord, might weave with an angelick skill
    A Damask Web of Velvet Verse thereby
    To deck thy Works up, all my Web would run
    To rags and jags: so snicksnarld to the thrum.

Thine are so rich: Within, Without. Refin'd.
    No workes like thine. No Fruits so sweete that grow
On th' trees of righteousness of Angell kinde
    And Saints, whose limbs reev'd with them bow down low.
    Should I search ore the Nutmeg Gardens shine
    Its fruits in flourish are but skegs to thine.

The Clove, when in its White-green'd blossoms shoots,
    Some Call the pleasantst s[c]ent the World doth show.
None Eye e're saw, nor nose e're smelt such Fruits
    My Lord, as thine, Thou Tree of Life in 'ts blow.
    Thou Rose of Sharon, Vallies Lilly true,
    Thy Fruits most sweet and glorious ever grew.

Thou art a Tree of Perfect nature trim
    Whose golden lining is of perfect Grace
Perfum'de with Deity unto the brim,
    Whose fruits, of the perfection, grow, of Grace.
    Thy Buds, thy Blossoms, and thy fruits adorne
    Thyselfe, and Works, more shining than the morn.

Art, natures Ape, hath many brave things done
    As th' Pyramids, the Lake of Meris vast
The Pensile Orchards built in Babylon,
    Psammitich's Labyrinth. (arts Cramping task)
    Archimedes his Engins made for war.
    Romes Golden House. Titus his Theater.

The Clock at Strasburgh, Dresdens Table-sight
    Regiamonts Fly of Steele about that flew.
Turrian's Wooden Sparrows in a flight.
    And th' Artificiall man Aquinas slew.
    Mark Scaliota's Lock and Key and Chain
    Drawn by a Flea, in our Queen Betties reign.

Might but my pen in natures Inventory
    Its progress make, 't might make such things to jump,
All which are but Inventions Vents or glory:
    Wits Wantonings, and Fancies frollicks plump:
    Within whose maws lies buried Times, and Treasures,
    Embalmed up in thick dawbd sinfull pleasures.

Nature doth better work than Art, yet thine
    Out vie both works of nature and of Art.
Natures Perfection and the perfect shine
    Of Grace attend thy deed in ev'ry part.
    A Thought, a Word, and Worke of thine, will kill
    Sin, Satan, and the Curse: and Law fulfill.

Thou art the Tree of Life in Paradise,
    Whose lively branches are with Clusters hung
Of Lovely fruits, and Flowers more sweet than spice.
    Bende down to us, and doe outshine the sun.
    Delightfull unto God, doe man rejoyce
    The pleasant'st fruits in all Gods Paradise.

Lord, feed mine eyes then with thy Doings rare,
    And fat my heart with these ripe fruites thou bear'st;
Adorn my Life well with thy works; make faire
    My Person with apparrell thou prepar'st.
    My Boughs shall loaded bee with fruits that spring
    Up from thy Works, while to thy praise I sing.

"PREFACE" TO GODS DETERMINATIONS TOUCHING HIS ELECT*

Text: Poems, *pp.* 387–388.

Infinity, when all things it beheld
In Nothing, and of Nothing all did build,
Upon what Base was fixt the Lath, wherein
He turn'd this Globe, and riggalld it so trim?
Who blew the Bellows of his Furnace Vast?
Or held the Mould wherein the world was Cast?
Who laid its Corner Stone? Or whose Command?
Where stand the Pillars upon which it stands?
Who lac'de and Fillitted the earth so fine,
With Rivers like green Ribbons Smaragdine?
Who made the Sea's its Selvedge, and it locks
Like a Quilt Ball within a Silver Box?
Who Spread its Canopy? Or Curtains Spun?
Who in this Bowling Alley bowld the Sun?
Who made it always when it rises set
To go at once both down, and up to get?
Who th' Curtain rods made for this Tapistry?
Who hung the twinckling Lanthorns in the Sky?
Who? who did this? or who is he? Why, know
It's Onely Might Almighty this did doe.
His hand hath made this noble worke which Stands
His Glorious Handywork not made by hands.
Who spake all things from nothing; and with ease
Can speake all things to nothing, if he please.
Whose little finger at his pleasure Can
   Out mete ten thousand worlds with halfe a Span:
   Whose Might Almighty can by half a looks

---

* *Gods Determinations* is Taylor's longest poem, in which, in the manner of a morality play, he dramatizes the structure of Puritan Theology.

Root up the rocks and rock the hills by th' roots.
Can take this mighty World up in his hande,
And shake it like a Squitchen or a Wand.
Whose single Frown will make the Heavens shake
Like as an aspen leafe the Winde makes quake.
Oh! what a might is this Whose single frown
Doth shake the world as it would shake it down?
Which All from Nothing set, from Nothing, All:
Hath All on Nothing set, lets Nothing fall.
Gave All to nothing Man indeed, whereby
Through nothing man all might him Glorify.
In Nothing then imbosst the brightest Gem
More pretious than all pretiousness in them.
But Nothing man did throw down all by Sin:
And darkened that lightsom Gem in him.
    That now his Brightest Diamond is grown
    Darker by far than any Coalpit Stone.

"HUSWIFERY"[3]

Text: Poems, p. 437.

Make me, O Lord, thy Spining Wheele compleate;
  Thy Holy Worde my Distaff make for mee.
Make mine Affections thy Swift Flyers neate
  And make my Soule thy holy Spoole to bee.
  My Conversation make to be thy Reele
  And reele the yarn thereon spun of thy Wheele.

Make me thy Loome then, knit therein this Twine:
  And make thy Holy Spirit, Lord, winde quills:
Then weave the Web thyselfe. The yarn is fine.
  Thine Ordinances make my Fulling Mills.
  Then dy the same in Heavenly Colours Choice,
  All pinkt with Varnisht Flowers of Paradise.

Then cloath therewith mine Understanding, Will,
Affections, Judgment, Conscience, Memory
My Words and Actions, that their shine may fill
My wayes with glory and thee glorify.
Then mine apparell shall display before yee
That I am Cloathd in Holy robes for glory.

ANOTHER UPON THE SAME*

Text: Poems, *p. 468.*

Make me thy Spinning Wheele of use for thee,
  Thy Grace my Distaffe, and my heart thy Spoole.
Turn thou the wheele: let mine Affections bee
  The flyers filling with thy yarne my soule.
  Then weave the web of Grace in mee, thy Loome
  And Cloath my soule therewith, its Glories bloome

Make mee thy Loome: thy Grace the warfe therein,
  My duties Woofe, and let thy word winde Quills.
The shuttle shoot. Cut off the ends my sins.
  Thy Ordinances make my fulling mills,
  My Life thy Web: and cloath me all my dayes
  With this Gold-web of Glory to thy praise.

---

* I.e., a variation upon the "Huswifery" metaphor.

THE EBB AND FLOW.

Text: Poems, *p.* 470.

When first thou on me Lord wrought'st thy Sweet Print,
  My heart was made thy tinder box.
  My 'ffections were thy tinder in't.
    Where fell thy Sparkes by drops.
Those holy Sparks of Heavenly Fire that came
Did ever catch and often out would flame.

But now my Heart is made thy Censar trim,
  Full of thy golden Altars fire,
  To offer up Sweet Incense in
    Unto thyselfe intire:
I finde my tinder scarce thy sparks can feel
That drop out from thy Holy flint and Steel.

Hence doubts out bud for feare thy fire in mee
  'S a mocking Ignis Fatuus
  Or lest thine Altars fire out bee,
    Its hid in ashes thus.
Yet when the bellows of thy Spirit blow
Away mine ashes, then thy fire doth glow.

"UPON THE SWEEPING FLOOD:
AUGUST 13 AND 14,
1683"

Text: Poems, *p.* 471.

Oh! that I'd had a tear to've quencht that flame
  Which did dissolve the Heavens above

Into those liquid drops that came
　　To drown our Carnall love.
Our cheeks were dry and eyes refusde to weep.
　　Tears bursting out ran down the skies darke Cheek.

Were th' Heavens sick? must wee their Doctors bee
　　And physick them with pills, our sin?
　　To make them purg and Vomit, see,
　　　　And Excrements out fling?
We've griev'd them by such Physick that they shed
Their Excrements upon our lofty heads.

Cotton Mather

(1663–1728)

EPITAPH ON SHUBAEL DUMMER, KILLED BY INDIANS, 1691

(1702)

Text: Magnalia Christi Americana
(*Hartford*, 1820), II, 531.

DUMMER the shepherd sacrific'd
By wolves, because the sheep he priz'd.
The orphans father, churches light,
The love of heav'n, of hell the spight.
The countries gapman, and the face
That shone, but knew it not, with grace.
Hunted by devils, but reliev'd
By Angels, and on high receiv'd
The martyr'd Pelican, who bled
Rather than leave his charge unfed.
A proper bird of paradise,
Shot, and flown thither in a trice.

Lord, hear the cry of righteous DUMMER'S wounds,
Ascending still against the salvage hounds,
That worry thy dear flocks, and let the cry
Add force to theirs that at thine altar lye.

Roger Woolcott

(1679–1767)

PSALM LXIV-6
THE HEART IS DEEP

Text: Poetical Meditations
(*New London, 1725*), *p. 12.*

> He that can trace a Ship making her way,
> Amidst the threatening Surges on the Sea;
> Or track a Towering Eagle in the Air,
> Or on a Rock find the Impressions there
> Made by a Serpents Footsteps. Who Surveys
> The Subtile Intreagues that a Young Man lays,
> In his Sly Courtship of an harmless Maid,
> Whereby his Wanton Amours are Convey'd
> Into her Breast; Tis he alone that can
> Find out the Cursed Policies of Man.

IV

THE VIRGINIA GENTLEMAN

Although the planting of Virginia was primarily an enterprise in financial speculation and empire building, we must not forget that for the seventeenth-century Englishman, the idea of empire was only a reflection of a larger, more inclusive idea— that of a divine mission to give order to the new world and to make it like the old. The shape of Virginia society and its notion of the gentleman who was to be at its center—both these must be understood as products at once of socioeconomic and intellectual history.

Gentlemen, yeomen-freemen, and indentured servants who came to Virginia intended to work the land according to the patterns of British farming. If gentlemen were being established on large estates, still there would be great opportunity for yeomen to operate small farms and even for indentured servants to work their way up to the status of small farmers. But Virginia society did not pattern itself thus. Conditions of soil, availability of land, the cheap labor of indentured servants, and ease of cultivation soon led to a one-crop economy. Tobacco was king. As it was discovered that it was impossible (and undesirable) to establish the diversified kind of farming that was known in England, the gentlemen took over more and more land. Yeomen on their small farms, finding it increasingly difficult to handle and ship their tobacco, discovering, moreover, that the single crop soon exhausted the small amounts of land they owned, could only give up and sell out to the gentlemen. Then, towards the end of the seventeenth century, with the discovery of an apparently limitless source of cheaper labor in Negro slaves, the need for indentured servants began to decrease. By the beginning of the eighteenth century, the gentlemen were almost completely in control.

Such a society—unified in its economy, controlled by the landed few—was bound to have the gentleman as its ideal. The gentleman had organized the society; the society, as it took shape around him, had made his existence not only possible but necessary. He was a kind of feudal lord with responsibilities above and below. Generally speaking, his blood was good but not aristocratic, upper-middle-class English. He was determined to establish in a kind of upper-middle-class country squirearchy, patterned after its British equivalent but adjusted to American social and economic conditions. He would realize, in his fashion, the Renaissance idea of the gentleman as the well-rounded man, in whom the religious and the secular—expressed in piety, learning, and conduct—were fused. Yet he did not have to be born the complete gentleman: he could make himself into such. Indeed, his ideal was the Renaissance ideal of *virtú* accommodated to his time and to his place. So he raised his crops and sold them; looked after his family, relatives, friends, and slaves; participated in politics; studied to make himself a good and useful man; and worshipped a God merciful and bounteous enough to give him Virginia. He might well be at once farmer, doctor, veterinarian, hunter, surveyor, political leader, and handyman. *Virtú* was the *virtú* of living fully and wisely and responsibly in his world.

The Virginia gentleman (and his Maryland and South Carolina counterpart) everywhere set the pattern for the southern gentleman. In the later eighteenth and early nineteenth centuries, yeomen and ex-indentured servants, frontiersmen and small farmers, moving to the south and to the west, would try to establish themselves in his image. As often as not, they became something else—even as he, feeling economic and ideological pressures, was eventually to romanticize and sectionalize himself into something else. What is important is that we understand his image as it existed before 1750 and look not only to its immediate influence but also to its development into the Jeffersons and Madisons in whom it found its fullest embodiment.

The selections here printed reveal that image variously. First, there is John Hammond's *Leah and Rachel*, which sets forth a frankly sanguine account of Virginia (and also Maryland) as a place in which the hand-working Englishman might realize all his true virtues. Second, there are two views, both more or less antagonistic, of Nathaniel Bacon, who tried in the 1670's to assert the independence and right of self-determination and self-protection of Virginia gentlemen pioneering on the frontier; here in "Bacon's Epitaph" above all, there is the noble tribute to the Virginia ideal—in whom "Mars and Minerva concurred."

Third, there are a Virginia gentleman's views of his America in the pieces from Byrd's *History of the Dividing Line* and the matter-of-fact self-portraiture in four weeks from his secret diary; in the case of the latter, it is rewarding to compare Byrd as diarist with Samuel Sewall, so to see the difference between the New England and the Virginia gentleman. (For Byrd as Augustan poet, see pp. 609–610.) And fourth, there is, in the chapters from Beverly's *History*, the Virginia gentleman's view of his own society. What is disclosed, in all, is a mind and an imagination which are secular, expansive, devout but not devoted, centered on the ideal of the best and most responsible life for the best and most responsible gentlemen. We are on our way to Jefferson's idea of the natural aristocrat.

Bibliographical Note. The best general study of the historical background is the section on Virginia in Wesley F. Craven's *The Southern Colonies in the Seventeenth Century* (Baton Rouge, 1949); the detailed critical bibliographies are especially valuable. A more specialized study of value is Thomas J. Wertenbaker's *The Old South* (New York, 1942). Most important for the understanding of the Virginia gentleman is L. B. Wright's *First Gentlemen of Virginia* (San Marino, 1940). For the later history and influence of this Virginia gentleman see W. J. Cash, *The Mind of the South* (New York, 1941) and R. J. Osterweis, *Romanticism and Rationalism in the Old South* (New Haven, 1949). A careful survey of the earliest Virginia writing is H. M. Jones, *The Literature of Virginia in the Seventeenth Century* (Boston, 1946). The most detailed bibliographical and historical survey, probably definitive, is in the relevant sections of Jay Hubbell's magisterial *The South in American Literature, 1607–1900* (Durham, N.C., 1954).

John Hammond

(*fl.* 1635–1656)

Bibliographical Note. The text here printed is taken from Peter Force, Tracts and Other Papers, III (Washington, 1844, reprinted New York, 1947).

LEAH AND RACHELL, OR THE TWO FRUITFULL SISTERS OF VIRGINIA AND MARY-LAND; THEIR PRESENT CONDITION IMPARTIALLY STATED AND RELATED

(1656)

It is the glory of every Nation to enlarge themselves, to encourage their own forraign attempts, and to be able to have of their own, within their own territories, as many several commodities as they can attain to, that so others may rather be beholding to them, then they to others; and to this purpose have′ Encouragements, Priviledges and Emunities been given to any Discoveries or Adventurers into remote Colonies, by all politique Common Wealths in the world.

But alas, we Englishmen (in all things else famous, and to other Countries terrible) do not onely faile in this, but vilifie, scandalize and cry down such parts of the unknown world, as have been found out, setled and made flourishing, by the charge, hazzard and diligence of their own brethren, as if because removed from us, we either account them people of another world or enemies.

This is too truly made good in the odiums and cruell slanders cast on those two famous Countries of *Virginia* and *Maryland*, whereby those Countries, not oncly arc many timcs at a stand, but are in danger to moulder away, and come in time to nothing; nor is there any thing but the fertility and natural gratefulnesse of them, left a remedy to prevent it.

To let our own Nation (whose common good I covet, and whose Common-wealths servant I am, as born to no other use) be made sensible of these injuries: I have undertaken in this Book to give the true state of those places, according to the condition they are now in; and to declare either to distressed or discontented, that they need not doubt because of any rumour detracting from their goodnesses, to remove and cast themselves and Fortunes upon those Countries, in which if I should deviate from the truth; I have at this present carping enemies in *London* enough, to contradict and cry down me and this, for Impostours. It is not long since I came from thence (God knows sore against my will) having lived there upward of one and twenty years; nor do I intend (by Gods assistance) to be long out of it again: and therefore can by experience, not hearsay (as *Bullock* and other lying Writters have done, who at randome or for their own private lucre have rendred their Books rediculous and themselves infamous lyars, nor will I like them, over extoll the places, as if they were rather Paradices than earthly habitations; but truly let ye know, what they are, and how the people there live.) Which when impartially viewed, will undoubtedly clear up those Foggy Mists, that hath to their own ruine blinded and kept off many from going thither, whose miseries and misfortunes by staying in *England* are much to be lamented, and much to be pittied.

In respect these two Sister Countries (though distinct Governments) are much of one nature, both for produce and manner of living; I shall only at present, Treat of the elder Sister *Virginia*, and in speaking of that include both: And ere I leave off, shall in particular rehearse the unnaturall usage *Mary-land* the younger Sister, hath had, not by *Virginia;* but by those Vipers she hath received and harboured with much kindnesse and hospitalitie.

The Country is reported to be an unhealthy place, a nest of Rogues, whores, desolute and rooking persons; a place of intolerable labour, bad usage and hard Diet, &c.

To Answer these several calumnies, I shall first shew what it was? next, what it is?

At the first settling and many years after, it deserved most of those aspersions (nor were they then aspersions but truths) it was not settled at the publique charge; but when found out, challenged, and maintained by Adventurers, whose avarice and inhumanity, brought in these inconveniences, which to this day brands *Virginia.*

Then were Jayls emptied, youth seduced, infamous women drilled in, the provisions all brought out of *England,* and that embezzelled by the Trustees (for they durst neither hunt fowl, nor Fish, for fear of the *Indian,* which they stood in aw of, their labour was almost perpetuall, their allowance of victual small, few or no cattle, no use of horses nor oxen to draw or carry, (which labours men supplyed themselves) all which caused a mortality; no civil courts of justice but under a Marshall law, no redresse of grievances, complaints were repaied with stripes, moneys with scoffes, tortures made delights, and in a word all and the worst that tyrany could inflict or act, which when complained of in *England:* (but so were they kept under that it was long ere they would suffer complaints to come home) the bondage was taken of, the people set free, and had lands a signed to each of them to live of themselves, and enjoy the benefit of their own industry; men then began to call what they laboured for their own, they fell to making themselves convenient housing to dwell in, to plant corne for their food, to range the wood for flesh, the rivers for fowle and fish, to finde out somwhat staple for supplie of cloathing, to continue a commerce, to purchase and breed cattle, &c. but the bud of this growing happinesse was again nipt by a cruell Massacre committed by the Natives, which again pull'd them back and kept them under, enforcing them to get into Forts (such as the infancy of those times afforded: they were taken off from planting; their provisions destroyed, their Cattle, Hogs, Horses, &c. kill'd up, and brought to such want and penury, that diseases grew rife, mortality exceeded; but receiving a supply of men, amunition and victuals out of *England*, they again gathered heart, pursued their enemies, and so often worsted them, that the *Indians* were glad to sue for peace, and they desirous of a cessation) consented to it.

They again began to bud forth, to spread further, to gather wealth, which they rather profusely spent (as gotten with ease then providently husbanded, or aimed at any publique good; or to make a Country for posterity; but from hand to mouth, and for a present being; neglecting discoveries, planting of Orchards, providing for the Winter preservation of their stocks, or thinking of any thing staple or firm; and whilest Tobacco, the onely Commodity they had to subsist on bore a price, they wholy and eagerly followed that, neglecting their very planting of Corn, and much relyed on *England* for the chiefest part of their provisions; so that being not alwayes amply supplied, they were often in such want, that their case and condition being related in *England*, it hindred and kept off many from going thither, who rather cast their eyes on the Barren and freezing soyle of *New-England*, than to joyn with such an indigent and sottish people, as were reported to be in *Virginia*.

Yet was not *Virginia* all this while without divers honest and vertuous inhabitants, who observing the general neglect and licensiousnesses there, caused Assemblies to be call'd and Laws to be made tending to the glory of God, the severe suppression of vices, and the compelling them not to neglect (upon strickt punishments) planting and tending such quantities of Corn, as would not onely serve themselves, their Cattle and Hogs plentifully, but to be enabled to supply *New-England* (then in want) with such proportions, as were extream reliefs, to them in their necessities.

From this industry of theirs and great plenty of Corn, (the main staffe of life) proceeded that great plenty of Cattel and Hogs, (now innumerable) and out of which not only *New-England* hath been stocked and relieved, but all other parts of the *Indies* inhabited by Englishmen.

The inhabitants now finding the benefit of their industries, began to look with delight on their increasing stocks: (as nothing more pleasurable then profit) to take pride in their plentifully furnished Tables, to grow not onely civil, but great observers of the Sabbath, to stand upon their reputations, and to be ashamed of that notorious manner of life they had formerly lived and wallowed in.

They then began to provide and send home for Gospel Ministers, and largely contributed for their maintenance; But *Virginia* savouring not handsomely in *England*, very few of good conversation would adventure thither, (as thinking it a place wherein surely the fear of God was not) yet many came, such as wore Black Coats, and could babble in a Pulpet, roare in a Tavern, exact from their Parishoners, and rather by their dissolutenesse destroy than feed their Flocks.

Loath was the Country to be wholy without Teachers, and therefore rather retain these then to be destitute; yet still endeavours for better in their places, which were obtained, and these Wolves in sheeps cloathing, by their Assemblies questioned, silenced, and some forced to depart the Country.

Then began the Gospel to flourish, civil, honourable, and men of great estates flocked in: famous buildings went forward, Orchards innumerable were planted and preserved; Tradesmen sct on work and encouraged, stable Commodities, as Silk, Flax, Pot-ashes, &c. of which I shall speak further hereafter, attempted on, and with good success brought to perfection; so that this Country which had a mean beginning, many back friends, two ruinous and bloody Massacres, hath by Gods grace out-grown all, and is become a place of pleasure and plenty.

And having briefly laid down the former state of *Virginia*, in its Infancy, and filth, and the occasion of its scandalous aspersions: I come to my main subject, its present Condition and Hapinesse (if any thing can be justly called happy in this transatory life (otherwise then as blessings which in the well using whereof, a future happinesse may be expected.)

I affirme the Country to be wholesome, healthy and fruitfull; and a modell on which industry may as much improve it self in, as in any habitable part of the World; yet not such a Lubberland as the Fiction of the land of Ease, is reported to be, nor such a V*topian* as Sr. *Thomas Moore* hath related to be found out.

In the Countries minority, and before they had well cleared the ground to let in ayre (which now is otherwise) many imputed the stifling of the wood to be the cause of such sicknesse; but I rather think the contrary; for divers new Rivers lately settled, where at their first comming upon them as woody as *James* Rivers, the first place they setled in, and yet those Rivers are as healthy as any former setled place in *Virginia* or *England* it self: I believe (and that not without reason) it was only want of such diet as best agreed with our English natures, good drinks and wholesome lodgings were the cause of so much sicknesses, as were formerly frequent, which we have now amended; and therefore enjoy better healths; to which I add, and that by experience since my comming into *England*, and many (if not all *Virginians* can do the like,) that change of ayre does much alter the state of our bodies: by which many travellers thither may expect some sickness, yet little danger of mortality.

A Geographicall description of the Country I shall not attempt (as having little skill in the Mathematicks) enough of that hath been formerly Written; nor is it a place now to learn to discover. I shall abhor to spirit over any; but go along with such as are voluntarily desirous to go thither, and lead them with my blunt relation (for truth knows little of eloquence) aboard the Ships thither bound, and carrying you into the Country, shew you the courtesie of the place, the disposition of the Inhabitants, the commodities, and give all sorts of people advice how and where to set down for their present benefit and future accommodation.

If any are minded to repair thither, if they are not in a capacity to defray their own charges (if they are I wish they might and so be at their own disposing) let them not be seduced by those mercinary spirits that know little of the place, nor aime at any good of theirs, but onely by foysting and flattering them to gain a reward of those they procure them for; beware them, for it is not only hab nab whether ye go to a good service or a bad, but scandalous to your selves to be so seduced, and it were good and very just that such vagabond people were severely punished, as great betrayers of their own Nation, for ye cannot

imagine but their are as well bad services as good; but I shall
shew ye if any happen into the hands of such crooked dispositions, how to order them and ease your selves, when I come to
treat of the justice of the Country, which many being ignorant
of suffer inconveniences, which by this they may prevent.

Let such as are so minded not rashly throw themselves upon
the voyage, but observe the nature, and enquire the qualities of
the persons with whom they ingage to transport themselves, or
if (as not acquainted with such as inhabit there, but go with
Merchants and Mariners, who transport them to others,) let
their covenant be such, that after their arrival they have a fort-
nights time assigned them to enquire of their Master, and make
choyce of such as they intend to expire their time with, nor let
that brand of selling of servants, be any discouragement to de-
ter any from going, for if a time must be served, it is all one
with whom it be served, provided they be people of honest repute, with which the Country is well replenished.

And be sure to have your contract in writing and under
hand and seal, for if ye go over upon promise made to do this or
that, or to be free or your own men, it signifies nothing, for by a
law of the Country (waving all promises) any one coming in,
and not paying their own passages, must serve if men or women
four years, if younger according to their years, but where an
Indenture is, that is binding and observing.

The usual allowance for servants is (besides their charge of
passage defrayed) at their expiration, a years provision of corne,
dubble apparrell, tooles necessary, and land according to the
custome of the Country, which is an old delusion, for there is
no land accustomary due to the servant, but to the Master, and
therefore that servant is unwise that will not dash out that custom in his covenant, and make that due of land absolutely his
own, which although at the present, not of so great consequence;
yet in few years will be of much worth, as I shall hereafter make
manifest.

When ye go aboard, expect the Ship somewhat troubled
and in a hurliburly, untill ye cleer the lands end; and that the
Ship is rummaged, and things put to rights, which many times
discourages the Passengers, and makes them wish the Voyage
unattempted: but this is but for a short season, and washes off

when at Sea, where the time is pleasantly passed away, though not with such choise plenty as the shore affords.

But when ye arrive and are settled, ye will find a strange alteration, an abused Country giving the lye in your own approbations to those that have calumniated it, and these infalable arguments may convince all incredible and obstinate opinions, concerning the goodnesse and delightfulnesse of the Country, that never any servants of late times have gone thither; but in their Letters to their Friends commend and approve of the place, and rather invite than disswade their acquaintance from comming thither. An other is this, that seldom (if ever) any that hath continued in *Virginia* any time, will or do desire to live in *England*, but post back with what expedition they can; although many are landed men in *England*, and have good Estates here, and divers wayes of preferments propounded to them, to entice and perswade their continuance.

The Country is as I said of a temperate nature, the dayes, in summer not so long as in *England*, in winter longer; it is somewhat hotter in *June*, *July* and *August* then here, but that heat sweetly allayed by a continual breaze of winde, which never failes to cool and refresh the labourer and traveller; the cold seldom approaches sencibly untill about *Christmas*, (although the last winter was hard and the worst I or any living there knew) and when winter comes, (which is such and no worse then is in *England*,) it continues two monthes seldom longer, often not so long and in that time although here seldom hardweather keep men from labour, yet there no work is done all winter except dressing their own victuals and making of fires.

The labour servants are put to, is not so hard nor of such continuance as Husbandmen, nor Handecraftmen are kept at in *England*, I said little or nothing is done in winter time, none ever work before sun rising nor after sun set, in the summer they rest, sleep or exercise themselves five houres in the heat of the day, Saturdayes afternoon is alwayes their own, the old Holidayes are observed and the Sabboath spent in good exercises.

The Women are not (as is reported) put into the ground to worke, but occupie such domestique imployments and houswifery as in *England*, that is dressing victuals, righting up the house, milking, imployed about dayries, washing, sowing, &c.

and both men and women have times of recreations, as much or more than in any part of the world besides, yet som wenches that are nasty, beastily and not fit to be so imployed are put into the ground, for reason tells us, they must not at charge be transported and then mantained for nothing, but those that prove so aukward are rather burthensome then servants desirable or usefull.

The Country is fruitfull, apt for all and more then *England* can or does produce, the usuall diet is such as in *England,* for the rivers afford innumerable sortes of choyce fish, (if they will take the paines to make wyers or hier the Natives, who for a small matter will undertake it,) winter and summer, and that in many places sufficient to serve the use of man, and to fatten hoggs, water-fowle of all sortes are (with admiration to be spoken of) plentifull and easie to be killed, yet by many degrees more plentifull in some places than in othersome, Deare all over the Country, and in many places so many, that venison is accounted a tiresom meat, wilde Turkeys are frequent, and so large that I have seen some weigh neer threescore pounds; other beasts there are whose flesh is wholsom and savourie, such are unknowne to us; and therefore I will not stuffe my book with superfluous relation of their names; huge Oysters and store in all parts where the salt-water comes.

The Country is exceedingly replenished with Neat cattle, Hoggs, Goats and Tame-fowle, but not many sheep; so that mutton is somewhat scarce, but that defect is supplied with store of Venison, other flesh and fowle; The Country is full of gallant Orchards, and the fruit generally more luscious and delightfull then here, witnesse the Peach and Quince, the latter may be eaten raw savourily, the former differs and as much exceeds ours as the best relished apple we have doth the crabb, and of both most excellent and comfortable drinks are made, Grapes in infinite manners grow wilde, so do Walnuts, Smalnuts, Chestnuts and abundance of excellent fruits, Plums and Berries, not growing or known in *England*; graine we have, both *English* and *Indian* for bread and Bear, and Pease besides *English* of ten several sorts, all exceeding ours in *England,* the gallant root of Potatoes are common, and so are all sorts of rootes, herbes and Garden stuffe.

It must needs follow then that diet cannot be scarce, since both rivers and woods affords it, and that such plenty of Cattle and Hoggs are every where, which yeeld beef, veal, milk, butter, cheese and other made dishes, porke, bacon, and pigs, and that as sweet and savoury meat as the world affords, these with the help of Orchards and Gardens, Oysters, Fish, Fowle and Venison, certainly cannot but be sufficient for a good diet and wholsom accommodation, considering how plentifully they are, and how easie with industry to be had.

Beare is indeed in some place constantly drunken, in other some, nothing but Water or Milk, and Water or Beverige; & that is where the goodwives, (if I may so call them) are negligent and idle; for it is not for want of Corn to make Malt with (for the Country affords enough) but because they are sloathfull and carelesse: but I hope this Item will shame them out of those humours, that they will be adjudged by their drink, what kinde of Housewives they are.

Those Servants that will be industrious may in their time of service gain a competent estate before their Freedomes, which is usually done by many, and they gaine esteeme and assistance that appear so industrious: There is no Master almost but will allow his Servant a parcell of clear ground to plant some Tobacco in for himself, which he may husband at those many idle times he hath allowed him and not prejudice, but rejoyce his Master to see it, which in time of Shipping he may lay out for commodities, and in Summer sell them again with advantage, and get a Sow-Pig or two, which any body almost will give him, and his Master suffer him to keep them with his own, which will be no charge to his Master, and with one years increase of them may purchase a Cow Calf or two, and by that time he is for himself; he may have Cattle, Hoggs and Tobacco of his own, and come to live gallantly; but this must be gained (as I said) by Industry and affability, not by sloth nor churlish behaviour.

And whereas it is rumoured that Servants have no lodging other then on boards, or by the Fire side, it is contrary to reason to believe it: First, as we are Christians; next as people living under a law, which compels as well the Master as the Servant to perform his duty; nor can true labour be either expected or exacted without sufficient cloathing, diet, and lodging;

all which both their Indentures (which must inviolably be observed) and the Justice of the Country requires.

But if any go thither, not in a condition of a Servant, but pay his or her passage, which is some six pounds: Let them not doubt but it is money well layd out (yet however let them not fail) although they carry little else to take a Bed along with them, and then few Houses but will give them entertainment, either out of curtesie, or on reasonable tearms; and I think it better for any that goes over free, and but in a mean condition, to hire himself for reasonable wages of Tobacco and Provision, the first year, provided he happen in an honest house, and where the Mistresse is noted for a good Housewife, of which there are very many (notwithstanding the cry to the contrary) for by that means he will live free of disbursment, have something to help him the next year, and be carefully looked to in his sicknesse (if he chance to fall sick) and let him so covenant that exceptions may be made, that he work not much in the hot weather, a course we alwayes take with our new hands (as they call them) the first year they come in.

If they are women that go after this manner, that is paying their own passages; I advise them to sojourn in a house of honest repute, for by their good carriage, they may advance themselves in marriage, by their ill, overthrow their fortunes; and although loose persons seldome live long unmarried if free; yet they match with as desolate as themselves, and never live handsomly or are ever respected.

For any that come over free, and are minded to dyet and quarter in another mans house, it matters not whether they know on what term or conditions they are there; for by an excellent Decree, made by Sir *William Berkly*, when Governour; (as indeed he was the Author of many good Laws:) It was ordered, that if any inhabitant received any stranger Merchant, or border into their houses, and did not condition in Writing with him or them so entertained on what tearms he received them, it should be supposed an invitation, an no satisfaction should be allowed or recovered in any Court of Justice; thereby giving notice that no stranger coming into the Country should be drilled in, or made a purchase of under colour of friendship: but that the Inhabitants at first coming shall let them know how they mean to deal with them, that if they like not the terms they may remove themselves at pleasure; a Law so good and commendable, that it is never like to be revoked or altered.

Now for those that carry over Families and estates with a determination to inhabit, my advice is that they neither sojourn for that will be chargeable; nor on the sudden purchase, for that may prove unfortunate; but that they for the first year hire a house (for seats are always to be hired) and by that means, they will not onely finde content and live at a cheap rate, but be acquainted in the Country and learn the worth and goodnesse of the Plantation they mean to purchase; and so not rashly intangle themselves in an ill bargain; or finde where a convenient parcell of Land is for their turns to be taken up.

Yet are the Inhabitants generally affable, courteous and very assistant to strangers (for what but plenty makes hospitality and good neighbourhood) and no sooner are they settled, but they will be visiting, presenting and advicing the stranger how to improve what they have, how to better their way of livelihood.

Justice is there duly and daily administred; hardly can any travaile two miles together, but they will finde a Justice, which hath power of himself to hear and determine mean differences, to secure and bind over notorious offenders, of which very few are in the Country.

In every County are Courts kept, every two moneths, and oftener if occasion require, in which Courts all things are determined without exceptions; and if any dislike the proceedings of those Courts, they have liberty to appeal to the Quarter Court, which is four times a year; and from thence to the Assembly, which is once or oftner every year: So that I am confident, more speedy Justice and with smaller charge is not in any place to be found.

Theft is seldome punished (as being seldome or never committed; for as the Proverb is, where there are no receivers, there are no thieves; and although Doores are nightly left open (especially in the Summer time) Hedges hanging full of Cloathes; Plate frequently used amongst all comers and goers (and there is good store of Plate in many houses) yet I never heard of any losse ever received either in Plate, Linnen, or any thing else out of their Houses all the time I inhabited there.

Indeed I have known some suffer for stealing of Hogs, (but not since they have been plentifull) and whereas Hogstealing was once punished with death, it is now made penal, and restitution given very amply to the owner thereof.

Cases of Murther are punished as in *England*, and Juries allowed, as well in Criminal causes, as in all other differences between party and party, if they desire it.

Servants complaints are freely harkened to, and (if not causlesly made) there Masters are compelled either speedily to amend, or they are removed upon second complaint to another service; and often times not onely set free, (if the abuse merit it) but ordered to give reparation and damage to their servant.

The Country is very full of sober, modest persons, both men and women, and many that truly fear God and follow that perfect rule of our blessed Saviour, to do as they would be done by; and of such a happy inclination is the Country, that many who in *England* have been lewd and idle, there in emulation or imitation (for example moves more then precept) of the industry of those they finde there, not onely grow ashamed of their former courses, but abhor to hear of them, and in small time wipe off those stains they have formerly been tainted with; yet I cannot but confesse, there are people wicked enough (as what Country is free) for we know some natures will never be reformed, but these must follow the Fryers rule, *Si non caste, tamen cante*; for if any be known, either to prophane the Lords day or his Name, be found drunk, commit whoredome, scandalize or disturb his neighbour, or give offence to the world by living suspiciously in any bad courses; there are for each of these, severe and wholsome laws and remedies made, provided and duly put in execution: I can confidently affirm, that since my being in *England*, which is not yet four moneths, I have been an eye and ear witnesse of more deceits and villanies (and such as modesty forbids me to utter) then I either ever saw or heard mention made of in *Virginia*, in my one and twenty years abroad in those parts.

And therefore those that shall blemish *Virginia* any more, do but like the Dog bark against the Moon, untill they be blind and weary; and *Virginia* is now in that secure growing condition, that like the Moon so barked at, she will passe on her

course, maugre all detractors, and a few years will bring it to
that glorious happinesse, that many of her calumniators, will
intercede to procure admittance thither, when it will be hard to
be attained to; for in smal time, little land will be to be taken
up; and after a while none at all; and as the Mulberry Trees
grows up, which are by every one planted, Tobacco will be laid
by, and we shall wholy fall to making of Silk (a Sample of
400l. hath already been sent for *England*, and approved of)
which will require little labour; and therefore shall have little
use of Servants; besides, Children increase and thrive so well
there, that they themselves will sufficiently supply the defect of
Servants: And in small time become a Nation of themselves
sufficient to people the Country: And this good policy is there
used; As the Children there born grow to maturity, and capable (as they are generally very capable and apt, they are still
preferred and put into authority, and carry themselves therein
civilly and discretly; and few there are but are able to give
some Portions with their daughters, more or lesse, according to
their abilities; so that many comming out of *England* have
raised themselves good fortunes there meerly by matching with
Maidens born in the Country.

And therefore I cannot but admire, and indeed much pitty
the dull stupidity of people necessitated in *England*, who rather
then they will remove themselves, live here a base, slavish, penurious life; as if there were a necessity to live and to live so,
choosing rather then they will forsake *England* to stuff *New-
Gate, Bridewell,* and other Jayles with their carkessies, nay
cleave to tyburne it selfe; and so bring confusion to their souls
horror and infamine to their kindred or posteritie, others itch
out their wearisom lives in reliance of other mens charities, an
uncertaine and unmanly expectation; some more abhorring such
courses betake themselve to almost perpetuall and restlesse
toyle and druggeries out of which (whilst their strength lasteth)
they (observing hard diets, earlie and late houres) make hard
shift to subsist from hand to mouth, untill age or sicknesse
takes them off from labour and directs them the way to beg-
gerie, and such indeed are to be pittied, relieved and provided
for.

I have seriously considered when I have (passing the

streets) heard the several Cryes, and noting the commodities, and the worth of them they have carried and cryed up and down; how possibly a livelihood could be exacted out of them, as to cry Matches, Smal-coal, Blacking, Pen and Ink, Thred-laces, and a hundred more such kinde of trifling merchandizes; then looking on the nastinesse of their linnen habits and bodies: I conclude if gain sufficient could be raised out of them for subsistance; yet their manner of living was degenerate and base; and their condition to be far below the meanest servant in *Virginia.*

The other day, I saw a man heavily loaden with a burden of Faggots on his back, crying, Dry Faggots, Dry Faggots; he travailed much ground, bawled frequently, and sweat with his burthen: but I saw none buy any, neer three houres I followed him, in which time he rested, I entered into discourse with him, offered him drink, which he thankfully accepted of (as desirous to learn the mistery of his trade) I enquired what he got by each burden when sold? he answered me three pence: I further asked him what he usually got a day? he replyed, some dayes nothing some dayes six pence; some time more, but seldome; me thought it was a pittifull life, and I admired how he could live on it; And yet it were dangerous to advise these wretches to better their conditions by travaile, for fear of the cry of, a spirit, a spirit.

The Country is not only plentifull but pleasant and profit-able, pleasant in regard of the brightnesse of the weather, the many delightfull rivers, on which the inhabitants are settled (every man almost living in sight of a lovely river) the abun-dance of game, the extraordinary good neighbour-hood and lov-ing conversation they have one with the other.

Pleasant in their building, which although for most part they are but one story besides the loft, and built of wood, yet contrived so delightfull, that your ordinary houses in England are not so handsome, for usually the rooms are large, daubed and whitelimed, glazed and flowered, and if not glazed win-dows, shutters which are made very pritty and convenient.

Pleasant in observing their stocks and flockes of Cattle, Hoggs, and Poultry, grazing, whisking and skipping in their sights, pleasant in having all things of their own, growing or breeding without drawing the peny to send for this and that, without which, in England they cannot be supplyed.

The manner of living and trading there is thus, each man almost lives a free-holder, nothing but the value of 12. d. a year to be paid as rent, for every 50. Acrees of land; firing cost nothing every man plants his own corne and neede take no care for bread: if any thing be bought, it is for cōmodity, exchanged presently, or for a day, payment is usuall made but once a year, and for that Bill taken (for accounts are not pleadable.)

In summer when fresh meat will not keep (seeing every man kils of his own, and quantities are inconvenient) they lend from one to another, such portions of flesh as they can spare, which is repaied again when the borrowers kils his.

If any fall sick, and cannot compasse to follow his crope which if not followed, will soon be lost, the adjoyning neighbour, will either voluntarily or upon a request joyn together, and work in it by spels, untill the honour recovers, and that gratis, so that no man by sicknesse loose any part of his years worke.

Let any travell, it is without charge, and at every house is entertainment as in a hostery, and with it hearty welcome are stranger entertained.

In a word, *Virginia* wants not good victual, wants not good dispositions, and as God hath freely bestowed it, they as freely impart with it, yet are there aswel bad natures as good.

The profit of the country is either by their labour, their stockes, or their trades.

By their labours is produced corne and Tobacco, and all other growing provisions, and this Tobacco however now low-rated, yet a good maintenance may be had out of it, (for they have nothing of necessity but cloathing to purchasse) or can this mean price of Tobacco long hold, for these reasons, First that in England it is prohibited, next that they have attained of late those sorts equall with the best Spanish, Thirdly that the sicknesse in Holland is decreasing, which hath been a great obstruction to the sail of Tobacco.

And lastly, that as the mulbery tree grows up, tobacco will be neglected and silke, flax, two staple commodities generally fallen upon.

Of the increase of cattle and hoggs, much advantage is made, by selling biefe, porke, and bacon, and butter &c. either to shipping, or to send to the Barbadoes, and other Islands, and he is a very poor man that hath not sometimes provision to put off.

By trading with Indians for Skine, Beaver, Furres and other commodities oftentimes good profits are raised; The Indians are in absolute subjection to the English, so that they both pay tribute to them and receive all their severall king from them, and as one dies they repaire to the English for a successor, so that none neede doubt it a place of securitie.

Several ways of advancement there are and imployments both for the learned and laborer, recreation for the gentry, traffique for the adventurer, congregations for the ministrie (and oh that God would stir, up the hearts of more to go over, such as would teach good doctrine, and not paddle in faction, or state matters; they could not want maintenance, they would find an assisting, an imbracing, a conforming people.)

It is knowne (such preferment hath this Country rewarded the industrious with) that some from being wool-hoppers and of as mean and meaner imployment in England have there grown great merchants, and attained to the most eminent advancements the Country afforded. If men cannot gaine (by diligence) states in those parts. I speake not only mine owne opinion, but divers others, and something by experience) it will hardly be done (unlesse by meere lucke as gamsters thrive, and other accidentals in any other part whatsoever.

Now having briefly set down the present state of *Virginia* not in fiction, but in realitie, I wish the juditious reader to consider what dislike can be had of the Country, or upon what grounds it is so infamously injured, I only therein covet to stop those blackmouthed babblers, that not only have and do abuse so noble a plantation, but abuse Gods great blessing in adding to England so flourishing a branch, in perswading many souls, rather to follow desparate and miserable courses in England, then to ingage in so honourable an undertaking as to travile and inhabite there; but to those I shall (if admonition will not worke on their recreant spirits) only say. Let him that *is filthie be filthie still.*

MARY-LANDS ADDITIONS

Having for 19. yeare served *Virginia* the elder sister, I casting my eye on Mary-land the younger, grew in amoured on her beauty, resolving like Jacob when he had first served for Leah, to begin a fresh service for Rachell.

Two year and upward have I enjoyed her company with delight and profit, but was enforced by reason of her unnatural disturbances to leave her weeping for her children & would not be comforted, because they were not; yet will I never totally forsake or be beaten off from her.

Twice hath she been deflowred by her own Inhabitants, stript, shorne and made deformed; yet such a naturall fertility and comelinesse doth she retain that she cannot but be loved, but be pittied; and although she would ever have vailed to *Virginia* as her elder, yet had not these two fatall mischiefs hapened, she would ere long have spread her self as largly, and produced as much in every respect as *Virginia* does or could doe.

Mary-land is a province not commonly knowne in England, because the name of *Virginia* includes or clouds it, it is a Country wholy belonging to that honorable Gentleman the Lord of *Baltamore*, granted him by Pattent under the broad Seal of England long since, and at his charge settled, granted for many reasons, and this for one; that *Virginia* having more land then they could manure or look after in convenient time, first the Duch came and tooke from the English much land which they still hold, next the Swead, who intrenched neerer and had not this Pattent came and prevented it, Dutch, Swead, French & other strangers had pend up our Nation with in the bounds of *Virginia*, whereas now they have now all *Mary-land*, as it were their own, it being only granted for the use of Brittaines and Irish.

It is (not an Island as is reported, but) part of that maine adjoyning to *Virginia*, only separated or parted from *Virginia*, by a river of ten miles broad, called *Patomack* river, the commodities and manner of living as in *Virginia*, the soyle somewhat more temporate (as being more Northerly) many stately and navigable rivers are contained in it, plentifully stored with wholsome springs, a rich and pleasant soile, and so that its extraordinary goodnes hath made it rather desired then envied, which hath been fatall to her (as beauty is often times to those that are endued with it) and that the reader may thoroughly be informed how she hath suffered. I shall in brief relate, and conclude.

It is to be understood that in the time of the late King; *Virginia* being whol for monarchy, and the last Country belonging to England that submitted to obedience of the Common-wealth of England. And there was in *Virginia* a certaine people congregated into a Church, calling themselves Independents, which daily encreasing, severall consultations were had by the state of that Coloney, how to suppresse and extinguish them, which was daily put in execution, as first their Pastor was banished, next their other Teachers, then many by informatiōs clapt up in prison, then generally disarmed) wch was very harsh in such a country where the heathen live round about them) by one Colonel *Samuel Mathews* then a Counsellor in *Virginia* and since Agent for *Virginia* to the then parliament, and lastly in a condition of banishment, so that they knew not in those streights how to dispose of themselves.

Mary-land (my present subject) was courted by them as a refuge, the Lord Proprietor and his Governor solicited to, and severall addresses and treaties made for their admittance & entertainment into that province, their conditions were pittied, their propositions were harkened to and agree on, which was that they should have convenient portions of land assigned them, libertie of conscience and priviledge to choose their owne officers, and hold courts within themselves, all was granted them, they had a whole County of the richest land in the province asigned them, & such as themselves made choyce of, the conditions of plantations (such as were common to all adventurers) were shewed and propounded to them, which they extreamly approved of, and nothing was in those conditions exacted from them, but appeales to the Provincial court, quit-rents, and an oath of fidelitie to the Proprietor: An assembly was called thoroughout the whole Country after their comming over (consisting aswell of themselves as the rest) and because there were some few papists that first inhabited these themselves, and others of being different judgments, an act passed that all professing in Jesus Christ should have equall justice, priviledges and benefits in that province, and that none on penaltie (mentioned) should disturb each other in their several professions, nor give the urging termes, either of Roundheads, sectarie, Independent, Jesuit, Papist, &c. Intending an absolute peace and union; the Oath of Fidelitie (although none other then such as every Lord of a manner requires from his tenant) was over hauled, and this clause added to it (provided it infring not the libertie of the conscience.)

They sat downe joyfully, followed their vocations chearfully, trad increased in their province, and divers others were by this incouraged and invited over from *Virginia*.

But these people finding themselves in a capacitie not only to capitulate, but to oversway, those that had so received and relieved them.

Began to pick quarrells, first with the Papists, next with the oath, and lastly declared their aversness to all conformalitie, wholy ayming (as themselves since confessed) to deprive the Lord proprietor of all his interest in that country, and make it their own: with unworthiness? What ingratitude? with unparalled inhumanitie was in these practices made obvious.

Amongst others that became tenants in this aforesaid distress was one *Richard Bennett* Merchant, who seated and settled amongst them, and so (not only owed obedience to that government, but) was obliged as a man received in his pretended distresse, to be a gratfull benefactor upon the setting forth of a fleet intended for the reducement of *Virginia*, the said B*ennet* and one *Claiborne* (a pestilent enemie to the welfaire of that province and the Lord Proprietor, although he had formerly submissively acknowledged he owed his forfeited life to the said proprietor, for dealing so favorably with him for his misdemeanors, as by his treacherous letters under his hand (now in print) is manifest, and many other acts of grace conferred on him, having a commission directed to them and others (who miscarried by sea) to reduce *Virginia* (not *Maryland*, for they were in obedience to the Common-wealth of

England, and great assistance to the said fleet) although they knew Mary-land to be excluded and dasht out of their Commission, yet because the commission mentioned the Bay of Chesapeack) in which Mary-land was (as well as Virginia) yet they were resolved to wreth and stretch their commission to the prejudice of Mary-land and becomming abbetters and confederats with those serpents that have been so taken in, presumed to alter the government and take away the governours Commission, putting in others in their place, viz. a Papist in cheife, and one more, who misgoverning the Country, they were excluded, and the former governor restored with an addition of Commissioners of their owne creatures, and as taking power from them, untill further knowledge from England, driving herein at their own interest.

The governour (so restored) being truly informed that their proceedings were illegal; held Courts and proceeds as if no such alteration had been made, issues out Writs (according to order) In the name of the Lord proprietor, but they require and command them to do it in the name of the Keepers of the Liberties of England, according to act of Parliament, to which answer sufficient was given, that they never were in opposition to the present power, they had taken the Engagement, & for the tenure or form of writs, they were not compelled by vertue of that act to make them other wise then they always had done, for by Patent from the late K. they had power to issue out in the Proprietors name, and never had used the Kings name at all, therefore that act requiring all Writs formerly issuing out in the late Kings name, now to rcvolve to the Keepers of the Liberties of England, was no way binding to them, who had never used the kings name at all.

But it was not religion, it was not punctilios they stood upon, it was that sweete, that rich, that large Country they aimed at; and therefore agrees amongst themselves to frame petitions, complaints, and subscriptions from those bandetoes to themselves (the said Bennet and Claiborne) to ease them of their pretended sufferings, and then come with arms, and againe make the Province their own, exalting themselves in all places of trust and command, totally expulsing the Governer, and all the hospitable Proprietors, Officers out of their places.

But when his Highnesse (not acquainted with these matchinations) had owned and under his hand and signet acknowledged Cap. *Will. Stone* (the former governor) Governor for the Lord *Baltamore* of his Province of *Mary-land,* he again endeavored to reasume the government, and fetched away the records from those usurpers, proclaimed peace to all not obstinate, and favorably received many submissives, who with seeming joy returned, bewailing their unworthy ingratitude & inhumanitie, blaming the unbridled ambition and base averice of those that had misled them.

The Province consists of foure Counties already inhabited, viz. St. *Maries, Calverton, An Arundal* and *Kent.* St. *Maries* and *Calverton* submitted, *An Arundall* and part of *Kent* opposed.

The Governor desirous to reclaim those opposing, takes a partie about 130. persons with. him, and sailes into those parts, one *Roger Heamans* who had a great ship under him, and who had promised to be instrumentall to the governor, to wind up those differences (being *Judas*-like, hired to joyn with those opposing Countries) and having the Governour and his vessells within reach of his Ordnance, perfidiously & contrary to his undertaking and ingagments, fires at them and enforces them to the first shore to prevent that mischief.

The next morning he sends messengers to those of *An Arundall* to treat, and messengers aboard that *Shittlecock Heamans,* but all were detained; and on the 25. of *March* last (being the next day and the Lords day) about 170. and odd of *Kent* and *Anne Arundall* came marching against them, *Heaman* fires a pace at them, and a small vessel of *New-England* under the command of one *John Cutts* comes neere the shore and seazes the boats. provision and amunition belonging to the Governour and his partie, and so in a nick, in a streight were they fallen upon.

The Governour being shot in many places yeilds on quarter, which was granted; but being in hold, was threatned (notwithstanding that quarter given) to be imediatly executed, unless he would writ to the rest to take quarter, which upon his request they did, twentie odd were killed in this skirmish, and all the rest prisoners on quarter, who were disarmed & taken into custodie.

But these formerly distressed supplicants for admittance, being now become High and Mighty States, and supposing their Conquest unquestionable, consult with themselves (notwithstanding their quarter given) to make their Conquest more absolute, by cutting off the heads of the Province, *viz.* the Governor, the Counsel and Commanders thereof: And so make themselves a Counsel of War, and condemn them to death: Foure were presently executed, scilicet, Mr. *William Eltonhead*, one of the Councel; Capt. *William Lewis*, Mr. *John Legate* Gentleman, and *John Pedro*; the rest at the importunity of some women, and resolution of some of their souldiers (who would not suffer their designe to take thorough effect, as being pricked in Conscience for their ingratitudes) were saved, but were Amerced, Fined and Plundred at their pleasures: And although this was prophetiquely foreseen by diverse eminent Merchants of *London*, who Petitioned his Highnesse for prevention, and that his Highnesse sent a gracious command to *Bennet*, and all others, not to disturb the Lord *Baltamores* Officers, nor People in *Mary-land*, but recalled all Power or pretence of Power from them; yet they still hold, and possesse (in defiance of so sacred a mandate) the said Province of *Maryland*, and sent an impious Agent home to Parlie whilest they plundred; but he hath long since given up his account to the great avenger of all injuries: Although sticklers (somewhat more powerfull, but by many degrees more brazen fac't then his spirit could bare him forth to appear) now labour to justifie these inhumanities, disorders, contempts, and rebellions; so that I may say with the Prophet *Jeremiah*; How doth the Citty sit solitary that was full of people? How is she become as a widdow? She that was great amongst the Nations, and Princesse amongst the Provinces? How is she become tributary. Thus have they brought to desolation, one of the happiest Plantations that ever *Englishmen* set foot in, and such a Country (that if it were again made formall) might harbor in peace and plenty all such as *England* shall have occasion to disburthen, or desire to forsake *England*.

A pious consideration of these distractions is by his High-nesse taking notice of, and these controversies are by him re-ferred to the Hearing, and Report of those two Honourable and judicious Gentlemen the Lords *Whitlock* and *Widdrington,* whose Pains and Moderation in Hearing, and mildly disputing indifferently the condition of these uproars, gives not onely hopes of relief, but have added to their renowns, by all those that (as observed) have been present at the severall Hearings, an account whereof will ere long be published in print.

Upon determination whereof, it must be concluded that a settlement will follow, and then many families will flock over to inhabit these ruines, the fertility of the Province will (in short time) make good (excepting the blood spilt which can never be recalled nor satisfied for.)

Let this be no discouragement to any to goe over, for it will now be more firmly settled then ever, and so throughly, setled that neither envy nor deceipt can again ever shake it.

And being so setled, I know no country (although I have travelled many) that I more affect, more esteem, that which profits delight, and here is both absolute profit, reall de-light; I shall forget my undertaking in the beginning of my booke, which was not to over extall the Country: for should I indeed give it its due commendations, I should seem to be suborn'd; but in few words, it is that Country in which I desire to spend the remnant of my dayes, in which I covet to make my grave.

This I have not written for profit, for it is known I have given away the copy, and therefore am the less to be mistrusted for a deluder, for popular applause I did it not, for in this pregnant age, my lines appear so harsh and disordered, that I would not have affixed my name to it, but in obedience to those commands that so require it, and to prevent the imputation of a libeller, the maine drift and scope I have herein aimed at, is to discover *Virginia* and *Mary-land,* and stand up in their just defences when culminated, to let many that pine in *England* know, they are to their ruines deluded, that are frighted from going thither, if their wayes of livelihood be not certaine in *England.*

Two Views
of Nathaniel Bacon

Bibliographical Note. The most important texts concerning Bacon and his Rebellion are collected in C. M. Andrews, ed. *Narratives of the Insurrections, 1675–1690* (New York, 1915); the selections here printed follow this edition, pp. 108–120, 74–77. On Bacon's Rebellion, see T. J. Wertenbaker, *Torchbearer of the Revolution* (Princeton, 1940).

from

SIR JOHN BERRY (1635—1690), COLONEL HERBERT JEFFREYS (d. 1678), AND FRANCIS MORYSON (FL. 1649—1677), A TRUE NARRATIVE OF THE LATE REBELLION IN VIRGINIA, BY THE ROYAL COMMISSIONERS (WRITTEN 1677)*

[Bacon's Character and Rise to Power]

The Murders, Rapines and outrages of the Indians became soe much the more Barbarous, fierce and frequent, by how much

---

* Reprinted from *Narratives of the Insurrections, 1675–1690*, edited by C. M. Andrews and used with permission of Barnes & Noble, Inc.

the more they perceived the Public Preparations of the English against them, Prosecuting their mischiefs upon the extreem Plantations thereby forcing many to dessert them to their Ruines, and destroying those that adventur'd to stay behind.

The unsatisfied People finding themselves still lyable to the Indian Crueltyes,[1] and the cryes of their wives and children growing grievous and intollerable to them, gave out in Speeches that they were resolved to Plant tobacco rather than pay the Tax for maintaining of Forts, and that the erecting of them was a great Grievance, Juggle and cheat, and of no more use or service to them than another Plantation with men at it, and that it was merely a Designe of the Grandees to engrosse all their Tobacco into their owne hands.

Thus the sense of this oppression and the dread of a comon approaching calamity made the giddy-headed multitude madd, and precipitated them upon that rash overture of Running out upon the Indians themselves, at their owne voluntary charge and hazard of their Lives and Fortunes, onely they first by Petition humbly craved leave or comission to be ledd by any comander or comanders as the Governor should please to appoint over them to be their Chieftaine or Generall. But instead of Granting this Petition the Governor by Proclamation under great Penalty forbad the like Petitioning for the future.

This made the People jealous that the Governor for the lucre of the Beaver and otter trade etc. with the Indians, rather sought to protect the Indians than them, Since after publick Proclamation prohibiting all trade with the Indians (they complaine) hee privately gave commission to some of his Friendes to truck with them, and that those persons furnished the Indians with Powder, Shott etc. soe that they were better provided than his Majestye's Subjects.

The People of Charles City County (neer Merchants

---

[1] Nathaniel Bacon (1647–1676), a planter on the Virginia frontier led other Virginians ostensibly against such "Indian Crueltyes." Because Governor Berkeley of Virginia would not give them enough support, Bacon's followers gradually followed him in a revolt against governmental authority. This selection, and the following, are from official reports on the Rebellion and its leader, who died by fever at the height of his success. His Rebellion virtually died with him.

TWO VIEWS OF NATHANIEL BACON 485

Hope) being denyed a Commission by the Governor although he was truly informed (as by a Letter of his to his Ma'tie he confesseth) of Several formidable Bodies of Indians coming downe on the heads of James River within 50 or 60 miles of the English Plantations, and knew not where the Storme would light, they begin to beat up drums for Volunteers to goe out against the Indians and soe continued Sundry dayes drawing into armes, the Magistrates being either soe remise or of the Same faction, that they suffered this disaster without contradiction or endeavouring to prevent soe dangerous a beginning and going on.

The Rout being got together now wanted nor waited for nothing but one to head and lead them out on their design. It soe happen'd that one Nathaniel Bacon Junr, a person whose lost and desperate fortunes had thrown him into that remote part of the world about 14 months before, and fram'd him fitt for such a purpose, as by the Sequel will appeare, which may make a short character of him no impertinent Digression.

Hee was a person whose erratique fortune had carryed and shewne him many Forraigne Parts, and of no obscure Family. Upon his first comming into Virginia hee was made one of the Councill, the reason of that advancement (all on a suddain) being best known to the Governour, which honor made him the more considerable in the eye of the Vulgar, and gave some advantage to his pernicious designes. Hee was said to be about four or five and thirty yeares of age, indifferent tall but slender, black-hair'd and of an ominous, pensive, melancholly Aspect, of a pestilent and prevalent Logical discourse tending to atheisme in most companyes, not given to much talke, or to make suddain replyes, of a most imperious and dangerous hidden Pride of heart, despising the wisest of his neighbours for their Ignorance, and very ambitious and arrogant. But all these things lay hidd in him till after hee was a councillor, and untill he became powerfull and popular.

Now this man being in Company with one Crews, Isham and Bird,[2] who growing to a highth of Drinking and making the Sadnesse of the times their discourse, and the Fear they all lived

---

[2] Father of William Byrd II.—*Andrews.*

in, because of the Susquahanocks who had settled a little above the Falls of James River, and comitted many murders upon them, among whom Bacon's overseer happen'd to be one, Crews and the rest persuaded Mr. Bacon to goe over and see the Soldiers on the other Side James river and to take a quantity of Rum with them to give the men to drinke, which they did, and (as Crews etc. had before laid the Plot with the Soldiers) they all at once in field shouted and cry'd out, a Bacon! a Bacon! a Bacon! w'ch taking Fire with his ambition and Spirit of Faction and Popularity, easily prevail'd on him to Resolve to head them, His Friends endeavouring to fix him the Faster to his Resolves by telling him that they would also goe along with him to take Revenge upon the Indians, and drink Damnation to their Soules to be true to him, and if hee could not obtain a Comission they would assist him as well and as much as if he had one; to which Bacon agreed.

This Forwardnesse of Bacons greatly cheer'd and animated the People, who looked upon him as the onely Patron of the Country and preserver of their Lives and Fortunes.

For he pretended and bosted what great Service hee would doe for the country, in destroying the Comon Enemy, securing their Lives and Estates, Libertyes, and such like fair frauds hee subtily and Secretly insinuated by his owne Instruments over all the country, which he seduced the Vulgar and most ignorant People to believe (two thirds of each county being of that Sort) Soe that theire whole hearts and hopes were set now upon Bacon. Next he charges the Governour as negligent and wicked, treacherous and incapable, the Lawes and Taxes as unjust and oppressive and cryes up absolute necessity of redress.

Thus Bacon encouraged the Tumult and as the unquiet crowd follow and adhere to him, he listeth them as they come in upon a large paper, writing their name circular wise, that their Ring-Leaders might not be found out.

Having conjur'd them into this circle, given them Brandy to wind up the charme, and enjoyn'd them by an oth to stick fast together and to him, and the othe being administered, he went and infected New Kent County ripe for Rebellion.

Bacon having gott about 300 men together in armes prepared to goe out against the Indians, the Governour and his Friends endeavour to divert his designes, but cannot.

Hee Proclames Bacon and his Followers Rebells and Mutineers for going forth against the Indians without a Commission, and (getting a company of Gentlemen together) the Governor marcheth up to the Falls of James River to pursue and take Bacon, or to Seize him at his Returne; but all in vaine, For Bacon had gott over the River with his Forces and hastning away into the woods, went directly and fell upon the Indians and killed some of them who were our best Friends of Indians and had fought ag't the Susquahanocks enemyes to the English.

The Governour having issued forth a Proclamation importing noe commerce with the reputed Indian Enemyes, Besides the cloggs and conditions w'ch were put on the Garrisons placed or to be Placed in the new erected Forts, enjoying them not to make any attempt upon the Indians untill they should first give the Governor an account thereof, and receive orders from him therein, Put many to a stand, made the People expostulate and say how shall wee know our enemyes from our Friends, are not the Indians all of a colour, and if wee must not defend ourselves before they oppose us, they may take their usual advantage of surprize, and soe destroy us ere wee are capable of making any resistance; Soe that after all that charge in erecting of Forts, after all the Troubles of the Congresse[3] of our forces, after all their toyle and diligence used in discovering the enemy (who are seldome to bee dealt with but in their owne way of surprize) the very point of Execution was to be determined of by a person residing in all likelihood at least a 100 miles distant from the Place of action, to the losse of opportunityes and utter discouragement of the soldiers and ourselves. Besides of what Security were these Forts like to be, when the Indians cutt off and destroy'd divers people within a small distance of the Forts and some of the very Soldiers in them, and they not daring to stir out to relieve any that were in danger and distresse, themselves being scarce secure upon the Place they were Posted on. Nor would the people understand any distinction of Friendly In-

---

[3] Bringing together.—*Andrews*.

dians and Indian Enemyes, for at that tyme it was impossible to distinguish one nation from another, they being deformed with Paint of many colors, and at best (say they) who is hee that can doe it, for there was never any open or free Trade among us that we might know them, But the whole Trade monopolized by the Governour and Grandees.

Soe the common cry and vogue of the Vulgar was, away with these Forts, away with these distinctions, wee will have warr with all Indians which come not in with their armes, and give Hostages for their Fidelity and to ayd against all others; we will spare none. and wee must bee hang'd for Rebells for killing those that will destroy us, let them hang us, wee will venture that rather than lye at the mercy of a Barbarous Enemy, and be murdered as we are etc. Thus went the ruder sort raging and exclaiming agt. the Indians, expressing the calamity that befell New England by them.[4] While the Governour was in the Upper Parts to wait Bacon's returne the people below began to draw into armes, and to declare against the Forts. Hee to appease the comotions of the People leaves off that designe and comes immediately back to his own house, and caused at his returne the Surry and other Forts to be forthwith dismantled, and dissolving the assembly that enacted them, gave the country a free new election, which new assembly were to be for the Settlement of the then distracted condition of Virginia.

At this new election (such was the Prevalency of Bacon's Party) that they chose instead of Freeholders, Free men that had but lately crept out of the condition of Servants (which were never before Eligible) for their Burgesses and such as were eminent abettors to Bacon, and for faction and ignorance fitt Representatives of those that chose them.

At the Same time Bacon being come back from his Indian march with a thousand braging lyes to the credulous Silly People of what feats he had perform'd, was by the Inhabitants of the county of Henrico chosen a Burgess, as was also Crews for the Same county.

The assembly being mett Bacon comes down in a sloope to James Towne. But the People being very Fond of him, would

---

[4] King Philip's War, 1675–1676.—*Andrews*.

not trust his person without a Guard, fearing some violence should be offered him by the Governour for what hee had already acted against his will, and Soe sent Forty armed men along in the Sloope with Bacon, coming somewhat neerer to Towne than Swanns Point dropt anchor and sent (as tis said) on Shore to the Governour to know if he might in safety come on shore, and sett as a Member etc. What answer was return'd we have not heard, onely what the Governor caused to be given him from the great guns that fired at the Sloope from the Towne Fort, soe that having gott his Sloope out of Gunshott, he lay higher up the River, and in the night tyme with a party of his men ventured on shore, and having had some conference (at Laurances house) with Laurance and Drumond came off again undiscovered. Several Propositions were made and some boats sent off to apprehend him but could effect nothing. Bacon endeavours to make his Escape up the River. In this Juncture Capt. Thomas Gardner Master of the Ship *Adam and Eve* being at Towne, having an order from the Governor to pursue and seize him, immediately got on Board his ship, and as Bacon returned up the River comanded his Sloope in by Firing at him from on Board, and soe tooke him and all his men Prisoners and brought them away to the Governor at Towne.

Bacon being delivered up Prisoner to the Governor by Capt. Gardner, the Governor lifting up his hands and eyes said in the hearing of many people, "Now I behold the greatest Rebell that ever was in Virginia," who (with a dejected look) made noe Reply, till after a short pause the Governour ask'd Bacon these words: "Sir, doe you continue to be a Gentleman, and may I take your word? if soe you are at Liberty upon your owne parrol."

Bacon feignes a most deep sense of shame and sorrow for his Guilt, and expresses the greatest kind of obligacion to Gratitude towards the Governour imaginable. And to make it looke the more reall and sincere drew up an humble Submission for and acknowledgem't of his soe late crimes and disobedience, imploring thereby the Governor's Pardon and Favor, which Bacon being in readyness to Present on his coming before the Governor hee told the Council then Sitting, "Now you shall see a Penitent Sinner."

Whereupon Bacon in very humble manner and with many low bowings of his Body approacht the Governor and on his knee gave up his Parasiticall Paper into the Governor's hands, and soe withdrew himself.

After a short while hee was sent for in againe and had his pardon confirmed to him, Is restor'd into favor and readmitted into the councell, to the wonder of all men.

Now Capt. Gardner instead of a Reward for the Service hee performed in taking and bringing away Bacon Prisoner was suffered to be fined 70 *lb.* damage for seizing him and the Sloope, although Capt. Gardner had discharged himself of her, the sd sloope being afterwards by a storme drove on shore and lost.[5]

However soe powerfull (it seems) was Bacon's interest in this new assembly that he procured a Public order to passe ag't Gardner for the payment of the 70 *lb.* where upon he threw Gardner into goale till he found Security for his Enlargement. But when they understand that the Governor had not onely sett him free, but readmitted him into the Councill, with Promise also of a commission to be given him to goe out against the Indians, the People were so well pacified for the present as that every man with great gladnesse return'd to his owne home.

Bacon attending at Towne for a Comission (w'ch the Governor is said to have promised him) and being delayed or putt off, was secretly whispered to by some of his Friends that those delayes would endanger his Life, and that if speedily he endeavour'd not to prevent it, there was a conspiracy to murder him on such a night; upon w'ch hee privately leaves the Towne. Now whether this was onely a rais'd rumor of Bacon's, or a reall truth wee cannot determine, but being rais'd after Bacon was gone we suppose it false.

Hee no sooner was come to the upper Parts of James River, but the impatient people run to him to ask how affairs Stood, exclaiming still more and more against the Indians, and desired to know if he had yet a comission, and understanding he had or could not obtaine any, they began to sett up their throats in one

---

[5] It is a wonder Sir Wm. Berkeley (being then in Towne) did not protect or preserve a Person he had imploy'd in so signal a Service.—*Marginal note in original.*

common kry of othes and curses and cry'd out aloud that they would either have a comission for Bacon that they might serve under his conduct or else they would pull downe the Towne or doe worse to some if they had it not, and if Bacon would go but with them they would gett him a commission. Thus the Raging Tumult came downe to Towne (Sitting the assembly) and Bacon at the head of them, having entred the Towne, hee Seises and secures the Principall Places and avenues, setts Sentinells and sends forth scouts, so that noe Place could bee more Securely guarded.

Having soe done, hee drawes up all his men in armes against the State house where the Governour councell and Burgesses were then assembled and Sitting, and sends in to the Assembly to know if now they would grant him a commission, which Sr. Wm. Berkeley utterly refused, and rising from his chair of judicature came downe to Bacon, and told him to his Face and before all his men that hee was a Rebell and a Traytor etc. and should have noe commission, and uncovering his naked Bosome before him, required that some of his men might shoot him, before ever he would be drawne to signe or consent to a commission for such a Rebell as Bacon, "Noe" (said the Governor) "lett us first try and end the difference singly between ourselves," and offer'd to measure swords with him; all the answer Bacon gave the Governor was, "Sir, I came not, nor intend to hurt a haire of your honor's head, and for your sword your Honor may please to putt it up, it shall rust in the scabbard before ever I shall desire you to drawe it. I come for a commission against the Heathen who dayly inhumanely murder us and spill our Brethrens Blood, and noe care is taken to prevent it," adding, "God damne my Blood, I came for a commission, and a commission I will have before I goe," and turning to his soldiers, said "Make ready and Present," which they all did. Some of the Burgesses looking out at the windows and seeing the soldiers in that posture of Firing cry'd out to them, "For God's sake hold your handes and forebear a little, and you shall have what you please." Much hurrying, solicitation and importunity is used on all sides to the Governor to grant Bacon a commission. At last the Governor consents, a commission is drawne up and sent him, he dislikes it, they pray him to draw or direct

one himself and the Governour should signe it. Whereupon
Bacon drawes up the contents of a commission according to his
owne mind, and returnes it to the Clerke, to prepare one by,
which is done, liked of and received.

After the Governor had signed the Principall Commission
to Bacon, hee is also pleas'd to sign 30 commissions more
[Blanke] for officers that were to serve under him.

But Bacon finding occasion for more, sent to Sir William
Berkley to signe others also, who said hee had signed enough
already, and bid him signe the rest himself if hee would.

The assembly also passe orders to raise or presse 1000 men,
and to raise Provisions etc. for this intended service ag't the
Indians wherein severell of the councell and assembly-members
were concern'd and acted in the promoting this designe, encour-
aging others to list themselves into Bacon's service, and particularly one Ballard who endeavoure'd to perswade some (who
scrupled the Legality of Bacon's commission) that it was fairly
and freely granted by Governor, Councill and Burgesses, this
Ballard being one of the councill, and of those that both tooke
and administer'd Bacon's Oath.

There was also an act of Indempnity pass'd to Bacon and
his party who committed the offence on the assembly, and a
Publick Letter of applause and approbation of Bacon's actions
and Loyalty writ to the King and signed by the Governor and
assembly. Which upon the Breaking up of this Session were
sent abroad and read among the Ignorant People who believ'd
thereby that all was well and nothing coming forth of a long
time to quash, contradict or disowne this Commission, Indempnity, Lre etc. granted to Bacon, But on the contrary other
comissions of the Governors own signing and seal'd with the
Publick seal of the Colony coming to them, they were the more
easily inclined to swallow down so fair a bait not seeing Rebellion at the end of it, and most men grew ambitious of the service as thinking it both safe and for the Publick good as having
the approbation of the Governor and assembly, at least there yet
appeared nothing to the contrary nor of a good while after.

Severall Volunteers and Reformadoes come in to list themselves under Bacon, and many were press'd into this service, till
at last having his complement of men, and all things else being

in readynesse according as the Assembly had provided for this
expedition, A general Rendezvous is appointed by Bacon at the
Falls of James River, where all things being well appointed for
the march, Bacon makes a speech to his men, Assuring them all
of his Loyalty to his Prince, declaring to them that his designe
was no other than merely to serve his King and country and to
cleere all suspicion of the contrary (if any were amongst them)
by what had bin by him already acted or Proclamed against him,
as also of what he said about the procuring his comission; hee
urges to them the reasons that induced it, the necessity of that
tyme that compell'd him, the negligence and coldnesse of others
that hated him and the cryes of his Brethrens blood that
alarm'd and waken'd him to this Publique revenge, using what
motives hee could to raise up the spirits of his men. And finally
before them all tooke the oath of allegiance and supremacy,
willing his soldiers also to doe the like, which having freely comply'd with Hee drew up an oath of Fidelity to himselfe, which
hee (as their head and Generall) required them to take; it comprehended the following contents or heads:

That they should not conceale any Plot or conspiracy of
hurt against his Person, but immediately reveale the same to
him or such others by whome he might come to the knowledge
of it.

That if any harme or damage was intended towards any of
his men, whether by surprizal or otherwise, or any conference
used, or councell kept about the Same, to discover it.

That noe commerce or correspondence should be had with
the Heathen, and if any knowne, to discover it.

That no news or information should be sent out least himself or army by such intelligence should be endanger'd either in
Repute or otherwise.

All Councells, Plotts and conspiracyes known of the Heathen, to discover them, etc.

Just now (even on the very night before their going out on
the intended march ag't the Indians) a messenger comes Post
from Gloster Countyes bringing Intelligence to Bacon, that the
Governor was there endeavouring to raise Forces to come and
surprize him and his men and that hee was resolved by Force
to take his extorted commission away from him, For that the

whole county had Petitioned ag't him as a Rebell and a Traytor etc.

This amusing message was noe sooner brought to Bacon, but immediately he causes the Drums to Beat and Trumpett to Sound for calling his men together to whome he spake after this manner:

Gentlemen and Fellow Soldiers: The Newes just now brought mee may not a little startle you as well as myselfe. But seeing it is not altogether unexpected, wee may the better beare it and provide our remedies. The Governour is now in Gloster County endeavouring to raise Forces against us, having Declared us Rebells and Traytors: if true, crimes indeed too great for Pardon; our consciences herein are our best witnesses, and theres soe conscious, as like cowards therefore they will not have the courage to face us. It is Revenge that hurryes them on without regard to the Peoples Safety, and had rather wee should be murder'd and our ghosts sent to our Slaughter'd country-men by their actings, than wee live to hinder them of their Interest with the heathen, and preserve the remaining part of our Fellow Subjects from their crueltyes. Now then wee must bee forced to turne our swords to our owne defence, or expose ourselves to their Mercyes, or Fortune of the woodes, whilest his majestyes country here lyes in Bloode and Wasting (like a candle) at both ends. How Incapable wee may be made (if wee should proceede) through Sicknesse, want of Provisions, Slaughter, wounds lesse or more, none of us is void of the Sense hereof.

Therefore while wee are sound at heart, unwearyed and not receiving damage by the fate of Warr, lett us descend to know the reasons why such Proceedings are used against us, That those whome they have raised for their Defence, to Preserve them against the Fury of the Heathen, they should thus seeke to Destroy, and to Betray our Lives whome they raised to Preserve theirs. If ever such Treachery was heard of, such wickednesse and inhumanity (and call all the former ages to Witnesse) and if any, that they suffered in like nature as wee are like by the sword and Ruines of warr.

But they are all damn'd Cowards, and you shall see they

will not dare to meete us in the Field to try the Justnesse of
our cause and soe we will downe to them etc.

To which they all cry'd "Amen, amen, wee are all ready and
will rather die in the Field than be hang'd like Roges, or Perish
in the woods, expos'd to the Favours of the mercylesse Indians."

How unhappy, unsuccessfull and how fatale this avocation
prov'd the consequence will but too Plainly Shewe. For Bacon
(then the hopes of the People) was just upon the Point of
marching out, and nothing could have call'd him back, or
turn'd the sword of a civil warr into the heart and bowels of the
country but soe ill-tymed a Project as this Prov'd.

from

THE BURWELL PAPERS
(WRITTEN 1676)

[Bacon's Death and His Memory]

Bacon haveing for som time bin beseiged by sickness, and now
not able to hould out any longer, all his strength, and provis-
sions being spent, surrendred up that Fort he was no longer able
to keepe, into the hands of that grim and all conquering Captaine, Death; after that he had implor'd the assistance of the
above mentioned Minester, for the well makeing his Artickles of
Rendition. The onely Religious duty (as they say) he was
observ'd to perform dureing these Intregues of affaires, in which
he was so considerable an actor, and soe much consearn'd, that
rather then he would decline the cause, he became so deeply
ingaged in, in the first rise there of, though much urged by
arguments of dehortations, by his nearest Relations and best
friends, that he subjected him selfe to all those inconvenences

that, singly, might bring a Man of a more Robust frame to his last hom. After he was dead he was bemoned in these following lines (drawne by the Man that waited upon his person, as it is said) and who attended his Corps to there Buriall place: But where depossited till the Generall day, not knowne, onely to those who are ressalutly silent in that particuler. There was many coppes of Verces made after his departure, calculated to the Lattitude of there affections who composed them; as a relish taken from both appetités I have here sent you a cuple.

Bacon's Epitaph, Made By His Man[6]

Death why soe crewill! what, no other way
To manifest thy splleene, but thus to slay
Our hopes of safety; liberty, our all
Which, through thy tyrany, with him must fall
To its late Caoss? Had thy riged force
Bin delt by retale, and not thus in gross
Griefe had bin silent: Now wee must complaine
Since thou, in him, hast more then thousand slane
Whose lives and safetys did so much depend
On him there lif, with him there lives must end.
  If't be a sin to thinke Death brib'd can bee
Wee must be guilty; say twas bribery
Guided the fatall shaft. Verginias foes,
To whom for secrit crimes just vengance owes
Disarved plagues, dreding their just disart
Corrupted Death by Parasscellcian[7] art
Him to destroy; whose well tride curage such,
There heartless harts, nor arms, nor strength could touch.
  Who now must heale those wounds, or stop that blood
The Heathen made, and drew into a flood?
Who i'st must pleade our Cause? nor Trump nor Drum
Nor Deputations; these alass are dumb,

---

[6] This poem may have been written by a Virginia planter, John Cotton. The manuscript, however, is anonymous.
[7] Medical or alchemical; from Paracelsus, the celebrated physican (1493–1541)—Andrews.

And Cannot speake. Our Arms (though nere so strong)
Will want the aide of his Commanding tongue,
Which Conquer'd more than Ceaser: He orethrew
Onely the outward frame; this Could subdue
The ruged workes of nature. Soules repleate
With dull Child could,[8] he'd annemate with heate
Drawne forth of reasons Lymbick. In a word
Marss and Minerva both in him Concurd
For arts, for arms, whose pen and sword alike,
As Catos did, may admireation strike
In to his foes; while they confess withall
It was there guilt stil'd him a Criminall.
Onely this differance doth from truth proceed:
They in the guilt, he in the name must bleed,
While none shall dare his Obseques to sing
In disarv'd measures, untill time shall bring
Truth Crown'd with freedom, and from danger free,
To sound his praises to posterity.
    Here let him rest; while wee this truth report,
Hee's gon from hence unto a higher Court
To pleade his Cause: where he by this doth know
Whether to Ceaser hee was friend, or foe.

Upon the Death of G. B.

    Whether to Ceaser he was Friend or Foe?
Pox take such Ignorance, do you not know?
Can he be Friend to Ceaser, that shall bring
The Arms of Hell, to fight against the King?
(Treason, Rebellion) then what reason have
Wee for to waite upon him to his Grave,
There to express our passions? Wilt not bee
Worss then his Crimes, to sing his Ellegie
In well tun'd numbers; where each Ella bcares
(To his Flagitious name) a flood of teares?
A name that hath more soules with sorrow fed,

---

[8] Chilled cold. In the next line, Lymbick for alembic.—*Andrews*.

Then reched [9] Niobe single teares ere shed;
A name that fil'd all hearts, all eares, with paine,
Untill blest fate proclamed, Death had him slane.
Then how can it be counted for a sin
Though Death (nay though my selfe) had bribed bin,
To guide the fatall shaft? we honour all
That lends a hand unto a T[r]ators fall.
What though the well paide Rochit soundly ply
And box the Pulpitt in to flatterey;
Urging his Rethorick, and straind elloquence,
T'adorne incoffin'd filth and excrements;
Though the Defunct (like ours) nere tride
A well intended deed untill he dide?
'Twill be nor sin, nor shame, for us, to say
A two fould Passion checker-workes this day
Of Joy and Sorow; yet the last doth move
On feete impotent, wanting strength to prove
(Nor can the art of Logick yeild releife)
How Joy should be surmounted, by our greife.
Yet that wee Grieve it cannot be denide,
But 'tis because he was, not cause he dide.
So wep the poore destresed Ilyum Dames
Hereing those nam'd, there Citty put in flames,
And Country ruing'd; If wee thus lament
It is against our present Joyes consent.
For if the rule, in Phisick, trew doth prove,
Remove the cause, th' effects will after move,
We have outliv'd our sorows, since we see
The Causes shifting, of our miserey.
    Nor is't a single cause, that's slipt away,
That made us warble out a well-a-day.
The Braines to plot, the hands to execute
Projected ills, Death Joyntly did nonsute
At his black Bar. And what no Baile could save
He hath commited Prissoner to the Grave;
From whence there's no repreive. Death keep him close
We have too many Divells still goe loose.

---

[9] Wretched.—*Andrews*.

Robert Beverly

(c. 1673–1722)

Bibliographical Note. Beverly's *History and Present State of Virginia* has been edited by L. B. Wright (Chapel Hill, 1947); the selections here printed follow this text, pp. 8–11, 271–274, 286–288, 308–319. The Introduction to Wright's edition furnishes a fine brief account of Beverly and his *History*.

from

THE HISTORY AND PRESENT STATE OF VIRGINIA*

(1705)

The Preface

'Tis agreed, that Travellers are of all Men, the most suspected of Insincerity. This does not only hold, in their private Conversations; but likewise in the *Grand Tours*, and Travels, with which they pester the Publick, and break the Bookseller. There are no Books, (the Legends of Saints always excepted,) so stuff'd with Poetical Stories, as Voyages; and the more distant the Countries lie, which they pretend to describe, the greater License those priviledg'd Authors take, in imposing upon the World. The *French* Travels are commonly more infamous on

---

* Reprinted from *History and Present State of Virginia* edited by L. B. Wright and published by the University of North Carolina Press.

this Account, than any other, which must be imputed to the strong Genius of that Nation to *Hyperbole,* and *Romance.* They are fond of dressing up every thing in their gay Fashion, from a happy Opinion, that their own *Fopperies* make any Subject more entertaining. The *English,* it must be granted, invent more within the Compass of Probability, and are contented to be less Ornamental, while they are more Sincere.

I make no Question, but the following Account will come in for its Share of this Imputation. I shall be reputed as arrant a Traveller as the rest, and my Credit, (like that of Women,) will be condemn'd for the Sins of my Company. However, I intreat the gentle Reader to be so just, as not to convict me upon bare Suspicion; let the Evidence be plain, or at least amount to a violent Presumption, and then I don't fear being acquitted. If an honest Author might be believ'd in his own Case, I wou'd solemnly declare, that I have not knowingly asserted any untrue Thing in the whole Book. On the contrary, I fear, I shall rather be accused of saying too much Truth, than too little. If I have had the Misfortune to have err'd in any Particular this Way, which yet I have used all imaginable Care to avoid, I hope the World, with all its Uncharitableness, will vouchsafe to forgive my Understanding.

If I might be so happy, as to settle my Credit with the Reader, the next Favour I wou'd ask of him, shou'd be, not to Criticize too unmercifully upon my Stile. I am an *Indian,* and don't pretend to be exact in my Language: But I hope the Plainness of my Dress, will give him the kinder Impressions of my Honesty, which is what I pretend to. Truth desires only to be understood, and never affects the Reputation of being finely equipp'd. It depends upon its own intrinsick Value, and, like Beauty, is rather conceal'd, than set off, by Ornament.

I wonder no Body has ever presented the World, with a tolerable Account of our *Plantations.* Nothing of that kind has yet appear'd, except some few General Descriptions, that have been calculated more for the Benefit of the Bookseller, than for the Information of Mankind. If I may judge of the rest, by what has been publish'd concerning *Virginia,* I will take the Liberty to say, that there's none of 'em either true, or so much as well invented. Such Accounts are as impertinent as ill Pictures, that resemble any Body, as much as the Persons they are drawn for. For my part, I have endeavour'd to hit the *Likeness;* though, perhaps, my *Colouring* may not have all the Life and Beauty I cou'd wish.

The Method I have taken in this Performance, is as follows. I have divided the Whole into Four distinct Parts. The first contains, a Chronological History, of the most remarkable Things that have happen'd in *Virginia,* ever since it was first seated by the *English.* It shows all the Wars with the *Indians,* and their Causes, all the Massacres, and other Disasters, occasion'd by the Resentment of the Natives. It likewise gives a faithful Account, of all the successive Governours of that Country, and their Administration, together with the principal Laws, that have been enacted in the Time of Each. In the doing of which, I have been carful to mention nothing, but what I can make good by very Authentique Testimony. So that if I have taken the Freedom, to represent the Mismanagements of several Gentlemen, it is their Fault, that acted such Irregularities, and not mine, that report them to the World. If Men will please to be unjust, run counter to the *Royal Instructions,* oppress the People, and offer Violence to all the *Laws* of a Country, they ought to be known, and abhorr'd by Mankind.

The Second Part treats of the Spontaneous Productions of that Country, and the Original State, wherein the *English* found it at their first Arrival. This is a very copious Subject, but I have handled it with more Brevity than it deserves, because I am conscious of my want of Skill in the *Works of Nature.* However I flatter my self, that what I have said, will be sufficient, to give a Handle to a more compleat Undertaking. The World had some Years ago an unhappy Loss, by the Death of Mr. *Banister,* who was making curious Collections for a *Natural History of* Virginia: But the sudden Death of that Gentleman, put an End to that excellent Design. He had great Talents that Way, and if he had liv'd a few Years longer, he wou'd have done Justice to so fine a Country, by describing it in all its Native Perfections.

The Third Part gives a true Account of the *Indians,* together with their Religion, Customs, and Government. There I have added Fourteen Copper Plates, to illustrate the Dress, and

Way of Living of the Natives, the Draughts of which were taken exactly from the Life. Herein, as well as throughout the whole Book, I have been very scrupulous, not to insert any thing, but what I can justifie, either by my own Knowledge, or by credible Information.

In the Fourth Part, I have represented the *English* Form of Government in that Country, with all the Publick Officers, their Business, and Salary. There I have mention'd many of their most material Laws, and Methods of proceeding. I have likewise shown the small Improvements, that the *English* have made, since they have been in Possession, and pointed at several great Advantages, which they might secure to themselves, by a due Spirit of Industry, and Management. I have everywhere made it my chief Business, to avoid *Partiality*; and therefore have fairly expos'd the Inconveniences, as well as proclaim'd the Excellencies of my Country.

This is the *Bill of Fare*, of what the Reader may expect to meet with in the following Discourse; and I shou'd be very happy, if he wou'd have the Goodness, to think it a tolerable Entertainment.

from

BOOK IV, "THE PRESENT STATE OF THE COUNTRY, AS TO THE POLICY OF THE GOVERNMENT, AND THE IMPROVEMENTS OF THE LAND."

Chapter X
Of the Servants and Slaves in Virginia

Their Servants, they distinguish by the Names of Slaves for Life, and Servants for a time.

Slaves are the Negroes, and their Posterity, following the condition of the Mother, according to the Maxim, *partus sequitur ventrem*. They are call'd Slaves, in respect of the time of their Servitude, because it is for Life.

Servants, are those which serve only for a few years, according to the time of their Indenture, or the Custom of the Country. The Custom of the Country takes place upon such as have no Indentures. The Law in this case is, that if such Servants be under Nineteen years of Age, they must be brought into Court, to have their Age adjudged; and from the Age they are judg'd to be of, they must serve until they reach four and twenty: But if they be adjudged upwards of Nineteen, they are then only to be Servants for the term of five Years.

The Male-Servants, and Slaves of both Sexes, are imployed together in Tilling and Manuring the Ground, in Sowing and Planting Tobacco, Corn, &c. Some Distinction indeed is made between them in their Cloaths, and Food; but the Work of both, is no other than what the Overseers, the Freemen, and the Planters themselves do.

Sufficient distinction is also made between the Female-Servants, and Slaves; for a White Woman is rarely or never put to work in the Ground, if she be good for any thing else: And to Discourage all Planters from using any Women so, their Law imposes the heaviest Taxes upon Female-Servants working in the Ground, while it suffers all other white Women to be absolutely exempted: Whereas on the other hand, it is a common thing to work a Woman Slave out of Doors; nor does the Law make any Distinction in her Taxes, whether her Work be Abroad, or at Home.

Because I have heard how strangely cruel, and severe, the Service of this Country is represented in some parts of *England*; I can't forbear affirming, that the work of their Servants, and Slaves, is no other than what every common Freeman do's. Neither is any Servant requir'd to do more in a Day, than his Overseer. And I can assure you with a great deal of Truth, that generally their Slaves are not worked near so hard, nor so many Hours in a Day, as the Husbandmen, and Day-Labourers in *England*. An Overseer is a Man, that having served his time, has acquired the Skill and Character of an experienced Planter, and is therefore intrusted with the Direction of the Servants and Slaves.

But to compleat this account of Servants, I shall give you a short Relation of the care their Laws take, that they be used as tenderly as possible.

By the Laws of Their Country

1. All Servants whatsoever, have their Complaints heard without Fee, or Reward; but if the Master be found Faulty, the charge of the Complaint is cast upon him, otherwise the business is done *ex Officio*.

2. Any Justice of Peace may receive the Complaint of a Servant, and order every thing relating thereto, till the next County Court, where it will be finally determin'd.

3. All Masters are under the Correction, and Censure of the County-Courts, to provide for their Servants, good and wholsome Diet, Clothing, and Lodging.

4. They are always to appear, upon the first Notice given of the Complaint of their Servants, otherwise to forfeit the Service of them, until they do appear.

5. All Servants Complaints are to be receiv'd at any time in Court, without Process, and shall not be delay'd for want of Form; but the Merits of the Complaint must be immediately inquir'd into by the Justices; and if the Master cause any delay therein, the Court may remove such Servants, if they see Cause, until the Master will come to Tryal.

6. If a Master shall at any time disobey an Order of Court, made upon any Complaint of a Servant; the Court is impower'd to remove such Servant forthwith to another Master, who will be kinder; Giving to the former Master the produce only, (after Fees deducted) of what such Servants shall be sold for by Publick Outcry.

7. If a Master should be so cruel, as to use his Servant ill, that is faln Sick, or Lame in his Service, and thereby render'd unfit for Labour, he must be remov'd by the Church-Wardens out of the way of such Cruelty, and boarded in some good Planters House, till the time of his Freedom, the charge of which must be laid before the next County-Court, which has

power to levy the same from time to time, upon the Goods and Chattels of the Master; After which, the charge of such Boarding is to come upon the Parish in General.

8. All hired Servants are intituled to these Priviledges.

9. No Master of a Servant, can make a new Bargain for Service, or other Matter with his Servant, without the privity and consent of a Justice of Peace, to prevent the Master's Over-reaching, or scareing such Servant into an unreasonable Complyance.

10. The property of all Money and Goods sent over thither to Servants, or carry'd in with them; is reserv'd to themselves, and remain intirely at their disposal.

11. Each Servant at his Freedom, receives of his Master fifteen Bushels of Corn, (which is sufficient for a whole year) and two new Suits of Cloaths, both Linnen and Woollen; and then becomes as free in all respects, and as much entituled to the Liberties, and Priviledges of the Country, as any other of the Inhabitants or Natives are.

12. Each Servant has then also a Right to take up fifty Acres of Land, where he can find any unpatented: But that is no great Privilege, for any one may have as good a right for a piece of Eight.

This is what the Laws prescribe in favour of Servants, by which you may find, that the Cruelties and Severities imputed to that Country, are an unjust Reflection. For no People more abhor the thoughts of such Usage, than the *Virginians,* nor take more precaution to prevent it.

Chapter XV
Of the People, Inhabitants of Virginia

I can easily imagine with *Sir Josiah Child,* that this, as well as all the rest of the Plantations, was for the most part at first peopled by Persons of low Circumstances, and by such as were willing to seek their Fortunes in a Foreign Country. Nor was it hardly possible it should be otherwise; for 'tis not likely that any Man of a plentiful Estate, should voluntarily abandon a happy Certainty, to roam after imaginary Advantages, in a New World. Besides which incertainty, he must have propos'd to

himself, to encounter the infinite Difficulties and Dangers, that
attend a New Settlement. These Discouragements were sufficient
to terrifie any Man, that cou'd live easy in *England*, from going to provoke his Fortune in a strange Land.

Those that went over to that Country first, were chiefly single Men, who had not the Incumbrance of Wives and Children
in *England;* and if they had, they did not expose them to the
fatigue and hazard of so long a Voyage, until they saw how it
should fare with themselves. From hence it came to pass, that
when they were setled there in a comfortable way of Subsisting
a Family, they grew sensible of the Misfortune of wanting
Wives, and such as had left Wives in *England*, sent for them;
but the single Men were put to their Shifts. They excepted
against the *Indian* Women, on account of their being *Pagans*,
and for fear they shou'd conspire with those of their own Nation, to destroy their Husbands. Under this Difficulty they had
no hopes, but that the Plenty in which they liv'd, might invite
Modest Women of small Fortunes, to go over thither from
England. However, they wou'd not receive any, but such as
cou'd carry sufficient Certificate of their Modesty, and good
Behaviour. Those if they were but moderately qualified in all
other Respects, might depend upon Marrying very well in those
Days, without any Fortune. Nay, the first Planters were so far
from expecting Money with a Woman, that 'twas a common
thing for them to buy a deserving Wife, at the price of 100
Pound, and make themselves believe, they had a hopeful bargain.

But this way of Peopling the Colony was only at first; for
after the advantages of the Climate, and the fruitfulness of the
Soil were well known, and all the dangers incident to Infant
Settlements were over, People of better Condition retir'd thither
with their Families, either to increase the Estates they had before, or else to avoid being persecuted for their Principles of
Religion, or Government.

Thus in the time of the Rebellion in *England*, several good
Cavalier Families went thither with their Effects, to escape the
Tyranny of the Usurper. And so again, upon the Restoration,
many People of the opposite Party took Refuge there, to shelter
themselves from the King's Resentment. But they had not

many of these last, because that Country was famous, for holding out the longest for the Royal Family, of any of the *English* Dominions; for which reason, the Roundheads went for the most part to *New-England*, as did most of those, that in the Reign of King *Charles* II. were molested on the account of their Religion, though some of these fell likewise to the share of *Virginia*. As for Malefactors condemn'd to Transportation, they have always receiv'd very few, and for many years last past, their Laws have been severe against them.

Chapter XXI
Of the recreations, and Pastimes Used in Virginia

For their Recreation, the Plantations, Orchards, and Gardens constantly afford 'em fragrant and delightful Walks. In their Woods and Fields, they have an unknown variety of Vegetables, and other rarities of Nature to discover and observe. They have Hunting, Fishing, and Fowling, with which they entertain themselves an hundred ways. Here is the most Good-nature, and Hospitality practis'd in the World, both towards Friends and Strangers: but the worst of it is, this Generosity is attended now and then, with a little too much Intemperance. The Neighbourhood is at much the same distance, as in the Country in *England:* but with this Advantage, that all the better sort of People have been abroad, and seen the World, by which means they are free from that stiffness and formality, which discover more Civility, than Kindness: And besides, the goodness of the Roads, and the fairness of the Weather, bring People oftener together.

The *Indians*, as I have already observ'd, had in their Hunting, a way of concealing themselves, and coming up to the Deer, under the blind of a Stalking-Head, in imitation of which, many People have taught their Horses to stalk it, that is, to walk gently by the Huntsman's side, to cover him from the sight of the Deer. Others cut down Trees for the Deer to browze upon, and lie in wait behind them. Others again set Stakes, at a certain distance within their Fences, where the Deer have been used to leap over into a Field of Peas, which they love extreamly; these Stakes they so place, as to run into the Body of the Deer, when he Pitches, by which means they Impale him.

They Hunt their Hares, (which are very numerous) a Foot, with Mungrils or swift Dogs, which either catch them quickly, or force them to hole in a hollow Tree, whither all their Hares generally tend, when they are closely pursued. As soon as they are thus hoed, and have crawl'd up into the Body of the Tree, the business is to kindle a Fire, and smother them with Smoak, till they let go their hold, and fall to the bottom stifled; from whence they take them. If they have a mind to spare their Lives, upon turning them loose, they will be as fit as ever to hunt at another time; for the mischief done them by the Smoak, immediately wears off again.

They have another sort of Hunting, which is very diverting, and that they call Vermine Hunting; It is perform'd a Foot, with small Dogs in the Night, by the Light of the Moon or Stars. Thus in Summertime they find abundance of Racoons, Opossums, and Foxes in the Corn-Fields, and about their Plantations: but at other times, they must go into the Woods for them. The Method is to go out with three or four Dogs, and as soon as they come to the place, they bid the Dogs seek out, and all the Company follow immediately. Where-ever a Dog barks, you may depend upon finding the Game; and this Alarm, draws both Men and Dogs that way. If this Sport be in the Woods, the Game by that time you come near it, is perhaps mounted to the top of an high Tree, and then they detach a nimble Fellow up after it, who must have a scuffle with the Beast, before he can throw it down to the Dogs; and then the Sport increases, to see the Vermine encounter those little Currs. In this sort of Hunting, they also carry their great Dogs out with them, because Wolves, Bears, Panthers, Wild-Cats, and all other Beasts of Prey, are abroad in the Night.

For Wolves they make Traps, and set Guns bated in the Woods, so that when he offers to seize the Bate, he pulls the Trigger, and the Gun discharges upon him. What *Elian* and *Pliny* write, of the Horses being benummed in their Legs, if they tread in the Track of a Wolf, does not hold good here; for I my self, and many others, have rid full Speed after Wolves in the Woods, and have seen live ones taken out of a Trap, and drag'd at a Horse's Tail; and yet those that follow'd on Horseback, have not perceived any of their Horses to falter in their pace.

They have many pretty devices besides the Gun, to take wild Turkeys; And among others, a Friend of mine invented a great Trap, wherein he at times caught many Turkeys, and particularly seventeen at one time, but he could not contrive it so, as to let others in after he had entrapped the first flock, until they were taken out.

The *Indian* Invention of Weirs in Fishing, is mightily improved by the English besides which, they make use of Seins, Trolls, Casting-Netts, Setting-Netts, Hand-fishing, and Angling, and in each find abundance of Diversion. I have set in the shade, at the Heads of the Rivers Angling, and spent as much time in taking the Fish off the Hook, as in waiting for their taking it. Like those of the *Euxine Sea*, they also Fish with Spilyards, which is a long Line staked out in the River, and hung with a great many Hooks on short strings, fasten'd to the main Line, about three or four Foot asunder. The only difference is, our Line is supported by Stakes, and theirs is buoyed up with Gourds.

Their Fowling is answerable to their Fishing for plenty of Game, in its proper Season, no Plantation being so ill stored, as to be without a great deal. They have a vast variety of it, several sorts of which, I have not yet mention'd, as Beaver, Otter, Squirrels, Partridges, Pigeons, and an infinite number of small Birds, &c.

The admirable Oeconomy of the Beavers, deserves to be particularly remember'd. They cohabit in one House, are incorparated in a regular Form of Government, something like Monarchy, and have over them a Superintendent, which the *Indians* call *Pericu*. He leads them out to their several Imployments, which consist in Felling of Trees, biting off the Branches, and cutting them into certain lengths, suitable to the business they design them for, all which they perform with their Teeth. When this is done, the Governor orders several of his Subjects to joyn together, and take up one of those Logs, which they must carry to their House or Damm, as occasion requires. He walks in State by them all the while, and sees that every one bear his equal share of the burden; while he bites with his Teeth, and lashes with his Tail, those that lag behind, and do not lend all their Strength. They commonly build their Houses in Swamps, and then to raise the Water to a convenient height, they make a Damm with Logs, and a binding sort of Clay, so firm, that though the Water runs continually over, it cannot wash it away. Within these Damms, they'l inclose Water enough to make a Pool, like a Mill-pond; and if a Mill happen to be built upon the same Stream, below their Damm, the Miller in a dry Season, finds it worth his while to cut it, to supply his Mill with Water. Upon which Disaster, the Beavers are so expert at their Work, that in one or two Nights time, they will repair the breach, and make it perfectly whole again. Sometimes they build their Houses in a broad Marsh, where the Tide ebbs and flows, and then they make no Damm at all. The Doors into their Houses are under Water. I have been at the Demolishing one of these Houses, that was found in a Marsh, and was surpriz'd to find it fortify'd with Logs, that were six Foot long, and ten Inches through, and had been carried at least one hundred and fifty yards. This House was three Stories high, and contain'd five Rooms, that is to say, two in the lower, and middle Stories, and but one at the top. These Creatures have a great deal of Policy, and know how to defeat all the Subtilty and Strategems of the Hunter, who seldom can meet with them, tho' they are in great numbers all over the Country.

There is yet another kind of Sport, which the young People take great Delight in, and that is, the Hunting of wild Horses; which they pursue sometimes with Dogs, and sometimes without. You must know they have many Horses foaled in the Woods of the Uplands, that never were in hand, and are as shy as any Savage Creature. These having no mark upon them, belong to him, that first takes them. However, the Captor commonly purchases these Horses very dear, by spoiling better in the pursuit; in which case, he has little to make himself amends, besides the pleasure of the Chace. And very often this is all he has for it, for the wild Horses are so swift, that 'tis difficult to catch them; and when they are taken, tis odds but their Grease is melted, or else being old, they are so sullen, that they can't be tam'd.

The Inhabitants are very Courteous to Travellers, who need no other Recommendation, but the being Human Creatures. A Stranger has no more to do, but to inquire upon the Road, where any Gentleman, or good House-keeper Lives, and there he may depend upon being received with Hospitality. This good Nature is so general among their People, that the Gentry when they go abroad, order their Principal Servant to entertain all Visitors, with every thing the Plantation affords. And the poor Planters, who have but one Bed, will every often sit up, or lie upon a Form or Couch all Night, to make room for a weary Traveller, to repose himself after his Journey.

If there happen to be a Churl, that either out of Covetousness, or Ill-nature, won't comply with this generous Custom, he has a mark of Infamy set upon him, and is abhorr'd by all. But I must confess, (and am heartily sorry for the occasion) that this good Neighbourhood has of late been much depraved by the present Governor, who practices, the detestable Politicks of governing by Parties; by which, Feuds and Heart-burnings have been kindled in the Minds of the People; and Friendship, Hospitality, and Good-Neighbourhood, have been extreamly discouraged.

Chapter XXII
Of the Natural Product of Virginia, and the Advantages of Their Husbandry

The extream fruitfulness of that Country, has been sufficiently shewn in the Second Book, and I think we may justly add, that in that particularly it is not exceeded by any other. No Seed is Sowed there, but it thrives, and most Plants are improved, by being Transplanted thither. And yet there's very little Improvement made among them, nor any thing us'd in Traffique, but Tobacco.

Besides all the natural Productions mention'd in the Second Book, you may take notice, that Apples from the Seed, never degenerate into Crabs, or Wildings there, but produce the same, or better Fruit than the Mother-Tree, (which is not so in *England,*) and are wonderfully improved by Grafting and Managing; yet there are very few Planters that graft at all, and much fewer that take any care to get choice Fruits.

The Fruit-Trees are wonderfully quick of growth, so that in six or seven years time from the Planting, a Man may bring an Orchard to bear in great plenty, from which he may make store of good Cyder, or distill great quantities of Brandy; for the Cyder is very strong, and yields abundance of in Spirit. Yet they have very few, that take any care at all for an Orchard; nay, many that have good Orchards, are so negligent of them, as to let them go to ruine, and expose the Trees to be torn, and barked by the Catle.

Peaches, Nectarines, and Apricocks, as well as Plums and Cherries, grow there upon Standard Trees. They commonly bear in three years from the Stone, and thrive so exceedingly, that they seem to have no need of Grafting or Inoculating, if any Body would be so good a Husband; and truly I never heard of any that did Graft either Plum, Nectarine, Peach or Apricock in that Country.

Peaches and Nectarines I believe to be Spontaneous somewhere or other on that Continent; for the *Indians* have, and ever had greater variety, and finer sorts of them than the *English.* The best sort of these cling to the Stone, and will not come off clear, which they call Plum-Nectarines, and Plum-Peaches, or Cling-Stones. Some of these are 12 or 13 Inches in the Girt. These sorts of Fruits are raised so easily there, that some good Husbands plant great Orchards of them, purposely for their Hogs; and others make a Drink of them, which they call Mobby, and either drink it as Cyder, or Distill it off for Brandy. This makes the best Spirit next to Grapes.

Grape-Vines of the *English Stock,* as well as those of their own Production, bear most abundantly, if they are suffered to run near the Ground, and increase very kindly by Slipping; yet very few have them at all in their Gardens, much less indeavour to improve them by cutting or laying. Indeed my Curiosity the last year, caused me to lay some of the white Muscadine, which came of a Stock removed thither from *England,* and they increased by this method to Admiration: I likewise set several

Slips of the cuttings of the same Vine, and the Major part of the Sets bore Grapes in perfection the first year, I remember I had seven full Bunches from one of them.

When a single Tree happens in clearing the Ground, to be left standing with a Vine upon it, open to the Sun and Air; that Vine generally produces as much as 4 or five others, that remain in the Woods. I have seen in this case, more Grapes upon one single Vine, than wou'd load a *London* Cart. And for all this, the People never remove any of them into their Gardens, but content themselves throughout the whole Country, with the Grapes they find thus wild; much less can they be expected to attempt the making of Wine or Brandy from the Grape.

The Almond, Pomgranate and Fig, ripen there very well, and yet there are not ten People in the Country, that have any of them in their Gardens, much less endeavour to preserve any of them for future spending, or to propagate them to make a Trade.

A Garden is no where sooner made than there, either for Fruits, or Flowers. Tulips from the Seed-flower the second year at farthest. All sorts of Herbs have there a perfection in their flavour, beyond what I ever tasted in a more *Northern* Climate. And yet they han't many Gardens in the Country, fit to bear that name.

All sorts of *English* Grain thrive, and increase there, as well as in any other part of the World as for Example, Wheat, Barley, Oats, Rye, Peas, Rape, &c. And yet they don't make a Trade of any of them. Their Peas indeed, are troubled with Wivels, which eat a Hole in them: But this Hole does neither dammage the Seed, nor make the Peas unfit for Boiling. And such as are sow'd late, and gather'd after *August,* are clear of that Inconvenience.

It is thought too much for the same Man, to make the Wheat, and grind it, bolt it, and bake it himself. And it is too great a charge for every Planter, who is willing to sow Barley, to build a Malt-House, and Brew-House too, or else to have no benefit of his Barley; nor will it answer, if he wou'd be at the Charge. These things can never be expected from a single Family: But if they had cohabitations, it might be thought worth attempting. Neither as they are now settled, can they find any certain Market for their other Grain, which if they had Towns, would be quite otherwise.

Rice has been tried there, and is found to grow as well, as in *Carolina*, or in any other part of the Earth: But it labours under the same inconvenience, the want of a Community, to husk and clean it; and after all, to take it off the Planters Hands.

I have related at large in the first Book, how Flax, Hemp, Cotton, and the Silk-Worms have thriven there, in the several essays made upon them; how formerly there was Incouragement given for making of Linnen, Silk, &c. and how all Persons not performing several things towards produceing of them were put under a Fine: But now all Incouragement of such things is taken away, and People are not only suffer'd to neglect them, but such as do go about them, are discouraged by their Governor, according to the Maxim laid down in the Memorials before recited.

Silk-grass is there spontaneous in many places, and may be cut several times in a Year. I need not mention what Advantage may be made of so useful a Plant, whose Fibres are as fine as Flax, and much stronger than Hemp. Mr. *Purchas* tells us, in his *Fourth Pilgrim*, Page 1786, That in the first Discovery of this part of the World, they presented Q. *Elizabeth* with a Piece of Grogram that had been made of it. And yet to this Day they make no manner of use of this Plant, no, not so much as the *Indians* did, before the *English* came among them, who then made their Baskets, Fishing Nets, and Lines, of it.

The Sheep increase well, and bear good Fleeces, but they generally are suffer'd to be torn off their Backs by Briers, and Bushes, instead of being shorn, or else are left rotting upon the Dunghil with their Skins.

Bees thrive there abundantly, and will very easily yield to the careful Huswife, two Crops of Honey in a Year, and besides lay up a Winter-store sufficient to preserve their Stocks.

The Beeves, when any Care is taken of them in the Winter, come to great Perfection. They have noble Marshes there, which, with the Charge of draining only, would make as fine

Pastures as any in the World; and yet there is not an hundred Acres of Marsh drained throughout the whole Country.

Hogs swarm like Vermine upon the Earth, and are often accounted such, insomuch that when an Inventory of any considerable Man's Estate is taken by the Executors, the Hogs are left out, and not listed in the Appraisement. The Hogs run where they list, and find their own Support in the Woods, without any Care of the Owner; and in many Plantations it is well, if the Proprietor can find and catch the Pigs, or any part of a Farrow, when they are young, to mark them; for if there be any markt in a Gang of Hogs, they determine the Property of the rest, because they seldom miss their Gangs; but as they are bred in Company, so they continue to the End.

The Woods produce great Variety of Incense and sweet Gums, which distil from several Trees; as also Trees bearing Honey, and Sugar, as before was mention'd: Yet there's no use made of any of them, either for Profit or Refreshment.

All sorts of Naval Stores may be produced there, as Pitch, Tar, Rosin, Turpentine, Plank, Timber, and all sorts of Masts, and Yards, besides Sails, Cordage, and Iron, and all these may be transported, by an easy Water-Carriage.

These and a Thousand other Advantages that Country naturally affords, which its Inhabitants make no manner of use of. They can see their Naval Stores daily benefit other People, who send thither to build Ships; while they, instead of promoting such Undertakings among themselves, and easing such as are willing to go upon them, allow them no manner of Encouragement, but rather the contrary. They receive no Benefit nor Refreshment from the Sweets, and precious things they have growing amongst them, but make use of the Industry of *England* for all such things.

What Advantages do they see the Neighbouring Plantations make of their Grain and Provisions, while they, who can produce them infinitely better, not only neglect the making a Trade thereof, but even a necessary Provision against an accidental Scarcity, contenting themselves with a supply of Food from hand to mouth, so that if it should please God, to send them an unseasonable Year, there wou'd not be found in the

Country, Provision sufficient to support the People for three Months extraordinary.

By reason of the unfortunate Method of the Settlement, and want of Cohabitation, they cannot make a beneficial use of their Flax, Hemp, Cotten, Silk, Silkgrass, and Wool, which might otherwise supply their Necessities, and leave the Produce of Tobacco to enrich them, when a gainful Market can be found for it.

Thus they depend altogether upon the Liberality of Nature, without endeavouring to improve its Gifts, by Art or Industry. They spunge upon the Blessings of a warm Sun, and a fruitful Soil, and almost grutch the Pains of gathering in the Bounties of the Earth. I should be asham'd to publish this slothful Indolence of my Countrymen, but that I hope it will rouse them out of their Lethargy, and excite them to make the most of all those happy Advantages which Nature has given them; and if it does this, I am sure they will have the Goodness to forgive me.

William Byrd II

(1674–1744)

Bibliographical Note. Byrd's published writings are collected in J. S. Bassett, ed., *The Writings of "Colonel William Byrd, of Westover in Virginia, Esqr"* (New York, 1901). Writings edited from manuscript are published in: W. K. Boyd, ed. *William Byrd's Histories of the Dividing Line Betwixt Virginia and North Carolina* (Raleigh, 1929); L. B. Wright and Marion Tinling, eds., *The Secret Diary of William Byrd of Westover, 1709–1712* (Richmond, 1941); Maude Woodfin, ed., *Another Secret Diary of William Byrd of Westover, 1739–1741, with Letters and Literary Exercises, 1696–1726* (Richmond, 1942). The text of the following selections follows Bassett's edition of *The Writings,* pp. 3–21, 44–47, 94–103, and the *Wright-Tinling* edition of *The Secret Diary,* pp. 457–469. The best biography of Byrd is R. C. Beatty, *William Byrd of Westover* (Boston, 1932); but it was written without knowledge of Byrd's *Secret History of the Dividing Line* (first published by Boyd) and of the Byrd diaries. The best sketch of Byrd as diarist is L. B. Wright and Marion Tinling, "William Byrd of Westover, an American Pepys," *South Atlantic Quarterly,* XXXIX (1940), 259–274.

from

THE HISTORY OF THE DIVIDING LINE: RUN IN THE YEAR 1728 (WRITTEN 1729)

[On the First Settlers of America]

Before I enter upon the Journal of the Line between Virginia and North Carolina, it will be necessary to clear the way to it, by shewing how the other British Colonies on the Main have, one after the other, been carved out of Virginia, by Grants from his Majesty's Royal Predecessors. All that part of the Northern American Continent now under the Dominion of the King of Great Britain, and Stretching quite as far as the Cape of Florida, went *at first under the General Name of Virginia.*

The only Distinction, in those early Days, was, that all the Coast to the Southward of Chesapeake Bay was called South Virginia, and all to the Northward of it, North Virginia.

The first Settlement of this fine Country was owing to that great Ornament of the British Nation, Sir Walter Raleigh, who obtained a Grant thereof from Queen Elizabeth of ever-glorious Memory, by Letters Patent, dated March the 25th, 1584.

But whether that Gentleman ever made a Voyage thither himself is uncertain; because those who have favour'd the Public with an Account of His Life mention nothing of it. However, thus much may be depended on, that Sir Walter invited sundry persons of Distinction to Share in his Charter, and join their Purses with his in the laudable project of fitting out a Colony to Virginia.

Accordingly, 2 Ships were Sent away that very Year, under the Command of his good Friends Amidas and Barlow, to take possession of the Country in the Name of his Roial Mistress, the Queen of England.

These worthy Commanders, for the advantage of the Trade Winds, shaped their Course first to the Charibbe Islands, thence stretching away by the Gulph of Florida, dropt Anchor not far from Roanoak Inlet. They ventured ashoar near that place upon an Island now called Colleton island, where they set up the Arms of England, and Claimed the Adjacent Country in Right of their Sovereign Lady, the Queen; and this Ceremony being duly performed, they kindly invited the neighboring Indians to traffick with them.

These poor people at first approacht the English with great Caution, having heard much of the Treachery of the Spaniards, and not knowing but these Strangers might be as treacherous as they. But, at length, discovering a kind of good nature in their looks, they ventured to draw near, and barter their Skins and Furs, for the Bawbles and Trinkets of the English.

These first Adventurers made a very profitable Voyage, raising at least a Thousand per cent. upon their Cargo. Amongst other Indian Commodities, they brought over Some of that bewitching Vegetable, Tobacco. And this being the first that ever came to England Sir Walter thought he could do no less than make a present of Some of the brightest of it to His Roial Mistress, for her own Smoaking.

The Queen graciously accepted of it, but finding her Stomach sicken after two or three Whiffs, it was presently whispered by the earl of Leicester's Faction, that Sir Walter had certainly Poison'd Her. But Her Majesty soon recovering her Disorder, obliged the Countess of Nottingham and all her Maids to Smoak a whole Pipe out amongst them.

As it happen'd some Ages before to be the fashion to Santer to the Holy Land, and go upon other Quixot Adventures, so it was now grown the Humour to take a Trip to America. The Spaniards had lately discovered Rich Mines in their Part of the West Indies, which made their Maritime Neighbours eager to do so too. This Modish Frenzy being still more In-flam'd by the Charming Account given of Virginia, by the first Adventurers, made many fond of removeing to such a Paradise.

Happy was he, and still happier She, that cou'd get them-selves transported, fondly expecting their Coarsest Utensils, in that happy place, would be of Massy Silver.

This made it easy for the Company to procure as many Volunteers as they wanted for their new Colony; but, like most other Undertakers who have no Assistance from the Public, they Starved the Design by too much Frugality; for, unwilling to Launch out at first into too much Expense, they Ship't off but few People at a Time, and Those but Scantily provided. The Adventurers were, besides, Idle and extravagant, and expected they might live without work in so plentiful a Country.

These Wretches were set Ashoar not far from Roanoak Inlet, but by some fatal disagreement, or Laziness, were either Starved or cut to Pieces by the Indians.

Several repeated Misadventures of this kind did, for some time, allay the Itch of Sailing to this New World; but the Dis-temper broke out again about the Year 1606. Then it happened that the Earl of Southampton and several other Persons, eminent for their Quality and Estates, were invited into the Company, who apply'd themselves once more to People the then almost abandon'd Colony. For this purpose they embarkt about an Hundred men, most of them Riprobates of good Familys, and related to some of the company, who were men of Quality and Fortune.

The Ships that carried them made a Shift to find a more direct way to Virginia, and ventured thro the Capes into the Bay of Chesapeak. The same Night they came to an Anchor at the Mouth of Powatan, the same as James River, where they built a Small Fort at a Place call'd Point Comfort.

This Settlement stood its ground from that time forward in spite of all the Blunders and Disagreement of the first Adventurers, and the many Calamitys that befel the Colony afterwards.

The six gentlemen who were first named of the company by the crown, and who were empowered to choose an annual President from among themselves, were always engaged in Factions and Quarrels, while the rest detested Work more than Famine. At this rate the Colony must have come to nothing, had it not been for the vigilance and Bravery of Capt. Smith, who struck a Terrour into all the Indians round about. This Gentleman took some pains to perswade the men to plant Indian corn, but they lookt upon all Labor as a Curse. They chose rather to depend upon the Musty Provisions that were sent from England: and when they fail'd they were forct to take more pains to Seek for Wild Fruits in the Woods, than they would have taken in tilling the Ground. Besides, this Exposd them to be knockt on the head by the Indians, and gave them Fluxes into the Bargain, which thind the Plantation very much. To Supply this mortality, they were reinforct the year following with a greater number of People, amongst which were fewer Gentlemen and more Labourers, who, however, took care not to kill themselves with Work.

These found the First Adventurers in a very starving condition, but relievd their wants with the fresh Supply they brought with them. From Kiquotan they extended themselves as far as James-Town, where like true Englishmen, they built a Church that cost no more than Fifty Pounds, and a Tavern that cost Five hundred.

They had now made peace with the Indians, but there was one thing wanting to make that peace lasting. The Natives coud, by no means, perswade themselves that the English were heartily their Friends, so long as they disdained to intermarry with them. And, in earnest, had the English consulted their own Security and the good of the Colony—Had they intended either to Civilize or Convert these Gentiles, they would have brought their Stomachs to embrace this prudent Alliance.

The Indians are generally tall and well-proportion'd, which may make full Amends for the Darkness of their Complexions. Add to this, that they are healthy & Strong, with Constitutions untainted by Lewdness, and not enfeebled by Luxury. Besides, Morals and all considered, I cant think the Indians were much greater Heathens than the first Adventurers, who, had they been good Christians, would have had the Charity to take this only method of converting the Natives to Christianity. For, after all that can be said, a sprightly Lover is the most prevailing Missionary that can be sent amongst these, or any other Infidels.

Besides, the poor Indians would have had less reason to Complain that the English took away their Land, if they had received it by way of Portion with their Daughters. Had such Affinities been contracted in the Beginning, how much Bloodshed had been prevented, and how populous would the Country have been, and, consequently, how considerable? Nor wou'd the Shade of the Skin have been any reproach at this day; for if a Moor may be washt white in 3 Generations, Surely an Indian might have been blancht in two.

The French, for their Parts, have not been so Squeamish in Canada, who upon Trial find abundance of Attraction in the Indians. Their late Grand Monarch thought it not below even the Dignity of a Frenchman to become one flesh with this People, and therefore Ordered 100 Livres for any of his Subjects, Man or Woman, that would intermarry with a Native.

By this piece of Policy we find the French Interest very much Strengthen'd amongst the Savages, and their Religion, such as it is, propagated just as far as their Love. And I heartily wish this well-concerted Scheme don't hereafter give the French an Advantage over his Majesty's good Subjects on the Northern Continent of America.

About the same time New England was pared off from Virginia by Letters Patent, bearing date April the 10th, 1608.[1] Several Gentlemen of the Town and Neighborhood of Plymouth obtain'd this Grant, with the Ld Chief Justice Popham at their Head.

Their Bounds were Specified to extend from 38 to 45 Degrees of Northern Latitude, with a Breadth of one Hundred Miles from the Sea Shore. The first 14 Years, this Company encounter'd many Difficulties, and lost many men, tho' far from being discouraged, they sent over Numerous Recruits of Presbyterians, every year, who for all that, had much ado to stand their Ground, with all their Fighting and Praying.

But about the year 1620, a Large Swarm of Dissenters fled thither from the Severities of their Stepmother, the Church. These Saints conceiving the same Aversion to the Copper Complexion of the Natives, with that of the first Adventurers to Virginia, would, on no Terms, contract Alliances with them, afraid perhaps, like the Jews of Old, lest they might be drawn into Idolatry by those Strange Women.

Whatever disgusted them I can't say, but this false delicacy creating in the Indians a Jealousy that the English were ill affected towards them, was the Cause that many of them were cut off, and the rest Exposed to various Distresses.

This Reinforcement was landed not far from Cape Codd, where, for their greater Security they built a Fort, and near it a Small Town, which in Honour of the Proprietors, was call'd New Plymouth. But they Still had many discouragements to Struggle with, tho' by being well Supported from Home, they by Degrees Triumph't over them all.

Their Brethren, after this, flockt over so fast, that in a few Years they extended the Settlement one hundred Miles along the Coast, including Rhode Island and Martha's Vineyard.

Thus the Colony throve apace, and was throng'd with large

---

[1] The charters of the London and the Plymouth companies were both dated April 10, 1606.—*Bassett*.

Detachments of Independents and Presbyterians, who thought themsclvcs persecuted at home.

Tho' these People may be ridiculd for some Pharisaical Particularitys in their Worship and Behaviour, yet they were very useful Subjects, as being Frugal and Industrious, giving no Scandal or bad Example, at least by any Open and Public Vices. By which excellent Qualities they had much the Advantage of the Southern Colony, who thought their being Members of the Establish't Church sufficient to Sanctifie very loose and Profligate Morals. For this Reason New England improved much faster than Virginia, and in Seven or Eight Years New Plimouth, like Switzerland, seemed too Narrow a Territory for its Inhabitants.

For this Reason, several Gentlcmen of Fortune purchas'd of the Company that Canton of New England now called Massachuset colony. And King James confirm'd the Purchase by his Royal Charter, dated March the 4th, 1628. In lcss than 2 years after, above 1000 of the Puritanical Sect removed thither with considerable Effects, and these were followed by such Crowds, that a Proclamation was issued in England, forbidding any more of his Majesty's Subjects to be Shipt off. But this had the usual Effect of things forbidden, and serv'd only to make the Wilful Independcnts flock over the faster. And about this time it was that Messrs. Hampden and Pym, and (some say) Oliver Cromwell, to show how little they valued the King's Authority, took a Trip to New England.

In the Year 1630, the famous City of Boston was built, in a Commodious Situation for Trade and Navigation, the same bcing on a Peninsula at the Bottom of Massachuset Bay.

This Town is now the most considerable of any on the British Continent, containing at least 8,000 houses and 40,000 Inhabitants. The Trade it drives, is very great to Europe, and to every Part of the West Indies, having near 1,000 Ships and lesser Vessels belonging to it.

Altho the Extent of the Massachuset Colony reach't near one Hundred and Ten Miles in Length, and half as much in Breadth, yet many of its Inhabitants, thinking they wanted Elbow-room, quitted their Old Seats in the Year 1636, and formed 2 New Colonies: that of Connecticut and New Haven.

These King Charles the 2d erected into one Government in 1664,[2] and gave them many Valuable Privileges, and among the rest, that of chusing their own Governors. The Extent of these united Colonies may be about Seventy Miles long and fifty broad.

Besides these several Settlements, there Sprang up still another, a little more Northerly, called New Hampshire. But that consisting of no more than two Counties, and not being in condition to Support the Charge of a Distinct Government, was glad to be incorporated with that of Massachuset, but upon Condition, however, of being Named in all Public Acts, for fear of being quite lost and forgot in the Coalition.

In like manner New Plymouth joyn'd itself to Massachuset, except only Rhode Island, which, tho' of small Extent, got itself erected into a Separate government by a Charter from King Charles the 2d, soon after the Restoration, and continues so to this day.

These Governments all continued in Possession of their Respective Rights and Privileges till the Year 1683, when that of Massachuset was made Void in England by a Quo Warranto.

In Consequence of which the King was pleased to name Sir Edmund Andros His first Governor of that Colony. This Gentleman, it seems, ruled them with a Rod of Iron till the Revolution, when they laid unhallowed Hands upon Him, and sent him Prisoner to England.

This undutiful proceeding met with an easy forgiveness at that happy Juncture. King William and his Royal Consort were not only pleasd to overlook this Indignity offered to their Governor, but being made sensible how unfairly their Charter had been taken away, most graciously granted them a new one.

By this some new Franchises were given them, as an Equivalent for those of Coining Money and Electing a governour, which were taken away. However, the other Colonies of Connecticut and Rhode Island had the luck to remain in Possession of their Original Charters, which to this Day have never been calld in Question.

The next Country dismembered from Virginia was New

---

[2] 1662.—*Bassett.*

Scotland, claimd by the Crown of England in Virtue of the first Discovery by Sebastian Cabot. By Colour of this Title, King James the first granted it to Sir William Alexander by Patent, dated September the 10th, 1621.

But this Patentee never sending any Colony thither, and the French believing it very Convenient for them, obtained a Surrender of it from their good Friend and Ally, king Charles the 2d, by the Treaty of Breda. And, to show their gratitude, they stirred up the Indians soon after to annoy their Neighbours of New England. Murders happened continually to his Majesty's Subjects by their Means, till Sr William Phipps took their Town of Port Royal, in the year 1690. But as the English are better at taking than keeping Strong Places, the French retook it soon, and remaind Masters of it till 1710, when General Nicholson wrested it, once more, out of their Hands.

Afterwards the Queen of Great Britain's Right to it was recognized and confirmed by the treaty of Utrecht.

Another Limb lopt off from Virginia was New York, which the Dutch seized very unfairly, on pretence of having Purchasd it from Captain Hudson, the first Discoverer. Nor was their way of taking Possession of it a whit more justifiable than their pretended Title.

Their West India Company tampered with some worthy English Skippers (who had contracted with a Swarm of English Dissenters to transport them to Hudson river) by no means to land them there, but to carry 'em some leagues more northerly.

This Dutch Finesse took Exactly, and gave the Company time soon after to seize the Hudson River for themselves. But Sr Samuel Argall, then governor of Virginia, understanding how the King's Subjects had been abused by these Republicans, marcht thither with a good Force, and obligd them to renounce all pretensions to that Country. The worst of it was, the Knight depended on their Parole to Ship themselves to Brasile, but took no measures to make this Slippery People as good as their Word.

No sooner was the good Governor retired, but the honest Dutch began to build Forts and strengthen themselves in their ill-gotten Possessions; nor did any of the King's Liege People take the trouble to drive these Intruders thence. The Civil War in England, And the Confusions it brought forth, allowed no Leisure to such distant Considerations. Tho tis strange that the Protector, who neg leced no Occasion to mortify the Dutch, did not afterwards call them to Account for this breach of Faith. However, after the Restoration, the King sent a Squadron of his Ships of War, under the Command of Sir Robert Carr, and reduced that Province to his Obedience.

Some time after, His Majesty was Pleasd to grant that Country to his Royal Highness, the Duke of York, by Letters Patent, dated March the 12th, 1664. But to shew the Modesty of the Dutch to the Life, tho they had no Shaddow of Right to New York, yet they demanded Surinam, a more valuable Country, as an Equivalent for it, and our able Ministers at that time had the Generosity to give it them.

But what wounded Virginia deepest was the cutting off MARYLAND from it, by Charter from King Charles the 1st, to sir George Calvert, afterwards Ld Baltimore, bearing date the 20th of June, 1632. The Truth of it is, it begat much Speculation in those days, how it came about that a good Protestant King should bestow so bountiful a Grant upon a Zealous Roman catholic. But 'tis probable it was one fatal Instance amongst many other of his Majesty's complaisance to the Queen.

However that happened, 'tis certain this Province afterwards provd a Commodious Retreat for Persons of that Communion. The Memory of the Gun-Powder-Treason-Plot was Still fresh in every body's mind, and made England too hot for Papists to live in, without danger of being burnt with the Pope, every 5th of November; for which reason Legions of them transplanted themselves to Maryland in Order to be Safe, as well from the Insolence of the Populace as the Rigour of the Government.

Not only the Gun-Powder-Treason, but every other Plot, both pretended and real, that has been trump't up in England ever Since, has helpt to People his Lordship's Propriety.

But what has provd most Serviceable to it was the Grand Rebellion against King Charles the 1st, when every thing that bore the least tokens of Popery was sure to be demolisht, and every man that Profest it was in Jeopardy of Suffering the same kind of Martyrdom the Romish Priests do in Sweden.

Soon after the Reduction of New York, the Duke was pleasd to grant out of it all that Tract of Land included between Hudson and Delaware Rivers, to the Lord Berkley and Sir George Carteret, by deed dated June the 24th, 1664. And when these Grantees came to make Partition of this Territory, His Lordsp's Moiety was calld West Jersey, and that to Sir George, East Jersey.

But before the Date of this Grant, the Swedes began to gain Footing in part of that Country; tho, after they saw the Fate of New York, they were glad to Submit to the King of England, on the easy Terms of remaining in their Possessions, and rendering a Moderate Quit-rent. Their Posterity continue there to this Day, and think their Lot cast in a much fairer Land than Dalicarlia.[3]

The Proprietors of New Jersey, finding more Trouble than Profit in their new Dominions, made over their Right to several other Persons, who obtain a fresh Grant from his Royal Highness, dated March 14th, 1682.

Several of the Grantees, being Quakers and Anababtists, faild not to encourage many of their own Perswasion to remove to this Peaceful Region, Amongst them were a Swarm of Scots Quakers, who were not tolerated to exercise the Gifts of the Spirit in their own Country.

Besides the hopes of being Safe from Persecution in this Retreat, the New Proprietors inveigled many over by this tempting Account of the Country: that it was a Place free from those 3 great Scourges of Mankind, Priests, Lawyers, and Physicians. Nor did they tell a Word of a Lye, for the People were yet too poor to maintain these Learned Gentlemen, who, every where, love to be paid well for what they do; and, like the Jews, cant breathe in a Climate where nothing is to be got.

The Jerseys continued under the Government of these Proprietors till the Year 1702, when they made a formal Surrender of the Dominion to the Queen, reserving however the Property of the Soil to themselves. So soon as the Bounds of New Jersey came to be distinctly laid off, it appeared that there was still a Narrow Slipe of Land, lying betwixt that Colony

---

[3] Name of a former province of Sweden.—*Bassett.*

and Maryland. Of this, William Penn, a Man of much Worldly Wisdom, and some Eminence among the Quakers, got early Notice, and, by the Credit he had with the Duke of York, obtained a Patent for it, Dated March the 4th, 1680.

It was a little Surprising to some People how a Quaker should be so much in the good Graces of a Popish Prince; tho, after all, it may be pretty well Accounted for. This Ingenious Person had not be bred a Quaker; but, in his Earlier days, had been a Man of Pleasure about the Town. He had a beautiful form and very taking Address, which made him Successful with the Ladies, and Particularly with a Mistress of the Duke of Monmouth. By this Gentlewoman he had a Daughter, who had Beauty enough to raise her to be a Dutchess, and continued to be a Toast full 30 Years.[4]

But this Amour had like to have brought our Fine Gentleman in Danger of a Duell, had he not discreetly shelterd himself under this peaceable Perswasion. Besides, his Father having been a Flag-Officer in the Navy, while the Duke of York was Lord High Admiral, might recommend the Son to his Favour. This piece of secret History I thought proper to mention, to wipe off the Suspicion of his having been Popishly inclind.

This Gentleman's first Grant confind Him within pretty Narrow Bounds, giving him only that Portion of Land which contains Buckingham, Philadelphia and Chester Counties. But to get these Bounds a little extended, He pusht His Interest still further with His Royal Highness, and obtain a fresh Grant of the three Lower Counties, called New-Castle, Kent and Sussex, which still remaind within the New York Patent, and had been luckily left out of the Grant of New Jersey.

The Six Counties being thus incorporated, the Proprietor dignifyd the whole with the Name of Pensilvania.

The Quakers flockt over to this Country in Shoals, being averse to go to Heaven the same way with the Bishops. Amongst them were not a few of good Substance, who went Vigorously upon every kind of Improvement; and thus much I may truly say in their Praise, that by Diligence and Frugality, For which

---

[4] This piece of London gossip seems not to have been recorded by any other contemporary.—*Bassett.*

this Harmless Sect is remarkable, and by haveing no Vices but such as are Private, they have in a few Years made Pensilvania a very fine Country.

The Truth is, they have observed exact Justice with all the Natives that border upon them; they have purchasd all their Lands from the Indians; and tho they paid but a Trifle for them, it has procured them the Credit of being more righteous than their Neighbours. They have likewise had the Prudence to treat them kindly upon all Occasions, which has savd them from many Wars and Massacres wherein the other Colonies have been indiscreetly involved. The Truth of it is, a People whose Principles forbid them to draw the Carnal Sword, were in the Right to give no Provocation.

[On the People of the North Carolina Frontier]

[March 10.] The Sabbath happen'd very opportunely to give some ease to our jaded People, who rested religiously from every work, but that of cooking the Kettle. We observed very few cornfields in our Walks, and those very small, which seem'd the Stranger to us, because we could see no other Tokens of Husbandry or Improvement. But, upon further Inquiry, we were given to understand People only made Corn for themselves and not for their Stocks, which know very well how to get their own Living.

Both Cattle and Hogs ramble in the Neighbouring Marshes and Swamps, where they maintain themselves the whole Winter long, and are not fetch'd home till the Spring. Thus these Indolent Wretches, during one half of the Year, lose the Advantage of the Milk of their cattle, as well as their Dung, and many of the poor Creatures perish in the Mire, into the Bargain, by this ill Management.

Some, who pique themselves more upon Industry than their Neighbours, will, now and then, in compliment to their Cattle, cut down a Tree whose Limbs are loaden with the Moss aforemention'd. The trouble wou'd be too great to Climb the Tree in order to gather this Provender, but the Shortest way (which in this Country is always counted the best) is to fell it, just like the Lazy Indians, who do the same by such

Trees as bear fruit, and so make one Harvest for all. By this bad
Husbandry Milk is so Scarce, in the Winter Season, that were
a Big-belly'd Woman to long for it, She would lose her Longing. And, in truth, I believe this is often the Case, and at the
same time a very good reason why so many People in this
Province are markt with a Custard Complexion.

The only Business here is raising of Hogs, which is manag'd
with the least Trouble, and affords the Diet they are most fond
of. The Truth of it is, the Inhabitants of N Carolina devour so
much Swine's flesh, that it fills them full of gross Humours. For
want too of a constant Supply of Salt, they are commonly
obliged to eat it Fresh, and that begets the highest taint of
Scurvy. Thus, whenever a Severe Cold happens to Constitutions
thus Vitiated, tis apt to improve into the Yaws, called there
very justly the country-Distemper. This has all the Symptoms of
the Pox, with this Aggravation, that no Preparation of Mercury
will touch it. First it seizes the Throat, next the Palate, and
lastly shews its spite to the poor Nose, of which tis apt in a
small time treacherously to undermine the Foundation.

This Calamity is so common and familiar here, that it
ceases to be a Scandal, and in the disputes that happen about
Beauty, the Noses have in some Companies much ádo to carry
it. Nay, tis said that once, after three good Pork years, a Motion had like to have been made in the House of Burgesses, that
a Man with a Nose shou'd be incapable of holding any Place of
Profit in the Province; which Extraordinary Motion could never
have been intended without Some Hopes of a Majority.

Thus, considering the foul and pernicious Effects of Eating
Swine's Flesh in a hot Country, it was wisely forbidden and
made an Abomination to the Jews, who liv'd much in the same
Latitude with Carolina.

11. We ordered the Surveyors early to their Business, who
were blesst with pretty dry Grounds for three Miles together.
But they paid dear for it in the next two, consisting of one continued frightfull Pocoson, which no Creatures but those of the
amphibious kind ever had ventur'd into before.

This filthy Quagmire did in earnest put the Men's Courage
to a Tryal, and tho' I can't say it made them lose their Patience,

WILLIAM BYRD II 531

yet they lost their Humour for Joking. They kept their Gravity like so many Spaniards, so that a Man might then have taken his Opportunity to plunge up to the Chin, without Danger of being laught at. However, this unusual composure of countenance could not fairly be call'd complaining.

Their Day's-Work ended at the Mouth of Northern's Creek, which empties itself into N W River; tho' we chose to Quarter a little higher up the River, near Mossy Point. This we did for the Convenience of an Old house to Shelter our Persons and Baggage from the rain, which threaten'd us hard. We judg'd the thing right, for there fell an heavy shower in the Night, that drove the most hardy of us into the House. Tho' indeed, our case was not much mended by retreating thither, because that Tenement having not long before been us'd as a Pork-Store, the Moisture of the Air dissolv'd the Salt that lay Scatter'd on the Floor, and made it as wet within Doors as without. However, the Swamps and Marshes we were lately accustom'd to had made such Beavers and Otters of us that Nobody caught the least cold.

We had encampt so early, that we found time in the Evening to walk near half a Mile into the Woods. There we came pon a Family of Mulattoes, that call'd themselvs free, tho' by the Shyness of the Master of the House, who took care to keep least in Sight, their Freedom seem'd a little Doubtful. It is certain many Slaves Shelter themselves in this Obscure Part of the World, nor will any of their righteous Neighbours discover them. On the Contrary, they find their Account in Settling such Fugitives on some out-of-the-way-corner of their Land, to raise Stocks for a mean and inconsiderable Share, well knowing their Condition makes it necessary for them to Submit to any Terms.

Nor were these worthy Borderers content to Shelter Runaway Slaves, but Debtors and Criminals have often met with the like Indulgence. But if the Government of North Carolina has encourag'd this unneighbourly Policy in order to increase their People, it is no more than what Ancient Rome did before them, which was made a City of Refuge for all Debtors and Fugitives, and from that wretched Beginning grew up in time to be Mistress of a great Part of the World. And, considering how Fortune delights in bringing great things out of Small, who knows but Carolina may, one time or other, come to be the Seat of some other great Empire?

[On the Indians and Relations with Them]

[April 7.] The Next day being Sunday, we order'd Notice to be sent to all the Neighbourhood that there wou'd be a Sermon at this Place, and an Opportunity of Christening their Children. But the Likelihood of Rain got the better of their Devotion, and what perhaps, Might Still be a Stronger motive of their Curiosity. In the Morning we dispatcht a runner to the Nottoway Town, to let the Indians know we intended them a Visit that Evening, and our honest Landlord was so kind as to be our Pilot thither, being about 4 Miles from his House.

Accordingly in the Afternoon we marcht in good Order to the Town, where the Female Scouts, station'd on an Eminence for that purpose, had no sooner spy'd us, but they gave Notice of our Approach to their Fellow-Citizens by continual Whoops and Cries, which cou'd not possibly have been more dismal at the Sight of their most implacable Enemys.

This Signal Assembled all their Great Men, who receiv'd us in a Body, and conducted us into the Fort. This Fort was a Square Piece of Ground, inclos'd with Substantial Puncheons, or Strong Palisades, about ten feet high, and leaning a little outwards, to make a Scalade more difficult.

Each side of the Square might be about 100 Yards long, with Loop-holes at proper Distances, through which they may fire upon the Enemy.

Within this Inclosure we found Bark Cabanes Sufficient to lodge all their people, in Case they should be obliged to retire thither. These Cabanes are no other but Close Arbours made of Saplings, arched at the top, and cover'd so well with Bark as to be proof against all Weather. The fire is made in the Middle, according to the Hibernian Fashion, the Smoak whereof finds no other Vent but at the Door, and so keeps the whole family Warm, at the Expense both of their Eyes and Complexion.

The Indians have no standing Furniture in their Cabanes but Hurdles to repose their Persons upon, which they cover with Mats or Deer-skins. We were conducted to the best Appartments in the Fort, which just before had been made ready for our Reception, and adorn'd with new Mats, that were sweet and clean.

The Young Men had Painted themselves in a Hideous Manner, not so much for Ornament as Terror. In that frightful Equipage they entertain'd us with Sundry War-Dances, wherein they endeavour'd to look as formidable as possible. The Instrument they danct to was an Indian-drum, that is, a large Gourd with a Skin bract tort over the Mouth of it. The Dancers all Sang to this Musick, keeping exact Time with their feet, while their Heads and Arms were screw'd into a thousand Menacing Postures.

Upon this occasion the Ladies had array'd themselves in all their finery. They were Wrapt in their Red and Blue Match-Coats, thrown so Negligently about them, that their Mehogony Skins appcar'd in Several Parts, like the Lacedaemonian Damsels of Old. Their Hair was breeded with white and Blue Peak, and hung gracefully in a large Roll upon their Shoulders.

This peak Consists of Small Cylinders cut out of a Conque-Shell, drill'd through and Strung like Beads. It serves them both for Money and Jewels, the Blue being of much greater Value than the White, for the same reason that Ethiopian Mistresses in France are dearer than French, because they are more Scarce. The Women wear Necklaces and Bracelets of these precious Materials, when they have a mind to appear lovely. Tho' their complexions be a little Sad-Colour'd, yet their Shapes are very Strait and well proportion'd. Their Faces are Seldom handsome, yet they have an Air of Innocence and Bashfulness, that with a little less dirt wou'd not fail to make them desirable. Such Charms might have had their full Effect upon Men who had been so long deprived of female conversation, but that the whole Winter's Soil was so crusted on the Skins of those dark Angels, that it requir'd a very strong Appetite to approach them. The Bear's oyl, with which they anoint their Persons all over, makes their skins Soft, and at the Same time protects them from every Species of Vermin that use to be troublesome to other uncleanly People.

We were unluckily so many, that they cou'd not well make

us the Complement of Bed-fellows, according to the Indian Rules of Hospitality, tho' a grave Matron whisper'd one of the Commissioners very civily in the Ear, that if her Daughter had been but one year Older, she should have been at his Devotion.

It is by no means a loss of Reputation among the Indians, for Damsels that are Single to have Intrigues with the Men; on the contrary, they count it an Argument of Superior Merit to be liked by a great Number of Gallants. However, like the Ladys that Game they are a little Mercenary in their Amours, and seldom bestow their Favours out of Stark Love and Kindness. But after these Women have once appropriated their Charms by Marriage, they are from thenceforth faithful to their Vows, and will hardly ever be tempted by an Agreeable Gallant, or be provokt by a Brutal or even by a fumbling Husband to go astray.

The little Work that is done among the Indians is done by the poor Women, while the men are quite idle, or at most employ'd only in the Gentlemanly Diversions of Hunting and Fishing.

In this, as well as in their Wars, they now use nothing but Fire-arms, which they purchase of the English for Skins. Bows and Arrows are grown into disuse, except only amongst their Boys. Nor is it ill Policy, but on the contrary very prudent, thus to furnish the Indians with Fire-Arms, because it makes them depend entirely upon the English, not only for their Trade, but even for their subsistence. Besides, they were really able to do more mischief, while they made use of Arrows, of which they wou'd let Silently fly Several in a Minute with Wonderful Dexterity, whereas now they hardly ever discharge their Fire-locks more than once, which they insidiously do from behind a Tree, and then retire as nimbly as the Dutch Horse us'd to do now and then formerly in Flanders.

We put the Indians to no expense, but only of a little Corn for our Horses, for which in Gratitude we cheer'd their hearts with what Rum we had left, which they love better than they do their Wives and Children.

Tho' these Indians dwell among the English, and see in what Plenty a little Industry enables them to live, yet they chuse to continue in their Stupid Idleness, and to Suffer all the

Inconveniences of Dirt, Cold, and Want, rather than to disturb their heads With care, or defile their Hands with labour.

The whole Number of People belonging to the Notoway Town, if you include Women and Children, amount to about 200. These are the only Indians of any consequence now remaining within the Limits of Virginia. The rest are either removed, or dwindled to a very inconsiderable number, either by destroying one another, or else by the Small-Pox and other Diseases. Tho' nothing has been so fatal to them as their ungovernable Passion for Rum, with which, I am sorry to say it, they have been but too liberally supply'd by the English that live near them.

And here I must lament the bad Success Mr. Boyle's Charity[5] has hitherto had towards converting any of these poor Heathens to Christianity. Many children of our Neighbouring Indians have been brought up in the College of William and Mary. They have been taught to read and write, and have been carefully Instructed in the Principles of the Christian Religion, till they came to be men. Yet after they return'd home, instead of civilizeing and converting the rest, they have immediately Relapt into Infidelity and Barbarism themselves.

And some of them too have made the worst use of the Knowledge they acquir'd among the English, by employing it against their Benefactors. Besides, as they unhappily forget all the good they learn, and remember the Ill, they are apt to be more vicious and disorderly than the rest of their Countrymen.

I ought not to quit this Subject without doing Justice to the great Prudence of Colo Spotswood in this Affair. That Gentleman was lieut Governor of Virginia when Carolina was engaged in a bloody War with the Indians. At that critical Time it was thought expedient to keep a Watchful Eye upon our Tributary Savages, who we knew had nothing to keep them to their Duty but their Fears.

Then it was that he demanded of each Nation a Competent Number of their great Men's Children to be sent to the College, where they serv'd as so many Hostages for the

---

[5] Money left by the scientist Robert Boyle was used to support a foundation in Indian education at the College of William and Mary.

good Behaviour of the Rest, and at the same time were themselves principled in the Christian Religion. He also Plac'd a School-Master among the Saponi Indians, at the salary of Fifty Pounds P Annum, to instruct their Children. The Person that undertook that Charitable work was Mr. Charles Griffin, a Man of good Family, who by the Innocence of his Life, and the Sweetness of his Temper, was perfectly well qualify'd for that pious undertaking. Besides, he had so much the Secret of mixing Pleasure with instruction, that he had not a Scholar, who did not love him affectionately.

Such Talents must needs have been blest with a Proportionable Success, had he not been unluckily remov'd to the College, by which he left the good work he had begun unfinisht. In short, all the Pains he had undertaken among the Infidels had no other Effect but to make them something cleanlier than other Indians are.

The Care Colo Spotswood took to tincture the Indian Children with Christianity produc'd the following Epigram, which was not publisht during his Administration, for fear it might then have lookt like flattery.

> Long has the Furious Priest assay'd in Vain,
> With Sword and Faggot, Infidels to gain,
> But now the Milder Soldier wisely tryes
> By Gentler Methods to unveil their Eyes.
> Wonders apart, he knew 'twere vain t'engage
> The fix'd Preventions of Misguided Age.
> With fairer Hopes he forms the Indian Youth
> To early Manners, Probity and Truth.
> The Lyon's whelp thus on the Lybian Shore
> Is tam'd and Gentled by the Artful Moor,
> Not the Grim Sire, inured to Blood before.

I am sorry I can't give a Better Account of the State of the Poor Indians with respect to Christianity, altho' a great deal of Pains has been and still continues to be taken with them. For my Part, I must be of Opinion, as I hinted before, that there is but one way of Converting these poor Infidels, and reclaiming them from Barbarity, and that is, Charitably to intermarry with them, according to the Modern Policy of the most Christian King in Canada and Louisiana.

Had the English done this at the first Settlement of the Colony, the Infidelity of the Indians had been worn out at this Day, with their Dark Complexions, and the Country had swarm'd with People more than it does with Insects.

It was certainly an unreasonable Nicety, that prevented their entering into so good-Natur'd an Alliance. All Nations of men have the same Natural Dignity, and we all know that very bright Talents may be lodg'd under a very dark Skin. The principal Difference between one People and another proceeds only from the Different Opportunities of Improvement.

The Indians by no means want understanding, and are in their Figure tall and well-proportion'd. Even their copper-colour'd Complexion wou'd admit of Blanching, if not in the first, at the farthest in the Second Generation.

I may safely venture to say, the Indian Women would have made altogether as Honest Wives for the first Planters, as the Damsels they us'd to purchase from aboard the Ships. It is Strange, therefore, that any good Christian Shou'd have refused a wholesome, Straight Bed-fellow, when he might have had so fair a Portion with her, as the Merit of saving her Soul.

8. We rested on our clean Mats very comfortably, tho' alone, and the next Morning went to the Toilet of some of the Indian Ladys, where, what with the Charms of their Persons and the Smoak of their Apartments, we were almost blinded. They offer'd to give us Silk-Grass Baskets of their own making, which we Modestly refused, knowing that an Indian present, like that of a Nun, is a Liberality put out to Interest, and a Bribe plac'd to the greatest Advantage.

Our Chaplain observ'd with concern, that the Ruffles of Some of our Fellow Travellers were a little discolour'd with pochoon, wherewith the good Man had been told those Ladies us'd to improve their invisible charms.

About 10 a Clock we marched out of Town in good order, & the War Captains saluted us with a Volley of Small-Arms. From thence we proceeded over Black-water Bridge to colo' Henry Harrisons, where we congratulated each other upon our Return into Christendom.

from

THE SECRET DIARY
OF WILLIAM BYRD
OF WESTOVER, 1709–1712*

[*Four Weeks in the Life of a Virginia Gentleman*]

[December 23, 1711]. I rose about 7 o'clock and read a chapter in Hebrew and some Greek in Homer. I said my prayers and ate boiled milk for breakfast. I wrote out a chronology of the Bible which the Governor lent me and did not go to church, God forgive me. About 12 o'clock Dr. Cocke came to me in order to go to Queen's Creek and we got on horseback about one and rode there and [found] them pretty well. The weather was cold and had hindered them from going to church likewise. We waited till 3 o'clock for dinner and then I ate some turkey and chine and after dinner we sat by a fire and chatted and were merry, without much scandal to our [talk]. The Doctor was very pleasant company, as he commonly is. We had some roast apples and wine, with which we diverted ourselves till about 10 o'clock and then we retired to our lodgings where I said my prayers and had good health, good thoughts, and good humor, thank God Almighty.

24. I rose about 7 o'clock but read nothing because all the company was up. However, I said my prayers and ate boiled milk for breakfast. It was very cold and had frozen very hard. However, about 10 we took leave and rode to Williamsburg. Mr. Bland came to my lodging and told me he had bought Mr. Brodnax's land for me that lay near the Falls and was to give him £165 for it. Then I went to the coffeehouse, where I met all my brothers of the Council that were in town. About 12

---

o'clock Colonel Ludwell and I went to the Governor's to learn from himself how long he intended to keep us and to persuade him to give leave to the House of Burgesses to adjourn for a month without their asking, which he at last consented to. He asked us to dine but we [. . .][6] to the rest of the Council and dined with them at the coffeehouse and I ate some beef for dinner. I paid all my debts and about 3 o'clock we went to the capitol to expect the coming of the Governor, who adjourned the assembly till the 24th of January and then we all took leave and went away and I went to Queen's Creek and surprised a good company there. I ate some toast and cider and roast apples and sat and chatted till 10 o'clock and then I recommended the company to the divine protection and said a short prayer and had good thoughts and good health and good humor, thank God Almighty.

25. I rose about 7 o'clock and read nothing because I prepared for my journey to Colonel Duke's. However I said my prayers and ate boiled milk for breakfast. The weather threatened snow but it did not frighten me from taking my leave about 11 o'clock, but before that I wrote a letter to Mr. C-s and enclosed to Mr. Graeme who was to go soon in the man-of-war. About 2 o'clock I got to Colonel Duke's and found both him and his old woman in good health, only the last was grown very deaf. We sat and talked till about 4 and then we went to dinner and I ate some wild duck. In the meantime the Colonel sent a negro man to see whether the river was open at my brother Duke's and he brought word it was, and therefore I took leave of the Colonel and his old countess and rode away to the river and with some difficulty got over as soon as it was dark. I found all well there and we drank a bottle of wine. About 9 o'clock I went to bed. I said my prayers and had good health, good thoughts, and good humor, thank God Almighty.

26. I rose about 7 o'clock and read nothing because I prepared for my journey. However I said my prayers and ate boiled milk for breakfast. It was cold and threatened rain or snow. About 9 I took leave and rode towards home and between

---

[6] The diary is transcribed from Byrd's shorthand. Hiatuses such as these, like occasional unexpanded abbreviations, represent problems of transcription.

Captain Stith's and home I met my wife and Mrs. Dunn going to Williamsburg to see what was become of me, but they turned back with me home where I found all well, thank God Almighty, except old Jane who was very ill of a fever. About 3 o'clock we went to dinner and I ate some wild goose. In the afternoon I looked about and found all things in good order. Mr. Anderson dined with me and after dinner gave old Jane the Sacrament. He stayed with me till the evening and then returned home. I inquired of my people how everything was and they told me well. Then I gave them some rum and cider to be merry with and afterwards read some Italian and wrote two letters to my overseers. I said my prayers and had good health, and good thoughts, and good humor, thank God Almighty. I rogered my wife [lustily].

27. I rose about 7 o'clock and read nothing because I put my things in order, but I wrote in my journal. I should have said my prayers but as soon as I had eaten boiled milk for breakfast Colonel Hill and Mrs. Anderson came to see us. My wife had [c-s] some of her [f-x]. The Colonel inquired how matters went below and I acquainted him with everything I knew concerning it. The weather was more moderate than it had been lately. Mr. Anderson would have come likewise but he was obliged to go to marry a couple of his parishioners. About 1 o'clock we went to dinner and I ate some roast beef. The company stayed with me till 4 o'clock and then went away. Then I danced my dance and said my prayers devoutly and then walked in my library because the ground was wet. In the evening I wrote in my journal and caused several of my people to be let blood by way of prevention. Then I read some Latin in Terence till 10 o'clock. I said my prayers and had good health, good thoughts, and good humor, thank God Almighty. I rogered my wife [lustily].

28. I rose about 7 o'clock and read two chapters in Hebrew and some Greek in Lucian. I said my prayers and ate boiled milk for breakfast. The weather was warm but cloudy. I danced my dance. I wrote some accounts and put several matters in order. Poor old Jane was very ill. We had several of the people let blood by way of prevention and Jenny for a sore throat. I ate boiled beef for dinner. In the afternoon settled several

accounts till the evening and then I took a walk about the plantation and found matters pretty well, thank God. At night I wrote in my journal and read some Latin in Terence till 10 o'clock. It snowed a little this evening. I said my prayers and had good health, good thoughts, and good humor, thank God Almighty. About 8 o'clock came Mr. G-r-l and George Smith by whom I learned that all was well at Falling Creek and the coal-pit.

29. I rose about 7 o'clock and read two chapters in Hebrew and some Greek in Lucian. I said my prayers and ate boiled milk for breakfast. I had abundance of talk with Mr. G-r-l about the affairs of Falling Creek and he told me some of his wants and so did George Smith, which I endeavored to supply as well as I could. I gave John G-r-l leave to go visit his mother. Poor old Jane died this morning about 9 o'clock and I caused her to be buried as soon as possible because she stank very much. It was not very cold today. I danced my dance. Mr. G-r-l and George Smith went away about 12 o'clock. I ate some broiled goose for dinner. In the afternoon I set my razor, and then went out to shoot with bow and arrow till the evening and then I ran to breathe myself and looked over everything. At night I read some Latin in Terence till about 10 o'clock. I said my prayers and had good health, good thoughts, and good humor, thank God Almighty.

30. I rose about 7 o'clock and read a chapter in Hebrew and three chapters in the Greek Testament. I said my prayers very devoutly and ate boiled milk for breakfast. The weather was very clear and warm so that my wife walked out with Mrs. Dunn and forgot dinner, for which I had a little quarrel with her and another afterwards because I was not willing to let her have a book out of the library. About 12 o'clock came Mr. Bland from Williamsburg but brought no news. He stayed to dinner and I ate some roast beef. In the afternoon we sat and talked till about 4 o'clock and then I caused my people to set him over the river and then I walked with the women about the plantation till they were very weary. At night we ate some eggs and drank some Virginia beer and talked very gravely without reading anything. However I said my prayers and spoke with all my people. I had good health, good

thoughts, and good humor, thank God Almighty. I danced my dance in the morning.

31. I rose about 7 o'clock and read a chapter in Hebrew and six leaves in Lucian. I said my prayers and ate boiled milk for breakfast. The weather continued warm and clear. I settled my accounts and wrote several things till dinner. I danced my dance. I ate some turkey and chine for dinner. In the afternoon I weighed some money and then read some Latin in Terence and then Mr. Mumford came and told me my man Tony had been very sick but he was recovered again, thank God. He told me Robin Bolling had been like to die and that he denied that he was the first to mention the imposition on skins which he certainly did. Then he and I took a walk about the plantation. When I returned I was out of humor to find the negroes all at work in our chambers. At night I ate some broiled turkey with Mr. Mumford and we talked and were merry all the evening. I said my prayers and had good health, good thoughts, and good humor, thank God Almighty. My wife and I had a terrible quarrel about whipping Eugene while Mr. Mumford was there but she had a mind to show her authority before company but I would not suffer it, which she took very ill; however for peace sake I made the first advance towards a reconciliation which I obtained with some difficulty and after abundance of crying. However it spoiled the mirth of the evening, but I was not conscious that I was to blame in that quarrel.

January, 1712

1. I lay abed till 9 o'clock this morning to bring my wife into temper again and rogered her by way of reconciliation. I read nothing because Mr. Mumford was here, nor did I say my prayers, for the same reason. However I ate boiled milk for breakfast, and after my wife tempted me to eat some pancakes with her. Mr. Mumford and I went to shoot with our bows and arrows but shot nothing, and afterwards we played at billiards till dinner, and when we came we found Ben Harrison there, who dined with us. I ate some partridge for dinner. In the after-

noon we played at billiards again and I won two bits. I had a
letter from Colonel Duke by H-e the bricklayer who came to
offer his services to work for me. Mr. Mumford went away in
the evening and John Bannister with him to see his mother.
I took a walk about the plantation and at night we drank some
mead of my wife's making which was very good. I gave the
people some cider and a dram to the negroes. I read some
Latin in Terence and had good health, good thoughts, and
good humor, thank God Almighty. I said my prayers.

2. I rose about 7 o'clock and read two chapters in Hebrew
and some Greek in Lucian. I said my prayers and ate boiled
milk for breakfast. I danced my dance. It rained pretty much in
the night and was cloudy this morning. I settled several accounts and wrote a letter to Colonel Duke. About 12 o'clock
came Colonel Eppes but could not stay because he was obliged
to go to court. A little before dinner came Ben Harrison in
his best clothes, because he happened to come yesterday in
his worst. He dined with us and I ate roast beef and before
we had done Colonel Hill and Mrs. Harrison came and the
Colonel ate some pudding with us, but Mrs. Harrison ate
nothing. They went away about 4 o'clock and then my wife
and I went to walk about the plantation and saw some young
trees that Tom had planted this day. At night I read some
Terence till almost 10 o'clock. I said my prayers and had good
health, good thoughts, and good humor, thank God Almighty.
My mulatto Jacky came from Falling Creek with a very sore
arm and told me all was well there, thank God.

3. I rose about 7 o'clock and read two chapters in Hebrew
and some Greek in Lucian. I said my prayers and ate boiled
milk for breakfast. I danced my dance and then settled several
accounts. The weather was very clear and cold. Mr. Bland's
sloop brought two hogsheads of cider and 66 hides from Williamsburg which were put ashore. I read some Latin till dinner
and then I ate some roast pork. I gave Anaka a good scolding
for letting Billy Brayne have a hole in his stocking. In the afternoon I set my razor and then went to prune the trees in the
young orchard and then I took a walk about the plantation
and my wife and Mrs. Dunn came to walk with me. At night

I read some Latin in Terence and then we drank some cider. I said my prayers and had good health, good thoughts, and good humor, thank God Almighty.

4. I rose about 7 o'clock and read two chapters in Hebrew and some Greek in Homer. I said my prayers and ate boiled milk for breakfast. I danced my dance and then settled several accounts. The weather was clear and warm. My wife was in-disposed with the colic but recovered pretty soon again, thank God, by the help of good drams of caraway water. I took a walk in the garden till dinner. I ate no meat this day but only fruit. In the afternoon I weighed some money and then went into the new orchard to trim some trees and stayed there till it was dark almost and then took a little walk about the plantation. In the evening Tom Turpin brought 30 hogs from the Falls and told me all was well, thank God. At night I read some Latin in Terence and said my prayers and had good health, good thoughts, and good humor, thank God Almighty. I ate some broiled turkey for supper.

5. I rose about 7 o'clock and read nothing because Tom Turpin was here. He came with 30 hogs from the Falls. He told me all was well above. I said my prayers and ate boiled milk for breakfast. I danced my dance. About 9 o'clock came Major Harrison and the captain of the "Pelican". I gave them a bottle of sack. Then we played at billiards and I won 7 shillings, and sixpence. About one o'clock we went to dinner and I ate some boiled beef. In the afternoon we were merry and made the Quaker captain drink the Queen's health on his knees. About 2 o'clock came my brother and sister Custis and sat down to dinner. They brought no news. My sister was much tired. In the evening the captain and Major Harrison went away to Mrs. Harrison's where I understood that Mr. Clayton was come. We drank a bottle of wine at night. This day a negro of mine at Falling Creek had a tree fall on his head and had his brains beat out. I neglected to say my prayers and had good health, good thoughts, and good humor, thank God Almighty.

6. I rose about 8 o'clock because my wife made me lie in bed and I rogered her. I read nothing and neglected to say my prayers but had boiled milk for breakfast. About 10 o'clock

came Mr. Clayton and brought me two English letters without any news because they were of an old date. I gave him a dram and about 11 o'clock we walked to church where we heard a good sermon from Mr. Anderson. I invited Colonel Hill to dine with me and ate wild goose for dinner. In the afternoon it rained so that Colonel Hill agreed to stay all night. In the evening we drank a supper bottle and were merry with nonsense but Colonel Hill's head ached a little. However it did not mar the supper or conversation. The Colonel is a man of good sense and good principles notwithstanding what has been said of him. I neglected to say my prayers but had good health, good thoughts, and good humor, thank God Almighty.

7. I rose about 7 o'clock and read nothing because we prepared to go to Colonel Hill's. I ate chocolate for breakfast. I said a short prayer. About 10 o'clock our ladies made a shift to get dressed, when we got on horseback and my horse was very frolicsome. The weather was cold and very clear. We called at Captain Llewellyn's and took Lew Eppes and his wife with us to Colonel Hill's, where we found all well. We were as merry as we could be, considering there was but little [w—]. About 2 o'clock we went to dinner and I ate some boiled pork for dinner. In the afternoon we went to see the ship and found them far advanced. Then we returned and saw my sloop bringing to at the Hundred, where my people left behind 50 bushels of wheat from G-r-l. In the evening we were very merry and the women offered violence to me because I would not dance and my wife quarrelled with her sister because she would not dance. About 10 o'clock we went to bed. I recommended myself and my family to the protection of Almighty God, and had good health, good thoughts, and good humor, thank God Almighty.

8. I rose about 7 o'clock and read a little in Horace. I neglected to say my prayers because the women came in with a dram of strong water of which I [drank] two drams. Then I left the women and went to the men and talked with them. About 9 o'clock came Colonel Frank Eppes to discourse with me concerning the rangers in the upper county and he told me nobody would accept of that place because the pay was too little. I ate some roast beef for breakfast contrary to my

custom. About 10 o'clock we went away home and found all well, thank God. We expected Mr. Clayton and Major Harrison from Prince George court and therefore we ordered dinner late. About 3 o'clock came Dr. Cocke and brought me some English letters, by which I learned there were plenipotentiaries appointed to agree about a peace, which God prosper. About 5 o'clock came Mr. Clayton, Major Harrison, and his brother Harry. We went to supper and I ate some boiled beef. We were very merry and I gave them some of my best wine. We played at cards and I won 15 shillings. I neglected to say my prayers because the company kept me up late but I had good health, good thoughts, and good humor, thank God Almighty. Parson Finney dined with us also and stayed all night.

9. I rose about 7 o'clock and found the weather exceedingly cold. I neglected to say my prayers because of the company. However I drank chocolate for breakfast and ate some cake. After breakfast we went to [p-l-y] and I won £10 at cards. About 10 o'clock Major Harrison and his brother Harry went away but the rest of the company was persuaded to stay a day longer, only Parson Finney, who went away likewise. Mr. Clayton and I took a walk till dinner and then I ate some roast mutton which was very good. My sloop went away this morning to Falling Creek. In the afternoon we were merry without drinking but did not venture out because of the [. . .] cold weather. In the evening Peter came from the Falls and told me all was well, thank God. We drank some of my best wine and were merry but would not let the women part from us. About 10 we ate some bread and cheese and drank a bottle on it, and about 11 we went to bed. My wife had got some cold and was disordered in her hip. I neglected to say my prayers but had good health, good thoughts, and good humor, thank God Almighty, only I was a little displeased at a story somebody had told the Governor that I had said that no Governor ought to be trusted with £20,000.[7] Little Peter brought a wild goose with him and two ducks.

10. I rose about 7 o'clock and found it terribly cold. My

---

[7] In order to carry on the war against the Tuscaroras, the Burgesses attempted to raise £20,000 by extraordinary taxes. . . . — *Wright-Tinling*.

wife was a little better. I neglected my prayers and ate boiled milk for breakfast but the company ate some chicken pie. About 11 o'clock my company took leave and went away and then I could do everything which too much company had hindered me from. I read this day no Hebrew nor Greek in Lucian but read my English letters and settled some accounts. Mr. Chamberlayne came from Appomattox and told me all was well there, thank God. He would dine with me whether I asked him or not and I ate roast beef. In the afternoon I weighed some money and settled some accounts till the evening and then took a walk about the plantation. Redskin Peter pretended he fell and hurt himself but it was dissimulation. I had a cow die this day. At night I read some Latin in Terence. Then I said my prayers and had good health, good thoughts, and good humor, thank God Almighty.

11. I rose about 7 o'clock and read two chapters in Hebrew and some Greek in Lucian. I said my prayers and ate boiled milk for breakfast. I danced my dance. It was not so cold as it has been because the wind came to south. My wife was a little indisposed with a cold. I settled several accounts and put many things in order till dinner. I ate some raspberries for dinner. In the afternoon I set my razor and then went into the new orchard and trimmed the trees till the evening and then I took a walk about the plantation. Redskin Peter was very well again after he had worn the bit 24 hours and went to work very actively. Before I came in I took a run for my health. At night I read some Latin in Terence. I said my prayers and had thoughts [sic], good health, and good humor, thank God Almighty.

12. I rose about 8 o'clock and read two chapters in Hebrew and some Greek in Lucian. I said my prayers devoutly and ate boiled milk for breakfast. I danced my dance. Jacky's arm was almost well, thank God. The weather was warm but the wind was northeast. My wife was well again, thank God, and went about again as usual. I read some Latin in Terence till dinner and then I ate some roast pork. In the afternoon I went into the orchard and trimmed the young trees till I was called away by one of the girls who told me that Mr. Peter Butts would speak with me. His business was to desire me to get a sheriff's

place for his brother and in order to persuade me to it told me several things of Ned [Goodrich] and how he had once hindered my man Tony from paying £30 for lying with an Indian wife. A man came from New Kent concerning a protested bill and he stayed here all night. In the evening I took a walk and at night read some Latin in Terence. I said my prayers and had good health, good thoughts, and good humor, thank God Almighty.

V

THE QUAKER

For us, as also for most colonial Americans, the prime significance of the Quaker movement lies in its radically individualistic protestantism. Quakers were willing to realize the fullest implications of protestant thinking; they found the very source of order in society in the sacred inviolability of the individual. That inviolability was literal, a divine categorical imperative which meant that man could live only by knowing himself in others and others in himself. He could not be an empire-builder; he could only show men the possibilities of empire within themselves. Everyman was his brother, as Everyman was somehow himself. So he preached; so he lived; so he died. And his way came to represent to those to whom he preached, those whom he often as not annoyed into toleration and love, the way of the radically-minded, simply-minded peacemaker— literally, as he called himself, the Friend of man.

The background of the Quaker movement, however, is wider than that of English protestantism. Behind English and American Quakerism there is also German pietism of the sixteenth and seventeenth centuries—that of Jacob Boehme in particular—and the neo-platonic revival of the seventeenth century. In pietism and neo-platonism emphasis was on the individual contact with divinity and on the faculty which was the means of that contact. The Quakers came to call this faculty the "Inner Light." Seeing by this Light, the first Friend, George Fox (1624–1691) travelled and preached anywhere and everywhere, "convincing" all those he could. He "convinced" William Penn in 1677; and in 1681–1682 Penn moved to found a colony in America for others who had come to believe as he had. Meantime Quakers had been at work in the colonies. In 1656 and 1657 they came to Massachusetts and were barbarously mistreated; for they represented to proper Puritans all the dangers of antinomianism, democracy, and surrender to the corrupt self. But the Quakers survived, even thrived, elsewhere in America. Pennsylvania was a success; while Quakers were in control of the colony, frontier relations with the Indians were more peaceful than anywhere in the colonies; Philadelphia became the center of American life. Yet in practical terms, the Quaker way was too simple. Gradually losing political power in the eighteenth century, the Quakers took on their permanent role as protesters, gadflies, and peacemakers. Trying to protect Indians and to end slavery, they became for Enlightened Americans and Europeans the symbol of all that was free, intelligent, and rational. But their belief remained in something beyond the reason, something which was from God, something, however, which led inevitably to freedom, intelligence, and reason.

Records of the Quaker enterprise in America are voluminous. For Quakers felt it part of their duty to record lives which were at all points spiritualized. Thus we have myriad Quaker journals of experiences. Indubitably the greatest of these is that of John Woolman. Woolman's journal not only records a Quaker life but captures in its informal, sensitive, quietly ordered style a Quaker sensibility. Here—as in the essay of William Penn which precedes it in this collection—is a Quaker conscience. In many ways, it is an American conscience; for the destiny of the Quaker has been to be an American conscience.

Bibliographical Note. Elbert Russel, *A History of Quakerism* (New York, 1943) is a general introduction to the subject. Rufus Jones, *The Quakers in the American Colonies* (London, 1911) is an extended and inclusive study; F. B. Tolles, *Meeting House and Counting House* (Chapel Hill, 1948) is an important and valuable special study of Philadelphia Quaker attempts to mediate between the claims of work and worship and to live fully in the world. Luella Wright, *The Literary Life of the Early Friends,* 1650–1725 (New York, 1932) furnishes the best available introduction to Quaker writings.

William Penn

(1644–1718)

Bibliographical Note. The best, but not complete, collection of Penn's writings is in 2 vols., *A Collection of the Works of William Penn* (London, 1726). There is no modern edition. The text of the selection which follows is from *Narratives of Early Pennsylvania, West Jersey, and Delaware, 1630–1707*, ed. A. C. Myers (New York, 1912), pp. 225–242. For Penn's life, see William Hull, *William Penn* (New York, 1937); for his social ideas, see E. C. O. Beatty, *William Penn as a Social Philosopher* (New York, 1939).

LETTER FROM WILLIAM PENN TO THE COMMITTEE OF THE FREE SOCIETY OF TRADERS
(1683)*

My Kind Friends;

The Kindness of yours by the Ship *Thomas and Anne*, doth much oblige me; for by it I perceive the Interest you take in my Health and Reputation, and the prosperous Beginnings of this Province, which you are so kind as to think may much depend upon them. In return of which, I have sent you a long Letter, and yet containing as brief an Account of My self, and the Affairs of this Province, as I have been able to make.

---

* Reprinted from *Narratives of Early Pennsylvania, West Jersey, and Delaware, 1630–1707*, edited by A. C. Myers and used with permission of Barnes & Noble, Inc.

In the first place, I take notice of the News you sent me, whereby I find some Persons have had so little Wit, and so much Malice, as to report my Death, and to mend the matter, dead a Jesuit too. One might have reasonably hop'd, that this Distance, like Death, would have been a protection against Spite and Envy; and indeed, Absence being a kind of Death, ought alike to secure the Name of the Absent as the Dead; because they are equally unable as such to defend themselves: But they that intend Mischief, do not use to follow good Rules to effect it. However, to the great Sorrow and Shame of the Inventors, I am still Alive, and No Jesuit, and I thank God, very well: And without Injustice to the Authors of this, I may venture to infer, That they that wilfully and falsly Report, would have been glad it had been So. But I perceive, many frivolous and Idle Stories have been Invented since my Departure from England, which perhaps at this time are no more Alive, than I am Dead.

But if I have been Unkindly used by some I left behind me, I found Love and Respect enough where I came; an universal kind Welcome, every sort in their way. For here are some of several Nations, as well as divers Judgments: Nor were the Natives wanting in this, for their Kings, Queens and Great Men both visited and presented me; to whom I made suitable Returns, etc.

For the Province, the general Condition of it take as followeth.

I. The Country it self in its Soyl, Air, Water, Seasons and Produce both Natural and Artificial is not to be despised. The Land containeth divers sorts of Earth, as Sand Yellow and Black, Poor and Rich: also Gravel both Loomy and Dusty; and in some places a fast fat Earth, like to our best Vales in England, especially by Inland Brooks and Rivers, God in his Wisdom having ordered it so, that the Advantages of the Country are divided, the Back-Lands being generally three to one Richer than those that lie by Navigable Waters. We have much of another Soyl, and that is a black Hasel Mould, upon a Stony or Rocky bottom.

II. The Air is sweet and clear, the Heavens serene, like the South-parts of France, rarely Overcast; and as the Woods come by numbers of People to be more clear'd, that it self will Refine.

III. The Waters are generally good, for the Rivers and Brooks have mostly Gravel and Stony Bottoms, and in Number hardly credible. We have also Mineral Waters, that operate in the same manner with Barnet and North-hall, not two Miles from Philadelphia.

IV. For the Seasons of the Year, having by God's goodness now lived over the Coldest and Hottest, that the Oldest Liver in the Province can remember, I can say something to an English Understanding.

1st, Of the Fall, for then I came in: I found it from the 24th of October, to the beginning of December, as we have it usually in England in September, or rather like an English mild Spring. From December to the beginning of the Moneth called March, we had sharp Frosty Weather; not foul, thick, black Weather, as our North-East Winds bring with them in England; but a Skie as clear as in Summer, and the Air dry, cold, piercing and hungry; yet I remember not, that I wore more Clothes than in England. The reason of this Cold is given from the great Lakes that are fed by the Fountains of Canada. The Winter before was as mild, scarce any Ice at all; while this for a few dayes Froze up our great River Delaware. From that Moneth to the Moneth called June, we enjoy'd a sweet Spring, no Gusts, but gentle Showers, and a fine Skie. Yet this I observe, that the Winds here as there, are more Inconstant Spring and Fall, upon that turn of Nature, than in Summer or Winter. From thence to this present Moneth, which endeth the Summer (commonly speaking) we have had extraordinary Heats, yet mitigated sometimes by Cool Breezese. The Wind that ruleth the Summer-season, is the South-West; but Spring, Fall and Winter, 'tis rare to want the wholesome North Wester seven dayes together: And whatever Mists, Fogs or Vapours foul the Heavens by Easterly or Southerly Winds, in two Hours time are blown away; the one is alwayes followed by the other: A Remedy that seems to have a peculiar Providence in it to the Inhabitants; the multitude of Trees, yet standing, being liable to retain Mists and Vapours, and yet not one quarter so thick as I expected.

V. The Natural Produce of the Country, of Vegetables, is Trees, Fruits, Plants, Flowers. The Trees of most note are, the black Walnut, Cedar, Cyprus, Chestnut, Poplar, Gumwood,

Hickery, Sassafrax, Ash, Beech and Oak of divers sorts, as Red, White and Black; Spanish Chestnut and Swamp, the most durable of all: of All which there is plenty for the use of man.

The Fruits that I find in the Woods, are the White and Black Mulbery, Chestnut, Wallnut, Plumbs, Strawberries, Cranberries, Hurtleberries and Grapes of divers sorts. The great Red Grape (now ripe) called by Ignorance, the Fox-Grape (because of the Relish it hath with unskilful Palates) is in it self an extraordinary Grape, and by Art doubtless may be Cultivated to an excellent Wine, if not so sweet, yet little inferior to the Frontimack, as it is not much unlike in taste, Ruddiness set aside, which in such things, as well as Mankind, differs the case much. There is a white kind of Muskedel, and a little black Grape, like the cluster-Grape of England, not yet so ripe as the other; but they tell me, when Ripe, sweeter, and that they only want skilful Vinerons to make good use of them: I intend to venture on it with my French man this season, who shews some knowledge in those things. Here are also Peaches, and very good, and in great quantities, not an Indian Plantation without them; but whether naturally here at first, I know not, however one may have them by Bushels for little; they make a pleasant Drink and I think not inferior to any Peach you have in England, except the true Newington. 'Tis disputable with me, whether it be best to fall to Fining the Fruits of the Country, especially the Grape, by the care and skill of Art, or send for forreign Stems and Sets, already good and approved. It seems most reasonable to believe, that not only a thing groweth best, where it naturally grows; but will hardly be equalled by another Species of the same kind, that doth not naturally grow there. But to solve the doubt, I intend, if God give me Life, to try both, and hope the consequence will be as good Wine as any European Countries of the same Latitude do yield.

VI. The Artificial Produce of the Country, is Wheat, Barley, Oats, Rye, Pease, Beans, Squashes, Pumkins, Water-Melons, Mus-Melons, and all Herbs and Roots that our Gardens in England usually bring forth.

VII. Of living Creatures; Fish, Fowl, and the Beasts of the Woods, here are divers sorts, some for Food and Profit, and some for Profit only: For Food as well as Profit, the Elk, as big as a small Ox, Deer bigger than ours, Beaver, Racoon, Rabbits, Squirrels, and some eat young Bear, and commend it. Of Fowl of the Land, there is the Turkey (Forty and Fifty Pound weight) which is very great; Phesants, Heath-Birds, Pidgeons and Partridges in abundance. Of the Water, the Swan, Goose, white and gray, Brands, Ducks, Teal, also the Snipe and Curloe, and that in great Numbers; but the Duck and Teal excel, nor so good have I ever eat in other Countries. Of Fish, there is the Sturgeon, Herring, Rock, Shad, Catshead, Sheepshead, Ele, Smelt, Pearch, Roach; and in Inland Rivers, Trout, some say Salmon, above the Falls. Of Shelfish, we have Oysters, Crabbs, Cockles, Concks, and Mushels; some Oysters six Inches long, and one sort of Cockles as big as the Stewing Oysters, they make a rich Broth. The Creatures for Profit only by Skin or Fur, and that are natural to these parts, are the Wild Cat, Panther, Otter, Wolf, Fox, Fisher, Minx, Musk-Rat; and of the Water, the Whale for Oyl, of which we have good store, and two Companies of Whalers, whose Boats are built, will soon begin their Work, which hath the appearance of a considerable Improvement. To say nothing of our reasonable Hopes of good Cod in the Bay.

VIII. We have no want of Horses, and some are very good and shapely enough; two Ships have been freighted to Barbadoes with Horses and Pipe-Staves, since my coming in. Here is also Plenty of Cow-Cattle, and some Sheep; the People Plow mostly with Oxen.

IX. There are divers Plants that not only the Indians tell us, but we have had occasion to prove by Swellings, Burnings, Cuts, etc., that they are of great Virtue, suddenly curing the Patient: and for smell, I have observed several, especially one, the wild Mirtle; the other I know not what to call, but are most fragrant.

X. The Woods are adorned with lovely Flowers, for colour, greatness, figure, and variety: I have seen the Gardens of London best stored with that sort of Beauty, but think they may be improved by our Woods: I have sent a few to a Person of Quality this Year for a tryal.

Thus much of the Country, next of the Natives or Aborigines.

XI. The *Natives* I shall consider in their Persons, Language, Manners, Religion and Government, with my sence of their

Original. For their Persons, they are generally tall, streight, well-built, and of singular Proportion; they tread strong and clever, and mostly walk with a lofty Chin: Of Complexion, Black, but by design, as the Gypsies in England: They grease themselves with Bears-fat clarified, and using no defence against Sun or Weather, their skins must needs be swarthy; Their Eye is little and black, not unlike a straight-look't Jew: The thick Lip and flat Nose, so frequent with East-Indians and Blacks, are not common to them; for I have seen as comely European-like faces among them of both, as on your side the Sea; and truly an Italian Complexion hath not much more of the White, and the Noses of several of them have as much of the Roman.

XII. Their Language is lofty, yet narrow, but like the Hebrew; in Signification full, like Short-hand in writing; one word serveth in the place of three, and the rest are supplied by the Understanding of the Hearer: Imperfect in their Tenses, wanting in their Moods, Participles, Adverbs, Conjunctions, Interjections: I have made it my business to understand it, that I might not want an Interpreter on any occasion: And I must say, that I know not a Language spoken in Europe, that hath words of more sweetness or greatness, in Accent and Emphasis, than theirs; for Instance, *Octorockon, Rancocas, Ozicton, Shakamacon, Poquerim*, all of which are names of Places, and have Grandeur in them: Of words of Sweetness, *Anna*, is Mother, *Issimus*, a Brother, *Netap*, Friend, *usque ozet*, very good; *pone*, Bread, *metse*, eat, *matta*, no, *hatta*, to have, *payo*, to come; *Sepassen, Passijon*, the Names of Places; *Tamane, Secane, Menanse, Secatereus*, are the names of Persons. If one ask them for anything they have not, they will answer, *mattá ne hattá*, which to translate is, not I have, instead of I have not.

XIII. Of their Customs and Manners there is much to be said; I will begin with Children. So soon as they are born, they wash them in Water, and while very young, and in cold Weather to chuse, they Plunge them in the Rivers to harden and embolden them. Having wrapt them in a Clout, they lay them on a straight thin Board, a little more than the length and breadth of the Child, and swadle it fast upon the Board to make it straight; wherefore all Indians have flat Heads; and thus they carry them at their Backs. The Children will go very young, at nine Moneths commonly; they wear only a small Clout round their Waste, till they are big; if Boys, they go a Fishing till ripe for the Woods, which is about Fifteen; then they Hunt, and after having given some Proofs of their Manhood, by a good return of Skins, they may Marry, else it is a shame to think of a Wife. The Girls stay with their Mothers, and help to hoe the Ground, plant Corn and carry Burthens; and they do well to use them to that Young, they must do when they are Old; for the Wives are the true Servants of their Husbands: otherwise the Men are very affectionate to them.

XIV. When the Young Women are fit for Marriage, they wear something upon their Heads for an Advertisement, but so as their Faces are hardly to be seen, but when they please: The Age they Marry at, if Women, is about thirteen and fourteen; if Men, seventeen and eighteen; they are rarely elder.

XV. Their Houses are Mats, or Barks of Trees set on Poles, in the fashion of an English Barn, but out of the power of the Winds, for they are hardly higher than a Man; they lie on Reeds or Grass. In Travel they lodge in the Woods about a great Fire, with the Mantle of Duffills they wear by day, wrapt about them, and a few Boughs stuck round them.

XVI. Their Diet is Maze, or Indian Corn, divers ways pre-pared: sometimes Roasted in the Ashes, sometimes beaten and Boyled with Water, which they call *Homine*; they also make Cakes, not unpleasant to eat: They have likewise several sorts of Beans and Pease that are good Nourishment; and the Woods and Rivers are their Larder.

XVII. If an European comes to see them, or calls for Lodg-ing at their House or *Wigwam* they give him the best place and first cut. If they come to visit us, they salute us with an *Itah* which is as much as to say, Good be to you, and set them down, which is mostly on the Ground close to their Heels, their Legs upright; may be they speak not a word more, but observe all Passages: If you give them any thing to eat or drink, well, for they will not ask; and be it little or much, if it be with Kindness, they are well pleased, else they go away sullen, but say nothing.

XVIII. They are great Concealers of their own Resent-ments, brought to it, I believe, by the Revenge that hath been practised among them; in either of these, they are not exceeded by the Italians. A Tragical Instance fell out since I came into the Country; A King's Daughter thinking her self slighted by her Husband, in suffering another Woman to lie down between them, rose up, went out, pluck't a Root out of the Ground, and ate it, upon which she immediately dyed; and for which, last Week he made an Offering to her Kindred for Attonement and liberty of Marriage; as two others did to the Kindred of their Wives, that dyed a natural Death: For till Widdowers have done so, they must not marry again. Some of the young Women are said to take undue liberty before Marriage for a Portion; but when marryed, chaste; when with Child, they know their Husbands no more, till delivered; and during their Moneth, they touch no Meat, they eat, but with a Stick, least they should defile it; nor do their Husbands frequent them, till that time be expired.

XIX. But in Liberality they excell, nothing is too good for their friend; give them a fine Gun, Coat, or other thing, it may pass twenty hands, before it sticks; light of Heart, strong Affections, but soon spent; the most merry Creatures that live, Feast and Dance perpetually; they never have much, nor want much: Wealth circulateth like the Blood, all parts partake; and though none shall want what another hath, yet exact Observers of Property. Some Kings have sold, others presented me with several parcels of Land; the Pay or Presents I made them, were not hoarded by the particular Owners, but the neighbouring Kings and their Clans being present when the Goods were brought out, the Parties chiefly concerned consulted, what and to whom they should give them? To every King then, by the hands of a Person for that work appointed, is a proportion sent, so sorted and folded, and with that Gravity, that is admirable. Then that King subdivideth it in like manner among his Dependents, they hardly leaving themselves an Equal share with one of their Subjects: and be it on such occasions, at Festivals, or at their common Meals, the Kings distribute, and to themselves last. They care for little, because they want but little; and the Reason is, a little contents them: In this they are sufficiently revenged on us; if they are ignorant of our Pleasures, they are also free from our Pains. They are not disquieted with Bills of Lading and Exchange, nor perplexed with Chancery-Suits and

Exchequer-Reckonings. We sweat and toil to live; their pleasure feeds them, I mean, their Hunting, Fishing and Fowling, and this Table is spread every where; they eat twice a day, Morning and Evening; their Seats and Table are the Ground. Since the European came into these parts, they are grown great lovers of strong Liquors, Rum especially, and for it exchange the richest of their Skins and Furs: If they are heated with Liquors, they are restless till they have enough to sleep; that is their cry, Some more, and I will go to sleep; but when Drunk, one of the most wretchedst Spectacles in the world.

XX. In sickness impatient to be cured, and for it give any thing, especially for their Children, to whom they are extreamly natural; they drink at those times a *Teran* or Decoction of some Roots in spring Water; and if they eat any flesh, it must be of the Female of any Creature; If they dye, they bury them with their Apparel, be they Men or Women, and the nearest of Kin fling in something precious with them, as a token of their Love: Their Mourning is blacking of their faces, which they continue for a year; They are choice of the Graves of their Dead; for least they should be lost by time, and fall to common use, they pick off the Grass that grows upon them, and heap up the fallen Earth with great care and exactness.

XXI. These poor People are under a dark Night in things relating to Religion, to be sure, the Tradition of it; yet they believe a God and Immortality, without the help of Metaphysicks; for they say, There is a great King that made them, who dwells in a glorious Country to the Southward of them, and that the Souls of the good shall go thither, where they shall live again. Their Worship consists of two parts, Sacrifice and *Cantico*. Their Sacrifice is their first Fruits; the first and fattest Buck they kill, goeth to the fire, where he is all burnt with a Mournful Ditty of him that performeth the Ceremony, but with such marvellous Fervency and Labour of Body, that he will even sweat to a foam. The other part is their *Cantico*, performed by round-Dances, sometimes Songs, then Shouts, two being in the middle that begin, and by Singing and Drumming on a Board direct the Chorus: Their Postures in the Dance are very Antick and differing, but all keep measure. This is done with equal Earnestness and Labour, but great appearance of Joy.

In the Fall, when the Corn cometh in, they begin to feast one another; there have been two great Festivals already, to which all come that will: I was at one my self; their Entertainment was a green Seat by a Spring, under some shady Trees, and twenty Bucks, with hot Cakes of new Corn, both Wheat and Beans, which they make up in a square form, in the leaves of the Stem, and bake them in the Ashes: And after that they fell to Dance, But they that go, must carry a small Present in their Money, it may be six Pence, which is made of the Bone of a Fish; the black is with them as Gold, the white, Silver; they call it all *Wampum.*

XXII. Their Government is by Kings, which they call *Sachema,* and those by Succession, but always of the Mothers side; for Instance, the Children of him that is now King, will not succeed, but his Brother by the Mother, or the Children of his Sister, whose Sons (and after them the Children of her Daughters) will reign; for no Woman inherits; the Reason they render for this way of Descent, is, that their Issue may not be spurious.

XXIII. Every King hath his Council, and that consists of all the Old and Wise men of his Nation, which perhaps is two hundred People. nothing of Moment is undertaken, be it War, Peace, Selling of Land or Traffick, without advising with them; and which is more, with the Young Men too. 'Tis admirable to consider, how Powerful the Kings are, and yet how they move by the Breath of their People. I have had occasion to be in Council with them upon Treaties for Land, and to adjust the terms of Trade; their Order is thus: The King sits in the middle of an half Moon, and hath his Council, the Old and Wise on each hand; behind them, or at a little distance, sit the younger Fry, in the same figure. Having consulted and resolved their business, the King ordered one of them to speak to me; he stood up, came to me, and in the Name of his King saluted me, then took me by the hand, and told me, That he was ordered by his King to speak to me, and that now it was not he, but the King that spoke, because what he should say, was the King's mind. He first pray'd me, To excuse them that they had not complyed with me the last time; he feared, there might be some fault in the Interpreter, being neither Indian nor English; besides, it was the Indian Custom to deliberate, and take up much time in

Council, before they resolve; and that if the Young People and Owners of the Land had been as ready as he, I had not met with so much delay. Having thus introduced his matter, he fell to the Bounds of the Land they had agreed to dispose of, and the Price, (which now is little and dear, that which would have bought twenty Miles, not buying now two.) During the time that this Person spoke, not a man of them was observed to whisper or smile; the Old, Grave, the Young, Reverend in their Deportment; they do speak little, but fervently, and with Elegancy: I have never seen more natural Sagacity, considering them without the help, (I was agoing to say, the spoil) of Tradition; and he will deserve the Name of Wise, that Outwits them in any Treaty about a thing they understand. When the Purchase was agreed, great Promises past between us of Kindness and good Neighbourhood, and that the Indians and English must live in Love, as long as the Sun gave light. Which done, another made a Speech to the Indians, in the Name of all the *Sachamakers* or Kings, first to tell them what was done; next, to charge and command them, To Love the Christians, and particularly live in Peace with me, and the People under my Government: That many Governours had been in the River, but that no Governour had come himself to live and stay here before; and having now such a one that had treated them well, they should never do him or his any wrong. At every sentence of which they shouted, and said, Amen, in their way.

XXIV. The Justice they have is Pecuniary: In case of any Wrong or evil Fact, be it Murther it self, they Attone by Feasts and Presents of their *Wampon*, which is proportioned to the quality of the Offence or Person injured, or of the Sex they are of: for in case they kill a Woman, they pay double, and the Reason they render, is, That she breedeth Children, which Men cannot do. 'Tis rare that they fall out, if Sober; and if Drunk, they forgive it, saying, It was the Drink, and not the Man, that abused them.

XXV. We have agreed, that in all Differences between us, Six of each side shall end the matter: Don't abuse them, but let them have Justice, and you win them: The worst is, that they are the worse for the Christians, who have propagated their Vices, and yielded them Tradition for ill, and not for good things. But as low an Ebb as they are at, and as glorious as their Condition looks, the Christians have not out-liv'd their sight with all their Pretensions to an higher Manifestation: What good then might not a good People graft, where there is so distinct a Knowledge left between Good and Evil? I beseech God to incline the Hearts of all that come into these parts, to out-live the Knowledge of the Natives, by a fixt Obedience to their greater Knowledge of the Will of God, for it were miserable indeed for us to fall under the just censure of the poor Indian Conscience, while we make profession of things so far transcending.

XXVI. For their Original, I am ready to believe them of the Jewish Race, I mean, of the stock of the Ten Tribes, and that for the following Reasons; first, They were to go to a Land not planted or known, which to be sure Asia and Africa were, if not Europe; and he that intended that extraordinary Judgment upon them, might make the Passage not uneasie to them, as it is not impossible in it self, from the Easter-most parts of Asia, to the Wester-most of America. In the next place, I find them of like Countenance and their Children of so lively Resemblance, that a man would think himself in Dukes-place or Berry-street[1] in London, when he seeth them. But this is not all, they agree in Rites, they reckon by Moons: they offer their first Fruits, they have a kind of Feast of Tabernacles; they are said to lay their Alter upon twelve Stones; their Mourning a year, Customs of Women, with many things that do not now occur.

So much for the Natives, next the Old Planters will be considered in this Relation, before I come to our Colony, and the Concerns of it.

XXVII. The first Planters in these parts were the Dutch, and soon after them the Sweeds and Finns. The Dutch applied themselves to Traffick, the Sweeds and Finns to Husbandry. There were some Disputes between them some years, the Dutch looking upon them as Intruders upon their Purchase and Possession, which was finally ended in the Surrender made by John Rizeing, the Sweeds Governour, to Peter Styvesant, Governour for the States of Holland, *Anno* 1655.

---

[1] . . . Jewish quarters.—*Myers.*

XXVIII. The Dutch inhabit mostly those parts of the Province, that lie upon or near to the Bay, and the Sweeds the Freshes of the River Delaware. There is no need of giving any Description of them, who are better known there then here; but they are a plain, strong, industrious People, yet have made no great progress in Culture or propagation of fruit-Trees, as if they desired rather to have enough, than Plenty or Traffick. But I presume, the Indians made them the more careless, by furnishing them with the means of Profit, to wit, Skins and Furs, for Rum, and such strong Liquors. They kindly received me, as well as the English, who were few, before the People concerned with me came among them; I must needs commend their Respect to Authority, and kind Behaviour to the English; they do not degenerate from the Old friendship between both Kingdoms. As they are People proper and strong of Body, so they have fine Children, and almost every house full; rare to find one of them without three or four Boys, and as many Girls; some six, seven and eight Sons: And I must do them that right, I see few Young men more sober and laborious.

XXIX. The Dutch have a Meeting-place for Religious Worship at New Castle, and the Sweedes three, one at Christina, one at Tenecum, and one at Wicoco, within half a Mile of this Town.

XXX. There rests, that I speak of the Condition we are in, and what Settlement we have made, in which I will be as short as I can; for I fear, and not without reason, that I have tryed your Patience with this long Story. The Country lieth bounded on the East, by the River and Bay of Delaware, and Eastern Sea; it hath the Advantage of many Creeks or Rivers rather, that run into the main River or Bay; some Navigable for great Ships, some for small Craft: Those of most Eminency are Christina, Brandywine, Skilpot, and Skulkill; any one of which have room to lay up the Royal Navy of England, there being from four to eight Fathom Water.

XXXI. The lesser Creeks or Rivers, yet convenient for Sloops and Ketches of good Burthen, are Lewis, Mespilion, Cedar, Dover, Cranbrook, Feversham, and Georges, below, and Chichester, Chester, Toacawny, Pemmapecka, Portquessin, Neshimenck and Pennberry in the Freshes; many lesser that admit

Boats and Shallops. Our People are mostly settled upon the upper Rivers, which are pleasant and sweet, and generally bounded with good Land. The Planted part of the Province and Territories is cast into six Counties, Philadelphia, Buckingham, Chester, New Castle, Kent and Sussex, containing about Four Thousand Souls. Two General assemblies have been held, and with such Concord and Dispatch, that they sate but three Weeks, and at least seventy Laws were past without one Dissent in any material thing. But of this more hereafter, being yet Raw and New in our Geer: However, I cannot forget their singular Respect to me in this Infancy of things, who by their own private Expenses so early consider'd Mine for the Publick, as to present me with an Impost upon certain Goods Imported and Exported: Which after my Acknowledgements of their Affection, I did as freely Remit to the Province and the Traders to it. And for the well Government of the said Counties, Courts of Justice are establisht in every County, with proper Officers, as Justices, Sheriffs, Clarks, Constables, etc., which Courts are held every two Moneths: But to prevent Law-Suits, there are three Peacemakers chosen by every County-Court, in the nature of common Arbitrators, to hear and end Differences betwixt man and man; and Spring and Fall there is an Orphan's Court in each County, to inspect, and regulate the Affairs of Orphans and Widdows.

XXXII. Philadelphia, the Expectation of those that are concern'd in this Province, is at last laid out to the great Content of those here, that are any wayes Interested therein; The Scituation is a Neck of Land, and lieth between two Navigable Rivers, Delaware and Skulkill, whereby it hath two Fronts upon the Water, each a Mile, and two from River to River. Delaware is a glorious River, but the Skulkill being an hundred Miles Boatable above the Falls, and its Course North-East toward the Fountain of Susquahannah (that tends to the Heart of the Province, and both sides our own) it is like to be a great part of the Settlement of this Age. I say little of the Town it self, because a *Platform* will be shewn you by my Agent, in which those who are Purchasers of me, will find their Names and Interests: But this I will say for the good Providence of God, that of all the many Places I have seen in the World, I remember not one better seated; so that it seems to me to have been appointed for a Town, whether we regard the Rivers, or the conveniency of the Coves, Docks, Springs, the loftiness and soundness of the Land and the Air, held by the People of these parts to be very good. It is advanced within less than a Year to about four Score Houses and Cottages, such as they are, where Merchants and Handicrafts, are following their Vocations as fast as they can, while the Country-men are close at their Farms; Some of them got a little Winter-Corn in the Ground last Season, and the generality have had a handsom Summer-Crop, and are preparing for their Winter-Corn. They reaped their Barley this Year in the Moneth called May; the Wheat in the Moneth following; so that there is time in these parts for another Crop of divers Things before the Winter-Season. We are daily in hopes of Shipping to add to our Number; for blessed be God, here is both Room and Accommodation for them; the Stories of our Necessity being either the Fear of our Friends, or the Scare-Crows of our Enemies; for the greatest hardship we have suffered, hath been Salt-Meat, which by Fowl in Winter, and Fish in Summer, together with some Poultery, Lamb, Mutton, Veal, and plenty of Venison the best part of the year, hath been made very passable. I bless God, I am fully satisfied with the Country and Entertainment I can get in it; for I find that particular Content which hath always attended me, where God in his Providence hath made it my place and service to reside. You cannot imagin, my Station can be at present free of more than ordinary business, and as such, I may say, It is a troublesom Work; but the Method things are putting in, will facilitate the Charge, and give an easier Motion to the Administration of Affairs. However, as it is some mens Duty to plow, some to sow, some to water, and some to reap; so it is the Wisdom as well as Duty of a man, to yield to the mind of Providence, and chearfully, as well as carefully imbrace and follow the Guidance of it.

XXXIII. For your particular Concern, I might entirely refer you to the Letters of the President of the Society; but this I will venture to say, Your Provincial Settlements both within and without the Town, for Scituation and Soil, are without Exception; Your City-Lot is an whole Street, and one side of a Street, from River to River, containing near one hundred Acers, not easily valued, which is besides your four hundred Acers in the City Liberties, part of your twenty thousand Acers in the Countery. Your Tannery hath such plenty of Bark, the Saw-Mill for Timber, the place of the Glass-house so conveniently posted for Water-carriage, the City-Lot for a Dock, and the Whalery for a sound and fruitful Bank, and the Town Lewis by it to help your People, that by Gods blessing the Affairs of the Society will naturally grow in their Reputation and Profit. I am sure I have not turned my back upon any Offer that tended to its Prosperity; and though I am ill at Projects, I have sometimes put in for a Share with her Officers, to countenance and advance her Interest. You are already informed what is fit for you further to do, whatsoever tends to the Promotion of Wine, and to the Manufacture of Linnen in these parts, I cannot but wish you to promote it; and the French People are most likely in both respects to answer that design: To that end, I would advise you to send for some Thousands of Plants out of France, with some able Vinerons, and People of the other Vocation: But because I believe you have been entertained with this and some other profitable Subjects by your President, I shall add no more, but to assure you, that I am heartily inclined to advance your just Interest, and that you will always find me

Your Kind Cordial Friend,

WILLIAM PENN

Philadelphia, the 16th of the
    6th Moneth, call'd August,
    1683.

John Woolman

(1720–1772)

The most complete edition of Woolman's *Journal* is that edited
from the original manuscripts by Amelia Gummere, *The Journal
and Essays of John Woolman* (New York, 1922). The text of the
selection which follows, however, is from the edition edited by
Vida D. Scudder in Everyman's Library (London, 1910), pp. 99–
110; this latter text in turn derives from the 1871 edition of John
Greenleaf Whittier, that best known in America. The best account
of Woolman's life, aside from his own interpretation of it in the
Journal, is in the introduction to the Gummere edition of *The
Journal and Essays*. A recent valuable interpretation is E. H. Cady,
John Woolman (New York, 1965).

from

THE JOURNAL

(1774)

[*Early Days*]

I have often felt a Motion of Love to leave some Hints in
Writing of my Experience of the Goodness of God; and now,
in the thirty-sixth Year of my Age, I begin this Work.

I was born in *Northampton,* in *Burlington* County, *West-
Jersey,* in the Year 1720; and before I was seven Years old
I began to be acquainted with the Operations of divine Love.
Through the Care of my Parents, I was taught to read nearly
as soon as I was capable of it; and, as I went from School one
seventh Day, I remember, while my Companions went to play
by the Way, I went forward out of Sight, and, sitting down,
I read the 22d Chapter of the *Revelations:* "He shewed me a
pure River of Water of Life, clear as Chrystal, proceeding out

of the Throne of God and of the Lamb, *etc.*" and, in reading it, my Mind was drawn to seek after that pure Habitation, which, I then believed, God had prepared for his Servants. The Place where I sat, and the Sweetness that attended my Mind, remain fresh in my Memory.

This, and the like gracious Visitations, had that Effect upon me, that when Boys used ill Language it troubled me; and, through the continued Mercies of God, I was preserved from it.

The pious Instructions of my Parents were often fresh in my Mind when I happened to be among wicked Children, and were of Use to me. My Parents, having a large Family of Children, used frequently, on first Days after Meeting, to put us to read in the holy Scriptures, or some religious Books, one after another, the rest sitting by without much Conversation; which, I have since often thought, was a good Practice. From what I had read and heard, I believed there had been, in past Ages, People who walked in Uprightness before God, in a Degree exceeding any that I knew, or heard of, now living: And the Apprehension of there being less Steadiness and Firmness, amongst People in this Age than in past Ages, often troubled me while I was a Child.

A Thing remarkable in my Childhood was, that once, going to a Neighbour's House, I saw, on the Way, a *Robin* sitting on her Nest, and as I came near she went off, but, having young ones, flew about, and with many Cries expressed her Concern for them; I stood and threw Stones at her, till, one striking her, she fell down dead: At first I was pleased with the Exploit, but after a few Minutes was seized with Horror, as having, in a sportive Way, killed an innocent Creature while she was careful for her Young: I beheld her lying dead, and thought these young ones, for which she was so careful, must now perish for want of their Dam to nourish them; and, after some painful Considerations on the Subject, I climbed up the Tree, took all the young Birds, and killed them; supposing that better than to leave them to pine away and die miserably: And believed, in this Case, that Scripture-proverb was fulfilled, "The tender Mercies of the Wicked are cruel." I then went on my Errand, but, for some Hours, could think of little else but the Cruelties I had committed, and was much troubled. Thus he, whose tender Mercies are over all his Works, hath placed a Principle in the human Mind, which incites to exercise Goodness towards every living Creature; and this being singly attended to, People become tender hearted and sympathising; but being frequently and totally rejected, the Mind becomes shut up in a contrary Disposition.

About the twelfth Year of my Age, my Father being abroad, my Mother reproved me for some Misconduct, to which I made an undutiful Reply; and, the next first Day, as I was with my Father returning from Meeting, he told me he understood I had behaved amiss to my Mother, and advised me to be more careful in future. I knew myself blameable, and in Shame and Confusion remained silent. Being thus awakened to a Sense of my Wickedness, I felt Remorse in my Mind, and, getting home, I retired and prayed to the Lord to forgive me; and do not remember that I ever, after that, spoke unhandsomely to either of my Parents, however foolish in some other Things.

Having attained the Age of sixteen Years, I began to love wanton Company; and though I was preserved from prophane Language, or scandalous Conduct, still I perceived a Plant in me which produced much wild Grapes; yet my merciful Father forsook me not utterly, but, at Times, through his Grace, I was brought seriously to consider my Ways; and the Sight of my Backslidings affected me with Sorrow; but, for want of rightly attending to the Reproofs of Instruction, Vanity was added to Vanity, and Repentance to Repentance: Upon the whole, my Mind was more and more alienated from the Truth, and I hastened toward Destruction. While I meditate on the Gulph towards which I travelled, and reflect on my youthful Disobedience, for these Things I weep, mine Eyes run down with Water.

Advancing in Age, the Number of my Acquaintances increased, and thereby my Way grew more difficult; though I had found Comfort in reading the holy Scriptures, and thinking on heavenly Things, I was now estranged therefrom: I knew I was going from the Flock of Christ, and had no Resolution to return; hence serious Reflections were uneasy to me, and youthful Vanities and Diversions my greatest Pleasure. Running in this Road I found many like myself; and we associated in that which is the reverse of true Friendship.

But in this swift Race it pleased God to visit me with Sickness, so that I doubted of recovering; and then did Darkness, Horror, and Amazement, with full Force, seize me, even when my Pain and Distress of Body was very great. I thought it would have been better for me never to have had a Being, than to see the Day which I now saw. I was filled with Confusion; and in great Affliction, both of Mind and Body, I lay and bewailed myself. I had not Confidence to lift up my Cries to God, whom I had thus offended; but, in a deep Sense of my great Folly, I was humbled before him; and, at length, that Word which is as a Fire and a Hammer, broke and dissolved my rebellious Heart, and then my Cries were put up in Contrition; and in the multitude of his Mercies I found inward Relief, and felt a close Engagement, that, if he was pleased to restore my Health, I might walk humbly before him.

After my Recovery, this Exercise remained with me a considerable Time; but, by Degrees, giving Way to youthful Vanities, they gained Strength, and, getting with wanton young People, I lost Ground. The Lord had been very gracious, and spoke Peace to me in the Time of my Distress; and I now most ungratefully turned again to Folly; on which Account, at Times, I felt sharp Reproof. I was not so hardy as to commit Things scandalous; but to exceed in Vanity, and promote Mirth, was my chief Study. Still I retained a Love for pious People, and their Company brought an Awe upon me. My dear Parents, several Times, admonished me in the Fear of the Lord, and their Admonition entered into my Heart, and had a good Effect for a Season; but, not getting deep enough to pray rightly, the Tempter, when he came, found Entrance. I remember once, having spent a Part of the Day in Wantonness, as I went to Bed at Night, there lay in a Window, near my Bed, a Bible, which I opened, and first cast my Eye on this Text, "We lie down in our Shame, and our Confusion covers us:" This I knew to be my Case; and, meeting with so unexpected a Reproof, I was somewhat affected with it, and went to Bed under Remorse of Conscience; which I soon cast off again.

Thus Time passed on: My Heart was replenished with Mirth and Wantonness, and pleasing Scenes of Vanity were presented to my Imagination, till I attained the Age of eighteen Years; near which Time I felt the Judgments of God, in my Soul, like a consuming Fire; and, looking over my past Life, the Prospect was moving.—I was often sad, and longed to be delivered from those Vanities; then again, my Heart was strongly inclined to them, and there was in me a sore Conflict: At Times I turned to Folly, and then again, Sorrow and Confusion took hold of me. In a while, I resolved totally to leave off some of my Vanities; but there was a secret Reserve, in my Heart, of the more refined Part of them, and I was not low enough to find true Peace. Thus, for some Months, I had great Troubles; there remaining in me an unsubjected Will, which rendered my Labours fruitless, till at length, through the merciful Continuance of heavenly Visitations, I was made to bow down in Spirit before the Lord. I remember one Evening I had spent some Time in reading a pious Author; and walking out alone, I humbly prayed to the Lord for his Help, that I might be delivered from all those Vanities which so ensnared me. Thus, being brought low, he helped me; and, as I learned to bear the Cross, I felt Refreshment to come from his Presence; but, not keeping in that Strength which gave Victory, I lost Ground again; the Sense of which greatly affected me; and I sought Desarts and lonely Places, and there, with Tears, did confess my Sins to God, and humbly craved Help of him. And I may say with Reverence, he was near to me in my Troubles, and in those Times of Humiliation opened my Ear to Discipline. I was now led to look seriously at the Means by which I was drawn from the pure Truth, and learned this, that, if I would live in the Life which the faithful Servants of God lived in, I must not go into Company as heretofore in my own Will; but all the Cravings of Sense must be governed by a divine Principle. In Times of Sorrow and Abasement these Instructions were sealed upon me, and I felt the Power of Christ prevail over selfish Desires, so that I was preserved in a good degree of Steadiness; and, being young, and believing at that Time that a single Life was best for me, I was strengthened to keep from such Company as had often been a Snare to me.

I kept steadily to Meetings; spent First-day Afternoons chiefly in reading the Scriptures and other good Books; and was early convinced in Mind, that true Religion consisted in an inward Life, wherein the Heart doth love and reverence God the Creator, and learns to exercise true Justice and Goodness, not only toward all Men, but also toward the brute Creatures.—That as the Mind was moved, by an inward Principle, to love God as an invisible incomprehensible Being, by the same Principle it was moved to love him in all his Manifestations in the visible World.—That, as by his Breath the Flame of Life was kindled in all animal sensible Creatures, to say we love God, and, at the same Time exercise Cruelty toward the least Creature, is a Contradiction in itself.

I found no Narrowness respecting Sects and Opinions; but believed, that sincere upright-hearted People, in every Society, who truly love God, were accepted of him.

As I lived under the Cross, and simply followed the Openings of Truth, my Mind, from Day to Day, was more enlightened; my former Acquaintance were left to judge of me as they would, for I found it safest for me to live in private, and keep these Things sealed up in my own Breast. While I silently ponder on that Change wrought in me, I find no Language equal to it, nor any Means to convey to another a clear Idea of it. I looked on the Works of God in this visible Creation, and an Awfulness covered me; my Heart was tender and often contrite, and universal Love to my Fellow-creatures increased in me: This will be understood by such as have trodden the same Path. Some Glances of real Beauty may be seen in their Faces, who dwell in true Meekness. There is a Harmony in the Sound of that Voice to which divine Love gives Utterance, and some Appearance of right Order in their Temper and Conduct, whose Passions are regulated; yet all these do not fully shew forth that inward Life to such as have

not felt it: But this white Stone and new Name is known
rightly to such only as have it.

. . . . .

[*White Men and Indians*]

In my Youth I was used to hard Labour; and, though I was
middling healthy, yet my Nature was not fitted to endure so
much as many others: So that, being often weary, I was prepared to sympathize with those whose Circumstances in Life,
as free Men, required constant Labour to answer the Demands
of their Creditors, and with others under Oppression. In the
Uneasiness of Body, which I have many Times felt by too
much Labour, not as a forced but as a voluntary Oppression,
I have often been excited to think on the original Cause of
that Oppression, which is imposed on many in the World:
And, the latter Part of the Time wherein I laboured on our
Plantation, my Heart, through the fresh Visitations of heavenly
Love, being often tender, and my leisure Time frequently spent
in reading the Life and Doctrines of our blessed Redeemer,
the Account of the Sufferings of Martyrs, and the History of
the first Rise of our Society, a Belief was gradually settled in
my Mind, that if such, as had great Estates, generally lived in
that Humility and Plainness which belongs to a *Christian* Life,
and laid much easier Rents and Interests on their Lands and
Monies, and thus led the Way to a right Use of Things, so
great a Number of People might be employed in Things useful,
that Labour, both for Men and other Creatures, would need
to be no more than an agreeable Employ; and divers Branches
of Business, which serve chiefly to please the natural Inclinations of our Minds, and which, at present, seem necessary to
circulate that Wealth which some gather, might, in this Way
of pure Wisdom, be discontinued. And, as I have thus considered these Things, a Query, at Times, hath arisen: Do I,
in all my Proceedings, keep to that Use of Things which is
agreeable to universal Righteousness? And then there hath
some Degree of Sadness, at Times, come over me, for that I

accustomed myself to some Things, which occasioned more Labour than I believe divine Wisdom intends for us.

From my early Acquaintance with Truth I have often felt an inward Distress, occasioned by the striving of a Spirit in me against the Operation of the heavenly Principle; and in this Circumstance have been affected with a Sense of my own Wretchedness, and in a mourning Condition felt earnest Longing for that divine Help, which brings the Soul into true Liberty; and sometimes, in this State, retiring into private Places, the Spirit of Supplication hath been given me; and, under a heavenly Covering, I have asked my gracious Father to give me a Heart in all Things resigned to the Direction of his Wisdom.

In visiting People of Note in the Society who had Slaves, and labouring with them in brotherly Love on that Account, I have seen, and the Sight hath affected me, that a Conformity to some Customs, distinguishable from pure Wisdom, has entangled many; and the Desire of Gain, to support these Customs, greatly opposed the Work of Truth: And sometimes, when the Prospect of the Work before me has been such, that in Bowedness of Spirit, I have been drawn into retired Places, and besought the Lord with Tears that he would take me wholly under his Direction, and shew me the Way in which I ought to walk, it hath revived, with Strength of Conviction, that, if I would be his faithful Servant, I must, in all Things, attend to his Wisdom, and be teachable; and so cease from all Customs contrary thereto, however used amongst religious People.

As he is the Perfection of Power, of Wisdom, and of Goodness, so, I believe, he hath provided, that so much Labour shall be necessary for Men's Support, in this World, as would, being rightly divided, be a suitable Employment of their Time; and that we cannot go into Superfluities, or grasp after Wealth in a Way contrary to his Wisdom, without having Connection with some Degree of Oppression, and with that Spirit which leads to Self-exaltation and Strife, and which frequently brings Calamities on Countries, by Parties contending about their Claims.

In the eleventh Month of the Year 1762, feeling an Engagement of Mind to visit some Families in *Mansfield*, I joined my beloved Friend, BENJAMIN JONES, and we spent a few Days together in that Service. In the second Month, 1763, I joined in Company with ELIZABETH SMITH and MARY NOBLE on a Visit to the Families of Friends at *Ancocas;* in both which Visits, through the baptizing Power of Truth, the sincere Labourers were often comforted, and the Hearts of Friends opened to receive us. And, in the fourth Month following, I accompanied some Friends in a Visit to the Families of Friends in *Mount-Holly,* in which my Mind was often drawn into an inward Awfulness, wherein strong Desires were raised for the everlasting Welfare of my Fellow-creatures; and, through the Kindness of our heavenly Father, our Hearts were, at Times, enlarged, and Friends invited, in the Flowings of divine Love, to attend to that which would settle them on the sure Foundation.

Having many Years felt Love in my Heart towards the Natives of this Land, who dwell far back in the Wilderness, whose Ancestors were the Owners and Possessors of the Land where we dwell; and who, for a very small Consideration, assigned their Inheritance to us; and, being at *Philadelphia,* in the eighth Month, 1761, in a Visit to some Friends who had Slaves, I fell in Company with some of those Natives who lived on the East Branch of the River *Susquehannah,* at an *Indian* Town called *Wehaloosing,* two hundred Miles from *Philadelphia,* and, in Conversation with them by an Interpreter, as also by Observations on their Countenances and Conduct, I believed some of them were measurably acquainted with that divine Power which subjects the rough and forward Will of the Creature: And, at Times, I felt inward Drawings toward a Visit to that Place, of which I told none except my dear Wife, until it came to some Ripeness; and, then, in the Winter, 1762, I laid it before Friends at our Monthly and Quarterly, and afterwards at our general Spring-meeting; and, having the Unity of Friends, and being thoughtful about an *Indian* Pilot, there came a Man and three Women from a little beyond that Town to *Philadelphia* on Business: And I, being informed thereof by Letter, met them in Town in the fifth Month, 1763; and, after some Conversation, finding they were sober People, I, by the Concurrence of Friends in that Place, agreed to join with them as Companions in their Return; and, on the seventh Day of the sixth Month following, we appointed to meet at SAMUEL FOULK's, at *Richland* in *Bucks* County. Now, as this Visit felt weighty, and was performed at a Time when Travelling appeared perilous, so the Dispensations of divine Providence, in preparing my Mind for it, have been memorable; and I believe it good for me to give some Hints thereof.

After I had given up to go, the Thoughts of the Journey were often attended with unusual Sadness; in which Times my Heart was frequently turned to the Lord with inward Breathings for his heavenly Support, that I might not fail to follow him wheresoever he might lead me: And, being at our Youths Meeting at *Chesterfield*, about a Week before the Time I expected to set off, I was there led to speak on that Prayer of our Redeemer to his Father: "I pray not that thou shouldest take them out of the World, but that thou shouldest keep them from the Evil." And, in attending to the pure Openings of Truth, I had to mention what he elsewhere said to his Father; "I know that thou hearest me at all Times:" So that, as some of his Followers kept their Places, and as his Prayer was granted, it followed necessarily that they were kept from Evil: And, as some of those met with great Hardships and Afflictions in this World, and at last suffered Death by cruel Men, it appears, that whatsoever befalls Men while they live in pure Obedience to God, as it certainly works for their Good, so it may not be considered an Evil as it relates to them. As I spake on this Subject, my Heart was much tendered, and great Awfulness came over me; and then, on the first Day of the next Week, being at our own Afternoon-meeting, and my Heart being enlarged in Love, I was led to speak on the Care and Protection of the Lord over his People, and to make mention of that Passage, where a Band of *Assyrians* endeavouring to take captive the Prophet, were disappointed; and how the Psalmist said, "The Angel of the Lord encampeth round about them that fear him." And thus, in true Love and Tenderness, I parted from Friends, expecting the next Morning, to proceed on my Journey, and, being weary, went early to Bed; and, after I had been asleep a short Time, I was awaked by a Man calling at my Door; and, arising, was invited to meet some Friends at a Publick-house in our Town, who came from *Philadelphia* so late, that Friends were generally gone to Bed: These Friends informed me, that an Express arrived the last Morning from *Pittsburgh*, and brought News that the *Indians* had taken a Fort from the *English* Westward, and slain and scalped *English* People in divers Places, some near the said *Pittsburgh*; and that some elderly Friends in *Philadelphia*, knowing the Time of my expecting to set off, had conferred together, and thought good to inform me of these Things, before I left Home, that I might consider them, and proceed as I believed best; so I, going again to Bed, told not my Wife till Morning. My Heart was turned to the Lord for his heavenly Instruction; and it was an humbling Time to me. When I told my dear Wife, she appeared to be deeply concerned about it; but, in a few Hours Time, my Mind became settled in a Belief, that it was my Duty to proceed on my Journey; and she bore it with a good Degree of Resignation. In this Conflict of Spirit, there were great Searchings of Heart, and strong Cries to the Lord, that no Motion might be, in the least Degree, attended to, but that of the pure Spirit of Truth.

The Subjects before-mentioned, on which I had so lately spoken in publick, were now very fresh before me; and I was brought inwardly to commit myself to the Lord, to be disposed of as he saw best. So I took Leave of my Family and Neighbours, in much Bowedness of Spirit, and went to our Monthly-meeting at *Burlington*; and, after taking Leave of Friends there, I crossed the River, accompanied by my Friends, ISRAEL and JOHN PEMBERTON; and, parting the next Morning with ISRAEL, JOHN bore me Company to SAMUEL FOULK'S, where I met the before-mentioned *Indians*, and we were glad to see each other: Here my Friend, BENJAMIN PARVIN, met me, and proposed joining as a Companion, we having passed some Letters before on the Subject; and now, on his Account, I had a sharp Trial; for, as the Journey appeared perilous, I thought, if he went chiefly to bear me Company, and we should be taken Captive, my having been the Means of drawing him into these Difficulties would add to my own Afflictions: So I told him my Mind freely, and let him know that I was resigned to go alone; but, after all, if he really believed it to be his Duty to go on, I believed his Company would be very comfortable to me: It was indeed a Time of deep Exercise, and BENJAMIN appeared to be so fastened to the Visit, that he could not be easy to leave me; so we went on, accompanied by our Friends, JOHN PEMBERTON, *and* WILLIAM LIGHTFOOT of *Pikeland,* and lodged at *Bethlehem;* and there, parting with JOHN, WILLIAM and we went forward on the ninth Day of the sixth Month, and got Lodging on the Floor of a House, about five Miles from *Fort-Allen:* Here we parted with WILLIAM; and at this Place we met with an *Indian* Trader, lately come from *Wioming;* and, in Conversation with him, I perceived that many white People do often sell Rum to the *Indians,* which, I believe, is a great Evil; first, they being thereby deprived of the Use of their Reason, and their Spirits violently agitated, Quarrels often arise, which end in Mischief; and the Bitterness and Resentments, occasioned hereby, are frequently of long Continuance; Again, their Skins and Furs, gotten through much Fatigue and hard Travels in Hunting, with which they intended to buy Clothing, when they become intoxicated, they often sell at a low Rate for more Rum; and afterward, when they suffer for want of the Necessaries of Life, are angry with those who, for the Sake of Gain, took the Advantage of their Weakness: Of this their Chiefs have often complained, at their Treaties with the *English.* Where cunning People pass Counterfeits, and impose that on others which is good for nothing, it is considered as a Wickedness; but, to sell that to People which we know does them Harm, and which often works their Ruin, for the Sake of Gain, manifests a hardened and corrupt Heart, and is an Evil, which demands the Care of all true Lovers of Virtue to suppress: And while my Mind, this Evening, was thus employed, I also remembered, that the People on the Frontiers, among whom this Evil is too common, are often poor; who venture to the Outside of a Colony, that they may live more independent on such as are wealthy, who often set high Rents on their Land: Being renewedly confirmed in a Belief, that, if all our Inhabitants lived according to sound

Wisdom, labouring to promote universal Love and Righteousness, and ceased from every inordinate Desire after Wealth,
and from all Customs which are tinctured with Luxury, the
Way would be easy for our Inhabitants, though much more
numerous than at present, to live comfortably on honest Employments, without having that Temptation they are often
under of being drawn into Schemes to make Settlements on
Lands which have not been purchased of the *Indians*, or of
applying to that wicked Practice of selling Rum to them.

On the tenth Day of the Month we set out early in the
Morning, and crossed the Western Branch of *Delaware*, called
the *Great Lehie*, near *Fort-Allen*; the Water being high, we
went over in a Canoe: Here we met an *Indian*, and had some
friendly Conversation with him, and gave him some Biscuit;
and he having killed a Deer, gave the *Indians* with us some
of it: Then, after travelling some Miles, we met several *Indian*
Men and Women with a Cow and Horse, and some Household Goods, who were lately come from their Dwelling at
Wioming, and going to settle at another Place; we made them
some small Presents, and, some of them understanding *English*,
I told them my Motive in coming into their Country, with
which they appeared satisfied: And, one of our Guides talking
a While with an ancient Woman concerning us, the poor old
Woman came to my Companion and me, and took her Leave
of us with an Appearance of sincere Affection. So, going on,
we pitched our Tent near the Banks of the same River, having
laboured hard in crossing some of those Mountains called the
Blue-Ridge; and, by the Roughness of the Stones, and the
Cavities between them, and the Steepness of the Hills, it
appeared dangerous; but we were preserved in Safety, through
the Kindness of him, whose Works in those mountainous
Desarts appeared awful: Toward whom my Heart was turned
during this Day's Travel.

Near our Tent, on the Sides of large Trees peeled for that
Purpose, were various Representations of Men going to, and
returning from the Wars, and of some killed in Battle; this
being a Path heretofore used by Warriours: And, as I walked
about viewing those *Indian* Histories, which were painted

mostly in red, but some in black; and thinking on the innumerable Afflictions which the proud, fierce, Spirit produceth in
the World; thinking on the Toils and Fatigues of Warriours,
travelling over Mountains and Desarts; thinking on their
Miseries and Distresses when wounded far from Home by their
Enemies; and of their Bruises and great Weariness in chasing
one another over the Rocks and Mountains; and of their
restless, unquiet, State of Mind, who live in this Spirit; and of
the Hatred which mutually grows up in the Minds of the
Children of those Nations engaged in War with each other:
During these Meditations, the Desire to cherish the Spirit of
Love and Peace amongst these People arose very fresh in me.
This was the first Night that we lodged in the Woods; and,
being wet with travelling in the Rain, the Ground, our Tent,
and the Bushes, which we proposed to lay under our Blankets,
being also wet, all looked discouraging; but I believed, that it
was the Lord who had thus far brought me forward, and that
he would dispose of me as he saw good; and therein I felt easy:
So we kindled a Fire, with our Tent open to it; and, with
some Bushes next the Ground, and then our Blankets, we
made our Bed, and, lying down, got some Sleep; and, in the
Morning, feeling a little unwell, I went into the River; the
Water was cold, but soon after I felt fresh and well.

The eleventh Day of the sixth Month, the Bushes being
wet, we tarried in our Tent till about eight o'Clock; when, going
on, we crossed a high Mountain supposed to be upwards of four
Miles over; the Steepness on the North Side exceeding all the
others. We also crossed two Swamps, and, it raining near Night,
we pitched our Tent and lodged.

About Noon, on our Way, we were overtaken by one of the
Moravian Brethren, going to *Wehaloosing*, and an *Indian* Man
with him, who could talk *English*; and we, being together while
our Horses ate Grass, had some friendly Conversation; but they,
travelling faster than we, soon left us. This *Moravian*, I understood, had spent some Time this Spring at *Wehaloosing*, and
was, by some of the *Indians*, invited to come again.

The twelfth Day of the sixth Month, and first of the Week,
it being a rainy Day, we continued in our Tent; and here I was

led to think on the Nature of the Exercise which hath attended me: Love was the first Motion, and thence a Concern arose to spend some Time with the *Indians,* that I might feel and understand their Life, and the Spirit they live in, if haply I might receive some Instruction from them, or they be in any Degree helped forward by my following the Leadings of Truth amongst them: And, as it pleased the Lord to make Way for my going at a Time when the Troubles of War were increasing, and when, by Reason of much wet Weather, Travelling was more difficult than usual at that Season, I looked upon it as a more favourable Opportunity to season my Mind, and bring me into a nearer Sympathy with them: And, as mine Eye was to the great Father of Mercies, humbly desiring to learn what his Will was concerning me, I was made quiet and content.

Our Guide's Horse, though hoppled, went away in the Night; after finding our own, and searching some Time for him, his Footsteps were discovered in the Path going back again, whereupon my kind Companion went off in the Rain, and, about seven Hours after, returned with him: And here we lodged again; tying up our Horses before we went to Bed, and loosing them to feed about Break of Day.

On the thirteenth Day of the sixth month, the Sun appearing, we set forward; and, as I rode over the barren Hills, my Meditations were on the Alterations of the Circumstances of the Natives of this Land since the Coming in of the *English.* The Lands near the Sea are conveniently situated for fishing; the Lands near the Rivers, where the Tides flow, and some above, are in many Places fertile, and not mountainous; while the Running of the Tides makes passing up and down easy with any Kind of Traffic. Those Natives have, in some Places, for trifling Considerations, sold their Inheritance so favourably situated; and, in other Places, been driven back by superior Forces: So that in many Places, as their Way of clothing themselves is now altered from what it was, and they, far remote from us, have to pass over Mountains, Swamps, and barren Desarts, Travelling is very troublesome, in bringing their Skins and furs to trade with us.

By the extending of *English* Settlements, and partly by

English Hunters, the wild Beasts, they chiefly depend on for a Subsistance, are not so plenty as they were; and People too often, for the Sake of Gain, open a Door for them to waste their Skins and Furs, in purchasing a Liquor which tends to the Ruin of them and their Families.

My own Will and Desires were now very much broken, and my Heart, with much Earnestness, turned to the Lord, to whom alone I looked for Help in the Dangers before me. I had a Prospect of the *English* along the Coast, for upwards of nine hundred Miles, where I had travelled; and the favourable Situation of the *English*, and the Difficulties attending the Natives in many Places, and the Negroes, were open before me; and a weighty and heavenly Care came over my Mind, and Love filled my Heart toward all Mankind, in which I felt a strong Engagement, that we might be obedient to the Lord, while, in tender Mercies, he is yet calling to us; and so attend to pure universal Righteousness, as to give no just Cause of Offence to the *Gentiles*, who do not profess *Christianity*, whether the Blacks from *Africa*, or the native Inhabitants of this Continent: And here I was led into a close laborious Enquiry, whether I, as an Individual, kept clear from all Things which tended to stir up, or were connected with Wars, either in this Land or *Africa*; and my Heart was deeply concerned, that, in future, I might in all Things keep steadily to the pure Truth, and live and walk in the Plainness and Simplicity of a sincere Follower of Christ. And, in this lonely Journey, I did, this Day, greatly bewail the Spreading of a wrong Spirit, believing, that the prosperous, convenient, Situation of the *English*, requires a constant Attention to divine Love and Wisdom to guide and support us in a Way answerable to the Will of that good, gracious, and almighty Being, who hath an equal Regard to all Mankind: And, here, Luxury and Covetousness, with the numerous Oppressions, and other Evils attending them, appeared very afflicting to me; and I felt in that which is immutable, that the Seeds of great Calamity and Desolation are sown and growing fast on this Continent: Nor have I Words sufficient to set forth that Longing I then felt, that we, who are placed along the Coast, and have tasted the Love and Goodness of God, might arise in his Strength; and, like faithful Messengers, labour to check the Growth of these Seeds, that they may not ripen to the Ruin of our Posterity.

. . . . .

VI

THE AMERICAN AS
AUGUSTAN POET

If, in the first half of the eighteenth century, colonial Americans could not produce a distinguished belles lettres, still they felt the need for one. Edward Taylor, it is true, was writing early in the century; yet his affinities in poetry as well as in religion were with the century before; and, like other Puritan poetry, his work derived its strength from a religious attitude alien to most Americans in his time. A Virginia gentleman such as William Byrd is more characteristic of his time than is Taylor. Byrd often indulged himself in flights of poetic fancy—but, as ten examples of his verse here printed show, only briefly and with no high seriousness; for him esthetic experience was that which adorned a gentleman's leisure. His way, indeed, points to the way of most other colonial poets of the first half of the eighteenth century. They wrote poems enough, even devout poems; they were, however, poems à la mode, to be taken only as seriously as the time spent on them would allow. Literature represented high culture. High culture, the culture of learned, imaginative leisure, came from England. Americans who wanted to be highly cultured aspired to be cultured Englishmen. Thus the American, if he was to be a poet, was an Augustan poet, or none. Literary nationalism was still in the very dim future.

The poetry is not distinguished, certainly; but it is often marked with wit and intelligence. We should take it seriously, but not with high seriousness. For we cannot afford to neglect it if we are to understand the nature of our colonial culture. It is a poetry of the kind which anonymous or pseudonymous Englishmen contributed to their *Gentleman's Magazine*. It represents all the proper modes—songs, satires, Miltonic imitations, and the like—in all the proper forms. It covers all the proper subject-matters—the foibles of colonial society, love for the classically named maiden, worship of the sublime deity, and celebration of neoclassical contentment. Yet we must read it not only for its imitativeness but for its significance to colonial Americans becoming conscious of their own need for imaginative maturity, happy to do in America what was done in England, determined, even in their leisure, to establish a civilization.

Bibliographical Note. There are no general studies of this period of American poetry except those in Tyler's *History* and the first volume of the *Literary History of the United States*; highly specialized studies are listed in the bibliographies in the third volume of the latter. The basis for general studies can now be found in Kenneth Silverman, ed., *Colonial American Poetry* (New York, 1968).

Ebenezer Cook

(*fl.* 1708–1732)

"THE SOT-WEED FACTOR"*
(1708)†

Text: The Sot-weed Factor: Or, a Voyage
to Maryland. A Satyr (*London,* 1708).
(*Cook published another,
toned-down version of this poem in 1731.*)

> Condemn'd by Fate to way-ward Curse,
> Of Friends unkind, and empty Purse;
> Plagues worse then fill'd *Pandora's* Box,
> I took my leave of *Albion's* Rocks:
> With heavy Heart, concern'd that I ⎫
> Was forc'd my Native Soil to fly,   ⎬
> And the *Old World* must bid good-buy. ⎭
> But Heav'n ordain'd it should be so,
> And to repine is vain we know:
> Freighted with Fools, from *Plymouth* sound,
> To *Mary-Land* our Ship was bound;
> Where we arriv'd in dreadful Pain,
> Shock'd by the Terrours of the Main;
> For full three Months, our wavering Boat,
> Did thro' the surley Ocean float,
> And furious Storms and threat'ning Blasts,

---

* Sot-weed: tobacco.
† The lettered footnotes are Cook's own.

Both tore our Sails and sprung our Masts:
Wearied, yet pleas'd, we did escape
Such Ills, we anchor'd at the (a) *Cape;*
But weighing soon, we plough'd the *Bay,*
To (b) *Cove* it in (c) *Piscato-way,*
Intending there to open Store,
I put myself and Goods a-shore:
Where soon repair'd a numerous Crew,
In Shirts and Drawers of (d) *Scotch-cloth* Blue.
With neither Stockings, Hat, nor Shooe.
These *Sot-weed* Planters Crowd the Shoar,
In Hue as tawny as a Moor:
Figures so strange, no God design'd,
To be a part of Humane Kind:
But wanton Nature, void of Rest,
Moulded the brittle Clay in Jest.
At last a Fancy very odd
Took me, this was the Land of *Nod;*
Planted at first, when Vagrant *Cain,*
His Brother had unjustly slain:
Then conscious of the Crime he'd done,
From Vengeance dire, he hither run;
And in a Hut supinely dwelt,
The first in *Furs* and *Sot-weed* dealt.
And ever since his Time, the Place,
Has harbour'd a destested Race;
Who when they cou'd not live at Home,
For Refuge to these Worlds did roam;
In hopes by Flight they might prevent,
The Devil and his fell intent;
Obtain from Tripple Tree repreive,
And Heav'n and Hell alike deceive:

(a) By the *Cape,* is meant the *Capes* of *Virginia,* the first Land on the Coast of *Virginia* and *Mary-Land.* [This and the following notes are Cook's.]
(b) To *Cove* is to lie at Anchor safe in Harbour.
(c) The Bay of *Piscato-way,* the usual place where our Ships come to an Anchor in *Mary-Land.*
(d) The Planters generally wear Blue *Linnen.*

But e're their Manners I display,
I think it fit I open lay
My Entertainment by the way;
That Strangers well may be aware on,
What homely Diet they must fare on.
To touch that Shoar, where no good Sense is found,
But Conversation's lost, and Manners drown'd.
I crost unto the other side,   ⎫
A River whose impetuous Tide,   ⎬
The Savage Borders does divide;   ⎭
In such a shining odd invention,
I scarce can give its due Dimention.
The *Indians* call this watry Waggon
(*e*) *Canoo*, a Vessel none can brag on;
Cut from a *Popular-Tree*, or *Pine*,
And fashion'd like a Trough for Swine:
In this most noble Fishing-Boat,
I boldly put myself a-float;
Standing Erect, with Legs stretch'd wide,
We paddled to the other side:
Where being Landed safe by hap,
As *Sol* fell into *Thetis* Lap.
A ravenous Gang bent on the stroul,
Of (*f*) Wolves for Prey, began to howl;
This put me in a pannick Fright,
Least I should be devoured quite:
But as I there a musing stood,
And quite benighted in a Wood,
A Female Voice pierc'd thro' my Ears,
Crying, *You Rogue drive home the Steers,*
I listen'd to th'attractive sound,   ⎫
And straight a Herd of Cattel found   ⎬
Drove by a Youth, and homewards bound: ⎭
Cheer'd with the sight, I straight thought fit,
To ask where I a Bed might get.
The surley Peasant bid me stay,

(*e*) A *Canoo* is an *Indian* Boat, cut out of the body of a Popler-Tree.
(*f*) Wolves are very numerous in *Mary-Land*.

And ask'd from whom (g) I'de run away.
Surpriz'd at such a saucy Word,
I instantly lugg'd out my Sword;
Swearing I was no Fugitive,
But from *Great-Britain* did arrive,
In hopes I better there might Thrive.
To which he mildly made reply,
I beg your Pardon, Sir, *that I*
Should talk to you Unmannerly;
But if you please to go with me
To yonder House, you'll welcome be.
Encountring soon the smoaky Seat,
The Planter old did thus me greet:
"Whether you come from Goal or Colledge,
"You're welcome to my certain Knowledge;
"And if you please all Night to stay,
"My Son shall put you in the way.
Which offer I most kindly took,
And for a Seat did round me look:
When presently amongst the rest,
He plac'd his unknown *English* Guest,
Who found them drinking for a whet,
A Cask of (h) Syder on the Fret,
Till Supper came upon the Table,
On which I fed whilst I was able.
So after hearty Entertainment,
Of Drink and Victuals without Payment;
For Planters Tables, you must know,
Are free for all that come and go.
While (i) Pon and Milk, with (k) Mush well stoar'd,
In wooden Dishes grac'd the Board;
With (l) Homine and Syder-pap,

(g) 'Tis supposed by the Planters, that all unknown Persons are run away from some Master.
(h) Syder-pap is a sort of Food made of Syder and small Homine, like our Oat-meal.
(i) Pon is Bread made of *Indian-Corn.*
(k) Mush is a sort of Hasty-pudding made with Water and *Indian* Flower.
(l) Homine is a Dish that is made of boiled *Indian*-Wheat, eaten with Molossus, or Bacon-Fat.

(Which scarce a hungry Dog wou'd lap)
Well stuff'd with Fat, from Bacon fry'd,
Or with *Molossus* dulcify'd.
Then out our Landlord pulls a Pouch,
As greasy as the Leather Couch
On which he sat, and straight begun,
To load with Weed his *Indian* Gun;
In length, scarce longer than ones Finger,
Or that for which the Ladies linger:
His Pipe smoak'd out with aweful Grace,
With aspect grave and solemn pace;
The reverend Sire walks to a Chest,
Of all his Furniture the best,
Closely confin'd within a Room,
Which seldom felt the weight of Broom;
From thence he lugs a Cag of Rum,
And nodding to me, thus begun:
I find, says he, you don't much care,
For this our *Indian* Country Fare;
But let me tell you, Friend of mine, ⎫
You may be glad of it in time, ⎬
Tho' now your Stomach is so fine; ⎭
And if within this Land you stay,
You'll find it true what I do say.
This said, the Rundlet up he threw,
And bending backwards strongly drew:
I pluck'd as stoutly for my part,
Altho' it made me sick at Heart,
And got so soon into my Head
I scarce cou'd find my way to Bed;
Where I was instantly convey'd
By one who pass'd for Chamber-Maid;
Tho' by her loose and sluttish Dress,
She rather seem'd a *Bedlam-Bess*:
Curious to know from whence she came,
I prest her to declare her Name.
She Blushing, seem'd to hide her Eyes,
And thus in Civil Terms replies;
In better Times, e'er to this Land,

I was unhappily Trapann'd;
Perchance as well I did appear,
As any Lord or Lady here,
Not then a Slave for twice two (m) Year.
My Cloaths were fashionably new,
Nor were my Shifts of Linnen Blue;
But things are changed now at the Hoe,
I daily work, and Bare-foot go,
In weeding Corn or feeding Swine,
I spend my melancholy Time.
Kidnap'd and Fool'd, I hither fled,
To shun a hated Nuptial (n) Bed,
And to my cost already find,
Worse Plagues than those I left behind.
Whate'er the Wanderer did profess,
Good-faith I cou'd not choose but guess
The Cause which brought her to this place,
Was supping e'er the Priest said Grace.
Quick as my Thoughts, the Slave was fled,
(Her Candle left to shew my Bed)
Which made of Feathers soft and good,
Close in the (o) Chimney-corner stood;
I threw me down expecting Rest,
To be in golden Slumbers blest:
But soon a noise disturb'd my quiet,
And plagu'd me with nocturnal Riot;
A Puss which in the ashes lay,
With grunting Pig began a Fray;
And prudent Dog, that Feuds might cease,
Most strongly bark'd to keep the Peace.
This Quarrel scarcely was decided,
By stick that ready lay provided;
But *Reynard* arch and cunning Loon,
Broke into my Appartment soon;

(m) 'Tis the Custom for Servants to be obliged for four Years to very servile Work; after which time they have their Freedom.
(n) These are the general Excuses made by *English* Women, which are sold, or sell themselves to *Mary-Land*.
(o) Beds stand in the Chimney-corner in this Country.

In hot pursuit of Ducks and Geese,
With fell intent the same to seize:
Their Cackling Plaints with strange surprize,
Chac'd Sleeps thick Vapours from my Eyes:
Raging I jump'd upon the Floar,
And like a Drunken Saylor Swore;
With Sword I fiercly laid about,
And soon dispers'd the Feather'd Rout:
The Poultry out of Window flew,
And *Reynard* cautiously withdrew:
The Dogs who this Encounter heard,
Fiercely themselves to aid me rear'd,
And to the Place of Combat run,
Exactly as the Field was won.
Fretting and hot as roasting Capon,
And greasy as a Flitch of Bacon;
I to the Orchard did repair,
To Breathe the cool and open Air;
Expecting there the rising Day,
Extended on a Bank I lay:
But Fortune here, that saucy Whore,
Disturb'd me worse and plagu'd me more,
Than she had done the night before.
Hoarse croaking (*p*) Frogs did 'bout me ring,
Such Peals the Dead to Life wou'd bring,
A Noise might move their Wooden King.
I stuff'd my Ears with Cotten white
For fear of being deaf out-right,
And curst the melancholy Night:
But soon my Vows I did recant,
And Hearing as a Blessing grant;
When a confounded Rattle-Snake,
With hissing made my Heart to ake:
Not knowing how to fly the Foe,
Or whether in the Dark to go;
By strange good Luck, I took a Tree,

(*p*) Frogs are called *Virginea* Bells, and make, (both in that Country and *Mary-Land*) during the Night, a very hoarse ungrateful Noise.

Prepar'd by Fate to set me free;
Where riding on a Limb a-stride,
Night and the Branches did me hide,
And I the Devil and Snake defy'd.
Not yet from Plagues exempted quite,
The curst Muskitoes did me bite;
Till rising Morn' and blushing Day,
Drove both my Fears and Ills away;
And from Night's Errors set me free.
Discharg'd from hospitable Tree;
I did to Planters Booth repair,
And there at Breakfast nobly Fare,
On rashier broil'd of infant Bear:
I thought the Cub delicious Meat,
Which ne'er did ought but Chesnuts eat;
Nor was young Orsin's flesh the worse,
Because he suck'd a Pagan Nurse.
Our Breakfast done, my Landlord stout,
Handed a Glass of Rum about;
Pleas'd with the Treatment I did find,
I took my leave of Oast so kind;
Who to oblige me, did provide,
His eldest Son to be my Guide,
And lent me Horses of his own,
A skittish Colt, and aged Rhoan,
The four-leg'd prop of his Wife *Joan.*
Steering our Barks in Trot or Pace,
We sail'd directly for a place
In *Mary-Land* of high renown,
Known by the Name of *Battle-Town.*
To view the Crowds did there resort,
Which Justice made, and Law their sport,
In that sagacious County Court:
Scarce had we enter'd on the way,
Which thro' thick Woods and Marshes lay:
But *Indians* strange did soon appear,
In hot persuit of wounded Deer;
No mortal Creature can express,
His wild fantastick Air and Dress;

His painted Skin in colours dy'd,
His sable Hair in Satchel ty'd,
Shew'd Savages not free from Pride:
His tawny Thighs, and Bosom bare,
Disdain'd a useless Coat to wear,
Scorn'd Summer's Heat, and Winters Air;
His manly Shoulders such as please,
Widows and Wives, were bath'd in Grease
Of Cub and Bear, whose supple Oil,
Prepar'd his Limbs 'gainst Heat or Toil.
Thus naked Pict in Battel faught,
Or undisguis'd his Mistress sought;
And knowing well his Ware was good,
Refus'd to screen it with a Hood;
His Visage dun, and chin that ne'er ⎤
Did Raizor feel or Scissers bear, ⎬
Or know the Ornament of Hair, ⎦
Look'd sternly Grim, surpriz'd with Fear,
I spur'd my Horse, as he drew near:
But Rhoan who better knew than I,
The little Cause I had to fly;
Seem'd by his solemn steps and pace,
Resolv'd I shou'd the Specter face,
Nor faster mov'd, tho' spur'd and lick'd,
Than *Balaam's* Ass by Prophet kick'd.
Kekicknitop (*q*) the Heathen cry'd:
How is it *Tom*. my Friend reply'd,
Judging from thence the Brute was civel,
I boldly fac'd the Courteous Devil;
And lugging out a Dram of Rum,
I gave his Tawny worship some:
Who in his language as I guess,
(My Guide informing me no less,)
Implored the (*r*) Devil, me to bless.

(*q*) *Kekichnitop* is an *Indian* Expression, and signifies no more than this, *How do you do?*
(*r*) These *Indians* worship the Devil, and pray to him as we do to God Almighty. 'Tis suppos'd, That *America* was peopl'd from *Scythia* or *Tartaria*, which Borders on *China*, by reason the *Tartarians* and *Americans* very much agree in their Manners, Arms and Government. Other Persons are

I thank'd him for his good Intent,
And forwards on my Journey went;
Discoursing as along I rode,
Whether this Race was framed by God
Or whether some Malignant pow'r,
Contriv'd them in an evil hour
And from his own Infernal Look;
Their Dusky form and Image took:
From hence we fell to Argument
Whence Peopled was this Continent,
My Friend suppos'd *Tartarians* wild,
Or *Chinese* from their Home exiled;
Wandring thro' Mountains hid with Snow,
And Rills did in the Vallies flow,
Far to the South of *Mexico:*
Broke thro' the Barrs which Nature cast,
And wide unbeaten Regions past,
Till near those Streams the humane deludge roll'd,
Which sparkling shin'd with glittering Sands of Gold;
And fetch (s) *Pizarro* from the (t) *Iberian* Shoar,
To Rob the Natives of their fatal Stoar.
I Smil'd to hear my young Logician,
Thus Reason like a Politician;
Who ne'rc by Fathers Pains and Earning
Had got at Mother *Cambridge* Learning;
Where Lubber youth just free from birch
Most stoutly drink to prop the Church;
Nor with (u) *Grey Groat* had taken Pains

---

of Opinion, that the *Chinese* first peopled the *West Indies*; imagining *China* and the Southern part of *America* to be contiguous. Others believe that the *Phoenicians* who were very skilful Mariners, first planted a Colony in the Isles of *America,* and supply'd the Persons left to inhabit there with Women and all other Necessaries; till either the Death or Shipwreck of the first Discoverers, or some other Misfortune occasioned the loss of the Discovery, which had been purchased by the Peril of the first Adventurers.
(s) *Pizzarro* was the Person that conquer'd *Peru;* a Man of a most bloody Disposition, base, treacherous, covetous, and revengeful.
(t) *Spanish* Shoar.
(u) There is a very bad Custom in some Colledges, of giving the Students A *Groat ad purgandas Rhenes,* which is usually employ'd to the use of the Donor.

To purge his Head and Cleanse his Reines:
And in obedience to the Colledge,
Had pleas'd himself with carnal Knowledge:
And tho' I lik'd the youngester's Wit,
I judg'd the Truth he had not hit;
And could not choose but smile to think
What they could do for Meat and Drink,
Who o'er so many Desarts ran,
With Brats and Wives in *Caravan*;
Unless perchance they'd got the Trick,
To eat no more than Porker sick;
Or could with well contented Maws,
Quarter like (*v*) Bears upon their Paws.
Thinking his Reasons to confute,
I gravely thus commenc'd Dispute,
And urg'd that tho'a *Chinese* Host,
Might penetrate this *Indian* Coast;
Yet this was certainly most true,
They never cou'd the Isles subdue;
For knowing not to steer a Boat,
They could not on the Ocean float,
Or plant their Sunburnt Colonies,
In Regions parted by the Seas:
I thence inferr'd (*w*) *Phoenicians* old,
Discover'd first with Vessels bold
These Western Shoars, and planted here,
Returning once or twice a Year,
With *Naval Stoars* and Lasses kind,
To comfort those were left behind;
Till by the Winds and Tempest toar
From their intended Golden Shoar;
They suffer'd Ship-wreck, or were drown'd,
And lost the World so newly found.
But after long and learn'd Contention,

(*v*) Bears are said to live by sucking of their *Paws*, according to the Notion of some Learned Authors.
(*w*) The *Phoenicians* were the best and boldest Saylors of Antiquity, and indeed the only *Persons*, in former Ages, who durst venture themselves on the Main Sea.

We could not finish our dissention;
And when that both had talk'd their fill,
We had the self same Notion still.
Thus Parson grave well read and Sage,
Does in dispute with Priest engage;
The one protests they are not Wise,
Who judge by (x) Sense and trust their Eyes;
And vows he'd burn for it at Stake,
That Man may God his Maker make;
The other smiles at his Religion,
And vows he's but a learned Widgeon:
And when they have empty'd all their stoar ⎫
From Books and Fathers, are not more   ⎬
Convinc'd or wiser than before.   ⎭
   Scarce had we finish'd serious Story,
But I espy'd the Town before me,
And roaring Planters on the ground,
Drinking of Healths in Circle round:
Dismounting Steed with friendly Guide,
Our Horses to a Tree we ty'd,
And forwards pass'd amongst the Rout,
To chuse convenient *Quarters* out:
But being none were to be found,
We sat like others on the ground
Carousing Punch in open Air
Till Cryer did the Court declare;
The planting Rabble being met,
Their Drunken Worships likewise set:
Cryer proclaims that Noise shou'd cease,
And streight the Lawyers broke the Peace.
Wrangling for Plantiff and Defendant,
I thought they ne'er wou'd make an end on't:
With nonsence, stuff and false quotations,
With brazen Lyes and Allegations;
And in the splitting of the Cause,

(x) The *Priests* argue, That our Senses in the point of *Transubstantiation* ought not to be believed, for tho' the Consecrated Bread has all the accidents of Bread, yet they affirm, 'tis the Body of Christ, and not Bread but Flesh and Bones.

They us'd such Motions with their Paws,
As shew'd their Zeal was strongly bent,
In Blows to end the Argument.
A reverend Judge, who to the shame
Of all the Bench, cou'd write his (y) Name;
At Petty-fogger took offence,
And wonder'd at his Impudence.
My Neighbour *Dash* with scorn replies,
And in the Face of Justice flies:
The Bench in fury streight divide,
And Scribbles take, or Judges side;
The Jury, Lawyers, and their Clyents,
Contending, fight like earth-born Gyants:
But Sheriff wily lay perdue,
Hoping Indictments wou'd ensue,
And when......................
A Hat or Wig fell in the way,
He seiz'd them for the *Queen* as stray:
The Court adjourn'd in usual manner,
In Battle Blood, and fractious Clamour,
I thought it proper to provide,
A Lodging for myself and Guide,
So to our Inn we march'd away,
Which at a little distance lay;
Where all things were in such Confusion,
I thought the World at its conclusion:
A Herd of Planters on the ground,
O'er-whelm'd with Punch, dead drunk we found:
Others were fighting and contending,
Some burnt their Cloaths to save the mending.
A few whose Heads by frequent use,
Could better bare the potent Juice,
Gravely debated State Affairs.
Whilst I most nimbly trip'd up Stairs;
Leaving my Friend discoursing oddly,
And mixing things Prophane and Godly:

(y) In the County-Court of *Mary-Land*, very few of the Justices of the *Peace* can write or read.

Just then beginning to be Drunk,
As from the Company I slunk,
To every Room and Nook I crept,
In hopes I might have somewhere slept;
But all the bedding was possest
By one or other drunken Guest:
But after looking long about,
I found an antient Corn-loft out,
Glad that I might in quiet sleep,
And there my bones unfractur'd keep.
I lay'd me down secure from Fray,
And soundly snoar'd till break of Day;
When waking fresh I sat upright,
And found my Shoes were vanish'd quite,
Hat, Wig, and Stockings, all were fled
From this extended *Indian* Bed:
Vext at the Loss of Goods and Chattel,
I swore I'd give the Rascal battel,
Who had abus'd me in this sort,
And Merchant Stranger made his Sport.
I furiously descended Ladder;
No Hare in *March* was ever madder:
In vain I search'd for my Apparel,
And did with Oast and Servants Quarrel;
For one whose Mind did much aspire
To (z) Mischief, threw them in the Fire:
Equipt with neither Hat nor Shooe,
I did my coming hither rue,
And doubtful thought what I should do:
Then looking round, I saw my Friend
Lie naked on a Tables end;
A Sight so dismal to behold,
One wou'd have judg'd him dead and cold;
When wringing of his bloody Nose,
By fighting got we may suppose;
I found him not so fast asleep,

(z) 'Tis the Custom of the Planters, to throw their own, or any other
Persons Hat, Wig, Shooes or Stockings in the Fire.

Might give his Friends a cause to weep:
Rise (*a*) *Oronooko*, rise, said I,
And from this *Hell* and *Bedlam* fly.
My Guide starts up, and in amaze,
With blood-shot Eyes did round him gaze;
At length with many a sigh and groan,
He went in search of aged Rhoan;
But Rhoan, tho' seldom us'd to faulter,
Had fairly this time slipt his Halter;
And not content all Night to stay
Ty'd up from Fodder, ran away:
After my Guide to ketch him ran,
And so I lost both Horse and Man;
Which Disappointment, tho' so great,
Did only Mirth and Jests create:
Till one more Civil than the rest,
In Conversation for the best,
Observing that for want of Rhoan,
I should be left to walk alone;
Most readily did me intreat,
To take a Bottle at his Seat;
A Favour at that time so great,
I blest my kind propitious Fate;
And finding soon a fresh supply,
Of Cloaths from Stoar-house kept hard by,
I mounted streight on such a Steed,
Did rather curb, than whipping need;
And straining at the usual rate,   ⎫
With spur of Punch which lay in Pate,   ⎬
E'er long we lighted at the Gate: ⎭
Where in an antient *Cedar* House,
Dwelt my new Friend, a (*b*) Cockerouse;
Whose Fabrick, tho' 'twas built of Wood,
Had many Springs and Winters stood;
When sturdy Oaks, and lofty Pines

(*a*) Planters are usually call'd by the Name of *Oronooko*, from their Planting *Oronooko-Tobacco*.
(*b*) Cockerouse, is a Man of Quality.

Were level'd with (c) Musmelion Vines,
And Plants eradicated were,
By Hurricanes into the air;
There with good Punch and apple Juice,
We spent our Hours without abuse:
Till Midnight in her sable Vest,
Persuaded Gods and Men to rest;
And with a pleasing kind surprize,
Indulg'd soft Slumbers to my Eyes.
Fierce (d) Æthon courser of the Sun,
Had half his Race exactly run;
And breath'd on me a fiery Ray,
Darting hot Beams the following Day,
When snug in Blanket white I lay:
But Heat and (e) Chinces rais'd the Sinner,
Most opportunely to his Dinner;
Wild Fowl and Fish delicious Meats,
As good as Neptune's Doxy eats,
Began our Hospitable Treat;
Fat Venson follow'd in the Rear,
And Turkies (f) wild Luxurious Chear:
But what the Feast did most commend,
Was hearty welcom from my Friend.
Thus having made a noble Feast;
And eat as well as pamper'd Priest,
Madera strong in flowing Bowls,
Fill'd with extream, delight our Souls;
Till wearied with a purple Flood,
Of generous Wine (the Giant's blood,
As Poets feign) away I made,
For some refreshing verdant Shade;
Where musing on my Rambles strange,
And Fortune which so oft did change;
In midst of various Contemplations

(c) Musmilleon Vines are what we call Muskmilleon Plants.
(d) Æthon is one of the Poetical Horses of the Sun.
(e) Chinces are a sort of Vermin like our Bugs in England.
(f) Wild Turkies are very good Meat, and prodigiously large in Maryland.

Of Fancies odd, and Meditations,
I slumber'd long. . . . .
Till hazy Night with noxious Dews,
Did Sleep's unwholsom Fetters lose:
With Vapours chil'd, and misty air,
To fire-side I did repair:
Near which a jolly Female Crew,
Were deep engag'd at *Lanctre-Looe*;
In Nightrails white, with dirty Mein,
Such Sights are scarce in *England* seen:
I thought them first some Witches bent,
On Black Designs in dire Convent.
Till one who with affected air,
Had nicely learn'd to Curse and Swear:
Cry'd Dealing's lost is but a Flam,
And vow'd by G-d she'd keep her *Pam*.
When dealing through the board had run,
They ask'd me kindly to make one;
Not staying often to be bid,
I sat me down as others did:
We scarce had play'd a Round about,
But that these *Indian* Froes fell out.
D—m you, says one, tho' now so brave,
I knew you late a Four Years Slave;
What if for Planters Wife you go,
Nature design'd you for the Hoe.
Rot you replies the other streight,
The Captain kiss'd you for his Freight;
And if the Truth was known aright,
And how you walk'd the Streets by night,
You'd blush (if one cou'd blush) for shame,
Who from *Bridewell* or *Newgate* came.
From Words they fairly fell to Blows,
And being loath to interpose,
Or meddle in the Wars of Punk,
Away to Bed in hast I slunk.
Waking next day, with aking Head,
And Thirst, that made me quit my Bed;
I rigg'd myself, and soon got up,

To cool my Liver with a Cup
Of (g) *Succahana* fresh and clear,
Not half so good as *English* Beer;
Which ready stood in Kitchin Pail,
And was in fact but *Adam's* Ale;
For Planters Cellars you must know,
Seldom with good *October* flow,
But Perry Quince and Apple Juice,
Spout from the Tap like any Sluce;
Untill the Cask's grown low and stale,
They're forc'd again to (h) Goad and Pail:
The soathing drought scarce down my Throat,
Enough to put a Ship a float,
With Cockerouse as I was sitting,
I felt a Feaver Intermitting;
A fiery Pulse beat in my Veins,
From Cold I felt resembling Pains:
This cursed seasoning I remember,
Who neither Swore nor kept his Word,
But cheated in the Fear of God;
And when his Debts he would not pay,
By Light within he ran away.
With this sly Zealot soon I struck
A Bargain for my *English* Truck,
Agreeing for ten thousand weight,
Of *Sot-weed* good and fit for freight,
Broad *Oronooko* bright and sound,
The growth and product of his ground;
In Cask that should contain compleat,
Five hundred of Tobacco neat.
The Contract thus betwixt us made,
Not well acquainted with the Trade,
My Goods I trusted to the Cheat,
Whose crop was then aboard the Fleet;
And going to receive my own,

(g) *Succahana* is Water.
(h) A *Goad* grows upon an *Indian* Vine, resembling a Bottle, when ripe it
is hollow; this the Planters make use of to drink water out of.

I found the Bird was newly flown:
Cursing this execrable Slave,
This damn'd pretended Godly Knave;
On due Revenge and Justice bent,
I instantly to Counsel went,
Unto an ambodexter (*i*) *Quack*,
Who learnedly had got the knack
Of giving Glisters, making Pills,
Of filling Bonds, and forging Wills;
And with a stock of Impudence,
Supply'd his want of Wit and Sense;
With Looks demure, amazing People,
No wiser than a Daw in Steeple;
My Anger flushing in my Face,
I stated the preceding Case:
And of my Money was so lavish,
That he'd have poyson'd half the Parish,
And hang'd his Father on a Tree,
For such another tempting Fee;
Smiling, said he, the Cause is clear,
I'll manage him you need not fear;
The Case is judg'd, good Sir, but look ⎤
In *Galen*, No—in my Lord *Cook*,   ⎬
I vow to God I was mistook: ⎦
I'll take out a Provincial Writ,
And Trounce him for his Knavish Wit;
Upon my Life we'll win the Cause,
With all the ease I cure the (*j*) *Yaws*:
Resolv'd to plague the holy Brother,
I set one Rogue to catch another;
To try the Cause then fully bent,
Up to (*k*) *Annapolis* I went,
A City Situate on a Plain,
Where scarce a House will keep out Rain;
The Buildings fram'd with Cyprus rare,

(*i*) This Fellow was an Apothecary, and turn'd an Attorney at Law.
(*j*) The *Yaws* is the *Pox*.
(*k*) The chief of *Maryland* containing about twenty four *Houses*.

Resembles much our *Southwark* Fair:
But Stranger here will scarcely meet,
With Market-place, Exchange, or Street;
And if the Truth I may report,
'Tis not so large as *Tottenham Court.*
St. *Mary's* once was in repute,   ⎤
Now here the Judges try the Suit,   ⎬
And Lawyers twice a Year dispute: ⎦
As oft the Bench most gravely meet,   ⎤
Some to get Drunk, and some to eat   ⎬
A swinging share of Country Treat.   ⎦
But as for Justice right or wrong,
Not one amongst the numerous throng,
Knows what they mean, or has the Heart,
To give his Verdict on a Stranger's part:
Now Court being call'd by beat of Drum,
The Judges left their Punch and Rum,
When Pettifogger Doctor draws,
His Paper forth, and opens Cause:
And least I shou'd the better get,
Brib'd *Quack* supprest his Knavish Wit.
So Maid upon the downy Field,
Pretends a Force, and Fights to yeild:
The Byast Court without delay,
Adjudg'd my Debt in Country Pay;
In (*l*) Pipe staves, Corn, or Flesh of Boar,
Rare Cargo for the *English* Shoar:
Raging with Grief, full speed I ran,
To joyn the Fleet at (*m*) *Kicketan;*
Embarqu'd and waiting for a Wind,
I left this dreadful Curse behind.

　　May Canniballs transported o'er the Sea
Prey on these Slaves, as they have done on me;
May never Merchant's, trading Sails explore

(*l*) There is a Law in this Country, the Plantiff may pay his Debt in
Country pay, which consists in the produce of his Plantation.
(*m*) The homeward bound Fleet meets here.

This Cruel, this Inhospitable Shoar;
But left abandon'd by the World to starve,
May they sustain the Fate they well deserve:
May they turn Savage, or as *Indians* Wild,
From Trade, Converse, and Happiness exil'd;
Recreant to Heaven, may they adore the Sun,
And into Pagan Superstitions run
For Vengence ripe..............
May Wrath Divine then lay those Regions wast
Where no Man's (*n*) Faithful, nor a Woman Chast.

(*n*) The Author does not intend by this, any of the *English* Gentlemen
resident there.

William Byrd II

(1674–1744)

"LONG HAS THE FURIOUS PRIEST"

Text: William K. Boyd, ed., William Byrd's Histories of the Dividing Line *(Raleigh, 1929), p. 120.*

Long has the Furious Priest assay'd in Vain,
With Sword and Faggot, Infidels to gain,
But now the Milder Soldier wisely tryes
By Gentler Methods to unveil their Eyes.
Wonders apart, he knew 'twere vain t'engage
The fix'd Preventions of Misguided Age.
With fairer Hopes he forms the Indian Youth
To early Manners, Probity and Truth.
The Lyon's whelp thus on the Libian Shore
Is tam'd and Gentled by the Artful Moor,
Not the Grim Sire, inured to Blood before.

A SONG

Text: Another Secret Diary of William Byrd of Westover 1739–1741, *ed., Maude H. Woodfin (Richmond, 1942), pp. 202–203.*

Sabina with an Angels face,
　　By Love ordain'd for Joy,
Seems of the Syren's cruel Race,
　　To Charm and then destroy.

With all the arts of Look and dress,
　　She fans the fatal fire:
Thro Pride, mistaken oft for Grace,
　　She bids the Swain expire.

The God of Love inrag'd to see,
　　The Nymph defy his flame;
Pronounc'd this merciless Decree,
　　Against the haughty Dame

Let Age with double speed oretake her;
　　Let Love the room of Pride supply;
And when the Fellows all forsake her,
　　Let her gnaw the sheets & dy.

Richard Lewis

(c. 1700–1734)

DESCRIPTION OF THE SPRING. A JOURNEY FROM PATAPSCO IN MARYLAND TO ANNAPOLIS, APRIL 4, 1730.

Text: The Gentleman's Magazine, II (*March*, 1732), 669–671.

AT length the *wintry* Horrors disappear,
And *April* views with Smiles the infant Year;
The grateful Earth from frosty Chains unbound,
Pours out its *vernal* Treasures all around,
Her Face bedeckt with Grass, with Buds the Trees are
   crown'd
In this soft Season, ere the Dawn of Day,
I mount my Horse, and lonely take my Way,
From woody Hills that shade *Patapsco's* Head
(In whose deep Vales he makes his stony Bed,
From whence he rushes with resistless Force,
Tho' huge rough Rocks retard his rapid Course,)
Down to *Annapolis*, on that smooth Stream
Which took from fair *Anne-Arundel* its Name.
   And now the *Star* that ushers in the Day,
'Begins to pale her ineffectual Ray.
The *Moon* with blunted Horns now shines less bright,
Her fading Face eclips'd with growing Light;
The fleecy Clouds with streaky Lustre glow,

And Day quits Heaven to view the Earth below.
O'er yon tall *Pines* the *Sun* shews half its Face,
And fires their floating Foliage with his Rays:
Now sheds aslant on Earth its lightsome Beams,
That trembling shine in many-colour'd Streams.
Slow-rising from the Marsh, the Mist recedes,
The Trees, emerging, rear their dewy Heads;
Their dewy Heads the *Sun* with Pleasure views,
And brightens into Pearls the pendent Dews.
  The *Beasts* uprising, quit their leafy Beds,
And to the cheerful *Sun* erect their Heads;
All joyful rise, except the filthy *Swine*,
On obscene Litter stretch'd they snore supine:
In vain the Day awakes, Sleep seals their Eyes,
Till Hunger breaks the Band and bids them rise.
Mean while the *Sun* with more exalted Ray,
From cloudless Skies distributes riper Day;
Thro' sylvan Scenes my Journey I pursue,
Ten thousand Beauties rising to my View;
Which kindle in my Breast poetic Flame,
And bid me my *Creator's* praise proclaim;
Tho' my low Verse ill-suits the noble Theme.
  Here various Flourets grace the teeming Plains,
Adorn'd by Nature's Hand with beauteous Stains.
First-born of *Spring*, here the *Pacone* appears,
Whose golden Root a silver Blossom rears.
In spreading Tufts, see there the *Crowfoot* blue,
On whose green Leaves still shines a globous Dew;
Behold the *Cinque-foil*, with its dazzling Dye
Of flaming yellow, wounds the tender Eye.
But there enclos'd the grassy *Wheat* is seen,
To heal the aching sight with cheerful Green.
  Safe in yon Cottage dwells the *Monarch Swain*,
His *Subject Flocks*, close grazing, hide the Plain;
For him they live; and die t'uphold his Reign.
Viands unbought his well-till'd Lands afford,
And smiling *Plenty* waits upon his Board;
Health shines with sprightly Beams around his Head.
And *Sleep*, with downy Wings, o'er shades his Bed,

His *Sons* robust his daily Labours share,
Patient of Toil, Companions of his Care.
And all their Toils with sweet Success are crown'd.
In graceful Ranks there *Trees* adorn the Ground,
The *Peach*, the *Plum*, the *Apple* here are found.
Delicious Fruits!—Which from their Kernels rise,
So fruitful is the Soil—so mild the Skies.
The lowly *Quince* yon sloping Hill o'er-shades,
Here lofty *Cherry-Trees* erect their Heads:
High in the Air each spiry Summit waves,
Whose Blooms thick-springing yield no space for Leaves;
Evolving Odours fill the ambient Air,
The *Birds* delighted to the Grove repair:
On ev'ry Tree behold a tuneful Throng,
The Vocal Vallies echo to their Song.
    But what is *He*, who perch'd above the rest,
Pours out such various Musick from his Breast!
His Breast, whose Plumes a cheerful White display,
His quiv'ring Wings are dress'd in sober Grey.
Sure all the *Muses* this their Bird inspire!
And he, alone, is equal to the Choir
Of warbling Songsters who around him play,
While, Echo like, *He* answers ev'ry Lay.
The chirping *Lark* now sings with sprightly Note
Responsive to her Strain *He* shapes his Throat.
Now the poor widow'd *Turtle* wails her Mate,
While in soft Sounds *He* cooes to mourn his Fate.
Oh sweet Musician, thou dost far excel
The soothing Song of pleasing *Philomel!*
Sweet is her Song, but in few Notes confin'd;
But thine, thou *Mimic* of the feath'ry Kind,
Runs thro' all Notes!—*Thou* only know'st them *All*,
At once the *Copy*—and th'Original.
    My *Ear* thus charm'd, my *Eye* with Pleasure sees
Hov'ring about the Flow'rs th' industrious *Bees*.
Like them in Size, the *Humming Bird* I view,
Like them, *He* sucks his Food, the Honey Dew,
With nimble Tongue, and Beak of jetty Hue.
He takes with rapid Whirl his noisy Flight,

His gemmy Plumage strikes the Gazer's Sight;
And as he moves his ever-flutt'ring Wings,
Ten thousand Colours he around him flings.
Now I behold the Em'rald's vivid Green,
Now scarlet, now a purple Die is seen;
In brightest Blue his Breast *He* now arrays,
Then strait his Plumes emit a golden Blaze.
Thus whirring round he flies, and varying still
He mocks the *Poet's* and the *Painter's* Skill;
Who may for ever strive with fruitless Pains,
To catch and fix those beauteous changeful Stains,
While Scarlet now, and now the Purple shines,
And Gold to Blue its transient Gloss resigns.
Each quits, and quickly each resumes its Place,
And ever-varying Dies each other chase.
Smallest of Birds, what Beauties shine in thee!
A living *Rainbow* on thy Breast I see.
   Oh had that *Bard,* in whose heart-pleasing Lines
The *Phoenix* in a Blaze of Glory shines,
Beheld those Wonders which are shewn in thee,
That Bird had lost his Immortality!
Thou in his Verse hadst stretch'd thy flutt'ring Wing
Above all other Birds,—their beauteous King.
   But now th' enclos'd Plantation I forsake,
And onwards thro' the Woods my Journey take:
The level Road, the longsome Way beguiles,
A blooming Wilderness around me smiles;
Here hardy *Oak,* there fragrant *Hick'ry* grows,
Their bursting Buds the tender Leaves disclose.
The tender Leaves in downy Robes appear,
Trembling, they seem to move with cautious Fear,
Yet new to Life, and Strangers to the Air.
Here stately *Pines* unite their whip'ring Heads,
And with a solemn Gloom embrown the Glades.
See there a green *Savana* open wide,
Thro' which smooth Streams in wanton Mazes glide,
Thick-branching Shrubs o'er hang the silver Streams,
Which scarcely deign t'admit the solar Beams.
   While with delight on this soft Scene I gaze,

The *Cattle* upward look, and cease to graze,
But into Covert run thro' various Ways.
And now the Clouds in black Assemblage rise,
And dreary Darkness overspreads the Skies,
Thro' which the Sun strives to transmit his Beams,
"But sheds his sickly Light in straggling Streams.
Hush'd is the Musick of the wood-land Choir,
Fore-knowing of the Storm, the Birds retire
For Shelter, and forsake the shrubby Plains,
And a dumb Horror thro' the Forest reigns;
In that lone House which opens wide its Door,
Safe may I tarry till the Storm is o'er.
    Hark how the *Thunder* rolls with solemn Sound!
And see the forceful *Lightning* dart a Wound
On yon tall Oak!—Behold its Top laid bare!
Its Body rent, and scatter'd thro' the Air
The Splinters fly!—Now—now the *Winds* arise,
From different Quarters of the low'ring Skies;
Forth issuing fierce, the *West* and *South* engage,
The waving Forest bends beneath their Rage:
But where the winding Valley checks their Course,
They roar and ravage with redoubled Force:
With circling sweep in dreadful Whirlwinds move
And from its Root tear up the gloomy Grove,
Down rushing fall the Trees, and beat the Ground
In Fragments flie the shatter'd Limbs around;
Tremble the Under-woods, the Vales resound.
    Follows, with patt'ring Noise, the icy *Hail*,
And *Rain*, fast falling, floods the lowly Vale.
Again the *Thunders* roll, the *Lightnings* fly,
And as they first disturb'd, now clear the Sky;
For lo! the *Gust* decreases by Degrees,
The dying *Winds* but sob amidst the Trees;
With pleasing Softness falls the silver Rain,
Thro' which at first faint gleaming o'er the Plain,
The Orb of Light scarce darts a wat'ry Ray
To gild the Drops that fall from ev'ry Spray;
But soon the dusky Vapours are dispell'd,
And thro' the Mist that late his Face conceal'd,

Bursts the broad *Sun,* triumphant in a Blaze
Too keen for Sight—Yon Cloud refracts his Rays;
The mingling Beams compose th' *ethereal Bow,*
How sweet, how soft, its melting Colours glow!
Gaily they shine, by heav'nly Pencils laid,
Yet vanish swift—How soon does *Beauty* fade!
    The *Storm* is past, my Journey I renew,
And a new Scene of Pleasure greats my View:
Wash'd by the copious Rain the gummy *Pine,*
Does cheerful, with unsully'd Verdure shine!
The *Dogwood* Flow'rs assume a snowy White,
The *Maple* blushing gratifies the Sight:
No verdant Leaves the lovely *Red-Bud* grace,
Carnation Blossoms now supply their Place.
The *Sassafras* unfolds its fragrant Bloom,
The *Vine* affords an exquisite perfume.
These grateful Scents wide-wafting thro' the Air
The smelling Sense with balmy Odours cheer.
And now the *Birds,* sweet singing, stretch'd their
    Throats,
And in one Choir unite their various Notes.
Nor yet unpleasing is the *Turtle's* Voice,
Tho' he complains while other Birds rejoice.
    These vernal Joys, all restless Thoughts controul,
And gently-soothing calm the troubled Soul.
    While such Delights my Senses entertain,
I scarce perceive that I have left the *Plain;*
'Till now the Summit of a *Mount* I gain:
Low at whose sandy Base the *River* glides.
Slow-rolling near their Height his languid Tides;
Shade above Shade, the Trees in rising Ranks,
Cloath with eternal Green his steepy Banks:
The Flood, well pleas'd, reflects their verdant Gleam
From the smooth Mirror of his limpid Stream.
    But see the *Hawk,* who with acute Survey,
Tow'ring in Air predestinates his Prey
Amid the Floods!—Down dropping from on high,
He strikes the *Fish,* and bears him thro' the Sky.
The Stream disturb'd no longer shews the Scene

That lately stain'd its silver Waves with green;
In spreading Circles roll the troubled Floods,
And to the Shores bear off the pictur'd Woods.
   Now looking round I view the out-stretch'd *Land,*
O'er which the Sight exerts a wide Command;
The fertile Vallies, and the naked Hills,
The Cattle feeding near the chrystal Rills;
The Lawns wide-op'ning to the sunny Ray,
And mazy Thickets that exclude the Day.
Awhile the Eye is pleas'd these Scenes to trace,
Then hurrying o'er the intermediate Space,
Far-distant Mountains dress'd in Blue appear,
And all their Woods are lost in empty Air.
   The *Sun* near setting now arrays his Head
In milder Beams, and lengthens ev'ry Shade.
The rising Clouds usurping on the Day
A bright Variety of Dies display;
About the wide Horizon swift they fly,
"And chase a Change of Colours round the Sky.
And now I view but half the *flaming Sphere,*
Now one faint Glimmer shoots along the Air;
And all his golden Glories disappear.
   Onwards the *Ev'ning* moves in Habit grey,
And for her Sister *Night* prepares the Way.
The plumy People seek their secret Nests,
To Rest repair the ruminating Beasts;
Now deep'ning Shades confess th' Approach of Night,
Imperfect Images elude the Sight:
From earthly Objects I remove mine Eye,
And view with Look erect the vaulted Sky,
Where dimly shining now the Stars appear,
At first thin-scatt'ring thro' the misty Air;
Till Night confirm'd, her jetty Throne ascends,
On her the *Moon* in cloudy State attends;
But soon unveil'd her lovely Face is seen,
And *Stars* unnumber'd wait around their Queen.
Rang'd by their *Maker's* Hand in just Array,
They march Majestic thro' th' ethereal Way.
   Are these bright Luminaries hung on high

Only to please with twinkling Rays our Eye?
Or may we rather count each *Star* a *Sun,*
Round which *full peopled Worlds* their Courses run?
Orb above Orb harmoniously they steer
Their various Voyages thro' Seas of Air.
   Snatch me some *Angel* to those high Abodes,
The Seats perhaps of *Saints* and *Demigods!*
Where such as bravely scorn'd the galling Yoke
Of *vulgar Error,* and her Fetters broke;
Where *Patriots,* who to fix the publick Good,
In Fields of Battle sacrific'd their Blood;
Where *pious Priests,* who Charity proclaim'd,
And *Poets* whom a *virtuous Muse* enflam'd;
Philosophers who strove to mend our Hearts,
And such as polish'd Life with *useful Arts,*
Obtain a Place; when by the Hand of Death
Touch'd, they retire from this poor Speck of Earth;
Their *Spirits* freed from bodily Alloy,
Perceive a Fore-tast of that endless Joy,
Which from Eternity hath been prepar'd,
To crown their Labours with a vast Reward.
While to these Orbs my wand'ring Thoughts aspire,
A falling *Meteor* shoots his lambent Fire,
Thrown from the heav'nly Space he seeks the Earth,
From whence he first deriv'd his humble Birth.
   The *Mind* advis'd by this instructive Sight,
Descending sudden from th' aereal Height,
Obliges me to view a different Scene,
Of more Importance to myself, tho' mean.
These distant Objects I no more pursue,
But turning inward my reflective View,
My working Fancy helps me to survey
In the just Picture of this *April Day,*
My Life o'er past,—a Course of thirty *Years,*
Blest with few Joys, perplex'd with num'rous Cares.
   In the dim Twilight of our *Infancy,*
Scarce can the Eye surrounding Objects see.
Then thoughtless *Childhood* leads us pleas'd and gay,
In Life's fair Morning thro' a flow'ry Way:

The *Youth* in Schools inquisitive of Good,
Science pursues thro' *Learning's* mazy Wood;
Whose lofty Trees, he, to his Grief perceives,
Are often bare of *Fruit*, and only fill'd with *Leaves:*
Thro' lonely wilds his tedious Journey lies,
At last a brighter Prospect cheers his Eyes;
Now the gay Fields of *Poetry* he views,
And joyous listens to the *tuneful Muse;*
Now *History* affords him vast Delight,
And opens lovely Landscapes to his Sight:
But ah! too soon this Scene of Pleasure flies;
And o'er his Head tempestuous Troubles rise,
He hears the Thunders roll, he feels the Rains,
Before a friendly Shelter he obtains;
And thence beholds with Grief the furious Storm
The *noon tide* Beauties of his *Life* deform:
He views the *painted Bow* in distant Skies;
Hence, in his Heart some Gleams of Comfort rise;
He hopes the *Gust* has almost spent its Force,
And that he safely may pursue his Course.
     Thus far *my Life* does with the *Day* agree,
Oh! may its coming Stage from Storms be free,
While passing thro' the World's most private Way,
With Pleasure I my *Maker's* Works survey;
Within my Heart let *Peace* a Dwelling find,
Let my *Good-will* extend to *all Mankind:*
Freed from *Necessity*, and blest with *Health;*
Give me *Content*, let others toil for *Wealth.*
In *busy* Scenes of Life let me exert
A *careful Hand*, and wear an *honest Heart;*
And suffer me my *leisure* Hours to spend,
With chosen *Books*, or a well-natur'd *Friend.*
Thus journeying on, as I advance in Age,
May I look back with Pleasure on my Stage;
And as the setting *Sun* withdrew his Light
To rise on other Worlds serene and bright,
Cheerful may I resign my vital Breath,
Nor anxious tremble at th' Approach of *Death;*
Which shall, I hope, but strip me of *my Clay,*

And to a better World my Soul convey.
 Thus musing, I my silent Moments spend,
Till to the *River's* Margin I descend,
From whence I may discern my *Journey's* End:
Annapolis adorns its further Shore,
To which the *Boat* attends to bear me o'er.
 And now the moving *Boat* the Flood divides,
While the *Stars* 'tremble on the floating Tides.
Pleas'd with the Sight again I raise mine Eye
To the bright Glories of the azure Sky;
And while these Works of God's creative Hand,
The *Moon* and *Stars*, that move at his Command
Obedient thro' their circling Course on high,
Employ my Sight,—struck with amaze I cry,
Almighty Lord! Whom Heav'n and Earth proclaim
The *Author* of their universal Frame,
Wilt thou vouchsafe to view the *Son of Man,*
The Creature, who but *Yesterday* began
Thro' animated Clay to draw his Breath,
To morrow doom'd a Prey to ruthless Death!
 Tremendous God! May I not justly fear,
That I, unworthy Object of thy Care,
Into this World by thy bright Presence tost,
Am in th' Immensity of *Nature* lost!
And that my Notions of the *World above,*
Are but Creations of my own *Self-Love!*
To feed my coward Heart, afraid to die,
With *fancied* Feasts of *Immortality!*
 These Thoughts, which thy amazing Works suggest,
Oh glorious *Father*, rack my troubled Breast.
 Yet, *Gracious God*, reflecting that my Frame
From *Thee* deriv'd in animating Flame,
And that whate'er I am, however mean,
By thy Command I enter'd on this Scene
Of Life—thy wretched *Creature of a Day*,
Condemn'd to travel thro' a tiresome Way;
Upon whose Banks (perhaps to cheer my Toil)
I see thin Verdures rise, and *Daisies* smile:
Poor Comforts these, my Pains t'alleviate!

While on my Head tempestuous Troubles beat.
And must I, when I quit this Earthly Scene,
Sink total into *Death*, and never rise again?
  No sure,—These *Thoughts* which in my Bosom roll,
Must issue from a *never-dying Soul*;
These active *Thoughts* that penetrate the Sky,
Excursive into dark Futurity;
Which hope eternal Happiness to gain,
Could never be bestow'd on *Man* in vain.
  To *Thee, O Father*, fill'd with fervent Zeal,
And sunk in humble Silence I appeal;
Take me, my great *Creator*, to *Thy Care*,
And gracious listen to my ardent Prayer!
  Supreme of Beings, omnipresent Pow'r,
My great Preserver from my natal Hour,
Fountain of Wisdom, boundless Deity,
Omniscient God, my Wants are known to *Thee*,
With Mercy look on mine Infirmity!
Whatever State thou shalt for me ordain,
Whether my Lot in Life be *Joy* or *Pain*;
Patient let me sustain thy wise Decree,
And learn to know *myself*, and *honour Thee*.

William Dawson

(1704–1752)

"HYMN TO THE MORNING"*
(1736)

Text: Poems on Several Occasions, 1736, *ed.*,
R. L. Rusk (*New York*, 1930), *pp.* 5–8.

   Awake, my Soul, and with the constant Morn,
Carol th' ALMIGHTY's Praise; awake and tune
The vocal Shell to sympathetic Sounds,
And heav'nly Consort. See! the radiant Sun
Stains with etherial Gold the varied *East,*
And vast Expanse; behold! with Giant stride
He advances ruddy, and with him returns
The sweet Vicissitude of Day, and all
The obsequious Train of filial Colours. Now
The vivid Green extends her welcome Sway
O'er the sequester'd Lawns, and smiling Meads:
And now the purpled V*iolet* resumes
Its costly Dye; and all th' extended Plains
Confess th' ALMIGHTY's Hand, of Ornament
Profuse. Behold! with fleshy *Pink* they smile
Enamel'd, and the *Daisy's* dwarfy Bloom
Of pallid Hue, and gorgeous *Marygold.*

   ON ev'ry grassy Sprig a pearly Drop
Hangs wav'ring, and with varied Ray proclaims

---

* Reprinted, as are the following poems by Dawson, by courtesy of the
Columbia University Press.

Its great Progenitor. The liquid Gem,
Pendent and tremulous, with rival Gleam
Mimicks the Lustre of its Parent Orb.
Vain Man's best Emblem! who with BORROW'D LIGHT
Which EV'RY TOUCH DESTROYS, against his GOD
Dares wage an impious and gigantic War.

    FROM downy Nest of artificial Weft
The sedulous Airlings rise, and to their Task
Hye joious. Or with gamesome Wing they cut
The yielding Fluent, and with transient Touch
Skim the moist Element in sportive Whirl:
Or else to studious Wand'rer's curious View
Delightful, they collect their grainy Food
And masticative Stones. But heark! the Grove,
Respondent to the tuneful Choir, resound
Celestial Symphony. The speckled *Thrush*
Of various Note, and *Blackbirds* piercing Sound,
Conjoin'd to *Philomela's* parting Lay,
Mournfully sweet, conspire to usher in
The pompous Morn. Nor shall my only Voice
Be wanting in the general Hymn: Of Song
Unskilful, yet with grateful Hand I'll touch
The trembling String, and chant th' ALMIGHTY's Praise.
Vagrant, like the industrious Bee, I'll cull
Nature's choice Sweets, and still with prying Ken
Descry the Wonders of her fruitful Womb.

    BUT see! the great Exemplar of my Verse,
The Lab'rer Bee, assiduous rise! Behold!
From waxen Cell and more inglorious Ease,
Active he hastens, and with hov'ring Buzz
Extracts mellific Juice. From Bloom to Bloom
He wanders dainty, and with nice Discern
Rejects each vulgar Sweet. Hail, mighty Chief!
Hyblaan Wand'rer, hail! Still may'st thou sip
The pure and elemental Dews; whilst I,
With daring Song, and more advent'rous Foot,
Attempt the steepy Heights, where MILTON first,
Great Chieftain, solitary trod; and taught

The list'ning World, what MICHAEL's potent Arm
In Fight could do, and human Wit atchieve.

"ANACREONTIQUE."
(1736)

Text: Poems on Several Occasions, *pp. 15–16.*

IF Gold protracts the merry Scene,
    And partial Death obeys its Pow'r;
With prudent Forecast, careful Mien,
    I'll amass the shining Store.

AND if his grisley Godship come,
    I'll divert the fatal Dart.
A Purse he wants—Behold the Sum—
    He'll scrape obsequious, and depart. ·

    BUT since reverseless Fates deny
    This Virtue to the glitt'ring Ore;
Tell me, Mortal, tell me, why
    Should I the gaudy Dust adore?

    THEN let the ruddy God advance,
    And some beauteous lovesome She;
With Mirth, and Joke, and Quirp, and Dance:
    These alone have Joys for me.

"SONG"

(1736)

Text: Poems on Several Occasions, *pp. 21–22.*

YOUNG Poets, in Love,
   Will call from above
Cytherea, drest all in her Graces and Airs;
And will tell their fond Dreams of *Ida's* soft Grove,
   Of Cupids, of Doves, and of Carrs.

SOME *Cloe* beside,
   Or *Sylvia* must hide
The Name of the Fair that possesses their Heart.
Thus fighting in Pomp of Poetical Pride,
   They vainly make Shew of their Art.

NO Poet am I,
   And no Dame of the Sky,
· No Fiction shall ever disgrace my bright Flame;
That the Truth is most beautiful, none will deny,
   When I tell them, that ——————— is her Name.

THEN fill up my Glass;
   Here's a Health to the Lass:
As for V*enus*, I fairly now bid you Adieu;
Since on her you can never reflect any Praise,
   I'll not labour to compliment you.

Mather Byles

(1707–1788)

"WRITTEN IN MILTON'S
PARADISE LOST"*
(1744)

Text: Poems on Several Occasions, 1744, *ed.,* C. L. Carlson (*New York,* 1940), *pp.* 25–34.

Had I, O had I all the tuneful Arts
Of lofty Verse; did ev'ry Muse inspire
My flowing Numbers, and adorn my Song!
Did Milton's Fire flash furious in my Soul;
Could I command the Harmony, the Force,
The glitt'ring Language, and the true Sublime
Whose mingled Beauties grace his glowing Lays,
Then should my Lines glide languishingly slow,
Or thundring roar, and rattle as they fleet,
Or, lovely-smiling, bud immortal Bloom,
As various as the Subjects they describe,
And imitate the Beauties which they mark.
Thus with ambitious Hand, I'd boldly snatch
A spreading Branch from his immortal Laurels.

But, O my Muse, where shall thy Song begin?
Or where conclude? ten thousand Glories charm
My ravish'd Heart, and dance before my Sight.

---

* Reprinted, as is the following poem by Byles, by courtesy of the Columbia University Press.

O Milton! I'm transported at thy Name!
My Soul takes Wing at once; or shoots away,
Born eager by a Tyde of Thought along

Sometimes big Fury swells thy awful Verse,
And rolling Thunder bursts along thy Lines.
Now Hell is open'd, and I see the Flames
Wide-waving, blazing high, and flutt'ring dance:
Now clanking Chains amaze my list'ning Ears,
And hideous Spectres skim before my Sight.
Or in my wild Imagination stare.

Here *Satan* rears his mighty Bulk on high,
And tow'rs amid th' infernal Legions; fill'd
With Pride, and dire Revenge; daring his Looks;
Rage heaves his lab'ring Breast, and all around
His fiery Eye-balls formidably roll,
And dart destructive Flames; with dreadful Blaze
The ruddy Ligh'ning rapid runs along,
And guilds the gloomy Regions of Despair,
With Streaks tremendous. Here assaults my Sight
The gressly Monster *Death,* He onward stalks
With horrid Strides, Hell trembles as he treads;
On his fierce Front a bold defiance low'rs;
Bent is his Brow, in his right Hand he shakes
His quiv'ring Lance. How fell the Fiend appears
In ev'ry Prospect, wrathful or serene?
Pleas'd, *horrible he grins a gastly Smile;*
And *Erebus* grows blacker as he Frowns.

But tell, immortal Muse, O Goddess! tell
The joyful Dread, the terrible Delight,
Which fill my Mind, when I behold the Ranks,
Th' embatt'led Ranks of mighty Cherubim,
In dreadful Quadrate croud the Plains of Heav'n.
I hear, I hear the Trumpets loud Alarms;
The keen Vibration cuts the yielding Air,
And the shril Clangors ring around the Sky.
I see the bold intrepid Cohorts move;
From ev'ry Scabbard flies a flaming Sword,

Wav'd by the mighty Combatants on high,
So flashing radiant from a gloomy Cloud,
Long Lightnings flourish with a livid Glare.
Now on at once th' immortal Hero's rush,
And with a sudden Onset shake the Field.
Hark! how confus'd Sounds thicken in the Air,
Mingling, tumultous, and perplex'd, and rough,
Of Shouts, and Groans, and grating Clang of Arms,
The twanging Bow, the Jav'lins deadly Hiss,
Loud-clashing Swords, and Spears encountring Spears.
Helms found on Helms, on Bucklers Bucklers ring.
Vast waving Wings high in the Air are heard,
Whilst loud-resounding Feet beat thick the Ground,
And all the jarring Sounds of War unite,
In direful Discord, and outragious Roar.
    Behold, my Muse, where Michael bends his Course,
Starts his swift Car, and bounds impetuous on,
With rapid Rage it rattles thro' the Ranks,
Smokes o'er the Field, and drives the War along.

    But who can tell the Raptures which I feel,
When fix'd in deep Astonishment, my Eyes
Behold Messiah, dread Messiah! arm'd
With all the dire Artillery of God?
Unnumber'd Seraphim around him throng,
Clap their expanded Wings, and shout aloud;
Heav'ns mighty Concave echo's to their Voice,
The everlasting Hills return the Sound.
Oh! how I feel the noble Ardor warm
My beating Breast, and thrill along my Veins!
My charging Spirits pour around my Heart;
My Eyes bright-sparkling with immortal Fires.
His flying Chariot shakes the tott'ring Sky,
Swift all the vast Expanse behind him rolls,
Resistless Thunders rattle from his Hand,
Devouring Lightnings shoot beneath his Feet,
Ten thousand Terrors thicken where he bends.
What Havock! What Confusion spreads the Plain!
What Myriads fall by his descending Bolts,

Dash'd to the Ground, and crush'd beneath his Wheels?
Tumult and Ruin, Horror, Rage and Death,
Play round his Sword, and shake their shaggy Wings:
Hell flames before him, wild Despair stalks on,
And Purple Vict'ry hovers o'er his Head.
Great GOD! what Vengeance kindled in thy Eyes!
What Thunders bellow'd! and what Lightnings blaz'd!
When *Satan*, daring Chief of all thy Foes!
Was seiz'd, as trembling and agast he stood,
Seiz'd by thy mighty Hand, and rais'd aloft,
Then headlong hurl'd down the high Steep of Heav'n?
At the dire Sight his bold compeers amaz'd,
Confounded, shiver ev'n amidst the Flames,
Forget to Fight, drop all their idle Arms,
Swift from thy Fury fly away, and down
Down from the tow'ring Battlements they rush
Precipitant, into the Dark profound,
Whilst *Chaos* loud rebellows to the Fall.
      No more—my fainting Muse folds up her Wings,
Unable to sustain so strong a Flight—
The Battle only Raphael should relate,
Or Milton in such Strains as Raphael sings.

      Let softer Subjects now command my Muse,
Let softer Numbers smoothly flow along,
And bloom, and blossom as the Ever-greens,
That deck the flow'ry Face of Paradise.
O Milton, *Eden* opens by thy Art,
And with redoubl'd Beauty wanton smiles.
I'm charm'd, I'm ravish'd, all my Soul dissolves,
I loose my Life amid the heav'nly Scenes;
That in gay Order from thy Pencil flow.
O beauteous Garden! O delightful Walks!
In you forever, ever will I stray,
Glide o'er thy flow'ry Vales, clumb thy fair Hills,
And thro' thy fragrant Lawns transported tread
I'd trace the mazy Windings of thy Bow'rs,
And in the Gloom of thy surrounding Groves
Ask the cool Shadow, and the fanning Breeze.

Here rising Perfume should regale my Smell,
And heav'nly Harmony transport my Ears;
While all the Trees around, to court a look,
Flourish luxuriant with unfading Charms.
Roses, and Violets, and Daffodils,
And gaudy Tulips of a thousand Dyes,
Shall spring profusely round; the Lilly too,
Ambitious, off its unsullied White,
To grace a Garland for fair Innocence.
Ye feather'd Songsters of the Spring, arise,
Display your spangled Plumes, where twinkling Gems,
With blended Beauties, cast a doubtful Blaze,
And, keenly-flashing, strike the Gazer's Sight.
Let your sweet Voices warble thro' the Grove,
While in concording Harmony I hear
The purling Murmurs of the bubbling Brooks
Mean time the embroider'd Banks on either Hand
Shall open all their everlasting Sweets,
Their verdant Honours, and their flow'ry Pride,
As the pure floating Volumes wind along.
Here the first Pair, divinely reign'd supream,
And sunk reclining on the flow'ry Turff.
Hail, happy *Adam*, Heav'n adorns thy Soul,
Full bless'd. And thou, immortal Mother, Hail!
O heav'nly-fair, divinely-beauteous *Eve!*
Thee to adorn what endless Charms conspire?
Caelestial Coral blushes on thy Lips,
No op'ning Rose glows with so bright a Bloom.
Thy Breath abroad diffusive Odor spreads,
A gay Carnation purple o'er thy Cheeks,
While thy fair Eyes roll around their radiant Orbs,
With winning Majesty, and nat'ral Art.
Thy waving Tresses on thy Shoulders play,
Flow loosely down, and wanton in the Wind.
You, am'rous *Zephires*, kiss her snowy Breast,
Flit softly by, and gently lift her Locks.
Forgive, fair Mother, O forgive thy Son,
Forgive his vain Redundance of Expression.
Fir'd by thy Beauty, and by Milton's Song.

Here could the ravish'd Fancy rove perpetual,
Amid the Raptures, the transporting Bliss,
That in soft Measures move for ever round.—

　But, O my Muse, shake off these idle Dreams,
Imaginary Trances! vain Illusions!
Count the gay Stars, and number all the Sands,
And ev'ry Drop that in the Ocean floats:
But never hope to sum th' unnumber'd Charms,
That swim before thy ever-ravish'd Eyes,
When they on thee, O Milton, give a glance.
In vain thou striv'st to lisp his lofty Praise;
Imperfect Accents flutter round thy Tongue,
And on thy Lips Unfinish'd, Milton dies.
His mighty Numbers tow'r above thy Sight,
Mock thy low Musick, and elude thy Strains.

"TO PICTORIO, ON THE SIGHT OF HIS PICTURES"
(1744)

Text: Poems on Several Occasions, 89–93.

　Ages our Land a barbarous Desart stood,
And savage Nations howl'd in ev'ry Wood;
No laurel'd Art o'er the rude Region smil'd,
　Nor bless'd Religion dawn'd admist the Wild;
Dulness and Tyranny confederate reign'd,
And Ignorance her gloomy State maintain'd.
　An hundred Journies now the Earth has run,
In annual Circles, round the central Sun,
Since the first ship the unpolish'd Letters bore
Thro' the wide Ocean to the barb'rous Shore.
Then Infant-Science made it's early Proof,

Honest, sincere, tho' unadorn'd, and rough;
Still thro' a Cloud the rugged Stranger shone,
Politeness, and the softer Arts unknown:
No heavenly Pencil the free Stroke could give,
Nor the warm Canvass felt its Colours live.
No moving Rhet'rick rais'd the ravish'd Soul,
Flourish'd in Flames, or heard it's Thunder roll;
Rough horrid Verse, harsh, grated thro' the Ear,
And jarring Discords tore the tortur'd Air;
Solid, and grave, and plain the Country stood,
Inelegant, and rigorously good.

Each Year, succeeding, the rude Rust devours,
And softer Arts lead on the following Hours;
The Tuneful Nine begin to touch the Lyre,
And flowing Pencils light the living Fire;
In the fair Page new Beauties learn to shine,
The Thoughts to brighten, and the Style refine,
Till the great Year the finish'd Period brought;
Pictorio painted, and Maecenas wrote.

Thy Fame, Pictorio, shall the Muse rehearse,
And sing her Sister-Art in softer Verse:
'Tis your's, great Master, in just Lines to trace
The rising Prospect, or the lovely Face.
In the fair Round to swell the glowing Cheek,
Give Thought to Shades, and teach the Paints to speak.
Touch'd by thy Hand, how *Sylvia's* Charms engage!
And *Flavia's* Features smile thro' ev'ry Age.
In *Clio's* Face, th' attentive Gazer spies
Minerva's reasoning Brow, and azure Eyes,
Thy Blush, *Belinda*, future Hearts shall warm,
And *Celia* shine in *Citherea's* Form.
In hoary Majesty, see Cato here;
Fix'd strong in Thought, there Newton's Lines appear;
Here in full Beauty blooms the charming Maid;
Here *Roman* Ruins nod their awful Head;
Here gloting Monks their am'rous Rights debate,
The *Italian* Master sits in easy State,

Vandike and Rubens show their rival Forms,
And Caesar flashes in the Blaze of Arms.

But cease, fond Muse, nor the rude Lays prolong,
A thousand Wonders must remain unsung;
Crowds of new Beings lift their wond'ring Heads,
In conscious Forms, and animated Shades.
What Sounds can speak, to ev'ry Figure just,
The breathing Statue, and the living Bust?
Landskips how gay! arise in ev'ry Light,
And fresh Creations rush upon the Sight;
Thro' fairy Scenes the roving Fancy strays,
Lost in the endless, visionary Maze.

Still, wondrous Artist, let thy Pencil flow,
Still, warm with Life, thy blended Colours glow,
Raise the ripe Blush, bid the quick Eye-balls roll
And call forth every Passion of the Soul.
Let thy soft Shades in mimick Figures play,
Steal on the Heart, and catch the Mind away.
Yet *Painter*, on the kindred Muse attend,
The Poet ever proves the Painter's Friend.
In the same Studies Nature we pursue,
I the description touch, the Picture you;
The same gay Scenes our beauteous Works adorn,
The purple Ev'ning, or the flamy Morn:
Now, with bold Hand, we strike the strong Design;
Mature in Thought, now soften every Line;
Now, unrestrain'd in freer Airs suprize,
And sudden, at our Word, new World's arise,
In gen'rous Passion let our Breasts conspire,
As is the Fancy's, be the Friendship's Fire;
Alike our Labour, and alike our Flame:
'Tis thine to raise the Shape; 'tis mine to fix the Name.

Benjamin Church

(1734–1776)

"THE CHOICE"

(1757)

Text: The Choice, A Poem After the Manner
of M. Pomfret (*Boston, 1757*).

IF youthful Fancy might it's Choice pursue,
And act as natural Reason prompts it to;
If Inclination could dispose our State,
And human Will might govern future Fate;
Remote From Grandeur, I'd be humbly wise,
And all the Glitter of a Court despise:
Unskill'd the Proud, or Vicious to commend,
To cringe to Insolence, or Fools attend;
Within myself contended and secure,
Above what mean Ambition can endure;
Nor yet so anxious to obtain a Name,
To bleed for Honor, in the Fields of Fame;
Empty Parade, is all that Heroes know,
Unless fair Vertue hover in the Show.

BUT in these Walls, where Heav'n has fix'd my stay,
One half of Life, I'd wish to breath away:
The Fall and Winter of each future Year,
I'd humbly hope to spend contented here;
'Mid the fierce Ravage of a wintry Storm,
Kind Friends to cheer me, moderate Wine to warm;

[634]

Securely happy we'd delude the Day,
And smile the Seasons chearfully away.

   NO needless Show my modest Dome should claim,
Neat and genteel without, within the same;
Decently furnish'd to content and please,
Sufficient for Necessity and Ease;
Vain is the Pomp of Prodigal Expence,
Frugality denotes the Man of sense;
My Doors the needy Stranger should befriend,
And Hospitality my Board attend;
With frugal Plenty be my Table spread,
Those, and those only whom I love be fed:
The Meek and Indigent my Banquet share,
Who love the Master, and approve the Fare;
Thy mellow Vintage *Lisbon!* should abound,
Pouring a mirthful Inspiration 'round;
While laughing *Bacchus* baths within the Bowl,
Love, Mirth and Friendship swallow up the Soul.

   I'D have few Friends, and those by Nature true,
Sacred to Friendship, and to Vertue too;
Tho' but to few an Intimate profest,
I'd be no Foe, nor useless to the Rest:
Each Friend belov'd requires a friendly Care,
Each Grief, Dejections, and his Fate to share;
For this my Choice should be to Bounds confin'd,
Nor with a Burst of Passion flood Mankind.
Above the Rest, one dear selected Friend,
Kind to advise and cautious to offend;
To Malice, Envy, and to Pride unknown,
Nor apt to censure Foibles, but his own;
Firm in Religion, in his Morals just,
Wise in discerning, and advising best;
Learn'd without Pedantry, in Temper kind,
Soft in his Manners, happy in his Mind;
Is there in whom, these social Virtues blend,
The Muse lisps Pollio, and she calls him Friend:
To him, when flush'd with Transport I'd repair,

His faithful Bosom should my Solace share;
To him I'd fly when Sorrows prove too great,
To him discover all the Stings of Fate:
His social Soul, should all my Pangs allay,
Tune every Nerve, and charm my Griefs away.

O, How I wish to join the friendly Throng,
Elude the Hours, and harmonize the Song;
Each generous Soul still sedulous to please,
With calm good Temper, and with mutual Ease;
Glad to receive and give, the keen Reply,
Nor Approbation to the Jest deny.

BUT at a decent hour with social Heart,
In Love, and Humor should my Friends depart:
Then to my Study, eager I'd repair,
And feast my Mind with new Refreshment there;
There plung'd in Tho't my active Mind should tread,
Through all the Labours of the learned Dead;
Homer, great Parent of Heroick Strains,
Virgil, whose Genius was improv'd with Pains;
Horace, in whom the Wit and Courtier join'd,
Ovid, the tender, amorous and refin'd;
Keen *Juvenal,* whose all-correcting Page
Lash'd daring Vice, and sham'd an unproud Age;
Expressive *Lucan,* who politely sung
With hum'rous *Martial* tickling as he stung;
Elaborate *Terence,* studious where he smil'd,
Familiar *Plautus,* regularly wild;
With frequest Visit these I would survey,
And read, and mediate the Hours away.

NOR these alone, should on my Shelves recline,
But awful *Pope!* majestically shine,
Unequall'd Bard! Who durst thy Praise engage?
Nor yet grown reverend with the Rust of Age;
Sure Heav'n alone thy Art unrival'd taught,
To think so well, so well express the Thought;
What Villain hears thee, but regrets the Smart?
But tears the lurking Demon from his Heart?

Virtue attends thee, with the best Applause,
Conscious Desert! great Victor in her Cause,
She faithful to thy Worth, thy Name shall grace
Beyond all Period and beyond all Space:
Go, shine a Seraph and thy Notes prolong
For Angels only merit such a Song!

 HAIL Briton's Genuis, *Milton!* deathless Name!
Blest with a full Satiety of Fame:
Who durst attempt Impertinence of Praise!
Or sap insidious thy eternal Bays?
For greater Song, or more exalted Fame,
Exceeds Humanity to make, or claim.
These to peruse, I'd oft forget to dine,
And suck Refection from each mighty Line,
Next Addison's great Labours should be join'd,
Prais'd by all Tongues and known to all Mankind:
With *Littleton* the tender, and correct,
And copious *Dryden*, glorious in Defect;
Now would I leave the great and pious *Young*,
Divinely fir'd, and sublime in Song.
Next would I add the unaffect'd *Gay*,
And gentle *Waller*, with his flowing Lay;
Last Nature-Limning Thompson should appear,
Who link'd Eternity within his Year.
These for Diverson, with the Comic Throng,
Should raise my Fancy, and improve my Song;
Extend my View, 'till op'ning Visions roll,
And all Piaeria bursts upon my Soul.

 BUT to inform the Mind, and mend the Heart,
Great *Tillotson* and *Butler*, light impart;
Sagacious *Newton*, with all Science blest,
And *Lock*, who always tho't and reason'd best.

 BUT LO! for real Worth, and true Desert,
Exhaustless Science, and extensive Art,
Boerhaave superior stands; in whom we find
The other Saviour of diseas'd Mankind;
Whose skilful Hand could almost Life create,

And make us leap the very Bounds of Fate;
Death, Tyrant Death, beholding his decline,
That *Boerhaave* would his Kingdom undermine,
Arm'd with his surest Shafts attack'd his Foe,
Who long eluded the repeated Throw,
At Length fatigu'd with Life, he bravely fell,
And Health with *Boerhaave* bad the World farewell.

THUS 'till the Year recedes I'd be employ'd,
Ease, Health and Friendship happily enjoy'd;
But when the Vernal Sun revolves it's Ray,
Melting hoar Winter with her Rage away,
When vocal Groves a gay perspective yield,
And a new Verdure springs from Field to Field;
With the first Larks I'd to the Plains retire,
For rural Pleasures are my chief Desire.

AH doubly blest! on native Verdure laid,
Whose Fields support him, and whose arbours Shade;
In his own Hermitage in Peace resides,
Fann'd by his Breeze, and slumbering by his Tides;
Who drinks a Fragrance from paternal Groves,
Nor lives ungrateful for the Life he loves.

I'D have a handsome Seat not far from Town,
The Prospect beautous, and the Taste my own;
The Fabrick modern, faultless the Design,
Not large, nor yet imoderately fine;
But neat Oeconomy my Mansion boast,
Nor should Convenience be in Beauty lost;
Each Part should speak superior Skill and Care,
And all the Artist be distinquish'd there.

ON some small Elevation should it stand,
And a free Prospect to the South command;
Where safe from Damps I'd snuff the wholesome Gale,
And Life and Vigour thro' the Lungs inhald;
Eastward my moderate Fields should wave with Grain,
Southward the Verdure of a broad Champaign;
Where gamesome Flocks and rampart Herds might play,
To the warm Sun-shine of the Vernal Day;

Northward, a Garden on a Slope should lye,
Finely adjusted to the nicest Eye;
In midst of This should stand a Cherry Grove,
A breezy, blooming Canopy of Love!
Whose blossom'd Boughs the timeful Choir should chear,
And pour Regalement on the Eye and Ear:
A gay Parterre the vivid Box should bound,
To waft a Fragrance thro' the Fields around;
Where blushing Fruits might tempt another *Eve*,
Without another Serpent to deceive.
Westward, I'd have a thick-set Forest grow,
Thro' which the bounded Sight should scarcely go;
Confus'dly rude, the Scen'ry should impart
A view of Nature unimprov'd by Art—

    RAPT in the soft retreat my anxious Breast,
Pants eager still for something unpossess'd;
Whence Springs this sudden Hope, this warm Desire?
To what Enjoyment would my Soul aspire?
'Tis Love! extends my Wishes, and my Care,
Eden was tasteless 'til an *Eve* was there:
Almightly Love! I own thy powerful Sway,
Resign my Soul, and willingly obey.

    GRANT me kind Heav'n! the Nymph still form'd to please,
Impassionate as Infants when at Ease;
Fair as the op'ning Rose; her Person small,
Artless as Parent *Eve* before her Fall;
Courteous as Angels, unreserv'dly kind,
Of modest Carriage, and the chastest Mind;
Her Temper sweet, her Conversation keen,
Not wildly gay, but soberly serene;
Not Talkative, nor apt to take Offence,
With Female Softness form'd to Manly Sense;
Her Dress and Language elegantly plain,
Not sluttish, forward, prodigal or vain;
Not proud of Beauty, nor elate with Praise,
Not fond to govern, but by *Choice* obeys;
True to my Arms in Body and in Soul,
As the touch'd Needle to the attractive Pole.

Caution, oppos'd to Charms like these were vain,
And Man would glory in the silken Chain;
Unlike the sensual Wish that burns and Stains,
But where the purest Admiration reigns;
Give me, O give me! such superior Love,
Before the Nectar of the God's above;
Then Time on downy Wings would steal away,
And Love still be the Business of the Day.

WHILE sporting Flocks in fond Rotations court
And to the Thicket Pair by Pair resort;
While toneful Birds in tender Murmurings plead,
Chanting their amorous Carolls through the Mead;
Link'd Arm in Arm we'd search the Twilight Grove,
Where all inspires with Harmony and Love:
Ye Boughs, your friendly Umbrage wide extend!
Guard from rude Eyes, and from the Sun defend:
Ye wanton Gales! pant gently on my Fair,
Thou Love-inspiring Goddess meet us there!
While soft-invited, and with Joy obey'd,
We press the Herbage, and improve the Shade.

BUT is th' Almighty ever bound to please?
Rul'd by my Wish, or studious of my Ease?
Shall I determine where his Frowns shall fall?
And fence my Grotto from the Lot of all!
Prostrate, his sovereign Wisdom I adore,
Intreat his Mercy, but I dare no more:
No constant Joys Mortality attend,
But Sorrows violate, and Cares offend;
Heav'n wisely mixt our Pleasures with Alloy,
And gilds our Sorrows, with a Ray of Joy;
Life without Storms a stagnant Pool appears,
And grows offensive with unruffled Years;
An active State, is Vertue's proper Sphere,
To do, and suffer is our duty here:
Foes to encounter, Vices to disdain,
Pleasures to shun, and Passions to restrain;
To fly Temptation's open, flowery Road,
And labour to be obstinately good.

THEN, blest is he who takes a calm Survey,
Of all th' Events that paint the checquer'd Day;
Content, that Blessing makes the Balance even,
And poizes Fortune, by the Scale of Heav'n.

I'LL let no future Ill my Peace destroy,
Or cloud the Aspect of a present Joy;
He who directed and dispenc'd the past,
O'er-rules the present, and shall guide the last:
If Providence a present Good has giv'n,
I clasp the Boon in Gratitude to Heav'n:
May Resignation fortify my Mind,
He cannot be unhappy that's resign'd.

GUARD my Repose thou Lord of all within!
An equal Temper, and a Soul serene;
O! teach me Patience when oppos'd to Wrong,
Restrain the mad'ning Heart, and curb the Tongue;
May Prudence govern, Piety controul,
All Slander, Rage and Bitterness of Soul;
Peace, Plenty, Health and Innocence be made,
The blissful Tenants of my tranquil Shade.

O LET me not maliciously comply,
To that curst Action that shall raise a Sigh;
Or cause the wretched Orphan to complain,
Or see the Widow's Tears, and see in vain;
From a remorseless Soul O set me free,
And prompt a Pang for every Wretch I see.

WHATEVER Station be for me design'd,
May Virtue be the Mistress of my Mind;
May I despise th' Abandon'd and the Base,
Tho' Opulent, or dignified with Place;
And spurn the Wretch who meanly lost to Shame,
Thinks Wealth or Place, a Substitute for Fame:
If Wisdom, Wealth or Honor, Heav'n lend,
Teach me those Talents happily to spend;
Nor make so blest, as I would wish to live,
Beyond those Moments Heav'n is pleas'd to give;

Then when Life trembles on the Verge of Rest,
And brings expended Minutes to the Test;
Absolve me Conscience, thou imperial Power!
O bless me with a self-approving Hour.

Joseph Dumbleton

(fl. 1750)

"THE PAPER-MILL.
INSCRIB'D TO MR. PARKS."*

Text: The American Magazine (*August 1744*),
p. 523, as reprinted in Colonial American Poetry,
ed., Kenneth Silverman (*New York, 1968*),
pp. 326–327.

    In nova, sert Animus, mutates dicere formas, Corpora;
OVID.

> THO' sage Philosophers have said,
> *Of nothing, can be nothing made:*
> Yet *much* thy Mill, O *Parks*, brings forth
> From what we reckon *nothing worth.*
> Hail kind *Machine!*—The Muse shall praise
> Thy Labours, that receive her Lays.
> Soon as the *Learn'd* denounce the War
> From pratling Box, or wrangling Bar,
> Straight, Pen and Paper range the Fight;
> They meet, they close, in Black & White.
> The Substances of what we think,
> Tho' born in *Thought*, must live in *Ink.*
> Whilst willing *Mem'ry* lends her Aid,
> She finds herself by *Time* betray'd.

---

* Reprinted with permission of the Hafner Publishing Company.

Nor can thy Name, Dear *Molly,* live
Without those Helps the Mill must give;
The Sheet now hastens to declare,
How lovely Thou, and—my Despair.

   Unwitting Youths, whom Eyes or Breast,
Involve in Sighs, and spoil of Rest;
Unskill'd to say their piteous Case,
But miss the Girl for want of *Brass,*
May paint their Anguish on the Sheet;
For Paper cannot blush, I weet.
And *Phillis,* (for Bissextile Year
Does only once in Four appear,
When Maids, in dread to lie alone
Have Leave to bid the Men *come on,*)
Each Day may write to lure the Youth
She longs to wed, or fool, or—both.

   Ye *Brave,* whose Deeds shall vie with Time,
Whilst Mill can turn, or Poet rhime,
Your Tatters hoard for future Quires;
So Need demands, so *Parks* desires.
(And long that gen'rous Patriot live
Who for soft Rags, hard Cash will give!)
'The Shirt, Cravat, the Cap again
Shall meet your Hands, with *Mails* from *Spain;*
The *Surplice,* which, when whole or new,
With Pride the Sexton's Wife could view,
Tho' worn by Time and gone to rack,
It quits its Rev'rend Master's Back;
The same again the Priest may see
Bound up in Sacred Liturgy.

   Ye *Fair,* renown'd in *Cupid's* Field,
Who fain would tell what Hearts you've kill'd;
Each Shift decay'd, lay by with Care;
Or Apron rubb'd to bits at—Pray'r,
One Shift ten Sonnets may contain,
To gild your Charms, and make you vain;
One Cap, a *Billet-doux* may shape.

As full of Whim, as when a Cap,
And modest 'Kerchiefs Sacred held
May sing the Breasts they once *conceal'd*.

Nice *Delia's* Smock, which, neat and whole,
No Man durst finger for his Soul;
Turn'd to *Gazette,* now all the Town,
May take it up, or smooth it down.
Whilst *Delia* may with it dispence,
And no Affront to Innocence.

The Bards, besure, their Aids will lend;
The Printer is the Poet's Friend;
Both cram the News, and stuff the Mills,
For Bards have Rags, and—little else.

"A RHAPSODY ON *RUM*"*

Text: The South Carolina Gazette, No. 776
(*March* 20, 1749), *as reprinted in* Colonial
American Poetry, *ed.,* Kenneth Silverman
(*New York,* 1968), *pp.* 327–328.

—*Ignigenamque* Vocant.   OVID.

GREAT Spirit hail!—Confusion's angry Sire,
And like thy Parent *Bacchus,* born of Fire:
The Goal's Decoy; the greedy Merchant's Lure;
Disease of Money, but Reflection's Cure.

We owe, great DRAM! the trembling Hand to thee,
The headstrong Purpose; and the feeble Knee;
The Loss of Honour; and the Cause of Wrong;

* Reprinted with permission of the Hafner Publishing Company.

The Brain enchanted; and the fault'ring Tongue;
Whilst Fancy flies before Thee unconfin'd,
Thou leav'st disabl'd Prudence far behind.

In thy Pursuit our Fields are left forlorn,
Whilst giant Weeds oppress the pigmy Corn:
Thou throw'st a Mist before the Planter's Eyes;
The Plough grows idle, and the Harvest dies.

By Thee refresh'd no cruel Norths we fear;
'Tis ever warm and calm when thou art near:
On the bare Earth for Thee expos'd we lie,
And brave the Malice of a weeping Skie.
And seem like those that did of old repent;
We sit in Ashes, and our Cloathes are rent.

From Thee a thousand flatt'ring Whims escape,
Like hasty Births, that ne'er have perfect Shape.
Thine Ideots seem in gay Delusion fair,
But born in Flame, they soon expire in Air.

O grand Deluder! such thy charming Art,
'Twere good we ne'er should meet, or ne'er should part:
Ever abscond, or ever tend our Call;
Leave us our Sense entire, or none at all.

George Webb

(1708?–   ?)

"BATCHELORS-HALL"*

Text: Batchelors-Hall (*Philadelphia, 1731*), *as
reprinted in* Colonial American Poetry, *ed., Kenneth
Silverman (New York, 1968), pp. 367–369.*

O SPRING, thou fairest season of the year,
How lovely soft, how sweet dost thou appear!
What pleasing landskips meet the gazing eye!
How beauteous nature does with nature vie:
Gay scenes around the fancy does invite,
And universal beauty prompts to write:
But chiefly that proud dome on *Delaware's* stream,
Of this my humble song the nobler theme,
Claims all the tribute of these rural lays,
And tunes ev'n my harsh voice to sing its praise.

 Say, goddess, tell me, for to thee is known,
What is, what was, and what shall e'er be done;
Why stands this dome erected on the plain;
For pleasure was it built, or else for gain:
For midnight revels was it ever thought,
Shall impious doctrines ever here be taught:
Or else for nobler purposes design'd,
To cheer the soul and cultivate the mind;

---

* Reprinted with permission of the Hafner Publishing Company.

With mutual love each glowing breast inspire,
Or cherish friendship's now degenerate fire:
Say, goddess, say, do thou the truth reveal,
Say what was the design, if good or ill.

Tir'd with the bus'ness of the noisy town,
The weary Batchelors their cares disown;
For this lov'd seat they all at once prepare,
And long to breath the sweets of country air;
On nobler thoughts their active minds employ,
And a select variety enjoy.
'Tis not a revel, or lascivious night,
That to this Hall the Batchelors invite;
Much less shall impious doctrines here be taught
Blush ye accusers at the very thought:
For other, O far other ends design'd,
To mend the heart, and cultivate the mind.
Mysterious nature here unveil'd shall be,
And knotty points of deep philosophy;
Whatever wonders undiscover'd are,
Deep hid in earth, or floating high in air,
Tho' in the darkest womb of night involv'd,
Shall by the curious searcher here be solv'd.
Close to the Dome a Garden shall be join'd,
A fit employment for a studious mind:
In our vast woods whatever simples grow,
Whose virtues none, or none but *Indians* know,
Within the confines of this Garden brought,
To rise with added lustre shall be taught;
Then cull'd with judgment each shall yield its juice,
Saliferous balsam to the sick man's use:
A longer date of life mankind shall boast,
And death shall mourn her ancient empire lost.

But yet sometimes the all-inspiring bowl
To laughter shall provoke, and cheer the soul;
The jocund tale to humour shall invite,
And dedicate to wit a jovial night:
Not the false wit the cheated World admires,

The mirth of sailors, or of country 'squires;
Nor the gay punster's, whose quick sense affords
Nought but a miserable play on words;
Nor the grave *Quidnunc's*, whose enquiring head;
With musty scraps of journals must be fed:
But condescending, genuine, apt and fit;
Good nature is the parent of true wit;
Tho' gay, not loose; tho' learned, yet still clear;
"Tho' bold, yet modest; human, tho' severe;
Tho' nobly thirsting after honest fame,
In spight of wit's temptation keeping friendship's name.

O friendship, heavenly flame! by far above
The ties of nature, or of dearer love:
How beauteous are thy paths! how well design'd,
To sooth wretched mortal's restless mind!
By thee inspir'd, we wear a soul sedate,
And cheerful tread the thorny paths of fate.

Then Musick too shall cheer this fair abode,
Musick, the sweetest of the gifts of God;
Musick, the language of propitious love;
Musick, that things inanimate can move.
Ye winds be hush'd, let no presumptuous breeze
Now dare to whistle thro' the rustling trees;
Thou *Delaware* a while forget to roar,
Nor dash thy foamy surge against the shore:
Be thy green nymphs upon thy surface found,
And let thy stagnant waves confess the sound:
Let thy attentive fishes all be nigh;
For fish were always friends to harmony:
Witness the Dolphin which *Arion* bore,
And landed safely on his native shore.

Let doting cynicks snarl, let noisy zeal
Tax this design with act or thought of ill;
Let narrow souls their rigid morals boast,
'Till in the shadowy name the vertue's lost;

Let envy strive their character to blast,
And fools despise the sweets they cannot taste;
This certain truth let the enquirer know,
It did from good and generous motives flow.

Jonathan Boucher

(1738–1804)

"ABSENCE, A PASTORAL: DRAWN FROM THE LIFE, FROM THE MANNERS, CUSTOMS AND PHRASEOLOGY OF PLANTERS (OR, TO SPEAK MORE PASTORALLY, OF THE RURAL SWAINS) INHABITING THE BANKS OF THE POTOMAC, IN MARYLAND."
(C.—1775)

Text: Glossary of Archaic & Provincial Words, ed. *Joseph Stevenson* (*London, 1833*), *pp. xlix-l.*

'Twas noon, when all alone young *Billsey*[1] sate
Aloan to dine, though hardly down to eat:
His *gammon* smok'd in vain,—the *coleworts* too,

---

[1] *Billsey:* this effeminate manner of pronouncing such names was at that time extremely common in the neighbourhood where this was written. [This and the following notes are Boucher's.]

Though all with *good clear fat* drench'd through and through:
For, ah! his love had *o'er the river* gone,
And left her swain—to eat and drink alone.

Why stays my *Mollsey* dear? at length he cries,
The big round drops a-streaming from his eyes:
Ah, idle rover, haste, oh hasten, home,
And, ere the cherries all be gone, O, come!
Green pease, my love, are just a-coming in,
And lamb, and quarter'd *shote*,[2] and goslings green;
How fast the season of good eating rolls!—
Our chickens, in a month, will be old fowls:
Love only fix'd, and without changing, stays;
Ah! He remains a chicken all his days.

Four *colour'd hogsheads*, late in week the last,
And ten besides, have, all, *inspection* past:
My *new crap's pitch'd*, from which I hope to *share*
At least *two thousand*, all good *notes*,[3] next year:
Accounts of sales are come, and highly please;
I've got my goods all home,—and cut my cheese.
In vain I thrive,—in vain the world looks gay,
Still, still I *hone*[4] for bliss, while *Mollsey* is away.

Till now ne'er *crazy*, in my bones no pains,
I *never took no truck*, nor doctor's *means*:
Hoddy and *brave*, my careless days I told;
All night I slept,—all day I ate and *loll'd*,
Save when, an ugly fever *brief about*,[5]
I caught it in my toe, just like the gout:
My doctor thought, the neighbours all can tell,
I'd no *election*[6] ever to get well.

---

[2] *Shote*: a young swine.
[3] *Notes*: at that time, no tobacco could be shipped till it had been examined by inspectors, publicly appointed; who, on finding it marketable, received it into their warehouses, and gave a *note* for the re-delivery of it, when demanded.
[4] *Hone*: long for.
[5] *Brief about*: probably a corruption for *rife about*.
[6] *Election*: likelihood, chance, &c.

Ah, would no greater pains I now endur'd!
My *Mollsey* nurs'd me, and I soon was cur'd.

    Strolling, last *fall*,[7] by yon *pacosen*[8] side,
Coil'd in a heap, a rattle-snake I spied:
Was it for me a *rompus*[9] then to make?
I'm *mad* [10] to see some people dread a snake:
Instant I caught a *chunk*,[11] and, at a blow,
To pieces *smash'd* [12] my notice-giving foe.
For this, if merit's aught, to go no higher,
I look to be a col'nel, or a 'squire:
But what are titles to a swain forlorn?
My *Mollsey's* gone, and I all honours scorn.

    In *twist-bud, thick-joint, bull-face, leather-coat*,[13]
I'd toil all day; or *fall*, and *mall*, and *tote*:[14]
Brown linen shirts, and cotton jackets wear,
Or only *wring-jaw*[15] drink, and '*simmon beer*;[16]
My *pone*, or *hoe-cake*, without salt, would eat,
And taste but once a week a bit of meat;
Could my *old woman*,[17] whilst I labour'd thus,
At night reward me with a *smouch*, or buss.

    For breakfast, *mush*[18] and *th' top o' milk's*[19] a treat,
Or *bonny clabber* with *molasses* sweet:

---

[7] The *fall*: autumn, the *fall* of the leaf.
[8] *Pacosen*: an Indian term for a swamp, or marsh.
[9] *Rompus*: an uproar.
[10] *Mad*: angry, vexed.
[11] *Chunk*: a short piece of wood; a thick stick; a bludgeon.
[12] *Smash'd*: beat to pieces.
[13] *Twist-bud*, &c.: All these are names for different kinds of tobacco.
[14] *Fall, mall*, and *tote*: i.e., *fall*, or cut down, a tree; split, or rive it, by means of *mallets* and wedges, into rails, clapboards, staves, shingles, firewood, or any other purpose for which it may be fit and wanted; and then *tote*, or carry it to some pile or heap, from whence it may be carted away.
[15] *Wring-Jaw*: hard cider.
[16] '*Simmon beer*: beer, made of the *Prunus sylvestris Virginiensis*, or *Persimmon*; a harsh and unpleasant plum, growing in great plenty, but when mellowed by the frosts, and baked into cakes, and then used as malt, yielding a palatable and rich, but heady beer.
[17] *Old woman*: a very common term of endearment in the midland colonies.
[18] *Mush*: hasty-pudding, made of Indian meal.
[19] *Top o' th' milk*: cream.

At dinner, let me that best *buck-skin*[20] dish,
Broth made of bacon, cream, and eke *cat-fish*
With *toss 'em boys*,[21] and *belly bacon* see,
Cushie,[22] and *dough-boys*,[23] and small *homony:*
At night *crab-lanthorn*,[24] and *fried cucumbers;*
Or *milk and peaches mash'd*, and *roasting-ears.*[25]
Sweet are these luscious cates, and sweet the day,
Ere long, when *water-millions* come in play:
But neither *clabber*, with *molasses* sweet,
Nor *mush*, nor *top o' th' milk* for morning treat;
Nor *cat-fish* broth, nor *paune*, with *toss 'em boys*,
Nor *middling*, garnish'd all with dainties nice;
Nor yet *crab-lanthorn*, with *fried cucumbers*,
Nor *milk and peaches mash'd*, nor *roasting-ears;*
Fog-drams[26] i' th' morn, or (better still) *egg-nogg*,[27]
At night *hot-suppings*, and at mid-day, *grogg*,
My palate can regale:—my *Mollsey's* gone,
And ev'ry dainty's naught, when ate alone.

Our *man-boy*,[28] Jack, did, in his *new-ground patch*,[29]
A *runaway* a' grabbling '*moodies*[30] catch:
The rogues escap'd, but all the '*moodies* I

---

[20] *Buckskins:* Natives of Virginia and Maryland are so called, in contradistinction to *outlandish* persons, or the natives of any other country.
[21] *Toss 'em boys:* chickens; so called, it is supposed, because when any unexpected guest is seen coming, a young negro is dispatched to procure more chickens, to be added to the dinner; and these chickens it is common to run down with his dog, whom he sets on, and encourages, by the phrase *Toss 'em, boys.*
[22] *Cushie:* a kind of pancake, made of Indian meal.
[23] *Dough-boys:* hard, or Norfolk dumplings; not seldom also made of Indian meal.
[24] *Crab-lanthorn:* To the best of my recollection, fried apples are so called.
[25] *Roasting-ears:* Indian corn, whilst still soft in the ear, is roasted, and eaten as a favourite delicacy; and indeed is delicious food.
[26] *Fog-drams: drams* resorted to on the pretence of their protecting from the danger of *fogs.*
[27] *Egg-nogg:* a heavy and unwholesome, but not unpalatable, strong drink, made of rum beaten up with the yolks of raw *eggs.*
[28] *Man-boy:* an hobbete-hoy, an *ephebus*, betwixt boyhood and manhood.
[29] *New-ground patch:* a piece of ground that had never been cultivated before; the *culta novalia* of Virgil.
[30] '*Moodies:* sweet potatoes; first brought from the Bermudas.

For *Mollsey*, in my *'tatoe-hole*, put by.
Ah, woe is me! these dainties are no more;
Some *bugs*[31] or grubs did every one devour:—
Just so have I been prey'd upon within;
For Absence is a worm that preys unseen.

Old Johnny Two-Shoes,—bless his honest soul!
Sent me a *'possum*,[32] dead indeed, but whole;
I never saw a finer with my eyes:—
All full of maggots in the *safe*[33] it lies:
These things won't keep; no more do I, of late,
Know how to keep out maggots from my pate.

Last *forest-ball*,[34] I felt like one forlorn,
Though *Ebo-Nan* was play'd, and then *Parch'd Corn*:[35]
When Nancy Wriggle slily did advance,
And, bent to shame me, ask'd me out to dance.
Humgh, humgh,[36] said I; and got upon the floor;
But, ah! I found my dancing days were o'er:
Thinking on *Mollsey*, oft I stood *stock still*,
Or danced a minuet, when they play'd a reel.

'Twas thus, in lowly and unletter'd strain,
Our shepherd long of Absence did complain;
When to his clap-board mansion he withdrew,
To eat, and loll, and sleep,—as he was wont to do.

---

[31] *Bugs:* Almost all insects in America are called *bugs;* excepting that particularly offensive insect, so noisome in beds, so called in London.
[32] A *'possum:* an opossum.
[33] A *safe:* a kind of cupboard.
[34] *Forest-ball:* this term is, in Virginia and Maryland, equivalent to *the country* in England, or to *landwart* in Scotland.
[35] *Ebo-Nan*, and *Parch'd Corn:* two favourite tunes, or jigs, among the negros are so called.
[36] *Humgh, humgh:* interjections denoting assent.

Nathaniel Evans

(1742–1767)

"TO BENJAMIN FRANKLIN, ESQ; L.L.D. *OCASIONED BY HEARING HIM PLAY ON THE HARMONICA.*"*

Text: Poems on Several Occasions (1772), *pp.* 108–109, *as reprinted in* Colonial American Poetry, *ed.* Kenneth Silverman (New York, 1968), *pp. 756–757.*

IN grateful wonder lost, long had we view'd   2 *ems*
Each gen'rous act thy patriot-soul pursu'd:
Our Little State resounds thy just applause,
And, pleas'd, from thee new fame and honour draws;
In thee those various virtues are combin'd,
That form the true pre-eminence of mind.

    What wonder struck us when we did survey
The lambent lightnings innocently play,
And down thy rods beheld the dreaded fire
In a swift flame descend—and then expire;
While the red thunders, roaring loud around,
Burst the black clouds, and harmless smite the ground.

---

* Reprinted with permission of the Hafner Publishing Company.

Blest use of art! apply'd to serve mankind,
The noble province of the sapient mind!
For this the soul's best faculties were giv'n,
To trace great nature's laws from earth to heav'n!

Yet not these themes alone thy thoughts command,
Each softer *science* owns thy fostering hand;
Aided by thee, Urania's heav'nly art,
With finer raptures charms the feeling heart;
Th'*Harmonica* shall join the sacred choir,
Fresh transports kindle, and new joys inspire—

Hark! the soft warblings, sounding smooth and clear,
Strike with celestial ravishment the ear,
Conveying inward, as they sweetly roll,
A tide of melting music to the soul;
And sure if aught of mortal-moving strain,
Can touch with joy the high angelic train,
'Tis this enchanting instrument of thine,
Which speaks in accents more than half divine!

VII

THE FRONTIERSMAN

The existence of a series of frontiers, as Frederick Jackson Turner and his followers have taught us, is one of the facts of American life. Indeed, the natural riches of the west, a land going unused, even the savage Indian—all these have seemed to cry out to eastern Americans for settlement and order, for "civilization," as believers in Manifest Destiny termed it. Pioneering has been one of the deepest of American drives. Yet movement to the west has always meant more than imposing eastern "civilization" on an "uncivilized" frontier; it has meant the creation of a new kind of life, new and overpowering awareness of the need for and the possibilities of freedom, independence, abundance, and economic, spiritual, and legal elbow-room. It has meant the creation of the frontier character.

We must view this character as the product of the meeting of the east and the west. Americans moving onto the frontier at once made their environment and were made by it. The Puritan Mrs. Rowlandson interpreted violence of her captivity by Indians as the sort of message that she, as a sinner, had been taught to expect from God; William Byrd interpreted the lubber-land North Carolinians among whom he travelled as creatures who had simply surrendered to or been overwhelmed by their frontier environment and thus as creatures not worthy of civilized consideration. However, the immediate sources of our tradition of the frontier character are not in such accounts as these. They are rather in the later eighteenth-century accounts of those hardy men who went into the Ohio country and beyond, made a new and special world for themselves, and so became the advance guard of that American civilization which was to follow them westward.

The two selections here printed exhibit two early stages in the creation of this frontier character. Croghan's diary is as direct an account of pre-civilized pioneering life as we likely could find—simple, straightforward, business-like, and realistic. Croghan, sent to "pacify" first Ohio and then Illinois Indians, scores a diplomatic success, is tomahawked in an Indian attack, is taken captive, is released, and again scores a diplomatic success. The stuff of his diplomacy is recorded as accounts, in all their ritualism, of Indian treaties, with Croghan's sympathetic yet superior response to them. The Boone narrative shows us what the American imagination was doing to an actual frontiersman—to a Boone who, though he was less a professional handler of Indians than Croghan, must have been fairly close to the actual Croghan. Cast in popular rhetoric, correctly religious, dramatically self-conscious, obviously doctored-up by its editor, it begins to make Boone into the ideal pioneer—the pioneer in whom more civilized and settled Americans believed, the pioneer who for them was bound to give up his life and new-found land to make way for their civilization. Here is the origin of the myth of Leatherstocking and of his sometimes heroic, sometimes villainous progeny—always men who at once create the law and are outside of it. Here, moreover, is one origin of the American obsession with the lonely hero, living dangerously, cut off from proper civilization. This Boone is not the "real" frontiersman, but rather the frontiersman whom Americans were creating so that they might comprehend themselves and what they might become as they moved west to clear the way for their new civilization.

Croghan's biographer reports that, after he had completed the mission dealt with in the journal reprinted here, Croghan wrote about his being tomahawked: "I got the stroke of a hatchett on the head, but my scull being pretty thick, the hatchett would not enter, so you may see a thick scull is of service on some occasions." Boone's biographer reports that in his old age Boone, living in the Missouri country, liked to have the Filson narrative read to him and would comment: "All true! Every word true! Not a lie in it!" The contrast is perhaps instructive.

Bibliographical Note. The classic essay on the meaning of the frontier in American culture is F. J. Turner's "The Significance of the Frontier in American History" (1920). Turner's essay is easily available, along with other essays pro and con, in *The Turner Thesis Concerning the Role of the Frontier in American History*, ed. G. R.

Taylor (New York, 1949). R. W. G. Vail, *The Voice of the Old Frontier* (Philadelphia, 1950) is important for its exhaustive bibliography of frontier writings. A study of American feelings about the Indian and his relation to their mission as civilizers is R. H. Pearce, *The Savages of America* (Baltimore, revised edition, 1965). Now the definitive study of the American understanding of the frontier is H. N. Smith, *Virgin Land* (Cambridge, 1950). See also Arthur K. Moore, *The Frontier Mind: A Cultural Analysis of the Kentucky Frontiersman* (Lexington, 1957).

George Croghan

(d. 1782)

Bibliographical Note. The text here printed is from R. G. Thwaites, *Early Western Travels, 1748–1846,* I (Cleveland, 1904), 126–166. Thwaites' text is a conflation of two journals Croghan kept, one personal, one official, with emphasis on the first. For a detailed analysis, see Thwaites' notes, which also supplement the journal with geographical, ethnological, and historical materials. On Croghan see Nicholas B. Wainwright, *George Croghan: Wilderness Diplomat* (Chapel Hill, 1959). A marvellous collection of Indian Treaties is Julian P. Boyd, ed., *Indian Treaties Printed by Benjamin Franklin, 1732–1762* (Philadelphia, 1938). Croghan figures in some of the Treaties Boyd collects.

A JOURNEY INTO THE OHIO AND ILLINOIS COUNTRY, 1765*

May 15, 1765.—I sent off from Fort Pitt with two batteaux, and encamped at Chartier's Island, in the Ohio, three miles below Fort Pitt.

16.—Being joined by the deputies of the Senecas, Shawnesse, and Delawares, that were to accompany me, we set off at seven o'clock in the morning, and at ten o'clock arrived at the Logs Town, an old settlement of the Shawnesse, about seventeen miles from Fort Pitt, where we put ashore, and viewed the remains of that village, which was situated on a

---

* Reprinted by permission of the publishers, the Arthur H. Clark Company.

high bank, on the south side of the Ohio river, a fine fertile country round it. At 11 o'clock we re-embarked and proceeded down the Ohio to the mouth of Big Beaver Creek, about ten miles below the Logs Town: this creek empties itself between two fine rich bottoms, a mile wide on each side from the banks of the river to the highlands. About a mile below the mouth of Beaver Creek we passed an old settlement of the Delawares, where the French, in 1756, built a town for that nation. On the north side of the river some of the stone chimneys are yet remaining; here the highlands come close to the banks and continue so for about five miles. After which we passed several spacious bottoms on each side of the river, and came to Little Beaver Creek, about fifteen miles below Big Beaver Creek. A number of small rivulets fall into the river on each side. From thence we sailed to Yellow Creek, being about fifteen miles from the last mentioned creek; here and there the hills come close to the banks of the river on each side, but where there are bottoms, they are very large, and well watered; numbers of small rivulets running through them, falling into the Ohio on both sides. We encamped on the river bank, and found a great part of the trees in the bottom are covered with grape vines. This day we passed by eleven islands, one of which being about seven miles long. For the most part of the way we made this day, the banks of the river are high and steep. The course of the Ohio from Fort Pitt to the mouth of Beaver Creek inclines to the north-west; from thence to the two creeks partly due West.

17th.—At 6 o'clock in the morning we embarked: and were delighted with the prospect of a fine open country on each side of the river as we passed down. We came to a place called the Two Creeks, about fifteen miles from Yellow Creek, where we put to shore; here the Senecas have a village on a high bank, on the north side of the river; the chief of this village offered me his service to go with me to the Illinois, which I could not refuse for fear of giving him offence, although I had a sufficient number of deputies with me already. From thence we proceeded down the river, passed many large, rich, and fine bottoms; the highlands being at a considerable distance from the river banks, till we came to the Buffalo Creek, being about ten miles below the Seneca village; and from Buffalo Creek, we proceeded down the river to Fat Meat Creek, about thirty miles. The face of the country appears much like what we met with before; large, rich, and well watered bottoms, then succeeded by the hills pinching close on the river; these bottoms, on the north side, appear rather low, and consequently subject to inundations, in the spring of the year, when there never fail to be high freshes in the Ohio, owing to the melting of the snows. This day we passed by ten fine islands, though the greatest part of them are small. They lay much higher out of the water than the main land, and of course less subject to be flooded by the freshes. At night we encamped near an Indian village. The general course of the river from the Two Creeks to Fat Meat Creek inclines to the southwest.

18th.—At 6 o'clock, A.M. we set off in our batteaux; the country on both sides of the river appears delightful; the hills are several miles from the river banks, and consequently the bottoms large; the soil, timber, and banks of the river, much like those we have before described; about fifty miles below Fat Meat Creek, we enter the long reach, where the river runs a straight course for twenty miles, and makes a delightful prospect; the banks continue high; the country on both sides, level, rich, and well watered. At the lower end of the reach we encamped. This day we passed nine islands, some of which are large, and lie high out of the water.

19th.—We decamped at six in the morning, and sailed to a place called the Three Islands, being about fifteen miles from our last encampment; here the highlands come close to the river banks, and the bottoms for the most part—till we come to the Muskingum (or Elk) river—are but narrow: this river empties itself into the Ohio about fifteen miles below the Three Islands; the banks of the river continue steep, and the country is level, for several miles back from the river. The course of the river from Fat Meat Creek to Elk River, is about southwest and by south. We proceeded down the river about fifteen miles, to the mouth of Little Conhawa River, with little or no alteration in the face of the country; here we encamped in a fine rich bottom, after having passed fourteen islands, some of them large, and mostly lying high out of the water. Here buffaloes, bears, turkeys, with all other kinds of wild game are extremely plenty. A good hunter, without much fatigue to himself, could here supply daily one hundred men with meat. The course of the Ohio, from Elk River to Little Conhawa, is about south.

20th.—At six in the morning we embarked in our boats, and proceeded down to the mouth of Hochocken or Bottle River, where we were obliged to encamp, having a strong head wind against us. We made but twenty miles this day, and passed by five very fine islands, the country the whole way being rich and level, with high and steep banks to the rivers. From here I despatched an Indian to the Plains of Scioto, with a letter to the French traders from the Illinois residing there, amongst the Shawnesse, requiring them to come and join me at the mouth of Scioto, in order to proceed with me to their own country, and take the oaths of allegiance to his Britannic Majesty, as they were now become his subjects, and had no right to trade there without license. At the same time I sent messages to the Shawnesse Indians to oblige the French to come to me in case of refusal.

21st.—We embarked at half past 8 o'clock in the morning, and sailed to a place called the Big Bend, about thirty-five miles below Bottle River. The course of the Ohio, from Little Conhawa River to Big Bend, is about south-west by south. The country hereabouts abounds with buffalo, bears, deer, and all sorts of wild game, in such plenty, that we killed out of our boats as much as we wanted. We proceeded down the river to the Buffalo Bottom, about ten miles from the beginning of the Big Bend, where we encamped. The country on both sides of the river, much the same as we passed the day before. This day we passed nine islands, all lying high out of the water.

22d.—At half an hour past 5 o'clock, set off and sailed to a place, called Alum Hill, so called from the great quantity of that mineral found there by the Indians; this place lies about ten miles from Buffalo Bottom; thence we sailed to the mouth of Great Conhawa River, being ten miles from the Alum Hill. The course of the river, from the Great Bend to this place, is mostly west; from hence we proceeded down to Little Guyondott River, where we encamped, about thirty miles from Great

Conhawa; the country still fine and level; the bank of the river high, with abundance of creeks and rivulets falling into it. This day we passed six fine islands. In the evening one of our Indians discovered three Cherokees near our encampment, which obliged our Indians to keep out a good guard the first part of the night. Our party being pretty strong, I imagine the Cherokees were afraid to attack us, and so ran off.

23d.—Decamped about five in the morning, and arrived at Big Guyondott, twenty miles from our last encampment: the country as of yesterday; from hence we proceeded down to Sandy River being twenty miles further; thence to the mouth of Scioto, about forty miles from the last mentioned river. The general course of the river from Great Conhawa to this place inclines to the south-west. The soil rich, the country level, and the banks of the river high. The soil on the banks of Scioto, for a vast distance up the country, is prodigious rich, the bottoms very wide, and in the spring of the year, many of them are flooded, so that the river appears to be two or three miles wide. Bears, deer, turkeys, and most sorts of wild game, are very plenty on the banks of this river. On the Ohio, just below the mouth of Scioto, on a high bank, near forty feet, formerly stood the Shawnesse town, called the Lower Town, which was all carried away, except three or four houses, by a great flood in the Scioto. I was in the town at the time, though the banks of the Ohio were so high, the water was nine feet on the top, which obliged the whole town to take to their canoes, and move with their effects to the hills. The Shawnesse afterwards built their town on the opposite side of the river, which, during the French war, they abandoned, for fear of the Virginians, and removed to the plains on Scioto. The Ohio is about one hundred yards wider here than at Fort Pitt, which is but a small augumentation, considering the great number of rivers and creeks, that fall into it during the course of four hundred and twenty miles; and as it deepens but very little, I imagine the water sinks, though there is no visible appearance of it. In general all the lands on the Scioto River, as well as the bottoms on Ohio, are too rich for any thing but hemp, flax, or Indian corn.

24th, 25th, and 26th.—Stayed at the mouth of Scioto,

waiting for the Shawnesse and French traders, who arrived here on the evening of the 26th, in consequence of the message I sent them from Hochocken, or Bottle Creek.

27th.—The Indians requested me to stay this day, which I could not refuse.

28th.—We set off: passing down the Ohio, the country on both sides the river level; the banks continue high. This day we came sixty miles; passed no islands. The river being wider and deeper, we drove all night.

29th.—We came to the little Miame River, having proceeded sixty miles last night.

30th.—We passed the Great Miame River, about thirty miles from the little river of that name, and in the evening arrived at the place where the Elephants' bones are found, where we encamped, intending to take a view of the place next morning. This day we came about seventy miles. The country on both sides level, and rich bottoms well watered.

31st.—Early in the morning we went to the great Lick, where those bones are only found, about four miles from the river, on the south-east side. In our way we passed through a fine timbered clear wood; we came into a large road which the Buffaloes have beaten, spacious enough for two waggons to go abreast, and leading straight into the Lick. It appears that there are vast quantities of these bones lying five or six feet under ground, which we discovered in the bank, at the edge of the Lick. We found here two tusks above six feet long; we carried one, with some other bones, to our boats, and set off. This day we proceeded down the river about eighty miles, through a country much the same as already described, since we passed the Scioto. In this day's journey we passed the mouth of the River Kentucky, or Holsten's River.

June 1st.—We arrived within a mile of the Falls of Ohio, where we encamped, after coming about fifty miles this day.

2d.—Early in the morning we embarked, and passed the Falls. The river being very low we were obliged to lighten our boats, and pass on the north side of a little island, which lays in the middle of the river. In general, what is called the Fall here, is no more than rapids; and in the least fresh, a batteau of any size may come and go on each side without any risk. This day we proceeded sixty miles, in the course of which we passed Pidgeon River. The country pretty high on each side of the River Ohio.

3d.—In the forepart of this day's course, we passed high lands; about mid-day we came to a fine, flat, and level country, called by the Indians the Low Lands; no hills to be seen. We came about eighty miles this day, and encamped.

4th.—We came to a place called the Five Islands; these islands are very long, and succeed one another in a chain; the country still flat and level, the soil exceedingly rich, and well watered. The highlands are at least fifty miles from the banks of the Ohio. In this day's course we passed about ninety miles, the current being very strong.

5th.—Having passed the Five Islands, we came to a place called the Owl River. Came about forty miles this day. The country the same as yesterday.

6th.—We arrived at the mouth of the Ouabache, where we found a breast-work erected, supposed to be done by the Indians. The mouth of this river is about two hundred yards wide, and in its course runs through one of the finest countries in the world, the lands being exceedingly rich, and well watered; here hemp might be raised in immense quantities. All the bottoms, and almost the whole country abounds with great plenty of the white and red mulberry tree. These trees are to be found in great plenty, in all places between the mouth of Scioto and the Ouabache: the soil of the latter affords this tree in plenty as far as Ouicatonon, and some few on the Miame River. Several large fine islands lie in the Ohio, opposite the mouth of the Ouabache, the banks of which are high, and consequently free from inundations; hence we proceeded down the river about six miles to encamp, as I judged some Indians were sent to way-lay us, and came to a place called the Old Shawnesse Village, some of that nation having formerly lived there. In this day's proceedings we came about seventy-six miles. The general course of the river, from Scioto to this place, is south-west.

7th.—We stayed here and despatched two Indians to the Illinois by land, with letters to Lord Frazer, an English officer, who had been sent there from Fort Pitt, and Monsieur St. Ange, the French commanding officer at Fort Chartres, and some speeches to the Indians there, letting them know of my arrival here; that peace was made between us and the Six Nations, Delawares, and Shawnesse, and of my having a number of deputies of those nations along with me, to conclude matters with them also on my arrival there. This day one of my men went into the woods and lost himself.

8th.—At day-break we were attacked by a party of Indians, consisting of eighty warriors of the Kiccapoos and Musquattimes, who killed two of my men and three Indians, wounded myself and all the rest of my party, except two white men and one Indian; then made myself and all the white men prisoners, plundering us of every thing we had. A deputy of the Shawnesse who was shot through the thigh, having concealed himself in the woods for a few minutes after he was wounded—not knowing but they were Southern Indians, who are always at war with the northward Indians—after discovering what nation they were, came up to them and made a very bold speech, telling them that the whole northward Indians would join in taking revenge for the insult and murder of their people; this alarmed those savages very much, who began excusing themselves, saying their fathers, the French, had spirited them up, telling them that the Indians were coming with a body of southern Indians to take their country from them, and enslave them; that it was this that induced them to commit this outrage. After dividing the plunder, (they left great part of the heaviest effects behind, not being able to carry them,) they set off with us to their village at Ouattonon, in a great hurry, being in dread of pursuit from a large party of Indians they suspected were coming after me. Our course was through a thick woody country, crossing a great many swamps, morasses, and beaver ponds. We traveled this day about forty-two miles.

9th.—An hour before day we set out on our march; passed through thick woods, some highlands, and small savannahs, badly watered. Traveled this day about thirty miles.

10th.—We set out very early in the morning, and marched through a high country, extremely well timbered, for three hours; then came to a branch of the Ouabache, which we crossed. The remainder of this day we traveled through fine rich bottoms, overgrown with reeds, which make the best pasture in the world, the young reeds being preferable to sheaf oats. Here is great plenty of wild game of all kinds. Came this day about twenty-eight, or thirty miles.

11th.—At day-break we set off, making our way through a thin woodland, interspersed with savannahs. I suffered extremely by reason of the excessive heat of the weather, and scarcity of water; the little springs and runs being dried up. Traveled this day about thirty miles.

12th.—We passed through some large savannahs, and clear woods; in the afternoon we came to the Ouabache; then marched along it through a prodigious rich bottom, overgrown with reeds and wild hemp; all this bottom is well watered, and an exceeding fine hunting ground. Came this day about thirty miles.

13th.—About an hour before day we set out; travcled through such bottoms as of yesterday, and through some large meadows, where no trees, for several miles togcther, are to be scen. Buffaloes, deer, and bears are here in great plenty. We traveled about twenty-six miles this day.

14th.—The country we traveled through this day, appears the same as described yesterday, excepting this afternoon's journey through woodland, to cut off a bend of the river. Came about twenty-seven miles this day.

15th.—We set out very early, and about one o'clock came to the Ouabache, within six or seven miles of Port Vincent. On my arrival there, I found a village of about eighty or ninety French families settled on the east side of this river, being one of the finest situations that can be found. The country is level and clear, and the soil very rich, producing wheat and tobacco. I think the latter preferable to that of Maryland or Virginia. The French inhabitants hereabouts, are an idle, lazy people, a parcel of renegadoes from Canada, and are much worse than the Indians. They took a secret pleasure at our misfortunes, and the moment we arrived, they came to the Indians, exchanging trifles for their valuable plunder. As the savages took from me a considerable quantity of gold and silver in specie, the French traders extorted ten half johannes[1] from them for one pound of

---

[1] A Portuguese coin worth about nine dollars.

vermilion. Here is likewise an Indian village of the Pyankeshaws, who were much displeased with the party that took me, telling them that "our and your chiefs are gone to make peace, and you have begun a war, for which our women and children will have reason to cry." From this post the Indians permitted me to write to the commander, at Fort Chartres, but would not suffer me to write to any body else, (this I apprehend was a precaution of the French, lest their villany should be perceived too soon,) although the Indians had given me permission to write to Sir William Johnson and Fort Pitt on our march, before we arrived at this place. But immediately after our arrival they had a private council with the French, in which the Indians urged, (as they afterwards informed me,) that as the French had engaged them in so bad an affair, which was likely to bring a war on their nation, they now expected a proof of their promise and assistance. Then delivered the French a scalp and part of the plunder, and wanted to deliver some presents to the Pyankeshaws, but they refused to accept of any, and declared they would not be concerned in the affair. This last information I got from the Pyankeshaws, as I had been well acquainted with them several years before this time.

Port Vincent is a place of great consequence for trade, being a fine hunting country all along the Ouabache, and too far for the Indians, which reside hereabouts, to go either to the Illinois, or elsewhere, to fetch their necessaries.

16th.—We were obliged to stay here to get some little apparel made up for us, and to buy some horses for our journey to Ouicatonon, promising payment at Detroit, for we could not procure horses from the French for hire; though we were greatly fatigued, and our spirits much exhausted in our late march, they would lend us no assistance.

17th.—At mid-day we set out; traveling the first five miles through a fine thick wood. We traveled eighteen miles this day, and encamped in a large, beautiful, well watered meadow.

18th and 19th.—We traveled through a prodigious large meadow, called the Pyankeshaw's Hunting Ground: here is no wood to be seen, and the country appears like an ocean: the ground is exceedingly rich, and partly overgrown with wild hemp; the land well watered, and full of buffalo, deer, bears, and all kinds of wild game.

20th and 21st.—We passed through some very large meadows, part of which belong to the Pyankeshaws on Vermilion River; the country and soil much the same as that we traveled over for these three days past, wild hemp grows here in abundance; the game very plenty: at any time, in half an hour we could kill as much as we wanted.

22nd.—We passed through part of the same meadow as mentioned yesterday; then came to a high woodland, and arrived at Vermilion River, so called from a fine red earth found here by the Indians, with which they paint themselves. About half a mile from the place where we crossed this river, there is a village of Pyankeshaws, distinguished by the addition of the name of the river. We then traveled about three hours, through a clear high woody country, but a deep and rich soil; then came to a meadow, where we encamped.

23d.—Early in the morning we set out through a fine meadow, then some clear woods; in the afternoon came into a very large bottom on the Ouabache, within six miles of Ouicatanon; here I met several chiefs of the Kickapoos and Musquattimes, who spoke to their young men who had taken us, and reprimanded them severely for what they had done to me, after which they returned with us to their village, and delivered us all to their chiefs.

The distance from port Vincent to Ouicatanon is two hundred and ten miles. This place is situated on the Ouabache. About fourteen French families are living in the fort, which stands on the north side of the river. The Kickapoos and the Musquattimes, whose warriors had taken us, live nigh the fort, on the same side of the river, where they have two villages; and the Ouicatanons have a village on the south side of the river. At our arrival at this post, several of the Wawcottonans, (or Ouicatonans) with whom I had been formerly acquainted, came to visit me, and seemed greatly concerned at what had happened. They went immediately to the Kickapoos and Musquattimes, and charged them to take the greatest care of us, till their chiefs should arrive from the Illinois, where they were gone to meet me some time ago, and who were entirely ignorant of this affair, and said the French had spirited up this party to go and strike us.

The French have a great influence over these Indians, and never fail in telling them many lies to the prejudice of his majesty's interest, by making the English nation odious and hateful to them. I had the greatest difficulties in removing these prejudices. As these Indians are a weak, foolish, and credulous people, they are easily imposed on by a designing people, who have led them hitherto as they pleased. The French told them that as the southern Indians had for two years past made war on them, it must have been at the instigation of the English, who are a bad people. However I have been fortunate enough to remove their prejudice, and, in a great measure, their suspicions against the English. The country hereabouts is exceedingly pleasant, being open and clear for many miles; the soil very rich and well watered; all plants have a quick vegetation, and the climate very temperate through the winter. This post has always been a very considerable trading place. The great plenty of furs taken in this country, induced the French to establish this post, which was the first on the Ouabache, and by a very advantageous trade they have been richly recompensed for their labor.

On the south side of the Ouabache runs a big bank, in which are several fine coal mines, and behind this bank, is a very large meadow, clear for several miles. It is surprising what false information we have had respecting this country: some mention these spacious and beautiful meadows as large and barren savannahs. I apprehend it has been the artifice of the French to keep us ignorant of the country. These meadows bear fine wild grass, and wild hemp ten or twelve feet high, which, if properly manufactured, would prove as good, and answer all the purposes of the hemp we cultivate.

July 1st—A Frenchman arrived from the Illinois with a Pipe and Speech from thence to the Kickapoos & Musquat-tamies, to have me Burnt, this Speech was said to be sent from a Shawanese Ind^n who resides at the Ilinois, & has been during the War, & is much attached to the French interest. As soon as this Speech was delivered to the Indians by the French, the Indians informed me of it in Council, & expressed their great concern for what had already happened, & told me they then sett me & my people at liberty, & assured me they despised the message sent them, and would return the Pipe & Belt to their Fathers the French, and enquire into the reason of such a message being sent them by one of his messengers, & desired me to stay with them 'till the Deputies of the Six Nations, Shawanese & Delawares arrived with Pondiac at Ouiatonon in order to settle matters, to w^h I consented.

From 4th to the 8th—I had several Conferences with the Wawiotonans, Pyankeeshas, Kickapoos & Musquatamies in which Conferences I was lucky enough to reconcile those Nations to his Majesties Interest & obtain their Consent and Approbation to take Possession of any Posts in their country which the French formerly possessed & an offer of their service should any Nation oppose our taking possession of it, all which they confirmed by four large Pipes.

11th—Mr Maisonville arrived with an Interpreter & a message to the Indians to bring me & my party to the Ilinois, till then I had no answer from M^r St. Ange to the letter I wrote him of the 16th June, as I wanted to go to the Ilinois, I desired the Chiefs to prepare themselves & set off with me as soon as possible.

12th—I wrote to General Gage & Sir William Johnson, to Col^o Campbell at Detroit, & Major Murray at Fort Pitt & Major Firmer at Mobiel or on his way to the Mississipi, & acquainted [them with] every thing that had happened since my departure from Ft. Pitt.

July 13th—The Chiefs of the Twightwees came to me from the Miamis and renewed their Antient Friendship with His Majesty & all his Subjects in America & confirmed it with a Pipe.

18th—I set off for the Ilinois with the Chiefs of all those Nations when by the way we met with Pondiac together with the Deputies of the Six Nations, Delawares & Shawanese, which accompanied Mr Frazier & myself down the Ohio & also Deputies with speeches from the four Nations living in the Ilinois Country to me & the Six Nations, Delawares & Shawanese, on which we return'd to Ouiatonon and there held another conference, in which I settled all matters with the Ilinois Indians—Pondiac & they agreeing to every thing the other Nations had done, all which they confirmed by Pipes & Belts, but told me the French had informed them that the English intended to take their Country from them, & give it to the Cherokees to settle on, & that if ever they suffered the English to take possession of their Country they would make slaves of them, that this was the reason of their Opposing the English hitherto from taking possession of *Fort Chartres* & induced them to tell Mr. La Gutrie & Mr Sinnott that they would not let the English come into their Country. But being informed since Mr Sinnott had retired by the Deputies of the Six Nations, Delawares & Shawanese, that every difference subsisting between them & the English was now settled, they were willing to comply as the other Nations their Brethren had done and desired that their Father the King of England might not look upon his taking possession of the Forts which the French had formerly possest as a title for his subjects to possess their Country, as they never had sold any part of it to the French, & that I might rest satisfied that whenever the English came to take possession they would receive them with open arms.

July 25th.—We set out from this place (after settling all matters happily with the natives) for the Miames, and traveled the whole way through a fine rich bottom, overgrown with wild hemp, alongside the Ouabache, till we came to Eel River, where we arrived the 27th. About six miles up this river is a small village of the Twightwee, situated on a very delightful spot of ground on the bank of the river. The Eel River heads near St. Joseph's, and runs nearly parallel to the Miames, and at some few miles distance from it, through a fine, pleasant country, and after a course of about one hundred and eighty miles empties itself into the Ouabache.

28th, 29th, 30th and 31st.—We traveled still along side the Eel River, passing through fine clear woods, and some good meadows, though not so large as those we passed some days before. The country is more overgrown with woods, the soil is sufficiently rich, and well watered with springs.

August 1st.—We arrived at the carrying place between the River Miames and the Ouabache, which is about nine miles long in dry seasons, but not above half that length in freshes. The head of the Ouabache is about forty miles from this place, and after a course of about seven hundred and sixty miles from the head spring, through one of the finest countries in the world, it empties itself into the Ohio. The navigation from hence to Ouicatanon, is very difficult in low water, on account of many rapids and rifts; but in freshes, which generally happen in the spring and fall, batteaux or canoes will pass, without difficulty, from here to Ouicatanon in three days, which is about two hundred and forty miles, and by land about two hundred and ten miles. From Ouicatanon to Port Vincent, and thence to the Ohio, batteaux and canoes may go at any season of the year. Throughout the whole course of the Ouabache the banks are pretty high, and in the river are a great many islands. Many shrubs and trees are found here unknown to us.

Within a mile of the Twightwee village, I was met by the chiefs of that nation, who received us very kindly. The most part of these Indians knew me, and conducted me to their village, where they immediately hoisted an English flag that I had formerly given them at Fort Pitt. The next day they held a council, after which they gave me up all the English prisoners they had, then made several speeches, in all which they expressed the great pleasure it gave them, to see the unhappy differences which embroiled the several nations in a war with their brethren, the English, were now so near a happy conclusion, and that peace was established in their country.

The Twightwee village is situated on both sides of a river, called St. Joseph's. This river, where it falls into the Miame river, about a quarter of a mile from this place, is one hundred yards wide, on the east side of which stands a stockade fort, somewhat ruinous.

The Indian village consists of about forty or fifty cabins, besides nine or ten French houses, a runaway colony from Detroit, during the late Indian war; they were concerned in it, and being afraid of punishment, came to this post, where ever since they have spirited up the Indians against the English. All the French residing here are a lazy, indolent people, fond of breeding mischief, and spiriting up the Indians against the English, and should by no means be suffered to remain here. The country is pleasant, the soil rich and well watered. After several conferences with these Indians, and their delivering me up all the English prisoners they had,—[blank space in MS.]

On the 6th of August we set out for Detroit, down the Miames river in a canoe. This river heads about ten miles from hence. The river is not navigable till you come where the river St. Joseph joins it, and makes a considerably large stream. Nevertheless we found a great deal of difficulty in getting our canoe over shoals, as the waters at this season were very low. The banks of the river are high, and the country overgrown with lofty timber of various kinds; the land is level, and the woods clear. About ninety miles from the Miames or Twightwee, we came to where a large river, that heads in a large lick, falls into the Miame river; this they call the Forks. The Ottawas claim this country, and hunt here, where game is very plenty. From hence we proceeded to the Ottawa village. This nation formerly lived at Detroit, but is now settled here, on account of the richness of the country, where game is always to be found in plenty. Here we were obliged to get out of our canoes, and drag them eighteen miles, on account of the rifts which interrupt the navigation. At the end of these rifts, we came to a village of the Wyondotts, who received us very kindly and from thence we proceeded to the mouth of the river, where it falls into Lake Erie. From the Miames to the lake is computed one hundred and eighty miles, and from the entrance of the river into the lake to Detroit, is sixty miles; that is, forty-two miles up the lake, and eighteen miles up the Detroit river to the garrison of that name. The land on the lake side is low and flat. We passed several large rivers and bays, and on the 16th of August, in the afternoon, we arrived at Detroit river. The country here is much higher than on the lake side; the river is about nine hundred yards wide, and the current runs very strong. There are several fine and large islands in this river, one of which is nine miles long; its banks high, and the soil very good.

17th.—In the morning we arrived at the fort, which is a large stockade, inclosing about eighty houses, it stands close on the north side of the river, on a high bank, commands a very pleasant prospect for nine miles above, and nine miles below the fort; the country is thick settled with French, their plantations are generally laid out about three or four acres in breadth on the river, and eighty acres in depth; the soil is good, producing plenty of grain. All the people here are generally poor wretches, and consist of three or four hundred French families, a lazy, idle people, depending chiefly on the savages for their subsistence; though the land, with little labor, produces plenty of grain, they scarcely raise as much as will supply their wants, in imitation of the Indians, whose manners and customs they have entirely adopted, and cannot subsist without them. The men, women, and children speak the Indian tongue perfectly well. In the last Indian war the most part of the French were concerned in it, (although the whole settlement had taken the oath of allegiance to his Britannic Majesty) they have, therefore, great reason to be thankful to the English clemency in not bringing them to deserved punishment. Before the late Indian war there resided three nations of Indians at this place: the Putawatimes, whose village was on the west side of the river, about one mile below the fort; the Ottawas, on the east side, about three miles above the Fort; and the Wyondotts, whose village lies on the east side, about two miles below the fort. The former two nations have removed to a considerable distance, and the latter still remain where they were, and are remarkable for their good sense and hospitality. They have a particular attachment to the Roman Catholic religion, the French, by their priests, having taken uncommon pains to instruct them.

During my stay here, I held frequent conferences with the different nations of Indians assembled at this place, with whom I settled matters to their general satisfaction.

August 17th—I arrived at Detroit where I found several small Tribes of Ottawas, Puttewatamies & Chipwas waiting in Consequence of Col⁰ Bradstreets Invitation to see him. Here I met M^r DeCouagne and Wabecomicat with a Deputation of Indians from Niagara, with Messages from Sir William Johnson to Pondiac & those Western Nations.

23ᵈ—Colo Campbell & I had a Meeting with the Twightwees, Wawiotonans, Pyankeshas, Kickapoos and Musquattamies, when they produced the several Belts sent them by Col⁰ Bradstreet, in consequence of which Invitation they came here.

Then they spoake to the Six Nations Delawares & Shawanese on several Belts & Pipes, beging in the most abject manner that they would forgive them for the ill conduct of their Young Men, to take Pity on their Women & Children & grant y^m peace.

They then spoake to the Col⁰ & me on several Pipes & Belts Expressing their great satisfaction at a firm and lasting Peace settled between their Bretheren the English, & the several Indian Nations in this Country, that they saw the heavy Clouds that hung over their heads for some time past were now dispersed, and that the Sun shone clear & bright, & that as their Father the King of England had conquered the French in that [this] Country & taken into his Friendship all the Indian Nations, they hoped for the future they would be a happy people, & that they should always have reason to call the English their Fathers & beged we would take pity on their Women & Children, & make up the difference subsisting between them and the Shawanese, Delawares & Six Nations, and said as they were come here in consequence of Col⁰ Bradstreet's Invitation, & that he had not met them they hoped their Fathers would pity their necessity & give them a little clothing, and a little rum to drink on the road, as they had come a great way to see their Fathers. Then the Wyondats spoake to the Shawanese, & all the Western Nations on severall Belts & strings, by which they exhorted the several Nations to behave themselves well to their Fathers the English, who had now taken them under their Protection, that if they did, they would be a happy People, that if they did not listen to the Councils of their Fathers, they must take the Consequences, having assured them that all Nations to the Sun rising had taken fast hold of their Fathers the English by the hand, & would follow their Advice, & do every thing they desired them, & never would let slip the Chain of Friendship now so happily renewed.

August 24ᵗʰ—We had another Meeting with the Several Nations, when the Wawiotonans, Twightwees, Pyankeshas, Kickapoos & Musquatamies made several speeches to Col⁰ Campbell & me, in presence of all the other Nations, when they promised to become the Children of the King of Great Britain & farther acknowledged that they had at Ouiatonon before they came there [here] given up the Soverignty of their Country to me for His Majesty, & promised to support his subjects in taking possession of all the Posts given up by the French their former Fathers, to the English, now their present Fathers, all which they confirmed with a Belt.

25th—We had another meeting with the same Indians, when Col° Campbell & I made them several speeches in answer to theirs of the 23 & 24th then delivered them a Road Belt in the name of Sir William Johnson Baronet, to open a Road from the rising to the setting of the Sun which we charged them to keep open through their Country & cautioned them to stop their Ears against the Storys or idle reports of evil minded People & continue to promote the good Works of Peace, all which they promised to do in a most sincere manner.

26th—Col° Campbell & I made those Nations some presents, when after taking leave of us, they sett off for their own Country well satisfied.

27th—We had a Meeting with Pondiac & all the Ottawa Tribes, Chipwaes & Puttewatamies wth the Hurons of this Place & the chiefs of those settled at Sandusky & the Miamis River, when we made them the following Speeches.

CHILDREN PONDIAC & ALL OUR CHILDREN THE OTTAWAS, PUTTEWATAMIES, CHIPWAYS & WYONDATTS: We are very glad to see so many of our Children here present at your Antient Council Fire, which has been neglected for some time past, since those high winds has arose & raised some heavy clouds over your Country, I now by this Belt dress up your Antient Fire & throw some dry wood upon it, that the blaze may ascend to the Clouds so that all Nations may see it, & know that you live in Peace & Tranquility with your Fathers the English.— A Belt.

By this Belt I disperse all the black clouds from over your heads, that the Sun may shine clear on your Women and Children, that those unborn may enjoy the blessings of this General Peace, now so happily settled between your Fathers the English & you & all your younger Bretheren to the Sun setting.— A Belt.

Children: By this Belt I gather up all the Bones of your deceased friends, & bury them deep in the ground, that the herbs & sweet flowers of the earth may grow over them, that we may not see them any more.—A Belt.

Children: with this Belt I take the Hatchet out of your Hands & I pluck up a large tree & bury it deep, so that it may never be found any more, & I plant the tree of Peace, where all our children may sit under & smoak in Peace with their Fathers.—A Belt.

Children: We have made a Road from the Sun rising to the Sun setting, I desire that you will preserve that Road good and pleasant to Travel upon, that we may all share the blessings of this happy Union. I am sorry to see our Children dispersed thro' the Woods, I therefore desire you will return to your Antient Settlements & take care of your Council Fire which I have now dressed up, & promote the good work of Peace.—A Belt.

After which Wapicomica delivered his Messages from Sir William Johnson to Pondiac & the rest of the several Chiefs.

Aug. 28th—We had a Meeting with Pondiac & the several Nations when Pondiac made the following Speeches.

FATHER: We have all smoaked out of the Pipe of Peace its your Childrens Pipe & as the War is all over, & the Great Spirit and Giver of light who has made the Earth & every thing therein, has brought us all together this day for our mutual good to promote the good Works of Peace, I declare to all Nations that I had settled my Peace with you before I came here, & now deliver my Pipe to be sent to Sir William Johnson that he may know I have made Peace, & taken the King of England for my Father, in presence of all the Nations now assembled, & whenever any of those Nations go to visit him, they may smoak out of it with him in Peace. Fathers we are oblidged to you for lighting up our old Council Fire for us, & desiring us to return to it, but we are now settled on the Miamis River, not far from hence, whenever you want us you will find us there ready to wait on you, the reason I choose to stay where we are now settled, is, that we love liquor, and did we live here as formerly, our People would be always drunk, which might occasion some quarrels between the Soldiers & them, this Father is all the reason I have for not returning to our old Settlements, & that we live so nigh this place, that when we want to drink, we can easily come for it.—Gave a large Pipe with a Belt of Wampum tied to it.

FATHER: Be strong and take pity on us your Children as our former Father did, 'tis just the Hunting Season of our children, our Fathers the French formerly used to credit his Children for powder & lead to hunt with, I request in behalf of all the Nations present that you will speak to the Traders now here to do the same, my Father, once more I request you will take pity on us & tell your Traders to give your Children credit for a little powder & lead, as the support of our Family's depend upon it, we have told you where we live, that whenever you want us & let us know it, we will come directly to you.—A Belt.

FATHER: You stoped up the Rum Barrel when we came here, 'till the Business of this Meeting was over, as it is now finished, we request you may open the barrel that your Children may drink & be merry.

August 29th—A Deputation of several Nations sett out from Detroit for the Ilinois Country with several Messages from me & the Wyondats, Six Nations, Delawares, Shawanese & other Nations, in answer to theirs delivered me at Ouiatonon.

30th—The Chiefs of the several Nations who are settled on the Ouabache returned to Detroit from the River Roche, where they had been encamped, & informed Colo Campbell & me, they were now going off for their own Country, & that nothing gave them greater pleasure, than to see that all the Western Nations & Tribes had agreed to a general Peace, & that they should be glad [to know] how soon their Fathers the English, would take possession of the Posts in their Country, formerly possessed by their late Fathers the French, to open a Trade for them, & if this could not be done this Fall, they desired that some Traders might be sent to their Villages to supply them for the Winter, or else they would be oblidged to go to the Ilinois and apply to their old Fathers the French for such necessarys as they might want.

They then spoke on a Belt & said Fathers, every thing is now settled, & we have agreed to your taking possession of the posts in our Country. we have been informed, that the English where ever they settle, make the Country their own, & you tell us that when you conquered the French they gave you this Country.—That no difference may happen hereafter, we tell you now the French never conquered us neither did they purchase a foot of our Country, nor have they a right to give it to you, we gave them liberty to settle for which they always rewarded us, & treated us with great Civility while they had it in their power, but as they are become now your people, if you expect to keep these Posts, we will expect to have proper returns from you.—A Belt.

Sept^br 2^d—The chiefs of the Wyondatts or Huron, came to me & said they had spoke last Summer to Sir Willm Johnson at Niagara about the lands, on which the French had settled near Detroit belonging to them, & desired I would mention again to him. they never had sold it to the French, & expected their new Fathers the English would do them justice, as the French were become one People with us.—A Belt.

4th—Pondiac with several chiefs of the Ottawas, Chippawaes & Potowatamies likewise complained that the French had settled part of their country, which they never had sold to them, & hoped their Fathers the English would take it into Consideration, & see that a proper satisfaction was made to them. That their Country was very large, & they were willing to give up such part of it, as was necessary for their Fathers the English, to carry on Trade at, provided they were paid for it, & a sufficient part of the Country left them to hunt on.—A Belt.

6th—The *Sagina* Indians came here, & made a speech on a Belt of Wampum expressing their satisfaction on hearing that a general Peace was made with all the Western Nations & with Pondiac, they desired a little Powder, Lead & a few knives to enable them to hunt on their way home, & a little rum to drink their new Fathers health.—A Belt.

9th—*Altewaky* and *Chamindiway* Chiefs of a Band of Ottawas from Sandusky with 20 Men came here and informed me that their late conduct had been peaceable, that on hearing there was a great Meeting of all Nations at this place, they came to hear what would be done, & on their way here they had been informed that a General Peace was settled with all Nations to the Sun setting, & they now came to assure us of their attachment to the English Interest, & beged for some Powder, Lead, some Blankets and a little rum to help them to return to their town. A String.

Septbr 11th—Col^o Campbell & I gave the above parties some presents & a little rum & sent them away well satisfied.

12th—The Grand Sautois came with his band and spoke as follows.

FATHER: You sent me a Belt from the Miamis, & as soon as I received it, I set off to meet you here, on my way I heard what had past between you & the several Tribes that met you here, you have had pity on them, & I beg in behalf of myself & the people of Chicago that you will have pity on us also. 'tis true we have been Fools, & have listened to evil reports, & the whistling of bad birds, we red people, are a very jealous and foolish people, & Father amongst you White People, there are bad people also, that tell us lyes & deceive us, which has been the occasion of what has past, I need not say much on this head, I am now convinced, that I have been wrong for some years past, but there are people who have behaved worse than I & my people, they were pardoned last year at this place, I hope we may meet with the same, that our Women & Children may enjoy the blessings of peace as the rest of our Bretheren the red people, & you shall be convinced by our future conduct that we will behave as well as any Tribe of Ind⁸ in this Country.—A Belt.

He then said that the St. Joseph Indians would have come along with him, but the English Prisoner which their Fathers want from them, was some distance off a hunting, & as soon as they could get him in, they would deliver him up and desire forgiveness.

14ᵗʰ—I had a private meeting with the grand Sautois when he told me he was well disposed for peace last Fall, but was then sent for to the Ilinois, where he met with Pondiac, & that then their Fathers the French told them, if they would be strong to keep the English out of possession of that Country but this Summer, That the King of France would send over an Army next Spring, to assist his Children the Indians, and that the King of Spain would likewise send troops to help them to keep the English out of their Country, that the English were a bad people, & had a design to cut off all the Indian Nations in this Country, & to bring the Southern Indians to live & settle there, this account made all the Indians very uneasy in their minds, & after holding a Council amongst themselves, they all determined to oppose the English, & not to suffer them to take Possession of the Ilinois, that for his part he behaved as ill as the rest to the English Officers that came there in the Spring, but since he had been better informed of the goodness of the English, & convinced the French had told lyes for the love of their Beaver, he was now determined with all his people to become faithfull to their new Fathers the English, & pay no regard to any stories the French should tell him for the future.

Sepr 15th—Col^o Campbell & I had a meeting with the Grand Sautois, at which we informed him of every thing that had past with the several Nations & Tribes & told him that we accepted him and his people in Friendship, & would forgive them as we had the rest of the Tribes, & forget what was past provided their future conduct should convince us of their sincerity, after which we gave them some presents, for which he returned thanks & departed very well satisfied.

19th—I received a letter by express from Col^o Reed acquainting me of Capt Sterlings setting out from Fort Pitt, with 100 men of the 42^d Reg^t to take possession of Fort Chartres in the Ilinois Country

20th—I sent of[f] Huron Andrew Express to Capt Sterling at the Ilinois, & with messages to the several Nations in that Country & those on the Ouabache, to acquaint them of Capt Starling's departure from Fort Pitt for the Ilinois Country.

25th—The Chiefs of the St Joseph Indians arrived and addressed themselves to Col^o Campbell & me as follows,

FATHERS: We are come here to see you, altho' we are not acquainted with you, we had a Father formerly, with whom we were very well acquainted, & never differed with him, you have conquered him some time ago, & when you came here first notwithstanding your hands were all bloody, you took hold of us by the hands, & used us well, & we thought we should be happy with our Fathers, but soon an unlucky difference happened, which threw us all in confusion, where this arose we don't know but we assure you, we were the last that entered into this Quarrel, the Ind^s from this place solicited us often to join them, but we would not listen to them, at last they got the better of our foolish young Warriors, but we never agreed to it, we knew it would answer no end, & often told our Warriors they were fools, if they succeeded in killing the few English in this Country, they could not kill them all because we knew you to be a great People.

Fathers: you have after all that has happened, received all

the several Tribes in this Country for your Children, we from St. Joseph's seem to be the last of your Children that come to you, we are no more than Wild Creatures to you Fathers in understanding therefore we request you'l forgive the past follies of our young people & receive us for your Children since you have thrown down our former Father on his back, we have been wandering in the dark like blind people, now you have dispersed all this darkness which hung over the heads of the several Tribes, & have accepted them for your Children, we hope you will let us partake with them of the light, that our Women & Children may enjoy Peace, & we beg you'l forget all that is past, by this belt we remove all evil thoughts from your hearts.—A Belt.

Fathers, When we formerly came to visit our late Fathers the French they always sent us home joyfull, & we hope you will have pity on our Women & Young Men who are in great Want of necessarys, & not let us return home to our Villages ashamed.

Col° Campbell & I made them the following answer.

CHILDREN: I have heard with attention what you have said, & am glad to hear that you have delivered up the Prisoners at Michillimakinac, agreeable to my desire, as the other Prisoner who I always thought belonged to your Nation does not, but the man who has him resides now in your Country, I must desire you'l do every thing in your Power to get him brought to me, nothing will give me greater pleasure than to promote the good Works of Peace, & make my Children the Indians happy as long as their own Conduct shall deserve it. I did not know what to think of your conduct for some time past, but to convince you of my sincere desire to promote Peace, I receive you as Children as I have done the other Nations, & hope your future Conduct may be such, as will convince me of your sincerity.—A Belt.

Children: Sometimes bad people take the liberty of stragling into your Country, I desire if you meet any such people to bring them immediately here, likewise I desire that none of your Young Men may steal any Horses out of this settlement as they have done formerly, we shall see always strict justice done to you, & expect the same from you, on that your own happiness depends, & as long as you continue to merit our friendship by good actions in promoting Peace & Tranquility between your

Young People & His Majesties Subjects, you may expect to be received here with open arms, & to convince you further of my sincerity, I give you some cloaths, powder, lead, vermillion & 2 cags of rum for your young People, that you may return home without shame as you desired.

Children, I take this oppertunity to tell you that your Fathers the English are gone down the Ohio from Fort Pitt to take possession the Ilinois, & desire you may acquaint all your people of it on your return home, & likewise desire you will stop your Ears against the Whistling of bad birds, & mind nothing else but your Hunting to support your Familys, that your Women & Children may enjoy the Blessing of Peace.—A Belt.

September 26th.—Set out from Detroit for Niagara; passed Lake Erie along the north shore in a birch canoe, and arrived the 8th of October at Niagara. The navigation of the lake is dangerous for batteaux or canoes, by reason the lake is very shallow for a considerable distance from the shore. The bank, for several miles, high and steep, and affords a harbor for a single batteau. The lands in general, between Detroit and Niagara, are high, and the soil good, with several fine rivers falling into the lake. The distance from Detroit to Niagara is computed three hundred miles.

John Filson

(c. 1747–1788)

Bibliographical Note. The text given below, apparently Filson's rewriting of notes dictated by Boone, was first published as the Appendix to Filson's *Kentucke* (Wilmington, Delaware, 1784). The whole has been reprinted in facsimile, with notes appended, ed. W. R. Jilson (Louisville, 1930); the text here printed follows Jilson's facsimile, pp. 49–92. The best life of Boone is John Bakeless, *Daniel Boone* (New York, 1939).

THE ADVENTURES
OF COL. DANIEL BOON;
CONTAINING A NARRATIVE
OF THE WARS OF KENTUCKE
(1784)

Curiosity is natural to the soul of man, and interesting objects have a powerful influence on our affections. Let these influencing powers actuate, by the permission or disposal of Providence, from selfish or social views, yet in time the mysterious will of Heaven is unfolded, and we behold our conduct, from whatsoever motives excited, operating to answer the important designs of heaven. Thus we behold Kentucke, lately an howling wilderness, the habitation of savages and wild beasts, become a fruitful field; this region, so favourably distinguished by nature, now become the habitation of civilization, at a period unparalled in history, in the midst of a raging war, and under all the disadvantages of emigration to a country so remote from the inhabited parts of the continent. Here; where the hand of violence shed the blood of the innocent; where the horrid yells of savages, and the groans of the distressed, sounded in our ears, we now hear the praises and adorations of our Creator; where wretched wigwams stood, the miserable abodes of savages, we behold the foundations of cities laid, that, in all probability, will rival the glory of the greatest upon earth. And we view Kentucke situated on the fertile banks of the great Ohio, rising from obscurity to shine with splendor, equal to any other of the stars of the American hemisphere.

The settling of this region well deserves a place in history. Most of the memorable events I have myself been exercised in; and, for the satisfaction of the public, will briefly relate the circumstances of my adventures, and scenes of life, from my first movement to this country until this day.

It was on the first of May, in the year 1769, that I resigned my domestic happiness for a time, and left my family and peaceable habitation on the Yadkin River, in North-Carolina, to wander through the wilderness of America, in quest of the country of Kentucke, in company with John Finley, John Stewart, Joseph Holden, James Monay, and William Cool. We proceeded successfully, and after a long and fatiguing journey through a mountainous wilderness, in a westward direction, on the seventh day of June following, we found ourselves on Red-River, where John Finley had formerly been trading with the Indians, and, from the top of an eminence, saw with pleasure the beautiful level of Kentucke. Here let me observe, that for some time we had experienced the most uncomfortable weather as a prelibation of our future sufferings. At this place we encamped, and made a shelter to defend us from the inclement season, and began to hunt and reconnoitre the country. We found every where abundance of wild beasts of all sorts, through this vast forest. The buffaloes were more frequent than I have seen cattle in the settlements, browzing on the leaves of the cane, or croping the herbage on those extensive plains, fearless, because ignorant, of the violence of man. Sometimes we saw hundreds in a drove, and the numbers about the salt springs were amazing. In this forest, the habitation of beasts of every kind natural to America, we practiced hunting with great success until the twenty-second day of December following.

This day John Stewart and I had a pleasing ramble, but fortune changed the scene in the close of it. We had passed through a great forest, on which stood myriads of trees, some gay with blossoms, others rich with fruits. Nature was here a series of wonders, and a fund of delight. Here she displayed her ingenuity and industry in a variety of flowers and fruits, beautifully coloured, elegantly shaped, and charmingly flavoured; and we were diverted with innumerable animals presenting themselves perpetually to our view.—In the decline of the day, near Kentucke river, as we ascended the brow of a small hill, a number of Indians rushed out of a thick canebrake upon us, and made us prisoners. The time of our sorrow was now arrived, and the scene fully opened. The Indians plundered us of what we had, and kept us in confinement seven days, treating us with common savage usage. During this time we discovered no uneasiness or desire to escape, which made them less suspicious of us; but in the dead of night, as we lay in a thick cane brake by a large fire, when sleep had locked up their senses, my situation not disposing me for rest, I touched my companion and gently awoke him. We improved this favourable opportunity, and departed, leaving them to take their rest, and speedily directed our course towards our old camp, but found it plundered, and the company dispersed and gone home. About this time my brother, Squire Boon, with another adventurer, who came to explore the country shortly after us, was wandering through the forest, determined to find me, if possible, and accidentally found our camp. Notwithstanding the unfortunate circumstances of our company, and our dangerous situation, as surrounded with hostile savages, our meeting so fortunately in the wilderness made us reciprocally sensible of the utmost satisfaction. So much does friendship triumph over misfortune, that sorrows and sufferings vanish at the meeting not only of real friends, but of the most distant acquaintances, and substitutes happiness in their room.

Soon after this, my companion in captivity, John Stewart, was killed by the savages, and the man that came with my

brother returned home by-himself. We were then in a dangerous, helpless situation, exposed daily to perils and death amongst
savages and wild beasts, not a white man in the country but
ourselves.

Thus situated, many hundred miles from our families in the
howling wilderness, I believe few would have equally enjoyed
the happiness we experienced. I often observed to my brother,
You see now how little nature requires to be satisfied. Felicity,
the companion of content, is rather found in our own breasts
than in the enjoyment of external things: And I firmly believe
it requires but a little philosophy to make a man happy in
whatsoever state he is. This consists in a full resignation to the
will of Providence; and a resigned soul finds pleasure in a path
strewed with briars and thorns.

We continued not in a state of indolence, but hunted every
day, and prepared a little cottage to defend us from the Winter
storms. We remained there undisturbed during the Winter; and
on the first day of May, 1770, my brother returned home to the
settlement by himself, for a new recruit of horses and ammunition, leaving me by myself, without bread, salt or sugar, without
company of my fellow creatures, or even a horse or dog. I confess
I never before was under greater necessity of exercising philosophy and fortitude. A few days I passed uncomfortably. The idea
of a beloved wife and family, and their anxiety upon the account
of my absence and exposed situation, made sensible impressions
on my heart. A thousand dreadful apprehensions presented
themselves to my view, and had undoubtedly disposed me to
melancholy, if further indulged.

One day I undertook a tour through the country, and the
diversity and beauties of nature I met with in this charming
season, expelled every gloomy and vexatious thought. Just at the
close of day the gentle gales retired, and left the place to the
disposal of a profound calm. Not a breeze shook the most tremulous leaf. I had gained the summit of a commanding ridge, and,
looking round with astonishing delight, beheld the ample plains,
the beauteous tracts below. On the other hand, I surveyed the
famous river Ohio that rolled in silent dignity, marking the
western boundary of Kentucke with inconceivable grandeur. At
a vast distance I beheld the mountains lift their venerable

brows, and penetrate the clouds. All things were still. I kindled
a fire near a fountain of sweet water, and feasted on the loin of
a buck, which a few hours before I had killed. The sullen shades
of night soon overspread the whole hemisphere, and the earth
seemed to gasp after the hovering moisture. My roving excursion
this day had fatigued my body, and diverted my imagination. I
laid me down to sleep, and I awoke not until the sun had chased
away the night. I continued this tour, and in a few days explored
a considerable part of the country, each day equally pleased as
the first. I returned again to my old camp, which was not dis-
turbed in my absence. I did not confine my lodging to it, but
often reposed in thick cane-brakes, to avoid the savages, who, I
believe, often visited my camp, but fortunately for me, in my
absence. In this situation I was constantly exposed to danger,
and death. How unhappy such a situation for a man tormented
with fear, which is vain if no danger comes, and if it does, only
augments the pain. It was my happiness to be destitute of this
afflicting passion, with which I had the greatest reason to be
affected. The prowling wolves diverted my nocturnal hours with
perpetual howlings; and the various species of animals in this
vast forest, in the daytime, were continually in my view.

Thus I was surrounded with plenty in the midst of want. I
was happy in the midst of dangers and inconveniences. In such
a diversity it was impossible I should be disposed to melancholy.
No populous city, with all the varieties of commerce and stately
structures, could afford so much pleasure to my mind, as the
beauties of nature I found here.

Thus, through an uninterrupted scene of sylvan pleasures, I
spent the time until the 27th day of July following, when my
brother, to my great felicity, met me, according to appointment,
at our old camp. Shortly after, we left this place, not thinking
it safe to stay there longer, and proceeded to Cumberland river,
reconnoitring that part of the country until March, 1771, and
giving names to the different waters.

Soon after, I returned home to my family with a determination to bring them as soon as possible to live in Kentucke, which
I esteemed a second paradise, at the risk of my life and fortune.

I returned safe to my old habitation, and found my family
in happy circumstances. I sold my farm on the Yadkin, and

what goods we could not carry with us; and on the twenty-fifth day of September, 1773, bade a farewell to our friends, and proceeded on our journey to Kentucke, in company with five families more, and forty men that joined us in Powel's Valley, which is one hundred and fifty miles from the now settled parts of Kentucke. This promising beginning was soon overcast with a cloud of adversity; for up on the tenth day of October, the rear of our company was attacked by a number of Indians, who killed six, and wounded one man. Of these my eldest son was one that fell in the action. Though we defended ourselves, and repulsed the enemy, yet this unhappy affair scattered our cattle, brought us into extreme difficulty, and so discouraged the whole company, that we retreated forty miles, to the settlement on Clench river. We had passed over two mountains, viz. Powels and Walden's, and were approaching Cumberland mountain when this adverse fortune overtook us. These mountains are in the wilderness, as we pass from the old settlements in Virginia to Kentucke, are ranged in S. west and N. east direction, are of a great length and breadth, and not far distant from each other. Over these, nature hath formed passes, that are less difficult than might be expected from a view of such huge piles. The aspect of these cliffs is so wild and horrid, that it is impossible to behold them without terror. The spectator is apt to imagine that nature had formerly suffered some violent convulsion; and that these are the dismemembered remains of the dreadful shock; the ruins, not of Persepolis or Palmyra, but of the world!

I remained with my family on Clench until the sixth of June, 1774, when I and one Michael Stoner were solicited by Governor Dunmore, of Virginia, to go to the Falls of the Ohio, to conduct into the settlement a number of surveyors that had been sent thither by him some months before; this country having about this time drawn the attention of many adventurers. We immediately complied with the Governor's request, and conducted in the surveyors, compleating a tour of eight hundred miles, through many difficulties, in sixty-two days.

Soon after I returned home, I was ordered to take the command of three garrisons during the campaign, which Governor Dunmore carried on against the Shawanese Indians: After the conclusion of which, the Militia was discharged from each garrison, and I being relieved from my post, was solicited by a number of North-Carolina gentlemen, that were about purchasing the lands lying on the S. side of Kentucke River, from the Cherokee Indians, to attend their treaty at Wataga, in March, 1775, to negotiate with them, and, mention the boundaries of the purchase. This I accepted, and at the request of the same gentlemen, undertook to mark out a road in the best passage from the settlement through the wilderness to Kentucke, with such assistance as I thought necessary to employ for such an important undertaking.

I soon began this work, having collected a number of enterprising men, well armed We proceeded with all possible expedition until we came within fifteen miles of where Boonsborough now stands, and where we were fired upon by a party of Indians that killed two, and wounded two of our number; yet, although surprised and taken at a disadvantage, we stood our ground. This was on the twentieth of March, 1775. Three days after, we were fired upon again, and had two men killed, and three wounded. Afterwards we proceeded on to Kentucke river without opposition; and on the first day of April began to erect the fort of Boonsborough at a salt lick, about sixty yards from the river, on the S. side.

On the fourth day, the Indians killed one of our men.—We were busily employed in building this fort, until the fourteenth day of June following, without any farther opposition from the Indians; and having finished the works, I returned to my family, on Clench.

In a short time, I proceeded to remove my family from Clench to this garrison; where we arrived safe without any other difficulties than such as are common to this passage, my wife and daughter being the first white women that ever stood on the banks of Kentucke river.

On the twenty-fourth day of December following we had one man killed, and one wounded, by the Indians, who seemed determined to persecute us for erecting this fortification.

On the fourteenth day of July, 1776, two of Col. Calaway's daughters, and one of mine, were taken prisoners near the fort. I immediately pursued the Indians, with only eight men, and on the sixteenth overtook them, killed two of the party, and recovered the girls. The same day on which this attempt was made, the Indians divided themselves into different parties, and attacked several forts, which were shortly before this time erected, doing a great deal of mischief. This was extremely distressing to the new settlers. The innocent husbandman was shot down, while busy cultivating the soil for his family's supply. Most of the cattle around the stations were destroyed. They continued their hostilities in this manner until the fifteenth of April, 1777, when they attacked Boonsborough with a party of above one hundred in number, killed one man, and wounded four—Their loss in this attack was not certainly known to us.

On the fourth day of July following, a party of about two hundred Indians attacked Boonsborough, killed one man, and wounded two. They besieged us forty-eight hours; during which time seven of them were killed, and at last, finding themselves not likely to prevail, they raised the siege, and departed.

The Indians had disposed their warriors in different parties at this time, and attacked the different garrisons to prevent their assisting each other, and did much injury to the distressed inhabitants.

On the nineteenth day of this month, Col. Logan's fort was besieged by a party of about two hundred Indians. During this dreadful siege they did a great deal of mischief, distressed the garrison, in which were only fifteen men, killed two, and wounded one. The enemies loss was uncertain, from the common practice which the Indians have of carrying off their dead in time of battle. Col. Harrod's fort was then defended by only sixty-five men, and Boonsborough by twenty-two, there being no more forts or white men in the country, except at the Falls, a considerable distance from these, and all taken collectively, were but a handful to the numerous warriors that were every where dispersed through the country, intent upon doing all the mischief that savage barbarity could invent. Thus we passed through a scene of sufferings that exceeds description.

On the twenty-fifth of this month a reinforcement of forty-five men arrived from North-Carolina, and about the twentieth of August following, Col. Bowman arrived with one hundred men from Virginia. Now we began to strengthen, and from hence, for the space of six weeks, we had skirmishes with Indians, in one quarter or other, almost every day.

The savages now learned the superiority of the Long Knife, as they call the Virginians, by experience; being out-generalled in almost every battle. Our affairs began to wear a new aspect, and the enemy, not daring to venture on open war, practiced secret mischief at times.

On the first day of January, 1778, I went with a party of thirty men to the Blue Licks, on Licking River, to make salt for the different garrisons in the country.

On the seventh day of February, as I was hunting, to procure meat for the company, I met with a party of one hundred and two Indians, and two Frenchmen, on their march against Boonsborough, that place being particularly the object of the enemy.

They pursued, and took me; and brought me on the eighth day to the Licks, where twenty-seven of my party were, three of them having previously returned home with the salt. I knowing it was impossible for them to escape, capitulated with the enemy, and, at a distance in their view, gave notice to my men of their situation, with orders not to resist, but surrender themselves captives.

The generous usage the Indians had promised before in my capitulation, was afterwards fully complied with, and we proceeded with them as prisoners to old Chelicothe, the principal Indian town, on Little Miami, where we arrived, after an uncomfortable journey, in very severe weather, on the eighteenth day of February, and received as good treatment as prisoners could expect from savages—On the tenth day of March following, I, and ten of my men, were conducted by forty Indians to Detroit, where we arrived the thirtieth day, and were treated by Governor Hamilton, the British commander at that post, with great humanity.

During our travels, the Indians entertained me well; and their affection for me was so great, that they utterly refused to leave me there with the others, although the Governor offered them one hundred pounds Sterling for me, on purpose to give me a parole to go home. Several English gentlemen there, being sensible of my adverse fortune, and touched with human sympathy, generously offered a friendly supply for my wants, which I refused, with many thanks for their kindness; adding, that I never expected it would be in my power to recompense such unmerited generosity.

The Indians left my men in captivity with the British at Detroit, and on the tenth day of April brought me towards Old Chelicothe, where we arrived on the twenty-fifth day of the same month. This was a long and fatiguing march, through an exceeding fertile country, remarkable for fine springs and streams of water. At Chelicothe I spent my time as comfortably as I could expect; was adopted, according to their custom, into a family where I became a son, and had a great share in the affection of my new parents, brothers, sisters, and friends. I was exceedingly familiar and friendly with them, always appearing as chearful and satisfied as possible, and they put great confidence in me. I often went a hunting with them, and frequently gained their applause for my activity at our shooting-matches. I was careful not to exceed many of them in shooting; for no people are more envious than they in this sport. I could observe, in their countenances and gestures, the greatest expressions of joy when they exceeded me; and, when the reverse happened, of envy. The Shawanese king took great notice of me, and treated me with profound respect, and entire friendship, often entrusting me to hunt at my liberty. I frequently returned with the spoils of the woods, and as often presented some of what I had taken to him, expressive of duty to my sovereign. My food and lodging was, in common, with them, not so good indeed as I could desire, but necessity made every thing acceptable.

I now began to meditate an escape, and carefully avoided their suspicions, continuing with them at Old Chelicothe until the first day of June following, and then was taken by them to the salt springs on Sciotha, and kept there, making salt, ten days. During this time I hunted some for them, and found the land, for a great extent about this river, to exceed the soil of Kentucke, if possible, and remarkably well watered.

When I returned to Chelicothe, alarmed to see four hundred and fifty Indians, of their choicest warriors, painted and

armed in a fearful manner, ready to march against Boonsborough, I determined to escape the first opportunity.

On the sixteenth, before sun-rise, I departed in the most
secret manner, and arrived at Boonsborough on the twentieth,
after a journey of one hundred and sixty miles; during which, I
had but one meal.

I found our fortress in a bad state of defence, but we proceeded immediately to repair our flanks, strengthen our gates
and posterns, and form double bastions, which we compleated
in ten days. In this time we daily expected the arrival of the
Indian army; and at length, one of my fellow prisoners, escaping
from them, arrived, informing us that the enemy had an account
of my departure, and postponed their expedition three weeks.—
The Indians had spies out viewing our movements, and were
greatly alarmed with our increase in number and fortifications.
The Grand Councils of the nations were held frequently, and
with more deliberation than usual. They evidently saw the approaching hour when the Long Knife would dispossess them of
their desirable habitations; and anxiously concerned for futurity,
determined utterly to extirpate the whites out of Kentucke. We
were not intimidated by their movements, but frequently gave
them proofs of our courage.

About the first of August, I made an incursion into the
Indian country, with a party of nineteen men, in order to surprise a small town up Sciotha, called Paint-Creek-Town. We
advanced within four miles thereof, where we met a party of
thirty Indians, on their march against Boonsborough, intending
to join the others from Chelicothe. A smart fight ensued betwixt
us for some time: At length the savages gave way, and fled. We
had no loss on our side: The enemy had one killed, and two
wounded. We took from them three horses, and all their baggage; and being informed, by two of our number that went to
their town, that the Indians had entirely evacuated it, we proceeded no further, and returned with all possible expedition
to assist our garrison against the other party. We passed by
them on the sixth day, and on the seventh, we arrived safe at
Boonsborough.

On the eighth, the Indian army arrived, being four hundred

and forty-four in number, commanded by Capt. Duquesne, eleven other Frenchmen, and some of their own chiefs, and marched up within view of our fort, with British and French colours flying; and having sent a summons to me, in his Britannick Majesty's name, to surrender the fort, I requested two days consideration, which was granted.

It was now a critical period with us.—We were a small number in the garrison:—A powerful army before our walls, whose appearance proclaimed inevitable death, fearfully painted, and marking their footsteps with desolation. Death was preferable to captivity; and if taken by storm, we must inevitably be devoted to destruction. In this situation we concluded to maintain our garrison, if possible. We immediately proceeded to collect what we could of our horses, and other cattle, and bring them through the posterns into the fort: And in the evening of the ninth, I returned answer, that we were determined to defend our fort while a man was living—Now, said I to their commander, who stood attentively hearing my sentiments, We laugh at all your formidable preparations: But thank you for giving us notice and time to provide for our defence. Your efforts will not prevail; for our gates shall for ever deny you admittance.—Whether this answer affected their courage, or not, I cannot tell; but, contrary to our expectations, they formed a scheme to deceive us, declaring it was their orders, from Governor Hamilton, to take us captives, and not to destroy us; but if nine of us would come out, and treat with them, they would immediately withdraw their forces from our walls and return home peaceably. This sounded grateful in our ears; and we agreed to the proposal.

We held the treaty within sixty yards of the garrison, on purpose to divert them from a breach of honour, as we could not avoid suspicions of the savages. In this situation the articles were formally agreed to, and signed; and the Indians told us it was customary with them, on such occasions, for two Indians to shake hands with every white-man in the treaty, as an evidence of entire friendship. We agreed to this also, but were soon convinced their policy was to take us prisoners.—They immediately grappled us; but, although surrounded by hundreds of savages, we extricated ourselves from them, and escaped all safe into the garrison, except one that was wounded, through a heavy fire from their army. They immediately attacked us on every side, and a constant heavy fire ensued between us day and night for the space of nine days.

In this time the enemy began to undermine our fort, which was situated sixty yards from Kentucke river. They began at the water-mark, and proceeded in the bank some distance, which we understood by their making the water muddy with the clay; and we immediately proceeded to disappoint their design, by cutting a trench a-cross their subterranean passage. The enemy discovering our counter-mine, by the clay we threw out of the fort, desisted from that stratagem: And experience now fully convincing them that neither their power nor policy could effect their purpose, on the twentieth day of August they raised the siege, and departed.

During this dreadful siege, which threatened death in every form, we had two men killed, and four wounded, besides a number of cattle. We killed of the enemy thirty-seven, and wounded a great number. After they were gone, we picked up one hundred and twenty-five pounds weight of bullets, besides what stuck in the logs of our fort; which certainly is a great proof of their industry. Soon after this, I went into the settlement, and nothing worthy of a place in this account passed in my affairs for some time.

During my absence from Kentucke, Col. Bowman carried on an expedition against the Shawanese, at Old Chelicothe, with one hundred and sixty men, in July, 1779. Here they arrived undiscovered, and a battle ensued, which lasted until ten o'clock, A.M. when Col. Bowman, finding he could not succeed at this time, retreated about thirty miles. The Indians, in the mean time, collecting all their forces, pursued and overtook him, when a smart fight continued near two hours, not to the advantage of Col. Bowman's party.

Col. Harrod proposed to mount a number of horse, and furiously to rush upon the savages, who at this time fought with remarkable fury. This desperate step had a happy effect, broke their line of battle, and the savages fled on all sides. In these two battles we had nine killed, and one wounded. The enemy's loss uncertain, only two scalps being taken.

On the twenty-second day of June, 1780, a large party of Indians and Canadians, about six hundred in number, commanded by Col. Bird, attacked Riddle's and Martin's stations, at the Forks of Licking River, with six pieces of artillery. They carried this expedition so secretly, that the unwary inhabitants did not discover them, until they fired upon the forts; and, not being prepared to oppose them, were obliged to surrender themselves miserable captives to barbarous savages, who immediately after tomahawked one man and two women, and loaded all the others with heavy baggage, forcing them along toward their towns, able or unable to march. Such as were weak and faint by the way, they tomahawked. The tender women, and helpless children, fell victims to their cruelty. This, and the savage treatment they received afterwards, is shocking to humanity, and too barbarous to relate.

The hostile disposition of the savages, and their allies, caused General Clark, the commandant at the Falls at the Ohio, immediately to begin an expedition with his own regiment, and the armed force of the country, against Pecaway, the principal town of the Shawanese, on a branch of Great Miami, which he finished with great success, took seventeen scalps, and burnt the town to ashes, with the loss of seventeen men.

About this time I returned to Kentucke with my family; and here, to avoid an enquiry into my conduct, the reader being before informed of my bringing my family to Kentucke, I am under the necessity of informing him that, during my captivity with the Indians, my wife, who despaired of ever seeing me again, expecting the Indians had put a period to my life, oppressed with the distresses of the country, and bereaved of me, her only happiness, had, before I returned, transported my family and goods, on horses, through the wilderness, amidst a multitude of dangers, to her father's house, in North-Carolina.

Shortly after the troubles at Boonsborough, I went to them, and lived peaceably there until this time. The history of my going home, and returning with my family, forms a series of difficulties, an account of which would swell a volume, and being foreign to my purpose, I shall purposely omit them.

I settled my family in Boonsborough once more; and shortly after, on the sixth day of October, 1780, I went in company with my brother to the Blue Licks; and, on our return home, we were fired upon by a party of Indians. They shot him, and pursued me, by the scent of their dog, three miles; but I killed the dog, and escaped. The Winter soon came on, and was very severe, which confined the Indians to their wigwams.

The severity of this Winter caused great difficulties in Kentucke. The enemy had destroyed most of the corn, the Summer before. This necessary article was scarce, and dear; and the inhabitants lived chiefly on the flesh of buffaloes. The circumstances of many were very lamentable: However, being a hardy race of people, and accustomed to difficulties and necessities, they were wonderfully supported through all their sufferings, until the ensuing Fall, when we received abundance from the fertile soil.

Towards Spring, we were frequently harassed by Indians; and, in May, 1782, a party assaulted Ashton's station, killed one man, and took a Negro prisoner. Capt. Ashton, with twenty-five men, pursued, and overtook the savages, and a smart fight ensued, which lasted two hours; but they being superior in number, obliged Captain Ashton's party to retreat, with the loss of eight killed, and four mortally wounded; their brave commander himself being numbered among the dead.

The Indians continued their hostilities; and, about the tenth of August following, two boys were taken from Major Hoy's station. This party was pursued by Capt. Holder and seventeen men, who were also defeated, with the loss of four men killed, and one wounded. Our affairs became more and more alarming. Several stations which had lately been erected in the country were continually infested with savages, stealing their horses and killing the men at every opportunity. In a field, near Lexington, an Indian shot a man, and running to scalp him, was himself shot from the fort, and fell dead upon his enemy.

Every day we experienced recent mischiefs. The barbarous savage nations of Shawanese, Cherokees, Wyandots, Tawas, Delawares, and several others near Detroit, united in a war against us and assembled their choicest warriors at old Chelicothe, to go on the expedition, in order to destroy us, and entirely depopulate the country. Their savage minds were inflamed to mischief by two abandoned men, Captains McKee and Girty.

These led them to execute every diabolical scheme; and, on the fifteenth day of August, commanded a party of Indians and Canadians, of about five hundred in number, against Briant's station, five miles from Lexington. Without demanding a surrender, they furiously assaulted the garrison, which was happily prepared to oppose them; and, after they had expended much ammunition in vain, and killed the cattle round the fort, not being likely to make themselves masters of this place, they raised the siege, and departed in the morning of the third day after they came, with the loss of about thirty killed, and the number of wounded uncertain.—Of the garrison four were killed, and three wounded.

On the eighteenth day Col. Todd, Col. Trigg, Major Harland, and myself, speedily collected one hundred and seventy-six men, well armed, and pursued the savages. They had marched beyond the Blue Licks to a remarkable bend of the main fork of Licking River, about forty-three miles from Lexington, as it is particularly represented in the map, where we overtook them on the nineteenth day. The savages observing us, gave way; and we, being ignorant of their numbers, passed the river. When the enemy saw our proceedings, having greatly the advantage of us in [our] situation, they formed the line of battle, as represented in the map, from one bend of Licking to the other, about a mile from the Blue Licks. An exceeding fierce battle immediately began, for about fifteen minutes, when we, being over-powered by numbers, were obliged to retreat, with the loss of sixty seven men; seven of whom were taken prisoners. The brave and much lamented Colonels Todd and Trigg, Major Harland and my second son, were among the dead. We were informed that the Indians, numbering their dead, found they had four killed more than we; and therefore, four of the prisoners they had taken, were, by general consent, ordered to be killed, in a most barbarous manner, by the young warriors, in order to train them up to cruelty; and then they proceeded to their towns.

On our retreat we were met by Col. Logan, hastening to join us, with a number of well armed men. This powerful assistance we unfortunately wanted in the battle; for, notwithstanding the enemy's superiority of numbers, they acknowledged that, if they had received one more fire from us, they should undoubtedly have given way. So valiantly did our small party fight, that, to the memory of those who unfortunately fell in the battle, enough of honour cannot be said. Had Col. Logan and his party been with us, it is highly probable we should have given the savages a total defeat.

I cannot reflect upon this dreadful scene, but sorrow fills my heart. A zeal for the defence of their country led these heroes to the scene of action, though with a few men to attack a powerful army of experienced warriors. When we gave way, they pursued us with the utmost eagerness, and in every quarter spread destruction. The river was difficult to cross, and many were killed in the flight, some just entering the river, some in the water, others after crossing in ascending the cliffs. Some escaped on horse-back, a few on foot; and, being dispersed every where, in a few hours, brought the melancholy news of this unfortunate battle to Lexington. Many widows were now made. The reader may guess what sorrow filled the hearts of the inhabitants, exceeding any thing that I am able to describe. Being reinforced, we returned to bury the dead, and found their bodies strewed every where, cut and mangled in a dreadful manner. This mournful scene exhibited a horror almost unparalleled: Some torn and eaten by wild beasts; those in the river eaten by fishes; all in such a putrified condition, that no one could be distinguished from another.

As soon as General Clark, then at the Falls of the Ohio, who was ever our ready friend, and merits the love and gratitude of all his country-men, understood the circumstances of this unfortunate action, he ordered an expedition, with all possible haste, to pursue the savages, which was so expeditiously effected, that we overtook them within two miles of their towns, and probably might have obtained a great victory, had not two of their number met us about two hundred poles before we come up. These returned quick as lightening to their camp with the alarming news of a mighty army in view. The savages fled in the utmost disorder, evacuated their towns, and reluctantly left their territory to our mercy. We immediately took possession of Old Chelicothe without opposition, being deserted by its inhabitants. We continued our pursuit through five towns on the

Miami rivers, Old Chelicothe, Pecaway, New Chelicothe, Will's Towns, and Chelicothe, burnt them all to ashes, entirely destroyed their corn, and other fruits, and every where spread a scene of desolation in the country. In this expedition we took seven prisoners and five scalps, with the loss of only four men, two of whom were accidentally killed by our own army.

This campaign in some measure damped the spirits of the Indians, and made them sensible of our superiority. Their connections were dissolved, their armies scattered, and a future invasion put entirely out of their power; yet they continued to practice mischief secretly upon the inhabitants, in the exposed parts of the country.

In October following, a party made an excursion into that district called the Crab Orchard, and one of them, being advanced some distance before the others, boldly entered the house of a poor defenceless family, in which was only a Negro man, a woman and her children, terrified with the apprehensions of immediate death. The savage, perceiving their defenceless situation, without offering violence to the family attempted to captivate the Negro, who, happily proved an over-match for him, threw him on the ground, and, in the struggle, the mother of the children drew an ax from a corner of the cottage, and cut his head off, while her little daughter shut the door. The savages instantly appeared, and applied their tomahawks to the door. An old rusty gun-barrel, without a lock, lay in a corner, which the mother put through a small crevice, and the savages, perceiving it, fled. In the mean time, the alarm spread through the neighbourhood; the armed men collected immediately, and pursued the savages into the wilderness. Thus Providence, by the means of this Negro, saved the whole of the poor family from destruction. From that time, until the happy return of peace between the United States and Great-Britain, the Indians did us no mischief. Finding the great king beyond the water disappointed in his expectations, and conscious of the importance of the Long Knife, and their own wretchedness, some of the nations immediately desired peace; to which, at present, they seem universally disposed, and are sending ambassadors to General Clark, at the Falls of the Ohio, with the minutes of their

Councils; a specimen of which, in the minutes of the Pian-kashaw Council, is subjoined.

To conclude, I can now say that I have verified the saying of an old Indian who signed Col. Henderson's deed. Taking me by the hand, at the delivery thereof, Brother, says he, we have given you a fine land, but I believe you will have much trouble in settling it.—My footsteps have often been marked with blood, and therefore I can truly subscribe to its original name. Two darling sons, and a brother, have I lost by savage hands, which have also taken from me forty valuable horses, and abundance of cattle. Many dark and sleepless nights have I been a companion for owls, separated from the chearful society of men, scorched by the Summer's sun, and pinched by the Winter's cold, an instrument ordained to settle the wilderness. But now the scene is changed: Peace crowns the sylvan shade.

What thanks, what ardent and ceaseless thanks are due to that all-superintending Providence which has turned a cruel war into peace, brought order out of confusion, made the fierce savages placid, and turned away their hostile weapons from our country! May the same Almighty Goodness banish the accursed monster, war, from all lands, with her hated associates, rapine and insatiable ambition. Let peace, descending from her native heaven, bid her olives spring amidst the joyful nations; and plenty, in league with commerce, scatter blessings from her copious hand.

This account of my adventures will inform the reader of the most remarkable events of this country.—I now live in peace and safety, enjoying the sweets of liberty, and the bounties of Providence, with my once fellow-sufferers, in this delightful country, which I have seen purchased with a vast expence of blood and treasure, delighting in the prospect of its being, in a short time, one of the most opulent and powerful states on the continent of North-America; which, with the love and gratitude of my country-men, I esteem a sufficient reward for all my toil and dangers.

DANIEL BOON

Fayette county, Kentucke.

Rinehart Editions